Seventh Edition

Principles of Information Security

Michael E. Whitman, *Ph.D., CISM, CISSP*
Herbert J. Mattord, *Ph.D., CISM, CISSP*

Information Security

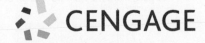
CENGAGE

Australia • Brazil • Canada • Mexico • Singapore • United Kingdom • United States

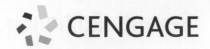

Principles of Information Security,
7th Edition
Michael E. Whitman and Herbert J. Mattord

SVP, Higher Education Product Management:
Erin Joyner

VP, Product Management: Thais Alencar

Product Director: Mark Santee

Associate Product Manager: Danielle Klahr

Product Assistant: Tom Benedetto

Executive Director, Learning: Natalie Skadra

Learning Designer: Mary Clyne

Vice President, Product Marketing: Jason Sakos

Portfolio Marketing Manager: Mackenzie Paine

Senior Director, Content Creation: Rebecca von
Gillern

Content Manager: Christina Nyren

Director, Digital Production Services: Krista
Kellman

Senior Digital Delivery Lead: Jim Vaughey

Developmental Editor: Dan Seiter

Production Service/Composition: SPi Global

Design Director: Jack Pendleton

Designer: Erin Griffin

Text Designer: Erin Griffin

Cover Designer: Erin Griffin

Cover image(s): Vandathai/Shutterstock.com

For product information and technology assistance, contact us at Cengage
**Customer & Sales Support, 1-800-354-9706
or support.cengage.com.**

For permission to use material from this text or product, submit all requests online at **www.cengage.com/permissions**.

Library of Congress Control Number: 2021909680

ISBN: 978-0-357-50643-1

Cengage
200 Pier 4 Boulevard
Boston, MA 02210
USA

Cengage is a leading provider of customized learning solutions with employees residing in nearly 40 different countries and sales in more than 125 countries around the world. Find your local representative at **www.cengage.com**.

To learn more about Cengage platforms and services, register or access your online learning solution, or purchase materials for your course, visit **www.cengage.com**.

Notice to the Reader

Publisher does not warrant or guarantee any of the products described herein or perform any independent analysis in connection with any of the product information contained herein. Publisher does not assume, and expressly disclaims, any obligation to obtain and include information other than that provided to it by the manufacturer. The reader is expressly warned to consider and adopt all safety precautions that might be indicated by the activities described herein and to avoid all potential hazards. By following the instructions contained herein, the reader willingly assumes all risks in connection with such instructions. The publisher makes no representations or warranties of any kind, including but not limited to, the warranties of fitness for particular purpose or merchantability, nor are any such representations implied with respect to the material set forth herein, and the publisher takes no responsibility with respect to such material. The publisher shall not be liable for any special, consequential, or exemplary damages resulting, in whole or part, from the readers' use of, or reliance upon, this material.

Printed at CLDPC, USA, 06-21

To Rhonda, Rachel, Alex, and Meghan, thank you for your loving support.

—MEW

To my grandchildren, Julie and Ellie; it is a wonderful life.

—HJM

Brief Contents

Table of Contents

Module 6

Legal, Ethical, and Professional Issues in Information Security 223

Module 7

Security and Personnel 261

Preface

The world continues to become ever more interconnected. As global information networks continue to expand, the interconnection of devices of every description becomes vital, as does the smooth operation of communication, computing, and automation solutions. However, ever-evolving threats such as malware and phishing attacks and the success of criminal and hostile government attackers illustrate weaknesses in the current technical landscape and the need to provide heightened security for information systems.

When attempting to secure current and planned systems and networks, organizations must draw on the current pool of information security and cybersecurity practitioners. However, to develop more secure computing environments in the future, these same organizations are counting on the next generation of professionals to have the correct mix of skills and experience to anticipate and manage the complex information security issues that will arise. Thus, improved texts with supporting materials, along with the efforts of college and university faculty, are needed to prepare students of technology to recognize the threats and vulnerabilities in existing systems and to learn to design and develop the secure systems needed.

The purpose of *Principles of Information Security, Seventh Edition*, is to continue to meet the need for a current, high-quality academic resource that surveys the full breadth of the information security and cybersecurity disciplines. Even today, there remains a lack of resources that provide students with a *balanced* introduction to the managerial and technical aspects of these fields. By specifically focusing our writing on the common body of knowledge, we hope to close this gap. Further, there is a clear need to include principles from criminal justice, political science, computer science, information systems, and other related disciplines to gain a clear understanding of information security and cybersecurity principles and formulate interdisciplinary solutions for system vulnerabilities. The essential tenet of this text is that information security and cybersecurity in the modern organization is a problem for management to solve, and not one that technology alone can address. In other words, an organization's information security has important economic consequences for which management will be held accountable.

Approach

Principles of Information Security, Seventh Edition, provides a broad review of the entire field of information security, background on many related elements, and enough detail to facilitate an understanding of the topic as a whole. The narrative covers the terminology of the field, the history of the discipline, and elementary strategies for managing an information security program.

Structure And Module Descriptions

Principles of Information Security, Seventh Edition, is structured to follow an approach that moves from the strategic aspects of information security to the operational—beginning with the external impetus for information security, moving through the organization's strategic approaches to governance, risk management, and regulatory compliance, and continuing with the technical and operational implementation of security in the organization. Our use of this approach is intended to provide a supportive but not overly dominant foundation that will guide instructors and students through the information domains of information security. To serve this end, the content is organized into 12 modules.

Module 1—Introduction to Information Security

The opening module establishes the foundation for understanding the broader field of information security. This is accomplished by defining key terms, explaining essential concepts, and reviewing the origins of the field and its impact on the understanding of information security.

Module 2—The Need for Information Security

Module 2 examines the business drivers behind the design process of information security analysis. It examines current organizational and technological security needs while emphasizing and building on the concepts presented in Module 1. One principal concept presented in this module is that information security is primarily a management issue rather than a technological one. To put it another way, the best practices within the field of information security involve applying technology only after considering the business needs.

The module also examines the various threats facing organizations and presents methods for ranking and prioritizing these threats as organizations begin their security planning process. The module continues with a detailed examination of the types of attacks that could result from these threats, and how these attacks could affect the organization's information systems. Module 2 also provides further discussion of the key principles of information security, some of which were introduced in Module 1: confidentiality, integrity, availability, authentication, identification, authorization, accountability, and privacy.

Module 3—Information Security Management

This module presents the different management functions within the field of information security and defines information security governance. It continues with management's role in the development, maintenance, and enforcement of information security policy, standards, practices, procedures, and guidelines. The module also explains data classification schemes, both military and private, as well as the security education, training, and awareness (SETA) program. The module concludes with discussions on information security blueprints.

Module 4—Risk Management

Before the design of a new information security solution can begin, information security analysts must first understand the current state of the organization and its relationship to information security. Does the organization have any formal information security mechanisms in place? How effective are they? What policies and procedures have been published and distributed to security managers and end users? This module explains how to conduct a fundamental information security assessment by describing procedures for identifying and prioritizing threats and assets as well as procedures for identifying what controls are in place to protect these assets from threats. The module also discusses the various types of control mechanisms and identifies the steps involved in performing the initial risk assessment. The module continues by defining risk management as the process of identifying, assessing, and reducing risk to an acceptable level and implementing effective control measures to maintain that level of risk. Module 4 concludes with a discussion of risk analysis and various types of feasibility analyses.

Module 5—Incident Response and Contingency Planning

This module examines the planning process that supports business continuity, disaster recovery, and incident response; it also describes the organization's role during incidents and specifies when the organization should involve outside law enforcement agencies. The module includes coverage of the subject of digital forensics.

Module 6—Legal, Ethical, and Professional Issues in Information Security

A critical aspect of the field is a careful examination of current legislation, regulation, and common ethical expectations of both national and international entities that provides important insights into the regulatory constraints that govern business. This module examines several key laws that shape the field of information security and examines the computer ethics to which those who implement security must adhere. This module also presents several common legal and ethical issues found in today's organizations, as well as formal and professional organizations that promote ethics and legal responsibility.

Module 7—Security and Personnel

The next area in the implementation stage addresses personnel issues. Module 7 examines both sides of the personnel coin: security personnel and security of personnel. It examines staffing issues, professional security credentials, and the implementation of employment policies and practices. The module also discusses how information security policy affects and is affected by consultants, temporary workers, and outside business partners.

Module 8—Security Technology: Access Controls, Firewalls, and VPNs

Module 8 provides a detailed overview of the configuration and use of technologies designed to segregate the organization's systems from the insecure Internet. This module examines the various definitions and categorizations of firewall technologies and the architectures under which firewalls may be deployed. The module discusses the rules and guidelines associated with the proper configuration and use of firewalls. Module 8 also discusses remote dial-up services and the security precautions necessary to secure access points for organizations still deploying this older technology. The module continues by presenting content filtering capabilities and considerations, and concludes by examining technologies designed to provide remote access to authorized users through virtual private networks.

Module 9—Security Technology: Intrusion Detection and Prevention Systems and Other Security Tools

Module 9 continues the discussion of security technologies by examining the concept of intrusion and the technologies necessary to prevent, detect, react, and recover from intrusions. Specific types of intrusion detection and prevention systems (IDPSs)—the host IDPS, network IDPS, and application IDPS—and their respective configurations and uses are presented and discussed. The module examines specialized detection technologies that are designed to entice attackers into decoy systems (and thus away from critical systems) or simply to identify the attacker's entry into these decoy areas. Such systems are known as honeypots, honeynets, and padded cell systems. The discussion also examines trace-back systems, which are designed to track down the true address of attackers who were lured into decoy systems. The module then examines key security tools that information security professionals can use to monitor the current state of their organization's systems and identify potential vulnerabilities or weaknesses in the organization's overall security posture. Module 9 concludes with a discussion of access control devices commonly deployed by modern operating systems and new technologies in the area of biometrics that can provide strong authentication to existing implementations.

Module 10—Cryptography

Module 10 continues the study of security technologies by describing the underlying foundations of modern cryptosystems as well as their architectures and implementations. The module begins by summarizing the history of cryptography and discussing the various types of ciphers that played key roles in that history. The module also examines some of the mathematical techniques that comprise cryptosystems, including hash functions. The module then extends this discussion by comparing traditional symmetric encryption systems with more modern asymmetric encryption systems and examining the role of asymmetric systems as the foundation of public-key encryption systems. Also covered are the cryptography-based protocols used in secure communications, including HTTPS, S/MIME, and SET. The module then discusses steganography and its emerging role as an effective means of hiding information. The module concludes by revisiting attacks on information security that are specifically targeted at cryptosystems.

Module 11—Implementing Information Security

The preceding modules provide guidelines for how an organization might design its information security program. Module 11 examines the elements critical to *implementing* this design. Key areas in this module include the bull's-eye model for implementing information security and a discussion of whether an organization should outsource components of its information security program. The module also discusses change management, program improvement, and additional planning for business continuity efforts.

Module 12—Information Security Maintenance

Last and most important is the discussion of maintenance and change. Module 12 describes the ongoing technical and administrative evaluation of the information security program that an organization must perform to maintain the security of its information systems. This module explores the controlled administration of changes to modern information systems to prevent the introduction of new security vulnerabilities. Special considerations needed for vulnerability analysis are explored, from Internet penetration testing to wireless network risk assessment. The module concludes with extensive coverage of physical security considerations.

Features

The following features exemplify our approach to teaching information security:

- *Information Security Professionals' Common Bodies of Knowledge*—Because the authors hold both the Certified Information Security Manager (CISM) and Certified Information Systems Security Professional (CISSP) credentials, those knowledge domains have had an influence in the design of this resource. Although care was taken to avoid producing a certification study guide, the authors' backgrounds ensure that their treatment of information security integrates the CISM and CISSP Common Bodies of Knowledge (CBKs).
- *Opening and Closing Scenarios*—Each module opens and closes with a short story that features the same fictional company as it encounters information security issues commonly found in real-life organizations. At the end of each module, a set of discussion questions provides students and instructors with opportunities to discuss the issues suggested by the story as well as offering an opportunity to explore the ethical dimensions of those issues.
- *Clearly Defined Key Terms*—Each key term is defined in a marginal note close to the term's first use. While the terms are referenced in the body of the text, the isolation of the definitions from the discussion allows a smoother presentation of the key terms and supports their standardization throughout all Whitman and Mattord works.
- *In-Depth Features*—Interspersed throughout the modules, these features highlight interesting topics and detailed technical issues, giving students the option of delving into information security topics more deeply.
- *Hands-On Learning*—At the end of each module, students will find a module summary and review questions as well as exercises. In the exercises, students are asked to research, analyze, and write responses to reinforce learning objectives, deepen their understanding of the reading, and examine the information security arena outside the classroom.

New To This Edition

- All graphics and tables are now in color.
- The newest relevant laws and industry trends are covered.
- The content on contingency planning and incident response has been significantly enhanced and moved into a module of its own to give additional emphasis to this critical topic.
- The risk management module has been updated to reflect recent industry changes in risk management methodology.
- The module that encompasses cryptography has been enhanced to include expanded coverage of blockchain and payment system security.
- Increased visibility for terminology used in the industry is provided by the prominent display of key terms throughout this resource and across the Whitman and Mattord series.
- Updated and additional "For More Information" boxes provide Web locations where students can find more information about the subjects being covered in the reading.

MindTap For *Principles of Information Security, Seventh Edition*

The complete text and supporting activities for *Principles of Information Security* are available on Cengage's MindTap platform. It gives you complete control of your course so you can provide engaging content, challenge every learner, and build student confidence. Customize interactive syllabi to emphasize high-priority topics, then add your own material or notes to the eBook as desired. This outcome-driven application gives you the tools needed to empower students and boost both understanding and performance.

Access Everything You Need in One Place

Cut down on prep with the preloaded and organized MindTap course materials. Teach more efficiently with interactive multimedia, assignments, and quizzes. Give your students the power to read, listen, and study on their phones so they can learn on their terms.

Empower Students to Reach Their Potential

Twelve distinct metrics give you actionable insights into student engagement. Identify topics that are troubling your class and instantly communicate with students who are struggling. Students can track their scores to stay motivated toward their goals. Together, you can be unstoppable.

Control Your Course—and Your Content

Get the flexibility to reorder textbook chapters, add your own notes, and embed a variety of content, including Open Educational Resources (OER). Personalize course content to your students' needs. They can even read your notes, add their own, and highlight key text to aid their learning.

Get a Dedicated Team, Whenever You Need Them

MindTap isn't just a tool; it's backed by a personalized team eager to support you. We can help set up your course and tailor it to your specific objectives, so you'll be ready to make an impact from day one. Know we'll be standing by to help you and your students until the final day of the term.

MindTap activities for Whitman and Mattord's *Principles of Information Security* are designed to help students master the skills they need in today's workforce. Research shows employers need critical thinkers, troubleshooters, and creative problem solvers to stay relevant in our fast-paced, technology-driven world. MindTap helps you achieve this with assignments and activities that provide hands-on practice, real-life relevance, and mastery of difficult concepts. Students are guided through assignments that progress from basic knowledge and understanding to more challenging problems.

All MindTap activities and assignments are tied to learning objectives. The hands-on exercises provide real-life application and practice. Readings and "Whiteboard Shorts" support the lecture, while "Security for Life" assignments encourage students to stay current and start practicing lifelong learning. Pre- and post-course assessments allow you to measure how much students have learned using analytics and reporting that make it easy to see where the class stands in terms of progress, engagement, and completion rates. Learn more at *www.cengage.com/mindtap/*.

Instructor Resources

Free to all instructors who adopt *Principles of Information Security* for their courses is a complete package of instructor resources accessible via single sign-on (SSO). Instructors can request an SSO account at *Cengage.com*.

Resources include the following:

- *Instructor's Manual*—This manual includes course objectives, key terms, teaching outlines and tips, quick quizzes, and additional information to help you plan and facilitate your instruction.
- *Solutions Manual*—This resource contains answers and explanations for all end-of-module review questions and exercises.
- *Cengage Testing Powered by Cognero*—A flexible, online system allows you to import, edit, and manipulate content from the text's test bank or elsewhere, including your own favorite test questions; create multiple test versions in an instant; and deliver tests from your LMS, your classroom, or wherever you want.
- *PowerPoint Presentations*—A set of Microsoft PowerPoint slides is included for each module. These slides are meant to be used as a teaching aid for classroom presentations, to be made available to students for module review, or to be printed for classroom distribution. Some tables and figures are included in the PowerPoint slides; however, all are available in the online instructor resources. Instructors are also at liberty to add their own slides.
- *Lab Exercises Available in the MindTap Edition and in the Instructor's Resource Kit (IRK)*—These exercises, written by the authors, can be used to provide technical experience in conjunction with the text. Contact your Cengage learning consultant for more information.
- *Readings and Cases*—Cengage also produced two texts by the authors—*Readings and Cases in the Management of Information Security* (ISBN-13: 9780619216276) and *Readings & Cases in Information Security: Law & Ethics* (ISBN-13: 9781435441576)—which make excellent companion texts. Contact your Cengage learning consultant for more information.
- *Curriculum Model for Programs of Study in Information Security/Cybersecurity*—In addition to the texts authored by this team, a curriculum model for programs of study in information security and cybersecurity is available from the Kennesaw State University (KSU) Institute for Cybersecurity Workforce Development (*https://cyberinstitute.kennesaw.edu/docs/ModelCurriculum-2021.pdf*). This document provides details on the authors' experiences in designing and implementing security coursework and curricula, as well as guidance and lessons learned.

Author Team

Michael Whitman and Herbert Mattord have jointly developed this text to merge knowledge from academic research with practical experience from the business world.

Michael E. Whitman, Ph.D., CISM, CISSP, is a Professor of Information Security and Assurance and the Executive Director of the KSU Institute for Cybersecurity Workforce Development *(cyberinstitute.kennesaw.edu)*. Dr. Whitman is an active researcher in information security, fair and responsible use policies, ethical computing, and curriculum development methodologies. He currently teaches graduate and undergraduate courses in information security and cybersecurity management. He has published articles in the top journals in his field, including *Information Systems Research, Communications of the ACM, Information and Management, Journal of International Business Studies,* and *Journal of Computer Information Systems.* Dr. Whitman is also the Co-Editor-in-Chief of the *Journal of Cybersecurity Education, Research and Practice.* Dr. Whitman is also the co-author of *Management of Information Security* and *Principles of Incident Response and Disaster Recovery,* among other works, all published by Cengage. Prior to his career in academia, Dr. Whitman was an officer in the United States Army, which included duties as Automated Data Processing Systems Security Officer (ADPSSO).

Herbert J. Mattord, Ph.D., CISM, CISSP, completed 24 years of IT industry experience as an application developer, database administrator, project manager, and information security practitioner before joining the faculty of Kennesaw State University in 2002. Dr. Mattord is the Director of Education and Outreach for the KSU Institute for Cybersecurity Workforce Development *(cyberinstitute.kennesaw.edu).* Dr. Mattord is also the Co-Editor-in-Chief of the *Journal of Cybersecurity Education, Research and Practice.* During his career as an IT practitioner, he has been an adjunct professor at Kennesaw State University, Southern Polytechnic State University in Marietta, Georgia, Austin Community College in Austin, Texas, and Texas State University: San Marcos. He currently teaches graduate and undergraduate courses in information security and cybersecurity. He was formerly the Manager of Corporate Information Technology Security at Georgia-Pacific Corporation, where much of the practical knowledge found in this resource was acquired. Dr. Mattord is also the co-author of *Management of Information Security, Principles of Incident Response and Disaster Recovery,* and other works, all published by Cengage.

Acknowledgments

The authors would like to thank their families for their support and understanding for the many hours dedicated to this project—hours taken away, in many cases, from family activities.

Contributors

Several people and organizations also provided materials for this resource, and we thank them for their contributions:

- The National Institute of Standards and Technology (NIST) is the source of many references, tables, figures, and other content used in many places in the text.

Reviewers

We are indebted to the following reviewers for their perceptive feedback during the module-by-module reviews of the text:

- Paul Witman, California Lutheran University
- Mia Plachkinova, Kennesaw State University

Special Thanks

The authors thank the editorial and production teams at Cengage. Their diligent and professional efforts greatly enhanced the final product:

- Dan Seiter, Developmental Editor
- Danielle Klahr, Associate Product Manager
- Christina Nyren, Content Manager

In addition, several professional organizations, commercial organizations, and individuals aided the development of the text by providing information and inspiration. The authors wish to acknowledge their contributions:

- Donn Parker
- Our colleagues in the Department of Information Systems and the Coles College of Business at Kennesaw State University

Our Commitment

The authors are committed to serving the needs of adopters and users of this resource. We would be pleased and honored to receive feedback on the text and supporting materials. You can contact us at *infosec@kennesaw.edu*.

Foreword

Information security is an art more than a science, and the mastery of protecting information requires multidisciplinary knowledge of a huge quantity of information plus experience and skill. You will find much of what you need here in this resource as the authors take you through the security systems development life cycle using real-life scenarios to introduce each topic. The authors provide their perspective from many years of real-life experience, combined with their academic approach for a rich learning experience expertly presented in this text. You have chosen the authors and this resource well.

Because you are reading this, you are most likely working toward a career in information security or at least have serious interest in information security. You must anticipate that just about everybody hates the constraints that security puts on their work. This includes both the good guys and the bad guys—except for malicious hackers who love the security we install as a challenge to be beaten. We concentrate on stopping the intentional wrongdoers because it applies to stopping the accidental ones as well. Security to protect against accidental wrongdoers is not good enough against those with intent.

I have spent 40 years of my life in a field that I found to be exciting and rewarding, working with computers and pitting my wits against malicious people, and you will too. Security controls and practices include logging on and off, using passwords, encrypting and backing up vital information, locking doors and drawers, motivating stakeholders to support security, and installing antivirus software.

These means of protection have no benefit except rarely, when adversities occur. Good security is in effect when nothing bad happens, and when nothing bad happens, who needs security? Nowadays, one reason we need security is because the law, regulations, and auditors say so—especially if we deal with the personal information of others, electronic money, intellectual property, and keeping ahead of the competition.

There is great satisfaction in knowing that your employer's information and systems are reasonably secure and that you are paid a good salary, are the center of attention in emergencies, and are applying your wits against the bad guys. This makes up for the downside of your security work. It is no job for perfectionists because you will almost never be fully successful, and there will always be vulnerabilities that you aren't aware of or that the bad guys discover first. Our enemies have a great advantage over us. They have to find only one vulnerability and one target to attack in a known place, electronically or physically at a time of their choosing, while we must defend from potentially millions of attacks against assets and vulnerabilities that are no longer in one computer room but are spread all over the world. It's like playing a game in which you don't know your opponents and where they are, what they are doing, or why they are doing it, and they are secretly changing the rules as they play. You must be highly ethical, defensive, secretive, and cautious. Bragging about the great security you are employing might tip off the enemy. Enjoy the few successes that you experience, for you will not even know about some of them.

Remember that when working in security, you are in a virtual army defending your employer and stakeholders from their enemies. From your point of view, the enemies will probably think and act irrationally, but from their perspective, they are perfectly rational, with serious personal problems to solve and gains to be made by violating your security. You are no longer just a techie with the challenging job of installing technological controls in systems and networks. Most of your work should be in assisting potential victims to protect themselves from information adversities and dealing with your smart but often irrational enemies, even though you rarely see or even identify them. I spent a major part of my security career hunting down computer criminals and interviewing them and their victims, trying to obtain insights to do a better job of defending from their attacks.

Likewise, you should use every opportunity to seek out attackers and understand what motivates their actions and how they operate. This experience gives you great cachet as a real and unique expert, even with minimal exposure to only a few enemies.

Comprehensiveness is an important part of the game you play for real stakes because the enemy will likely seek the easiest way to attack vulnerabilities and assets that you haven't fully protected yet or even know exist. For example, a threat that is rarely found on threat lists is endangerment of assets—putting information assets in harm's way. Endangerment is also one of the most common violations by security professionals when they reveal too much about their security and loss experience.

You must be thorough and meticulous and document everything pertinent, in case your competence is questioned and to meet the requirements of the Sarbanes–Oxley Law. Keep your documents safely locked away. Documentation is important so that when adversity hits and you lose the game, you will have proof of being diligent in spite of the loss. Otherwise, your career could be damaged, or at least your effectiveness will be diminished.

For example, if the loss occurred because management failed to give you an adequate budget and support for security you knew you required, you need to have documented that failure before the incident occurred. Don't brag about how great your security is, because it can always be beaten. Keep and expand checklists for everything: threats, vulnerabilities, assets, key potential victims, suspects of wrongdoing, security supporters and nonsupporters, attacks, enemies, criminal justice resources, auditors, regulators, and legal counsel. To assist your stakeholders, who are the front-line defenders of their information and systems, identify what they must protect and know the real extent of their security.

Make sure that upper management and other people to whom you report understand the nature of your job and its limitations.

Use the best possible security practices yourself to set a good example. You will have a huge collection of sensitive passwords to do your job. Find a way to keep these credentials accessible yet secure—maybe with a smartphone app. Know as much as possible about the systems and networks in your organization, and have access to experts who know the rest. Make good friends of local and national criminal justice officials, your organization's lawyers, insurance risk managers, human resources people, facilities managers, and auditors. Audits are one of the most powerful controls your organization has. Remember that people hate security and must be properly motivated by penalties and rewards to make it work. Seek ways to make security invisible or transparent to stakeholders while keeping it effective. Don't recommend or install controls or practices that stakeholders won't support, because they will beat you every time by making it look like the controls are effective when they are not—a situation worse than no security at all.

One of the most exciting parts of the job is the insight you gain about the inner workings and secrets of your organization, its business, and its culture. As an information security consultant, I was privileged to learn about the culture and secrets of more than 250 of the largest corporations throughout the world. I had the opportunity to interview and advise the most powerful business executives, if only for a few minutes of their valuable time. You should always be ready with a "silver bullet," a high-impact solution to recommend in your short time with top management for the greatest benefit of enterprise security.

Carefully learn the limits of management's security appetites. Know the nature of the business, whether it is a government department or a hotly competitive business. I once found myself in a meeting with a board of directors intensely discussing the protection of their greatest trade secret, the manufacturing process of their new disposable diapers.

Finally, we come to the last important bit of advice. Be trustworthy and develop mutual trust among your peers. Your most important objectives are not just risk reduction and increased security. They also include diligence to avoid negligence and endangerment, compliance with all of the laws and standards, and enablement when security becomes a competitive or budget issue. To achieve these objectives, you must develop a trusting exchange of the most sensitive security intelligence among your peers so you'll know where your organization stands relative to other enterprises. But be discreet and careful about it. You need to know the generally accepted and current security solutions. If the information you exchange is exposed, it could ruin your career and others, and could create a disaster for your organization. Your personal and ethical performance must be spotless, and you must protect your reputation at all costs.

Pay particular attention to the ethics section of this resource. I recommend that you join the Information Systems Security Association, become active in it, and become professionally certified as soon as you are qualified. My favorite certification is the Certified Information Systems Security Professional (CISSP) from the International Information System Security Certification Consortium.

Donn B. Parker, CISSP Retired
Sunnyvale, California

Introduction to Information Security

Upon completion of this material, you should be able to:

1. Define information security
2. Discuss the history of computer security and explain how it evolved into information security
3. Define key terms and critical concepts of information security
4. Describe the information security roles of professionals within an organization

Do not figure on opponents not attacking; worry about your own lack of preparation.

—The Book of Five Rings

Opening Scenario

For Amy, the day began like any other at the Sequential Label and Supply Company (SLS) help desk. Taking calls and helping office workers with computer problems was not glamorous, but she enjoyed the work; it was challenging and paid well enough. Some of her friends in the industry worked at bigger companies, some at cutting-edge tech companies, but they all agreed that jobs in information technology were a good way to pay the bills.

The phone rang, as it did about four times an hour. The first call of the day, from a worried user hoping Amy could help him out of a jam, seemed typical. The call display on her monitor showed some of the facts: the user's name, his phone number and department, where his office was on the company campus, and a list of his past calls to the help desk.

"Hi, Bob," she said. "Did you get that document formatting problem squared away?"

"Sure did, Amy. But now I have another issue I need your help with."

"Sure, Bob. Tell me about it."

"Well, my PC is acting weird," Bob said. "When I open my e-mail app, my mailbox doesn't respond to the mouse or the keyboard."

"Did you try a reboot yet?"

"Sure did. But the program wouldn't close, and I had to turn my PC off. After it restarted, I opened my e-mail again, and it's just like it was before—no response at all. The other stuff is working OK, but really, really slowly. Even my Web browser is sluggish."

"OK, Bob. We've tried the usual stuff we can do over the phone. Let me open a case, and I'll have a tech contact you for remote diagnosis as soon as possible."

Amy looked up at the help desk ticket status monitor on the wall at the end of the room. She saw that only two technicians were currently dispatched to user support, and because it was the day shift, four technicians were available. "Shouldn't be long at all, Bob."

She hung up and typed her notes into the company's trouble ticket tracking system. She assigned the newly generated case to the user dispatch queue, which would page the user support technician with the details in a few minutes.

A moment later, Amy looked up to see Charlie Moody, the senior manager of the server administration team, walking briskly down the hall. He was being trailed by three of his senior technicians as he made a beeline from his office to the room where the company servers were kept in a carefully controlled environment. They all looked worried.

Just then, Amy's screen beeped to alert her of a new e-mail. She glanced down. The screen beeped again—and again. It started beeping constantly. She clicked the envelope icon, and after a short delay, the mail window opened. She had 47 new e-mails in her inbox. She opened one from Davey Martinez in the Accounting Department. The subject line said, "Wait till you see this." The message body read, "Funniest joke you'll see today." Davey often sent her interesting and funny e-mails, and she clicked the file attachment icon to open the latest joke.

After that click, her PC showed the Windows "please wait" cursor for a second and then the mouse pointer reappeared. Nothing happened. She clicked the next e-mail message in the queue. Nothing happened. Her phone rang again. She clicked the icon on her computer desktop to activate the call management software and activated her headset. "Hello, Help Desk, how can I help you?" She couldn't greet the caller by name because her computer had not responded.

"Hello, this is Erin Williams in Receiving."

Amy glanced down at her screen. Still no tracking system. She glanced up to the tally board and was surprised to see the inbound-call counter tallying up waiting calls like digits on a stopwatch. Amy had never seen so many calls come in at one time.

"Hi, Erin," Amy said. "What's up?"

"Nothing," Erin answered. "That's the problem." The rest of the call was a replay of Bob's, except that Amy had to jot notes down on a legal pad. She couldn't notify the user support team either. She looked at the ticket status monitor again. It had gone dark. No numbers at all.

Then she saw Charlie walking quickly down the hall from the server room. His expression had changed from worried to frantic.

Amy picked up the phone again. She wanted to check with her supervisor about what to do now. There was no dial tone.

Introduction To Information Security

Every organization, whether public or private and regardless of size, has information it wants to protect. It could be customer information, product or service information, and/or employee information. Regardless of the source, it is the organization's job to protect the information to the best of its ability. Organizations have a responsibility to all its stakeholders to protect that information. Unfortunately, there aren't enough security professionals to go around. As a result, everyone in the organization must have a working knowledge of how to protect the information assigned to them and how to assist in preventing the unauthorized disclosure, damage, or destruction of that information. After all, if you're not part of the solution, you're part of the problem.

This module's opening scenario illustrates that information risks and controls may not be in balance at SLS. Though Amy works in a technical support role to help users with their problems, she did not recall her training about malicious e-mail attachments, such as worms or viruses, and fell victim to this form of attack herself. Understanding how malicious software (malware) might be the cause of a company's problems is an important skill for information technology (IT) support staff as well as users. SLS's management also showed signs of confusion and seemed to have no idea how to contain this kind of incident. If you were in Amy's place and were faced with a similar situation, what would you do? How would you react? Would it occur to you that something far more insidious than a technical malfunction was happening at your company? As you explore the modules of this book and learn more about information security, you will become more capable of answering these questions. But, before you can begin studying details about the discipline of information security, you must first know its history and evolution.

The history of information security begins with the concept of **computer security**. The need for computer security arose during World War II when the first mainframe computers were developed and used to aid computations for communication code-breaking messages from enemy cryptographic devices like the Enigma, shown in Figure 1-1. Multiple levels of security were implemented to protect these devices and the missions they served. This required new processes as well as tried-and-true methods needed to maintain data confidentiality. Access to sensitive military locations, for example, was controlled by means of badges, keys, and the facial recognition of authorized personnel by security guards. The growing need to maintain national security eventually led to more complex and technologically sophisticated computer security safeguards.

computer security

In the early days of computers, this term specified the protection of the physical location and assets associated with computer technology from outside threats, but it later came to represent all actions taken to protect computer systems from losses.

During these early years, information security was a straightforward process composed predominantly of physical security and simple document classification schemes. The primary threats to security were physical theft of equipment, espionage against products of the systems, and sabotage. One of the first documented security problems that fell outside these categories occurred in the early 1960s, when a systems administrator was working on a MOTD (message of the day) file while another administrator was editing the password file. A software glitch mixed the two files, and the entire password file was printed to every output file.[1]

The 1960s

During the Cold War, many more mainframe computers were brought online to accomplish more complex and sophisticated tasks. These mainframes required a less cumbersome process of communication than mailing magnetic tapes between computer centers. In response to this need, the U.S. Department of Defense's Advanced Research Projects Agency (ARPA) began examining the feasibility of a redundant, networked communications system to support the military's exchange of information. In 1968, Dr. Larry Roberts developed the ARPANET project, which evolved into what we now know as the Internet. Figure 1-2 is an excerpt from his program plan.

 For more information on Dr. Roberts, including links to his recorded presentations, visit the Internet Hall of Fame at *www.internethalloffame.org/inductees/lawrence-roberts*.

Earlier versions of the German code machine Enigma were first broken by the Poles in the 1930s. The British and Americans managed to break later, more complex versions during World War II. The increasingly complex versions of the Enigma, especially the submarine or *Unterseeboot* version of the Enigma, caused considerable anguish to Allied forces before finally being cracked. The information gained from decrypted transmissions was used to anticipate the actions of German armed forces. "Some ask why, if we were reading the Enigma, we did not win the war earlier. One might ask, instead, when, if ever, we would have won the war if we hadn't read it."

Source: © kamilpetran/Shutterstock.com.[2]

Figure 1-1   The Enigma

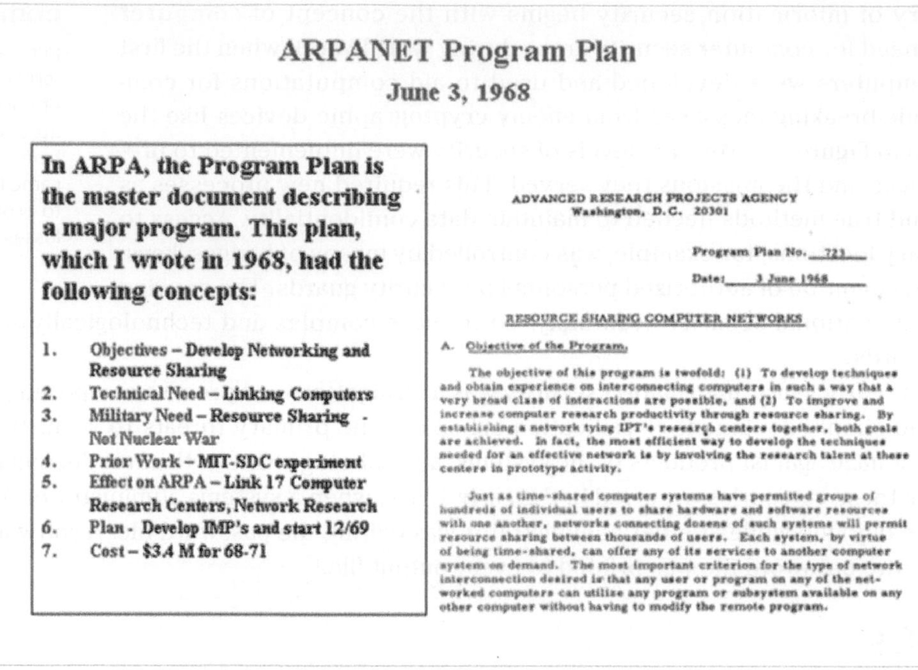

Source: Courtesy of Dr. Lawrence Roberts. Used with permission.[3]

ARPANET Program Plan

June 3, 1968

In ARPA, the Program Plan is the master document describing a major program. This plan, which I wrote in 1968, had the following concepts:

1. Objectives – **Develop Networking and Resource Sharing**
2. Technical Need – **Linking Computers**
3. Military Need – **Resource Sharing** - Not Nuclear War
4. Prior Work – **MIT-SDC experiment**
5. Effect on ARPA – **Link 17 Computer Research Centers, Network Research**
6. Plan - Develop IMP's and start 12/69
7. Cost – $3.4 M for 68-71

ADVANCED RESEARCH PROJECTS AGENCY
Washington, D.C. 20301

Program Plan No. 723

Date: 3 June 1968

RESOURCE SHARING COMPUTER NETWORKS

A. Objective of the Program.

The objective of this program is twofold: (1) To develop techniques and obtain experience on interconnecting computers in such a way that a very broad class of interactions are possible, and (2) To improve and increase computer research productivity through resource sharing. By establishing a network tying IPT's research centers together, both goals are achieved. In fact, the most efficient way to develop the techniques needed for an effective network is by involving the research talent at these centers in prototype activity.

Just as time-shared computer systems have permitted groups of hundreds of individual users to share hardware and software resources with one another, networks connecting dozens of such systems will permit resource sharing between thousands of users. Each system, by virtue of being time-shared, can offer any of its services to another computer system on demand. The most important criterion for the type of network interconnection desired is that any user or program on any of the networked computers can utilize any program or subsystem available on any other computer without having to modify the remote program.

Figure 1-2   Development of the ARPANET

The 1970s and '80s

During the next decade, ARPANET became more popular and saw wider use, increasing the potential for its misuse. In 1973, Internet pioneer Robert M. Metcalfe (pictured in Figure 1-3) identified fundamental problems with ARPANET security. As one of the creators of Ethernet, a dominant local area networking protocol, he knew that individual remote sites did not have sufficient controls and safeguards to protect data from unauthorized remote users. Other problems abounded, including vulnerability of password structure and formats, lack of safety procedures for dial-up connections, and nonexistent user identification and authorizations. Phone numbers were widely distributed and openly publicized on the walls of phone booths, giving hackers easy access to ARPANET. Because of the range and frequency of computer security violations and the explosion in the numbers of hosts and users on ARPANET, network security was commonly referred to as network insecurity.[4] For a timeline that includes seminal studies of computer security, see Table 1-1.

Security that went beyond protecting physical computing devices and their locations effectively began with a single paper published by the RAND Corporation in February 1970 for the Department of Defense. RAND Report R-609 attempted to define the multiple controls and mechanisms necessary for the protection of a computerized data processing system. The document was classified for almost 10 years, and is now considered to be the paper that started the study of computer security.

The security—or lack thereof—of systems sharing resources inside the Department of Defense was brought to the attention of researchers in the spring and summer of 1967. At that time, systems were being acquired at a rapid rate, and securing them was a pressing concern both for the military and defense contractors.

Source: U.S. Department of Commerce. Used with permission.

Figure 1-3   Dr. Metcalfe receiving the National Medal of Technology

Table 1-1   Key Dates in Information Security

Date	Document
1968	Maurice Wilkes discusses password security in *Time-Sharing Computer Systems*.
1970	Willis H. Ware authors the report "Security Controls for Computer Systems: Report of Defense Science Board Task Force on Computer Security—RAND Report R-609," which was not declassified until 1979. It became known as the seminal work identifying the need for computer security.
1973	Schell, Downey, and Popek examine the need for additional security in military systems in *Preliminary Notes on the Design of Secure Military Computer Systems*.
1975	The Federal Information Processing Standards (FIPS) examines DES (Digital Encryption Standard) in the *Federal Register*.
1978	Bisbey and Hollingworth publish their study "Protection Analysis: Final Report," which discussed the Protection Analysis project created by ARPA to better understand the vulnerabilities of operating system security and examine the possibility of automated vulnerability detection techniques in existing system software.[5]
1979	Morris and Thompson author "Password Security: A Case History," published in the *Communications of the Association for Computing Machinery* (ACM). The paper examined the design history of a password security scheme on a remotely accessed, time-sharing system.
	Dennis Ritchie publishes "On the Security of UNIX" and "Protection of Data File Contents," which discussed secure user IDs, secure group IDs, and the problems inherent in the systems.
1982	The U.S. Department of Defense Computer Security Evaluation Center publishes the first version of the Trusted Computer Security (TCSEC) documents, which came to be known as the Rainbow Series.
1984	Grampp and Morris write "The UNIX System: UNIX Operating System Security." In this report, the authors examined four "important handles to computer security": physical control of premises and computer facilities, management commitment to security objectives, education of employees, and administrative procedures aimed at increased security.[6]
	Reeds and Weinberger publish "File Security and the UNIX System Crypt Command." Their premise was: "No technique can be secure against wiretapping or its equivalent on the computer. Therefore, no technique can be secure against the system administrator or other privileged users . . . the naive user has no chance."[7]
1992	Researchers for the Internet Engineering Task Force, working at the Naval Research Laboratory, develop the Simple Internet Protocol Plus (SIPP) Security protocols, creating what is now known as IPSEC security.

In June 1967, ARPA formed a task force to study the process of securing classified information systems. The task force was assembled in October 1967 and met regularly to formulate recommendations, which ultimately became the contents of RAND Report R-609. The document was declassified in 1979 and released as *Security Controls for Computer Systems: Report of Defense Science Board Task Force on Computer Security—RAND Report R-609-1*.[8] The content of the two documents is identical with the exception of two transmittal memorandums.

 For more information on the RAND Report, visit www.rand.org/pubs/reports/R609-1.html.

RAND Report R-609 was the first widely recognized published document to identify the role of management and policy issues in computer security. It noted that the wide use of networking components in military information systems introduced security risks that could not be mitigated by the routine practices then used to secure these systems. Figure 1-4 shows an illustration of computer network vulnerabilities from the 1979 release of this document. This paper signaled a pivotal moment in computer security history—the scope of computer security expanded significantly from the safety of physical locations and hardware to include the following:

- Securing the data
- Limiting random and unauthorized access to that data
- Involving personnel from multiple levels of the organization in information security

Computer Network Vulnerabilities

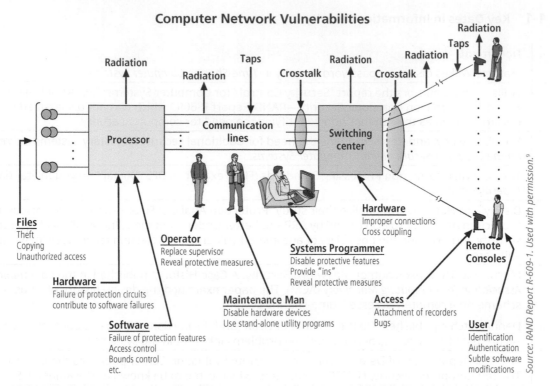

Figure 1-4   Illustration of computer network vulnerabilities from RAND Report R-609

MULTICS

Much of the early research on computer security centered on a system called Multiplexed Information and Computing Service (MULTICS). Although it is now obsolete, MULTICS is noteworthy because it was the first operating system to integrate security into its core functions. It was a mainframe, time-sharing operating system developed in the mid-1960s by a consortium of General Electric (GE), Bell Labs, and the Massachusetts Institute of Technology (MIT).

 For more information on the MULTICS project, visit *web.mit.edu/multics-history.*

In 1969, not long after the restructuring of the MULTICS project, several of its developers (Ken Thompson, Dennis Ritchie, Rudd Canaday, and Doug McIlroy) created a new operating system called UNIX. While the MULTICS system implemented multiple security levels and passwords, the UNIX system did not. Its primary function, text processing, did not require the same level of security as that of its predecessor. Not until the early 1970s did even the simplest component of security, the password function, become a component of UNIX.

In the late 1970s, the microprocessor brought the personal computer (PC) and a new age of computing. The PC became the workhorse of modern computing, moving it out of the data center. This decentralization of data processing systems in the 1980s gave rise to networking—the interconnecting of PCs and mainframe computers, which enabled the entire computing community to make all its resources work together.

In the early 1980s, TCP (the Transmission Control Protocol) and IP (the Internet Protocol) were developed and became the primary protocols for the ARPANET, eventually becoming the protocols used on the Internet to this day. During the same time frame, the hierarchical Domain Name System, or DNS, was developed. The first dial-up Internet service provider (ISP)—The World, operated by Standard Tool & Die—came online, allowing home users to access the Internet. Prior to that, vendors like CompuServe, GEnie, Prodigy, and Delphi had provided dial-up access for online computer services, while independent bulletin board systems (BBSs) became popular for sharing information among their subscribers.

 For more information on the history of the Internet, visit *www.livescience.com/20727-internet-history.html.*

In the mid-1980s, the U.S. government passed several key pieces of legislation that formalized the recognition of computer security as a critical issue for federal information systems. The Computer Fraud and Abuse Act of 1986 and the Computer Security Act of 1987 defined computer security and specified responsibilities and associated penalties. These laws and others are covered in Module 6.

In 1988, the Defense Advanced Research Projects Agency (DARPA) within the Department of Defense created the Computer Emergency Response Team (CERT) to address network security.

The 1990s

At the close of the 20th century, networks of computers became more common, as did the need to connect them to each other. This gave rise to the Internet, the first global network of networks. The Internet was made available to the general public in the 1990s after decades of being the domain of government, academia, and dedicated industry professionals. The Internet brought connectivity to virtually all computers that could reach a phone line or an Internet-connected local area network (LAN). After the Internet was commercialized, the technology became pervasive, reaching almost every corner of the globe with an expanding array of uses.

Since its inception as ARPANET, a tool for sharing Defense Department information, the Internet has become an interconnection of millions of networks. At first, these connections were based on de facto standards because industry standards for interconnected networks did not exist. These de facto standards did little to ensure the security of information, though some degree of security was introduced as precursor technologies were widely adopted and became industry standards. However, early Internet deployment treated security as a low priority. In fact, many problems that plague e-mail on the Internet today result from this early lack of security. At that time, when all Internet and e-mail users were presumably trustworthy computer scientists, mail server authentication and e-mail encryption did not seem necessary. Early computing approaches relied on security that was built into the physical environment of the data center that housed the computers. As networked computers became the dominant style of computing, the ability to physically secure a networked computer was lost, and the stored information became more exposed to security threats.

In 1993, the first DEFCON conference was held in Las Vegas. Originally, it was established as a gathering for people interested in information security, including authors, lawyers, government employees, and law enforcement officials. A compelling topic was the involvement of hackers in creating an interesting venue for the exchange of information between two adversarial groups—the "white hats" of law enforcement and security professionals and the "black hats" of hackers and computer criminals.

In the late 1990s and into the 2000s, many large corporations began publicly integrating security into their organizations. Antivirus products became extremely popular, and information security began to emerge as an independent discipline.

2000 to Present

Today, the Internet brings millions of unsecured computer networks and billions of computer systems into continuous communication with each other. The security of each computer's stored information is contingent on the security level of every other computer to which it is connected. Recent years have seen a growing awareness of the need to improve information security, as well as a realization that information security is important to national defense. The growing threat of cyberattacks has made governments and companies more aware of the need to defend the computerized control systems of utilities and other critical infrastructure. Other growing concerns are the threat of countries engaging in information warfare and the possibility that business and personal information systems could become casualties if they are undefended. Since 2000, Sarbanes–Oxley and other laws related to privacy and corporate responsibility have affected computer security.

The attack on the World Trade Centers on September 11, 2001, resulted in major legislation changes related to computer security, specifically to facilitate law enforcement's ability to collect information about terrorism. The USA PATRIOT Act of 2001 and its follow-up laws are discussed in Module 6.

The 21st century also saw the massive rise in mobile computing, with smartphones and tablets possessing more computing power than early-era mainframe systems. Embedded devices have seen the creation of computing built into everyday objects in the Internet of Things (IoT). Each of these networked computing platforms brings its own set of security issues and concerns as they are connected into networks with legacy platforms and cloud-based service delivery systems. Technology that is supposed to be seamless turns out to have many connection points, each with its own set of security and reliability vulnerabilities. The emergence of tools to deal with now-routine threats at large scale has led to the development of complete solutions for unified threat management, data loss prevention, and security information and event management. The solutions will be explored in more detail in later modules.

Wireless networking, and the risks associated with it, has become ubiquitous and pervasive, with widely available connectivity providing ready access to the Internet as well as local networks that are usually ill-prepared for access by the public. This opens the local net as well as the Internet to a constant threat of anonymous attacks from very large numbers of people and devices.

The threat environment has grown from the semiprofessional hacker defacing Web sites for amusement to professional cybercriminals maximizing revenue from theft and extortion, as well as government-sponsored cyberwarfare groups striking military, government, and commercial targets by intent and by opportunity. The attack sources of today are well-prepared and are attacking all connected public and private systems and users.

What Is Security?

Security is protection. Protection from adversaries—those who would do harm, intentionally or otherwise—is the ultimate objective of security. National security, for example, is a multilayered system that protects the sovereignty of a state, its people, its resources, and its territory. Achieving the appropriate level of security for an organization also requires a multifaceted system. A successful organization should have multiple layers of security in place to protect its people, operations, physical infrastructure, functions, communications, and information.

The Committee on National Security Systems (CNSS) defines **information security** as the protection of information and its critical elements, including the systems and hardware that use, store, and transmit the information.[10] Figure 1-5 shows that information security includes the broad areas of information security management, data security, and **network security**. The CNSS model of information security evolved from a concept developed by the computer security industry called the C.I.A. triad. The **C.I.A. triad** (see Figure 1-6) has been the standard for computer security in both industry and government since the development of the mainframe. This standard is based on the three characteristics of information that give it value to organizations: confidentiality, integrity, and availability. The security of these three characteristics is as important today as it has always been, but the C.I.A. triad model is generally viewed as no longer adequate in addressing the constantly changing environment. The threats to the confidentiality, integrity, and availability of information have evolved into a vast collection of events, including accidental or intentional damage, destruction, theft, unintended or unauthorized modification, or other misuse from human or nonhuman threats. This vast array of

security

A state of being secure and free from danger or harm; also, the actions taken to make someone or something secure.

information security

Protection of the confidentiality, integrity, and availability of information assets, whether in storage, processing, or transmission, via the application of policy, education, training and awareness, and technology.

network security

A subset of communications security; the protection of voice and data networking components, connections, and content.

C.I.A. triad

The industry standard for computer security since the development of the mainframe; the standard is based on three characteristics that describe the attributes of information that are important to protect: confidentiality, integrity, and availability.

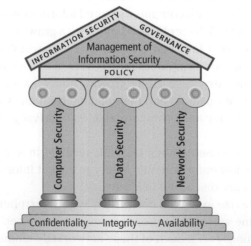

Figure 1-5   Components of information security

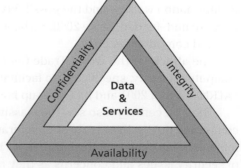

Figure 1-6   The C.I.A. triad

constantly evolving threats has prompted the development of a more robust model that addresses the complexities of the current information security environment. The expanded model consists of a list of critical characteristics of information, which are described in the next section. C.I.A. triad terminology is used in this module because of the breadth of material that is based on it.

Key Information Security Concepts

This book uses many terms and concepts that are essential to any discussion of information security. Some of these terms are illustrated in Figure 1-7; all are covered in greater detail in subsequent modules.

- **Access**—A subject or object's ability to use, manipulate, modify, or affect another subject or object. Authorized users have legal access to a system, whereas hackers must gain illegal access to a system. Access controls regulate this ability.

- **Asset**—The organizational resource that is being protected. An asset can be logical, such as a Web site, software information, or data; or an asset can be physical, such as a person, computer system, hardware, or other tangible object. Assets, particularly information assets, are the focus of what security efforts are attempting to protect.

- **Attack**—An intentional or unintentional act that can damage or otherwise compromise information and the systems that support it. Attacks can be active or passive, intentional or unintentional, and direct or indirect. Someone who casually reads sensitive information not intended for his or her use is committing a passive attack. A hacker attempting to break into an information system is an intentional attack. A lightning strike that causes a building fire is an unintentional attack. A direct attack is perpetrated by a hacker using a PC to break into a system. An indirect attack is a hacker compromising a system and using it to attack other systems—for example, as part of a botnet (slang for *robot network*). This group of compromised computers, running software of the attacker's choosing, can operate autonomously or under the attacker's direct control to attack systems and steal user information or conduct distributed denial-of-service attacks. Direct attacks originate from the threat itself. Indirect attacks originate from a compromised system or resource that is malfunctioning or working under the control of a threat.

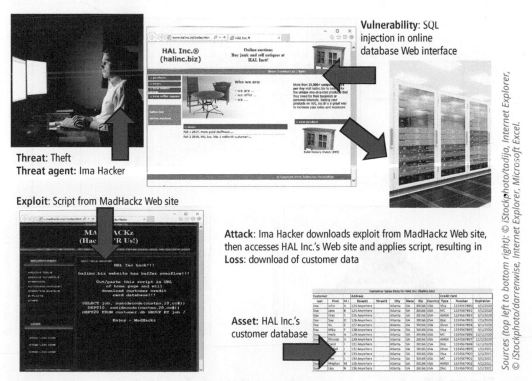

Figure 1-7   Key concepts in information security

- **Control, safeguard, or countermeasure**—Security mechanisms, policies, or procedures that can successfully counter attacks, reduce risk, resolve vulnerabilities, and otherwise improve security within an organization. The various levels and types of controls are discussed more fully in the following modules.
- **Exploit**—A technique used to compromise a system. This term can be a verb or a noun. Threat agents may attempt to exploit a system or other information asset by using it illegally for their personal gain. Or, an exploit can be a documented process to take advantage of a vulnerability or exposure, usually in software, that is either inherent in the software or created by the attacker. Exploits make use of existing software tools or custom-made software components.
- **Exposure**—A condition or state of being exposed; in information security, exposure exists when a vulnerability is known to an attacker.
- **Loss**—A single instance of an information asset suffering damage or destruction, unintended or unauthorized modification or disclosure, or denial of use. When an organization's information is stolen, it has suffered a loss.
- **Protection profile** or **security posture**—The entire set of controls and safeguards—including policy, education, training and awareness, and technology—that the organization implements to protect the asset. The terms are sometimes used interchangeably with the term *security program*, although a security program often comprises managerial aspects of security, including planning, personnel, and subordinate programs.
- **Risk**—The probability of an unwanted occurrence, such as an adverse event or loss. Organizations must minimize risk to match their risk appetite—the quantity and nature of risk they are willing to accept.
- **Subjects** and **objects of attack**—A computer can be either the subject of an attack—an agent entity used to conduct the attack—or the object of an attack: the target entity. See Figure 1-8. A computer can also be both the subject and object of an attack. For example, it can be compromised by an attack (object) and then used to attack other systems (subject).
- **Threat**—Any event or circumstance that has the potential to adversely affect operations and assets. The term *threat source* is commonly used interchangeably with the more generic term *threat*. The two terms are technically distinct, but to simplify discussion, the text will continue to use the term *threat* to describe threat sources.
- **Threat agent**—The specific instance or a component of a threat. For example, the threat source of "trespass or espionage" is a category of potential danger to information assets, while "external professional hacker" (like Kevin Mitnick, who was convicted of hacking into phone systems) is a specific threat agent. A lightning strike, hailstorm, or tornado is a threat agent that is part of the threat source known as "acts of God/acts of nature."

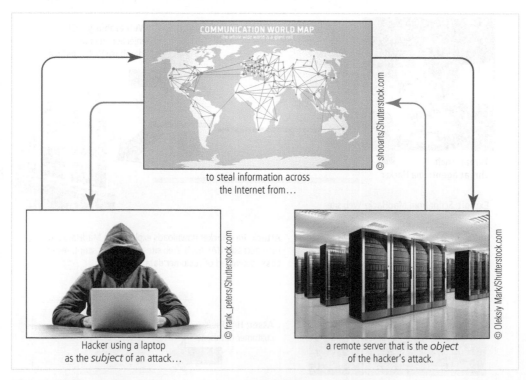

to steal information across
the Internet from...

Hacker using a laptop
as the *subject* of an attack...

a remote server that is the *object*
of the hacker's attack.

Figure 1-8 Computer as the subject and object of an attack

- **Threat event**—An occurrence of an event caused by a threat agent. An example of a threat event might be damage caused by a storm. This term is commonly used interchangeably with the term *attack*.
- **Threat source**—A category of objects, people, or other entities that represents the origin of danger to an asset—in other words, a category of threat agents. Threat sources are always present and can be purposeful or undirected. For example, threat agent "hackers," as part of the threat source "acts of trespass or espionage," purposely threaten unprotected information systems, while threat agent "severe storms," as part of the threat source "acts of God/acts of nature," incidentally threaten buildings and their contents.
- **Vulnerability**—A potential weakness in an asset or its defensive control system(s). Some examples of vulnerabilities are a flaw in a software package, an unprotected system port, and an unlocked door. Some well-known vulnerabilities have been examined, documented, and published; others remain latent (or undiscovered).

Critical Characteristics of Information

The value of information comes from the characteristics it possesses. When a characteristic of information changes, the value of that information either increases or, more commonly, decreases. Some characteristics affect information's value to users more than others, depending on circumstances. For example, timeliness of information can be a critical factor because information loses much or all of its value when delivered too late. Though information security professionals and end users share an understanding of the characteristics of information, tensions can arise when the need to secure information from threats conflicts with the end users' need for unhindered access to it. For instance, end users may perceive two-factor authentication in their login—which requires an acknowledgment notification on their smartphone—to be an unnecessary annoyance. Information security professionals, however, may consider two-factor authentication necessary to ensure that only authorized users access the organization's systems and data. Each critical characteristic of information—that is, the expanded C.I.A. triad—is defined in the following sections.

Confidentiality

Confidentiality ensures that *only* users with the rights, privileges, and need to access information are able to do so. When unauthorized individuals or systems view information, its confidentiality is breached. To protect the confidentiality of information, you can use several measures, including the following:

- Information classification
- Secure document storage
- Application of general security policies
- Education of information custodians and end users

Confidentiality, like most characteristics of information, is interdependent with other characteristics and is closely related to the characteristic known as privacy. The relationship between these two characteristics is covered in more detail in Module 6. The value of confidentiality is especially high for personal information about employees, customers, or patients. People who transact with an organization expect that their personal information will remain confidential, whether the organization is a federal agency, such as the Internal Revenue Service, a healthcare facility, or a business. Problems arise when companies disclose confidential information. Sometimes this disclosure is intentional, but disclosure of confidential information also happens by mistake—for example, when confidential information is mistakenly e-mailed to someone *outside* the organization rather than to someone *inside* it.

Other examples of confidentiality breaches include an employee throwing away a document that contains critical information without shredding it, or a hacker who successfully breaks into an internal database of a Web-based organization and steals sensitive information about its clients, such as names, addresses, and credit card numbers.

As a consumer, you give up pieces of personal information in exchange for convenience or value almost daily. By using a "members" card at a grocery store, you disclose some of your spending habits. When you fill out an online survey, you exchange pieces of your personal history for access to online privileges. When you sign up for a free magazine, Web resource, or free software application, you provide **personally identifiable information (PII)**. The bits and pieces of personal information you

confidentiality

An attribute of information that describes how data is protected from disclosure or exposure to unauthorized individuals or systems.

personally identifiable information (PII)

Information about a person's history, background, and attributes that can be used to commit identity theft; typically includes a person's name, address, Social Security number, family information, employment history, and financial information.

integrity

An attribute of information that describes how data is whole, complete, and uncorrupted.

disclose may be copied, sold, replicated, distributed, and eventually coalesced into profiles and even complete dossiers of you and your life.

Integrity

Information has **integrity** when it is in its expected state and can be trusted. The integrity of information is threatened when it is exposed to corruption, damage, destruction, or other disruption of its authentic state. Corruption can occur while information is being stored or transmitted. Many computer viruses and worms are designed with the explicit purpose of corrupting data. For this reason, a key method for detecting a virus or worm is to look for changes in file integrity, as shown by the file size. Another key method of assuring information integrity is file hashing, in which a file is read by a special algorithm that uses the bit values in the file to compute a single large number called a hash value. The hash value for any combination of bits is unique.

If a computer system performs the same hashing algorithm on a file and obtains a different number than the file's recorded hash value, the file has been compromised and the integrity of the information is lost. Information integrity is the cornerstone of information systems because information is of no value or use if users cannot verify its integrity. File hashing and hash values are examined in detail in Module 10.

File corruption is not necessarily the result of external forces, such as hackers. Noise in the transmission media, for instance, can also cause data to lose its integrity. Transmitting data on a circuit with a low voltage level can alter and corrupt the data. Redundancy bits and check bits can compensate for internal and external threats to the integrity of information. During each transmission, algorithms, hash values, and error-correcting codes ensure the integrity of the information. Data whose integrity has been compromised is retransmitted.

Unfortunately, even the routine use of computers can result in unintended changes to files as the equipment degrades, software malfunctions, or other "natural causes" occur.

Unintentional Disclosures

The number of unintentional information releases due to malicious attacks is substantial. Millions of people lose information to hackers and malware-focused attacks annually. However, organizations occasionally lose, misplace, or inadvertently release information in an event not caused by hackers or other electronic attacks.

In 2020, Virgin Media, a communications company, left more than 900,000 users' information unsecured for almost a year after one of its databases was misconfigured by employees. Also in 2020, more than 5.2 million customers of Marriott International were exposed in a data breach resulting from the misuse of two employees' credentials. This disclosure occurred not two years after Marriott's reservation database was breached, exposing more than 383 million guests and resulting in the loss of more than five million passport numbers.[11]

The Georgia Secretary of State gave out more than six million voters' private information, including Social Security numbers, in a breach that occurred in late 2015. The breach was found to have been caused by an employee who failed to follow established policies and procedures, and resulted in the employee being fired. While the agency claimed it recovered all copies of the data that were sent to 12 separate organizations, it was still considered a data breach.

In January 2008, GE Money, a division of General Electric, revealed that a data backup tape with credit card data from approximately 650,000 customers and more than 150,000 Social Security numbers went missing from a records management company's storage facility. Approximately 230 retailers were affected when Iron Mountain, Inc., announced it couldn't find a magnetic tape.[12]

In February 2005, the data aggregation and brokerage firm ChoicePoint revealed that it had been duped into releasing personal information about 145,000 people to identity thieves in 2004. The perpetrators used stolen identities to create ostensibly legitimate business entities, which then subscribed to ChoicePoint to acquire the data fraudulently. The company reported that the criminals opened many accounts and recorded personal information, including names, addresses, and identification numbers. They did so without using any network or computer-based attacks; it was simple fraud. The fraud was feared to have allowed the perpetrators to arrange hundreds of identity thefts.

The giant pharmaceutical organization Eli Lilly and Co. released the e-mail addresses of 600 patients to one another in 2001. The American Civil Liberties Union (ACLU) denounced this breach of privacy, and information technology industry analysts noted that it was likely to influence the public debate on privacy legislation. The company claimed the mishap was caused by a programming error that occurred when patients who used a specific drug produced by Lilly signed up for an e-mail service to access company support materials.

These are but a few of the multitudes of data breaches that occur regularly in the world, day in and day out. Wikipedia maintains a list of the more well-known breaches at *https://en.wikipedia.org/wiki/List_of_data_breaches*.

 For more details on information losses caused by attacks, visit Wikipedia.org and search on the terms "data breach" and "timeline of computer security hacker history."

Availability

Availability enables authorized users—people or computer systems—to access information without interference or obstruction and to receive it in the required format. Consider, for example, research libraries that require identification before entrance. Librarians protect the contents of the library so that they are available only to authorized patrons. The librarian must accept a patron's identification before the patron has free access to the book stacks. Once authorized patrons have access to the stacks, they expect to find the information they need in a usable format and familiar language. In this case, the information is bound in a book that is written in English.

Accuracy

Information has **accuracy** when it is free from mistakes or errors and has the value that the end user expects. If information has been intentionally or unintentionally modified, it is no longer accurate. Consider a checking account, for example. You assume that the information in your account is an accurate representation of your finances. Incorrect information in the account can result from external or internal errors. If a bank teller, for instance, mistakenly adds or subtracts too much money from your account, the value of the information is changed. Or, you may accidentally enter an incorrect amount into your account register. Either way, an inaccurate bank balance could cause you to make other mistakes, such as bouncing a check that overdraws your account.

Authenticity

Information is **authentic** when it is in the same state in which it was created, placed, stored, or transferred. Consider for a moment some common assumptions about e-mail. When you receive e-mail, you assume that a specific individual or group created and transmitted the e-mail—you assume you know its origin. This is not always the case. E-mail spoofing, the act of sending an e-mail message with a modified field, is a problem for many people today because the modified field often is the address of the originator. Spoofing the sender's address can fool e-mail recipients into thinking that the messages are legitimate traffic, thus inducing them to open e-mail they otherwise might not have.

Utility

The **utility** of information is its usefulness. In other words, information has value when it can serve a purpose. If information is available but is not in a meaningful format to the end user, it is not useful. For example, U.S. Census data can quickly become overwhelming and difficult for a private citizen to interpret; however, for a politician, the same data reveals information about residents in a district—such as their race, gender, and age. This information can help form a politician's campaign strategy or shape their policies and opinions on key issues.

Possession

The **possession** of information is the quality or state of ownership or control. Information is said to be in one's possession if one obtains it, independent of format or other characteristics. While a breach of confidentiality always results in a breach

availability
An attribute of information that describes how data is accessible and correctly formatted for use without interference or obstruction.

accuracy
An attribute of information that describes how data is free of errors and has the value that the user expects.

authenticity
An attribute of information that describes how data is genuine or original rather than reproduced or fabricated.

utility
An attribute of information that describes how data has value or usefulness for an end purpose.

possession
An attribute of information that describes how the data's ownership or control is legitimate or authorized.

McCumber Cube

A graphical representation of the architectural approach used in computer and information security; commonly shown as a cube composed of 3×3×3 cells, similar to a Rubik's Cube.

of possession, a breach of possession does not always lead to a breach of confidentiality. For example, assume a company stores its critical customer data using an encrypted file system. An employee who has quit decides to take a copy of the tape backups and sell the customer records to the competition. The removal of the tapes from their secure environment is a breach of possession. Because the data is encrypted, neither the former employee nor anyone else can read it without the proper decryption methods; therefore, there is no breach of confidentiality. Today, people who are caught selling company secrets face increasingly stiff fines and a strong likelihood of jail time. Also, companies are growing more reluctant to hire people who have demonstrated dishonesty in their past. Another example might be that of a ransomware attack in which a hacker encrypts important information and offers to provide the decryption key for a fee. The attack would result in a breach of possession because the owner would no longer have possession of the information.

CNSS Security Model

The definition of information security in this text is based in part on the National Training Standard for Information Systems Security Professionals, NSTISSI No. 4011 (1994). The hosting organization is CNSS, which is responsible for coordinating the evaluation and publication of standards related to the protection of National Security Systems (NSS). CNSS was originally called the National Security Telecommunications and Information Systems Security Committee (NSTISSC) when established in 1990 by National Security Directive (NSD) 42, *National Policy for the Security of National Security Telecommunications and Information Systems*. The outdated CNSS standards are expected to be replaced by a newer document from the National Institute of Standards and Technology (NIST) called Special Publication (SP) 800-16 Rev. 1 (2014), "A Role-Based Model for Federal Information Technology/Cyber Security Training," in the near future.

> (i) For more information on CNSS and its standards, see *www.cnss.gov/CNSS/issuances/Instructions.cfm*.

The model, which was created by John McCumber in 1991, provides a graphical representation of the architectural approach widely used in computer and information security; it is now known as the **McCumber Cube**.[13] As shown in Figure 1-9, the McCumber Cube shows three dimensions. When extrapolated, the three dimensions of each axis become a 3×3×3 cube with 27 cells representing areas that must be addressed to secure today's information systems. To ensure comprehensive system security, each of the 27 areas must be properly addressed. For example, the intersection of technology, integrity, and storage requires a set of controls or safeguards that address the need to use *technology* to protect the *integrity* of information while in *storage*. One such control might be a system for detecting host intrusion that protects the integrity of information by alerting security administrators to the potential

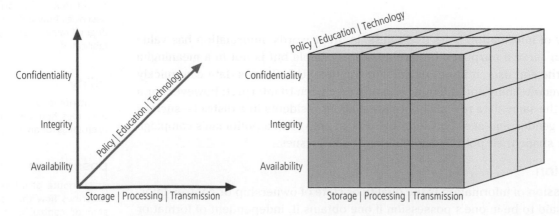

Figure 1-9 The McCumber Cube[14]

modification of a critical file. A common omission from such a model is the need for guidelines and policies that provide direction for the practices and implementations of technologies. The need for policy is discussed in subsequent modules of this book.

Components Of An Information System

As shown in Figure 1-10, an **information system (IS)** is much more than computer hardware and software; it includes multiple components, all of which work together to support personal and professional operations. Each of the IS components has its own strengths and weaknesses, as well as its own characteristics and uses. Each component of the IS also has its own security requirements.

Software

The software component of an IS includes applications (programs), operating systems, and assorted command utilities. Software is perhaps the most difficult IS component to secure. The exploitation of errors in software programming accounts for a substantial portion of the attacks on information. The IT industry is rife with reports warning of holes, bugs, weaknesses, or other fundamental problems in software. In fact, many facets of daily life are affected by buggy software, from smartphones that crash to flawed automotive control computers that lead to recalls.

Software carries the lifeblood of information through an organization. Unfortunately, software programs are often created under the constraints of project management, which limit time, costs, and manpower. Information security is all too often implemented as an afterthought rather than developed as an integral component from the beginning. In this way, software programs become an easy target of accidental or intentional attacks.

Hardware

Hardware is the physical technology that houses and executes the software, stores and transports the data, and provides interfaces for the entry and removal of information from the system. **Physical security** policies deal with hardware as a physical

information system (IS)

The entire set of software, hardware, data, people, procedures, and networks that enable the use of information resources in the organization.

physical security

The protection of material items, objects, or areas from unauthorized access and misuse.

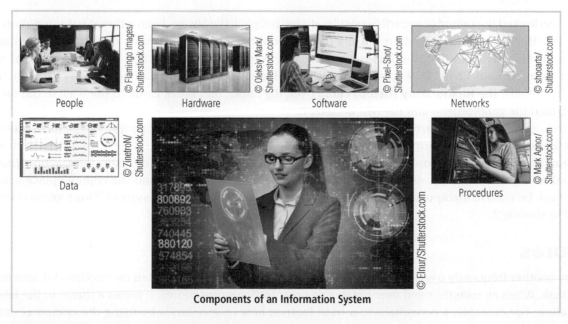

People   Hardware   Software   Networks

Data   Procedures

Components of an Information System

Figure 1-10   Components of an information system

asset and with the protection of physical assets from harm or theft. Applying the traditional tools of physical security, such as locks and keys, restricts access to and interaction with the hardware components of an information system. Securing the physical location of computers and the computers themselves is important because a breach of physical security can result in a loss of information. Unfortunately, most information systems are built on hardware platforms that cannot guarantee any level of information security if unrestricted hardware access is possible.

Before September 11, 2001, laptop thefts in airports were common. A two-person team worked to steal a computer as its owner passed it through the conveyor scanning devices. The first perpetrator entered the security area ahead of an unsuspecting target and quickly went through. Then, the second perpetrator waited behind until the target placed the computer on the baggage scanner. As the computer was whisked through, the second perpetrator slipped ahead of the victim and entered the metal detector with a substantial collection of keys, coins, and the like, slowing the detection process and allowing the first perpetrator to grab the computer and disappear in a crowded walkway.

While the security response to September 11 did tighten the security process at airports, hardware can still be stolen in offices, coffee houses, restaurants, and other public places. Although laptops and notebook computers might be worth a few thousand dollars, the information stored on them can be worth a great deal more to disreputable organizations and individuals. Consider that unless plans and procedures are in place to quickly revoke privileges on stolen devices like laptops, tablets, and smartphones, the privileged access that these devices have to cloud-based data stores could be used to steal information that is many times more valuable than the device itself.

Data

Data stored, processed, and transmitted by a computer system must be protected. Data is often the most valuable asset of an organization and therefore is the main target of intentional attacks. Systems developed in recent years are likely to make use of database management systems. When used properly, they should improve the security of the data and the applications that rely on the data. Unfortunately, many system development projects do not make full use of a database management system's security capabilities, and in some cases, the database is implemented in ways that make it less secure than traditional file systems. Because data and information exist in physical form in many organizations as paper reports, handwritten notes, and computer printouts, the protection of physical information is as important as the protection of electronic, computer-based information. As an aside, the terms *data* and *information* are used interchangeably today. Information was originally defined as *data with meaning,* such as a report or statistical analysis. For our purposes, we will use the term *information* to represent both unprocessed data and actual information.

People

Though often overlooked in computer security considerations, people have always been a threat to information security. Legend has it that around 200 B.C., a great army threatened the security and stability of the Chinese empire. So ferocious were the Hun invaders that the Chinese emperor commanded the construction of a great wall that would defend against them. Around 1275 A.D., Kublai Khan finally achieved what the Huns had been trying for more than a thousand years. Initially, the Khan's army tried to climb over, dig under, and break through the wall. In the end, the Khan simply bribed the gatekeeper—and the rest is history.

Whether this event actually occurred or not, the timeless moral to the story is that people can be the weakest link in an organization's information security program. Unless policy, education and training, awareness, and technology are properly employed to prevent people from accidentally or intentionally damaging or losing information, they will remain the weakest link. Social engineering can prey on the tendency to cut corners and the commonplace nature of human error. It can be used to manipulate people to obtain access information about a system. This topic is discussed in more detail in Module 2.

Procedures

Procedures are another frequently overlooked component of an IS. Procedures are written instructions for accomplishing a specific task. When an unauthorized user obtains an organization's procedures, it poses a threat to the integrity of the information. For example, a consultant to a bank learned how to wire funds by using the computer center's procedures, which were readily available. By taking advantage of a security weakness (lack of authentication), the bank consultant ordered millions of dollars to be transferred by wire to his own account. Lax security procedures caused the loss of more than $10 million before the situation was corrected. Most organizations distribute procedures to employees so they can access the information system, but many of these companies often fail to provide proper education for using the procedures safely. Educating employees about safeguarding procedures is as important as physically securing the information system. After all, procedures are information in their own right. Therefore, knowledge of procedures, as with all critical information, should be disseminated among members of an organization on a need-to-know basis.

Networks

Networking is the IS component that moves data and information between the components of the information system and has created much of the need for increased computer and information security. Prior to networking, physical security was the dominant focus when protecting information. When information systems are connected to each other to form LANs, and these LANs are connected to other networks such as the Internet, new security challenges rapidly emerge. Networking technology is accessible to organizations of every size. Applying the traditional tools of physical security, such as locks and keys, to restrict access to the system's hardware components is still important. However, when computer systems are networked, this approach is no longer enough. Steps to provide network security such as installing and configuring firewalls are essential, as is implementing intrusion detection systems to make system owners aware of ongoing compromises.

 The definition of what an information system is and the roles that it plays has been getting some attention in industry and academia. As information systems have become the core elements of most organizations' ongoing operations, do they still need to be considered anything other than the way companies do all of their business?

For another view of what makes an information system, and to better understand how we might approach improving its security, you can read this article at Technopedia: *www.techopedia.com/definition/24142/information-system-is*.

Security And The Organization

Security has to begin somewhere in the organization, and it takes a wide range of professionals to support a diverse information security program. The following sections discuss the development of security as a program and then describe typical information security responsibilities of various professional roles in an organization.

Balancing Information Security and Access

Even with the best planning and implementation, it is impossible to obtain perfect information security. Information security cannot be absolute: It is a process, not a goal. You can make a system available to anyone, anywhere, anytime, through any means. However, such unrestricted access poses a danger to the security of the information. On the other hand, a completely secure information system would not allow anyone access. To achieve balance—that is, to operate an information system that satisfies users and security professionals—the security level must allow reasonable access yet protect against threats. Figure 1-11 shows some of the competing voices that must be considered when balancing information security and access.

Because of today's security concerns and issues, an information system or data processing department can get too entrenched in the management and protection of systems. An imbalance can occur when the needs of the end user are undermined by obsessive focus on protecting and administering the information systems. Information security technologists and end users must recognize that both groups share the same overall goals of the organization—to ensure that data is available when, where, and how it is needed, with minimal delays or obstacles. In an ideal world, this level of availability can be met even after addressing concerns about loss, damage, interception, or destruction.

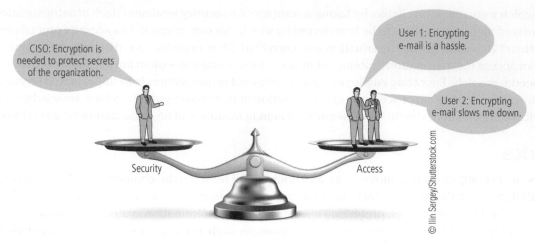

Figure 1-11   Balancing information security and access

Approaches to Information Security Implementation

The implementation of information security in an organization must begin somewhere and cannot happen overnight. Securing information assets is an incremental process that requires coordination, time, and patience. Information security can begin as an attempt by systems administrators to improve the security of their systems by working together. This is often referred to as a **bottom-up approach**. The key advantage of the bottom-up approach is the technical expertise of individual administrators. By working with information systems on a day-to-day basis, these administrators possess in-depth knowledge that can greatly enhance the development of an information security system. They know and understand the threats to their systems and the mechanisms needed to protect them successfully. Unfortunately, the bottom-up approach seldom works because it lacks critical features such as participant support and organizational staying power.

The **top-down approach** has a higher probability of success. With this approach, the project is formally designed and supported by upper-level managers who issue policies, procedures, and processes, dictate the goals and expected outcomes, and determine accountability for each required action. This approach has strong upper management support, a dedicated champion, usually dedicated funding, a clear planning and implementation process, and the means of influencing organizational culture. The most successful kind of top-down approach also involves a formal development strategy known as a systems development life cycle.

For any organization-wide effort to succeed, management must buy into and fully support it. The role of the champion—typically an executive such as a chief information officer (CIO) or the vice president of information technology (VP-IT)—in this effort cannot be overstated. The champion moves the project forward, ensures that it is properly managed, and pushes for acceptance throughout the organization. Without this high-level support, many mid-level administrators fail to make time for the project or dismiss it as a low priority. The involvement and support of end users is also critical to the success of this type of project. Users are most directly affected by the process and outcome of the project and must be included in the information security process. Key end users should be assigned to a joint application development (JAD) team. To succeed, the JAD must have staying power. It must be able to survive employee turnover and should not be vulnerable to changes in the personnel team that is developing the information security system. This means the processes and procedures must be documented and integrated into the organizational culture. They must be adopted and promoted by the organization's management.

The organizational hierarchy and its relationship to the bottom-up and top-down approaches are illustrated in Figure 1-12.

bottom-up approach

A method of establishing security policies and/or practices that begins as a grassroots effort in which systems administrators attempt to improve the security of their systems.

top-down approach

A methodology of establishing security policies and/or practices that is initiated by upper management.

Security Professionals

Because information security is best initiated from the top down, senior management is the key component and the vital force for a successful implementation of an information security program. However, administrative support is also essential to developing and executing specific security policies and procedures, and of course, technical expertise is essential to implementing the details of the information security program.

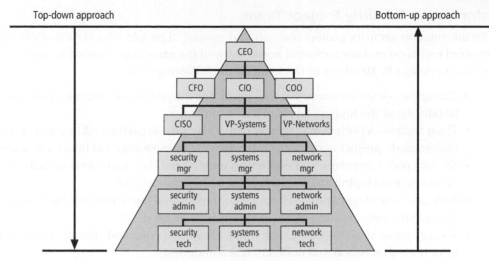

Figure 1-12   Approaches to information security implementation

Senior Management

The senior technology officer is typically the **chief information officer (CIO)**, although other titles such as vice president of information, VP of information technology, and VP of systems may be used. The CIO is primarily responsible for advising the chief executive officer, president, or company owner on strategic planning that affects the management of information in the organization. The CIO translates the strategic plans of the entire organization into strategic information plans for the information systems or information technology division of the organization. Once this is accomplished, CIOs work with subordinate managers to develop tactical and operational plans for the division and to enable planning and management of the systems that support the organization.

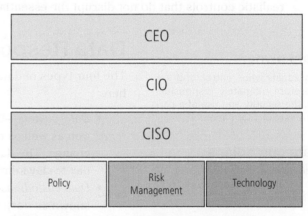

Figure 1-13   The CISO's place and roles

The **chief information security officer (CISO)** has primary responsibility for the assessment, management, and implementation of information security in the organization. The CISO may also be referred to as the manager for IT security, the security administrator, or by a similar title. The CISO usually reports directly to the CIO, although in larger organizations, one or more layers of management might exist between the two. However, the recommendations of the CISO to the CIO must be given equal if not greater priority than other technology and information-related proposals. The most common placement of CISOs in organizational hierarchies, along with their assigned roles and responsibilities, is illustrated in Figure 1-13. Note that the placement and accountabilities of the CISO have been the subject of debate across the industry for decades.[15]

 An emerging trend is the "Virtual CISO." Many consulting organizations are offering this as a service to clients as a means to gain the advantages of having a CISO's perspective on solving security problems without the complexities and expense of hiring a dedicated executive.

You can look into what a vCISO is and does with a short reading session on the Web. Start with an article by Doug Drinkwater from *CSO Magazine* at *www.csoonline.com/article/3259926/what-is-a-virtual-ciso-when-and-how-to-hire-one.html*.

chief information officer (CIO)

An executive-level position that oversees the organization's computing technology and strives to create efficiency in the processing and access of the organization's information.

chief information security officer (CISO)

The title typically assigned to the top information security manager in an organization.

Information Security Project Team

The information security project team should consist of people who are experienced in one or multiple facets of the required technical and nontechnical areas. Many of the same skills needed to manage and implement security are also needed to design it. Members of the team fill the following roles:

- *Champion*—A senior executive who promotes the project and ensures its support, both financially and administratively, at the highest levels of the organization
- *Team leader*—A project manager who may also be a departmental line manager or staff unit manager, and who understands project management, personnel management, and information security technical requirements
- *Security policy developers*—People who understand the organizational culture, existing policies, and requirements for developing and implementing successful policies
- *Risk assessment specialists*—People who understand financial risk assessment techniques, the value of organizational assets, and the security methods to be used
- *Security professionals*—Dedicated, trained, and well-educated specialists in all aspects of information security from both a technical and nontechnical standpoint
- *Systems administrators*—People with the primary responsibility for administering systems that house the information used by the organization
- *End users*—Those whom the new system will most directly affect. Ideally, a selection of users from various departments, levels, and degrees of technical knowledge assist the team in focusing on the application of realistic controls that do not disrupt the essential business activities they seek to safeguard.

Data Responsibilities

The four types of data ownership and their respective responsibilities are outlined here:

- *Data owners*—**Data owners** usually determine the level of data classification as well as the changes to that classification required by organizational change. The data owners work with subordinate managers to oversee the day-to-day administration of the data.
- *Data custodians*—Working directly with data owners, **data custodians** (also known as **data stewards**) are responsible for the information and the systems that process, transmit, and store it. Depending on the size of the organization, this may be a dedicated position, such as the CISO, or it may be an additional responsibility of a systems administrator or other technology manager. The duties of a data custodian often include overseeing data storage and backups, implementing the specific procedures and policies laid out in the security policies and plans, and reporting to the data owner.
- *Data trustees*—**Data trustees** are individuals appointed by data owners to oversee the management of a particular set of information and to coordinate with data custodians for its storage, protection, and use. Because data owners are typically top-level executives and managers too busy to oversee the management of their data, they will typically appoint a senior subordinate as a data trustee to handle those responsibilities.
- *Data users*—Everyone in the organization is responsible for the security of data, so **data users** are included here as all individuals or end users with access to information and thus an information security role.

data owners

Individuals who control, and are therefore ultimately responsible for, the security and use of a particular set of information.

data custodians

Individuals who are responsible for the storage, maintenance, and protection of information.

data stewards

See *data custodians*.

data trustees

Individuals who are assigned the task of managing a particular set of information and coordinating its protection, storage, and use.

data users

Internal and external stakeholders (customers, suppliers, and employees) who interact with information in support of their organization's planning and operations.

community of interest

A group of individuals who are united by similar interests or values within an organization and who share a common goal of helping the organization to meet its objectives.

Communities of Interest

Each organization develops and maintains its own unique culture and values. Within each organizational culture, one or more **communities of interest** usually develop and evolve. While an organization can have many different communities of interest, this book identifies the three that are most common and that have roles and responsibilities in information security. In theory, each role must complement the other, but this is often not the case in practice.

Information Security Management and Professionals

The roles of information security professionals are aligned with the goals and mission of the information security community of interest. These job functions and organizational roles focus on protecting the organization's information systems and stored information from attacks.

Information Technology Management and Professionals

The community of interest made up of IT managers and skilled professionals in systems design, programming, networks, and other related disciplines has many of the same objectives as the information security community. However, its members focus more on costs of system creation and operation, ease of use for system users, and timeliness of system creation, as well as transaction response time. The goals of the IT community and the information security community are not always in complete alignment, and depending on the organizational structure, this may cause conflict.

Organizational Management and Professionals

The organization's general management team and the rest of the personnel in the organization make up the other major community of interest. This large group is almost always made up of subsets of other interests as well, including executive management, production management, human resources, accounting, and legal staff, to name just a few. The IT community often categorizes these groups as users of information technology systems, while the information security community categorizes them as security subjects. In fact, this community serves as the greatest reminder that all IT systems and information security objectives exist to further the objectives of the broad organizational community. The most efficient IT systems operated in the most secure fashion ever devised have no value if they are not useful to the organization as a whole.

Information Security: Is It An Art Or A Science?

Given the level of complexity in today's information systems, the implementation of information security has often been described as a combination of art and science. System technologists, especially those with a gift for managing and operating computers and computer-based systems, have long been suspected of using more than a little magic to keep the systems running as expected. In information security, such technologists are sometimes called *security artisans*.[16] Everyone who has studied computer systems can appreciate the anxiety most people feel when faced with complex technology. Consider the inner workings of the computer: With the mind-boggling functions performed by the 1.4 billion transistors found in a CPU, the interaction of the various digital devices over the local networks and the Internet, and the memory storage units on the circuit boards, it's a miracle that computers work at all.

Security as Art

The administrators and technicians who implement security can be compared to a painter applying oils to canvas. A touch of color here, a brush stroke there, just enough to represent the image the artist wants to convey without overwhelming the viewer—or in security terms, without overly restricting user access. There are no hard and fast rules regulating the installation of various security mechanisms, nor are there many universally accepted complete solutions. While many manuals exist to support individual systems, no manual can help implement security throughout an entire interconnected system. This is especially true given the complex levels of interaction among users, policy, and technology controls.

Security as Science

Technology developed by computer scientists and engineers—which is designed for rigorous performance levels—makes information security a science as well as an art. Most scientists agree that specific conditions cause virtually all actions in computer systems. Almost every fault, security hole, and systems malfunction is a result of the interaction of specific hardware and software. If the developers had sufficient time, they could resolve and eliminate all of these faults.

The faults that remain are usually the result of technology malfunctioning for any of a thousand reasons. There are many sources of recognized and approved security methods and techniques that provide sound technical security advice. Best practices, standards of due care, and other tried-and-true methods can minimize the level of guesswork necessary to secure an organization's information and systems.

Security as a Social Science

A third view to consider is information security as a social science, which integrates components of art and science and adds another dimension to the discussion. Social science examines the behavior of people as they interact with systems, whether they are societal systems or, as in this context, information systems. Information security begins and ends with the people inside the organization and the people who interact with the system, intentionally or otherwise.

There is a long-standing joke in IT that is sometimes told when a user has the experience of using a system that is not performing as expected: "It's not a bug, it's a feature!" This situation occurs when a system performs as it was designed but not as users anticipated, or when users simply don't have the skills or knowledge to make full use of the system. The same is true when an attacker learns of unintended ways to use systems, not by taking advantage of defects in a system, but by taking advantage of *unintended* functions or operations. Although the science of the system may be exact, its use or misuse—the human side of systems—is not.

End users who need the very information that security personnel are trying to protect may be the weakest link in the security chain. By understanding some behavioral aspects of organizational science and change management, security administrators can greatly reduce the levels of risk caused by end users and create more acceptable and supportable security profiles. These measures, coupled with appropriate policy and training issues, can substantially improve the performance of end users and result in a more secure information system.

Closing Scenario

The next day at SLS found everyone on the technical support team busy and focused on the unified threat management system as they restored computer systems to their former state and validated the virus and worm control systems. Amy found herself learning how to reinstall desktop computer operating systems and applications as SLS made a heroic effort to recover from the attack of the previous day.

Discussion Questions

1. Do you think this event was caused by an insider or an outsider? Explain your answer.
2. Other than installing malware control software, what can SLS do to prepare for the next incident?
3. Do you think this attack was the result of malware? Explain your answer.

Ethical Decision Making

Often an attacker crafts e-mail attacks containing malware designed to take advantage of the curiosity or even greed of the recipients. Imagine that the message body Amy saw in the e-mail from Davey had been "See our managers' salaries and SSNs" instead of "Funniest joke you'll see today."

1. Would it be ethical for Amy to open such a file?
2. If such an e-mail came in, what would be the best action to take?

Selected Readings

- *Beyond Fear* by Bruce Schneier, 2006, Springer-Verlag, New York. This book is an excellent look at the broader areas of security. Of special note is Chapter 4, "Systems and How They Fail," which describes how systems are often implemented and how they might be vulnerable to threats and attacks.
- *Fighting Computer Crime* by Donn B. Parker, 1983, Macmillan Library Reference.
- *Seizing the Enigma: The Race to Break the German U-Boat Codes, 1939–1943* by David Kahn, 1991, Houghton Mifflin.
- Glossary of Terms Used in Security and Intrusion Detection by SANS Institute. This glossary can be accessed online at *www.sans.org/resources/glossary.php*.
- RFC 2828–Internet Security Glossary from the Internet RFC/STD/FYI/BCP Archives. This glossary can be accessed online at *www.faqs.org/rfcs/rfc2828.html*.
- SP 800-12, "An Introduction to Computer Security: The NIST Handbook." This document can be accessed online at *http://csrc.nist.gov/publications/nistpubs/800-12/handbook.pdf*.

Module Summary

- Information security evolved from the early field of computer security.
- Security is protection from danger. A successful organization should have multiple layers of security in place to protect its people, operations, physical infrastructure, functions, communications, and information.
- Information security is the protection of information assets that use, store, or transmit information through the application of policy, education, and technology.
- The critical characteristics of information, including confidentiality, integrity, and availability (the C.I.A. triad), must be protected at all times. This protection is implemented by multiple measures that include policies, education, training and awareness, and technology.
- Information systems are made up of the major components of hardware, software, data, people, procedures, and networks.
- Upper management drives the top-down approach to security implementation, in contrast with the bottom-up approach or grassroots effort, in which individuals choose security implementation strategies.
- The control and use of data in the organization is accomplished by the following parties:
  - Data owners, who are responsible for the security and use of a particular set of information
  - Data custodians, who are responsible for the storage, maintenance, and protection of the information
  - Data trustees, who are appointed by data owners to oversee the management of a particular set of information and to coordinate with data custodians for its storage, protection, and use
  - Data users, who work with the information to perform their daily jobs and support the mission of the organization
- Each organization has a culture in which communities of interest are united by similar values and share common objectives. The three communities in information security are general management, IT management, and information security management.
- Information security has been described as both an art and a science, and it comprises many aspects of social science as well.

Review Questions

1. What is the difference between a threat agent and a threat source?
2. What is the difference between vulnerability and exposure?
3. What is a loss in the context of information security?
4. What type of security was dominant in the early years of computing?
5. What are the three components of the C.I.A. triad? What are they used for?
6. If the C.I.A. triad is incomplete, why is it so commonly used in security?

7. Describe the critical characteristics of information. How are they used in the study of computer security?

8. Identify the six components of an information system. Which are most directly affected by the study of computer security? Which are most commonly associated with its study?

9. What is the McCumber Cube, and what purpose does it serve?

10. Which paper is the foundation of all subsequent studies of computer security?

11. Why is the top-down approach to information security superior to the bottom-up approach?

12. Describe the need for balance between information security and access to information in information systems.

13. How can the practice of information security be described as both an art and a science? How does the view of security as a social science influence its practice?

14. Who is ultimately responsible for the security of information in the organization?

15. What is the relationship between the MULTICS project and the early development of computer security?

16. How has computer security evolved into modern information security?

17. What was important about RAND Report R-609?

18. Who decides how and when data in an organization will be used or controlled? Who is responsible for seeing that these decisions are carried out?

19. Who should lead a security team? Should the approach to security be more managerial or technical?

20. Besides the champion and team leader, who should serve on an information security project team?

Exercises

1. Look up "the paper that started the study of computer security." Prepare a summary of the key points. What in this paper specifically addresses security in previously unexamined areas?

2. Assume that a security model is needed for the protection of information in your class. Using the CNSS model, examine each of the cells and write a brief statement on how you would address the three components of each cell.

3. Using the Web, identify the chief executive officer (CEO), chief information officer (CIO), chief information security officer (CISO), and systems administrator for your school. Which of these people represents the data owner? Which represents the data custodian?

4. Using the Web, find a large company or government agency that is familiar to you or located in your area. Try to find the name of the CEO, the CIO, and the CISO. Which was easiest to find? Which was hardest?

5. Using the Web, find out more about Kevin Mitnick. What did he do? Who caught him? Write a short summary of his activities and explain why he is infamous.

References

1. Salus, Peter. "Net Insecurity: Then and Now (1969–1998)." Sane '98 Online. November 19, 1998. Accessed June 15, 2020, from *www.sane.nl/events/sane98/aftermath/salus.html*.

2. Bletchley Park Trust and kamilpetran/Shutterstock.com.

3. Roberts, Larry. "Program Plan for the ARPANET." Provided by Dr. Roberts on February 8, 2004.

4. Salus, Peter. "Net Insecurity: Then and Now (1969–1998)." Sane '98 Online. November 19, 1998. Accessed June 15, 2020, from *www.sane.nl/events/sane98/aftermath/salus.html*.

5. Bisbey, Richard II, and Hollingworth, Dennis. "Protection Analysis: Final Report." May 1978. ISI/SR-78-13, USC/Information Sciences Institute. Marina Del Rey, CA 90291.

6. Grampp, F. T., and Morris, R. H. "UNIX Operating System Security." *AT&T Bell Laboratories Technical Journal* 63, no. 8 (1984): 1649–1672.

7. Reeds, J. A., and Weinberger, P.J. "The UNIX System: File Security and the UNIX System Crypt Command." *AT&T Bell Laboratories Technical Journal* 63, no. 8 (1984): 1673–1683.

8. Ware, Willis. "Security Controls for Computer Systems: Report of Defense Science Board Task Force on Computer Security." RAND Online. October 10, 1979. Accessed June 15, 2020, from *www.rand.org/pubs/reports/R609-1.html*.

9. Ibid.

10. National Security Telecommunications and Information Systems Security. National Training Standard for Information Systems Security (Infosec) Professionals. File 4011. June 20, 1994. Accessed July 14, 2020, from *www.cnss.gov/CNSS/issuances/Instructions.cfm*.

11. Mihalcik, C. "Marriott Discloses New Data Breach Impacting 5.2 Million Guests." C|Net. Accessed July 9, 2020, from *www.cnet.com/news/marriott-discloses-new-data-breach-impacting-5-point-2-million-guests/*.

12. Claburn, Thomas. "GE Money Backup Tape with 650,000 Records Missing at Iron Mountain." Accessed June 22, 2020, from *www.informationweek.com/ge-money-backup-tape-with-650000-records-missing-at-iron-mountain/d/d-id/1063500?*.

13. McCumber, John. "Information Systems Security: A Comprehensive Model." Proceedings of the 14th National Computer Security Conference, National Institute of Standards and Technology, Baltimore, MD, October 1991.

14. Ibid.

15. Hayes, Mary. "Where the Chief Security Officer Belongs." *InformationWeek*, no. 877 (25 February 2002): 38.

16. Parker, D. B. *Fighting Computer Crime*. 1998. New York: Wiley Publishing, 189.

The Need for Information Security

Upon completion of this material, you should be able to:

1. Discuss the need for information security
2. Explain why a successful information security program is the shared responsibility of the entire organization
3. List and describe the threats posed to information security and common attacks associated with those threats
4. List the common information security issues that result from poor software development efforts

Our bad neighbor makes us early stir-rers, which is both healthful and good husbandry.

—William Shakespeare, King Henry, in Henry V, Act 4, Scene 1

Opening Scenario

Fred Chin, CEO of Sequential Label and Supply (SLS), leaned back in his leather chair and propped his feet up on the long mahogany table in the conference room where the SLS Board of Directors had just adjourned from their quarterly meeting.

"What do you think about our computer security problem?" he asked Gladys Williams, the company's chief information officer (CIO). He was referring to the outbreak of a malicious worm on the company's computer network the previous month.

Gladys replied, "I think we have a real problem, and we need to put together a real solution. We can't sidestep this with a quick patch like last time." Six months ago, most of the systems on the company network had been infected with a virus program that came from an employee's personal USB drive. To prevent this from happening again, all users in the company were now prohibited from using personal devices on corporate systems and networks.

Fred wasn't convinced. "Can't we just allocate additional funds to the next training budget?"

Gladys shook her head. "You've known for some time now that this business runs on technology. That's why you hired me as CIO. I've seen this same problem at other companies, and I've been looking into our information security issues. My staff and I have some ideas to discuss with you. I've asked Charlie Moody to come in today to talk about it. He's waiting to speak with us."

When Charlie joined the meeting, Fred said, "Hello, Charlie. As you know, the Board of Directors met today. They received a report on the costs and lost production from the malware outbreak last month, and they directed us to improve the security of our technology. Gladys says you can help me understand what we need to do about it."

"To start with," Charlie said, "Instead of simply ramping up our antivirus solution or throwing resources at an endpoint protection product, we need to start by developing a formal information security program. We need a thorough review of our policies and practices, and we need to establish an ongoing risk management program. Then we can explore the technical options we have. There are some other things that are part of the process as well, but this is where I think we should start."

"Sounds like it is going to be complicated … and expensive," said Fred.

Charlie looked at Gladys and then answered, "Well, there will probably be some extra expenses for specialized hardware and software, and we may have to slow down some of our product development projects a bit, but this approach will call more for a change in our attitude about security than just a spending spree. I don't have accurate estimates yet, but you can be sure we'll put cost-benefit worksheets in front of you before we commit any funds."

Fred thought about this for a few seconds. "Okay. What's our next step?"

Gladys answered, "First, we need to initiate a project plan to develop our new information security program. We'll use our usual systems development and project management approach. There are a few differences, but we can easily adapt our current models. We'll need to reassign a few administrators to help Charlie with the new program. We'd also like a formal statement to the entire company identifying Charlie as our new chief information security officer and asking all of the department heads to cooperate with his new information security initiatives."

"Information security? What about computer security?" asked Fred.

Charlie responded, "Information security includes computer security, plus all the other things we use to do business: securing our information, networks, operations, communications, personnel, and intellectual property. Even our paper records need to be factored in."

"I see," Fred said. "Okay, Mr. Chief Information Security Officer." Fred held out his hand for a congratulatory handshake. "Bring me the draft project plan and budget in two weeks. The audit committee of the Board meets in four weeks, and we'll need to report our progress then."

Introduction To The Need For Information Security

Unlike any other business or information technology program, the primary mission of an information security program is to ensure that **information assets**—information and the systems that house them—are protected and thus remain safe and useful. Organizations expend a lot of money and thousands of hours to maintain their information assets. If threats to these assets didn't exist, those resources could be used exclusively to improve the systems that contain, use, and transmit the information. However, the threat of attacks on information assets is a constant concern, and the need for information security grows along with the sophistication of the attacks. While some organizations lump both information and systems under their definition of an information asset, others prefer to separate the true information-based assets (data, databases, data sets, and the applications that use data) from their **media**—the technologies that access, house, and carry the information. For our purposes, we will include both data and systems assets in our use of the term. Similarly, we'll use the term *information* to describe both **data** and **information**, as for most organizations the terms can be used interchangeably.

Organizations must understand the environment in which information assets reside so their information security programs can address actual and potential problems. This module describes the environment and identifies the threats to it, the organization, and its information.

Information security performs four important functions for an organization:

- Protecting the organization's ability to function
- Protecting the data and information the organization collects and uses, whether physical or electronic
- Enabling the safe operation of applications running on the organization's IT systems
- Safeguarding the organization's technology assets

information asset

The focus of information security; information that has value to the organization and the systems that store, process, and transmit the information.

media

As a subset of information assets, the systems, technologies, and networks that store, process, and transmit information.

data

Items of fact collected by an organization; includes raw numbers, facts, and words.

information

Data that has been organized, structured, and presented to provide additional insight into its context, worth, and usefulness.

Business Needs First

There is a long-standing saying in information security: When security needs and business needs collide, business wins. Without the underlying business to generate revenue and use the information, the information may lose value, and there would be no need for it. If the business cannot function, information security becomes less important. The key is to balance the needs of the organization with the need to protect information assets, realizing that business needs come first. This is not to say that information security should be casually ignored whenever there is a conflict, but to stress that decisions associated with the degree to which information assets are protected should be made carefully, considering both the business need to use the information and the need to protect it.

Protecting Functionality

The three communities of interest defined in Module 1—general management, IT management, and information security management—are each responsible for facilitating the information security program that protects the organization's ability to function. Although many business and government managers shy away from addressing information security because they perceive it to be a technically complex task, implementing information security has more to do with *management* than *technology*. Just as managing payroll involves management more than mathematical wage computations, managing information security has more to do with risk management, policy, and its enforcement than the technology of its implementation. As the noted information security author Charles Cresson Wood writes:

> *In fact, a lot of [information security] is good management for information technology. Many people think that a solution to a technology problem is more technology. Well, not necessarily. ... So a lot of my work, out of necessity, has been trying to get my clients to pay more attention to information security as a management issue in addition to a technical issue, information security as a people issue in addition to the technical issue.[1]*

Each of an organization's communities of interest must address information security in terms of business impact and the cost of business interruption rather than isolating security as a technical problem.

Protecting Data That Organizations Collect and Use

Without data, an organization loses its record of transactions and its ability to deliver value to customers. Any business, educational institution, or government agency that operates within the modern context of connected and responsive services relies on information systems. Even when transactions are not online, information systems and the data they process enable the creation and movement of goods and services. Therefore, protecting data *in transmission, in processing*, and *at rest* (*storage*) is a critical aspect of information security. The value of data motivates attackers to steal, sabotage, or corrupt it. An effective information security program implemented by management protects the integrity and value of the organization's data.

Organizations store much of the data they deem critical in **databases**, managed by specialized software known as a database management system (DBMS). **Database security** is accomplished by applying a broad range of control approaches common to many areas of information security. Securing databases encompasses most of the topics covered in this textbook, including managerial, technical, and physical controls. *Managerial controls* include policy, procedure, and governance. *Technical controls* used to secure databases rely on knowledge of access control, authentication, auditing, application security, backup and recovery, encryption, and integrity controls. *Physical controls* include the use of data centers with locking doors, fire suppression systems, video monitoring, and physical security guards.

The fundamental practices of information security have broad applicability in database security. One indicator of this strong degree of overlap is that the International Information System Security Certification Consortium (ISC)², the organization that evaluates candidates for many prestigious information security certification programs, allows experience as a database administrator to count toward the experience requirement for the Certified Information Systems Security Professional (CISSP).

Enabling the Safe Operation of Applications

Today's organizations are under immense pressure to acquire and operate integrated, efficient, and capable applications. A modern organization needs to create an environment that safeguards these applications, particularly those that are important elements of the organization's infrastructure—operating system platforms, certain

database

A collection of related data stored in a structured form and usually managed by specialized systems.

database security

A subset of information security that focuses on the assessment and protection of information stored in data repositories.

operational applications, electronic mail (e-mail), and instant messaging (IM) applications, like text messaging (short message service, or SMS). Organizations acquire these elements from a service provider, or they implement their own. Once an organization's infrastructure is in place, management must continue to oversee it and not relegate its management to the IT department.

Safeguarding Technology Assets in Organizations

To perform effectively, organizations must employ secure infrastructure hardware appropriate to the size and scope of the enterprise. For instance, a small business may get by in its start-up phase using a small-scale firewall, such as a *small office/home office (SOHO)* device.

In general, as an organization grows to accommodate changing needs, more robust technology solutions should replace security technologies the organization has outgrown. An example of a robust solution is a commercial-grade, unified security architecture device, complete with intrusion detection and prevention systems, public key infrastructure (PKI), and virtual private network (VPN) capabilities. Modules 8 through 10 describe these technologies in more detail.

Information technology continues to add new capabilities and methods that allow organizations to solve business information management challenges. In recent years, we have seen the emergence of the Internet and the Web as new markets. Cloud-based services, which have created new ways to deliver IT services, have also brought new risks to organizational information, additional concerns about the ways these assets can be threatened, and concern for how they must be defended.

Information Security Threats And Attacks

Around 500 B.C., the Chinese general Sun Tzu Wu wrote *The Art of War*, a military treatise that emphasizes the importance of knowing yourself as well as the threats you face.[2] To protect your organization's information, you must (1) know yourself—that is, be familiar with the information to be protected and the systems that store, transport, and process it—and (2) know your enemy; in other words, the threats you face. To make sound decisions about information security, management must be informed about the various threats to an organization's people, applications, data, and information systems. As discussed in Module 1, a threat represents a potential risk to an information asset, whereas an *attack* represents an ongoing act against the asset that could result in a loss. Threat agents damage or steal an organization's information or physical assets by using **exploits** to take advantage of *vulnerabilities* where controls are not present or no longer effective. Unlike threats, which are always present, attacks exist only when a specific act may cause a loss. For example, the *threat* of damage from a thunderstorm is present throughout the summer in many places, but an *attack* and its associated risk of loss exist only for the duration of an actual thunderstorm. The following sections discuss each of the major types of threats and corresponding attacks facing modern information assets.

 For more information on *The Art of War*, check out MIT's Classics page at *http://classics.mit.edu/Tzu/artwar.html*.

To investigate the wide range of threats that pervade the interconnected world, many researchers have collected information on threats and attacks from practicing information security personnel and their organizations. While the categorizations may vary, threats are relatively well researched and understood.

4.8 Billion Potential Hackers

There is wide agreement that the threat from external sources increases when an organization connects to the Internet. The number of Internet users continues to grow; about 62 percent of the world's almost 7.8 billion people—that is, more than 4.8 billion people—have some form of Internet access, a dramatic increase over the 49.2 percent reported as recently as 2015. Table 2-1 shows Internet usage by continent. Since the time this data was collected in mid-2020, the world population has continued to grow, with an expected increase in Internet usage. Therefore, a typical organization with an online connection to its systems and information faces an ever-increasing pool of potential hackers.

exploit

A technique used to compromise a system; may also describe the tool, program, or script used in the compromise.

Table 2-1 World Internet Usage[3]

World Regions	Population (2020 Est.)	Population % of World	Internet Users (6/30/2020)	Penetration Rate (% Pop.)	Growth 2000–2020	Internet World %
Africa	1,340,598,447	17.2%	566,138,772	42.2%	12,441%	11.7%
Asia	4,294,516,659	55.1%	2,525,033,874	58.8%	2,109%	52.2%
Europe	834,995,197	10.7%	727,848,547	87.2%	592%	15.1%
Latin America/ Caribbean	654,287,232	8.4%	467,817,332	71.5%	2,489%	9.7%
Middle East	260,991,690	3.3%	184,856,813	70.8%	5,527%	3.8%
North America	368,869,647	4.7%	332,908,868	90.3%	208%	6.9%
Oceania/Australia	42,690,838	0.5%	28,917,600	67.7%	279%	0.6%
WORLD TOTAL	7,796,949,710	100.0%	4,833,521,806	62.0%	1,239%	100.0%

Notes: Internet usage and world population estimates are as of July 20, 2020.

Other Studies of Threats

Several studies in recent years have examined the threats and attacks to information security. One of the most recent studies, conducted in 2015, found that 67.1 percent of responding organizations suffered malware infections.

More than 98 percent of responding organizations identified malware attacks as a threat, with 58.7 percent indicating they were a significant or severe threat. Malware was identified as the second-highest threat source behind electronic phishing/spoofing.[4]

Table 2-2 shows these and other threats from internal stakeholders. Table 2-3 shows threats from external stakeholders. Table 2-4 shows general threats to information assets.

Table 2-2 Rated Threats from Internal Sources in 2015 SEC/CISE Survey of Threats to Information Protection[5]

From Employees or Internal Stakeholders	Not a Threat 1	2	3	4	A Severe Threat 5	Comp. Rank
Inability/unwillingness to follow established policy	6.6%	17.2%	33.6%	26.2%	16.4%	66%
Disclosure due to insufficient training	8.1%	23.6%	29.3%	25.2%	13.8%	63%
Unauthorized access or escalation of privileges	4.8%	24.0%	31.2%	31.2%	8.8%	63%
Unauthorized information collection/data sniffing	6.4%	26.4%	40.0%	17.6%	9.6%	60%
Theft of on-site organizational information assets	10.6%	32.5%	34.1%	12.2%	10.6%	56%
Theft of mobile/laptop/tablet and related/ connected information assets	15.4%	29.3%	28.5%	17.9%	8.9%	55%
Intentional damage or destruction of information assets	22.3%	43.0%	18.2%	13.2%	3.3%	46%
Theft or misuse of organizationally leased, purchased, or developed software	29.6%	33.6%	21.6%	10.4%	4.8%	45%
Web site defacement	43.4%	33.6%	16.4%	4.9%	1.6%	38%
Blackmail of information release or sales	43.5%	37.1%	10.5%	6.5%	2.4%	37%

Table 2-3 Rated Threats from External Sources in 2015 SEC/CISE Survey of Threats to Information Protection[6]

From Outsiders or External Stakeholders	Not a Threat 1	2	3	4	A Severe Threat 5	Comp. Rank
Unauthorized information collection/data sniffing	6.4%	14.4%	21.6%	32.8%	24.8%	71%
Unauthorized access or escalation of privileges	7.4%	14.0%	26.4%	31.4%	20.7%	69%
Web site defacement	8.9%	23.6%	22.8%	26.8%	17.9%	64%
Intentional damage or destruction of information assets	14.0%	32.2%	18.2%	24.8%	10.7%	57%
Theft of mobile/laptop/tablet and related/connected information assets	20.5%	25.4%	26.2%	15.6%	12.3%	55%
Theft of on-site organizational information assets	21.1%	24.4%	25.2%	17.9%	11.4%	55%
Blackmail of information release or sales	31.1%	30.3%	14.8%	14.8%	9.0%	48%
Disclosure due to insufficient training	34.5%	21.8%	22.7%	13.4%	7.6%	48%
Inability/unwillingness to follow established policy	33.6%	29.4%	18.5%	6.7%	11.8%	47%
Theft or misuse of organizationally leased, purchased, or developed software	31.7%	30.1%	22.8%	9.8%	5.7%	46%

Table 2-4 Perceived Threats to Information Assets in 2015 SEC/CISE Survey of Threats to Information Protection[7]

General Threats to Information Assets	Not a Threat 1	2	3	4	A Severe Threat 5	Comp. Rank
Electronic phishing/spoofing attacks	0.8%	13.1%	16.4%	32.0%	37.7%	79%
Malware attacks	1.7%	12.4%	27.3%	36.4%	22.3%	73%
Unintentional employee/insider mistakes	2.4%	17.1%	26.8%	35.8%	17.9%	70%
Loss of trust due to information loss	4.1%	18.9%	27.0%	22.1%	27.9%	70%
Software failures or errors due to unknown vulnerabilities in externally acquired software	5.6%	18.5%	28.2%	33.9%	13.7%	66%
Social engineering of employees/insiders based on social media information	8.1%	14.6%	32.5%	34.1%	10.6%	65%
Social engineering of employees/insiders based on other published information	8.9%	19.5%	24.4%	32.5%	14.6%	65%
Software failures or errors due to poorly developed, internally created applications	7.2%	21.6%	24.0%	32.0%	15.2%	65%
SQL injections	7.6%	17.6%	31.9%	29.4%	13.4%	65%

(continues)

Table 2-4   Perceived Threats to Information Assets in 2015 SEC/CISE Survey of Threats to Information Protection[7] (*Continued*)

General Threats to Information Assets	Not a Threat 1	2	3	4	A Severe Threat 5	Comp. Rank
Social engineering of employees/insiders based on organization's Web sites	11.4%	19.5%	23.6%	31.7%	13.8%	63%
Denial of service (and distributed DoS) attacks	8.2%	23.0%	27.9%	32.8%	8.2%	62%
Software failures or errors due to known vulnerabilities in externally acquired software	8.9%	23.6%	26.8%	35.8%	4.9%	61%
Outdated organizational software	8.1%	28.2%	26.6%	26.6%	10.5%	61%
Loss of trust due to representation as source of phishing/spoofing attack	9.8%	23.8%	30.3%	23.0%	13.1%	61%
Loss of trust due to Web defacement	12.4%	30.6%	31.4%	19.8%	5.8%	55%
Outdated organizational hardware	17.2%	34.4%	32.8%	12.3%	3.3%	50%
Outdated organization data format	18.7%	35.8%	26.8%	13.8%	4.9%	50%
Inability/unwillingness to establish effective policy by management	30.4%	26.4%	24.0%	13.6%	5.6%	48%
Hardware failures or errors due to aging equipment	19.5%	39.8%	24.4%	14.6%	1.6%	48%
Hardware failures or errors due to defective equipment	17.9%	48.0%	24.4%	8.1%	1.6%	46%
Deviations in quality of service from other provider	25.2%	38.7%	25.2%	7.6%	3.4%	45%
Deviations in quality of service from data communications provider/ISP	26.4%	39.7%	23.1%	7.4%	3.3%	44%
Deviations in quality of service from telecommunications provider/ISP (if different from data provider)	29.9%	38.5%	18.8%	9.4%	3.4%	44%
Loss due to other natural disaster	31.0%	37.9%	23.3%	6.9%	0.9%	42%
Loss due to fire	26.2%	49.2%	21.3%	3.3%	0.0%	40%
Deviations in quality of service from power provider	36.1%	43.4%	12.3%	5.7%	2.5%	39%
Loss due to flood	33.9%	43.8%	19.8%	1.7%	0.8%	38%
Loss due to earthquake	41.7%	35.8%	15.0%	6.7%	0.8%	38%

Common Attack Pattern Enumeration and Classification (CAPEC)

A tool that security professionals can use to understand attacks is the Common Attack Pattern Enumeration and Classification (CAPEC) Web site hosted by Mitre—a nonprofit research and development organization sponsored by the U.S. government. This online repository can be searched for characteristics of a particular attack or simply browsed by professionals who want additional knowledge of how attacks occur procedurally.

 For more information on CAPEC, visit *http://capec.mitre.org*, where contents can be downloaded or viewed online.

The 12 Categories Of Threats

The scheme shown in Table 2-5 consists of 12 general categories of threats that represent a clear and present danger to an organization's people, information, and systems. Each organization must prioritize the threats it faces based on the particular security situation in which it operates, its organizational strategy regarding risk, and the exposure levels of its assets. Module 4 covers these topics in more detail. You may notice that many of the attack examples in Table 2-5 could be listed in more than one category. For example, an attack performed by a hacker to steal customer data falls into the category of "theft," but it can also be preceded by "espionage or trespass," as the hacker illegally accesses the information. The theft may also be accompanied by Web site defacement actions to delay discovery, qualifying it for the category of "sabotage or vandalism." As mentioned in Module 1, these are technically *threat sources*, but for simplicity's sake, they are described here as threats.

Compromises to Intellectual Property

Many organizations create or support the development of **intellectual property (IP)** as part of their business operations. (You will learn more about IP in Module 6.) IP includes *trade secrets, copyrights, trademarks,* and *patents.* IP is protected by copyright law and other laws, carries the expectation of proper attribution or credit to its source, and potentially requires the acquisition of permission for its use, as specified in those laws. For example, use of some IP may require specific payments or royalties before a song can be used in a movie or before the distribution of a photo in a publication. The unauthorized appropriation of IP constitutes a threat to information security—for example, when employees take an idea they developed at work and use it to make money for themselves. Employees may have access privileges to a variety of IP, including purchased and developed software and organizational information, as many employees typically need to use IP to conduct day-to-day business.

intellectual property (IP)

Original ideas and inventions created, owned, and controlled by a particular person or organization; IP includes the representation of original ideas.

software piracy

The unauthorized duplication, installation, or distribution of copyrighted computer software, which is a violation of intellectual property.

Software Piracy

Organizations often purchase or lease the IP of other organizations and must abide by a purchase or licensing agreement for its fair and responsible use. The most common IP breach is **software piracy**. Because most software is licensed to an individual

Table 2-5 The 12 Categories of Threats to Information Security[8]

Category of Threat	Attack Examples
Compromises to intellectual property	Piracy, copyright infringement
Deviations in quality of service	Internet service provider (ISP), power, or WAN service problems
Espionage or trespass	Unauthorized access and/or data collection
Forces of nature	Fire, floods, earthquakes, lightning
Human error or failure	Accidents, employee mistakes
Information extortion	Blackmail, information disclosure
Sabotage or vandalism	Destruction of systems or information
Software attacks	Viruses, worms, macros, denial of service
Technical hardware failures or errors	Equipment failure
Technical software failures or errors	Bugs, code problems, unknown loopholes
Technological obsolescence	Antiquated or outdated technologies
Theft	Illegal confiscation of equipment or information

user, its use is restricted to a single installation or to a designated user in an organization. If a user copies the program to another computer without securing another license or transferring the license, the user has violated the copyright. The nearby feature describes a classic case of this type of copyright violation. While you may note that the example is from 1997, which seems a long time ago, it illustrates that the issue remains significant today.

Software licenses are strictly enforced by regulatory and private organizations, and software publishers use several control mechanisms to prevent copyright infringement. In addition to laws against software piracy, two watchdog organizations investigate allegations of software abuse: the Software and Information Industry Association (SIIA) at *www.siia.net*, formerly known as the Software Publishers Association, and the Business Software Alliance (BSA) at *www.bsa.org*. BSA estimates that approximately 37 percent of software installed on personal computers globally, as reported in the 2018 findings, was not properly licensed. This number is only slightly lower than the 39 percent reported in the 2016 BSA global study; however, the majority of countries in the study indicate unlicensed rates in excess of 50 percent. Furthermore, BSA estimates an increased risk of malware for systems using unlicensed software.[9] Figure 2-1 shows the BSA's software piracy reporting Web site.

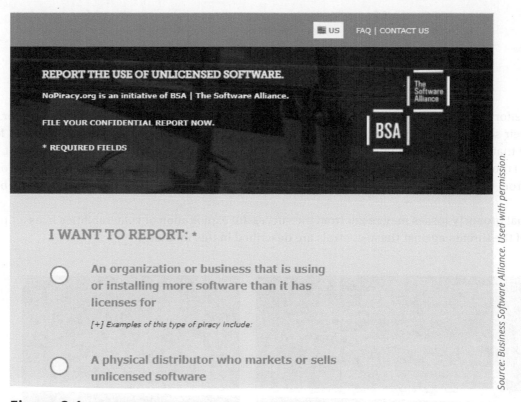

Source: Business Software Alliance. Used with permission.

Figure 2-1   BSA's software piracy reporting Web site

Copyright Protection and User Registration

A number of technical mechanisms—digital watermarks, embedded code, copyright codes, and even the intentional placement of bad sectors on software media—have been used to enforce copyright laws. The most common tool is a unique software registration code in combination with an end-user license agreement (EULA) that usually pops up during the installation of new software, requiring users to indicate that they have read and agree to conditions of the software's use. Figure 2-2 shows a license agreement from Microsoft for an Office 365 subscription.[10]

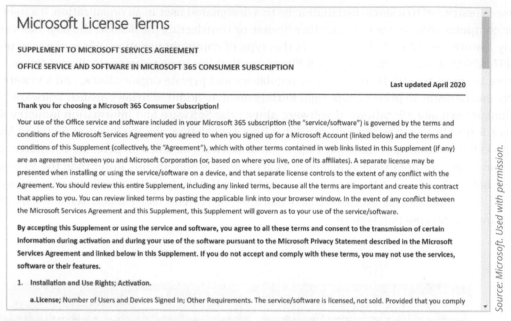

Figure 2-2 Microsoft Office software license terms

Another effort to combat piracy is online registration. Users who install software are often asked or even required to register their software to complete the installation, obtain technical support, or gain the use of all features. Some users believe that this process compromises personal privacy because they never know exactly what information is obtained from their computers and sent to the software manufacturer. Figure 2-3 shows an example of online software registration from the Steam game client. Steam requires the user to create an account and log in to it before registering software.

Intellectual property losses may result from the successful exploitation of vulnerabilities in asset protection controls. Many of the threats against these controls are described in this module.

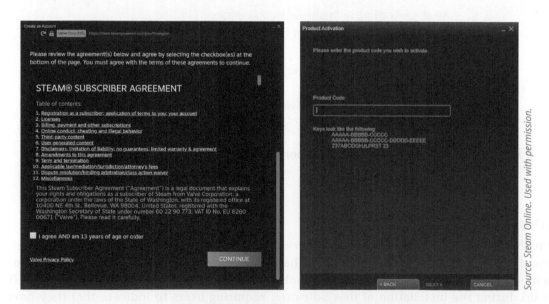

Figure 2-3 Steam subscriber agreement and product registration

Violating Software Licenses

Adapted from "Bootlegged Software Could Cost Community College"[11]
By Natalie Patton, *Las Vegas Review Journal*, September 18, 1997

Ever heard of the software police? The Washington-based Software Publishers Association (SPA) copyright watchdogs were tipped off that a community college in Las Vegas, Nevada, was using copyrighted software in violation of the software licenses. The SPA spent months investigating the report. Academic Affairs Vice President Robert Silverman said the college was prepared to pay some license violation fines, but was unable to estimate the total amount of the fines. The college cut back on new faculty hires and set aside more than $1.3 million in anticipation of the total cost.

The audit was intensive, and it examined every computer on campus, including faculty machines, lab machines, and the college president's computer. Peter Beruk, SPA's director of domestic antipiracy cases, said the decision to audit a reported violation is only made when there is overwhelming evidence to win a lawsuit, as the SPA has no policing authority and can only bring civil actions. Most investigated organizations settle out of court and agree to pay the fines to avoid costly court battles.

The process begins with an anonymous tip, usually from someone inside the organization. Of the hundreds of tips the SPA receives each week, only a handful are selected for on-site visits. If the audited organizations have license violations, they are required to destroy illegal software copies, repurchase software they want to keep (at double the retail price), and pay the proper licensing fees for the software they used illegally.

In this case, the community college president suggested the blame for the college's violations belonged to faculty and students who may have downloaded illegal copies of software from the Internet or installed software on campus computers without permission. Some of the faculty suspected that the problem lay with the qualifications and credibility of the campus technology staff. The president promised to put additional staff and rules in place to prevent future license violations.

Deviations in Quality of Service

An organization's information system depends on the successful operation of many interdependent support systems, including power grids, data and telecommunications networks, parts suppliers, service vendors, and even janitorial staff and garbage haulers. Any of these support systems can be interrupted by severe weather, intentional or accidental employee actions, or other unforeseen events. Deviations in quality of service can result from such accidents as a backhoe taking out the organization's Internet connection or phone lines. The backup provider may be online and in service but may be able to supply only a fraction of the bandwidth the organization needs for full service. This degradation of service is a form of **availability disruption**. Irregularities in Internet service, communications, and power supplies can dramatically affect the availability of information and systems.

Internet Service Issues

In organizations that rely heavily on the Internet and the World Wide Web to support continued operations, ISP failures can considerably undermine the availability of information. Many organizations have sales staff and telecommuters working at remote locations. When these off-site employees cannot contact the host systems, they must use manual procedures to continue operations. The U.S. government's Federal Communications Commission (FCC) maintains a Network Outage Reporting System (NORS), which according to FCC regulation 47 C.F.R. Part 4, requires communications providers to report outages that disrupt communications at certain facilities, like emergency services and airports.

When an organization places its Web servers in the care of a Web hosting provider, that provider assumes responsibility for all Internet services and for the hardware and operating system software used to operate the Web site. These Web hosting services are usually arranged with a **service level agreement (SLA)**. When a service provider fails to meet the terms of the SLA, the provider may accrue fines

availability disruption

An interruption or disruption in service, usually from a service provider, which causes an adverse event within an organization.

service level agreement (SLA)

A document or part of a document that specifies the expected level of service from a service provider, including provisions for minimum acceptable availability and penalties or remediation procedures for downtime.

uptime

The percentage of time a particular service is available.

downtime

The percentage of time a particular service is not available.

to cover losses incurred by the client, but these payments seldom cover the losses generated by the outage. Vendors may promote high availability or **uptime** (or low **downtime**), but Figure 2-4 shows even an availability that seems acceptably high can cost the average organization a great deal. In August 2013, for example, the *Amazon.com* Web site went down for 30 to 40 minutes, costing the company between $3 million and $4 million. Another widely reported disruption was the Mirai botnet event in 2016, a massive attack that disrupted Internet access in parts of Europe and the United States.

> (i) If you suspect that a widely used Internet service is down, you can check its status at *https://downdetector.com/*.

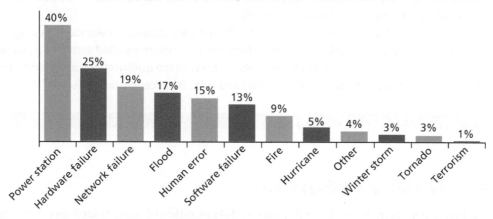

What are the top causes of downtime?

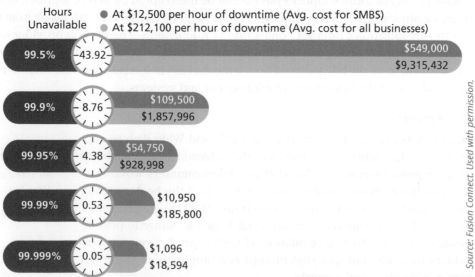

Breakdown of downtime

Source: Fusion Connect. Used with permission.

Figure 2-4   Average cost of downtime according to Fusion Connect[12]

Communications and Other Service Provider Issues

Other utility services can affect organizations as well. Among these are telephone, water, wastewater, trash pickup, cable television, natural or propane gas, and custodial services. The loss of these services can impair the ability of an organization to function. For instance, most facilities require water service to operate an air-conditioning system. Even in Minnesota in February, air-conditioning systems help keep a modern facility operating. If a wastewater system fails, an organization might be prevented from allowing employees into the building. While several online utilities allow an organization to compare pricing options from various service providers, only a few show a comparative analysis of availability or downtime.

Power Irregularities

Irregularities from power utilities are common and can lead to fluctuations such as power excesses, power shortages, and power losses. These fluctuations can pose problems for organizations that provide inadequately conditioned power for their information systems equipment. In the United States, we are supplied 120-volt, 60-cycle power, usually through 15- and 20-amp circuits. Europe as well as most of Africa, Asia, South America, and Australia use 230-volt, 50-cycle power. With the prevalence of global travel by organizational employees, failure to properly adapt to different voltage levels can damage computing equipment, resulting in a loss. When power voltage levels vary from normal, expected levels, such as during a **blackout**, **brownout**, **fault**, **noise**, **sag**, **spike**, or **surge**, an organization's sensitive electronic equipment—especially networking equipment, computers, and computer-based systems, which are vulnerable to fluctuations—can be easily damaged or destroyed. With small computers and network systems, power-conditioning options such as surge suppressors can smooth out spikes. The more expensive uninterruptible power supply (UPS) can protect against spikes and surges as well as sags and even blackouts of limited duration.

Espionage or Trespass

Espionage or trespass is a well-known and broad category of electronic and human activities that can breach the confidentiality of information. When an unauthorized person gains access to information an organization is trying to protect, the act is categorized as espionage or trespass. Attackers can use many different methods to access the information stored in an information system. Some information-gathering techniques are legal—for example, using a Web browser to perform market research. These legal techniques are collectively called **competitive intelligence**. When information gatherers employ techniques that cross a legal or ethical threshold, they are conducting **industrial espionage**. Many countries that are considered allies of the United States engage in industrial espionage against American organizations. When foreign governments are involved, these activities are considered espionage and a threat to national security.

blackout

A long-term interruption (outage) in electrical power availability.

brownout

A long-term decrease in quality of electrical power availability.

fault

A short-term interruption in electrical power availability.

noise

The presence of additional and disruptive signals in network communications or electrical power delivery.

sag

A short-term decrease in electrical power availability.

spike

A short-term increase in electrical power availability, also known as a *swell*.

surge

A long-term increase in electrical power availability.

competitive intelligence

The collection and analysis of information about an organization's business competitors through legal and ethical means to gain business intelligence and competitive advantage.

industrial espionage

The collection and analysis of information about an organization's business competitors, often through illegal or unethical means, to gain an unfair competitive advantage; also known as *corporate spying*.

 For more information about industrial espionage in the United States, visit the National Counterintelligence and Security Center at *www.dni.gov/index.php/ncsc-home*. Look through the resources for additional information on top issues like economic espionage, cyber threats, and insider threats.

Figure 2-5 Shoulder surfing

Some forms of espionage are relatively low-tech. One example, called **shoulder surfing**, is pictured in Figure 2-5. This technique is used in public or semipublic settings when people gather information they are not authorized to have. Instances of shoulder surfing occur at computer terminals, desks, and ATMs; on a bus, airplane, or subway, where people use smartphones and tablets; and in other places where employees may access confidential information. Shoulder surfing flies in the face of the unwritten etiquette among professionals who address information security in the workplace: If you can see another person entering personal or private information into a system, look away as the information is entered. Failure to do so constitutes not only a breach of etiquette but an affront to privacy and a threat to the security of confidential information.

To avoid shoulder surfing, try not to access confidential information when another person is present. People should limit the number of times they access confidential data, and should do it only when they are sure nobody can observe them. Users should be constantly aware of the presence of others when accessing sensitive information.

shoulder surfing

The direct, covert observation of individual information or system use.

trespass

Unauthorized entry into the real or virtual property of another party.

hacker

A person who accesses systems and information without authorization and often illegally.

expert hacker

A hacker who uses extensive knowledge of the inner workings of computer hardware and software to gain unauthorized access to systems and information, and who often creates automated exploits, scripts, and tools used by other hackers; also known as an *elite hacker*.

novice hacker

A relatively unskilled hacker who uses the work of expert hackers to perform attacks; also known as a neophyte, n00b, newbie, script kiddie, or packet monkey.

Hackers

Acts of **trespass** can lead to unauthorized real or virtual actions that enable information gatherers to enter premises or systems without permission. Controls sometimes mark the boundaries of an organization's virtual territory. These boundaries give notice to trespassers that they are encroaching on the organization's cyberspace. Sound principles of authentication and authorization can help organizations protect valuable information and systems. These control methods and technologies employ multiple layers or factors to protect against unauthorized access and trespass.

The classic perpetrator of espionage or trespass is the **hacker**, who is frequently glamorized in fictional accounts as a person who stealthily manipulates a maze of computer networks, systems, and data to find information that solves the mystery and heroically saves the day. However, the true life of the hacker is far more mundane. The profile of the typical hacker has shifted from that of a 13- to 18-year-old male with limited parental supervision who spends all of his free time on the computer; by comparison, modern hackers have fewer known attributes (see Figure 2-6). In the real world, a hacker frequently spends long hours examining the types and structures of targeted systems and uses skill, guile, or fraud to attempt to bypass controls placed on information owned by someone else.

Hackers possess a wide range of skill levels, as with most technology users. However, most hackers are grouped into two general categories: the **expert hacker** and the **novice hacker**. The expert hacker is usually a master of several programming languages, networking protocols, and operating systems, and exhibits a mastery of the technical environment of the chosen targeted system. As described in the nearby feature "Hack *PCWeek*," expert hackers are extremely talented and usually devote extensive time and energy attempting to break into other people's information systems. Even though this example occurred several years ago, it illustrates that systems and networks are still attacked and compromised using the same techniques.

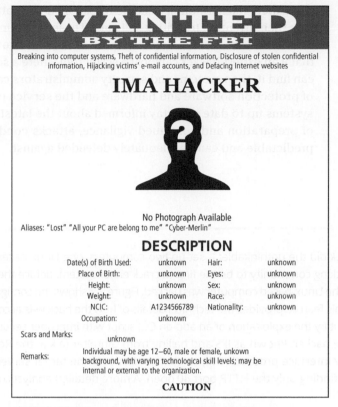

WANTED
BY THE FBI

Breaking into computer systems, Theft of confidential information, Disclosure of stolen confidential information, Hijacking victims' e-mail accounts, and Defacing Internet websites

IMA HACKER

No Photograph Available
Aliases: "Lost" "All your PC are belong to me" "Cyber-Merlin"

DESCRIPTION

Date(s) of Birth Used:	unknown	Hair:	unknown
Place of Birth:	unknown	Eyes:	unknown
Height:	unknown	Sex:	unknown
Weight:	unknown	Race:	unknown
NCIC:	A1234566789	Nationality:	unknown
Occupation:	unknown		

Scars and Marks: unknown

Remarks: Individual may be age 12–60, male or female, unkown background, with varying technological skill levels; may be internal or external to the organization.

CAUTION

Figure 2-6   Contemporary hacker profile

In 2017, the Singapore Ministry of Defense invited hackers to test its publicly accessible system for vulnerabilities. In March 2016, General Motors (GM) invited computer researchers to look for vulnerabilities in the software used in its vehicles and Web site, offering a reward to anyone who found an undocumented issue. In April 2015, the U.S. government did the same thing, inviting hackers to "Hack the Pentagon," of all places—a program that continues to this day. This type of "bug bounty" program is an effort to convince both ethical and unethical hackers to help rather than hinder organizations in their security efforts. Other companies that recently invited such attacks include Tesla Motors, Inc., the ride-share company Uber, and Google.

Once an expert hacker chooses a target system, the likelihood is high that he or she will successfully enter the system. Fortunately for the many poorly protected organizations in the world, there are substantially fewer expert hackers than novice hackers.

A new category of hacker has emerged over the last few years. The **professional hacker** seeks to conduct attacks for personal benefit or the benefit of an employer, which is typically a crime organization or illegal government operation (see the section on cyberterrorism). The professional hacker should not be confused with the **penetration tester** (or **pen tester**), who has authorization from an organization to test its information systems and network defense and is expected to provide detailed reports of the findings. The primary differences between professional hackers and penetration testers are the *authorization* provided and the ethical professionalism displayed.

professional hacker

A hacker who conducts attacks for personal financial benefit or for a crime organization or foreign government; not to be confused with a penetration tester.

penetration tester

An information security professional with authorization to attempt to gain system access in an effort to identify and recommend resolutions for vulnerabilities in those systems; also known as a *pen tester*.

pen tester

See *penetration tester*.

 For more information about hacking, see the master's thesis of Steven Kleinknecht, "Hacking Hackers: Ethnographic Insights into the Hacker Subculture—Definition, Ideology and Argot," which you can find online either by searching on the title or by going to *https://macsphere.mcmaster.ca/handle/11375/10956*.

script kiddies

Novice hackers who use expertly written software to attack a system; also known as skids, skiddies, or script bunnies.

packet monkey

A novice hacker who uses automated exploits to engage in denial-of-service attacks.

Expert hackers often become dissatisfied with attacking systems directly and turn their attention to writing software. These programs are automated exploits that allow novice hackers to act as **script kiddies** or **packet monkeys**. The good news is that if an expert hacker can post a script tool where a script kiddie or packet monkey can find it, then systems and security administrators can find it, too. The developers of protection software and hardware and the service providers who keep defensive systems up to date also stay informed about the latest in exploit scripts. As a result of preparation and continued vigilance, attacks conducted by scripts are usually predictable and can be adequately defended against.

Hack *PCWeek*

On September 20, 1999, *PCWeek* did the unthinkable: It set up two computers, one Linux-based, one Windows NT-based, and challenged members of the hacking community to be the first to crack either system, deface the posted Web page, and claim a $1,000 reward. Four days later, the Linux-based computer was hacked. Figure 2-7 shows the configuration of *www.hackpcweek.com*, which is no longer functional. This feature provides the technical details of how the hack was accomplished not by a compromise of the root operating system, but by the exploitation of an add-on CGI script with improper security checks.

In just under 20 hours, the hacker, known as JFS and hailing from Gibraltar (a.k.a. the Rock), used his advanced knowledge of the Common Gateway Interface protocol (CGI) to gain control over the target server. He began as most attackers do, with a standard port scan, finding only the HTTP port 80 open. A more detailed analysis of the Web servers revealed no additional information.

> Port scanning reveals TCP-based servers, such as telnet, FTP, DNS, and Apache, any of which are potential access points for an attacker, wrote Pankaj Chowdhry in PCWeek. Further testing revealed that most of the potentially interesting services refused connections, with JFS speculating that TCP Wrappers was used to provide access control. The Web server port, 80/TCP, had to be open for Web access to succeed. JFS next used a simple trick. If you send GET X HTTP/1.0 to a Web server, it will send back an error message (unless there is a file named X) along with the standard Web server header. The header contains interesting facts, such as the type and version of the Web server, and sometimes the host operating system and architecture.... As the header information is part of the Web server standard, you can get this from just about any Web server, including IIS.[13]

JFS then methodically mapped out the target, starting with the directory server, using the publicly offered WWW pages. He identified commercial applications and scripts. Because he had learned nothing useful with the networking protocol analyses, he focused on vulnerabilities in the dominant commercial application served on the system, PhotoAds. He was able to access the source code, as it was offered with the product's sale. With this knowledge, JFS was able to find, identify, and look at the environment configuration script, but little else.

JFS then started his effort to exploit known server-side vulnerabilities such as the use of script includes and mod_PERL embedded commands. When that did not pan out with his first attempt, he kept on, trying the process with every field to find that a PERL regexp was in place to filter out most input before it was processed. JFS was able to locate just one user-assigned variable that wasn't being screened properly for malformed content. This single flaw encouraged him to keep up his effort.

JFS had located an ENV variable in the HTTP REFERER that was left unprotected. He first tried to use it with a server-side include or mod_PERL embedded command to launch some code of his choosing. However, these services were not configured on the machine.

JFS continued to poke and prod through the system configuration, looking specifically for vulnerabilities in the PhotoAds CGI scripts. He then turned his attention to looking at open() and system() calls. Dead end.

JFS tried post commands, but the Web server stripped out one of the necessary components of the hack string, the % sign, making the code fail to function. He then tried uploading files, but the file name variable was again being filtered by a regexp, and they were just placed into a different directory and renamed anyway. He eventually gave up trying to get around the rename function.

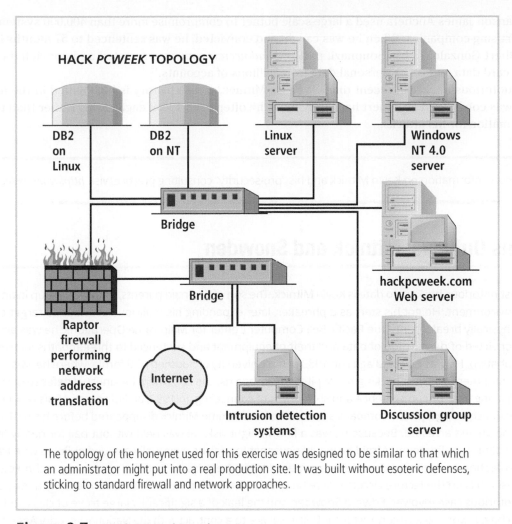

HACK *PCWEEK* TOPOLOGY

DB2 on Linux

DB2 on NT

Linux server

Windows NT 4.0 server

Bridge

Raptor firewall performing network address translation

Bridge

Internet

hackpcweek.com Web server

Intrusion detection systems

Discussion group server

The topology of the honeynet used for this exercise was designed to be similar to that which an administrator might put into a real production site. It was built without esoteric defenses, sticking to standard firewall and network approaches.

Figure 2-7   Hack *PCWeek* topology

After extensive work to create a C-based executable and smuggle it into the server, constantly battling to minimize the file size to the 8,190-byte restriction imposed on the get command, JFS hit another dead end, and turned his attention to gaining root access.

"Using the bugtraq service, he found a cron exploit for which patches hadn't been applied," Chowdhry wrote. "He modified the hack to get a suidroot. This got him root access—and the ability to change the home page to the chilling: 'This site has been hacked. JFS was here.'"[14]

Game over.

 To learn more about one of the leading vulnerability sharing Web sites, you can examine Bugtraq at *www.securityfocus.com*, which provides information on many of the latest security vulnerabilities.

There are a few well-documented cases of unskilled hackers getting caught. In February 2000, Michael Calce, a.k.a. Mafiaboy, a 15-year-old Canadian, was responsible for a series of widely publicized denial-of-service attacks on prominent Web sites. He pleaded guilty to 56 counts of computer mischief and was sentenced to eight months of open custody (house arrest), to one year of probation with restricted Internet access, and to pay $250 to charity. His downfall came from his inability to delete the system logs that tracked his activity and his need to brag about his exploits in chat rooms.[15]

In 2005, Jeanson James Ancheta used a large-scale botnet to compromise more than 400,000 systems that he then rented to advertising companies. When he was caught and convicted, he was sentenced to 57 months in prison.[16]

In 2015, Albert Gonzalez, a.k.a. Soupnazi, part of *Shadowcrew.com*, was arrested and convicted of hacking and stealing credit card data and other personal data from millions of accounts.[17]

The most notorious hacker in recent times is Kevin Mitnick, whose history is highlighted in the nearby feature. While Mitnick was considered an expert hacker by most, he often used social engineering rather than technical skills to collect information for his attacks.

 For more information on Kevin Mitnick and his "pro-security" consulting practice, visit *http://mitnicksecurity.com/*.

Notorious Outlaws: Mitnick and Snowden

Among the most notorious hackers to date is Kevin Mitnick. The son of divorced parents, Mitnick grew up in an unremarkable middle-class environment. He got his start as a phreaker, later expanding his malicious activities to target computer companies. After physically breaking into the Pacific Bell Computer Center for Mainframe Operations, he was arrested. Mitnick, then 17, was convicted of destruction of data and theft of equipment and sentenced to three months in juvenile detention and a year's probation. He was arrested again in 1983 at the University of Southern California, where he was caught breaking into Pentagon computers. His next hacking battle pitched him against the FBI, where his unusual defense of computer addiction resulted in a one-year prison sentence and six months of counseling. In 1992, an FBI search of his residence resulted in charges of illegally accessing a phone company's computer, but this time Mitnick disappeared before his trial. In 1995, he was finally tracked down and arrested. Because he was a known flight risk, he was held without bail for nearly five years, eight months of it in solitary confinement. Afraid he would never get to trial, he eventually pleaded guilty to wire fraud, computer fraud, and intercepting communications. He was required to get permission to travel or use any technology until January 2003. His newest job is on the lecture circuit, where he speaks out in support of information security and against hacking.[18]

Another notorious case involved Edward Snowden and the leak of a significantly large trove of classified intelligence. In 2009, Snowden began working as a contractor for Dell in service to a contract with the National Security Agency. In April 2012, Snowden began collecting classified documents that described the U.S. government's activities in amassing intelligence that purportedly included proscribed surveillance of the domestic activities of U.S. citizens. After consulting with several journalists in early 2013, he changed employers, working at the NSA as a contractor for Booz Allen Hamilton. He began sending copies of NSA documents and other documents to the journalists he had met. In June 2013, Snowden was fired by Booz Allen Hamilton and fled from Hawaii to Hong Kong, and the government charges against him began to mount. The public debate about Snowden and NSA wiretap and surveillance activities continues—some perceive Snowden as a traitor, releasing critical national intelligence to the nation's adversaries, while others view him as a patriot, pursuing an ideal in uncovering unconstitutional government misadventure.[19]

Escalation of Privileges

Once an attacker gains access to a system, the next step is to increase his or her privileges (**privilege escalation**). While most accounts associated with a system have only rudimentary "use" permissions and capabilities, the attacker needs administrative (a.k.a. admin) or "root" privileges. These privileges allow attackers to access information, modify the system itself to view all information in it, and hide their activities by modifying system logs. The escalation of privileges is a skill set in and of itself. However, just as novice hackers can use tools to gain access, they can use tools to escalate privileges.

One aggravating circumstance occurs when legitimate users accumulate unneeded privileges as they go about their assignments, having new privileges added for work tasks while keeping privileges they no longer need. Even over a short time, users can collect many unneeded privileges that an attacker could

privilege escalation

The unauthorized modification of an authorized or unauthorized system user account to gain advanced access and control over system resources.

exploit if a user's credentials were compromised. Many organizations periodically review privileges and remove those that are no longer needed.

A common example of privilege escalation is called **jailbreaking** or **rooting**. Owners of certain smartphones can download and use a set of specialized tools to gain control over system functions, often against the original intentions of the designers. The term *jailbreaking* is more commonly associated with Apple's iOS devices, while the term *rooting* is more common with Android-based devices. Apple's tight controls over its iOS operating system prohibited other developers from creating applications for iOS devices. In 2010, the U.S. Copyright Office issued a statement specifying that jailbreaking a smartphone was legal as a special exemption under the Digital Millennium Copyright Act, but jailbreaking a tablet (such as the iPad) was not.[20] Apple continues to insist that jailbreaking its devices violates the warranty and thus should not be attempted.

Hacker Variants

Other terms for system rule breakers may be less familiar. The term **cracker** is now commonly associated with software copyright bypassing and password decryption. With the removal of the copyright protection, software can be easily distributed and installed. With the decryption of user passwords from stolen system files, user accounts can be illegally accessed. In current usage, the terms *hacker* and *cracker* both denote criminal intent.

Phreakers grew in fame in the 1970s when they developed devices called *blue boxes* that enabled them to make free calls from pay phones. Later, *red boxes* were developed to simulate the tones of coins falling in a pay phone, and finally *black boxes* emulated the line voltage. With the advent of digital communications, these boxes became practically obsolete. Even with the loss of the colored box technologies, however, phreakers continue to cause problems for all telephone systems.

In addition to the "Hack *PCWeek*" competition described earlier in this module, numerous other "hacker challenges" are designed to provide targets to people who want to test their hacking abilities. For example, *www.hackthissite.org* promotes a "free, safe, and legal training ground for hackers to test and expand their hacking skills."[21] It is interesting that a site designed to support hacking requires user registration and compliance with a legal disclaimer.

Password Attacks

Password attacks fall under the category of espionage or trespass just as lock picking falls under breaking and entering. Attempting to guess or reverse-calculate a password is often called **cracking**. There are several alternative approaches to password cracking:

- Brute force
- Dictionary
- Rainbow tables
- Social engineering

The application of computing and network resources to try every possible password combination is called a **brute force password attack**. If attackers can narrow the field of target accounts, they can devote more time and resources to these accounts. This is one reason to always change the password of the manufacturer's default administrator account.

Brute force password attacks are rarely successful against systems that have adopted the manufacturer's recommended security practices. Controls that limit the number of unsuccessful access attempts within a certain time are very effective against brute force attacks. As shown in Table 2-6, the strength of a password determines its ability to withstand a brute force attack. Using best practice policies like the **10.4 password rule** and systems that allow case-sensitive passwords can greatly enhance their strength.

---

jailbreaking

Escalating privileges to gain administrator-level or root access control over a smartphone operating system; typically associated with Apple iOS smartphones. See also *rooting*.

rooting

Escalating privileges to gain administrator-level control over a computer system (including smartphones); typically associated with Android OS smartphones. See also *jailbreaking*.

cracker

A hacker who intentionally removes or bypasses software copyright protection designed to prevent unauthorized duplication or use.

phreakers

A hacker who manipulates the public telephone system to make free calls or disrupt services.

cracking

Attempting to reverse-engineer, remove, or bypass a password or other access control protection, such as the copyright protection on software (see *cracker*).

brute force password attack

An attempt to guess a password by attempting every possible combination of characters and numbers in it.

10.4 password rule

An industry recommendation for password structure and strength that specifies passwords should be at least 10 characters long and contain at least one of the following four elements: an uppercase letter, one lowercase letter, one number, and one special character.

Table 2-6   Password Strength

Case-insensitive Passwords Using a Standard Alphabet Set (No Numbers or Special Characters)		
Password Length	**Odds of Cracking: 1 in (based on number of characters ^ password length):**	**Estimated Time to Crack***
8	208,827,064,576	0.36 seconds
9	5,429,503,678,976	9.27 seconds
10	141,167,095,653,376	4.02 minutes
11	3,670,344,486,987,780	1.74 hours
12	95,428,956,661,682,200	1.89 days
13	2,481,152,873,203,740,000	49.05 days
14	64,509,974,703,297,200,000	3.5 years
15	1,677,259,342,285,730,000,000	90.9 years
16	43,608,742,899,428,900,000,000	2,362.1 years
Case-sensitive Passwords Using a Standard Alphabet Set with Numbers and 20 Special Characters		
Password Length	**Odds of Cracking: 1 in (based on number of characters ^ password length):**	**Estimated Time to Crack***
8	2,044,140,858,654,980	1.0 hours
9	167,619,550,409,708,000	3.3 days
10	13,744,803,133,596,100,000	271.7 days
11	1,127,073,856,954,880,000,000	61.0 years
12	92,420,056,270,299,900,000,000	5,006.0 years
13	7,578,444,614,164,590,000,000,000	410,493.2 years
14	621,432,458,361,496,000,000,000,000	33,660,438.6 years
15	50,957,461,585,642,700,000,000,000,000	2,760,155,968.2 years
16	4,178,511,850,022,700,000,000,000,000,000	226,332,789,392.1 years

Note: Modern workstations are capable of using multiple CPUs, further decreasing time to crack, or simply splitting the workload among multiple systems.

Estimated Time to Crack is based on a 2020-era Intel i9-10900X 10 Core CPU performing 585 Dhrystone GFLOPS (giga/billion floating point operations per second) at 5.2 GHz (overclocked).

The **dictionary password attack**, or simply *dictionary attack*, is a variation of the brute force attack that narrows the field by using a dictionary of common passwords and includes information related to the target user, such as names of relatives or pets, and familiar numbers such as phone numbers, addresses, and even Social Security numbers. Organizations can use similar dictionaries to disallow passwords during the reset process and thus guard against passwords that are easy to guess. In addition, rules requiring numbers and special characters in passwords make the dictionary attack less effective.

A far more sophisticated and potentially much faster password attack is possible if the attacker can gain access to an encrypted password file, such as the Security Account Manager (SAM) data file. While these password files contain hashed representations of users' passwords—not the actual passwords, and thus cannot be used by themselves—the hash values for a wide variety of passwords can be looked up in a database known as a **rainbow table**. These plain text files can be quickly searched, and a hash value and its corresponding plaintext value can be easily located. Module 10, "Cryptography," describes plaintext, ciphertext, and hash values in greater detail.

dictionary password attack

A variation of the brute force password attack that attempts to narrow the range of possible passwords guessed by using a list of common passwords and possibly including attempts based on the target's personal information.

rainbow table

A table of hash values and their corresponding plaintext values that can be used to look up password values if an attacker is able to steal a system's encrypted password file.

Did you know that a space can change how a word is used? For example, "plaintext" is a special term from the field of cryptography that refers to textual information a cryptosystem will transmit securely as ciphertext. It is plaintext before it is encrypted, and it is plaintext after it is decrypted, but it is ciphertext in between. However, the phrase "plain text" is a term from the field of information systems that differentiates the text characters you type from the formatted text you see in a document. For more information about cryptosystems and cryptography, see Module 10.

Social Engineering Password Attacks

While social engineering is discussed in detail later in the section called "Human Error or Failure," it is worth mentioning here as a mechanism to gain password information. Attackers posing as an organization's IT professionals may attempt to gain access to systems information by contacting low-level employees and offering to help with their computer issues. After all, what employee doesn't have issues with computers? By posing as a friendly help-desk or repair technician, the attacker asks employees for their usernames and passwords, and then uses the information to gain access to organizational systems. Some even go so far as to resolve the user's issues. Social engineering is much easier than hacking servers for password files.

Forces of Nature

Forces of nature, sometimes called acts of God, can present some of the most dangerous threats because they usually occur with little warning and are beyond the control of people. These threats, which include events such as fires, floods, earthquakes, landslides, mudslides, windstorms, sandstorms, solar flares, and lightning as well as volcanic eruptions and insect infestations, can disrupt not only people's lives but the storage, transmission, and use of information. Severe weather was suspected in three 2008 outages in the Mediterranean that affected Internet access to the Middle East and India.

Natural disasters also include pandemics, such as the 2020 COVID-19 outbreak. At the time of this writing, the pandemic was still under way, and many small businesses were shut down, some never to reopen. The majority of the world's infrastructure continues to function, but if the virus had been more deadly, its global impact could have been even more disastrous. Knowing a region's susceptibility to certain natural disasters is a critical planning component when selecting new facilities for an organization or considering the location of off-site data backup.

Because it is not possible to avoid threats from forces of nature, organizations must implement controls to limit damage and prepare contingency plans for continued operations, such as disaster recovery plans, business continuity plans, and incident response plans. These threats and plans are discussed in detail in Module 5, "Contingency Planning and Incident Response."

Another term you may encounter, *force majeure*, can be translated as "superior force," which includes forces of nature as well as civil disorder and acts of war.

Fire

A structural fire can damage a building with computing equipment that comprises all or part of an information system. Damage can also be caused by smoke or by water from sprinkler systems or firefighters. This threat can usually be mitigated with fire casualty insurance or business interruption insurance.

Floods

Water can overflow into an area that is normally dry, causing direct damage to all or part of the information system or the building that houses it. A flood might also disrupt operations by interrupting access to the buildings that house the information system. This threat can sometimes be mitigated with flood insurance or business interruption insurance.

Earthquakes

An earthquake is a sudden movement of the earth's crust caused by volcanic activity or the release of stress accumulated along geologic faults. Earthquakes can cause direct damage to the information system or, more often, to the building that houses it. They can also disrupt operations by interrupting access to the buildings that house the information system. In 2006, a large earthquake just off the coast of Taiwan severed several underwater communications cables, shutting down Internet access for more than a month in China, Hong Kong, Taiwan, Singapore, and other countries throughout the Pacific Rim. In 2013, major earthquakes and the resulting tsunami severed cables around Japan. In 2016, several undersea cables around Singapore were damaged, resulting in substantial loss of communications capacity to the island. In the United States, earthquakes impacted the country from Alaska to North Carolina in 2020. Most cause some damage to property. Losses due to earthquakes can sometimes be mitigated with casualty insurance or business interruption insurance, but earthquakes usually are covered by a separate policy.

Lightning

Lightning is an abrupt, discontinuous natural electric discharge in the atmosphere. Lightning usually damages all or part of the information system and its power distribution components. It can also cause fires or other damage to the building that houses the information system, and it can disrupt operations by interfering with access to those buildings. In 2012, a lightning strike to a communications cable near Fort Wayne, Indiana, left almost 100,000 residents without phone and Internet access. Damage from lightning can usually be prevented with specialized lightning rods placed strategically on and around the organization's facilities and by installing special circuit protectors in the organization's electrical service. Losses from lightning may be mitigated with multipurpose casualty insurance or business interruption insurance.

Landslides, Mudslides, and Avalanches

The downward slide of a mass of earth, rock, or snow can directly damage the information system or, more likely, the building that houses it. Landslides, mudslides, and avalanches also disrupt operations by interfering with access to the buildings that house the information system. This threat can sometimes be mitigated with casualty insurance or business interruption insurance.

Tornados and Severe Windstorms

A tornado is a rotating column of air that can be more than a mile wide and whirl at destructively high speeds. Usually accompanied by a funnel-shaped downward extension of a cumulonimbus cloud, tornados can directly damage all or part of the information system or, more likely, the building that houses it. Tornadoes can also interrupt access to the buildings that house the information system. Wind shear is a much smaller and linear wind effect, but it can have similar devastating consequences. These threats can sometimes be mitigated with casualty insurance or business interruption insurance.

Hurricanes, Typhoons, and Tropical Depressions

A severe tropical cyclone that originates in equatorial regions of the Atlantic Ocean or Caribbean Sea is referred to as a hurricane, and one that originates in eastern regions of the Pacific Ocean is called a typhoon. Many hurricanes and typhoons originate as tropical depressions—collections of multiple thunderstorms under specific atmospheric conditions. Excessive rainfall and high winds from these storms can directly damage all or part of the information system or, more likely, the building that houses it. Organizations in coastal or low-lying areas may suffer flooding as well. These storms may also disrupt operations by interrupting access to the buildings that house the information system. This threat can sometimes be mitigated with casualty insurance or business interruption insurance.

Tsunamis

A tsunami is a very large ocean wave caused by an underwater earthquake or volcanic eruption. These events can directly damage the information system or the building that houses it. Organizations in coastal areas may experience tsunamis. They may also disrupt operations through interruptions in access or electrical power to the buildings that house the information system. This threat can sometimes be mitigated with casualty insurance or business interruption insurance.

While you might think a tsunami is a remote threat, much of the world's coastal area is under some threat from such an event. In 2011, the Fukushima Daiichi nuclear disaster resulted from an earthquake and subsequent tsunami; the disruption to the Japanese economy directly and indirectly affected much of the world. The United States coastline has exposure to tsunamis caused by severe earthquakes or landslides that might begin across the Atlantic Ocean, Pacific Ocean, or the Gulf of Mexico.

The earthquake that shook Alaska in 2020 was expected to result in a significant tsunami. The U.S. Coast Guard was mobilized, and the coastal regions were warned. Fortunately, the resulting tsunami only reached about a foot high, almost indistinguishable from normal wave patterns.

To read about technology used to save lives after tsunamis, visit the Web site of NOAA's National Weather Service U.S. Tsunami Warning Center. From there, you can find out how state-of-the-art satellite, computer, and network systems are used to notify people in the country about emergency tsunami events. You can see the Web page at *www.tsunami.gov.*

Electrostatic Discharge

Electrostatic discharge (ESD), also known as static electricity, is usually little more than a nuisance. However, the mild static shock we receive when walking across a carpet can be costly or dangerous when it ignites flammable mixtures and damages costly electronic components. An employee walking across a carpet on a cool, dry day can generate up to 12,000 volts of electricity. Humans cannot detect static electricity until it reaches around 1,500 volts. When it encounters technology, especially computer hard drives, ESD can be catastrophic, as damage can be caused by as little as 10 volts.[22]

Static electricity can draw dust into clean-room environments or cause products to stick together. The cost of ESD-damaged electronic devices and interruptions to service can be millions of dollars for critical systems. ESD can also cause significant loss of production time in information processing. Although ESD can disrupt information systems, it is not usually an insurable loss unless covered by business interruption insurance.

Dust Contamination

Some environments are not friendly to the hardware components of information systems. Accumulation of dust and debris inside systems can dramatically reduce the effectiveness of cooling mechanisms and potentially cause components to overheat. Some specialized technology, such as CD or DVD optical drives, can suffer failures due to excessive dust contamination. Because it can shorten the life of information systems or cause unplanned downtime, this threat can disrupt normal operations.

Solar Activity

While most of us are protected by the earth's atmosphere from the more dramatic effects of solar activity, such as radiation and solar flares, our communications satellites bear the brunt of such exposure. Extreme solar activity can affect power grids, however, as in Quebec in 1989, when solar currents in the magnetosphere affected power lines, blowing out electric transformers and power stations. Business communications that are heavily dependent on satellites should consider the potential for disruption.

Human Error or Failure

This category includes acts performed without intent or malicious purpose or in ignorance by an authorized user. When people use information assets, mistakes happen. Similar errors happen when people fail to follow established policy. Inexperience, improper training, and incorrect assumptions are just a few things that can cause human error or failure. Regardless of the cause, even innocuous mistakes can produce extensive damage. In 2017, an employee debugging an issue with the Amazon Web Services (AWS) billing system took more servers down than he was supposed to, resulting in a chain reaction that took down several large Internet sites. It took time to restart the downed systems, resulting in extended outages for several online vendors, while other sites were unable to fully operate due to unavailable AWS services.[23]

In 1997, a simple keyboarding error caused worldwide Internet outages:

> *In April 1997, the core of the Internet suffered a disaster. Internet service providers lost connectivity with other ISPs due to an error in a routine Internet router-table update process. The resulting outage effectively shut down a major portion of the Internet for at least twenty minutes. It has been estimated that about 45 percent of Internet users were affected. In July 1997, the Internet went through yet another more critical global shutdown for millions of users. An accidental upload of a corrupt database to the Internet's root domain servers occurred. Because this provides the ability to address hosts on the Net by name (i.e., eds.com), it was impossible to send e-mail or access Web sites within the .com and .net domains for several hours. The .com domain comprises a majority of the commercial enterprise users of the Internet.[24]*

social engineering

The process of using interpersonal skills to convince people to reveal access credentials or other valuable information to an attacker.

One of the greatest threats to an organization's information security is its own employees, as they are the threat agents closest to the information. Because employees use data and information in everyday activities to conduct the organization's business, their mistakes represent a serious threat to the confidentiality, integrity, and availability of data—even, as Figure 2-8 suggests, relative to threats from outsiders. Employee mistakes can easily lead to revelation of classified data, entry of erroneous data, accidental deletion or modification of data, storage of data in unprotected areas, and failure to protect information. Leaving classified information in unprotected areas, such as on a desktop, on a Web site, or even in the trash can, is as much a threat as a person who seeks to exploit the information, because the carelessness can create a vulnerability and thus an opportunity for an attacker. However, if someone damages or destroys data on purpose, the act belongs to a different threat category.

In 2014, New York's Metro-North railroad lost power when one of its two power supply units was taken offline for repairs. Repair technicians apparently failed to note the interconnection between the systems, resulting in a two-hour power loss. Similarly, in 2016, Telstra customers in several major cities across Australia lost communications for more than two hours due to an undisclosed human error.

Human error or failure often can be prevented with training, ongoing awareness activities, and controls. These controls range from simple activities, such as requiring the user to type a critical command twice, to more complex procedures, such as verifying commands by a second party. An example of the latter is the performance of key recovery actions in PKI systems. Many military applications have robust, dual-approval controls built in. Some systems that have a high potential for data loss or system outages use expert systems to monitor human actions and request confirmation of critical inputs.

Humorous acronyms are commonly used when attributing problems to human error. They include PEBKAC (problem exists between keyboard and chair), PICNIC (problem in chair, not in computer), and ID-10-T error (idiot).

Social Engineering

In the context of information security, **social engineering** is used by attackers to gain system access or information that may lead to system access. There are several social engineering techniques, which usually involve a perpetrator posing as a person who is higher in the organizational hierarchy than the victim. To prepare for this false representation, the perpetrator already may have used social engineering tactics against others in the organization to collect seemingly unrelated information that, when used together, makes the false representation more credible. For instance, anyone can check a company's Web site or even call the main switchboard to get the name of the CIO; an attacker may then obtain even more information by calling others in the company and falsely asserting his or her authority by mentioning the CIO's name. Social engineering attacks may involve people posing as new employees or as current employees requesting assistance to prevent getting fired. Sometimes attackers threaten, cajole, or beg to sway the

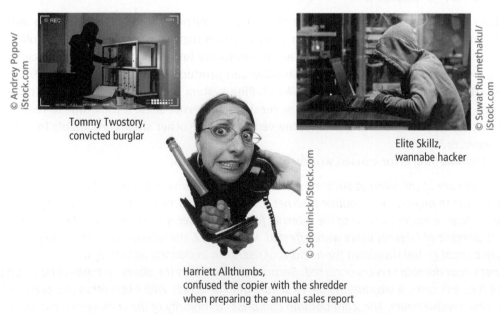

Tommy Twostory,
convicted burglar

Harriett Allthumbs,
confused the copier with the shredder
when preparing the annual sales report

Elite Skillz,
wannabe hacker

© Andrey Popov/
iStock.com

© Sdominick/iStock.com

© Suwat Rujimethakul/
iStock.com

Figure 2-8   The biggest threat—acts of human error or failure

target. The infamous hacker Kevin Mitnick, whose exploits are detailed earlier in this module, once stated:

> *People are the weakest link. You can have the best technology; firewalls, intrusion-detection systems, biometric devices … and somebody can call an unsuspecting employee. That's all she wrote, baby. They got everything.*[25]

Business E-Mail Compromise (BEC)

A new type of social engineering attack has surfaced in the last few years. **Business e-mail compromise (BEC)** combines the exploit of social engineering with the compromise of an organization's e-mail system. An attacker gains access to the system either through another social engineering attack or technical exploit, and then proceeds to request that employees within the organization, usually administrative assistants to high-level executives, transfer funds to an outside account or purchase gift cards and send them to someone outside the organization. According to the FBI, almost 24,000 BEC complaints were filed in 2019, with projected losses of more than $1.7 billion. Reporting these crimes quickly is the key to a successful resolution. The FBI Internet Crime Complaint Center's Recovery Asset Team has made great strides in freezing and recovering finances that are stolen through these types of scams, as long as they are reported quickly and the perpetrators are inside the United States.[26]

Advance-Fee Fraud

Another social engineering attack called the **advance-fee fraud (AFF)**, internationally known as the 4-1-9 fraud, is named after a section of the Nigerian penal code. The perpetrators of 4-1-9 schemes often use the names of fictitious companies, such as the Nigerian National Petroleum Company. Alternatively, they may invent other entities, such as a bank, government agency, long-lost relative, lottery, or other nongovernmental organization. See Figure 2-9 for a sample letter used for this type of scheme.

The scam is notorious for stealing funds from credulous people, first by requiring them to participate in a proposed money-making venture by sending money up front, and then by soliciting an endless series of fees. These 4-1-9 schemes are even suspected to involve kidnapping, extortion, and murder. According to The 419 Coalition, more than $100 billion has been swindled from victims as of 2020.[27]

 You can go to the Advance Fee Fraud Coalition's Web site to see how the Nigerian Government's Economic and Financial Crimes Commission is fighting AFF and 4-1-9 crimes. Visit *https://efccnigeria.org/efcc/*.

Phishing

Many other attacks involve social engineering. One such attack is described by the Computer Emergency Response Team/Coordination Center (CERT/CC):

> *CERT/CC has received several incident reports concerning users receiving requests to take an action that results in the capturing of their password. The request could come in the form of an e-mail message, a broadcast, or a telephone call. The latest ploy instructs the user to run a "test" program, previously installed by the intruder, which will prompt the user for his or her password. When the user executes the program, the user's name and password are e-mailed to a remote site.*
> *These messages can appear to be from a site administrator or root. In reality, they may have been sent by an individual at a remote site, who is trying to gain access or additional access to the local machine via the user's account.*[28]

While this attack may seem crude to experienced users, the fact is that *many* e-mail users have fallen for it. These tricks and similar variants are called **phishing** attacks. They gained national recognition with the AOL phishing attacks that were widely reported in the late 1990s, in which attackers posing as AOL technicians

---

business e-mail compromise (BEC)

A social engineering attack involving the compromise of an organization's e-mail system followed by a series of forged e-mail messages directing employees to transfer funds to a specified account, or to purchase gift cards and send them to an individual outside the organization.

advance-fee fraud (AFF)

A form of social engineering, typically conducted via e-mail, in which an organization or some third party indicates that the recipient is due an exorbitant amount of money and needs only to send a small advance fee or personal banking information to facilitate the transfer.

phishing

A form of social engineering in which the attacker provides what appears to be a legitimate communication (usually e-mail), but it contains hidden or embedded code that redirects the reply to a third-party site in an effort to extract personal or confidential information.

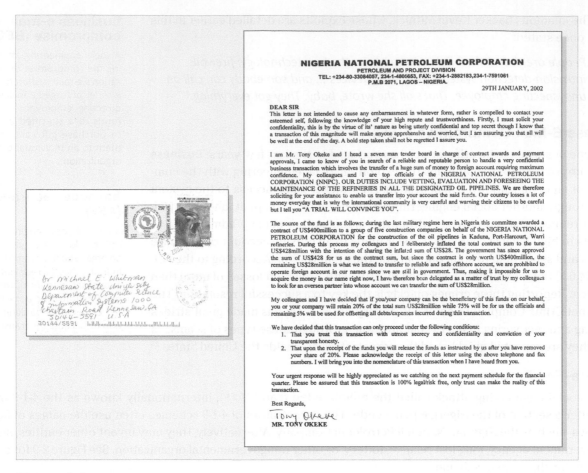

Figure 2-9   Example of a Nigerian 4-1-9 fraud letter

attempted to get login credentials from AOL subscribers. The practice became so widespread that AOL added a warning to all official correspondence that no AOL employee would ever ask for password or billing information. Variants of phishing attacks can leverage their purely social engineering aspects with a technical angle, such as that used in pharming, spoofing, and redirection attacks, as discussed later in this module.

Another variant is **spear phishing**. While normal phishing attacks target as many recipients as possible, a spear phisher sends a message to a small group or even one person. The message appears to be from an employer, a colleague, or other legitimate correspondent. This attack sometimes targets users of a certain product or Web site. When this attack is directed at a specific person, it is called spear phishing. When the intended victim is a senior executive, it may be called *whaling* or *whale phishing*.

Phishing attacks use two primary techniques, often in combination with one another: URL manipulation and Web site forgery. In Uniform Resource Locator (URL) manipulation, attackers send an HTML-embedded e-mail message or a hyperlink whose HTML code opens a forged Web site. For example, Figure 2-10 shows an e-mail that appears to have come from Regions Bank. Phishers typically use the names of large banks or retailers because potential targets are more likely to have accounts with them. In Figure 2-11, the link appears to be to RegionsNetOnline, but the HTML code actually links the user to a Web site in Poland. This is a very simple example; many phishing attackers use sophisticated simulated Web sites in their e-mails, usually copied from actual Web sites. Companies that are commonly used in phishing attacks include banks, lottery organizations, and software companies like Microsoft, Apple, and Google.

In the forged Web site shown in Figure 2-11, the page looks legitimate; when users click either of the bottom two buttons—Personal Banking Demo or Enroll in RegionsNet—they are directed to the authentic bank Web page. The Access Accounts button, however, links to another simulated page that looks just like the real bank login Web page.

spear phishing

A highly targeted phishing attack.

When victims type their banking ID and password, the attacker records that information and displays a message that the Web site is now offline. The attackers can use the recorded credentials to perform transactions, including fund transfers, bill payments, or loan requests.

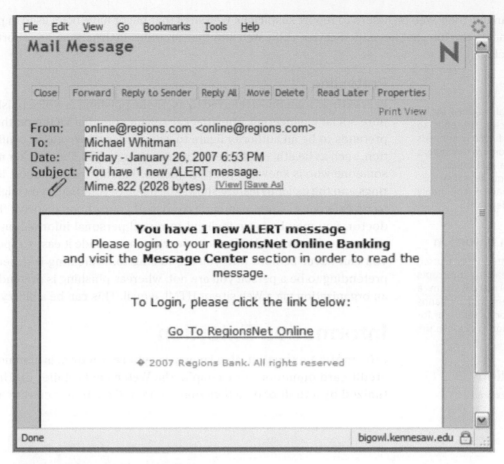

Figure 2-10   Phishing example: lure

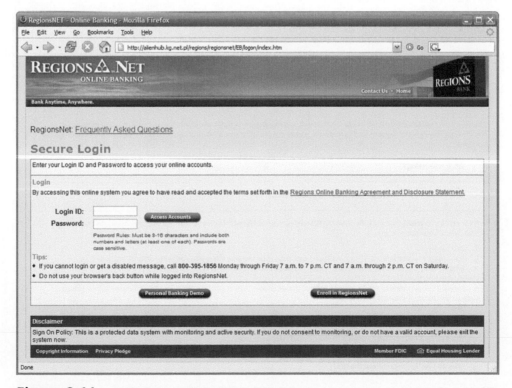

Figure 2-11   Phishing example: fake Web site

People can use their Web browsers to report suspicious Web sites that might have been used in phishing attacks. Figure 2-12 shows the Internal Revenue Service (IRS) Web site that provides instructions on reporting IRS-spoofed phishing attacks.

pretexting

A form of social engineering in which the attacker pretends to be an authority figure who needs information to confirm the target's identity, but the real object is to trick the target into revealing confidential information; commonly performed by telephone.

information extortion

The act of an attacker or trusted insider who steals or interrupts access to information from a computer system and demands compensation for its return or for an agreement not to disclose the information.

cyberextortion

See *information extortion*.

Pretexting

Pretexting, sometimes referred to as phone phishing or voice phishing (*vishing*), is pure social engineering. The attacker calls a potential victim on the telephone and pretends to be an authority figure to gain access to private or confidential information, such as health, employment, or financial records. The attacker may impersonate someone who is known to the potential victim only by reputation. If your telephone rings and the caller ID feature shows the name of your bank, you might be more likely to reveal your account number. Likewise, if your phone displays the name of your doctor, you may be more inclined to reveal personal information than you might otherwise. Be careful; VOIP phone services have made it easy to spoof caller ID, and you can never be sure who you are talking to. Pretexting is generally considered pretending to be a person you are not, whereas phishing is pretending to represent an organization via a Web site or HTML e-mail. This can be a blurry distinction.

Information Extortion

Information extortion, also known as **cyberextortion**, is common in the theft of credit card numbers. For example, the Web-based retailer CD Universe was victimized by a theft of data files that contained customer credit card information.

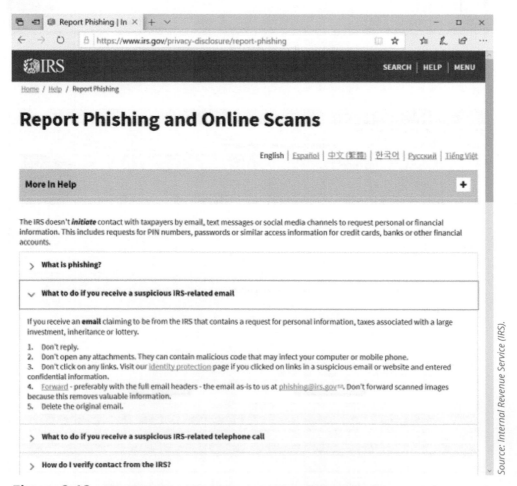

Figure 2-12   IRS phishing and online scams reporting Web site

The culprit was a Russian hacker named Maxus who hacked the online vendor and stole several hundred thousand credit card numbers. When the company refused to pay the $100,000 blackmail, he posted the card numbers to a Web site, offering them to the criminal community. His Web site became so popular he had to restrict access.[29]

Another incident of extortion occurred in 2008 when pharmacy benefits manager Express Scripts, Inc., fell victim to a hacker who demonstrated that he had access to 75 customer records and claimed to have access to millions more. The perpetrator demanded an undisclosed amount of money. The company notified the FBI and offered a $1 million reward for the arrest of the perpetrator. Express Scripts notified the affected customers, as required by various state laws. The company was obliged to pay undisclosed expenses for the notifications and was required to buy credit monitoring services for its customers in some states.[30]

In 2010, Anthony Digati allegedly threatened to conduct a spam attack on the insurance company New York Life. He reportedly sent dozens of e-mails to company executives threatening to conduct a negative image campaign by sending more than six million e-mails to people throughout the country. He then demanded approximately $200,000 to stop the attack, and next threatened to increase the demand to more than $3 million if the company ignored him. His arrest thwarted the spam attack.[31]

In 2012, a programmer from Walachi Innovation Technologies allegedly broke into the organization's systems and changed the access passwords and codes, locking legitimate users out of the system. He then reportedly demanded $300,000 in exchange for the new codes. A court order eventually forced him to surrender the information to the organization. In Russia, a talented hacker created malware that installed inappropriate materials on an unsuspecting user's system, along with a banner threatening to notify the authorities if a bribe was not paid. At 500 rubles (about $17), victims in Russia and other countries were more willing to pay the bribe than risk prosecution by less considerate law enforcement.[32]

Ransomware

The latest type of attack in this category is known as **ransomware**. Ransomware is a malware attack on the host system that denies access to the user and then offers to provide a key to allow access back to the user's system and data for a fee. There are two types of ransomware: lockscreen and encryption. Lockscreen ransomware denies access to the user's system simply by disabling access to the desktop and preventing the user from bypassing the ransom screen that demands payment. Encryption ransomware is far worse, in that it encrypts some or all of a user's hard drive and then demands payment. (See Figure 2-13.) Common phishing mechanisms to get a user to download ransomware include pop-ups indicating that illegal information or malware was detected on the user's system, threatening to notify law enforcement, or offering to delete the offending material if the user clicks a link or button.

In 2013, a virus named CryptoLocker made the headlines as one of the first examples of this new type of malware. More than $100 million in losses were attributed to this ransomware before U.S. federal agents, working with law enforcement from other countries, identified the culprits and seized their systems. The hackers behind CryptoLocker also ran Gameover Zeus Botnet, a server farm that used other hackers to spread the malware. The leader of the hacker group was the Russian hacker Evgeniy Mikhailovich Bogachev, a.k.a. Slavik, who is still at large and still listed on the FBI's Cyber Most Wanted.[33]

In 2017, the ransomware WannaCry made the headlines as it swept through cyberspace, locking systems and demanding payments in Bitcoin. The ransomware attack was cut short when a researcher discovered a flaw in the attack that contained a *kill switch*, preventing the attack from spreading. Software companies like Microsoft quickly issued patches that further stopped the infection. Several governments asserted that the North Korean government was behind the attack.[34]

In 2019, the FBI's Internet Crime Complaint Center received more than 2,000 complaints identified as ransomware, with estimated losses of almost $9 million.[35]

ransomware
Computer software specifically designed to identify and encrypt valuable information in a victim's system in order to extort payment for the key needed to unlock the encryption.

 For a list of prominent ransomware investigations and arrests, visit *www.technology.org/2016/11/21/ ransomware-authors-arrest-cases/*.

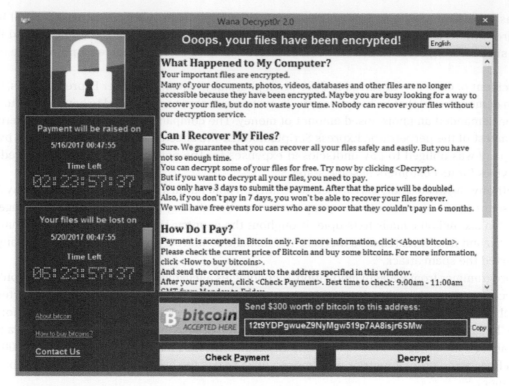

Figure 2-13   Ransomware notification screen

Sabotage or Vandalism

This category of threat involves the deliberate sabotage of a computer system or business or acts of vandalism to destroy an asset or damage the image of an organization. These acts can range from petty vandalism by employees to organized sabotage against an organization.

Although they might not be financially devastating, attacks on the image of an organization are serious. Vandalism to a Web site can erode consumer confidence, diminishing an organization's sales, net worth, and reputation. For example, in the early hours of July 13, 2001, a group known as Fluffi Bunni left its mark on the home page of the SysAdmin, Audit, Network, and Security (SANS) Institute, a cooperative research and education organization. This event was particularly embarrassing to SANS Institute management because the organization provides security instruction and certification. The defacement read, "Would you really trust these guys to teach you security?"[36] At least one member of the group was subsequently arrested by British authorities.

Online Activism

There are innumerable reports of hackers accessing systems and damaging or destroying critical data. Hacked Web sites once made front-page news, as the perpetrators intended. The impact of these acts has lessened as the volume has increased. The Web site that acts as the clearinghouse for many hacking reports, *attrition.org*, has stopped cataloging all Web site defacements because the frequency of such acts has outstripped the ability of the volunteers to keep the site up to date.[37]

Compared to Web site defacement, vandalism within a network is more malicious in intent and less public. Today, security experts are noticing a rise in another form of online vandalism: **hacktivist** or **cyberactivist** operations. For example, in November 2009, a group calling itself "antifascist hackers" defaced the Web site of Holocaust denier and Nazi sympathizer David Irving. They also released his private e-mail correspondence, secret locations of events on his speaking tour, and detailed information about people attending those events, among them members of various white supremacist organizations. This information was posted on the Web site WikiLeaks, an organization that publishes sensitive and classified information provided by anonymous sources.[38]

hacktivist

A hacker who seeks to interfere with or disrupt systems to protest the operations, policies, or actions of an organization or government agency.

cyberactivist

See *hacktivist*.

Leveraging online social media resources can sometimes cross over into unethical or even illegal territory. For example, activists engage in a behavior known as **doxing** to locate or steal confidential and personal records and then release them publicly to embarrass political opponents.

Figure 2-14 illustrates how Greenpeace, a well-known environmental activist organization, once used its Web presence to recruit cyberactivists.

Cyberterrorism and Cyberwarfare

A much more sinister form of activism—related to hacking—is **cyberterrorism**, practiced by **cyberterrorists**. The United States and other governments are developing security measures intended to protect critical computing and communications networks as well as physical and power utility infrastructures.

> *In the 1980s, Barry Collin, a senior research fellow at the Institute for Security and Intelligence in California, coined the term "cyberterrorism" to refer to the convergence of cyberspace and terrorism. Mark Pollitt, special agent for the FBI, offers a working definition: "Cyberterrorism is the premeditated, politically motivated attack against information, computer systems, computer programs, and data which result in violence against noncombatant targets by subnational groups or clandestine agents."[39]*

Cyberterrorism has thus far been largely limited to acts such as the defacement of NATO Web pages during the war in Kosovo. Some industry observers have taken the position that cyberterrorism is not a real threat, but instead is merely hype that distracts from more concrete and pressing information security issues that do need attention.

doxing

A practice of using online resources to find and then disseminate compromising information, perhaps without lawful authority, with the intent to embarrass or harm the reputation of an individual or organization. The term originates from *dox*, an abbreviation of *documents*.

cyberterrorism

The conduct of terrorist activities via networks or Internet pathways.

cyberterrorist

A hacker who attacks systems to conduct terrorist activities via networks or Internet pathways.

Figure 2-14 Cyberactivists wanted

However, further instances of cyberterrorism have begun to surface. According to Dr. Mudawi Mukhtar Elmusharaf at the Computer Crime Research Center, "on October 21, 2002, a distributed denial-of-service (DDoS) attack struck the 13 root servers that provide the primary road map for all Internet communications. Nine servers out of these 13 were jammed. The problem was taken care of in a short period of time."[40] While this attack was significant, the results were not noticeable to most users of the Internet. A news report shortly after the event noted that "the attack, at its peak, only caused 6 percent of domain name service requests to go unanswered [… and the global] DNS system normally responds almost 100 percent of the time."[41]

Internet servers were again attacked on February 6, 2007, with four Domain Name System (DNS) servers targeted. However, the servers managed to contain the attack. It was reported that the U.S. Department of Defense was on standby to conduct a military counterattack if the cyberattack had succeeded.[42] In 2011, China confirmed the existence of a nation-sponsored cyberterrorism organization known as the Cyber Blue Team, which is used to infiltrate the systems of foreign governments.

Government officials are concerned that certain foreign countries are "pursuing cyberweapons the same way they are pursuing nuclear weapons."[43] Some of these cyberterrorist attacks are aimed at disrupting government agencies, while others seem designed to create mass havoc with civilian and commercial industry targets. However, the U.S. government conducts its own **cyberwarfare** actions, having reportedly targeted overseas efforts to develop nuclear enrichment plants by hacking into and destroying critical equipment, using the infamous Stuxnet worm to do so.[44]

 For more information about the evolving threat of cyberwarfare, visit a leading think tank, the RAND Corporation, to read research reports and commentary from leaders in the field (*www.rand.org/topics/cyber-warfare.html*).

Positive Online Activism

Not all online activism is negative. Social media outlets, such as Facebook, Twitter, and YouTube, are commonly used to perform fund-raising, raise awareness of social issues, gather support for legitimate causes, and promote involvement. Modern business organizations try to leverage social media and online activism to improve their public image and increase awareness of socially responsible actions.

Software Attacks

cyberwarfare

Formally sanctioned offensive operations conducted by a government or state against information or systems of another government or state; sometimes called information warfare.

Deliberate software attacks occur when an individual or group designs and deploys software to attack a system. This attack can consist of specially crafted software that attackers trick users into installing on their systems. This software can be used to overwhelm the processing capabilities of online systems or to gain access to protected systems by hidden means.

Malware

malware

Computer software specifically designed to perform malicious or unwanted actions.

malicious code

See *malware*.

malicious software

See *malware*.

zero-day attack

An attack that makes use of malware that is not yet known by the antimalware software companies.

Malware, also referred to as **malicious code** or **malicious software**, includes the viruses, worms, and other scripts and applications designed to harm a target computer system. Other attacks that use software, like redirect attacks and denial-of-service attacks, also fall under this threat. These software components or programs are designed to damage, destroy, or deny service to targeted systems. Note that the terminology used to describe malware is often not mutually exclusive; for instance, Trojan horse malware may be delivered as a virus, a worm, or both.

Malicious code attacks include the execution of viruses, worms, Trojan horses, and active Web scripts with the intent to destroy or steal information. The most state-of-the-art malicious code attack is the polymorphic worm, or multivector worm. These attack programs use up to six known attack vectors to exploit a variety of vulnerabilities in common information system devices. Many successful malware attacks are completed using techniques that are widely known; some have been in use for years. When an attack makes use of malware that is not yet known by the antimalware software companies, it is said to be a **zero-day attack**.

Other forms of malware include covert software applications—bots, spyware, and **adware**—that are designed to work out of users' sight or be triggered by an apparently innocuous user action. Bots are often the technology used to implement Trojan horses, logic bombs, back doors, and spyware.[45] **Spyware** is placed on a computer to secretly gather information about the user and report it. One type of spyware is a Web bug, a tiny graphic that is referenced within the Hypertext Markup Language (HTML) content of a Web page or e-mail to collect information about the user viewing the content. Another form of spyware is a tracking cookie, which is placed on users' computers to track their activity on different Web sites and create a detailed profile of their behavior.[46] Each of these hidden code components can be used to collect user information that could then be used in a social engineering or identity theft attack.

 For more information about current events in malware, visit the U.S. Computer Emergency Readiness Team (US-CERT) Web site, and go to its Current Activity page at *https://us-cert.cisa.gov/ncas/current-activity*. US-CERT is part of the Department of Homeland Security.

Table 2-7 draws on three surveys to list some of the malware that has had the biggest impact on computer users to date. While this table may seem out of date, the values still hold up as of mid-2020. It seems that newer malware cannot break into the all-time top 10, possibly because of the proliferation of malware variants and do-it-yourself malware kits. It's hard for any one new piece of malware to "break out" when so many variations are in play. It seems we are entering the days of precisely targeted malware.

Viruses

A computer **virus** consists of code segments (programming instructions) that perform malicious actions. This code behaves much like a virus pathogen that attacks animals and plants, using the cell's own replication machinery to propagate the attack beyond the initial target. The code attaches itself to an existing program and takes control of the program's access to the targeted computer. The virus-controlled target program then carries out the virus plan by replicating itself into additional targeted systems. Often, users unwittingly help viruses get into a system. Opening infected e-mail or some other seemingly trivial action

adware

Malware intended to provide undesired marketing and advertising, including pop-ups and banners on a user's screens.

spyware

Any technology that aids in gathering information about people or organizations without their knowledge.

virus

A type of malware that is attached to other executable programs and, when activated, replicates and propagates itself to multiple systems, spreading by multiple communications vectors.

Table 2-7   The Most Dangerous Malware Attacks to Date[47,48,49]

Malware	Type	Year	Estimated Number of Systems Infected	Estimated Financial Damage
CIH, a.k.a. Chernobyl	Memory-resident virus	1998	Unknown	$250 million
Melissa	Macro virus	1999	Unknown	$300 million to $600 million
ILOVEYOU	Virus	2000	10% of Internet	$5.5 billion
Klez (and variants)	Virus	2001	7.2% of Internet	$19.8 billion
Code Red (and CR II)	Worm	2001	400,000 servers	$2.6 billion
Nimda	Multivector worm	2001	Unknown	Unknown
Sobig F	Worm	2003	1 million	$3 billion
SQL Slammer, a.k.a. Sapphire	Worm	2003	75,000	$950 million to $1.2 billion
MyDoom	Worm	2004	2 million	$38 billion
Sasser	Worm	2004	500,000 to 700,000	Unknown
Nesky	Virus	2004	Less than 100,000	Unknown
Storm Worm	Trojan horse virus	2006	10 million	Unknown
Leap-A/Oompa-A	Virus	2006	Unknown (Apple)	Unknown
Conficker	Worm	2009	15 million	Unknown
Stutznet	Worm	2009	~200,000	Unknown

macro virus

A type of virus written in a specific language to target applications that use the language, and activated when the application's product is opened; typically affects documents, slideshows, e-mails, or spreadsheets created by office suite applications.

boot virus

Also known as a boot sector virus, a type of virus that targets the boot sector or Master Boot Record (MBR) of a computer system's hard drive or removable storage media.

memory-resident virus

A virus that is capable of installing itself in a computer's operating system, starting when the computer is activated, and residing in the system's memory even after the host application is terminated; also known as a resident virus.

non-memory-resident virus

A virus that terminates after it has been activated, infected its host system, and replicated itself; does not reside in an operating system or memory after executing and is also known as a non-resident virus.

can cause anything from random messages appearing on a user's screen to the destruction of entire hard drives. Just as their namesakes are passed among living bodies, computer viruses are passed from machine to machine via physical media, e-mail, or other forms of computer data transmission. When these viruses infect a machine, they may immediately scan it for e-mail applications or even send themselves to every user in the e-mail address book.

One of the most common methods of virus transmission is via e-mail attachment files. Most organizations block e-mail attachments of certain types and filter all e-mail for known viruses. Years ago, viruses were slow-moving creatures that transferred viral payloads through the cumbersome movement of diskettes from system to system. Now computers are networked, and e-mail programs prove to be fertile ground for computer viruses unless suitable controls are in place. The current software marketplace has several established vendors, such as Symantec Norton AntiVirus, Kaspersky Anti-Virus, AVG AntiVirus, and McAfee VirusScan, which provide applications to help control computer viruses. Microsoft's Malicious Software Removal Tool is freely available to help users of Windows operating systems remove viruses and other types of malware. Many vendors are moving to software suites that include antivirus applications and provide other malware and nonmalware protection, such as firewall protection programs.

Viruses can be classified by how they spread themselves. Among the most common types of information system viruses are the **macro virus**, which is embedded in automatically executing macro code used by word processors, spreadsheets, and database applications, and the **boot virus**, which infects the key operating system files in a computer's boot sector. Viruses can also be described by how their programming is stored and moved. Some are found as binary executables, including .exe or .com files; as interpretable data files, such as command scripts or a specific application's document files; or both.

Alternatively, viruses may be classified as **memory-resident viruses** or **non-memory-resident viruses**, depending on whether they persist in a computer system's memory after they have been executed. Resident viruses are capable of reactivating when the computer is booted and continuing their actions until the system is shut down, only to restart the next time the system is booted.

In 2002, the author of the Melissa virus, David L. Smith of New Jersey, was convicted in U.S. federal court and sentenced to 20 months in prison, a $5,000 fine, and 100 hours of community service upon release.[50]

 For more information on computer criminals and their crimes and convictions, visit *http://en.wikipedia.org* and search on "List of Computer Criminals."

Viruses and worms can use several attack vectors to spread copies of themselves to networked peer computers, as illustrated in Table 2-8.

Worms

Named for the tapeworm in John Brunner's novel *The Shockwave Rider*, a computer **worm** can continue replicating itself until it completely fills available resources, such as memory, hard drive space, and network bandwidth. Read the nearby feature about Robert Morris to learn how much damage a worm can cause. Code Red, Sircam, Nimda ("admin" spelled backwards), and Klez are classic examples of a class of worms that combine multiple modes of attack into a single package. Newer malware that includes features of worms and viruses will usually contain multiple exploits that can use any predefined distribution vector to programmatically distribute the worm. (See the description of polymorphic threats later in this section for more details.)

worm

A type of malware that is capable of activation and replication without being attached to an existing program.

Table 2-8   Attack Replication Vectors

Vector	Description
IP scan and attack	The infected system scans a range of IP addresses and service ports and targets several vulnerabilities known to hackers or left over from previous exploits, such as Code Red, Back Orifice, or PoizonBox.
Web browsing	If the infected system has write access to any Web pages, it makes all Web content files infectious, including .html, .asp, .cgi, and other files. Users who browse to those pages infect their machines.
Virus	Each affected machine infects common executable or script files on all computers to which it can write, which spreads the virus code to cause further infection.
Unprotected shares	Using vulnerabilities in file systems and in the way many organizations configure them, the infected machine copies the viral component to all locations it can reach.
Mass mail	By sending e-mail infections to addresses found in the address book, the affected machine infects many other users, whose mail-reading programs automatically run the virus program and infect even more systems.
Simple Network Management Protocol (SNMP)	SNMP is used for remote management of network and computer devices. By using the widely known and common passwords that were employed in early versions of this protocol, the attacking program can gain control of the device. Most vendors have closed these vulnerabilities with software upgrades.

Robert Morris and the Internet Worm[51]

In November 1988, Robert Morris, Jr. made history. He was a postgraduate student at Cornell who invented a self-prop-agating program called a worm. He released it onto the Internet, choosing to send it from the Massachusetts Institute of Technology (MIT) to conceal the fact that the worm was designed and created at Cornell. Morris soon discovered that the program was reproducing itself and then infecting other machines at a much greater speed than he had envisaged. The worm had a bug.

Many machines across the United States and the world stopped working or became unresponsive. When Morris realized what was occurring, he reached out for help. He contacted a friend at Harvard, and they sent a message to system administrators at Harvard that described the problem and requested guidance for how to disable the worm. However, because the networks involved were jammed from the worm infection, the message was delayed and had no effect. It was too little too late. Morris' worm had infected many computers, including those at academic institutions, military sites, and commercial concerns. The estimated cost of the infection and the aftermath was estimated at roughly $200 per site.

The worm that Morris created took advantage of flaws in the sendmail program. These widely known faults allowed debug features to be exploited, but few organizations had taken the trouble to update or patch the flaws. Staff at the University of California, Berkeley and MIT had copies of the program and reverse-engineered them to determine how it functioned. After working nonstop for about 12 hours, the teams of programmers devised a method to slow down the infection. Another method was discovered at Purdue University and widely published. Ironically, the response was hampered by the clogged state of the e-mail infrastructure caused by the worm. After a few days, things slowly started to regain normalcy, and everyone wondered where the worm had originated. Morris was identified as its author in an article in the *New York Times*, even though his identity was not confirmed at that time.

Morris was convicted under the Computer Fraud and Abuse Act and sentenced to a fine, probation, community service, and court costs. His appeal was rejected in March 1991.

Even though it happened long ago, the outbreak of Nimda in September 2001 still serves as an example of how quickly and widely malware can spread. It used five of the six vectors shown in Table 2-8 to spread itself with startling speed. TruSecure Corporation, an industry source for information security statistics and solutions, reported that Nimda spread across the Internet address space of 14 countries in less than 25 minutes.[52]

The Klez worm delivered a double-barreled payload: It had an attachment that contained the worm, and if the e-mail was viewed on an HTML-enabled browser, it attempted to deliver a macro virus. News-making attacks, such as MyDoom and Netsky, are variants of the multifaceted attack worms and viruses that exploit weaknesses in leading operating systems and applications.

The complex behavior of worms can be initiated with or without the user downloading or executing the file. Once the worm has infected a computer, it can redistribute itself to all e-mail addresses found on the infected system. Furthermore, a worm can deposit copies of itself onto all Web servers that the infected system can reach; users who subsequently visit those sites become infected. Worms also take advantage of open shares found on the network in which an infected system is located. The worms place working copies of their code onto the server so that users of the open shares are likely to become infected.

In 2003, Jeffrey Lee Parson, an 18-year-old high school student from Minnesota, was arrested for creating and distributing a variant of the Blaster worm called W32.Blaster-B. He was sentenced to 18 months in prison, three years of supervised release, and 100 hours of community service.[53] The original Blaster worm was reportedly created by a Chinese hacker group.

Trojan horses are frequently disguised as helpful, interesting, or necessary pieces of software, such as the readme. exe files often included with shareware or freeware packages. Like their namesake in Greek legend, once Trojan horses are brought into a system, they become activated and can wreak havoc on the unsuspecting user. Figure 2-15 outlines a typical Trojan horse attack. Around January 20, 1999, Internet e-mail users began receiving messages with an attachment of a

Trojan horse

A malware program that hides its true nature and reveals its designed behavior only when activated.

polymorphic threat

Malware that over time changes the way it appears to antivirus software programs, making it undetectable by techniques that look for preconfigured signatures.

Trojan horse program named Happy99.exe. When the e-mail attachment was opened, a brief multimedia program displayed fireworks and the message "Happy 1999." While the fireworks display was running, the Trojan horse program was installing itself into the user's system. The program continued to propagate itself by following up every e-mail the user sent with a second e-mail to the same recipient and with the same attack program attached. A newer variant of the Trojan horse is an attack known as *SMiShing*, in which the victim is tricked into downloading malware onto a mobile phone via a text message. SMiShing is an abbreviation for SMS phishing.

One of the biggest challenges to fighting viruses and worms has been the emergence of polymorphic threats. A **polymorphic threat** actually evolves, changing its size and other external file characteristics to elude detection by antivirus software programs.

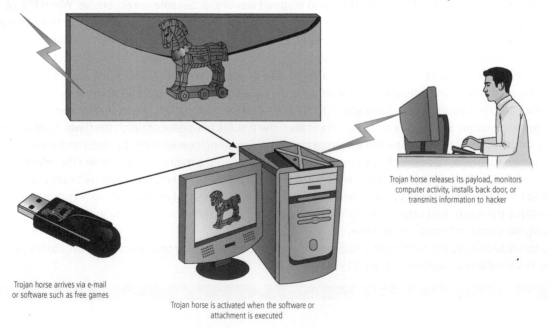

Trojan horse arrives via e-mail
or software such as free games

Trojan horse is activated when the software or
attachment is executed

Trojan horse releases its payload, monitors
computer activity, installs back door, or
transmits information to hacker

Figure 2-15   Trojan horse attacks

As frustrating as viruses and worms are, perhaps more time and money are spent resolving **malware hoaxes**. Well-meaning people can disrupt the harmony and flow of an organization when they send group e-mails warning of supposedly dangerous viruses that don't exist. When people fail to follow virus-reporting procedures in response to a hoax, the network becomes overloaded and users waste time and energy forwarding the warning message to everyone they know, posting the message on bulletin boards, and trying to update their antivirus protection software. Some hoaxes are the chain letters or chain e-mails of the day, which are designed to annoy or bemuse the reader. They are known as "weapons of mass distraction." One of the most prominent virus hoaxes was the 1994 "Goodtimes virus," which reportedly was transmitted in an e-mail with the header "Good Times" or "goodtimes."[54] The virus never existed, and thousands of hours of employee time were wasted retransmitting the e-mail, effectively creating a denial of service.

At one time, hoaxes amounted to little more than pranks, although occasionally a sting was attached. For example, the Teddy Bear hoax tricked users into deleting necessary operating system files, which made their systems stop working. Recently, criminals have been able to monetize the hoax virus by claiming that systems are infected with malware and then selling a cure for a problem that does not exist. The perpetrator of the hoax may then offer to sell a fake antivirus program to correct the fake malware.

Several Internet resources enable people to research viruses and determine if they are fact or fiction.

> ⓘ For the latest information on virus hoaxes, download the article "Virus Hoaxes—Are They Just a Nuisance?" from *www.sans.org/reading-room/whitepapers/malicious/paper/30*.
> For a more entertaining approach to the latest virus, worm, and hoax information, visit the Hoax-Slayer Web site at *www.hoax-slayer.com*.

Back Doors

Using a known or newly discovered access mechanism, an attacker can gain access to a system or network resource through a **back door**. Viruses and worms can have a payload that installs a back door or **trap door** component in a system, allowing the attacker to access the system at will with special privileges. Examples of such payloads include Subseven and Back Orifice.

Sometimes these doors are left behind by system designers or maintenance staff; such a door is referred to as a **maintenance hook**.[55] More often, attackers place a back door into a system or network they have compromised, making their return to the system that much easier the next time. A trap door is hard to detect because the person or program that places it often makes the access exempt from the system's usual audit logging features and makes every attempt to keep the back door hidden from the system's legitimate owners.

Denial-of-Service (DoS) and Distributed Denial-of-Service (DDoS) Attacks

In a **denial-of-service (DoS) attack**, the attacker sends a large number of connection or information requests to a target (see Figure 2-16). So many requests are made that the target system becomes overloaded and cannot respond to legitimate requests for service. The system may crash or simply become unable to perform ordinary functions. In a **distributed denial-of-service (DDoS) attack**, a coordinated stream of requests is launched against a target from many locations at the same time. Most DDoS attacks are preceded by a preparation phase in which many systems, perhaps thousands, are compromised. The compromised machines are turned into **bots** or **zombies**, machines that are directed remotely by the attacker (usually via a transmitted command) to participate in the attack. DDoS attacks are more difficult to defend

---

malware hoax

A message that reports the presence of nonexistent malware and wastes valuable time as employees share the message.

back door

A malware payload that provides access to a system by bypassing normal access controls or an intentional access control bypass left by a system designer to facilitate development.

trap door

See *back door*.

maintenance hook

See *back door*.

denial-of-service (DoS) attack

An attack that attempts to overwhelm a computer target's ability to handle incoming communications, prohibiting legitimate users from accessing those systems.

distributed denial-of-service (DDoS) attack

A form of attack in which a coordinated stream of requests is launched against a target from multiple locations at the same time using bots or zombies.

bot

An abbreviation of *robot*, an automated software program that executes certain commands when it receives a specific input; also known as a *zombie*.

zombie

See *bot*.

against, and currently there are no controls that any single organization can apply. There are, however, some cooperative efforts to enable DDoS defenses among groups of service providers; an example is the "Consensus Roadmap for Defeating Distributed Denial of Service Attacks."[56] To use a popular metaphor, DDoS is considered a weapon of mass destruction on the Internet. The MyDoom worm attack in February 2004 was intended to be a DDoS attack against *www.sco.com*, the Web site of a vendor for a UNIX operating system. Allegedly, the attack was payback for the SCO Group's perceived hostility toward the open-source Linux community.[57]

Any system connected to the Internet and providing TCP-based network services (such as a Web server, FTP server, or mail server) is vulnerable to DoS attacks. DoS attacks can also be launched against routers or other network server systems if these hosts enable other TCP services, such as echo.

Prominent in the history of notable DoS attacks are those conducted by Michael Calce (a.k.a. Mafiaboy) on *Amazon.com*, *CNN.com*, *ETrade.com*, *ebay.com*, *Yahoo.com*, *Excite.com*, and *Dell.com* in February 2000. These software-based attacks lasted approximately four hours and reportedly resulted in millions of dollars in lost revenue.[58] The British ISP CloudNine is believed to be the first business "hacked out of existence" by a DoS attack in January 2002. This attack was similar to the DoS attacks launched by Mafiaboy.[59] In January 2016, a group calling itself New World Hacking attacked the BBC's Web site. If the scope of the attack is verified, it would qualify as the largest DDoS attack in history, with an attack rate of 602 Gbps (gigabits per second). The group also hit Donald Trump's campaign Web site on the same day.[60]

In October 2016, a massive DDoS attack took down several Web sites, including Airbnb, Etsy, Github, Netflix, Reddit, Spotify, Twitter, and Vox, by attacking their common DNS service provider. While the initial attack only lasted hours, the sites experienced issues for the rest of the day.[61]

E-Mail Attacks

While many consider **spam** a trivial nuisance rather than an attack, it has been used as a means of enhancing malicious code attacks. In March 2002, there were reports of malicious code embedded in MP3 files that were included as attachments to spam.[62] The most significant consequence of spam, however, is the waste of computer and human resources. Many organizations attempt to cope with the flood of spam by using e-mail filtering technologies. Other organizations simply tell users of the mail system to delete unwanted messages.

spam

Undesired e-mail, typically commercial advertising transmitted in bulk.

mail bomb

An attack designed to overwhelm the receiver with excessive quantities of e-mail.

A form of e-mail attack that is also a DoS attack is called a **mail bomb**. It can be accomplished using traditional e-mailing techniques or by exploiting various technical flaws in the Simple Mail Transport Protocol (SMTP). The target of the attack receives an unmanageably large volume of unsolicited e-mail. By sending large e-mails with forged header information, attackers can take advantage of poorly

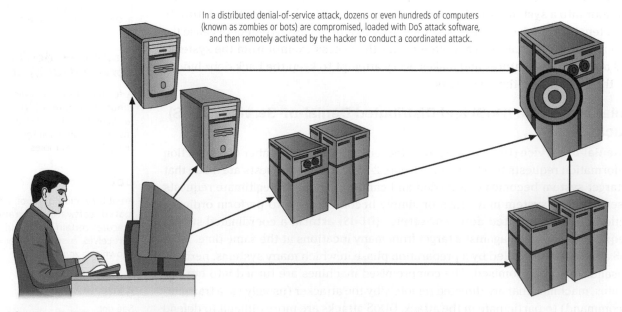

In a denial-of-service attack, a hacker compromises a system and uses that system to attack the target computer, flooding it with more requests for services than the target can handle.

In a distributed denial-of-service attack, dozens or even hundreds of computers (known as zombies or bots) are compromised, loaded with DoS attack software, and then remotely activated by the hacker to conduct a coordinated attack.

Figure 2-16   Denial-of-service attacks

configured e-mail systems on the Internet and trick them into sending many e-mails to an address of the attackers' choice. If many such systems are tricked into participating, the target e-mail address is buried under thousands or even millions of unwanted e-mails.

Although phishing attacks occur via e-mail, they are much more commonly associated with a method of social engineering designed to trick users to perform an action, rather than simply making the user a target of a DoS e-mail attack.

Communications Interception Attacks

Common software-based communications attacks include several subcategories designed to intercept and collect information in transit. These types of attacks include sniffers, spoofing, pharming, and man-in-the-middle attacks. The emergence of the Internet of Things (IoT)—the addition of communications and interactivity to everyday objects—increases the possibility of these types of attacks. Our automobiles, appliances, and entertainment devices have joined our smartphones in being interconnected and remotely controlled. The security of these devices has not always been a primary concern. IoT devices are now integrated intimately into our everyday lives and are proving to be difficult to secure, because they are often difficult or impossible to update and may not allow embedded passwords to be changed. The use of IoT devices poses significant privacy risks when they cannot be properly secured.

A **packet sniffer** (or simply **sniffer**) can monitor data traveling over a network. Sniffers can be used both for legitimate network management functions and for stealing information. Unauthorized sniffers can be extremely dangerous to a network's security because they are virtually impossible to detect and can be inserted almost anywhere. This feature makes them a favorite weapon in the hacker's arsenal. Sniffers often work on TCP/IP networks. Sniffers add risk to network communications because many systems and users send information on local networks in clear text. A sniffer program shows all the data going by, including passwords, the data inside files (such as word-processing documents), and sensitive data from applications.

Attackers want to mask their sources, so they frequently use some sort of **spoofing** to hide themselves. In **IP spoofing**, hackers use a variety of techniques to obtain trusted IP addresses and then modify packet headers (see Figure 2-17) to insert these forged addresses. Newer routers and firewall arrangements can offer protection against IP spoofing.

packet sniffer

A software program or hardware appliance that can intercept, copy, and interpret network traffic.

sniffer

See *packet sniffer*.

spoofing

The use of a communications identifier, such as a phone number, network address, or e-mail address, that is not accurately assigned to the source.

IP spoofing

A technique for gaining unauthorized access to computers using a forged or modified source IP address to give the perception that messages are coming from a trusted host.

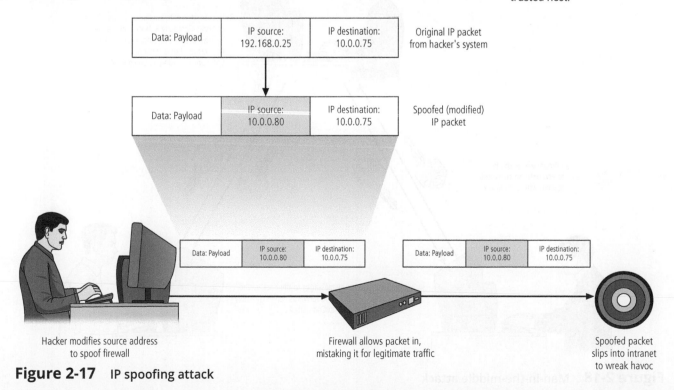

Figure 2-17   IP spoofing attack

pharming

The redirection of legitimate user Web traffic to illegitimate Web sites with the intent to collect personal information.

Domain Name System (DNS) cache poisoning

The intentional hacking and modification of a DNS database to redirect legitimate traffic to illegitimate Internet locations; also known as DNS spoofing.

man-in-the-middle

A group of attacks whereby a person intercepts a communications stream and inserts himself in the conversation to convince each of the legitimate parties that he is the other communications partner; some of these attacks involve encryption functions.

TCP hijacking

A form of man-in-the-middle attack whereby the attacker inserts himself into TCP/IP-based communications.

session hijacking

See *TCP hijacking*.

Pharming attacks often use Trojans, worms, or other virus technologies to attack an Internet browser's address bar so that the valid URL the user types is modified to be that of an illegitimate Web site. A form of pharming called **Domain Name System (DNS) cache poisoning** targets the Internet DNS system, corrupting legitimate data tables.

The key difference between pharming and *phishing* is that the latter requires the user to actively click a link or button to redirect to the illegitimate site, whereas pharming attacks modify the user's traffic without the user's knowledge or active participation.

In the well-known **man-in-the-middle** attack, an attacker monitors (or sniffs) packets from the network, modifies them, and inserts them back into the network. In a **TCP hijacking** attack, also known as **session hijacking**, the attacker uses address spoofing to impersonate other legitimate entities on the network. It allows the attacker to eavesdrop as well as to change, delete, reroute, add, forge, or divert data. A variant of TCP hijacking involves the interception of an encryption key exchange, which enables the hacker to act as an invisible man in the middle—that is, an eavesdropper—on encrypted communications. Figure 2-18 illustrates these attacks by showing how a hacker uses public and private encryption keys to intercept messages. You will learn more about encryption keys in Module 10.

Technical Hardware Failures or Errors

Technical hardware failures or errors occur when a manufacturer distributes equipment containing a known or unknown flaw. These defects can cause the system to perform outside of expected parameters, resulting in unreliable service or lack of availability. Some errors are terminal—that is, they result in the unrecoverable loss of the equipment. Some errors are intermittent in that they only manifest themselves periodically, resulting in faults that are not easily repeated. Thus, equipment can sometimes stop working or work in unexpected ways. Murphy's law (yes, there really was a Murphy) holds that if something can possibly go wrong, it will.[63] In other words, it's not a question *if* something will fail, but *when*.

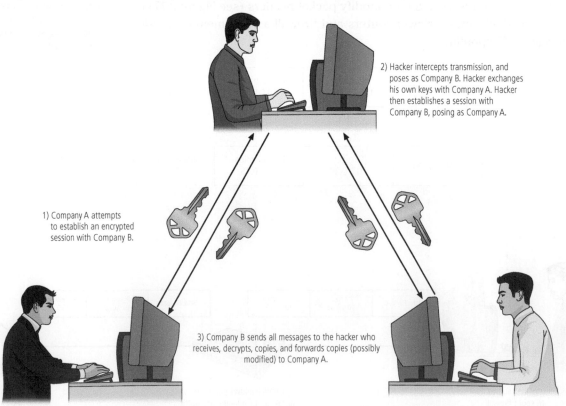

2) Hacker intercepts transmission, and poses as Company B. Hacker exchanges his own keys with Company A. Hacker then establishes a session with Company B, posing as Company A.

1) Company A attempts to establish an encrypted session with Company B.

3) Company B sends all messages to the hacker who receives, decrypts, copies, and forwards copies (possibly modified) to Company A.

Figure 2-18 Man-in-the-middle attack

The Intel Pentium CPU Failure

One of the best-known hardware failures is that of the Intel Pentium II chip (similar to the one shown in Figure 2-19), which had a defect that resulted in a calculation error under certain circumstances. Intel initially expressed little concern for the defect and stated that it would take an inordinate amount of time to identify a calculation that would interfere with the reliability of results. Yet, within days after the chip's defect was announced, popular computing journals were publishing a simple calculation (the division of 4,195,835 by 3,145,727 within a spreadsheet) that determined whether a machine contained the defective chip and thus the floating-point operation bug. The Pentium floating-point division bug (FDIV) led to a public-relations disaster for Intel that resulted in its first-ever chip recall and a loss of more than $475 million. A few months later, disclosure of another bug, known as the Dan-0411 flag erratum, further eroded the chip manufacturer's public image.[64] In 1998, Intel released its Xeon chip and discovered it also had hardware errors.

Figure 2-19   Intel chip

Intel said, "All new chips have bugs, and the process of debugging and improving performance inevitably continues even after a product is in the market."[65]

Mean Time Between Failure

In hardware terms, failures are measured in **mean time between failure (MTBF)** and **mean time to failure (MTTF)**. While MTBF and MTTF are sometimes used interchangeably, MTBF presumes that the item can be repaired or returned to service, whereas MTTF presumes the item must be replaced. From a repair standpoint, MTBF = MTTF + MTTD + MTTR, where MTTD examines **mean time to diagnose** and MTTR calculates **mean time to repair**. The most commonly failing piece of computer hardware is the hard drive, which currently has an average MTBF of approximately 500,000 hours. Hard drive vendors report they are converting from MTBF for hard drives to a new measure, **annualized failure rate**, which is based on the manufacturer's product and warranty data. So, instead of a 500,000 hour MTBF, you could have an AFR of 0.5 percent.

Technical Software Failures or Errors

Large quantities of computer code are written, debugged, published, and sold before all their bugs are detected and resolved. Sometimes, combinations of certain software and hardware reveal new failures that range from bugs to untested failure conditions. Sometimes these bugs are not errors but purposeful shortcuts left by programmers for benign or malign reasons. Collectively, shortcut access routes into programs that bypass security checks are called trap doors, and they can cause serious security breaches.

Software bugs are so commonplace that entire Web sites are dedicated to documenting them. Among the most popular is Bugtraq, found at *www.securityfocus.com*, which provides up-to-the-minute information on the latest security vulnerabilities as well as a thorough archive of past bugs.

The OWASP Top 10

The Open Web Application Security Project (OWASP) was founded in 2001 as a non-profit consortium dedicated to helping organizations create and operate software applications they could trust. Every three years or so, OWASP publishes a list of "Top 10 Web Application Security Risks" along with an OWASP Developer's Guide. The current OWASP Top 10 consists of the following:

1. Injection
2. Broken authentication
3. Sensitive data exposure
4. XML external entities (XXE)

---

mean time between failure (MTBF)

The average amount of time between hardware failures, calculated as the total amount of operation time for a specified number of units divided by the total number of failures.

mean time to failure (MTTF)

The average amount of time until the next hardware failure.

mean time to diagnose (MTTD)

The average amount of time a computer repair technician needs to determine the cause of a failure.

mean time to repair (MTTR)

The average amount of time a computer repair technician needs to resolve the cause of a failure through replacement or repair of a faulty unit.

annualized failure rate (AFR)

The probability of a failure of hardware based on the manufacturer's data of failures per year.

5. Broken access control
6. Security misconfiguration
7. Cross-site scripting (XSS)
8. Insecure deserialization
9. Insufficient logging & monitoring
10. Insecure direct object references[66]

This list is virtually unchanged since 2010. Many of these items are described in detail in the following section.

 For more information on the top 10 software vulnerabilities or the OWASP project, visit *www.owasp.org*.

The Deadly Sins in Software Security

Some software development failures and errors result in software that is difficult or impossible to deploy in a secure fashion. The most common of these failures have been identified as "deadly sins in software security."[67] These problem areas in software development were originally categorized by John Viega, upon request of Amit Youran, who at the time was the director of the Department of Homeland Security's National Cyber Security Division. These problem areas are described in the following sections. The first four "sins" are focused on Web applications.

SQL Injection   SQL injection occurs when developers fail to properly validate user input before using it to query a relational database. For example, a fairly innocuous program fragment might expect the user to input a user ID and then perform a SQL query against the USERS table to retrieve the associated name:

```
Accept USER-ID from console;
SELECT USERID, NAME FROM USERS WHERE USERID = USER-ID;
```

This is very straightforward SQL syntax; when used correctly, it displays the user ID and name. The problem is that the string accepted from the user is passed directly to the SQL database server as part of the SQL command. What if an attacker enters the string "JOE OR 1 = 1"? This string includes some valid SQL syntax that will return all rows from the table where the user ID is either "JOE" or "1 = 1." Because one is always equal to one, the system returns all user IDs and names. The possible effects of the hacker's "injection" of SQL code into the program are not limited to improper access to information—what if the attacker included SQL commands to drop the USERS table or even shut down the database?

Web Server-Related Vulnerabilities (XSS, XSRF, and Response Splitting)   One of the issues in programming Web-based applications is bugs that affect either the client side or the server side. Server-side **cross-site scripting** involves introducing security bugs that infect clients that connect to the site. Cross-site scripting allows the attacker to acquire valuable information, such as account credentials, account numbers, or other critical data. Often an attacker encodes a malicious link and places it in the target server, making it look less suspicious. After the data is collected by the hostile application, it sends what appears to be a valid response from the intended server. Cross-site request forgery (XSRF or CSRF) attacks cause users to attack servers they access legitimately, on behalf of an outside attacker. For example, on banking Web sites, this could include changing a fund transfer account number to the attacker's account number. HTTP response splitting involves the unvalidated redirection of data into a Web-based application from an unvalidated source, such as an HTTP request, or as part of an HTTP response header, and possibly contains malicious characters that have not been checked for.

Web Client-Related Vulnerability (XSS)   The same cross-site scripting attacks that can infect a server can also be used to attack Web clients. Client-side cross-site scripting errors can cause problems that allow an attacker to send malicious code to the user's computer by inserting the script into an otherwise normal Web site. The user's Web browser, not knowing the code is malicious, runs it and inadvertently infects the client system. Some code can read a user's Web information, such as his or her Web history, stored cookies or session tokens, or even stored passwords.

cross-site scripting (XSS)

A Web application fault that occurs when an application running on a Web server inserts commands into a user's browser session and causes information to be sent to a hostile server.

Use of Magic URLs and Hidden Forms   HTTP is a stateless protocol in which computer programs on either end of the communication channel cannot rely on a guaranteed delivery of any message. This makes it difficult for software developers to track a user's exchanges with a Web site over multiple interactions. Too often, sensitive state information is included in hidden form fields on the HTML page or simply included in a "magic" URL. (For example, the authentication ID is passed as a parameter in the URL for the exchanges that will follow.) If this information is stored as plain text, an attacker can harvest the information from a magic URL as it travels across the network or use scripts on the client to modify information in hidden form fields. Depending on the structure of the application, the harvested or modified information can be used in spoofing or hijacking attacks, or to change the way the application operates. For example, if an item's price is kept in a hidden form field, the attacker could arrange to buy that item for one cent.

Buffer Overrun   The next set of "sins" is focused on implementation. For example, buffers are used to manage mismatches in the processing rates between two entities involved in a communication process. During a **buffer overrun**, an attacker can make the target system execute instructions or take advantage of some other unintended consequence of the failure. Sometimes this is limited to a DoS attack. In any case, data on the attacked system loses integrity. In 1998, Microsoft encountered the following buffer overflow problem:

> *Microsoft acknowledged that if you type a res://URL (a Microsoft-devised type of URL) which is longer than 256 characters in Internet Explorer 4.0, the browser will crash. No big deal, except that anything after the 256th character can be executed on the computer. This maneuver, known as a buffer overrun, is just about the oldest hacker trick in the book. Tack some malicious code (say, an executable version of the Pentium-crashing FooF code) onto the end of the URL, and you have the makings of a disaster.*[68]

One of the marks of effective software is the ability to catch and resolve exceptions—unusual situations that require special processing. If the program doesn't manage exceptions correctly, the software may not perform as expected. Exceptions differ from errors in that exceptions are considered expected but irregular situations at runtime, while errors are mistakes in the running program that can be resolved only by fixing the program.

Format String Problems   Computer languages often are equipped with built-in capabilities to reformat data while they output it. The formatting instructions are usually written as a "format string." Unfortunately, some programmers may use data from untrusted sources as a format string. An attacker may embed characters that are meaningful as formatting directives (such as %x, %d, %p, etc.) into malicious input. If this input is then interpreted by the program as formatting directives (such as an argument to the C printf function), the attacker may be able to access information or overwrite very targeted portions of the program's stack with data of the attacker's choosing.

Integer Bugs (Overflows/Underflows)   Although mathematical calculation theoretically can deal with numbers that contain an arbitrary number of digits, the binary representations used by computers are of a particular fixed length. The programmer must anticipate the size of the numbers to be calculated in any given part of the program. An **integer bug** can result when a programmer does not validate the inputs to a calculation to verify that the integers are of the expected size. For example, adding 1 to 32,767 should produce 32,768, but in computer arithmetic with 16-bit signed integers, the erroneous result is –32,768. An underflow can occur, for example, when you subtract 5 from negative 32,767, which returns the incorrect result +32,764, because the largest negative integer that can be represented in 16 bits is negative 32,768.

> *Integer bugs fall into four broad classes: overflows, underflows, truncations, and signedness errors. Integer bugs are usually exploited indirectly—that is, triggering an integer bug enables an attacker to corrupt other areas of memory, gaining control of an application. The memory allocated for a value could be exceeded, if that value is greater than expected, with the extra bits written into other locations. The system may then experience unexpected consequences, which could be miscalculations, errors, crashing, or other problems. Even though integer bugs are often used to build a buffer overflow or other memory corruption attack, integer bugs are not just a special case of memory corruption bugs.*[69]

C++ Catastrophes   C++ is a programming language that has been around since the 1980s. In recent years, issues have arisen that cause concern from a security perspective. The first of these issues is the compromise of a function pointer, which is a way to reference executable code in memory. Many operating systems have APIs that use these pointers to control the execution of code. If these pointers are corrupted, control of the flow of the program can be interrupted

buffer overrun

An application error that occurs when more data is sent to a program buffer than it is designed to handle.

integer bug

A class of computational error caused by methods that computers use to store and manipulate integer numbers; this bug can be exploited by attackers.

and redirected. The second issue can occur if a C++ class has a virtual method containing a virtual function pointer table. Overwriting the class allows alteration of the virtual table pointer, which again allows the attacker to take over the flow of the program.[70]

Catching Exceptions   Exceptions are errors in the execution of a program. How the program handles these errors can allow the program either to close safely or to continue in an unstable and potentially insecure manner. Attackers learn about programs that don't handle errors well and figure out how to intentionally introduce an error, allowing them to seize control of the application in its post-error state. Learning how to properly manage "try-catch" blocks to handle exceptions is a critical skill in programming, and even the best programmers run across unexpected conditions that result in systems problems. This "sin" is closely related to several others that deal with system or program errors.

Command Injection   The problem of **command injection** is caused by a developer's failure to ensure that command input is validated before it is used in the program. Perhaps the simplest example can be demonstrated using the Windows command shell:

```
@echo off
set /p myVar="Enter the string>"
set someVar=%myVar%
echo
```

These commands ask the user to provide a string and then simply set another variable to the value and display it. However, an attacker could use the command chaining character "&" to append other commands to the string the user provides (Hello&del*.*).

Failure to Handle Errors   What happens when a system or application encounters a scenario that it is not prepared to handle? Does it attempt to complete the operation (reading or writing data or performing calculations)? Does it issue a cryptic message that only a programmer could understand, or does it simply stop functioning? Failure to handle errors can cause a variety of unexpected system behaviors. Programmers are expected to anticipate problems and prepare their application code to handle them. This category focuses on those errors rather than exceptions, which were described earlier.

Information Leakage   One of the most common methods of obtaining inside and classified information is directly or indirectly from one person, usually an employee. A famous World War II military poster warned that "loose lips sink ships," emphasizing the risk to naval deployments from enemy attack if sailors, Marines, or their families disclosed the movements of U.S. vessels. A widely shared fear was that the enemy had civilian operatives waiting in bars and shops at common Navy ports of call, just waiting for the troops to drop hints about where they were going and when. By warning employees against disclosing information, organizations can protect the secrecy of their operation.

Race Conditions   A race condition is a failure of a program that occurs when an unexpected ordering of events in its execution results in a conflict over access to a system resource. This conflict does not need to involve streams of code inside the program because current operating systems and processor technology automatically break a program into multiple threads that can be executed simultaneously. If the threads that result from this process share any resources, they may interfere with each other. A race condition occurs, for example, when a program creates a temporary file and an attacker can replace it between the time it is created and the time it is used. A race condition can also occur when information is stored in multiple memory threads if one thread stores information in the wrong memory location, either by accident or intent.

Poor Usability   Employees prefer doing things the easy way. When faced with an "official way" of performing a task and an "unofficial way"—which is easier—they prefer the latter. The best solution to address this issue is to provide only one way—the secure way! Integrating security and usability, adding training and awareness, and ensuring solid controls all contribute to the security of information. Allowing users to choose easier solutions by default will inevitably lead to loss.

command injection

An application error that occurs when user input is passed directly to a compiler or interpreter without screening for content that may disrupt or compromise the intended function.

Not Updating Easily   As developers create applications, they try to catch all of the errors and bugs in the programs. With the extreme complexity of modern applications, and with the expected dramatic increase in complexity of future applications, it's not always possible to catch all of the errors before the product needs to go to market. The current method of handling this issue is to release patches and updates after the product is in the hands of the consumers. Updates themselves introduce a security risk, as attackers could interrupt and swap out legitimate updates or patches with malware or their own program alterations. Applications that don't update cleanly and securely thus introduce a security risk for the organization. The aspects of change management discussed in later modules in this book also affect this sin, as the ability to test and roll back changes is critical in case an update or patch results in unexpected issues.

Executing Code with Too Much Privilege   Computers talk to other computers and are users in their own rights. As users, they must have privileges to access program and data on other computers. When systems are set up with excessive privileges, they can create security issues. Just like users, systems and applications should only have the least privilege they need to do the job. Developers may initially assign higher-level privileges in the development of an application and then may forget to lower those privileges. If attackers can compromise a system with these high-level privileges, they can use that access to take over other systems. One of the greatest concerns in this area occurs when individuals download and run code from public sources, like Web sites. Because you didn't develop the code or pay a professional vendor for it, you can't be certain that the code doesn't contain malicious components like back doors or data exfiltration components.

Failure to Protect Stored Data   Protecting stored data is a large enough issue to be the core subject of this entire text. Programmers are responsible for integrating access controls into programs and keeping secret information out of them. Access controls, the subject of later modules, regulate who, what, when, where, and how users and systems interact with data. Failure to properly implement sufficiently strong access controls makes the data vulnerable. Overly strict access controls hinder business users in the performance of their duties, and as a result, the controls may be administratively removed or bypassed. The integration of secret information—such as the "hard coding" of passwords, encryption keys, or other sensitive information—can put that information at risk of disclosure.

The Sins of Mobile Code   In this context, mobile code is an application, applet, macro, or script that may be imbedded in another application or document and thus downloaded and executed without the user even knowing, and especially without consenting. Office suite tools are notorious for using macros, and third parties could insert malicious content into existing office documents shared by users. Web pages also use mobile code with embedded scripts, programs, and applets. Java has come under fire lately for its susceptibility to attack, to the point that many programs won't use Java. The same approach has been taken with ActiveX and Adobe Flash plug-ins. Mobile code in organizational applications should be reviewed and tested carefully to ensure that security vulnerabilities from the code don't cause problems.

Use of Weak Password-Based Systems   The next set of sins involve the use of cryptography. For example, failure to require sufficient password strength and to control incorrect password entry is a serious security issue. Password policy can specify the acceptable number and type of characters, the frequency of mandatory changes, and even the reusability of old passwords. Similarly, a system administrator can regulate the permitted number of incorrect password entries that are submitted and further improve the level of protection. Systems that do not validate passwords, or that store passwords in easily accessible locations, are ripe for attack.

Weak Random Numbers   Most modern cryptosystems, like many other computer systems, use random number generators. However, a decision support system that uses random and pseudorandom numbers for Monte Carlo method forecasting does not require the same degree of rigor and the same need for true randomness as a system that seeks to implement cryptographic procedures. These "random" number generators use a mathematical algorithm based on a seed value and another system component (such as the computer clock) to simulate a random number. Those who understand the workings of such a "random" number generator can predict particular values at particular times.

Using Cryptography Incorrectly   A wide variety of issues fall into this category. Cryptography is a powerful tool to protect information, especially information that may travel outside the organization's protective networks and systems. Using untested or undertested cryptographic algorithms and programs can cause issues. Using weak crypto keys or reusing the same crypto keys can cause issues, as can sending crypto keys through the same medium as the encrypted messages. The challenges of using cryptography correctly require the organization to carefully review and implement its technologies before trusting them to carry its sensitive data.

Failure to Protect Network Traffic   The final set of "sins" focuses on issues associated with networking. For example, with the growing popularity of wireless networking comes a corresponding increase in the risk that wirelessly transmitted data will be intercepted. Most wireless networks are installed and operated with little or no protection for the information that is broadcast between the client and the network wireless access point. This is especially true of public networks found in coffee shops, bookstores, and hotels. Without appropriate encryption such as that afforded by WPA, attackers can intercept and view your data. Traffic on a wired network is also vulnerable to interception in some situations. On networks using hubs instead of switches, any user can install a packet sniffer and collect communications to and from users on that network. Periodic scans for unauthorized packet sniffers and unauthorized connections to the network, as well as general awareness of the threat, can mitigate this problem.

Improper Use of PKI, Especially SSL   Public key infrastructure (PKI), described in Module 10, is currently the gold standard for securing network communications. One of the biggest challenges in PKI is certificate management. There is a great deal of "trust" associated with the use of PKI, and a lot of that trust is manifested in certificates that must be properly passed around between systems, like an ID card, so that access can be granted. The mishandling of PKI certificates can cause issues, including improper validation of credentials. As a result, a person or system that should get access doesn't, and a person or system that shouldn't have access may get it. Many programs in PKI also revolve around the use of Secure Sockets Layer (SSL), which programmers use to transfer sensitive data, such as credit card numbers and other personal information, between a client and server. While most programmers assume that using SSL guarantees security, they often mishandle this technology. SSL and its successor, Transport Layer Security (TLS), both need certificate validation to be truly secure. Failure to use Hypertext Transfer Protocol Secure (HTTPS) to validate the certificate authority and then the certificate itself, or failure to validate the information against a certificate revocation list (CRL), can compromise the security of SSL traffic. You will learn much more about cryptographic controls in Module 10.

Trusting Network Name Resolution   The DNS is a function of the World Wide Web that converts a URL like *www .cengage.com* into the IP address of the Web server host. This distributed model is vulnerable to attack or "poisoning." DNS cache poisoning involves compromising a DNS server and then changing the valid IP address associated with a domain name into one the attacker chooses, usually a fake Web site designed to obtain personal information or one that accrues a benefit to the attacker—for example, redirecting shoppers from a competitor's Web site. Such attacks are usually more sinister, however; for instance, a simulated banking site used for a phishing attack might harvest online banking information.

How does someone get this fake information into the DNS server? Aside from a direct attack against a root DNS server, most attempts are made against primary and secondary DNS servers, which are local to an organization and part of the distributed DNS system. Other attacks attempt to compromise the DNS servers further up the DNS distribution mode—those of ISPs or backbone connectivity providers. The DNS relies on a process of automated updates that can be exploited. Attackers most commonly compromise segments of the DNS by attacking the name of the name server and substituting their own DNS primary name server, by incorrectly updating an individual record, or by responding before an actual DNS can. In the last type of attack, the attacker tries to discover a delay in a name server or to introduce a delay, as in a DoS attack. When the delay is in place, the attacker can set up another server to respond as if it were the actual DNS server, before the real DNS server can respond. The client accepts the first set of information it receives and is directed to that IP address.

Neglecting Change Control   One of the topics associated with an earlier version of "deadly sins" that has fallen off the newer list is more of a managerial topic, and is worthy of discussion. Developers use a process known as change control to ensure that the working system delivered to users represents the intent of the developers. Early in the development process, change control ensures that developers do not work at cross purposes by altering the same programs or parts of programs at the same time. Once the system is in production, change control processes ensure that only authorized changes are introduced and that all changes are adequately tested before being released.

Technological Obsolescence

Antiquated or outdated infrastructure can lead to unreliable and untrustworthy systems. Management must recognize that when technology becomes outdated, there is a risk of losing data integrity from attacks. Management's strategic planning should always include an analysis of the technology currently in use. Ideally, proper planning by management should prevent technology from becoming obsolete, but when obsolescence is clear, management must take immediate action. IT professionals play a large role in the identification of probable obsolescence.

Recently, the software vendor Symantec retired support for a legacy version of its popular antivirus software, and organizations that wanted continued product support were obliged to upgrade immediately to a different version of antivirus software. In organizations where IT personnel had kept management informed of the coming retirement, these replacements were made more promptly and at lower cost than in organizations where the software had become obsolete.

Perhaps the most significant case of technology obsolescence in recent years is Microsoft's Windows XP. This desktop operating system was dominant in the market for many years, beginning in 2001. The OS evolved over time to be used in multiple variations such as XP Pro and XP Home, it had feature and capability upgrades in three service packs, and it even made the transition to new processors with a 64-bit edition. It was superseded in the corporation's lineup of desktop operating systems by Microsoft Vista in January 2007. However, it retained a large following of users and remained in widespread use for many years. Microsoft discontinued support for Windows XP in April 2014. Many industries and organizations built critical elements of their business systems and even their infrastructure control systems on top of Windows XP, or they used it as an embedded operating system inside other systems, such as automated teller machines and power generating and control systems. Similar issues seem to follow other Windows variants, as users get comfortable with a particular OS and then seem reluctant to upgrade to a newer version.

Figure 2-20 shows other examples of obsolete technology, including removable storage media in 8-inch, 5-inch, and 3.5-inch formats as well as open-reel magnetic tape.

Theft

The threat of **theft** is a constant. The value of information is diminished when it is copied without the owner's knowledge. Physical theft can be controlled easily using a wide variety of measures, from locked doors to trained security personnel and the installation of alarm systems. Electronic theft, however, is a more complex problem to manage and control. When someone steals a physical object, the loss is easily detected; if it has any importance at all, its absence is noted. When electronic information is stolen, the crime is not always readily apparent. If thieves are clever and cover their tracks carefully, the crime may remain undiscovered until it is too late.

Theft is often an overlapping category with software attacks, espionage or trespass, information extortion, and compromises to intellectual property. A hacker or other individual threat agent could access a system and commit most of these offenses by downloading a company's information and then threatening to publish it if not paid.

The increasing use of mobile technology, including smartphones, tablet PCs, and laptops, increases the risk of data theft. More disconcerting than the loss of data is the chance that the user has allowed the mobile device to retain account credentials, allowing the thief to use legitimate access to get into business or personal accounts that belong to the victim.

theft

The illegal taking of another's property, which can be physical, electronic, or intellectual.

Figure 2-20   Obsolete technologies

Closing Scenario

Shortly after the SLS Board of Directors meeting, Charlie was named chief information security officer to fill a new leadership position created to report to the CIO, Gladys Williams. The primary role of the new position is to provide leadership for SLS's efforts to improve its information security profile.

Discussion Questions

1. Before the discussion at the start of this module, how did Fred, Gladys, and Charlie each perceive the scope and scale of the new information security effort? Did Fred's perception change after the discussion?
2. How should Fred measure success when he evaluates Gladys' performance for this project? How should he evaluate Charlie's performance?
3. Which of the threats discussed in this module should receive Charlie's attention early in his planning process?

Ethical Decision Making

1. Suppose Charlie has made great progress in planning to improve the security program at the company. After many weeks of planning and careful implementation, a formal plan is ready for presentation to the Board of Directors. Gladys asks Charlie to prepare a written report and a presentation for Gladys to give to the Board. Gladys edits the presentation to make it seem that she prepared the work herself with Fred's assistance, but without any mention of Charlie's contributions. Is Gladys acting ethically? What may be some consequences of her actions?
2. Suppose that SLS has implemented the policy prohibiting use of personal USB drives at work. Also, suppose that Davey Martinez brought in the USB drive he had used to store last month's accounting worksheet. When he plugged in the drive, the worm outbreak started again and infected two servers. When Charlie finds out about this violation of policy, he confronts Davey and gives him a verbal dressing down that includes profanity and threats. Is Charlie acting ethically?

Selected Readings

- The journal article "Enemy at the Gates: Threats to Information Security," by Michael Whitman, was published in *Communications of the ACM* in August 2003, on pages 91–96. An abstract is available from the ACM Digital Library at *www.acm.org*. Journal access may be available through your local library.
- *The Art of War* by Sun Tzu. Many translations and editions are widely available, both print and online.
- *24 Deadly Sins of Software Security: Programming Flaws and How to Fix Them*, by M. Howard, D. LeBlanc, and J. Viega, is published by McGraw-Hill/Osborne Publishing.

Module Summary

- Information security performs four important functions to ensure that information assets remain safe and useful: protecting the organization's ability to function, enabling the safe operation of applications implemented on the organization's IT systems, protecting the data an organization collects and uses, and safeguarding the organization's technology assets.
- To make sound decisions about information security, management must be informed about threats to its people, applications, data, and information systems, and the attacks they face.

- Threats are any events or circumstances that have the potential to adversely affect operations and assets. An attack is an intentional or unintentional act that can damage or otherwise compromise information and the systems that support it. A vulnerability is a potential weakness in an asset or its defensive controls.
- Threats or dangers facing an organization's people, information, and systems fall into the following categories:
  - *Compromises to intellectual property*—Intellectual property, such as trade secrets, copyrights, trademarks, or patents, are intangible assets that may be attacked via software piracy or the exploitation of asset protection controls.
  - *Deviations in quality of service*—Organizations rely on services provided by others. Losses can come from interruptions to those services.
  - *Espionage or trespass*—Asset losses may result when electronic and human activities breach the confidentiality of information.
  - *Forces of nature*—A wide range of natural events can overwhelm control systems and preparations to cause losses to data and availability.
  - *Human error or failure*—Losses to assets may come from intentional or accidental actions by people inside and outside the organization.
  - *Information extortion*—Stolen or inactivated assets may be held hostage to extract payment of ransom.
  - *Sabotage or vandalism*—Losses may result from the deliberate sabotage of a computer system or business, or from acts of vandalism. These acts can either destroy an asset or damage the image of an organization.
  - *Software attacks*—Losses may result when attackers use software to gain unauthorized access to systems or cause disruptions in systems availability.
  - *Technical hardware failures or errors*—Technical defects in hardware systems can cause unexpected results, including unreliable service or lack of availability.
  - *Technical software failures or errors*—Software used by systems may have purposeful or unintentional errors that result in failures, which can lead to loss of availability or unauthorized access to information.
  - *Technological obsolescence*—Antiquated or outdated infrastructure can lead to unreliable and untrustworthy systems that may result in loss of availability or unauthorized access to information.
  - *Theft*—Theft of information can result from a wide variety of attacks.

Review Questions

1. Why is information security a management problem? What can management do that technology cannot?

2. Why is data the most important asset an organization possesses? What other assets in the organization require protection?

3. Which management groups are responsible for implementing information security to protect the organization's ability to function?

4. Has the implementation of networking technology, such as the cloud, created more or less risk for businesses that use information technology? Why?

5. What is information extortion? Describe how such an attack can cause losses, using an example not found in the text.

6. Why are employees among the greatest threats to information security?

7. How can you protect against shoulder surfing?

8. How has the perception of the hacker changed over recent years? What is the profile of a hacker today?

9. What is the difference between a skilled hacker and an unskilled hacker, other than skill levels? How does the protection against each differ?

10. What are the various types of malware? How do worms differ from viruses? Do Trojan horses carry viruses or worms?

11. Why does polymorphism cause greater concern than traditional malware? How does it affect detection?

12. What is the most common violation of intellectual property? How does an organization protect against it? What agencies fight it?

13. What are the various forces of nature? Which type might be of greatest concern to an organization in Las Vegas? Jakarta? Oklahoma City? Amsterdam? Miami? Tokyo?

14. How is technological obsolescence a threat to information security? How can an organization protect against it?

15. Does the intellectual property owned by an organization usually have value? If so, how can attackers threaten that value?

16. What are the types of password attacks? What can a systems administrator do to protect against them?

17. What is the difference between a denial-of-service attack and a distributed denial-of-service attack? Which is more dangerous? Why?

18. For a sniffer attack to succeed, what must the attacker do? How can an attacker gain access to a network to use the sniffer system?

19. What methods would a social engineering hacker use to gain information about a user's login ID and password? How would these methods differ depending on the user's position in the company?

20. What is a buffer overflow, and how is it used against a Web server?

Exercises

1. Consider that an individual threat agent, like a hacker, can be a factor in more than one threat category. If a hacker breaks into a network, copies a few files, defaces a Web page, and steals credit card numbers, how many different threat categories does the attack fall into?

2. Using the Web, research Mafiaboy's exploits. When and how did he compromise sites? How was he caught?

3. Search the Web for "The Official Phreaker's Manual." What information in this manual might help a security administrator to protect a communications system?

4. This module discussed many threats and vulnerabilities to information security. Using the Web, find at least two other sources of information about threats and vulnerabilities. Begin with *www.securityfocus.com* and use a keyword search on "threats."

5. Using the categories of threats mentioned in this module and the various attacks described, review several current media sources and identify examples of each threat.

References

1. Wood, Charles C. *Information Security Policies Made Easy*. 10th Edition. InformationShield. 2008.
2. Sun-Tzu Wu. "Sun Tzu's The Art of War." Translation by the Sonshi Group. Accessed May 31, 2016, from *www.sonshi.com/sun-tzu-art-of-war-translation-original.html*.
3. Internet World Stats. "Internet Usage Statistics: The Internet Big Picture, World Internet Users and Population Stats." Accessed July 14, 2020, from *www.internetworldstats.com/stats.htm*.
4. Whitman, M., and Mattord, H. 2015 SEC/CISE Threats to Information Protection Report. Security Executive Council. *www.securityexecutivecouncil.com*.
5. Ibid.
6. Ibid.
7. Ibid.
8. Whitman, M., and Mattord, H. "Threats to Information Security Revisited." *Journal of Information Systems Security* 8, no. 1 (2012): 21, 41. *www.jissec.org/*.
9. Business Software Alliance. "Software Management: Security Imperative, Business Opportunity." 2018. Accessed July 14, 2020, from *https://gss.bsa.org/wp-content/uploads/2018/05/2018_BSA_GSS_Report_en.pdf*.
10. Microsoft. "Microsoft License Terms." Accessed August 10, 2020, from *www.microsoft.com/en-us/useterms*.

11. Patton, Natalie. "Bootlegged Software Could Cost Community College." Las Vegas Review Journal Online. September 18, 1997. Accessed May 24, 2016, from *http://nl.newsbank.com/nl-search/we/Archives?.*

12. Fusion Connect. "Infographic: The Cost of Downtime." Accessed August 12, 2020, from *www.fusionconnect. com/blog/blog-archive/infographic-the-cost-of-downtime/?megapath.*

13. Chowdhry, Pankaj. "The Gibraltar Hack: Anatomy of a Break-in." *PCWeek* 16, no. 41 (1999): 1, 22.

14. Ibid.

15. Rosencrance, Linda. "Teen Hacker 'Mafiaboy' Sentenced." ComputerWorld Online. Accessed May 24, 2016, from *www.computerworld.com/article/2583318/security0/teen-hacker-mafiaboy-sentenced.html.*

16. Kaspersky. "Top 10 Most Notorious Hackers of All Time." Accessed August 10, 2020, from *www.kaspersky. com/resource-center/threats/top-ten-greatest-hackers.*

17. Ibid.

18. Mitnick, K., and Simon, W. *The Art of Deception: Controlling the Human Element of Security.* Wiley Publishing, Inc., Indianapolis, 2002.

19. "Edward Snowden: A Timeline." NBC News. Accessed May 23, 2016, from *www.nbcnews.com/feature/ edward-snowden-interview/edward-snowden-timeline-n114871.*

20. Goldman, David. "Jailbreaking iPhone Apps is Now Legal." CNN Money. July 26, 2010. Accessed August 10, 2020, from *http://money.cnn.com/2010/07/26/technology/iphone_jailbreaking/.*

21. Hackthissite.org. Accessed August 10, 2020, from *www.hackthissite.org/.*

22. Webopedia. "Static Electricity and Computers." Accessed August 10, 2020, from *www.webopedia.com/ DidYouKnow/Computer_Science/static.asp.*

23. Del Rey, Jason. "Amazon's Massive AWS Outage Was Caused by Human Error." Vox. Accessed August 11, 2020, from *www.vox.com/2017/3/2/14792636/amazon-aws-internet-outage-cause-human-error-incorrect-command.*

24. Kennedy, James T. "Internet Intricacies: Don't Get Caught in the Net." *Contingency Planning & Management* 3, no. 1: 12.

25. Abreu, Elinor. "Hacker Kevin Mitnick speaks out." CNN. Accessed August 10, 2020, from *www.cnn. com/2000/TECH/computing/09/29/open.mitnick.idg/.*

26. FBI Internet Crime Complaint Center. "2019 Internet Crime Report." Accessed August 11, 2020, from *https://pdf.ic3.gov/2019_IC3Report.pdf.*

27. The 419 Coalition. Accessed August 11, 2020, from *https://419coalition.org/.*

28. CERT Advisory CA-1991-03. "Unauthorized Password Change Requests Via Email Messages." Accessed August 10, 2020, from *https://resources.sei.cmu.edu/asset_files/WhitePaper/1991_019_001_496244.pdf.*

29. "Rebuffed Internet Extortionist Posts Stolen Credit Card Data." CNN Online. January 10, 2000.

30. Lewis, Truman. "Express Scripts Extortion Scheme Widens." *Consumer Affairs.* September 30, 2009. Accessed August 10, 2020, from *www.consumeraffairs.com/news/index/2009/09/.*

31. Gendar, Alison. "Anthony Digati arrested for allegedly threatening New York Life with email spam attack." March 8, 2010. Accessed August 10, 2020, from *www.nydailynews.com/news/money/ anthony-digati-arrested-allegedly-threatening-new-york-life-email-spam-attack-article-1.173739.*

32. Wlasuk, Alan. "Cyber-Extortion—Huge Profits, Low Risk." *Security Week.* July 13, 2012. Accessed August 10, 2020, from *www.securityweek.com/cyber-extortion-huge-profits-low-risk.*

33. Leger, Donna Leinwand, and Johnson, Kevin. "Federal Agents Knock Down Zeus Botnet, CryptoLocker." *USA Today.* June 2, 2014. Accessed August 11, 2020, from *www.usatoday.com/story/news/ nation/2014/06/02/global-cyber-fraud/9863977/.*

34. Fruhlinger, Josh. "What Is WannaCry Ransomware, How Does It Infect, and Who Was Responsible?" CSO Online. August 30, 2018. Accessed August 10, 2020, from *www.csoonline.com/article/3227906/what-is-wann-acry-ransomware-how-does-it-infect-and-who-was-responsible.html.*

35. FBI Internet Crime Complaint Center. "2019 Internet Crime Report." Accessed August 11, 2020, from *https://pdf.ic3.gov/2019_IC3Report.pdf.*

36. Bridis, Ted. "British Authorities Arrest Hacker Wanted as Fluffi Bunni." April 29, 2003. Accessed August 10, 2020, from *www.securityfocus.com/news/4320*.

37. Costello, Sam. "Attrition.org Stops Mirroring Web Site Defacements." ComputerWorld Online. May 22, 2001. Accessed August 10, 2020, from *www.computerworld.com/article/2582627/attrition-org-stops-mirroring-web-site-defacements.html*.

38. Infoshop News. "Fighting the Fascists Using Direct Action Hacktivism." March 28, 2010. Accessed May 24, 2016, from *www.anarchistnews.org/content/fighting-fascists-using-direct-action-hacktivism*.

39. Denning, Dorothy E. "Activism, Hacktivism, and Cyberterrorism: The Internet as a Tool for Influencing Foreign Policy." Info War Online. February 4, 2000. Accessed August 10, 2020, from *www.iwar.org.uk/cyberterror/resources/denning.htm*.

40. Elmusharaf, M. "Cyber Terrorism: The New Kind of Terrorism." Computer Crime Research Center Online. April 8, 2004. Accessed August 10, 2020, from *www.crime-research.org/articles/Cyber_Terrorism_new_kind_Terrorism*.

41. Lemos, R. "Assault on Net Servers Fails." C|Net *News.com*. October 22, 2002. Accessed August 10, 2020, from *www.cnet.com/news/assault-on-net-servers-fails/*.

42. Messmer, Ellen. "U.S. Cyber Counterattack: Bomb 'Em One Way or the Other." February 8, 2007. Accessed August 10, 2020, from *www.networkworld.com/article/2294945/u-s–cyber-counterattack–bomb–em-one-way-or-the-other.html*.

43. Perlroth, Nicole, and Sanger, David. "Cyberattacks Seem Meant to Destroy, Not Just Disrupt." March 28, 2013. Accessed August 11, 2020, from *www.nytimes.com/2013/03/29/technology/corporate-cyberattackers-possibly-state-backed-now-seek-to-destroy-data.html*.

44. Ibid.

45. Redwine, Samuel T., Jr. (Editor). *Software Assurance: A Guide to the Common Body of Knowledge to Produce, Acquire, and Sustain Secure Software*. Version 1.1. U.S. Department of Homeland Security. September 2006.

46. Ibid.

47. Strickland, Jonathon. "10 Worst Computer Viruses of All Time." *How Stuff Works*. Accessed August 11, 2020, from *http://computer.howstuffworks.com/worst-computer-viruses2.htm#page=1*.

48. Rochford, Louisa. "The Worst Computer Viruses in History." *CEO Today*. Accessed August 11, 2020, from *www.ceotodaymagazine.com/2019/06/the-worst-computer-viruses-in-history*.

49. Weinberger, Sharon. "Top Ten Most-Destructive Computer Viruses." *Smithsonian*. Accessed August 11, 2020, from *www.smithsonianmag.com/science-nature/top-ten-most-destructive-computer-viruses-159542266*.

50. U.S. Department of Justice Press Release. "Creator of Melissa Computer Virus Sentenced to 20 Months in Federal Prison." Accessed August 11, 2020, from *www.justice.gov/archive/criminal/cybercrime/press-releases/2002/melissaSent.htm*.

51. Kehoe, Brendan P. *Zen and the Art of the Internet*, 1st Edition. January 1992. Accessed August 11, 2020, from *https://legacy.cs.indiana.edu/docproject/zen/zen-1.0_10.html#SEC91*.

52. TruSecure. "TruSecure Successfully Defends Customers Against Goner Virus." TruSecure Online. December 18, 2001. Accessed May 24, 2016, from *www.thefreelibrary.com/TruSecure+Successfully+Defends+Customers+Against+Goner+Virus.-a080877835*.

53. McCarthy, Jack. "Blaster Worm Author Gets Jail Time." *InfoWorld*. January 28, 2005. Accessed August 11, 2020, from *www.infoworld.com/t/business/blaster-worm-author-gets-jail-time-441*.

54. Jones, Les. "GoodTimes Virus Hoax Frequently Asked Questions." December 12, 1998. Accessed August 11, 2020, from *http://fgouget.free.fr/goodtimes/goodtimes.html*.

55. SANS Institute. "Glossary of Security Terms." SANS Institute Online. Accessed August 11, 2020, from *www.sans.org/security-resources/glossary-of-terms/*.

56. SANS Institute. "Consensus Roadmap for Defeating Distributed Denial of Service Attacks: A Project of the Partnership for Critical Infrastructure Security." SANS Institute Online. February 23, 2000. Accessed August 11, 2020, from *www.sans.org/dosstep/roadmap*.

57. Trend Micro. WORM_MYDOOM.A. Accessed May 24, 2016, from *www.trendmicro.com/vinfo/us/ threat-encyclopedia/archive/malware/worm_mydoom.a.*

58. Richtel, Matt. "Canada Arrests 15-Year-Old In Web Attack." *The New York Times.* April 20, 2000.

59. "How CloudNine Wound Up in Hell." Wired Online. February 1, 2002. Accessed August 11, 2020, from *www. wired.com/2002/02/how-cloudnine-wound-up-in-hell/.*

60. Korolov, M. "Last Week's DDoS Against the BBC May Have Been the Largest in History." CSO Online. Accessed August 11, 2020, from *www.csoonline.com/article/3020292/cyber-attacks-espionage/ddos-attack- on-bbc-may-have-been-biggest-in-history.html.*

61. O'Brien, Sara Ashley. "Widespread Cyberattack Takes Down Sites Worldwide." CNN Business. October 21, 2016. Accessed August 11, 2020, from *https://money.cnn.com/2016/10/21/technology/ddos-attack-popular- sites/index.html.*

62. Pearce, James. "Security Expert Warns of MP3 Danger." ZDNet News Online. March 18, 2002. Accessed August 12, 2020, from *www.zdnet.com/article/security-expert-warns-of-mp3-danger/.*

63. "Murphy's Laws Site." Accessed August 12, 2020, from *www.murphys-laws.com/.*

64. Wolfe, Alexander. "Intel Preps Plan to Bust Bugs in Pentium MPUs." *Electronic Engineering Times*, no. 960 (June 1997): 1.

65. Taylor, Roger. "Intel to Launch New Chip Despite Bug Reports." *Financial Times* (London), no. 25 (June 1998): 52.

66. OWASP. "Top 10 Web Application Security Risks." Accessed August 12, 2020, from *https://owasp.org/ www-project-top-ten/.*

67. Howard, M., LeBlanc, D., and Viega, J. *24 Deadly Sins of Software Security: Programming Flaws and How to Fix Them.* 2010. New York: McGraw-Hill/Osborne.

68. Spanbauer, Scott. "Pentium Bug, Meet the IE 4.0 Flaw." *PC World* 16, no. 2 (February 1998): 55.

69. Brumley, D., Tzi-cker, C., Johnson, R., Lin, H., and Song, D. "RICH: Automatically Protecting Against Integer- Based Vulnerabilities." Accessed August 12, 2020, from *https://sites.cs.ucsb.edu/~rachel.lin/papers/Rich. pdf.*

70. Howard, M., LeBlanc, D., and Viega, J. *24 Deadly Sins of Software Security: Programming Flaws and How to Fix Them.* 2010. New York: McGraw-Hill/Osborne.

Information Security Management

Upon completion of this material, you should be able to:

1. Describe the different management functions with respect to information security

2. Define *information security governance* and list the expectations of the organization's senior management with respect to it

3. Describe management's role in the development, maintenance, and enforcement of information security policy, standards, practices, procedures, and guidelines

4. List the elements in an effective security education, training, and awareness program and describe a methodology for effectively implementing security policy in the organization

5. Explain what an information security blueprint is, identify its major components, and explain how it supports the information security program

> *Begin with the end in mind.*
>
> — Stephen Covey, Author of
> *Seven Habits of Highly
> Effective People*

Opening Scenario

Charlie had a problem. Well, to be precise, Janet Kinneck had a problem, and now Charlie had to deal with it.

Janet, the vice president of social media market development in the SLS Marketing unit, had appeared on the monthly abuse report. Charlie had started having the security operations team prepare this report, based on the network activity for the prior month. All SLS employees consented to this monitoring whenever they used the company's network.

SLS had a pretty liberal policy in place that described how and when employees could use company computers and networks for their own personal reasons. Charlie had convinced CEO Fred Chin and the other senior executives that employees had lives that filtered over into the workplace and that the minor costs of the company network's incidental use for personal matters, within certain boundaries, were well worth the improved productivity that resulted. It was those "certain boundaries" that they were dealing with now.

Charlie looked at the report and the data it contained once more and picked up his phone to call Gladys Williams, the CIO. He had considered whether this meeting should involve Fred, but he decided it fit better with Gladys' role. She could always decide to bring Fred in if she determined that his presence was needed.

Gladys picked up, saying, "Hi, Charlie, what's up?"

He replied, "Hey, Gladys, we have an issue with that new monthly abuse report we are implementing." Gladys knew the report, as she had helped in its creation. She knew what was coming next because she was to be informed when employees above a specific rank were involved.

Charlie continued, "Well, anyway, it looks like we have an issue with Janet Kinneck in Marketing. Near as I can tell without a forensic examination of her computer, she's running a commercial sports gaming league out of her office on the sixth floor."

Gladys thought for a second and replied, "That doesn't sound like an acceptable use to me."

Introduction To The Management Of Information Security

An organization's information security effort succeeds only when it operates in conjunction with the organization's information security policy. An information security program begins with policy, standards, and practices, which are the foundation for the information security program and its blueprint. The creation and maintenance of these elements require coordinated planning. The role of planning in modern organizations is hard to overemphasize. All but the smallest organizations engage in some planning, from strategic planning to manage the future direction of the organization to the operational day-to-day planning to control the use and allocation of resources.

As part of the organization's management team, the InfoSec management team operates like all other management units. However, the InfoSec management team's goals and objectives differ from those of the IT and general management communities in that the InfoSec management team is focused on the secure operation of the organization. In fact, some of the InfoSec management team's goals and objectives may be contrary to or require resolution with the goals of the IT management team, as *the primary focus of the IT group is to ensure the effective and efficient processing of information, whereas the primary focus of the InfoSec group is to ensure the confidentiality, integrity, and availability of information.*

Security, by its very nature, will slow down the information flow into, through, and out of an organization as information is validated, verified, and assessed against security criteria. Because the chief information security officer (CISO) in charge of the security management team typically reports directly to the chief information officer (CIO), who is responsible for the IT function, issues and prioritization conflicts can arise unless upper management intervenes.

Because InfoSec management oversees a specialized program, certain aspects of its managerial responsibility are unique. These unique functions, which are known as "the six Ps" (planning, policy, programs, protection, people, and project management), are discussed throughout this book and briefly described in the following sections.

Planning

Planning in InfoSec management is an extension of the basic planning mentioned later in this module. Included in the InfoSec planning model are activities necessary to support the design, creation, and implementation of InfoSec strategies within the planning environments of all organizational units, including IT. Because the InfoSec strategic plans must support not only the IT department's use and protection of information assets but those of the entire organization, it is imperative that the CISO work closely with all senior managers in developing InfoSec strategy. The business strategy is translated into the IT strategy. The strategies of other business units and the IT strategy are then used to develop the InfoSec strategy. Just as the CIO uses the IT objectives gleaned from the business unit plans to create the organization's IT strategy, the CISO develops InfoSec objectives from the IT and other business units to create the organization's InfoSec strategy.

The IT strategy and that of the other business units provides critical information used for InfoSec planning as the CISO gets involved with the CIO and other executives to develop the strategy for the next level down. The CISO then works with the appropriate security managers to develop operational security plans. These security managers consult with security technicians to develop tactical security plans. Each of these plans is usually coordinated across the business and IT functions of the enterprise and placed into a master schedule for implementation. The overall goal is to create plans that support long-term achievement of the overall organizational strategy. If all goes as expected, the entire collection of tactical plans accomplishes the operational goals and the entire collection of operational goals accomplishes the subordinate strategic goals; this helps to meet the strategic goals and objectives of the organization as a whole.

Several types of InfoSec plans and planning functions exist to support routine operations as well as activities and responses that are not part of the normal operating environment. Routine planning includes that for policy, personnel issues, technology rollouts, risk management, and security programs. Plans and functions that go beyond the routine include planning for incident response, business continuity, disaster recovery, and crisis management. Each of these plans has unique goals and objectives, yet each can benefit from the same methodical approach. These planning areas are discussed in detail in Module 4.

Another basic planning consideration unique to InfoSec is the location of the InfoSec department within the organization structure. This topic is discussed in Module 7.

Policy

In InfoSec, there are three general policy categories, which are discussed in greater detail later in this module:

- *Enterprise information security policy (EISP)*—Developed within the context of the strategic IT plan, this sets the tone for the InfoSec department and the InfoSec climate across the organization. The CISO typically drafts the program policy, which is usually supported and signed by the CIO or the CEO.
- *Issue-specific security policies (ISSPs)*—These are sets of rules that define acceptable behavior within a specific organizational resource, such as e-mail or Internet usage.
- *Systems-specific policies (SysSPs)*—A merger of technical and managerial intent, SysSPs include both the managerial guidance for the implementation of a technology as well as the technical specifications for its configuration.

Programs

InfoSec operations that are specifically managed as separate entities are called "programs." An example would be a security education, training, and awareness (SETA) program or a risk management program. SETA programs provide critical information to employees to maintain or improve their current levels of security knowledge. Risk management programs include the identification, assessment, and control of risks to information assets. Other programs that may emerge include a physical security program, complete with fire protection, physical access, gates, and guards. Some organizations with specific regulations may have additional programs dedicated to client/customer privacy, awareness, and the like. Each organization will typically have several security programs that must be managed.

Protection

The protection function is executed via a set of risk management activities, as well as protection mechanisms, technologies, and tools. Each of these mechanisms or safeguards represents some aspect of the management of specific controls in the overall InfoSec plan.

People

People are the most critical link in the InfoSec program. This area encompasses security personnel (the professional information security employees), the security of personnel (the protection of employees and their information), and aspects of the SETA program mentioned earlier.

Projects

Whether an InfoSec manager is asked to roll out a new security training program or select and implement a new firewall, it is important that the process be managed as a project. The final element for thoroughgoing InfoSec management is the application of a project management discipline to all elements of the InfoSec program. Project management involves identifying and controlling the resources applied to the project, as well as measuring progress and adjusting the process as progress is made toward the goal.

strategic planning

The process of defining and specifying the long-term direction (strategy) to be taken by an organization, and the allocation and acquisition of resources needed to pursue this effort.

goals

A term sometimes used synonymously with *objectives*; the desired end of a planning cycle.

strategic plan

The documented product of strategic planning; a plan for the organization's intended strategic efforts over the next several years.

objectives

A term sometimes used synonymously with *goals*; the intermediate states obtained to achieve progress toward a goal or goals.

governance, risk management, and compliance (GRC)

An approach to information security strategic guidance from a board of directors' or senior management perspective that seeks to integrate the three components of information security governance, risk management, and regulatory compliance.

governance

The set of responsibilities and practices exercised by the board and executive management with the goal of providing strategic direction, ensuring that objectives are achieved, ascertaining that risks are managed appropriately, and verifying that the enterprise's resources are used responsibly.

corporate governance

Executive management's responsibility to provide strategic direction, ensure the accomplishment of objectives, oversee that risks are appropriately managed, and validate responsible resource use.

information security governance

The application of the principles and practices of corporate governance to the information security function, emphasizing the responsibility of the board of directors and/or senior management for the oversight of information security in the organization.

Information Security Planning And Governance

Strategic planning sets the long-term direction to be taken by the organization and each of its component parts. Strategic planning should guide organizational efforts and focus resources toward specific, clearly defined **goals**. After an organization develops a general strategy, it generates an overall **strategic plan** by extending that general strategy into plans for major divisions. Each level of each division then translates those plan **objectives** into more specific objectives for the level below. To execute this broad strategy, the executive team must first define individual responsibilities. (The executive team is sometimes called the organization's C-level, as in CEO, COO, CFO, CIO, and so on.)

Information Security Leadership

The leadership of the information security function that delivers strategic planning and corporate responsibility is best accomplished using an approach industry refers to as **governance, risk management, and compliance (GRC)**. GRC seeks to integrate these three previously separate responsibilities into one holistic approach that can provide sound executive-level strategic planning and management of the InfoSec function. The subjects themselves are neither new nor unique to InfoSec; however, recognition of the need to integrate the three at the board or executive level is becoming increasingly important to practitioners in the field. Note that the management of risk is not limited to an organization's information security. Although organizations increasingly seem to manage their risk challenges with an integrated InfoSec approach focused on GRC, many types of organizations face many types of risk and have developed specific strategies to manage them.

InfoSec objectives must be addressed at the highest levels of an organization's management team in order to be effective and offer a sustainable approach. In organizations with formal boards of directors, the boards should be the basis for **governance** review and oversight. For organizations that have a parent organization, the executive management of the parent should be the basis. For organizations that don't have either, this strategic oversight must stem from a formal governance board consisting of executive management from across the organization—usually the chief executive officer (CEO) or president and their immediate subordinate executives.

Just like governments, corporations and other organizations have guiding documents—corporate charters or partnership agreements—as well as appointed or elected leaders or officers, and planning and operating procedures. These elements in combination provide **corporate governance**.

When security programs are designed and managed as a technical specialty in the IT department, they are less likely to be effective. A broader view of InfoSec encompasses all of an organization's information assets, including IT assets. These valuable commodities must be protected regardless of how the information is processed, stored, or transmitted, and with a thorough understanding of the risks and benefits.

Each operating unit within an organization also has controlling customs, processes, committees, and practices. The information security group's leadership monitors and manages all organizational structures and processes that safeguard information. **Information security governance** then applies these principles and management structures to the information security function.

According to the Corporate Governance Task Force (CGTF), the organization should engage in a core set of activities suited to its needs to guide the development and implementation of the InfoSec governance program:

- Conduct an annual InfoSec evaluation, the results of which the CEO should review with staff and then report to the board of directors.
- Conduct periodic risk assessments of information assets as part of a risk management program.
- Implement policies and procedures based on risk assessments to secure information assets.
- Establish a security management structure to assign explicit individual roles, responsibilities, authority, and accountability.
- Develop plans and initiate actions to provide adequate InfoSec for networks, facilities, systems, and information.
- Treat InfoSec as an integral part of the system life cycle.
- Provide InfoSec awareness, training, and education to personnel.
- Conduct periodic testing and evaluation of the effectiveness of InfoSec policies and procedures.
- Create and execute a plan for remedial action to address any InfoSec inefficiencies.
- Develop and implement incident response procedures.
- Establish plans, procedures, and tests to provide continuity of operations.
- Use security best practices guidance, such as the ISO 27000 series, to measure InfoSec performance.[1]

The CGTF framework defines the responsibilities of the board of directors and trustees, the senior organizational executive (for example, the CEO), executive team members, senior managers, and all employees and users.

ISO 27014:2013 is the ISO 27000 series standard for Governance of Information Security. This remarkably short document (11 pages) provides brief recommendations for the assessment of an information security governance program. The standard specifies six high-level "action-oriented" information security governance principles:

1. Establish organization-wide information security.
2. Adopt a risk-based approach.
3. Set the direction of investment decisions.
4. Ensure conformance with internal and external requirements.
5. Foster a security-positive environment.
6. Review performance in relation to business outcomes.[2]

The standard also promotes five governance processes, which should be adopted by the organization's executive management and its governing board. These processes are illustrated in Figure 3-1 and described in the following list.

- *Evaluate*—Review the status of current and projected progress toward organizational information security objectives and make a determination whether modifications of the program or its strategy are needed to keep on track with strategic goals.
- *Direct*—The board of directors provides instruction for developing or implementing changes to the security program. This could include modification of available resources, structure of priorities of effort, adoption of policy, recommendations for the risk management program, or alteration to the organization's risk tolerance.
- *Monitor*—The review and assessment of organizational information security performance toward goals and objectives by the governing body. Monitoring is enabled by ongoing performance measurement.
- *Communicate*—The interaction between the governing body and external stakeholders, where information on organizational efforts and recommendations for change are exchanged.
- *Assure*—The assessment of organizational efforts by external entities like certification or accreditation groups, regulatory agencies, auditors, and other oversight entities, in an effort to validate organizational security governance, security programs, and strategies.[3]

According to the Information Technology Governance Institute (ITGI), information security governance includes all of the accountabilities and methods undertaken by the board of directors and executive management to provide the following:

- Strategic direction
- Establishment of objectives

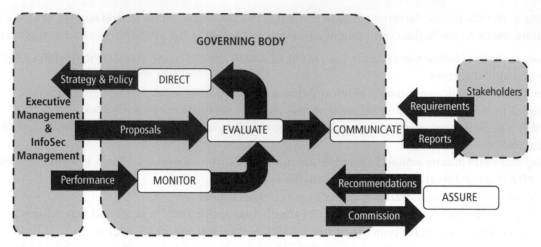

Figure 3-1   ISO/IEC 27014:2013 governance processes[4]

Source: R. Mahncke, Australian eHealth Informatics and Security Conference, December 2013.

- Measurement of progress toward those objectives
- Verification that risk management practices are appropriate
- Validation that the organization's assets are used properly[5]

Figure 3-2 illustrates the responsibilities of various people within an organization for information security governance.

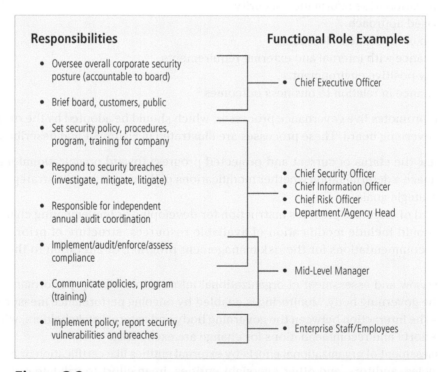

Figure 3-2   Information security governance roles and responsibilities

Source: This information is derived from the Corporate Governance Task Force Report, "Information Security Governance: A Call to Action," April 2004, National Cyber Security Task Force.

Information Security Governance Outcomes

Effective communication among stakeholders is critical to the structures and processes used in governance at every level, and especially in information security governance. It requires the development of constructive relationships, a common language, and a commitment to the objectives of the organization.

The five goals of information security governance are as follows:

1. *Strategic alignment of information security with business strategy to support organizational objectives*
2. *Risk management by executing appropriate measures to manage and mitigate threats to information resources*
3. *Resource management by using information security knowledge and infrastructure efficiently and effectively*
4. *Performance measurement by measuring, monitoring, and reporting information security governance metrics to ensure that organizational objectives are achieved*
5. *Value delivery by optimizing information security investments in support of organizational objectives*[6]

Planning Levels

Once the organization's overall strategic plan is translated into strategic plans for each major division or operation, the next step is to translate these plans into tactical objectives that move toward reaching specific, measurable, achievable, and time-bound accomplishments. The process of strategic planning seeks to transform broad, general, sweeping statements into more specific and applied objectives. Strategic plans are used to create **tactical plans**, which in turn are used to develop **operational plans**.

Tactical planning focuses on undertakings that will be completed within one or two years. The process of tactical planning breaks each strategic goal into a series of incremental objectives. Each objective in a tactical plan should be specific and should have a delivery date within a year of the plan's start. Budgeting, resource allocation, and personnel are critical components of the tactical plan. Tactical plans often include project plans and resource acquisition planning documents (such as product specifications), project budgets, project reviews, and monthly and annual reports. The CISO and security managers use the tactical plan to organize, prioritize, and acquire resources necessary for major projects and to provide support for the overall strategic plan.

Managers and employees use **operational planning** derived from tactical planning to organize the ongoing, day-to-day performance of tasks. An operational plan includes the necessary tasks for all relevant departments as well as communication and reporting requirements, which might include weekly meetings, progress reports, and other associated tasks. These plans must reflect the organizational structure, with each subunit, department, or project team conducting its own operational planning and reporting. Frequent communication and feedback from the teams to the project managers and/or team leaders, and then up to the various management levels, will make the planning process more manageable and successful.

Planning and the CISO

The first priority of the CISO and the information security management team is the creation of a strategic plan to accomplish the organization's information security objectives. While each organization may have its own format for the design and distribution of a strategic plan, the fundamental elements of planning share characteristics across all types of enterprises. The plan is an evolving statement of how the CISO and various elements of the organization will implement the objectives of the enterprise information security policy (EISP), as you will learn later in this module.

As a clearly directed strategy flows from top to bottom, a systematic approach is required to translate it into a program that can inform and lead all members of the organization. Strategic plans formed at the highest levels of the organization are used to create an overall corporate strategy. As lower levels of the organizational hierarchy are involved (moving down the hierarchy), the plans from higher levels are evolved into more detailed, concrete planning. So, higher-level plans are translated into more specific plans for intermediate layers of management. That layer of

---

tactical plan

The documented product of tactical planning; a plan for the organization's intended tactical efforts over the next few years.

operational plan

The documented product of operational planning; a plan for the organization's intended operational efforts on a day-to-day basis for the next several months.

tactical planning

The actions taken by management to specify the intermediate goals and objectives of the organization in order to obtain specified strategic goals, followed by estimates and schedules for the allocation of resources necessary to achieve those goals and objectives.

operational planning

The actions taken by management to specify the short-term goals and objectives of the organization in order to obtain specified tactical goals, followed by estimates and schedules for the allocation of resources necessary to achieve those goals and objectives.

strategic planning by function (such as financial, IT, and operations strategies) is then converted into tactical planning for supervisory managers and eventually provides direction for the operational plans undertaken by non-management members of the organization. This multilayered approach encompasses two key objectives: general strategy and overall strategic planning. First, general strategy is translated into specific strategy; second, overall strategic planning is translated into lower-level tactical and operational planning.

Information security, like information technology, must support more than its own functions. All organizational units will use information, not just IT-based information, so the information security group must understand and support the strategic plans of all business units. This role may sometimes conflict with that of the IT department, as IT's role is the efficient and effective delivery of information and information resources, while the role of information security is the protection of all information assets.

 For more information on information security planning, read NIST Special Publication (SP) 800-18, Rev. 1, which is available from the NIST SP Web site at *https://csrc.nist.gov/publications/sp.*

Information Security Policy, Standards, And Practices

policy

Instructions that dictate certain behavior within an organization.

standard

A detailed statement of what must be done to comply with policy, sometimes viewed as the rules governing policy compliance.

de facto standard

A standard that has been widely adopted or accepted by a public group rather than a formal standards organization.

de jure standard

A standard that has been formally evaluated, approved, and ratified by a formal standards organization.

guidelines

Nonmandatory recommendations the employee may use as a reference in complying with a policy.

procedures

Step-by-step instructions designed to assist employees in following policies, standards, and guidelines.

practices

Examples of actions that illustrate compliance with policies.

Management from all communities of interest, including general staff, information technology, and information security, must make **policy** the basis for all information security planning, design, and deployment. Policies direct how issues should be addressed and how technologies should be used. Policies do not specify the proper operation of equipment or software—this information should be placed in the standards, procedures, and practices of users' manuals and systems documentation. In addition, *policy should never contradict law; policy must be able to stand up in court, if challenged; and policy must be properly administered through dissemination and documented acceptance.* Otherwise, an organization leaves itself exposed to significant liability.

Good security programs begin and end with policy. Information security is primarily a management problem, not a technical one, and policy is a management tool that obliges personnel to function in a manner that preserves the security of information assets. Security policies are the least expensive control to execute but the most difficult to implement *properly*. They have the lowest cost in that their creation and dissemination require only the time and effort of the management team. Even if the management team hires an outside consultant to help develop policy, the costs are minimal compared to those of technical controls.[7]

Policy as the Foundation for Planning

Policies function like laws in an organization because they dictate acceptable and unacceptable behavior there, as well as the penalties for failure to comply. Like laws, policies define what is right and wrong, the penalties for violating policy, and the appeal process. **Standards**, on the other hand, are more detailed statements of what must be done to comply with policy. They have the same requirements for compliance as policies. Standards may be informal or part of an organizational culture, as in **de facto standards**. Or, standards may be published, scrutinized, and ratified by a group, as in formal or **de jure standards**. Practices, procedures, and guidelines effectively explain how to comply with policy.

Table 3-1 and Figure 3-3 show the relationships among policies, standards, **guidelines**, **procedures**, and **practices**. These relationships are further examined in the nearby feature.

Table 3-1   Relationship between Policies, Standards, Practices, Procedures, and Guidelines

Policy	"Use strong passwords, frequently changed."
Standard	"The password must be at least 10 characters with at least one of each of these: uppercase letter, lowercase letter, number, and special character."
Practice	"According to *Passwords Today*, most organizations require employees to change passwords at least every six months."
Procedure	"In order to change your password, first click the Windows Start button; then ..."
Guideline	"We recommend you don't use family or pet names, or parts of your Social Security number, employee number, or phone number in your password."

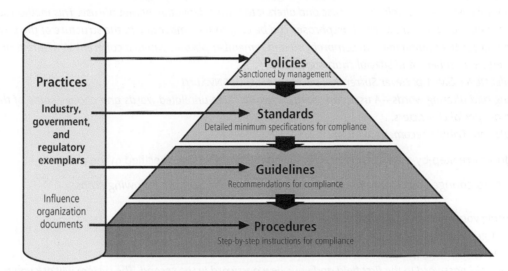

Figure 3-3   Policies, standards, guidelines, and procedures

Policies, Practices, Standards, Guidelines, and Procedures

The relationships among these terms, even when carefully defined, sometimes confuse the reader. The following examples are provided for assistance. Note that many organizations may use the terms differently and publish documents they identify as policy, which may be a combination of what this text defines as policy, standards, or procedures.

The initial statement of intent is the policy.

> *Policy: Employees must use strong passwords on their accounts. Passwords must be changed regularly and protected against disclosure.*

The standard provides specifics to help employees comply with the policy.

> *Standard: Passwords must be at least 10 characters long and incorporate at least one lowercase letter, one uppercase letter, one numerical digit (0–9), and one special character permitted by our system (&%$#@!). Passwords must be changed every 90 days and must not be written down or stored on insecure media.*

The practice identifies other reputable organizations and agencies that offer recommendations the organization may have adopted or adapted.

> *Practice: US-CERT recommends the following:*
>
> * *Use a minimum password length of 15 characters for administrator accounts.*
> * *Require the use of alphanumeric passwords and symbols.*
> * *Enable password history limits to prevent the reuse of previous passwords.*

- *Prevent the use of personal information as passwords, such as phone numbers and dates of birth.*
- *Use a minimum password length of 8 characters for standard users.*
- *Disable local machine credential caching if not required through the use of a Group Policy Object (GPO).*
- *Deploy a secure password storage policy that provides password encryption.*[8]

Guidelines provide examples and recommendations to assist users in complying with the new policy.

Guidelines: In order to create strong yet easy-to-remember passwords, consider the following recommendations from NIST SP 800-118: "Guide to Enterprise Password Management" (draft), April 2009:

- *Mnemonic method—A user selects a phrase and extracts a letter of each word in the phrase (such as the first letter or second letter of each word), adding numbers or special characters or both.*
  - *Example: "May the force be with you always, young Jedi" becomes Mtfbwya-yJ*
- *Altered passphrases—A user selects a phrase and alters it to form a derivation of that phrase. This method supports the creation of long, complex passwords. Passphrases can be easy to remember due to the structure of the password: It is usually easier for the human mind to comprehend and remember phrases within a coherent structure than a string of random letters, numbers, and special characters.*
  - *Example: Never Give Up! Never Surrender! becomes Nv.G.Up!-Nv.Surr!*
- *Combining and altering words—A user can combine two or three unrelated words and change some of the letters to numbers or special characters.*
  - *Example: Jedi Tribble becomes J3d13bbl*

Finally, procedures are step-by-step instructions for accomplishing the task specified in the policy.

Procedures: To change your login password on our system, perform the following steps:

1. *Log in using your current (old) password.*
2. *On your organizational portal home page, click the [Tools] Menu option.*
3. *Select [Change Password].*
4. *Enter your old password in the first field and your new password in the second. The system will ask you to confirm your new password to prevent you from mistyping it.*
5. *The system will then report that your password has been updated and ask you to log out and log back in with your new password.*

Do not write your new password down. If you own a smartphone, you may request that your department purchase an approved password management application like eWallet for storing passwords.

As stated earlier, many organizations combine their policy and standards in the same document and then provide directions or a Web link to a page with guidelines and procedures.

The meaning of the term *security policy* depends on the context in which it is used. Governmental agencies view security policy in terms of national security and national policies to deal with foreign states. A security policy can also communicate a credit card agency's method for processing credit card numbers. In general, a security policy is a set of rules that protects an organization's assets. An **information security policy** provides rules for protection of the organization's information assets.

Management must define three types of security policy, according to SP 800-14 of the National Institute of Standards and Technology (NIST):

information security policy

Written instructions provided by management that inform employees and others in the workplace about proper behavior regarding the use of information and information assets.

1. Enterprise information security policies
2. Issue-specific security policies
3. Systems-specific security policies

NIST SP 800-14 will be discussed in greater detail later in this module.

Enterprise Information Security Policy

An **enterprise information security policy (EISP)** is also known as a general security policy, organizational security policy, IT security policy, or information security policy. The EISP is an executive-level document, usually drafted by or in cooperation with the organization's chief information officer. This policy is usually two to 10 pages long and shapes the philosophy of security in the IT environment. The EISP usually needs to be modified only when there is a change in the strategic direction of the organization.

The EISP guides the development, implementation, and management of the security program. It sets out the requirements that must be met by the information security blueprint. It defines the purpose, scope, constraints, and applicability of the security program. It also assigns responsibilities for the various areas of security, including systems administration, maintenance of the information security policies, and the practices and responsibilities of users. Finally, it addresses legal compliance. According to NIST, the EISP typically addresses compliance in two areas:

- General compliance to ensure that an organization meets the requirements for establishing a program and assigning responsibilities therein to various organizational components
- The use of specified penalties and disciplinary action[9]

When the EISP has been developed, the CISO begins forming the security team and initiating necessary changes to the information security program.

> **enterprise information security policy (EISP)**
>
> The high-level information security policy that sets the strategic direction, scope, and tone for all of an organization's security efforts; also known as a security program policy, general security policy, IT security policy, high-level InfoSec policy, or simply an InfoSec policy.

EISP Elements

Although the specifics of EISPs vary among organizations, most EISP documents should include the following elements:

- An overview of the corporate philosophy on security
- Information on the structure of the information security organization and people who fulfill the information security role
- Fully articulated responsibilities for security that are shared by all members of the organization (employees, contractors, consultants, partners, and visitors)
- Fully articulated responsibilities for security that are unique to each role within the organization

The components of a good EISP are shown in Table 3-2. For examples of EISP documents and recommendations for how to prepare them, we recommend using *Information Security Policies Made Easy* by Charles Cresson Wood, published by Information Shield. While the current version is relatively expensive, prior editions are widely available as used books and in libraries around the world.

Issue-Specific Security Policy

As an organization supports routine operations by executing various technologies and processes, it must instruct employees on their proper use. In general, the **issue-specific security policy**, or **ISSP**, (1) addresses specific areas of technology as listed here, (2) requires frequent updates, and (3) contains a statement about the organization's position on a specific issue.[10] An ISSP may cover the following topics, among others:

> **issue-specific security policy (ISSP)**
>
> An organizational policy that provides detailed, targeted guidance to instruct all members of the organization in the use of a resource, such as one of its processes or technologies.

- E-mail
- Use of the Internet and World Wide Web
- Specific minimum configurations of computers to defend against worms and viruses
- Prohibitions against hacking or testing organization security controls
- Home use of company-owned computer equipment
- Use of personal equipment on company networks (BYOD: bring your own device)
- Use of telecommunications technologies, such as fax and phone
- Use of photocopy equipment

Table 3-2   Components of the EISP[11]

Component	Description
Statement of Purpose	Answers the question "What is this policy for?" Provides a framework that helps the reader understand the intent of the document. Can include text such as the following: "This document will:
	• Identify the elements of a good security policy
	• Explain the need for information security
	• Specify the various categories of information security
	• Identify the information security responsibilities and roles
	• Identify appropriate levels of security through standards and guidelines
	This document establishes an overarching security policy and direction for our company. Individual departments are expected to establish standards, guidelines, and operating procedures that adhere to and reference this policy while addressing their specific and individual needs."
Information Security Elements	Defines information security. For example:
	"Protecting the confidentiality, integrity, and availability of information while in processing, transmission, and storage, through the use of policy, education and training, and technology ..."
	This section can also lay out security definitions or philosophies to clarify the policy.
Need for Information Security	Provides information on the importance of information security in the organization and the legal and ethical obligation to protect critical information about customers, employees, and markets.
Information Security Responsibilities and Roles	Defines the organizational structure designed to support information security within the organization. Identifies categories of people with responsibility for information security (IT department, management, users) and those responsibilities, including maintenance of this document.
Reference to Other Information Standards and Guidelines	Lists other standards that influence this policy document and are influenced by it, perhaps including relevant federal laws, state laws, and other policies.

- Use of portable storage devices such as USB memory sticks, backpack drives, game players, music players, and any other device capable of storing digital files
- Use of cloud-based storage services that are not self-hosted by the organization or engaged under contract; such services include Google Drive, Dropbox, and Microsoft OneDrive
- Use of networked infrastructure devices, "intelligent assistants" such as Google Assistant and Amazon Echo, and accompanying devices usually classified as the Internet of Things (IoT)
- Use of programmable logic controller (PLC) devices and associated control protocols with corporate data networks and production-focused industrial networks

For examples of ISSP policies and recommendations for how to prepare them, we recommend using *Information Security Policies Made Easy* by Charles Cresson Wood, published by Information Shield. The book includes a wide variety of working policy documents and can assist in defining which are needed and how to create them.

Several approaches are used to create and manage ISSPs within an organization. Three of the most common are as follows:

- Independent ISSP documents, each tailored to a specific issue
- A single comprehensive ISSP document that covers all issues
- A modular ISSP document that unifies policy creation and administration while maintaining each specific issue's requirements

The independent ISSP document typically has a scattershot effect. Each department responsible for an application of technology creates a policy governing its use, management, and control. This approach may fail to cover all necessary issues and can lead to poor policy distribution, management, and enforcement.

The single comprehensive ISSP is centrally managed and controlled. With formal procedures for the management of ISSPs in place, the comprehensive policy approach establishes guidelines for overall coverage of necessary issues and clearly identifies processes for the dissemination, enforcement, and review of these guidelines. Usually, these policies are developed by the people responsible for managing the information technology resources. Unfortunately, these policies tend to overgeneralize the issues and skip over vulnerabilities.

The optimal balance between the independent and comprehensive ISSP is the modular ISSP. It is also centrally managed and controlled, but it is tailored to individual technology issues. The modular approach provides a balance between issue orientation and policy management. The policies created with this approach comprise individual modules, each created and updated by people responsible for the issues addressed. These people report to a central policy administration group that incorporates specific issues into an overall comprehensive policy.

Table 3-3 is an outline of a sample ISSP, which can be used as a model. An organization should start with this structure and add specific details that dictate security procedures not covered by these general guidelines.

Table 3-3   Components of an ISSP[12]

Components of an ISSP
1.   Statement of policy
a. Scope and applicability
b. Definition of technology addressed
c. Responsibilities
2.   Authorized access and usage of equipment
a. User access
b. Fair and responsible use
c. Protection of privacy
3.   Prohibited use of equipment
a. Disruptive use or misuse
b. Criminal use
c. Offensive or harassing materials
d. Copyrighted, licensed, or other intellectual property
e. Other restrictions
4.   Systems management
a. Management of stored materials
b. Employee monitoring
c. Virus protection
d. Physical security
e. Encryption
5.   Violations of policy
a. Procedures for reporting violations
b. Penalties for violations
6.   Policy review and modification
a. Scheduled review of policy procedures for modification
b. Legal disclaimers
7.   Limitations of liability
a. Statements of liability
b. Other disclaimers as needed

Source: Whitman, Townsend, and Aalberts, Communications of the ACM.

The components of each major category of a typical ISSP are discussed in the following sections. Even though the details may vary from policy to policy and some sections of a modular policy may be combined, it is essential for management to address and complete each section.

Statement of Policy

The policy should begin with a clear statement of purpose—in other words, what exactly is this policy supposed to accomplish? Consider a policy that covers the issue of fair and responsible Internet use. The introductory section of this policy should address the following questions: What is the scope of this policy? Who does this policy apply to? Who is responsible and accountable for policy implementation? What technologies and issues does it address?

Authorized Access and Usage of Equipment

This section of the policy statement addresses *who* can use the technology governed by the policy and *what* it can be used for. Remember that an organization's information systems are its exclusive property, and users have no rights of use. Each technology and process is provided for business operations. Use for any other purpose constitutes misuse of equipment. This section defines "fair and responsible use" of equipment and other organizational assets and should address key legal issues, such as protection of personal information and privacy.

Prohibited Use of Equipment

Unless a particular use is clearly prohibited, the organization cannot penalize its employees for misuse. For example, the following can be prohibited: personal use, disruptive use or misuse, criminal use, offensive or harassing materials, and infringement of copyrighted, licensed, or other intellectual property. As an alternative approach, sections 2 and 3 of Table 3-3 can be collapsed into a single category called "Appropriate Use." Many organizations use such an ISSP section to cover both categories.

Systems Management

The systems management section of the ISSP policy statement focuses on the users' relationship to systems management. Specific rules from management include regulating the use of e-mail, the storage of materials, the authorized monitoring of employees, and the physical and electronic scrutiny of e-mail and other electronic documents. It is important that all such responsibilities are assigned either to the systems administrator or the users; otherwise, both parties may infer that the responsibility belongs to the other.

Violations of Policy

The people to whom the policy applies must understand the penalties and repercussions of violating it. Violations of policy should carry penalties that are appropriate—neither draconian nor overly lenient. This section of the policy statement should contain not only specific penalties for each category of violation, but instructions for how people in the organization can report observed or suspected violations. Many people think that powerful employees in an organization can retaliate against someone who reports violations. Allowing anonymous submissions is often the only way to convince users to report the unauthorized activities of more influential employees.

Policy Review and Modification

Because any document is only useful if it is up to date, each policy should contain procedures and a timetable for periodic review. As the organization's needs and technologies change, so must the policies that govern their use. This section should specify a methodology for reviewing and modifying the policy to ensure that users do not begin circumventing it as it grows obsolete.

Limitations of Liability

If an employee is caught conducting illegal activities with the organization's equipment or assets, management does not want the organization held liable. The policy should state that if employees violate a company policy or any law using company technologies, the company will not protect them, and the company is not liable for their actions. In fact, many organizations assist in the prosecution of employees who violate laws when their actions violate policies. It is assumed that such violations occur without knowledge or authorization by the organization.

Systems-Specific Security Policy (SysSP)

While issue-specific policies are formalized as written documents readily identifiable as policy, **systems-specific security policies (SysSPs)** sometimes have a different look. SysSPs often function as standards or procedures to be used when configuring or maintaining systems. For example, a SysSP might describe the configuration and operation of a network firewall. This document could include a statement of managerial intent; guidance to network engineers on the selection, configuration, and operation of firewalls; and an access control list that defines levels of access for each authorized user. SysSPs can be separated into two general groups, **managerial guidance SysSPs** and **technical specifications SysSPs**, or they can be combined into a single policy document that contains elements of both.

Managerial Guidance SysSPs

A managerial guidance SysSP document is created by management to guide the implementation and configuration of technology and to address the behavior of employees in ways that support information security. For example, while the method for configuring a firewall belongs in the technical specifications SysSP, the firewall's configuration must follow guidelines established by management. An organization might not want its employees to access the Internet via the organization's network, for instance; in that case, the firewall should be configured accordingly.

Firewalls are not the only technology that may require systems-specific policies. Any system that affects the confidentiality, integrity, or availability of information must be assessed to evaluate the trade-off between improved security and restrictions.

Systems-specific policies can be developed at the same time as ISSPs, or they can be prepared in advance of their related ISSPs. Before management can craft a policy informing users what they can do with certain technology and how to do it, system administrators might have to configure and operate the system. Some organizations may prefer to develop ISSPs and SysSPs in tandem so that operational procedures and user guidelines are created simultaneously.

Technical Specifications SysSPs

While a manager can work with a systems administrator to create managerial policy, as described in the preceding section, the systems administrator in turn might need to create a policy to implement the managerial policy. Each type of equipment requires its own set of policies, which are used to translate management's intent for the technical control into an enforceable technical approach. For example, an ISSP may require that user passwords be changed quarterly; a systems administrator can implement a technical control within a specific application to enforce this policy. There are two general methods of implementing such technical controls: access control lists and configuration rules.

Access Control Lists An **access control list (ACL)** consists of details about user access and use permissions and privileges for an organizational asset or resource, such as a file storage system, software component, or network communications device. ACLs focus on assets and the users who can access and use them. A **capabilities table** is similar to an ACL, but it focuses on users, the assets they can access, and what they can do with those assets. In some systems, capability tables are called user profiles or user policies.

These specifications frequently take the form of complex matrices rather than simple lists or tables, resulting in an **access control matrix** that combines the information in ACLs and capability tables.

---

systems-specific security policies (SysSPs)

Organizational policies that often function as standards or procedures to be used when configuring or maintaining systems. SysSPs can be separated into two general groups—managerial guidance and technical specifications—but may be written as a single unified SysSP document.

managerial guidance SysSP

A policy that expresses management's intent for the acquisition, implementation, configuration, and management of a particular technology, written from a business perspective.

technical specifications SysSP

A policy that expresses technical details for the acquisition, implementation, configuration, and management of a particular technology, written from a technical perspective; usually includes details on configuration rules, systems policies, and access control.

access control list (ACL)

Specifications of authorization that govern the rights and privileges of users to a particular information asset; includes user access lists, matrices, and capabilities tables.

capabilities table

A lattice-based access control with rows of attributes associated with a particular subject (such as a user).

access control matrix

An integration of access control lists (focusing on assets) and capability tables (focusing on users) that results in a matrix with organizational assets listed in the column headings and users listed in the row headings; contains ACLs in columns for a particular device or asset and capability tables in rows for a particular user.

As illustrated in Figures 3-4 and 3-5, both Microsoft Windows and Linux systems translate ACLs into sets of configurations that administrators use to control access to their systems.

The level of detail may differ from system to system, but in general, ACLs can restrict access for a specific user, computer, time, or duration—even a specific file. This specificity provides powerful control to the administrator. In general, ACLs regulate the following:

- *Who* can use the system
- *What* authorized users can access
- *When* authorized users can access the system
- *Where* authorized users can access the system

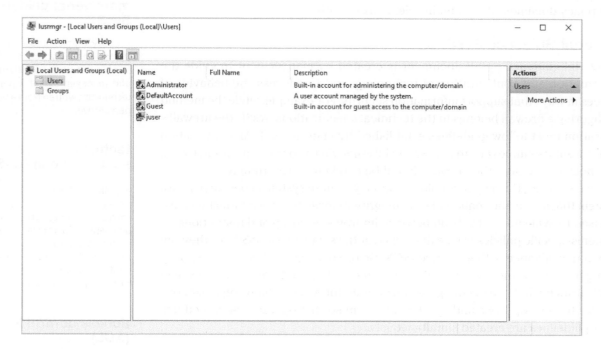

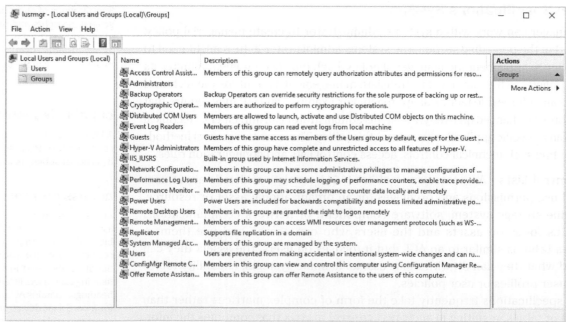

Figure 3-4 Microsoft Windows use of ACLs

Source: Microsoft.

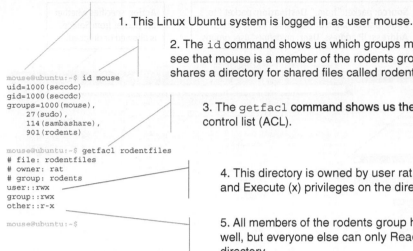

```
                                    1. This Linux Ubuntu system is logged in as user mouse.

                                    2. The id command shows us which groups mouse is in. You can
                                    see that mouse is a member of the rodents group. This group
                                    shares a directory for shared files called rodentfiles.
mouse@ubuntu:~$ id mouse
uid=1000(seccdc)
gid=1000(seccdc)
groups=1000(mouse),
     27(sudo),                     3. The getfacl command shows us the directory file's access
     114(sambashare),             control list (ACL).
     901(rodents)

mouse@ubuntu:~$ getfacl rodentfiles
# file: rodentfiles
# owner: rat
# group: rodents                   4. This directory is owned by user rat, who has Read (r), Write (w),
user::rwx                          and Execute (x) privileges on the directory and all files in it.
group::rwx
other::r-x

mouse@ubuntu:~$                    5. All members of the rodents group have these privileges as
                                    well, but everyone else can only Read and Execute files in the
                                    directory.
```

Figure 3-5 Linux use of ACLs

Source: Linux.

The *who* of ACL access may be determined by a person's identity or membership in a group. Restricting *what* authorized users are permitted to access—whether by type (printers, files, communication devices, or applications), name, or location—is achieved by adjusting the resource privileges for a person or group to Read, Write, Create, Modify, Delete, Compare, or Copy. To control *when* access is allowed, some organizations implement time-of-day and day-of-week restrictions for certain network or system resources. To control *where* resources can be accessed, many network-connected assets block remote usage and have some levels of access that are restricted to locally connected users, such as restrictions by computer MAC address or network IP address. When these various ACL options are applied concurrently, the organization can govern how its resources can be used.

Configuration Rule Policies Configuration rules (or policies) govern how a security system reacts to the data it receives. Rule-based policies are more specific to the operation of a system than ACLs, and they may or may not deal with users directly. Many security systems—for example, firewalls, intrusion detection and prevention systems (IDPSs), and proxy servers, all of which you will learn about in Modules 8 and 9—use specific configuration scripts that represent the configuration rule policy to determine how the system handles each data element they process. The examples in Figures 3-6 and 3-7 show how network security policy has been implemented by a Palo Alto firewall's rule set and by Ionx Verisys (File Integrity Monitoring) in a host-based IDPS rule set.

> **configuration rules**
>
> The instructions a system administrator codes into a server, networking device, or security device to specify how it operates.

Combination SysSPs

Many organizations create a single document that combines the managerial guidance SysSP and the technical specifications SysSP. While this document can be somewhat confusing to casual users, it is practical to have the guidance from managerial and technical perspectives in a single place. If this approach is used, care should be taken to clearly articulate the required actions. Some might consider this type of policy document a procedure, but it is actually a hybrid that combines policy with procedural guidance to assist implementers of the system being managed. This approach is best used by organizations that have multiple technical control systems of different types and by smaller organizations that want to document policy and procedure in a compact format.

Developing and Implementing Effective Security Policy

How policy is developed and implemented can help or hinder its usefulness to the organization. If an organization takes punitive action on an effective policy, the individual(s) affected may sue the organization, depending on its action in implementing the penalties or other actions defined in the policy. Employees terminated for violating poorly designed and implemented policies could sue their organization for wrongful termination. In general, policy is only enforceable and legally defensible if it is properly designed, developed, and implemented using a process that assures repeatable results.

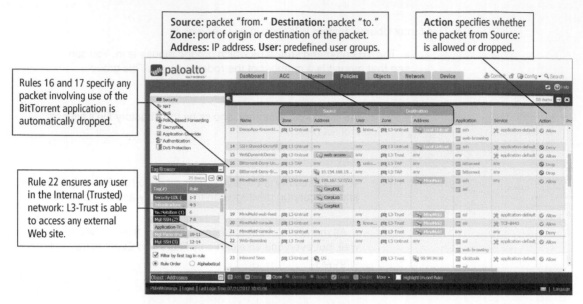

Figure 3-6   Sample Palo Alto firewall configuration rules

Source: Palo Alto Software, Inc.

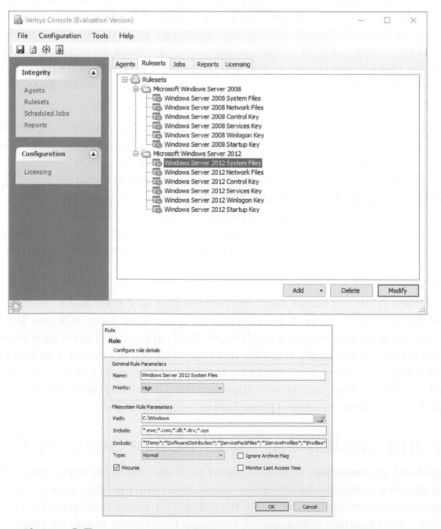

Figure 3-7   Ionx Verisys (File Integrity Monitor) use of rules

Source: Ionx.

For policies to be effective and legally defensible, the following must be done properly:

1. *Development*—Policies must be written using industry-accepted practices and formally approved by management.
2. *Dissemination*—Policies must be distributed using all appropriate methods.
3. *Review*—Policies must be readable and read by all employees.
4. *Comprehension*—Policies must be understood by all employees.
5. *Compliance*—Policies must be formally agreed to by act or affirmation.
6. *Enforcement*—Policies must be uniformly applied to all employees.

We will examine each of these stages in the sections that follow. Before we do, however, you should realize that almost every organization has a set of existing policies, standards, procedures, and/or practices. This installed base of guidance may not always have been prepared using an approach that delivers consistent or even usable results. Most of the situations you find yourself in will involve more policy maintenance than policy development. Prior to implementation, policy should be reviewed by the organization's legal counsel to ensure it is acceptable within the limits of the law and that implementation of the policy and its corresponding penalties would, in fact, be defensible in the event of a legal dispute.

Developing Information Security Policy

It is often useful to view policy development as a three-part project. In the first part of the project, policy is designed and written (or, in the case of an outdated policy, redesigned and rewritten). In the second part, a senior manager or executive at the appropriate level and the organization's legal counsel review and formally approve the document. In the third part of the development project, management processes are established to distribute and enforce the policy within the organization. The first part is an exercise in project management, whereas the latter two parts require adherence to good business practices and legal regulation.

Writing a policy is not always as easy as it seems. However, the prudent security manager always scours available resources (including the Web) for examples that may be adapted to the organization. Seldom will the manager find the perfect policy, ready to be implemented. Some online vendors sell blank policies that you can customize to your organization. In any event, it is important that the organization respect the intellectual property of others when developing policy. If parts of another organization's policy are adapted, appropriate attribution must be made. Most policies contain a reference section where the author may list any policies used in the development of the current document. Even policies that are purchased from policy vendors or developed from a book on writing policies may require some level of attribution. It is recommended that any policies adapted from outside sources are thoroughly summarized to prevent the need for direct quotations, which can detract from the message the policy is attempting to convey—that "our organization" wants employees to be effective and efficient without undue distractions.

Policy Distribution

While it might seem straightforward, getting the policy document into the hands of employees can require a substantial investment by the organization to be effective. The most common alternatives are hard copy and electronic distribution. Hard copy distribution involves either directly handing or mailing a copy to each employee or posting the policy in a publicly accessible location. Posting a policy on a bulletin board or other public area may be insufficient unless another policy requires the employees to read the bulletin board on a specified schedule.

Distribution by internal or external mail may still not guarantee that the individual receives the document. Unless the organization can prove that the policy reached its target audience, it cannot be enforced. Unlike in law, ignorance of policy, where policy is inadequately distributed, is considered an acceptable excuse. Distribution of classified policies—those containing confidential information—requires additional levels of controls, in the labeling of the document, in the dissemination and storage of new policy, and in the collection and destruction of older versions to ensure the confidentiality of the information contained within the policy documents themselves.

Another common method of dissemination is by electronic means: e-mail, newsletter, intranet, or document management systems. Perhaps the easiest way is to post policies on a secure intranet in HTML or PDF (Adobe Acrobat) form. The organization must still enable a mechanism to prove distribution, such as an auditing log for tracking when users access the documents. As an alternative delivery mechanism, e-mail has advantages and disadvantages. While it is easy to send a document to an employee and even track when the employee opens the e-mail, e-mail tracking may not be sufficient as proof that the employee downloaded and actually read any attached policies, and the document can get lost in an avalanche of spam, phishing attacks, or other unwanted e-mail. The best method is through electronic policy management software, as described in the section on automated tools. Electronic policy management software not only assists in the distribution of policy documents, it supports the assessment of comprehension and evaluation of compliance.

Policy Review

Barriers to employees reading policies can arise from literacy or language issues. A surprisingly large percentage of the workforce is considered functionally illiterate. According to Macrotrends, a full 1 percent of people 15 and older living in the United States cannot read and write with understanding. Based on statistics from 2020, that means more than 3.28 million adults in the United States are considered illiterate.[13] Many jobs do not require literacy skills—for example, custodial staff, groundskeepers, or production line workers. Because such workers can still pose risks to InfoSec, they must be made familiar with policy even if it must be read to them. Visually impaired employees also require additional assistance, either through audio or large-type versions of the document.

A contributing factor to the literacy issue is that the number of non-English-speaking residents in the United States continues to climb. According to 2018 U.S. Census data, more than 67 million residents speak a language other than English at home.[14] However, language challenges are not restricted to organizations with locations in the United States. Multinational organizations also must deal with the challenges of gauging reading levels of foreign citizens. Simple translations of policy documents, while a minimum requirement, necessitate careful monitoring. Translation issues have long created challenges for organizations.

Policy Comprehension

Simply making certain that a copy of the policy gets to employees in a form they can review may not ensure that they truly understand what the policy requires of them. Comprehension involves two aspects of policy administration: (1) the target audience can understand the policy, and (2) the organization has assessed how well they understand it.

To be certain that employees can understand the policy, the document must be written at an appropriate reading level, with minimal technical jargon or management terminology. The readability statistics supplied by most productivity suite applications—such as Microsoft Word—can help determine the current reading level of a policy. The Flesch Reading Ease test evaluates writing on a scale of 1–100. The higher the score, the easier it is to understand the writing. For most corporate documents, a score of 60 to 70 is preferred. The Flesch–Kincaid Grade Level test evaluates writing on a U.S. grade-school level. While a 13th-grade level (freshman in college) may be appropriate for a textbook, it is too high for organizational policy intended for a broad audience. For most corporate documents, a score of 7.0 to 8.0 is preferred.

The next step is to use some form of assessment to gauge how well employees understand the policy's underlying issues. Quizzes and other forms of examination can be employed to assess quantitatively which employees understand the policy by earning a minimum score (e.g., 70 percent) and which employees require additional training and awareness efforts before the policy can be enforced. Quizzes can be conducted in either hard copy or electronic formats. The electronic policy management systems mentioned earlier can assist in the assessment of employee performance on policy comprehension.

Policy Compliance

Policy compliance means the employee must agree to the policy. According to Whitman in "Security Policy: From Design to Maintenance": Policies must be agreed to by act or affirmation. Agreement by act occurs when the employee performs an action, which requires them to acknowledge understanding of the policy prior to use of a technology or organizational resource. Network banners, end-user license agreements (EULAs), and posted warnings can serve to meet this burden of proof. However, these approaches in and of themselves may not be sufficient. Only through direct collection of a signature or the equivalent digital alternative can the organization prove that it has obtained an agreement to comply with policy, which also demonstrates that the previous conditions have been met.[15]

What if an employee refuses explicitly to agree to comply with policy? Can the organization deny access to information that the individual needs to do his or her job? While this situation has not yet been adjudicated in the legal system, it seems clear that failure to agree to a policy is tantamount to refusing to work and thus may be grounds for termination. Organizations can avoid this dilemma by incorporating policy confirmation statements into employment contracts, annual evaluations, or other documents necessary for the individual's continued employment.

Policy Enforcement

The final component of the design and implementation of effective policies is uniform and impartial enforcement. As in law enforcement, policy enforcement must be able to withstand external scrutiny. Because this scrutiny may occur during legal proceedings—for example, in a civil suit contending wrongful termination— organizations must establish high standards of due care with regard to policy management. For instance, if policy mandates that all employees wear identification badges in a clearly visible location and select members of management decide they are not required to follow this policy, any actions taken against other employees will not withstand legal challenges. If an employee is punished, censured, or dismissed as a result of a refusal to follow policy and is subsequently able to demonstrate that the policies are not uniformly applied or enforced, the organization may find itself facing punitive as well as compensatory damages.

One forward-thinking organization found a way to enlist employees in the enforcement of policy. After the organization had just published a new ID badge policy, the manager responsible for the policy was seen without his ID. One of his employees chided him in jest, saying, "You must be a visitor here, since you don't have an ID. Can I help you?" The manager smiled and promptly produced his ID, along with a $20 bill, which he presented to the employee as a reward for vigilant policy enforcement. Soon, the entire staff was routinely challenging anyone without a badge.[16]

Policy Development and Implementation Using the SDLC

Like any major project, a policy development or redevelopment project should be well planned, properly funded, and aggressively managed to ensure that it is completed on time and within budget. One way to accomplish this goal is to use a systems development life cycle (SDLC). The following discussion expands the use of a typical SDLC model by discussing the tasks that could be included in each phase of the SDLC during a policy development project.

Investigation Phase   During the investigation phase, the policy development team or committee should attain the following:

- Support from senior management because any project without it has a reduced chance of success. Only with the support of top management will a specific policy receive the attention it deserves from the intermediate-level managers who must implement it and from the users who must comply with it.
- Support and active involvement of IT management, specifically the CIO. Only with the CIO's active support will technology-area managers be motivated to participate in policy development and support the implementation efforts to deploy it once created.
- Clear articulation of goals. Without a detailed and succinct expression of the goals and objectives of the policy, broken into distinct expectations, the policy will lack the structure it needs to obtain full implementation.
- Participation of the correct individuals from the communities of interest affected by the recommended policies. Assembling the right team, by ensuring the participation of the proper representatives from the groups that will be affected by the new policies, is very important. The team must include representatives from the legal department, the human resources department, and end users of the various IT systems covered by the policies, as well as a project champion with sufficient stature and prestige to accomplish the goals of the project and a capable project manager to see the project through to completion.
- A detailed outline of the scope of the policy development project and sound estimates for the cost and scheduling of the project.

Analysis Phase   The analysis phase should produce the following:

- A new or recent risk assessment or IT audit documenting the current InfoSec needs of the organization. This risk assessment should include any loss history, as well as past lawsuits, grievances, or other records of negative outcomes from InfoSec areas.
- The gathering of key reference materials, including any existing policies. Sometimes policy documents that affect InfoSec will be housed in the human resources department as well as the accounting, finance, legal, or corporate security departments.
- The policy development committee must determine the fundamental philosophy of the organization when it comes to policy. This will dictate the general development of all policies, but in particular, the format to be used in the crafting of all ISSPs. This philosophy typically falls into one of two groups:

- ○ *"That which is not permitted is prohibited."* Also known as the "whitelist" approach, this is the more restrictive of the two, and focuses on creating an approach where specific authorization is provided for various actions and behaviors; all other actions and behaviors (and uses) are prohibited or at least require specific permissions. This approach can impede normal business operations if appropriate options emerge but cannot be incorporated into policy until subsequent revisions are made.
- ○ *"That which is not prohibited is permitted."* Also known as the "blacklist" approach, this alternate approach specifies what actions, behaviors, and uses are prohibited and then allows all others by default. While easier to implement, this approach can result in issues as more and more areas that should be prohibited are discovered by users.

Design Phase   The first task in the design phase is the drafting of the actual policy document. While this task can be done by a committee, it is most commonly done by a single author. This document should incorporate all the specifications and restrictions from the investigation and analysis phases. This can be a challenging process, but you do not have to come up with a good policy document from scratch. A number of resources are at your disposal, including the following:

- *The Web*—You can search for other similar policies. The point here is not to advocate wholesale copying of these policies but to encourage you to look for ideas for your own policy. For example, dozens of policies available on the Web describe fair and responsible use of various technologies. What you may not find, however, are policies that relate to sensitive internal documents or processes.
- *Government sites*—Sites such as *http://csrc.nist.gov* contain numerous sample policies and policy support documents, including SP 800-100, "Information Security Handbook: A Guide for Managers." While these policies are typically applicable to federal government Web sites, you may be able to adapt some sections to meet your organization's needs.
- *Professional literature*—Several authors have published books on the subject. Of particular note is Charles Cresson Wood's *Information Security Policies Made Easy* series, which not only provides more than 1,000 pages of policies, it makes those policies available in electronic format, complete with permission to use them in internal documents. Exercise caution when using such resources, however; it is extremely easy to take large sections of policy and end up with a massive, unwieldy document that is neither publishable nor enforceable.
- *Peer networks*—Other InfoSec professionals must write similar policies and implement similar plans. Attend meetings like those offered by the Information Systems Security Association (*www.issa.org*) or the Information Systems Audit and Control Association (*www.isaca.org*), and ask your peers.
- *Professional consultants*—Policy is one area of InfoSec that can certainly be developed in-house. However, if your organization does not have the requisite expertise, or if your team simply cannot find the time to develop your own policy, then hiring an outside consultant may be your best option. Keep in mind that no consultant can know your organization as well as you do; you may decide to have the consultant design generic policies that you can then adapt to your specific needs.

Next, the development team or committee reviews the work of the primary author and makes recommendations about its revision. Once the committee approves the document, it goes to the approving manager or executive for sign-off.

Implementation Phase   In the implementation phase, the team must create a plan to distribute and verify the distribution of the policies. Members of the organization must explicitly acknowledge that they have received and read the policy (compliance). Otherwise, an employee can claim never to have seen a policy, and unless the manager can produce strong evidence to the contrary, any enforcement action, such as dismissal for inappropriate use of the Web, can be overturned and punitive damages might be awarded to the former employee. The simplest way to document acknowledgment of a written policy is to attach a cover sheet that states "I have received, read, understood, and agreed to this policy." The employee's signature and date provide a paper trail of his or her receipt of the policy.

Some situations preclude a formal documentation process. Take, for instance, student use of campus computer labs. Most universities have stringent policies on what students can and cannot do in a computer lab. These policies are usually posted on the Web, in the student handbook, in course catalogs, and in several other locations, including bulletin boards in the labs. For the policies to be enforceable, however, some mechanism must be established that records the student's acknowledgment of the policy. This is frequently accomplished with a banner screen that displays a brief statement warning the user that the policy is in place and that use of the system constitutes acceptance of the policy. The user must then click an OK button or press a key to get past the screen. However, this method can be ineffective if the acknowledgment screen does not require any unusual action to move past it. Most acknowledgment screens require that the user click a specific button, press a function key, or type text to agree to the terms of the EULA. Some even require the user to scroll down to the bottom of the EULA screen before the "I accept" button is activated. Similar methods are used on network and computer logins to reinforce acknowledgment of the system use policy.

A stronger mechanism to document and ensure comprehension is a compliance assessment, such as a short quiz, to make sure that users both read the policy and understand it. A minimum score is commonly established before the employee is certified to be "in compliance." Coupled with a short training video, the compliance quiz is the current industry best practice for policy implementation and compliance.

The design phase should also include specifications for any automated tool used for the creation and management of policy documents, as well as revisions to feasibility analysis reports based on improved costs and benefits as the design is clarified. During the implementation phase, the policy development team ensures that the policy is properly distributed, read, understood, and agreed to by those to whom it applies, and that their understanding and acceptance of the policy are documented.

Maintenance Phase   During the maintenance phase, the policy development team monitors, maintains, and modifies the policy as needed to ensure that it remains effective as a tool to meet changing threats. The policy should have a built-in mechanism through which users can report problems—preferably on an anonymous basis through a Web form monitored either by the organization's legal team or a committee assigned to collect and review such content. It is in this phase that the last component of effective policy development—uniform enforcement—comes into play. The organization should make sure that everyone is required to follow the policy equally and that policies are not implemented differently in different areas or hierarchies of the organization.

When the policy comes up for schedule review, the development committee reassembles, reviews any submitted recommendations, and begins the process anew, as described in the next section.

Policy Management

Policies are living documents that must be managed. It is unacceptable to create such an important set of documents and then shelve them. These documents must be properly distributed, read, understood, agreed to, uniformly applied, and managed. How they are managed should be specified in the policy management section of the issue-specific policy described earlier. Good management practices for policy development and maintenance make for a more resilient organization. For example, all policies, including security policies, undergo tremendous stress when corporate mergers and divestitures occur. In such situations, employees are faced with uncertainty and many distractions. System vulnerabilities can arise, for instance, if incongruent security policies are implemented in different parts of a newly merged organization. When two companies merge but retain separate policies, the difficulty of implementing security controls increases. Likewise, when one company with unified policies splits in two, each new company may require different policies.

To remain viable, security policies must have a responsible manager, a schedule of reviews, a method for making recommendations for reviews, and a policy issuance and revision date.

Responsible Manager

Just as information systems and information security projects must have champions and managers, so must policies. The policy manager is often called the **policy administrator**. Note that the policy administrator does not necessarily have to be proficient in the relevant technology. While practicing information security professionals require extensive technical knowledge, policy management and policy administration require only a moderate technical background. It is good practice, however, for policy administrators to solicit input both from technically adept information security experts and from business-focused managers in each community of interest when revising security policies. The administrator should also notify all affected members of the organization when the policy is modified.

> **policy administrator**
> An employee responsible for the creation, revision, distribution, and storage of a policy in an organization.

It is disheartening when a policy that required hundreds of staff hours to develop and document is ignored. Thus, someone must be responsible for placing the policy and all subsequent revisions into the hands of people who are accountable for its implementation. The policy administrator must be clearly identified in the policy document as the primary point of contact for additional information or suggested revisions to the policy.

sunset clause

A component of policy or law that defines an expected end date for its applicability.

Schedule of Reviews

Policies can only retain their effectiveness in a changing environment if they are periodically reviewed for currency and accuracy and then modified accordingly. Policies that are not kept current can become liabilities as outdated rules are enforced (or not) and new requirements are ignored. To demonstrate due diligence, an organization must actively seek to meet the requirements of the market in which it operates. This applies to government, academic, and nonprofit organizations as well as private, for-profit organizations. A properly organized schedule of reviews should be defined and published as part of the document. Typically, a policy should be reviewed at least annually to ensure that it is still an effective control.

Review Procedures and Practices

To facilitate policy reviews, the policy manager should implement a mechanism by which people can comfortably make recommendations for revisions, whether via e-mail, office mail, or an anonymous drop box. If the policy is controversial, anonymous submission of recommendations may be the best way to encourage staff opinions. Many employees are intimidated by management and hesitate to voice honest opinions about a policy unless they can do so anonymously. Once the policy has come up for review, all comments should be examined, and management-approved improvements should be implemented. In reality, most policies are drafted by a single responsible employee and then reviewed by a higher-level manager, but even this method does not preclude the collection and review of employee input.

Policy, Review, and Revision Dates

The simple action of dating the policy is often omitted. When policies are drafted and published without dates, confusion can arise. If policies are not reviewed and kept current, or if members of the organization are following undated versions, disastrous results and legal headaches can ensue. Such problems are particularly common in a high-turnover environment. Therefore, the policy must contain the date of origin and the date(s) of any reviews and/or revisions. If the policy is reviewed and considered up to date, a review date is applied to the document. If it is reviewed and determined to need updating, a revision date is applied once the update is complete. Some policies may also need a **sunset clause** that indicates their expiration date, particularly if the policies govern information use in short-term business associations. Establishing a policy end date prevents a temporary policy from mistakenly becoming permanent, and it also enables an organization to gain experience with a given policy before adopting it permanently.

Automated Policy Management

In recent years, a new category of software has emerged for the management of information security policies. This type of software was developed in response to the needs of information security practitioners. While many software products can meet the need for a specific technical control, software now can automate some of the busywork of policy management. Automation can streamline the repetitive steps of writing policy, tracking the workflow of policy approvals, publishing policy once it is written and approved, and tracking when employees have read the policy. Using techniques from computer-based training and testing, an organization can train staff members and improve its awareness program.

Security Education, Training, And Awareness Program

security education, training, and awareness (SETA)

A managerial program designed to improve the security of information assets by providing targeted knowledge, skills, and guidance for an organization's employees.

Once your organization has defined the policies that will guide its security program, it is time to implement a **security education, training, and awareness (SETA)** program. The SETA program is the responsibility of the CISO and is a control measure designed to reduce incidents of accidental security breaches by employees. Employee errors are among the top threats to information assets, so it is well worth developing programs to combat this threat. SETA programs are designed to supplement the general education and training programs that many organizations use to educate staff about information security. For example, if an organization detects that many employees are opening questionable e-mail attachments, those employees must be retrained. As a matter of good practice, systems development life cycles must include user training during the implementation phase. Practices used to take control of the security and privacy of online data are sometimes called *cyber hygiene.*

The SETA program consists of three distinct elements: security education, security training, and security awareness. An organization may not be able or willing to undertake all three of these elements, and it may outsource elements to local educational institutions. The purpose of SETA is to enhance security by doing the following:

- Improving awareness of the need to protect system resources
- Developing skills and knowledge so computer users can perform their jobs more securely
- Building in-depth knowledge as needed to design, implement, or operate security programs for organizations and systems[17]

Table 3-4 compares the features of security education, training, and awareness within the organization.

Table 3-4   Comparative Framework of SETA[18]

	Awareness	Training	Education
Attribute	Seeks to teach members of the organization *what* security is and what the employee should do in some situations	Seeks to train members of the organization *how* they should react and respond when threats are encountered in specified situations	Seeks to educate members of the organization as to *why* it has prepared in the way it has and why the organization reacts in the ways it does
Level	Offers basic *information* about threats and responses	Offers more detailed *knowledge* about detecting threats and teaches skills needed for effective reaction	Offers the background and depth of knowledge to gain *insight* into how processes are developed and enables ongoing improvement
Objective	Members of the organization can *recognize* threats and formulate simple responses	Members of the organization can mount effective responses using learned *skills*	Members of the organization can engage in active defense and use *understanding* of the organization's objectives to make continuous improvement
Teaching methods	• Media videos • Newsletters • Posters • Informal training	• Formal training • Workshops • Hands-on practice	• Theoretical instruction • Discussions/seminars • Background reading
Assessment	True/false or multiple choice (identify learning)	Problem solving (apply learning)	Essay (interpret learning)
Impact timeframe	Short-term	Intermediate	Long-term

Source: NIST SP 800-12.

Security Education

Everyone in an organization needs to be trained and made aware of information security, but not everyone needs a formal degree or certificate in information security. When management agrees that formal education is appropriate, an employee can investigate courses in continuing education from local institutions of higher learning. Several universities have formal coursework in information security. For people who are interested in researching formal information security programs, resources are available, such as the DHS/NSA-designated National Centers of Academic Excellence program (see *www.iad.gov/NIETP/index.cfm*). This program identifies universities that have had their coursework and practices in information security reviewed and found to meet national standards. Other local resources can also provide information on security education, such as Kennesaw State University's Institute for Cybersecurity Workforce Development (*https://cyberinstitute.kennesaw.edu*).

Security Training

Security training provides employees with detailed information and hands-on instruction to prepare them to perform their duties securely. Management of information security can develop customized in-house training or outsource the training program.

Alternatives to formal training programs are industry training conferences and programs offered through professional agencies such as SANS (*www.sans.org*), (ISC)² (*www.isc2.org*), and ISSA (*www.issa.org*). All of these agencies are described in other modules. Many of these programs are too technical for the average employee, but they may be ideal for the continuing education requirements of information security professionals.

A new venue for security training for both security professionals and the average end user is Massive Open Online Courses (MOOCs), which are available from a number of vendors, including Coursera (*www.coursera.org*). Many of these courses are free to enroll in, and a certificate of completion is provided upon payment of a nominal fee. The list of available topics ranges from the traditional academic introduction to security to technical topics and general information.

Several resources for conducting SETA programs offer assistance in the form of sample topics and structures for security classes. For organizations, the Computer Security Resource Center at NIST provides several useful documents free of charge in its special publications area (*http://csrc.nist.gov*).

Security Awareness

A security awareness program is one of the least frequently implemented but most beneficial programs in an organization. A security awareness program is designed to keep information security at the forefront of users' minds. These programs don't have to be complicated or expensive. Good programs can include newsletters, security posters (see Figure 3-8 for an example), videos, bulletin boards, flyers, and trinkets. Trinkets can include security slogans printed on mouse pads, coffee cups, T-shirts, pens, or any object frequently used during the workday that reminds employees of security. In addition, a good security awareness program requires a dedicated person who is willing to invest time and effort to promoting the program, and a champion willing to provide the needed financial support.

The security newsletter is the most cost-effective method of disseminating security information and news to employees. Newsletters can be distributed via hard copy, e-mail, or intranet. Topics can include new threats to the organization's information assets, the schedule for upcoming security classes, and the addition of new security personnel. The goal is to keep the idea of information security in users' minds and to stimulate users to care about security. If a security awareness program is not actively implemented, employees may begin to neglect security matters, and the risk of employee accidents and failures is likely to increase.

Figure 3-8   SETA awareness posters

Information Security Blueprint, Models, And Frameworks

Once an organization has developed its information security policies and standards, the information security community can begin developing the blueprint for the information security program. The organization's policy will guide the selection and development of the blueprint, and the organization will use the blueprint to guide the implementation of the rest of the security program. This **information security blueprint** is the plan and basis for the design, selection, and implementation of all security program elements, including policies, risk management programs, education and training programs, technological controls, and program maintenance.

The blueprint is the organization's detailed implementation of an **information security framework**. The blueprint specifies tasks and the order in which they are to be accomplished, just as an architect's blueprint serves as the design template for the construction of a building. The framework is the philosophical foundation from which the blueprint is designed, like the style or methodology in which an architect was trained.

In choosing the framework to use for an information security blueprint, the organization should consider adapting or adopting a recognized or widely accepted **information security model** backed or promoted by an established security organization or agency. This exemplar framework can outline steps for designing and implementing information security in the organization. Several published information security frameworks from government agencies and other sources are presented later in this module. Because each information security environment is unique, the security team may need to modify or adapt pieces from several frameworks. Experience teaches that what works well for one organization may not precisely fit another.

information security blueprint

In information security, a framework or security model customized to an organization, including implementation details.

information security framework

In information security, a specification of a model to be followed during the design, selection, and initial and ongoing implementation of all subsequent security controls, including information security policies, security education and training programs, and technological controls.

information security model

A well-recognized information security framework, usually promoted by a government agency, standards organization, or industry group.

The ISO 27000 Series

One of the most widely referenced security models is *Information Technology—Code of Practice for Information Security Management*, which was originally published as British Standard BS7799. In 2000, this code of practice was adopted as ISO/IEC 17799, an international standard framework for information security by the International Organization for Standardization (ISO) and the International Electrotechnical Commission (IEC). The standard has been regularly revised and updated, and today it consists of an entire portfolio of standards related to the design, implementation, and management of an "information security management system." The version released in 2000 was revised in 2005 to become ISO 17799:2005, and it was then renamed as ISO 27002 in 2007 to align it with ISO 27001.

While the details of the ISO/IEC 27000 series are available only to those who purchase the standard, its structure and general organization are well known and are becoming increasingly significant for all who work in information security. For a summary description of the structure of the most recent standard, ISO 27002:2013, see Table 3-5.

Here is the stated purpose of ISO/IEC 27002, as derived from its ISO/IEC 17799 origins:

> *ISO/IEC 27002:2013 gives guidelines for organizational information security standards and information security management practices, including the selection, implementation, and management of controls, taking into consideration the organization's information security risk environment(s).*
>
> *It is designed to be used by organizations that intend to:*
>
> > *1. Select controls within the process of implementing an information security management system based on ISO/IEC 27001;*
> >
> > *2. Implement commonly accepted information security controls;*
> >
> > *3. Develop their own information security management guidelines.[19]*

Table 3-5   The Sections of ISO/IEC 27002:2013[20]

ISO 27002:2013 Contents	
Foreword	
0.	Introduction
1.	Scope
2.	Normative references
3.	Terms and definitions
4.	Structure of this standard
5.	Information security policies
6.	Organization of information security
7.	Human resource security
8.	Asset management
9.	Access control
10.	Cryptography
11.	Physical and environmental security
12.	Operations security
13.	Communication security
14.	System acquisition, development, and maintenance
15.	Supplier relationships
16.	Information security incident management
17.	Information security aspects of business continuity management
18.	Compliance
Bibliography	

Source: Compiled from various sources.

ISO/IEC 27002:2013 is focused on a broad overview of the various areas of security. It provides information on 14 security control clauses and addresses 35 control objectives and more than 110 individual controls. Its companion document, ISO/IEC 27001:2018, provides information for how to implement ISO/IEC 27002 and set up an information security management system (ISMS). ISO/IEC 27001's primary purpose is to be used as a standard so organizations can adopt it to obtain certification and build an information security program; ISO 27001 serves better as an assessment tool than as an implementation framework. ISO 27002 is for organizations that want information about implementing security controls; it is not a standard used for certification. Figure 3-9 illustrates the ISO 27001 process.

In the United Kingdom, correct implementation of both volumes of these standards had to be determined by a BS7799-certified evaluator before organizations could obtain ISMS certification and accreditation. When the standard first came out, several countries, including the United States, Germany, and Japan, refused to adopt it, claiming that it had fundamental problems:

- The global information security community had not defined any justification for a code of practice identified in ISO/IEC 17799.
- The standard lacked the measurement precision associated with a technical standard.
- There was no reason to believe that ISO/IEC 17799 was more useful than any other approach.
- It was not as complete as other frameworks.
- The standard was hurriedly prepared given the tremendous impact its adoption could have on industry information security controls.[21]

The ISO/IEC 27000 series is becoming increasingly important in the field, especially among global organizations. Many certification bodies and corporate organizations are complying with it or will someday be expected to comply with it.

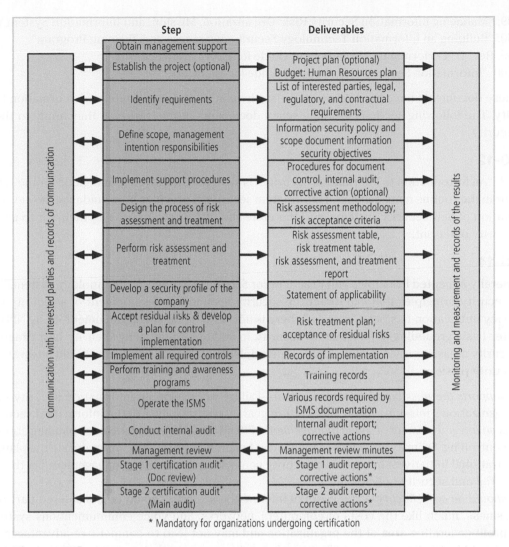

Figure 3-9 ISO/IEC 27001:2013 major process steps[22]

Source: 27001 Academy: ISO 27001 and ISO 22301 Online Consultation Center.

 For more details on current and proposed ISO/IEC 27000 series documents, visit the ISO 27001Security Web site. Gary Hinson, author/owner of the site, reports that the ISO 27000 suite has more than 70 standards planned, with approximately 61 published. For a complete list, visit *www.iso27001security.com/html/iso27000.html*.

NIST Security Models

Other approaches to security are described in the many documents available from the NIST Computer Security Resource Center (*http://csrc.nist.gov*). Because the NIST documents are publicly available at no charge and have been for some time, they have been broadly reviewed by government and industry professionals, and were among the references cited by the U.S. government when it decided not to select the ISO/IEC 17799 (now 27000 series) standards. The following NIST documents can assist in the design of a security framework:

- SP 800-12, Rev. 1: "An Introduction to Information Security"
- SP 800-18, Rev. 1: "Guide for Developing Security Plans for Federal Information Systems"
- SP 800-30, Rev. 1: "Guide for Conducting Risk Assessments"
- SP 800-37, Rev. 2: "Risk Management Framework for Information Systems and Organizations: A System Life Cycle Approach for Security and Privacy"

- SP 800-39: "Managing Information Security Risk: Organization, Mission, and Information System View"
- SP 800-50: "Building an Information Technology Security Awareness and Training Program"
- SP 800-55, Rev. 1: "Performance Measurement Guide for Information Security"
- SP 800-100: "Information Security Handbook: A Guide for Managers"

Many of these documents have been referenced elsewhere in this book as sources of information for the management of security. The following sections examine select documents in this series as they apply to the blueprint for information security.

NIST SP 800-12

SP 800-12, Rev. 1, "An Introduction to Information Security," is an excellent reference and guide for the security manager or administrator in the routine management of information security. It provides little guidance, however, for the design and implementation of new security systems, and therefore should be used only as a precursor to understanding an information security blueprint.

NIST SP 800-14

SP 800-14, "Generally Accepted Principles and Practices for Securing Information Technology Systems," provides best practices and security principles that can direct the security team in the development of a security blueprint. Even though this legacy publication has been "retired," there is not yet a replacement document in the NIST SP series that provides a better basic grounding in information security. In addition to detailing security best practices across the spectrum of security areas, it provides philosophical principles that the security team should integrate into the entire information security process:

- *Security supports the mission of the organization*—Failure to develop an information security system based on the organization's mission, vision, and culture guarantees the failure of the information security program.
- *Security is an integral element of sound management*—Effective management includes planning, organizing, leading, and controlling. Security enhances management functions by providing input during the planning process for organizational initiatives. Information security controls support sound management via the enforcement of managerial and security policies.
- *Security should be cost-effective*—The costs of information security should be considered part of the cost of doing business, much like the costs of computers, networks, and voice communications systems. Security is not a profit-generating area of the organization and may not lead to competitive advantages. Information security should justify its own costs. The use of security measures that do not justify their cost must have a strong business justification, such as a legal requirement.
- *Systems owners have security responsibilities outside their own organizations*—Whenever systems store and use information from customers, patients, clients, partners, or others, the security of this information becomes the responsibility of the systems' owners. These owners are expected to diligently work with each other to assure the confidentiality, integrity, and availability of the entire value chain of their interconnected systems.
- *Security responsibilities and accountability should be made explicit*—Policy documents should clearly identify the security responsibilities of users, administrators, and managers. To be legally binding, the policies must be documented, disseminated, read, understood, and agreed to by all involved members of the organization. As noted in Module 6, ignorance of the law is no excuse, but ignorance of policy is. Organizations should also provide information about relevant laws in issue-specific security policies.
- *Security requires a comprehensive and integrated approach*—Security personnel alone cannot effectively implement security. As emphasized throughout this textbook, *security is everyone's responsibility*. The three communities of interest—information technology management and professionals; information security management and professionals; and users, managers, administrators, and other stakeholders—should participate in the process of developing a comprehensive information security program.
- *Security should be periodically reassessed*—Information security that is implemented and then ignored is considered negligent because the organization has not demonstrated due diligence. Security is an ongoing process. To be effective against a constantly shifting set of threats and a changing user base, the security process must be periodically repeated. Continuous analyses of threats, assets, and controls must be conducted and new blueprints developed. Only thorough preparation, design, implementation, vigilance, and ongoing maintenance can secure the organization's information assets.

- *Security is constrained by societal factors*—Several factors influence the implementation and maintenance of security controls and safeguards, including legal demands, shareholder requirements, and even business practices. For example, security professionals generally prefer to isolate information assets from the Internet, which is the leading avenue of threats to the assets, but the business requirements of the organization may preclude this control measure.

NIST SP 800-18, Rev. 1

SP 800-18, Rev. 1, "Guide for Developing Security Plans for Federal Information Systems," can be used as the foundation for a comprehensive security blueprint and framework. This publication provides detailed methods for assessing, designing, and implementing controls and plans for applications of varying size. SP 800-18, Rev. 1, can serve as a useful guide to the activities described in this module and as an aid in the planning process. It also includes templates for major application security plans. As with any publication of this scope and magnitude, SP 800-18, Rev. 1, must be customized to fit the particular needs of an organization.

NIST and the Risk Management Framework

NIST's approach to managing risk in the organization, titled the Risk Management Framework (RMF), emphasizes the following:

- *Building information security capabilities into federal information systems through the application of state-of-the-practice management, operational, and technical security controls*
- *Maintaining awareness of the security state of information systems on an ongoing basis through enhanced monitoring processes*
- *Providing essential information to help senior leaders make decisions about accepting risk to an organization's operations and assets, individuals, and other organizations arising from the use of information systems*

The RMF has the following characteristics:

- *Promotes the concept of near real-time risk management and ongoing information system authorization through the implementation of robust continuous monitoring*
- *Encourages the use of automation to provide senior leaders with necessary information to make cost-effective, risk-based decisions about information systems that support an organization's core missions and business functions*
- *Integrates information security into the enterprise architecture and system development life cycle*
- *Emphasizes the selection, implementation, assessment, and monitoring of security controls and the authorization of information systems*
- *Links risk management processes at the information system level to risk management processes at the organization level through a risk executive function*
- *Establishes responsibility and accountability for security controls deployed within an organization's information systems and inherited by those systems (i.e., common controls).*[23]

The NIST Risk Management Framework is discussed in detail in Module 4, "Risk Management."

The NIST Cybersecurity Framework

In early 2014, NIST published a new Cybersecurity Framework in response to Executive Order 13636 from President Obama. NIST's mandate was to create a voluntary framework that provides an effective approach to "manage cybersecurity risk for those processes, information, and systems directly involved in the delivery of critical infrastructure services."[24] The resulting framework, which is designed specifically to be vendor-neutral, closely resembles the other approaches described in this textbook, but it provides additional structure to the process, if not detail. The NIST framework builds on and works closely with the RMF described in the previous section. The framework document represents the integration of previously discussed special publications from NIST, in a form that makes the framework easier to understand and enables organizations to implement an information security improvement program.

The intent of the framework is to allow organizations to: "1) Describe their current cybersecurity posture; 2) Describe their target state for cybersecurity; 3) Identify and prioritize opportunities for improvement within the context of a continuous and repeatable process; 4) Assess progress toward the target state; and 5) Communicate among internal and external stakeholders about cybersecurity risk."[25]

The NIST framework consists of three fundamental components:

- *The framework core*—This is a set of information security activities an organization is expected to perform, as well as their desired results. These core activities are as follows:
  - *"Identify*—Develop the organizational understanding to manage cybersecurity risk to systems, assets, data, and capabilities.
  - *Protect*—Develop and implement the appropriate safeguards to ensure delivery of critical infrastructure services.
  - *Detect*—Develop and implement the appropriate activities to identify the occurrence of a cybersecurity event.
  - *Respond*—Develop and implement the appropriate activities to take action regarding a detected cybersecurity event.
  - *Recover*—Develop and implement the appropriate activities to maintain plans for resilience and to restore any capabilities or services that were impaired due to a cybersecurity event."
- *The framework tiers*—The framework then provides a self-defined set of tiers so organizations can relate the maturity of their security programs and implement corresponding measures and functions. The four tiers include the following:
  - *Tier 1: Partial*—In this category, an organization does not have formal risk management practices, and security activities are relatively informal and ad hoc.
  - *Tier 2: Risk Informed*—Organizations in this category have developed but not fully implemented risk management practices, and have just begun their formal security programs, so security is not fully established across the organization.
  - *Tier 3: Repeatable*—Organizations in this category not only have risk management practices formally established, they have documented policy implemented. The organization has begun a repeatable security program to improve its approach to information protection and proactively manage risk to information assets.
  - *Tier 4: Adaptive*—The most mature organization falls into this tier. The organization not only has well-established risk management and security programs, it can quickly adapt to new environments and threats. The organization is experienced at managing risk and responding to threats and has integrated security completely into its culture.
- *The framework profile*—Organizations are expected to identify which tier their security programs most closely match and then use corresponding recommendations within the framework to improve their programs. This framework profile is then used to perform a gap analysis—comparing the current state of information security and risk management to a desired state, identifying the difference, and developing a plan to move the organization toward the desired state. This approach is identical to the approaches outlined elsewhere in this text.

Using the materials provided in the NIST framework, organizations are encouraged to follow a seven-step approach to implementing or improving their risk management and information security programs:

Step 1: Prioritize and scope—The organization identifies its business/mission objectives and high-level organizational priorities. With this information, the organization makes strategic decisions regarding cybersecurity implementations and determines the scope of systems and assets that support the selected business line or process.

Step 2: Orient—Once the scope of the cybersecurity program has been determined for the business line or process, the organization identifies related systems and assets, regulatory requirements, and overall risk approach. The organization then identifies threats to, and vulnerabilities of, those systems and assets.

Step 3: Create a current profile—The organization develops a current profile by indicating which category and subcategory outcomes from the framework core are currently being achieved.

Step 4: Conduct a risk assessment—This assessment could be guided by the organization's overall risk management process or previous risk assessment activities. The organization analyzes the operational environment in order to discern the likelihood of a cybersecurity event and the impact that the event could have on the organization.

Step 5: Create a target profile—The organization creates a target profile that focuses on the assessment of the framework categories and subcategories describing the organization's desired cybersecurity outcomes.

Step 6: Determine, analyze, and prioritize gaps—The organization compares the current profile and the target profile to determine gaps. Next it creates a prioritized action plan to address those gaps that draws upon mission drivers, a cost-benefit analysis, and understanding of risk to achieve the outcomes in the target profile. The organization then determines resources necessary to address the gaps.

Step 7: Implement action plan—The organization determines which actions to take in regards to the gaps, if any, identified in the previous step. It then monitors its current cybersecurity practices against the target profile.[26]

As you will learn in Module 11 while studying the SDLC waterfall methodology, the preceding steps are designed to be an iterative process that gradually moves the organization closer to a Tier 4 security level and results in a better approach to risk management and information protection.

NIST also provides a "Roadmap for Improving Critical Infrastructure Cybersecurity,"[27] which provides supplemental guidance for the framework and insights into its future development and refinement as an evolutionary, living document.

 For more information on the NIST Cybersecurity Framework, visit the NIST Web site at *www.nist.gov/cyberframework*.

Other Sources of Security Frameworks

Many public and private organizations promote solid best security practices. Professional societies often provide information on best practices for their members. The Technology Manager's Forum (*www.techforum.com*) has an annual best practice award in several areas, including information security. The Information Security Forum (*www.securityforum.org*) has a free publication titled "Standard of Good Practice for Information Security," which outlines information security best practices.

Many organizations hold seminars and classes on best practices for implementing security; in particular, the Information Systems Audit and Control Association (*www.isaca.org*) hosts regular seminars. The International Association of Professional Security Consultants (*www.iapsc.org*) has a listing of best practices. At a minimum, information security professionals can peruse Web portals for posted security best practices. Several free portals dedicated to security have collections of best practices, such as SearchSecurity.com and NIST's Computer Resources Center.

Design of the Security Architecture

To inform the discussion of information security program architecture and to illustrate industry best practices, the following sections outline a few key components of security architecture. Many of these components are examined in detail in later modules of the book, but this overview can help you assess whether a framework and blueprint are on target to meet an organization's needs.

Spheres of Security

The spheres of security, shown in Figure 3-10, are the foundation of the security framework. Generally speaking, the spheres of security illustrate how information is under attack from a variety of sources. The right side of Figure 3-10 illustrates the ways in which internal users access information. For example, users can access hard copies of documents and information directly. Information, as the most important asset in this model, is at the center of the sphere. Information is always at risk from attacks whenever it is accessible by people or computer systems. Networks and the Internet are indirect threats, as exemplified by the fact that a person attempting to access information from the Internet must traverse local networks.

The left side of Figure 3-10 illustrates that a layer of protection must exist between each layer of the sphere of use. For example, "Policy and law" and "Education and training" are protections placed between people and the information. Controls are also implemented between systems and the information, between networks and the computer systems, and between the Internet and internal networks. This reinforces the concept of defense in depth. A variety of controls can

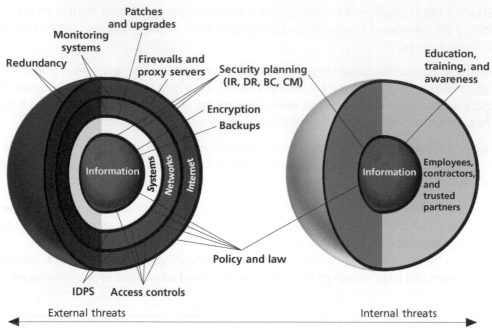

Figure 3-10   Spheres of security

be used to protect the information. The items of control shown in the figure are not intended to be comprehensive, but they illustrate some of the safeguards that can protect the systems closer to the center of the sphere. Because people can directly access each ring as well as the information at the core of the model, the side of the sphere of protection that attempts to control access by relying on people requires a different approach to security than the side that uses technology. The members of the organization must become a safeguard that is effectively trained, implemented, and maintained, or they too will present a threat to the information.

managerial controls

Information security safeguards that focus on administrative planning, organizing, leading, and controlling, and that are designed by strategic planners and implemented by the organization's security administration; they include governance and risk management.

Information security is designed and implemented in three layers: policies, people (education, training, and awareness programs), and technology. These layers are commonly referred to as PPT. Each layer contains controls and safeguards to protect the information and information system assets that the organization values. But, before any technical controls or other safeguards can be implemented, the policies that define the management philosophies behind the security process must be in place.

Levels of Controls

operational controls

Information security safeguards focusing on lower-level planning that deals with the functionality of the organization's security; they include disaster recovery planning, incident response planning, and SETA programs.

Information security safeguards provide three levels of control: managerial, operational, and technical. **Managerial controls** set the direction and scope of the security process and provide detailed instructions for its conduct. In addition, these controls address the design and implementation of the security planning process and security program management. They also address risk management and security control reviews (as described in Module 4), describe the necessity and scope of legal compliance, and set guidelines for the maintenance of the entire security life cycle.

Operational controls address personnel security, physical security, and the protection of production inputs and outputs. In addition, operational controls guide the development of education, training, and awareness programs for users, administrators, and management. Finally, they address hardware and software systems maintenance and the integrity of data.

technical controls

Information security safeguards that focus on the application of modern technologies, systems, and processes to protect information assets; they include firewalls, virtual private networks, and IDPSs.

Technical controls are the tactical and technical implementations of security in the organization. While operational controls address specific operating issues, such as developing and integrating controls into the business functions, technical controls include logical access controls, such as identification, authentication, authorization, accountability (including audit trails), cryptography, and the classification of assets and users.

Defense in Depth

A basic tenet of security architectures is the layered implementation of security. To achieve **defense in depth**, an organization must establish multiple layers of security controls and safeguards, which can be organized into policy, training and education, and technologies, as shown in the CNSS model presented in Module 1. While policy itself may not prevent attacks, it certainly prepares the organization to handle them; when coupled with other layers, policy can deter attacks. For example, the layer of training and education can help defend against attacks enabled by employee ignorance and social engineering. Technology is also implemented in layers, with detection equipment working in tandem with reaction technology behind access control mechanisms. **Redundancy** can be implemented at several points throughout the security architecture, such as in firewalls, proxy servers, and access controls. Figure 3-11 illustrates the concept of building controls in multiple and sometimes redundant layers. The figure shows firewalls and prevention IDPSs that use both packet-level rules (shown as the packet header in the diagram) and content analysis (shown as a database icon with the caption 0100101011). More information on firewalls and intrusion detection systems is presented in Modules 8 and 9, respectively.

defense in depth

A strategy for the protection of information assets that uses multiple layers and different types of controls to provide optimal protection; typically, implementation of many different types of controls.

redundancy

The use of multiple types and instances of technology that prevent the failure of one system from compromising the security of information; typically, multiple instances of the same type of control.

security perimeter

The boundary in the network within which an organization attempts to maintain security controls for securing information from threats from untrusted network areas.

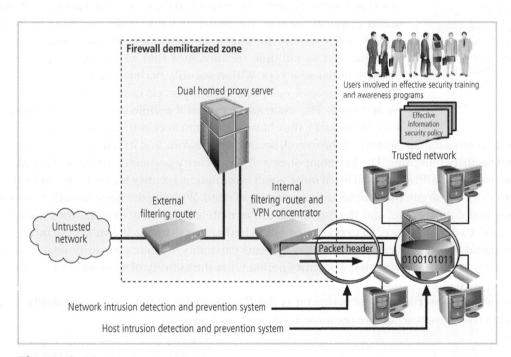

Figure 3-11　Defense in depth

Security Perimeter

A perimeter is a boundary of an area. A **security perimeter** is the border of security that protects all internal systems from outside threats, as pictured in Figure 3-12. Unfortunately, the perimeter does not protect against internal attacks from employee threats or on-site physical threats. In addition, the emergence of mobile computing devices, telecommuting, and cloud-based functionality has made the definition and defense of the perimeter increasingly more difficult. This has led some security experts to declare the security perimeter extinct and call for an increased focus on improved system-level security and active policing of networked assets. An organization can have both an

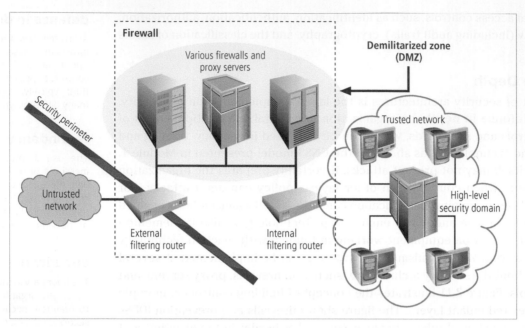

Figure 3-12 Security perimeters and domains

security domain

An area of trust within which information assets share the same level of protection; communication between these trust areas requires evaluation of communications traffic.

electronic security perimeter, usually at the exterior network or Internet connection, and a physical security perimeter, usually at the entrance to the organization's offices. Both require perimeter security. Security perimeters can effectively be implemented as multiple technologies that segregate the protected information from potential attackers. Within security perimeters, the organization can establish **security domains**, each with differing levels of security, between which traffic must be screened. The assumption is that if people have access to one system within a security domain, they have authorized access to all systems within that domain. The security perimeter is an essential element of the overall security framework, and its implementation details are the core of the completed security blueprint. The key components of the security perimeter are firewalls, DMZs (demilitarized zones), proxy servers, and IDPSs. You will learn more about information security technologies in Modules 8, 9, and 10.

Many security experts argue that the security perimeter is dead. With the dramatic growth in popularity of cloud-based computing and data storage, and the continued use of mobile computing devices, they argue that there is no "inside" or "outside" to organizations' networks anymore. Whether this is true is the subject of much debate. With the extensive use of cloud-based services to deliver key systems capability, including security-related functions, there is a growing movement toward realizing that a security perimeter is the entirety of an organization's network presence, anywhere and everywhere the company's data is, and that the use of defense in depth is still a valid approach to protecting it. Whether you subscribe to the "perimeter is dead" philosophy or not, the responsibility for protecting the organization's data using every available resource is still alive and well.

Closing Scenario

Janet stood up from the conference table and left the room.

The meeting had not lasted long, considering how significant its impact would be on Janet's life. Two officers from the corporate security team waited in the hallway to walk her to her office and collect her personal possessions, which were already in a box at her administrative assistant's desk. Her access card, phone, tablet, and laptop were already turned in, and every password she had ever used at SLS had been deactivated.

She was not looking forward to explaining this to her family.

The meeting in the room continued.

Fred asked, "Are we sure this was our only course? This seems harsh to me."

Janet's superior, the senior vice president of marketing, nodded and said, "I have to say that I agree. Janet was a solid performer and will be difficult, and expensive, to replace."

Charlie added, "I know what you mean. Jamie Hyack, the network engineer, is the same, except he chose to enable Janet's network access for her rotisserie league server without approval, without change control, and putting the company's entire network at risk. He had to go."

Gladys took a breath and said, "Sadly, this was needed. We cannot have two tiers of enforcement in our application of policy. If we do not enforce this policy requirement on executives, how can we be expected to have compliance from other employees?"

She continued, "As Charlie pointed out when we decided on this course of action, we have to enforce the policy we have in place. We can make changes to it that we feel better about and enforce those changes in the future."

Discussion Questions

1. Does this application of policy seem harsh to you? What alternatives might be implemented in policy to make it enforceable and perhaps less stringent than in this example?
2. Are there other punishments that might be enacted for situations like this? How might you propose structuring the policy to clarify what levels of punishment are appropriate?

Ethical Decision Making

The policies that organizations put in place are similar to laws, in that they are directives for how to act properly. Like laws, policies should be impartial and fair, and are often founded on ethical and moral belief systems of the people who create them.

In some cases, especially when organizations expand into foreign countries, they experience a form of culture shock when the laws of their new host country conflict with their internal policies. For example, suppose that SLS has expanded its operations into France. Setting aside any legal requirements that SLS make its policies conform to French law, does SLS have an ethical imperative to modify its policies across the company in all of its locations to better meet the needs of its stakeholders in the new country?

Suppose SLS has altered its policies for all operations in France and that the changes are much more favorable to employees—such as a requirement to provide childcare and eldercare services at no cost to employees. Is SLS under any ethical burden to offer the same benefit to employees in its home country?

Selected Readings

Many excellent sources of additional information are available in the area of information security. The following can add to your understanding of this module's content:

- "Information Security Governance: Guidance for Boards of Directors and Executive Management," available by searching at *www.isaca.org*.
- "Information Security Governance: A Call to Action," available from *www.cccure.org/Documents/Governance/InfoSec-Gov4_04.pdf*.
- *Information Security Policies Made Easy*, Version 12, by Charles Cresson Wood and Dave Lineman. 2012. Information Shield.
- *Management of Information Security*, by Michael E. Whitman and Herbert J. Mattord. 2019. Cengage Learning.
- *Principles of Incident Response and Disaster Recovery*, by Michael E. Whitman and Herbert J. Mattord. 2020. Cengage Learning.

Module Summary

- Information security governance is the application of the principles of corporate governance to the information security function. These principles include executive management's responsibility to provide strategic direction, ensure the accomplishment of objectives, oversee that risks are appropriately managed, and validate responsible resource use.
- Management must use policies as the basis for all information security planning, design, and deployment. Policies direct how issues should be addressed and technologies should be used.
- Standards are more detailed than policies and describe the steps that must be taken to conform to policies.
- Management must define three types of security policies: general or security program policies, issue-specific security policies, and systems-specific security policies.
- The enterprise information security policy (EISP) should be a driving force in the planning and governance activities of the organization as a whole.
- Information security policy is best disseminated in a comprehensive security education, training, and awareness (SETA) program. A security awareness program is one of the least frequently implemented but most beneficial programs in an organization. A security awareness program is designed to keep information security at the forefront of users' minds.
- Several published information security frameworks by government organizations, private organizations, and professional societies supply information on best practices for their members.
- One of the foundations of security architectures is the layered implementation of security. This layered approach is referred to as defense in depth.

Review Questions

1. How do the InfoSec management team's goals and objectives differ from those of the IT and general management communities?
2. What is included in the InfoSec planning model?
3. List and briefly describe the general categories of information security policy.
4. Briefly describe strategic planning.
5. List and briefly describe the levels of planning.
6. What is governance in the context of information security management?
7. What are the differences between a policy, a standard, and a practice? Where would each be used?
8. What is an EISP, and what purpose does it serve?
9. Who is ultimately responsible for managing a technology? Who is responsible for enforcing policy that affects the use of a technology?
10. What is needed for an information security policy to remain viable?
11. How can a security framework assist in the design and implementation of a security infrastructure?
    What is information security governance? Who in the organization should plan for it?
12. Where can a security administrator find information on established security frameworks?
13. What is the ISO 27000 series of standards? Which individual standards make up the series?
14. What documents are available from the NIST Computer Security Resource Center (CSRC), and how can they support the development of a security framework?
15. What Web resources can aid an organization in developing best practices as part of a security framework?
16. Briefly describe management, operational, and technical controls, and explain when each would be applied as part of a security framework.
17. What is defense in depth?
18. Define and briefly explain the SETA program and what it is used for.
19. What is the purpose of the SETA program?
20. What is security training?
21. What is a security awareness program?

Exercises

1. Search the Web for examples of issue-specific security policies. What types of policies can you find? Using the format provided in this module, draft a simple issue-specific policy that outlines fair and responsible use of computers at your college, based on the rules and regulations of your institution. Does your school have a similar policy? Does it contain all the elements listed in the text?
2. Using a graphics program, design several security awareness posters on the following themes: updating antivirus signatures, protecting sensitive information, watching out for e-mail viruses, prohibiting the personal use of company equipment, changing and protecting passwords, avoiding social engineering, and protecting software copyrights. What other themes can you imagine?
3. Search the Web for security education and training programs in your area. Keep a list and see which program category has the most examples. See if you can determine the costs associated with each example. Which do you think would be more cost-effective in terms of both time and money?

References

1. Corporate Governance Task Force. "Information Security Governance: A Call to Action." National Cyber Security Partnership, 2004.
2. Mahncke, R. "The Applicability of ISO/IEC 27014:2013 for Use Within General Medical Practice." Australian eHealth Informatics and Security Conference. December 2–4, 2013, Edith Cowan University, Perth, Western Australia. Accessed August 25, 2020, from *http://ro.ecu.edu.au/aeis/12*.
3. International Organization for Standardization. ISO/IEC 27014, "Information Technology—Security Techniques—Governance of Information Security." Accessed August 25, 2020, from *www.iso.org/obp/ ui/#iso:std:iso-iec:27014:ed-1:v1:en*.
4. Mahncke, R. "The Applicability of ISO/IEC 27014:2013 for Use Within General Medical Practice." Australian eHealth Informatics and Security Conference. December 2–4, 2013, Edith Cowan University, Perth, Western Australia. Accessed August 25, 2020, from *http://ro.ecu.edu.au/aeis/12*.
5. "Information Security Governance: A Call to Action," 2nd ed. 2006. Rolling Meadows, IL: IT Governance Institute.
6. Information Technology Governance Institute (ITGI). "Information Security Governance: Guidance for Information Security Managers." Accessed October 11, 2016, from *www.isaca.org*.
7. Wood, Charles Cresson. "Integrated Approach Includes Information Security." *Security* 37, no. 2 (February 2000): 43–44.
8. US-CERT. "Security Recommendations to Prevent Cyber Intrusions." Accessed August 24, 2020, from *https://us-cert.cisa.gov/ncas/alerts/TA11-200A*.
9. Nieles, M., Dempsey, K., and Pillitteri, V. SP 800-12, Rev. 1, "An Introduction to Information Security" (Draft). National Institute of Standards and Technology. Accessed August 25, 2020, from *https://csrc.nist. gov/CSRC/media/Publications/sp/800-12/rev-1/draft/documents/sp800_12_r1_draft.pdf*.
10. Derived from several sources, the most notable being The Washington University in St. Louis, Office of Information Security. Accessed August 24, 2020, from *https://informationsecurity.wustl.edu/policies/*.
11. Whitman, Michael E., Townsend, Anthony M., and Aalberts, Robert J. "Considerations for an Effective Telecommunications Use Policy." *Communications of the ACM* 42, no. 6 (June 1999): 101–109.
12. Ibid.

13. Macrotrends. "U.S. Literacy Rate 1990-2020." Accessed August 25, 2020, from *www.macrotrends.net/countries/USA/united-states/literacy-rate*.

14. Zeigler, K., and Camarota, S. "67.3 Million in the United States Spoke a Foreign Language at Home in 2018." Center for Immigration Studies. Accessed August 25, 2020, from *https://cis.org/Report/673-Million-United-States-Spoke-Foreign-Language-Home-2018*.

15. Whitman, Michael E. "Security Policy: From Design to Maintenance." Information Security Policies and Strategies—An Advances in MIS Monograph. Goodman, S., Straub, D., and Zwass, V. (eds). 2008. Armonk NY: M. E. Sharp, Inc.

16. Ibid.

17. Nieles, M., Dempsey, K., and Pillitteri, V. SP 800-12, Rev. 1, "An Introduction to Information Security." National Institute of Standards and Technology. Accessed August 25, 2020, from *https://csrc.nist.gov/publications/detail/sp/800-12/rev-1/final*.

18. Ibid.

19. ISO. "Abstract." Accessed August 25, 2020, from *www.iso.org/standard/54533.html*.

20. Compiled from a number of sources, including "ISO/IEC 27002:2013 Information Technology—Security Techniques—Code of Practice for Information Security Controls." Accessed August 25, 2020, from *www.iso27001security.com/html/27002.html*. Also, "Introduction to ISO 27002." Accessed August 25, 2020, from *www.27000.org/iso-27002.htm*.

21. National Institute of Standards and Technology. "Information Security Management, Code of Practice for Information Security Management." ISO/IEC 17799. December 6, 2001. Geneva, Switzerland.

22. Adapted from diagram of ISO 27001:2013 implementation process. Accessed August 25, 2020, from *https://advisera.com/27001academy/free-downloads/*.

23. National Institute of Standards and Technology. SP 800-37, Rev. 2, "Risk Management Framework for Information Systems and Organizations: A System Life Cycle Approach for Security and Privacy." Accessed August 26, 2020, from *https://csrc.nist.gov/publications/detail/sp/800-37/rev-2/final*.

24. National Institute of Standards and Technology. "Framework for Improving Critical Infrastructure Cybersecurity," version 1.0. February 12, 2014. Accessed August 26, 2020, from *www.nist.gov/cyberframework*.

25. Ibid.

26. Ibid.

27. National Institute of Standards and Technology. "Roadmap for Improving Critical Infrastructure Cybersecurity," version 1.1. April 25, 2019. Accessed August 26, 2020, from *www.nist.gov/system/files/documents/2019/04/25/csf-roadmap-1.1-final-042519.pdf*.

Risk Management

Upon completion of this material, you should be able to:

1. Define risk management and describe its importance
2. Explain the risk management framework and process model, including major components
3. Define risk appetite and explain how it relates to residual risk
4. Describe how risk is identified and documented
5. Discuss how risk is assessed based on likelihood and impact
6. Describe various options for a risk treatment strategy
7. Discuss conceptual frameworks for evaluating risk controls and formulating a cost-benefit analysis
8. Compare and contrast the dominant risk management methodologies

Once we know our weaknesses, they cease to do us any harm.

— G. C. (Georg Christoph) Lichtenberg (1742–1799), German Physicist, Philosopher

Opening Scenario

Charlie Moody called the meeting to order. The conference room was full of developers, systems analysts, and IT managers, as well as staff and management from sales and other departments.

"All right everyone, let's get started. Welcome to the kickoff meeting of our new risk management project team, the Sequential Label and Supply Information Security Task Force. We're here today to talk about our objectives and to review the initial work plan."

"Why is my department here?" asked the sales manager. "Isn't security the IT department's responsibility?"

Charlie explained, "Well, we used to think so, but we've come to realize that information security is about managing the risk of using information, which involves almost everyone in the company. To make our systems more secure, we need the participation of representatives from all departments."

Charlie continued, "I hope everyone managed to read the packets I sent out last week describing the legal requirements we face in our industry and the background articles on threats and attacks. Today we'll begin the process of identifying and classifying all of the information technology risks that face our organization. This includes everything from fires and floods that could disrupt our business to hackers who might try to steal our data or prevent us from accessing our own systems.

"Once we identify and classify the risks facing our assets, we can discuss how to reduce or eliminate these risks by establishing controls. Which controls we actually apply will depend on the costs and benefits of each control."

"Wow, Charlie!" said Amy Windahl, a member of the help-desk team, from the back of the room. "I'm sure we need to do it—I was hit by the last attack, just as everyone here was—but we have dozens of systems."

"It's more like hundreds," said Charlie. "That's why we have so many people on this team, and why the team includes members of every department."

Charlie continued, "Okay, everyone, please open your packets and take out the project plan with the work list showing teams, tasks, and schedules. Any questions before we start reviewing the work plan?"

Introduction To Risk Management

The upper management of an organization is responsible for overseeing, enabling, and supporting the structuring of IT and information security functions to defend its information assets. Part of upper management's information security governance requirement is the establishment and support of an effective risk management (RM) program. The IT community must serve the information technology needs of the entire organization and at the same time leverage the special skills and insights of the InfoSec community in supporting the RM program. The InfoSec team must lead the way with skill, professionalism, and flexibility as it works with other communities of interest to balance the usefulness and security of information systems, as well as evaluating and controlling the risks facing the organization's information assets.

In the early days of IT, corporations used computer systems mainly to gain a definitive advantage over the competition. Establishing a superior business model, method, or technique enabled an organization to provide a product or service that created a *competitive advantage*. In the modern business environment, however, all competitors have reached a certain level of technological competence and resilience. IT is now readily available to all organizations that make the investment, allowing them to react quickly to changes in the market. In this highly competitive environment, organizations cannot expect the implementation of new technologies to provide a competitive lead over others in the industry. Instead, the concept of *avoidance of competitive disadvantage*—working to prevent falling behind the competition—has emerged. Effective IT-enabled organizations quickly absorb relevant emerging technologies not just to gain or maintain competitive advantage, but to avoid loss of market share from an inability to maintain the highly responsive services required by their stakeholders.

To keep up with the competition, organizations must design and create safe environments in which their business processes and procedures can function. These environments must maintain confidentiality and privacy and assure the integrity of an organization's data—objectives that are met by applying the principles of risk management. As an aspiring information security professional, you will play a key role in risk management.

This module explores a variety of risk management approaches and provides a discussion of how risk is identified and assessed. The module includes a section on selecting and implementing effective control strategies for the protection of information assets in the modern organization.

Sun Tzu and the Art of Risk Management

In Module 1, you learned about the C.I.A. triad. Each of the three elements in the triad is an essential part of every organization's ability to sustain long-term competitiveness. When an organization depends on IT-based systems to remain viable, InfoSec and the discipline of **risk management** must become an integral part of the economic basis for making business decisions. These decisions are based on trade-offs between the costs of applying information system controls and the benefits of using secured, available systems.

Chinese general Sun Tzu Wu's quote, referenced earlier in this book, also has direct relevance to risk management:

> *If you know the enemy and know yourself, you need not fear the result of a hundred battles. If you know yourself but not the enemy, for every victory gained you will also suffer a defeat. If you know neither the enemy nor yourself, you will succumb in every battle.*[1]

Consider the similarities between information security and warfare. Information security managers and technicians are the defenders of information. The many threats discussed in Module 2 constantly attack the defenses surrounding information assets. Defenses are built in layers by placing safeguards behind safeguards. The defenders attempt to prevent, protect, detect, and recover from a seemingly endless series of attacks. Moreover, those defenders are legally prohibited from deploying offensive tactics, so the attackers have no need to expend resources on defense. While the defenders need to win every battle, the attackers only need to win once. To be victorious, defenders must know themselves and their enemy.

risk management

The process of identifying risk, assessing its relative magnitude, and taking steps to reduce it to an acceptable level.

Know Yourself

You must identify, examine, and understand the current information and systems in your organization. To protect *information assets*, which were defined earlier in this book as information and the systems that use, store, and transmit information, you must know what those assets are, where they are, how they add value to the organization, and the vulnerabilities to which they are susceptible. Once you know what you have, you can identify what you are already doing to protect it. Just because a control is in place does not necessarily mean that the asset is protected. Frequently, organizations implement control mechanisms but then neglect the necessary periodic review, revision, and maintenance. The policies, education and training programs, and technologies that protect information must be carefully maintained and administered to ensure that they remain effective.

Know the Enemy

Having identified your organization's assets and weaknesses, you move on to Sun Tzu's second step: Know the enemy. This means identifying, examining, and understanding the *threats* facing the organization. You must determine which threat aspects most directly affect the security of the organization and its information assets, and then use this information to create a list of threats, each one ranked according to the importance of the information assets that it threatens.

The Risk Management Framework

Risk management involves discovering and understanding answers to some key questions about the risk associated with an organization's information assets:

1. Where and what is the risk (risk identification)?
2. How severe is the current level of risk (risk analysis)?
3. Is the current level of risk acceptable (risk evaluation)?
4. What do I need to do to bring the risk to an acceptable level (risk treatment)?

The term **risk assessment** is commonly used to describe the entire set of activities associated with the first three questions, while **risk treatment** (or **risk control**) describes the fourth. Here, we will examine these activities individually to ensure that the distinctions between these stages are clear. InfoSec in an organization exists primarily to manage the risk to information assets stemming from the use of information. Managing risk is a key responsibility for every manager within an organization. Well-developed risk management programs rely on formal and repeatable processes. The coverage of risk management in this text was developed based on an extensive assessment of best practices in industry and government and of international standards. The international standard most closely aligned with the findings of this assessment—ISO 31000—was selected and adapted to facilitate ease of presentation and discussion.

Risk management is a complex operation that requires a formal methodology, much like the systems development life cycle (SDLC) discussed in Module 11. Figure 4-1 explores the entire approach to RM, which involves two key areas: the **RM framework** and the **RM process**. The RM framework is the overall structure of the strategic planning and design for the entirety of the organization's RM efforts. The RM process is the implementation of risk management, as specified in the framework. In other words, the RM framework (planning) guides the RM process (doing), which conducts the processes of risk evaluation and remediation. The RM framework assesses the RM process, which in turn assesses risk in the organization's information assets.

The RM framework and the RM process are continuous improvement activities. That means they are ongoing, repetitive, and designed to continually assess current performance to improve future RM results. The RM framework repeatedly assesses and improves how the RM process is evaluating and reacting to risk. The framework also continuously assesses and improves how well the planning and review activities are being performed—the framework itself. As an example, in a manufacturing plant, executives oversee the measurement of product quality and manufacturing

risk assessment

The identification, analysis, and evaluation of risk as initial parts of risk management.

risk treatment

The application of safeguards or controls to reduce the risks to an organization's information assets to an acceptable level.

risk control

See *risk treatment*.

RM framework

The overall structure of the strategic planning and design for the entirety of the organization's RM efforts.

RM process

The identification, analysis, evaluation, and treatment of risk to information assets, as specified in the RM framework.

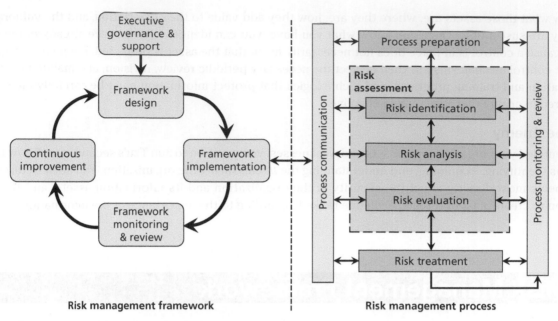

Figure 4-1   The risk management framework and process

productivity (the results and the equivalent of the RM process) while also assessing the effectiveness of the management processes used to structure manufacturing (the equivalent of the RM framework).

The left side of Figure 4-1 illustrates the major activities associated with the RM framework. As you have seen with other major InfoSec initiatives, this framework is developed and reviewed by an executive team led by a champion and organized using effective project management methods. Organizations that have existing RM programs may be able to adapt their operations to the methodology shown here, with minimum impact on their current efforts. Organizations that do not have formal RM programs—or have programs that are unsuccessful, inefficient, or ineffective—need to begin the process from scratch. The RM framework consists of five key stages:

1. Executive governance and support
2. Framework design
3. Framework implementation
4. Framework monitoring and review
5. Continuous improvement

While this framework is provided as an example of how to perform risk management in the organization, it is not by any means the only way to do RM. Each organization must decide for itself what works best from the multiple options available. The model shown here is adapted to be in alignment with an ISO standard, while others are based on industry standards or proprietary models.

It would not be difficult for an organization to take the general recommendations of this RM framework and process and adapt it to fit the details of another methodology. Only those involved in the process know what's best for their organizations.

The Roles of the Communities of Interest

Each community of interest has a role to play in managing the risks that an organization encounters. Because members of the information security community best understand the threats and attacks that introduce risk into the organization, they often take a leadership role in addressing risk to information assets. Management and users, when properly trained and kept aware of the threats the organization faces, play a part in early detection and response.

Management must also ensure that sufficient time, money, personnel, and other resources are allocated to the information security and information technology groups to meet the organization's security needs. Users work with systems and data and are therefore well positioned to understand the value these information assets offer the organization.

Users also understand which assets are the most valuable. The information technology community of interest must build secure systems and operate them safely. For example, IT operations ensure good backups to control the risk of data loss due to hard drive failure. The IT community can provide both valuation and threat perspectives to management during the risk management process. The information security community of interest must pull it all together in the risk management process.

All communities of interest must work together to address all levels of risk, which range from disasters that can devastate the whole organization to the smallest employee mistakes. The three communities of interest—InfoSec, IT, and general management—are also responsible for the following:

- Evaluating current and proposed risk controls
- Determining which control options are cost-effective for the organization
- Acquiring or installing the needed controls
- Ensuring that the controls remain effective

Because threats to assets are constantly changing, all three communities of interest must conduct periodic managerial reviews or audits, with general management usually providing oversight and access to information retained outside the IT department. The first managerial review is of the asset inventory. On a regular basis, management must ensure that the completeness and accuracy of the asset inventory is verified, usually through an IT audit. In addition, IT and information security must review and verify threats and vulnerabilities in the asset inventory, as well as current controls and mitigation strategies. They must also review the cost-effectiveness of each control and revisit decisions for deploying controls. Furthermore, managers at all levels must regularly verify the ongoing effectiveness of every deployed control. For example, a business manager might assess control procedures by periodically walking through the office after the workday ends, ensuring that all classified information is locked up, that all workstations are shut down, that all users are logged off, and that offices are secured. Managers may further ensure that no sensitive information is discarded in trash or recycling bins. Such controls are effective ways for managers and employees alike to ensure that no information assets are placed at risk. Other controls include following policy, promoting training and awareness, and employing appropriate technologies.

The RM Policy

As mentioned in Module 3, policy communicates management's intent for the outcome of an organization's effort. For RM program development and implementation, the project leader, in cooperation with the governance group, drafts a risk management policy. This policy converts the instructions and perspectives provided to the RM framework team by the governance group into cohesive guidance that structures and directs all subsequent risk management efforts within the organization.

The RM policy, much like the enterprise information security policy (EISP), is a strategic document that formalizes much of the intent of the governance group. While no two policies are identical, most include the following sections:

- *Purpose and scope*—What is this policy for and to whom does it apply?
- *RM intent and objectives*—What is the general view of RM by the governance group, and how will that be translated into goals and objectives for RM for the entire organization?
- *Roles and responsibilities*—A list of the assignments and expectations for each constituent responsible for the RM program. These lists should specify who will be involved (usually by position) and what their involvement is by group:
  - Oversight and governance group
  - RM framework development team
  - RM process implementation team (if different from framework)
  - Business units
  - IT department
  - Information security group

    For example: *The chief information security officer will serve as project team leader for the RM framework development team and is responsible for ensuring completion of the framework and implementation of the process within the timelines, budgets, and other constraints specified …*

- *Resource requirements*—A list of the resources allocated to the support of RM as a program and to the framework and process teams. The resource list should be compatible with the roles and responsibilities specified earlier.
- *Risk appetite and tolerances*—A summary of the expectations and preferences of executive management regarding the level of risk the organization is willing to tolerate.
- *RM program development guidelines*—Organization-specific instructions to guide the development and implementation of the RM effort. These could include a need to comply with specific regulations, to follow a particular methodology (which could either be incorporated into this RM project or in place of it), and any other special considerations the governance team wants to make known.
- *Special instructions and revision information*—Guidelines for the planned review and revision of the policy document, including information on "who," "how," and "when."
- *References to other key policies, plans, standards, and guidelines*—A list of key documents (internal or external) that the organization should remain cognizant of during the development and implementation of the RM program.

Framework Design

In this stage, the framework team begins designing the RM process by which the organization will understand its current levels of risk and determine what, if anything, it needs to do to bring those levels down to an acceptable level in alignment with the risk appetite specified earlier in the process. Designing the RM program means defining and specifying the detailed tasks to be performed by the framework team and the process team. Once the framework itself has been designed and completed at least one iteration, most of the work of the framework team involves oversight of the process rather than developing the framework.

As you will learn later in this module, a wide variety of methodologies are available for conducting risk management. At this stage, the organization may simply select an "off-the-shelf" implementation of such a methodology, which it can use as is or adapt to its needs. The organization may even decide to develop its own methodology. Whatever it does, this is the phase of the RM framework in which the entire RM program is decided and the corresponding details are specified.

In addition to coordinating with the governance group on the tasks outlined in the previous section, the framework team must also formally document and define the organization's risk appetite and draft the **risk management (RM) plan**.

Defining the Organization's Risk Tolerance and Risk Appetite

As the governance group communicates its intent to the RM framework development team, it also needs to communicate its general perspective on what level of risk is acceptable and what risk must be reduced or resolved in some fashion. In other words, the RM framework team needs to understand and be able to determine whether the level of controls identified at the end of the risk process results in a level of risk that management can accept. The amount of risk that remains after all current controls are implemented is **residual risk**. The organization may very well reach this point in the risk management process, examine the documented residual risk and simply state, "Yes, the organization can live with that," and then document everything for the next risk management review cycle.

The difficulty lies in the process of formalizing exactly what the organization "can live with." This process is the heart of **risk appetite**. Documenting risk appetite as part of the RM framework development effort is often a vague and poorly understood proposition.

According to KPMG, a global network of professional firms providing audit, tax, and advisory services:

A well-defined risk appetite should have the following characteristics:

- *Reflective of strategy, including organizational objectives, business plans, and stakeholder expectations.*

---

risk management (RM) plan

A document that contains specifications for the implementation and conduct of RM efforts.

residual risk

The risk to information assets that remains even after current controls have been applied.

risk appetite

The quantity and nature of risk that organizations are willing to accept as they evaluate the trade-offs between perfect security and unlimited accessibility.

- *Reflective of all key aspects of the business.*
- *Acknowledges a willingness and capacity to take on risk.*
- *Is documented as a formal risk appetite statement.*
- *Considers the skills, resources, and technology required to manage and monitor risk exposures in the context of risk appetite.*
- *Is inclusive of a tolerance for loss or negative events that can be reasonably quantified.*
- *Is periodically reviewed and reconsidered with reference to evolving industry and market conditions.*
- *Has been approved by the board.*[2]

The KPMG approach to defining risk appetite involves understanding the organization's strategic objectives, defining risk profiles for each major current organizational activity and future strategic plan, and defining a **risk tolerance** (or **risk threshold**) for each profile.

Risk tolerance works hand in glove with risk appetite, as it more clearly defines the range of acceptable risk for each initiative, plan, or activity. If an administrator is asked what level of attack success and loss he or she is willing to accept for a particular system, the answer should provide insight into the risk threshold for that system, as well as that for the data it stores and processes. If the answer to the question is "absolutely none," the administrator has a **zero-tolerance risk exposure** for the system and requires the highest level of protection. A realistic tolerance usually falls somewhere between "sporadic hardware/software issues" and "total destruction."

The synthesis of risk thresholds becomes the risk appetite for the organization. Risk thresholds are more tactical or operational in nature, and the risk appetite is more strategic. The final result of risk assessment is the formalization of risk appetite in the **risk appetite statement**, which is part of the RM framework policy.

Framework Implementation

Once the framework team has finished designing the RM program (framework and process), it begins implementing the program. As with any major project, this involves specifying the project manager for the process and laying out the detailed implementation methodology. The RM process, which is specified in the right half of Figure 4-1, provides general steps to follow in the conduct of risk evaluation and remediation and is designed to be intentionally vague so it can be adapted to any one of the methodologies available.

The implementation of the RM plan, specifically including the RM process, could be based on several traditional IT implementation methods and is likely to be influenced by the organization's risk appetite:

- The organization may distribute the plan to all mid- to upper-level managers for a *desk check* prior to deployment.
- The organization could *pilot-test* the plan in a small area to gauge initial issues and success prior to deployment across the entire organization.
- The organization may use a *phased approach* in which only a portion of the RM program is initially implemented, such as initial meetings with key managers or initial inventory of information assets.
- The bold organization with a larger risk appetite may simply choose a *direct cutover* (also known as a cold-turkey conversion) in which the new RM project is launched in totality across the entire organization.

Whatever rollout method is selected, it is important for the RM framework team to carefully monitor, communicate, and review the implementation so it can detect and address issues before they become threatening to the viability of the program, as discussed in the next section.

Framework Monitoring and Review

After the initial implementation and as the RM effort proceeds, the framework team continues to monitor the conduct of the RM process while simultaneously reviewing the utility and relative success of the framework planning function itself. In the first few iterations, the framework team will examine how successful it was in designing and implementing

risk tolerance

The assessment of the amount of risk an organization is willing to accept for a particular information asset, typically synthesized into the organization's overall risk appetite.

risk threshold

See *risk tolerance*.

zero-tolerance risk exposure

An extreme level of risk tolerance whereby the organization is unwilling to allow any successful attacks or suffer any loss to an information asset.

risk appetite statement

A formal document developed by the organization that specifies its overall willingness to accept risk to its information assets, based on a synthesis of individual risk tolerances.

the RM framework, plan, and RM process, and what issues required adjustments of the plan. The framework itself only exists as a methodology to design and implement the process, so once the framework is documented in the RM plan, the success of the process becomes the greatest concern. Success or failure in the framework's planning process may be relatively simple to resolve if addressed early, but issues downstream in the actual RM process may require redesign all the way back up to the framework and then modification of the RM plan. Performance measures, which are described in detail in Module 12, are often used to collect data about the RM process and determine its relative success or failure. The results of these assessments are used in the continuous improvement stage, which is described next.

Once the RM process is implemented and operating, the framework team is primarily concerned with the monitoring and review of the RM process cycle. However, until the framework and plan are implemented and operational, the framework team is also concerned with oversight of the RM framework and plan. The governance group also expects regular feedback on the entire RM program, including information about the relative success and progress of both the framework and process activities.

The Risk Management Process

During the implementation phase of the RM framework, the RM plan guides the implementation of the RM process, in which risk evaluation and remediation of key assets are conducted. The three communities of interest must work together to address every level of risk, ranging from full-scale disasters (whether natural or human-made) to the smallest mistake made by an employee. To do so, representatives from each community collaborate to be actively involved in RM process activities. This process uses the specific knowledge and perspective of the team to complete the following tasks:

- Establishing the context, which includes understanding both the organization's internal and external operating environments and other factors that could impact the RM process.
- Identifying risk, which includes the following:
  - Creating an inventory of information assets
  - Classifying and organizing those assets meaningfully
  - Assigning a value to each information asset
  - Identifying threats to the cataloged assets
  - Pinpointing vulnerable assets by tying specific threats to specific assets
- Analyzing risk, which includes the following:
  - Determining the likelihood that vulnerable systems will be attacked by specific threats
  - Assessing the relative risk facing the organization's information assets so that risk management and control activities can focus on assets that require the most urgent and immediate attention
  - Calculating the risks to which assets are exposed in their current setting
  - Looking in a general way at controls that might come into play for identified vulnerabilities and ways to control the risks that the assets face
  - Documenting and reporting the findings of risk identification and assessment
- Evaluating the risk to the organization's key assets and comparing identified uncontrolled risks against its risk appetite:
  - Identifying individual risk tolerances for each information asset
  - Combining or synthesizing these individual risk tolerances into a coherent risk appetite statement
- Treating the unacceptable risk:
  - Determining which treatment/control strategy is best considering the value of the information asset and which control options are cost-effective
  - Acquiring or installing the appropriate controls
  - Overseeing processes to ensure that the controls remain effective
- Summarizing the findings, which involves stating the conclusions of the identification, analysis, and evaluation stages of risk assessment in preparation for moving into the stage of controlling risk by exploring methods to further mitigate risk where applicable or desired

RM Process Preparation—Establishing the Context

As the RM process team convenes, it is initially briefed by representatives of the framework team and possibly by the governance group. These groups seek to provide executive guidance for the work to be performed by the RM process team, and to ensure that the team's efforts are in alignment with managerial intent, as documented in the RM policy and plan. The group is briefed on its responsibilities and set to its work. The plan is reviewed and individual assignments given.

The *context* in this phase is the understanding of the external and internal environments the RM team will be interacting with as it conducts the RM process. It also means understanding the RM process as defined by the framework team and having the internal knowledge and expertise to implement it. Finally, it means ensuring that all members of the RM process team understand the organization's risk appetite statement and can use the risk appetite to translate that statement into the appropriate risk treatment when the time comes.

NIST's Special Publication (SP) 800-30, Rev. 1, "Guide for Conducting Risk Assessments," recommends preparing for the risk process by performing the following tasks:

- Identify the purpose of the assessment;
- Identify the scope of the assessment;
- Identify the assumptions and constraints associated with the assessment;
- Identify the sources of information to be used as inputs to the assessment; and
- Identify the risk model and analytic approaches (i.e., assessment and analysis approaches) to be employed during the assessment.[3]

External Context

Understanding the external context means understanding the impact the following external factors could have on the RM process, its goals, and its objectives:

- *The business environment*—Customers, suppliers, competitors
- *The legal/regulatory/compliance environment*—Laws, regulations, industry standards
- *The threat environment*—Threats, known vulnerabilities, attack vectors
- *The support environment*—Government agencies like NIST and DHS, professional associations like ISSA, and service agencies such as SecurityFocus
- Perhaps other factors known to the subject-matter experts that make up the team

These factors should influence the organization's conduct of the RM process, its assessment methods, its findings, and most importantly, its decisions when treating risk.

Internal Context

The internal context is the understanding of internal factors that could impact or influence the RM process:

- The organization's governance structure (or lack thereof)
- The organization's internal stakeholders
- The organization's culture
- The maturity of the organization's information security program
- The organization's experience in policy, planning, and risk management in general

Risk Assessment: Risk Identification

The first operational phase of the RM process is the identification of risk. As a reminder, risk assessment includes risk identification as well as risk analysis and risk determination. **Risk identification** begins with the process of self-examination. As Sun Tzu stated, the organization must know itself to understand the risk to its information assets and where that risk resides. At this stage, managers must (1) identify the organization's information assets, (2) classify them, (3) categorize them into useful groups, and (4) prioritize them by overall importance. This can be a daunting task, but it must be done to identify weaknesses and the threats they present.

risk identification

The recognition, enumeration, and documentation of risks to an organization's information assets.

The RM process team must initially confirm or define the categories and classifications to be used for the information assets, once identified. Some organizations prefer to collect the inventory first and then see what natural categories and classifications emerge; those areas are discussed later in this module. Once the risk management team has its organization formalized, it begins with the first major task of risk identification.

Identification of Information Assets

The risk identification process begins with the identification and cataloging of information assets, including people, procedures, data, software, hardware, and networking elements. This step should be done without prejudging the value of each asset; values will be assigned later in the process.

One of the toughest challenges in the RM process is identifying information assets with precision for the purposes of risk management. In the most general sense, an *information asset* is any asset that collects, stores, processes, or transmits information, or any collection, set, or database of information that is of value to the organization. For these purposes, the terms *data* and *information* are commonly used interchangeably. In some RM efforts, the information and its supporting technology—hardware, software, data, and personnel—are defined separately, and the decision whether to include a specific category or component is made by the RM process team.

Some commercial RM applications simplify the decision by separating information assets from *media*. Media in this context include hardware, integral operating systems, and utilities that collect, store, process, and transmit information, *leaving only the data and applications designed to directly interface with the data as information assets for the purposes of RM*. When the application interfaces with an external database or data file (data set), each is treated as a separate, independent information asset. When an application has data that is integral to its operations, it is treated as a single information asset.

By separating components that are much easier to replace (hardware and operating systems) from the information assets that are in some cases almost irreplaceable, the RM effort becomes much more straightforward. After all, what is the organization most concerned with? Is it the physical server used to host a critical application? Or is it the application and its data? Servers, switches, routers, and most host technologies are relatively interchangeable. If a server dies, the organization simply replaces it and then reloads the applications and data that give that server purpose in the organization. If an application dies, the replacement effort may be much more substantial than simply reinstalling an off-the-shelf application. Most core applications are heavily customized or even custom-developed for a particular purpose. This is not to insinuate that some assets don't have value to the organization, but that they are not necessarily integral to an RM program.

Some organizations choose to focus narrowly on their initial RM process and then add information assets in later iterations. They may begin with data and core applications, add communications software, operating systems, and supporting utilities, and finally add physical assets. *The bottom line is that the RM process team should decide and define exactly what constitutes an information asset for the purposes of the RM effort, so it can effectively and efficiently manage the scope and focus of the effort.*

Table 4-1 shows a model outline of some information assets the organization may choose to incorporate into its RM effort. These assets are categorized as follows:

- The people asset can be divided into internal personnel (employees) and external personnel (nonemployees). Insiders can be further divided into employees who hold trusted roles and therefore have correspondingly greater authority and accountability, and regular staff members who do not have any special privileges. Outsiders consist of other users who have access to the organization's information assets; some of these users are trusted, and some are untrusted.
- Procedures can be information assets because they are used to create value for the organization. They can be divided into (1) IT and business standard procedures and (2) IT and business-sensitive procedures. Sensitive procedures have the potential to enable an attack or to otherwise introduce risk to the organization. For example, the procedures used by a telecommunications company to activate new circuits pose special risks because they reveal aspects of the inner workings of a critical process, which can be subverted by outsiders for the purpose of obtaining unbilled, illicit services.
- The data asset includes information in all states: transmission, processing, and storage. This is an expanded use of the term *data*, which is usually associated with data sets and databases, as well as the full range of information used by modern organizations.

Table 4-1   Organizational Assets Used in Systems

Information System Components	Risk Management Components	Example Risk Management Components
People	Internal personnel	Trusted employees
	External personnel	Other staff members
		People we trust outside our organization
		Strangers
Procedures	Procedures	IT and business-standard procedures
		IT and business-sensitive procedures
Data	Data/information	Transmission
		Processing
		Storage
Software	Software	Applications
		Operating systems
		Utilities
		Security components
Hardware	Hardware	Systems and peripherals
		Security devices
		Network-attached process control devices and other embedded systems (Internet of Things)
Networking	Networking	Local area network components
		Intranet components
		Internet or extranet components
		Cloud-based components

- Software can be divided into applications, operating systems, utilities, and security components. Software that provides security controls may fall into the operating systems or applications category but is differentiated by the fact that it is part of the InfoSec control environment and must therefore be protected more thoroughly than other systems components.
- Hardware can be divided into (1) the usual systems devices and their peripherals and (2) the devices that are part of InfoSec control systems. The latter must be protected more thoroughly than the former.
- Networking components can include networking devices (such as firewalls, routers, and switches) and the systems software within them, which is often the focal point of attacks, with successful attacks continuing against systems connected to the networks. Of course, most of today's computer systems include networking elements. You will have to determine whether a device is primarily a computer or primarily a networking device. A server computer that is used exclusively as a proxy server or bastion host may be classified as a networking component, while an identical server configured as a database server may be classified as hardware. For this reason, networking devices should be considered separately rather than combined with general hardware and software components.

In some corporate models, this list may be simplified into three groups: people, processes, and technology. Regardless of which model is used in the development of risk assessment methods, an organization should ensure that all its information resources are properly identified, assessed, and managed for risk.

As mentioned previously, the entire set of assets in some risk management programs is divided into RM information assets, such as applications, application-based data, other independent data sets or collections, and media—essentially anything that can collect, store, process, or transmit data. The media are used for grouping access to the asset but are not valued and evaluated as a critical function of the risk identification step. This simplistic approach may be best for organizations just starting out in RM.

Identifying Hardware, Software, and Network Assets Many organizations use asset inventory systems to keep track of their hardware, network, and software components. Numerous applications are available, and it is up to the chief information security officer (CISO) or chief information officer (CIO) to determine which application best serves the needs of the organization. Organizations that do not use an off-the-shelf inventory system must create an equivalent manual or automated process. Automated systems are valuable because hardware is already identified by model, make, and location. Note that the number of items and large quantity of data for each item will quickly overwhelm any manual system and might stress poorly designed automated inventory systems.

Whether automated or manual, the inventory process requires a certain amount of planning. Most importantly, you must determine which attributes of each of these information assets should be tracked. That determination will depend on the needs of the organization and its risk management efforts as well as the preferences and needs of the InfoSec and IT communities. When deciding which attributes to track for each information asset, consider the following list of potential attributes:

- *Name*—Some organizations may have several names for the same product, and each of them should be cross-referenced in the inventory. By having redundant names for its assets, the organization gains flexibility and allows different units to have their own designations. However, the different names should be cross-listed as synonyms in inventory, and one of the asset names should be designated as the authoritative name. No matter how many names you track or how you select a name, always provide a definition of the asset in question. A recommended practice is to adopt naming standards that do not convey critical information to potential system attackers. For instance, a server named CASH_1 or HQ_FINANCE may entice attackers.
- *Asset tag*—This is used to facilitate the tracking of physical assets. Asset tags are unique numbers assigned to assets and permanently affixed to tangible assets during the acquisition process.
- *Internet Protocol (IP) address*—This attribute may be useful for network devices and servers at some organizations, but it rarely applies to software. This practice is limited when the organization uses the Dynamic Host Configuration Protocol (DHCP) within TCP/IP, which reassigns IP numbers to devices as needed. In such cases, there is no value in using IP numbers as part of the asset-identification process.
- *Media Access Control (MAC) address*—As per the TCP/IP standard, all network-interface hardware devices have a unique number called the MAC address (also called an "electronic serial number" or a "hardware address"). The network operating system uses this number to identify specific network devices. The client's network software uses the address to recognize traffic that it needs to process. In most settings, MAC addresses can be a useful way to track connectivity, but they can be spoofed by some hardware/software combinations.
- *Asset type*—This attribute describes the function of each asset. For hardware assets, a list of possible asset types that includes servers, desktops, networking devices, and test equipment should be developed. For software assets, the organization should develop a list that includes operating systems, custom applications by type (accounting, human resources, or payroll, to name a few), and packaged applications and/or specialty applications (such as firewall programs). The degree of specificity is determined by the needs of the organization. Asset types can be recorded at two or more levels of specificity by first recording one attribute that classifies the asset at a high level and then adding attributes for more detail. For example, one server might be listed as follows:

DeviceClass = S (server)
DeviceOS = Win16 (Windows 2016)
DeviceCapacity = AS (Advanced Server)

- *Serial number*—This is a number that uniquely identifies a specific device. Some software vendors also assign a software serial number to each instance of the program licensed by the organization.
- *Manufacturer name*—This attribute can be useful for analyzing threat outbreaks when specific manufacturers announce specific vulnerabilities.
- *Manufacturer's model or part number*—This number identifies exactly what the asset is, and can be very useful in the later analysis of vulnerabilities because some threats apply only to specific models of certain devices and/or software components.

- *Software version, update revision, or FCO number*—This attribute includes information about software and firmware versions and, for hardware devices, the current field change order (FCO) number. An FCO occurs when a manufacturer performs an upgrade to a hardware component at the customer's premises. Tracking this information is particularly important when inventorying networking devices that function mainly through the software running on them.
- *Software licensing data*—The nature and number of an organization's software licenses, as well as where they are deployed, can be a critically important asset. Because licenses for software products are often tied to specific version numbers, geographic locations, or even specific users, this data may require specialized efforts to track.
- *Physical location*—This attribute does not apply to software elements. Nevertheless, some organizations may have license terms that indicate where software can be used. This may include systems leased at remote locations, often described as being "in the cloud."
- *Logical location*—This attribute specifies where an asset can be found on the organization's network. The logical location is most applicable to networking devices and indicates the logical network segment that houses the device.
- *Controlling entity*—This refers to the organizational unit that controls the asset. In some organizations, a remote location's on-site staff could be placed in control of network devices; in other organizations, a central corporate group might control all the network devices.

Consider carefully what should be tracked for specific assets. Often, larger organizations find that they can effectively track only a few valuable facts about the most critical information assets. For instance, a company may track only an IP address, server name, and device type for its mission-critical servers. The organization might forgo additional attribute tracking on all devices and completely omit the tracking of desktop or laptop systems.

Identifying People, Procedures, and Data Assets Human resources, documentation, and data information assets are not as readily identified and documented as hardware and software. Responsibility for identifying, describing, and evaluating these information assets should be assigned to managers who possess the necessary knowledge, experience, and judgment. As these assets are identified, they should be recorded via a reliable data-handling process like the one used for hardware and software.

The record-keeping system should be flexible, allowing you to link assets to attributes based on the nature of the information asset being tracked. Basic attributes for various classes of assets include the following:

People
- Position name/number/ID—Avoid names; use position titles, roles, or functions
- Supervisor name/number/ID—Avoid names; use position titles, roles, or functions
- Security clearance level
- Special skills

Procedures
- Description
- Intended purpose
- Software/hardware/networking elements to which the procedure is tied
- Location where procedure documents are stored for reference
- Location where documents are stored for update purposes

Data
- Classification
- Owner/creator/manager
- Size of data structure
- Data organization used (for example, hierarchical, sequential, or relational)
- Online or offline; if online, whether accessible from outside the organization or not
- Physical location
- Media access method (for example, through user client desktops, laptops, or mobile media)
- Backup procedures, timeline, and backup storage locations

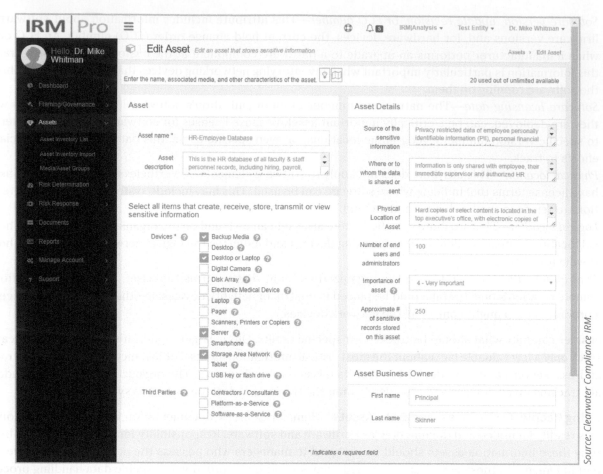

Figure 4-2   Clearwater IRM information asset description

As you will learn later in the text, a number of applications can assist with the collection, organization, and management of these inventories. As shown in Figure 4-2, Clearwater Compliance's Information Risk Management (CC | IRM) application has detailed fields in its asset inventory list to assist in the inventory and description of information assets.

Classifying and Categorizing Information Assets   Once the initial inventory is assembled, you must determine whether its asset categories are meaningful to the organization's risk management program. Such a review may cause managers to further subdivide the categories presented in Table 4-1 or create new categories that better meet the needs of the risk management program. For example, if the category "Internet components" is deemed too general, it could be further divided into subcategories of servers, networking devices (routers, hubs, switches), protection devices (firewalls, proxies), and cabling.

The inventory should also reflect the sensitivity and security priority assigned to each information asset. A **data classification scheme** should be developed (or reviewed, if already in place) that categorizes these information

data classification scheme

A formal access control methodology used to assign a level of confidentiality to an information asset and thus restrict the number of people who can access it.

assets based on their sensitivity and security needs. Consider the following classification scheme for an information asset: confidential, internal, and public. *Confidential* describes assets that must be protected as critical to the operations and reputation of the organization, such as strategic and marketing plans. *Internal* would describe assets that are for official use and should not be released to the public, like an internal phone directory or memorandum. *Public* would describe anything that can be shared with the general public, like Web content. Each of these classification categories designates the level of protection needed for an information asset. Some asset types, such as personnel, may require an alternative classification scheme that identifies the InfoSec processes used by the asset type. For example, based on need-to-know and right-to-update policies, an employee might be given a certain level of security clearance, which identifies the level of information that individual is authorized to use.

For organizations that need higher levels of security for very sensitive data, such as research and development (R&D) data, additional levels can be added above "confidential." Classification categories must be *comprehensive* and *mutually exclusive*. "Comprehensive" means that all assets fit into a category; "mutually exclusive" means that each asset fits in only one category. A comprehensive scheme is important for ensuring that all assets are included if they fit in multiple locations.

Assessing the Value of Information Assets   As each information asset is identified, categorized, and classified, a relative value must be assigned to it. Relative values are comparative judgments intended to ensure that the most valuable information assets are given the highest priority when managing risk. It may be impossible to know in advance—in absolute economic terms—what losses will be incurred if an asset is compromised; however, a relative assessment helps to ensure that the higher-value assets are protected first.

As each information asset is assigned to its proper category, posing the following basic questions can help you develop the weighting criteria to be used for information asset valuation or impact evaluation.

- *How critical is the asset to the success of the organization?* When determining the relative importance of each information asset, refer to the organization's mission statement or statement of objectives. From this source, determine which assets are essential for meeting the organization's objectives, which assets support the objectives, and which are merely adjuncts.
- *How much does the information asset contribute to revenue generation?* The relative value of an information asset depends on how much revenue it generates—or, in the case of a nonprofit organization, how critical it is to service delivery. Some organizations have different systems in place for each line of business or service they offer. Which of these assets plays the biggest role in generating revenue or delivering services?
- *How much does the information asset contribute to profit generation?* Managers should evaluate how much profit depends on a particular asset. For instance, at Amazon.com, some servers support the book sales operations, others support the auction process, and still others support the customer book review database. Which of these servers contributes the most to profitability? Although important, the review database server does not directly generate profits. Note the distinction between revenues and profits: Some systems on which revenues depend operate on thin or nonexistent margins and do not generate profits after expenses are paid. In nonprofit organizations, you can determine what percentage of the agency's clientele receives services from the information asset being evaluated.
- *How expensive is the information asset to replace?* Sometimes an information asset acquires special value because it is unique. Organizations must control the risk of loss or damage to such unique assets—for example, by buying and storing a backup device. These storage devices must be periodically updated and tested, of course.
- *How expensive is the information asset to protect?* Some assets are by their nature difficult to protect, and formulating a complete answer to this question may not be possible until the risk identification phase is complete, because the costs of controls cannot be computed until the controls are identified. However, you can still make a preliminary assessment of the relative difficulty of establishing controls for each asset.
- *How much embarrassment or liability would the asset's loss or compromise cause?* Almost every organization is aware of its image in the local, national, and international spheres. Loss or exposure of some assets would prove especially embarrassing. Microsoft's image, for example, was tarnished when an employee's computer system became a victim of the QAZ Trojan horse and a version of Microsoft Office was stolen as a result.[4]

You can use a worksheet such as the one shown in Table 4-2 to collect the answers to the preceding list of questions for later analysis. You may also need to identify and add other institution-specific questions to the evaluation process.

Throughout this module, numbers are assigned to example assets to illustrate the concepts being discussed. This highlights one of the challenging issues in risk management. While other industries use actuarially derived sources to make estimates, InfoSec risk management lacks such data. Many organizations use a variety of estimating methods to assess values. Some in the industry question the use of "guesstimated" values in calculations with other estimated

Table 4-2   Sample Asset Classification Scheme

System Name: SLS E-Commerce

Date Evaluated: February 2022

Evaluated By: D. Jones

Information assets	Data classification	Impact to profitability
Information Transmitted:		
EDI Document Set 1 — Logistics BOL to outsourcer (outbound)	Confidential	High
EDI Document Set 2 — Supplier orders (outbound)	Confidential	High
EDI Document Set 2 — Supplier fulfillment advice (inbound)	Confidential	Medium
Customer order via SSL (inbound)	Confidential	Critical
Customer service request via e-mail (inbound)	Private	Medium
DMZ Assets:		
Edge router	Public	Critical
Web server #1 — Home page and core site	Public	Critical
Web server #2 — Application server	Private	Critical

Notes: BOL: Bill of Lading

DMZ: Demilitarized Zone

EDI: Electronic Data Interchange

SSL: Secure Sockets Layer

values, claiming this degree of uncertainty undermines the entire risk management endeavor. Research in this field is ongoing, and you are encouraged to study the sections later in this module that discuss alternative techniques for qualitative risk management. Figure 4-3 illustrates a simplistic method that can be used to value an information asset by determining its "importance," as shown in the Clearwater Compliance IRM application.

Prioritizing (Rank-Ordering) Information Assets

The final step in the risk identification process is to prioritize, or rank-order, the assets. This goal can be achieved by using a weighted table analysis similar to the one shown in Table 4-3 and discussed elsewhere in this text. In this process, each information asset is listed in the first column. Next, the relevant criteria that the organization wants to use to value the assets are listed in the top row. Next, each criterion is assigned a weight or value that typically sums to 1.0, 10, 100, or some other value that is easy to sum. The use of these weights is what gives this analysis its name. Next, the organization assigns a value to each asset, again using a scale of 0 to 1, 0 to 5, 0 to 10, or 0 to 100, based on the particular criteria value. Table 4-3 uses values from 0 to 5, corresponding to a simple scale of 1 = not important to 5 = critically important (zero is used to indicate "not applicable"). Finally, each information asset's cell values are multiplied by the criteria weights and then summed to create the weighted score for that information asset. Sorting the table by the weighted score results in a prioritized list of information assets. Such tables can be used as a method of valuing information assets by ranking various assets based on criteria specified by the organization. This method may prove to be much more straightforward than a raw estimation based on some other more ambiguous assessment.

threat assessment

An evaluation of the threats to information assets, including a determination of their likelihood of occurrence and potential impact of an attack.

Threat Assessment

As mentioned at the beginning of this module, the goal of risk identification is to assess the circumstances and setting of each information asset to reveal any vulnerabilities. Armed with a properly classified inventory, you can assess potential weaknesses in each information asset—a process known as **threat assessment**. If you

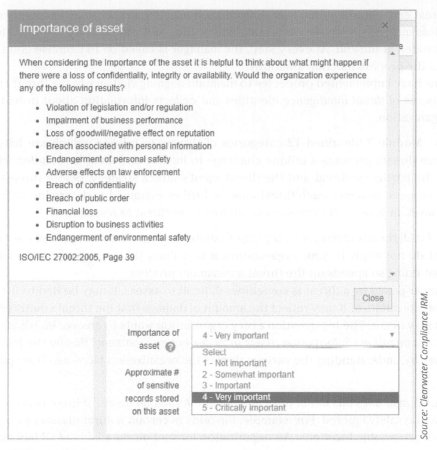

Figure 4-3   Clearwater IRM information asset importance

Table 4-3   Weighted Table Analysis of Information Assets

#	Criterion ⟶ Criterion Weight ⟶ Information Asset ↓	Impact on Revenue 0.3	Impact on Profitability 0.4	Impact on Reputation 0.3	TOTAL (1.0)	Importance (0-5; Not Applicable to Critically Important)
1	Customer order via SSL (inbound)	5	5	5	5	Critically Important
2	EDI Document Set 1— Logistics bill of lading to outsourcer (outbound)	5	5	3	4.4	Very Important
3	EDI Document Set 2— Supplier orders (outbound)	4	5	4	4.4	Very Important
4	Customer service request via e-mail (inbound)	3	3	5	3.6	Very Important
5	EDI Document Set 3—Supplier fulfillment advice (inbound)	3	3	2	2.7	Important
						4.5 - 5: Critically Important 3.5 - 4.4: Very Important 2.5 - 3.4: Important 1.5 - 2.4: Somewhat Important 0.5 - 1.4: Not Important 0 - 0.4: Not Applicable

assume that every threat can and will attack every information asset, then the project scope becomes too complex. To make the process less unwieldy, each step in threat identification and vulnerability identification is managed separately and then coordinated at the end. At every step, the manager is called on to exercise good judgment and draw on experience to make the process function smoothly.

Some organizations have implemented processes to maintain ongoing vigilance in the threat environment in which they operate. This process of *threat intelligence* identifies and collects information about potential threats that may present risk to the organization.

Identifying Threats   Module 2 identified 12 categories of threats to InfoSec, which are listed alphabetically in Table 4-4. Each of these threats presents a unique challenge to InfoSec and must be handled with specific controls that directly address the particular threat and the threat agent's attack strategy. Before threats can be assessed in the risk identification process, however, each threat must be further examined to determine its potential to affect the targeted information asset. In general, this process is referred to as threat assessment.

Assessing Threats   Not all threats endanger every organization, of course. Examine each of the categories in Table 4-4 and eliminate any that do not apply to your organization. It is unlikely that an organization can eliminate an entire category of threats, but doing so speeds up the threat assessment process.

The amount of danger posed by a threat is sometimes difficult to assess. It may be tied to the probability that the threat will attack the organization, or it may reflect the amount of damage that the threat could create or the frequency with which the attack may occur. The big question every organization wants to answer is: *Which threats represent the greatest danger to this organization's information assets in its current environment?* Posing the following questions can help you find an answer by understanding the various threats the organization faces and their potential effects on an information asset:

- *How much actual danger does this threat represent to our information assets?* If there is no actual danger, a perceived threat can be safely ignored. For example, the odds of certain natural disasters vary greatly based on an organization's geographic locations. An organization located on the plains of Oklahoma shouldn't worry about tidal waves, mudslides, or other events that are extremely uncommon in that region. Similarly, an organization that doesn't use a particular software or hardware package doesn't need to worry about threats to vulnerabilities in those items.

Table 4-4   Threats to Information Security

Threat	Examples
Compromises to intellectual property	Software piracy or other copyright infringement
Deviations in quality of service from service providers	Fluctuations in power, data, and other services
Espionage or trespass	Unauthorized access and/or data collection
Forces of nature	Fire, flood, earthquake, lightning, etc.
Human error or failure	Accidents, employee mistakes, failure to follow policy
Information extortion	Blackmail threat of information disclosure
Sabotage or vandalism	Damage to or destruction of systems or information
Software attacks	Malware: viruses, worms, macros, denial of services, or script injections
Technical hardware failures or errors	Hardware equipment failure
Technical software failures or errors	Bugs, code problems, loopholes, back doors
Technological obsolescence	Antiquated or outdated technologies
Theft	Illegal confiscation of equipment or information

Source: CACM.

- *Is this threat internal or external?* Some threat environments require different approaches, while some defenses address threats from multiple environments. Understanding the potential source of a threat helps to prioritize it.

- *How probable is an attack by this threat?* Determining the probability that an attack will occur from a threat includes understanding how widely known the attack is (pervasiveness) and how many threat agents can execute the attack.

- *How probable is a successful attack by this threat?* A threat with a low probability of success is less concerning than one with a high probability of success. Some of the attacks conducted by threats require extremely complicated attack exploits or highly sophisticated attack skills. The more complicated the exploit or the more expert the attacker must be for the attack to occur, the less the organization should worry about it. In summary, the previous question asks, "Could I be attacked by this threat?" while this question asks, "In an attack, would this threat be able to access my information assets?"

- *How severe would the loss be if this threat is successful in attacking?* Of equal concern is understanding what damage could result from a successful attack by a threat. A threat with a high probability of success that would cause only minor damage is of less concern than a threat with a lower chance of success that would create a much greater loss to the organization.

- *How prepared is the organization to handle this threat?* If the organization is ill prepared to handle an attack from a specific threat, it should give priority to that threat in its preparations and planning. This issue becomes increasingly important when rolling out new technologies, starting new business ventures, or making any other change in the organization in which the InfoSec function finds itself in new competitive and threat environments.

- *How expensive is it to protect against this threat?* Another factor that affects the danger posed by a particular threat is the amount it would cost to protect against that threat. Some threats carry a nominal cost to protect against (for example, malicious code), while others are very expensive, as in protection from forces of nature. Especially in small to medium-sized businesses (SMBs), the budget may be insufficient to cover all the defensive strategies the organization would like to implement; as a result, some threat prioritization simply may boil down to available funds. Here again, the manager ranks, rates, or attempts to quantify the level of danger associated with protecting against a particular threat by using the same techniques used for calculating recovery costs.

- *How expensive is it to recover from a successful attack by this threat?* One of the calculations that guides corporate spending on controls is the cost of recovery operations if an attack occurs and is successful. At this preliminary phase, it is not necessary to conduct a detailed assessment of the costs associated with recovering from a particular attack. Instead, organizations often create a subjective ranking or listing of the threats based on recovery costs. Alternatively, an organization can assign a rating for each threat on a scale of 1 to 5, where a 1 represents inexpensive recovery costs and a 5 represents extremely expensive costs. If the information is available, a raw value such as $5,000, $10,000, or $2 million can be assigned. In other words, the goal at this phase is to provide a rough assessment of the cost to recover normal business operations if the attack interrupts them.

You can use both quantitative and qualitative measures to rank values. The preceding questions can be used as categories in a weighted table analysis of threats, like the asset analysis described previously. Because information in this case is preliminary, the organization may simply want to identify threats that top the list for each question.

The preceding list of questions may not cover everything that affects risk assessment. An organization's specific guidelines or policies should influence the process and will inevitably require that some additional questions be answered.

Prioritizing Threats   Just as it did with information assets, the organization should conduct a weighted table analysis with threats. The organization should list the categories of threats it faces and then select categories that correspond to the questions of interest described earlier. Next, it assigns a weighted value to each question category and then assigns a value to each threat with respect to each question category. The result is a prioritized list of threats the organization can use to determine the relative severity of each threat facing its assets. In extreme cases, the organization may want to perform such an assessment of each threat by asset, if the severity of each threat is different depending on the nature of the information asset under evaluation.

Vulnerability Assessment Once the organization has identified and prioritized both its information assets and the threats facing those assets, it can begin to compare information assets to threats. This review leads to the creation of a list of vulnerabilities that remain potential risks to the organization. What are vulnerabilities? They are specific avenues that threat agents can exploit to attack an information asset. In other words, they are chinks in the asset's armor—a flaw or weakness in an information asset, security procedure, design, or control that can be exploited accidentally or on purpose to breach security. For example, Table 4-5 analyzes the threats to a DMZ router and its possible vulnerabilities.

A list like the one in Table 4-5 should be created for each information asset to document its vulnerability to each possible or likely attack. This list is usually long and shows all the vulnerabilities of the information asset. Some threats manifest themselves in multiple ways, yielding multiple vulnerabilities for that asset-threat pair. Of necessity, the process of listing vulnerabilities is somewhat subjective and is based on the experience and knowledge of the people who create the list. Therefore, the process works best when groups of people with diverse backgrounds work together in a series of brainstorming sessions. For instance, the team that reviews the vulnerabilities for networking equipment should include networking specialists, the systems management team that operates the network, InfoSec risk specialists, and even technically proficient users of the system.

Table 4-5 Vulnerability Assessment of a DMZ Router

Threat	Possible Vulnerabilities
Compromises to intellectual property	Router has little intrinsic value, but other assets protected by this device could be attacked if it is compromised.
Espionage or trespass	Router has little intrinsic value, but other assets protected by this device could be attacked if it is compromised.
Forces of nature	All information assets in the organization are subject to forces of nature unless suitable controls are provided.
Human error or failure	Employees or contractors may cause an outage if configuration errors are made.
Information extortion	Router has little intrinsic value, but other assets protected by this device could be attacked if it is compromised.
Quality-of-service deviations from service providers	Unless suitable electrical power conditioning is provided, failure is probable over time.
Sabotage or vandalism	IP is vulnerable to denial-of-service attacks. Device may be subject to defacement or cache poisoning.
Software attacks	IP is vulnerable to denial-of-service attacks. Outsider IP fingerprinting activities can reveal sensitive information unless suitable controls are implemented.
Technical hardware failures or errors	Hardware could fail and cause an outage. Power system failures are always possible.
Technical software failures or errors	Vendor-supplied routing software could fail and cause an outage.
Technological obsolescence	If it is not reviewed and periodically updated, a device may fall too far behind its vendor support model to be kept in service.
Theft	Router has little intrinsic value, but other assets protected by this device could be attacked if it is stolen.

The TVA Worksheet

At the end of the risk identification process, an organization should have (1) a prioritized list of assets and (2) a prioritized list of threats facing those assets. Prioritized lists should be developed using a technique like the weighted table analysis discussed earlier.

The organization should also have a working knowledge of the vulnerabilities that exist between each threat and each asset. These lists serve as the starting point for the next step in the risk management process: risk assessment. The prioritized lists of assets and threats can be combined into a threats-vulnerabilities-assets (TVA) worksheet, in preparation for the addition of vulnerability and control information during risk assessment. Along one axis lies the prioritized set of assets. Table 4-6 shows the placement of assets along the horizontal axis, with the most important asset at the left. The prioritized list of threats is placed along the vertical axis, with the most important or most dangerous threat listed at the top. The resulting grid provides a convenient method of examining the "exposure" of assets, allowing a simple vulnerability assessment. We now have a starting point for our risk assessment, along with the other documents and forms.

Before you begin the risk analysis process, it may be helpful to create a list of the TVA "triples" to facilitate your examination of the severity of the vulnerabilities. For example, between Threat 1 and Asset 1, there may or may not be a vulnerability. After all, not all threats pose risks to all assets. If a pharmaceutical company's most important asset is its research and development database and that database resides on a stand-alone network (one that is not connected to the Internet), then there may be no vulnerability to external hackers. If the intersection of T1 and A1

Table 4-6 The TVA Worksheet

	Asset 1	Asset 2	Asset 3	...	...	...	...	...	...	Asset n
Threat 1	T1V1A1 T1V2A1 T1V3A1 ...	T1V1A2 T1V2A2 ...	T1V1A3 ...	T1V1A4 ...						
Threat 2	T2V1A1 T2V2A1 ...	T2V1A2 ...	T2V1A3 ...							
Threat 3	T3V1A1 ...	T3V1A2 ...								
Threat 4	T4V1A1 ...									
Threat 5										
Threat 6										
...										
...										
Threat n										

Legend: Priority of effort	1	2	3	4	5	6	7	8	...	

These bands of controls should be continued through all asset-threat pairs.

has no vulnerability, then the risk assessment team simply crosses out that box. It is much more likely, however, that one or more vulnerabilities exist between the two, and as these vulnerabilities are identified, they are categorized as follows:

> T1V1A1—Vulnerability 1 that exists between Threat 1 and Asset 1
>
> T1V2A1—Vulnerability 2 that exists between Threat 1 and Asset 1
>
> T2V1A1—Vulnerability 1 that exists between Threat 2 and Asset 1 … and so on.

In the risk analysis phase discussed in the next section, not only are the vulnerabilities examined, the assessment team analyzes any existing controls that protect the asset from the threat or mitigate the losses that may occur. Cataloging and categorizing these controls is the next step in the risk identification process.

There is a key delineator here between risk identification and risk analysis: In developing the TVA spreadsheet, the organization is performing risk identification simply by determining whether an asset is at risk from a threat and identifying any vulnerabilities that exist. The extent to which the asset is at risk falls under risk analysis. The fine line between the two is part of the reason that many organizations follow the methodology outlined in Figure 4-1 described earlier in this module, but they merge risk identification, risk analysis, and risk evaluation into one logical process and just call it risk assessment.

Risk Assessment: Risk Analysis

Assessing the relative risk for each vulnerability is accomplished via a process called **risk analysis**. Risk analysis assigns a risk rating or score to each specific vulnerability. While this number does not mean anything in absolute terms, it enables you to gauge the relative risk associated with each vulnerable information asset, and it facilitates the creation of comparative ratings later in the risk treatment process.

Estimating risk is not an exact science. Some practitioners use calculated values for risk estimation, whereas others rely on broader methods of estimation. The NIST approach to assessing risk, shown in Figure 4-4, illustrates how the components discussed in this section work together to provide overall risk assessment activities based on the NIST risk management framework. While very similar to the risk framework discussed in this module, there are variations in the NIST model that should prove relatively easy to adapt to this model or vice versa. This section discusses the understanding of risk analysis; pay close attention to the NIST model because it illustrates the integration of the analysis with the understanding of the threats discussed previously.

risk analysis

A determination of the extent to which an organization's information assets are exposed to risk.

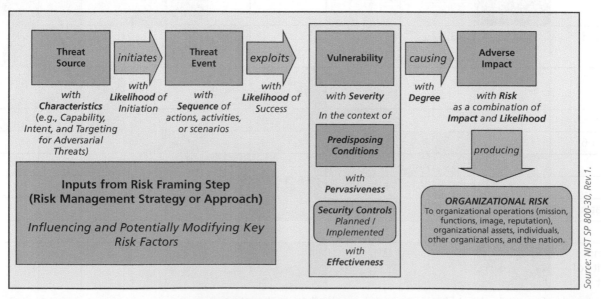

Figure 4-4   NIST generic risk model with key risk factors

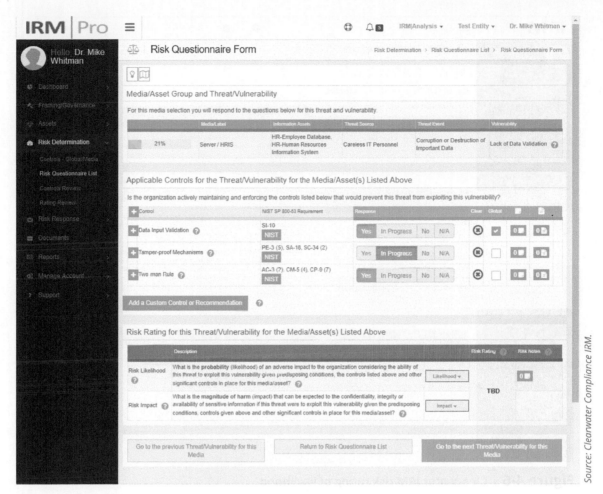

Figure 4-5   Clearwater IRM risk questionnaire form

Source: Clearwater Compliance IRM.

The goal is to develop a repeatable method to evaluate the relative risk of each vulnerability that has been identified and added to the list. Other modules describe how to determine more precise costs that may be incurred from vulnerabilities that lead to losses as well as projected expenses for the controls that reduce the risks. You can use the simpler risk model used by Clearwater and shown in Figure 4-5 to evaluate the risk for each information asset. The next section describes the factors used to calculate the relative risk for each vulnerability, based on existing controls, and the likelihood and impact of a threat event. Figure 4-5 also illustrates the Clearwater IRM approach to risk determination (their methodology for risk analysis), which uses a series of risk questionnaires to examine the threats and vulnerabilities facing each information asset. At the top of this figure is the listed information asset, which was cataloged previously. In the middle is the recommended generic control implementation, which is discussed in the next section. The bottom of the figure displays the risk rating based on the NIST likelihood and impact methodology, which is also described in the following sections.

Mitigation of Applicable Controls

If a vulnerability is fully managed by an existing control, it can be set aside. If it is partially controlled, you can estimate what percentage of the vulnerability has been controlled. A simplistic approach involves determining what recommended controls have been implemented as part of the security program, and describing the level of implementation, as shown in Figure 4-6. This figure displays the set of controls from NIST SP 800-53, Revision 4, "Security and Privacy Controls for Federal Information Systems and Organizations," when determining whether the information asset's general vulnerabilities have been protected by existing applied controls. Note that this information does not include application-specific vulnerabilities, such as those inherent in a computer's operating system. The organization must research those vulnerabilities independently of the NIST recommendations to ensure complete understanding of the issues.

Source: Clearwater Compliance IRM.

Figure 4-6   Clearwater IRM risk rating of likelihood

Determining the Likelihood of a Threat Event

Likelihood is the overall rating—a numerical value on a defined scale—of the *probability* that a specific vulnerability will be exploited or attacked. This attempt is commonly referred to as a threat event, as described in Module 1. According to NIST's SP 800-30, Rev. 1:

> *The likelihood of occurrence is a weighted risk factor based on an analysis of the probability that a given threat is capable of exploiting a given vulnerability (or set of vulnerabilities). The likelihood risk factor combines an estimate of the likelihood that the threat event will be initiated with an estimate of the likelihood of impact (i.e., the likelihood that the threat event results in adverse impacts). For adversarial threats, an assessment of likelihood of occurrence is typically based on: (i) adversary intent; (ii) adversary capability; and (iii) adversary targeting. For other than adversarial threat events, the likelihood of occurrence is estimated using historical evidence, empirical data, or other factors.[5]*

A simple method of assessing risk likelihood is to score the event on a rating scale, similar to the one shown in Table 4-7 and in the Clearwater IRM software in Figure 4-6.

Using this scale, the likelihood of a system being damaged by a water leak could be rated as 1, while the likelihood of receiving at least one e-mail that contains a virus or worm in the next year would be rated as 5. You could also choose to use a different number scale, such as 1 to 10 or 1 to 100, depending on the granularity needed by the organization's process. Whatever rating system you employ for assigning likelihood, use professionalism, experience, and judgment to determine the rating—and use it consistently. Whenever possible, use external

likelihood

The probability that a specific vulnerability within an organization will be attacked by a threat.

Table 4-7   Risk Likelihood

Rank	Description	Percent Likelihood	Example
0	Not Applicable	0% likely in the next 12 months	Will never happen
1	Rare	5% likely in the next 12 months	May happen once every 20 years
2	Unlikely	25% likely in the next 12 months	May happen once every 10 years
3	Moderate	50% likely in the next 12 months	May happen once every 5 years
4	Likely	75% likely in the next 12 months	May happen once every year
5	Almost Certain	100% likely in the next 12 months	May happen multiple times a year

Source: Clearwater Compliance IRM.

references for likelihood values, after reviewing and adjusting them for your specific circumstances. For many asset/vulnerability combinations, existing sources have already determined their likelihood. For example:

- The likelihood of a fire has been estimated actuarially for each type of structure.
- The likelihood that a given e-mail will contain a virus or worm has been researched.
- The number of network attacks can be forecast depending on how many network addresses the organization has been assigned.

Assessing Potential Impact on Asset Value

Once the probability of an attack by a threat has been evaluated, the organization typically looks at the possible **impact** or *consequences* of a successful attack. A feared consequence is the loss of asset value. As mentioned in the section on assessing threats, the impact of an attack (most often as a loss in asset value) is of great concern to the organization in determining where to focus its protection efforts. The weighted tables used in risk identification can help organizations better understand the magnitude of a successful breach. Another good source of information is popular media venues that report on successful attacks in other organizations.

> *The level of impact from a threat event is the magnitude of harm that can be expected to result from the consequences of unauthorized disclosure of information, unauthorized modification of information, unauthorized destruction of information, or loss of information or information system availability. Such harm can be experienced by a variety of organizational and non-organizational stakeholders, including, for example, heads of agencies, mission and business owners, information owners/stewards, mission/business process owners, information system owners, or individuals/groups in the public or private sectors relying on the organization—in essence, anyone with a vested interest in the organization's operations, assets, or individuals, including other organizations in partnership with the organization, or the Nation. Organizations make explicit: (i) the process used to conduct impact determinations; (ii) assumptions related to impact determinations; (iii) sources and methods for obtaining impact information; and (iv) the rationale for conclusions reached with regard to impact determinations.[6]*

Most commonly, organizations create multiple scenarios to better understand the potential impact of a successful attack. Using a "worst case/most likely outcome" approach is common. In this approach, organizations begin by speculating on the worst possible outcome of a successful attack by a particular threat, given the organization's current protection mechanisms. Once the organization frames this worst-case scenario, it moves on to determine the most likely outcome. The organization uses this approach in most of its planning and assessment activities. The use of a risk impact value like the one used for risk likelihood—ranging from 0 to 5—is shown in Table 4-8 and in Clearwater's application in Figure 4-7.

Once the risk impact has been documented for all TVA triples, it is useful for organizations to retain this information because it can also be used during contingency planning, as you will learn in Module 5. Attack scenarios play a key role in understanding how the organization needs to react to a successful attack, particularly in its plans for incident response, disaster recovery, and business continuity. Crafting

impact

An understanding of the potential consequences of a successful attack on an information asset by a threat.

Table 4-8 Risk Impact

Rank	Description	Example	# of Records	Productivity Hours Lost	Financial Impact
0	Not applicable threat	No impact	N/A	N/A	N/A
1	Insignificant	No interruption, no exposed data	0	0	0
2	Minor	Multi-minute interruption, no exposed data	0	2	$20,000
3	Moderate	Multi-hour interruption, minor exposure of data	499	4	$175,000
4	Major	One-day interruption, exposure of data	5,000	8	$2,000,000
5	Severe	Multi-day interruption, major exposure of sensitive data	50,000	24	$20,000,000

Source: Clearwater Compliance IRM.

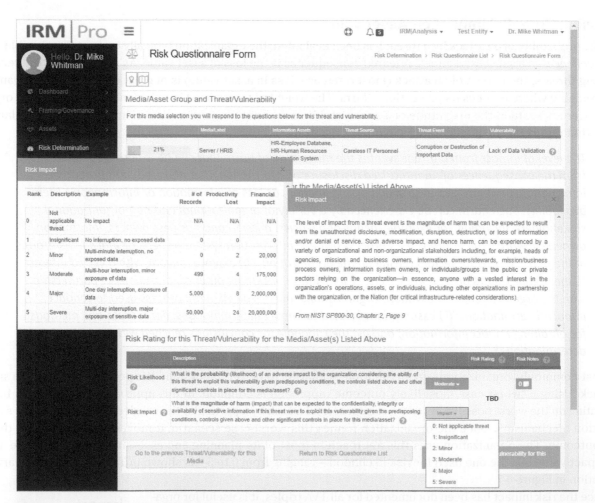

Figure 4-7 Clearwater IRM rating of risk impact

Source: Clearwater Compliance IRM.

this information at the assessment stage and forwarding it to the contingency planning management team for use in that process save the organization time and effort.

Aggregation

If the RM process begins to overwhelm an SMB, the RM team can begin merging together or aggregating groups of assets, threats, and their associated risks into more general categories. As described in NIST 800-30, Rev. 1:

> Organizations may use risk aggregation to roll up several discrete or lower-level risks into a more general or higher-level risk. Organizations may also use risk aggregation to efficiently manage the scope and scale of risk assessments involving multiple information systems and multiple mission/business processes with specified relationships and dependencies among those systems and processes... In general, for discrete risks (e.g., the risk associated with a single information system supporting a well-defined mission/business process), the worst-case impact establishes an upper bound for the overall risk to organizational operations, assets, and individuals.[7]

Aggregation is one tool to assist in the RM process; others include using simpler methodologies with more qualitative approaches (although the method shown here is relatively simplistic) or purchasing applications that guide the organization through the entire process.

Uncertainty

It is not possible to know everything about every vulnerability, such as the likelihood of an attack against an asset or how great an impact a successful attack would have on the organization. The degree to which a current control can reduce risk is also subject to estimation error. A factor that accounts for **uncertainty** must always be considered; it consists of an estimate made by the manager using good judgment and experience.

> Uncertainty is inherent in the evaluation of risk, due to such considerations as: (i). limitations on the extent to which the future will resemble the past; (ii). imperfect or incomplete knowledge of the threat (e.g., characteristics of adversaries, including tactics, techniques, and procedures); (iii). undiscovered vulnerabilities in technologies or products; and (iv). unrecognized dependencies, which can lead to unforeseen impacts. Uncertainty about the value of specific risk factors can also be due to the step in the RMF or phase in the system development life cycle at which a risk assessment is performed. For example, at early phases in the system development life cycle, the presence and effectiveness of security controls may be unknown, while at later phases in the life cycle, the cost of evaluating control effectiveness may outweigh the benefits in terms of more fully informed decision making. Finally, uncertainty can be due to incomplete knowledge of the risks associated with other information systems, mission/business processes, services, common infrastructures, and/or organizations. The degree of uncertainty in risk assessment results, due to these different reasons, can be communicated in the form of the results (e.g., by expressing results qualitatively, by providing ranges of values rather than single values for identified risks, or by using visual representations of fuzzy regions rather than points).[8]

Risk Determination

Once the likelihood and impact are known, the organization can perform risk determination using a formula that seeks to quantify certain risk elements. In this formula, risk equals likelihood of threat event (attack) occurrence multiplied by impact (or consequence), plus or minus an element of uncertainty. To see how this equation works, consider the following scenario:

- Information asset 1 faced with threat 1 is at risk with general vulnerability 1. The risk rating for T1V1A1 (or A1V1T1 if you prefer) has been assigned a Likelihood value of 3 and an Impact value of 5. You estimate that assumptions and data are 90 percent accurate (uncertainty of ±10%). The resulting risk rating is 15 ± 1.5, so your risk rating range is 13.5 to 16.5 on a 25-point scale.

uncertainty

The state of having limited or imperfect knowledge of a situation, making it less likely that organizations can successfully anticipate future events or outcomes.

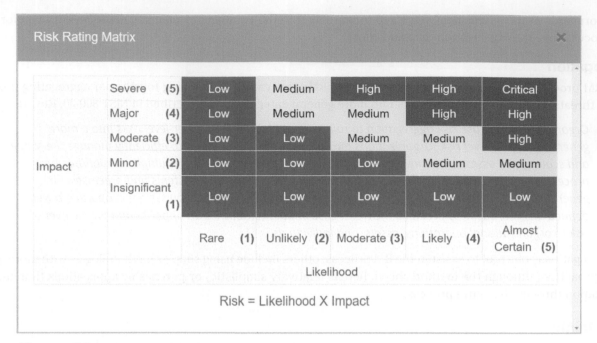

Figure 4-8 Clearwater IRM risk rating matrix

Source: Clearwater Compliance IRM.

- Information asset 2 faced with threat 2 is at risk with general vulnerabilities 2 and 3. The risk rating for T2V2A2 has a Likelihood rating of 4 and an Impact rating of 4. The risk rating for T2V3A2 has a Likelihood rating of 3 and an Impact rating of 2. You estimate that assumptions and data are 80 percent accurate. The resulting risk rating for T2V2A2 is 16 ± 3.2 (range of 12.8–19.2). The risk rating for T2V3A2 is 6 ± 1.2 (range of 4.8–7.2).

Most organizations simply accept the uncertainty factor and go with a simpler formula: Likelihood × Impact. The results provide a range of risk ratings from 1 to 25, as shown in Figure 4-8.

The results of this analysis can be summarized in a risk rating worksheet, as shown in Table 4-9. This document is an extension of the TVA spreadsheet discussed earlier; it shows only the assets and relevant vulnerabilities. A review of this worksheet reveals similarities to the weighted factor analysis worksheet depicted earlier in Table 4-3. Table 4-9 illustrates a weighted spreadsheet that calculates risk vulnerability for a number of information assets, using the simpler model of ignoring uncertainty. The columns in the worksheet are as follows:

- *Asset*—List each vulnerable asset.
- *Vulnerability*—List each uncontrolled vulnerability.
- *Likelihood*—State the likelihood of the realization of the vulnerability by a threat agent, as indicated in the vulnerability analysis step. (In our example, the potential values range from 0 to 5.)
- *Impact*—Show the results for this asset from the weighted factor analysis worksheet. (In our example, this value is also a number from 0 to 5.)
- *Risk-rating factor*—Enter the figure calculated by multiplying the asset impact and its likelihood. (In our example, the calculation yields a number ranging from 0 to 25.)

Looking at Table 4-9, you may be surprised that the most pressing risk requires making the Web server or servers more robust and ensuring that the organization is contracting with a reliable ISP with high availability. The high likelihood and severe impact of such an exploit make the risk to this specific information asset/vulnerability pair the most severe of those shown in the table. Figure 4-9 illustrates the same information, as developed in the Clearwater IRM application for each set of media, assets, threats, and vulnerabilities. This information illustrates the intent of the entire process of identifying assets, matching them to vulnerabilities, and assessing the relative risks for each pair. Once the most pressing pair is identified, it becomes the pair that would most benefit the organization to remedy.

Table 4-9   Risk Rating Worksheet

Asset	Vulnerability	Likelihood	Impact	Risk-Rating Factor
Customer service request via e-mail (inbound)	E-mail disruption due to hardware failure	3	3	9
Customer service request via e-mail (inbound)	E-mail disruption due to software failure	4	3	12
Customer order via SSL (inbound)	Lost orders due to Web server hardware failure	2	5	10
Customer order via SSL (inbound)	Lost orders due to Web server or ISP service failure	4	5	20
Customer service request via e-mail (inbound)	E-mail disruption due to SMTP mail relay attack	1	3	3
Customer service request via e-mail (inbound)	E-mail disruption due to ISP service failure	2	3	6
Customer service request via e-mail (inbound)	E-mail disruption due to power failure	3	3	9
Customer order via SSL (inbound)	Lost orders due to Web server denial-of-service attack	1	5	5
Customer order via SSL (inbound)	Lost orders due to Web server software failure	2	5	10
Customer order via SSL (inbound)	Lost orders due to Web server buffer overrun attack	1	5	5

The biggest problem in using a more complex quantitative approach to risk determination is the huge amount of "guesstimation" that must occur to develop discrete values. Very few concrete examples exist to provide the likelihood for a particular threat attack on a more granular scale (say, from 1 to 100), and even fewer examples allow the organization to determine the exact impact on an asset's value from a successful attack (again on a 1–100 scale). For the most part, professionals will tell you "It depends." When precise values are unknowable and a method like the one shown here is employed in a consistent fashion, it allows making decisions on a relative basis.

Any time a calculation is based on pure quantitative numbers of this caliber, the value of the outcome is immediately suspect because the numbers used in the calculations are most likely general estimates. As a result, more and more organizations are turning to qualitative or semi-qualitative assessments, as illustrated in the RM framework and process discussed in this module.

Risk Evaluation

Once the risk ratings are calculated for all TVA triples, the organization needs to decide whether it can live with the analyzed level of risk—in other words, the organization must determine its risk appetite. This is the **risk evaluation** stage. Knowing that a particular threat/vulnerability/asset triple is a 16 out of a maximum of 25 is a start, but is that good or bad? The organization must translate its risk appetite from the general statement developed by the RM framework team (and based on guidance from the governance group) into a numerical value it can compare to each analyzed risk.

As shown in Figure 4-10, the default risk threshold value is set to a level of 10 in the Clearwater Compliance IRM application, but that value can be easily modified by the RM process team. The value is then used by the software to filter TVAs that do not exceed the value, allowing the process team to focus its efforts on TVAs that do exceed the value. Therefore, assets with vulnerabilities ranked below the risk appetite settings are not shown on the Risk Treatment screen and do not have to be addressed by the organization.

While this may seem to be a minor step in the overall risk assessment task, it is a crucial one. There could be severe consequences to the risk analyst or RM process team member who codes this value too high, leaving key information assets exposed.

risk evaluation

The process of comparing an information asset's risk rating to the numerical representation of the organization's risk appetite or risk threshold to determine if risk treatment is required.

Figure 4-9   Clearwater IRM risk ratings

Source: Clearwater Compliance IRM.

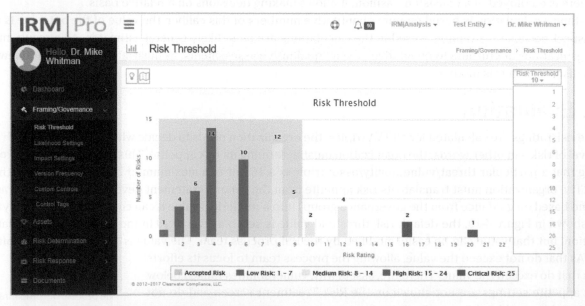

Figure 4-10   Clearwater IRM risk threshold

Source: Clearwater Compliance IRM.

In the first few iterations of the RM process, the value should be set to a conservative level in the range of 6 to 8, requiring the team to address the risk ratings of assets it might otherwise ignore if the default values were accepted or if a higher level of risk threshold were selected. After the team gains expertise with the process, it can easily adjust this value and streamline the process, with fewer TVAs to review throughout the cycle. The average information asset has more than 50 general vulnerabilities to review in the current Clearwater IRM application, so the fewer TVAs the team has to review, the faster it can address those rated as having insufficient levels of current controls.

Once the organization has addressed vulnerabilities that apply generally to multiple classes of assets, it may want to revisit the list of hardware- and OS-specific vulnerabilities, which are available on published sites such as Bugtraq (*www.securityfocus.com*) and US-CERT (*www.us-cert.gov*). When these specific risks for particular assets are included, the organization can then evaluate the previous risk ratings developed by the RM process team to address all identified vulnerabilities.

Documenting the Results of Risk Assessment

The efforts to compile risks into a comprehensive list allow the organization to make informed choices from the best available information. It is also of value for future iterations of the process to document the results in a reusable form. As efforts to compile and assess risk are completed, the results of these steps are documented for current and future use in the list of deliverables, as shown in Table 4-10.

While the organization may require additional deliverables, the table lists the minimum required to fully document the operations of the RM process team and provide continuity for future iterations.

Evaluating Risk

Once the risk has been identified and its relative severity against the value of the information asset has been evaluated, the organization must decide whether the current level of risk is acceptable or something must be done. If the RM process team completes its analysis and shares its findings with the framework team and/or governance group, and the executive decision makers state, "We can live with that," then the process moves on to the monitoring and review function, where the organization keeps an eye on the assets, the threat environment, and known vulnerabilities list for a trigger to restart the RM process anew. If the decision makers indicate that they are not comfortable with the current level of risk, then the next stage of the RM process begins: risk treatment.

In most organizations, engaging in risk treatment is not a simple decision. Instead, it requires extensive input from the RM process team, along with recommendations and cost estimates. This decision process typically requires a formal presentation in which the RM process team provides multiple options if the current level of risk is not acceptable. Deciding whether the current level of risk is acceptable is not a clear-cut choice; rather, it will be a value judgement. Although the governance team provides guidance for general risk appetite, it seldom comes to a simple mathematical comparison, as in "Our risk appetite is a level 10, and the current level of risk in this particular information asset is a 9, so we recommend 'live with it.'"

Table 4-10   Risk Assessment Deliverables

Deliverable	Purpose
Information asset and classification worksheet	Assembles information about information assets, their sensitivity levels, and their value to the organization
Information asset value weighted table analysis	Rank-orders each information asset according to criteria developed by the organization
Threat severity weighted table analysis	Rank-orders each threat to the organization's information assets according to criteria developed by the organization
TVA controls worksheet	Combines the output from the information asset identification and prioritization with the threat identification and prioritization, identifies potential vulnerabilities in the "triples," and incorporates extant and planned controls
Risk ranking worksheet	Assigns a risk-rating ranked value to each TVA triple, incorporating likelihood, impact, and possibly a measure of uncertainty

Another factor that makes this process even more challenging is that the solution for one information asset may positively or negatively affect the level of risk in other information assets. If the simple solution to protect a critical asset is to upgrade the organization's firewall or hire additional firewall administrators, that decision could prove substantially expensive but could very positively impact many other information assets. On the other hand, if the recommendation is to remove an information asset from the threat environment—for example, replacing an overly complex firewall implementation with a simpler alternative that is easier to manage—other information assets could be negatively impacted. The bottom line is that once the risk is known, it requires extensive deliberation and understanding before the "yea or nay" decision is made.

Another step performed during risk evaluation is the prioritization of effort for the treatment of risk, which occurs in the next step of the RM process. The organization can use the asset weighted table analysis performed earlier in the process to make this prioritization, or it can delay the ranking until it has a better understanding of the expected costs and benefits of the various treatment options. Many organizations choose a two-pronged approach, developing a draft listing of treatment priorities and then confirming or adjusting that list once the expected costs and benefits are understood.

There is also the chance that the organization may think it does not have enough information to decide whether to treat the residual risk in a particular information asset and may need to request additional information. If this decision is reached by the RM process team, the framework team, or the governance group, then the conduct of additional investigation falls under the risk evaluation phase.

Risk Treatment/Risk Response

After the risk management (RM) process team has identified, analyzed, and evaluated the level of risk currently inherent in its information assets (risk assessment), it then must treat the risk that is deemed unacceptable when it exceeds the organization's risk appetite. This process is also known as risk response or risk control. As risk treatment begins, the organization has a list of information assets with currently unacceptable levels of risk; the appropriate strategy must be selected and then applied for each asset. In this section, you will learn how to assess risk treatment strategies, estimate costs, weigh the relative merits of the available alternatives, and gauge the benefits of various treatment approaches. Treating risk begins with an understanding of what risk treatment strategies are and how to formulate them. The chosen strategy may include applying additional or newer controls to some or all of the assets and vulnerabilities identified in earlier steps. Once the project team for InfoSec development has identified the information assets with unacceptable levels of risk, the team must choose one of four basic strategies to treat the risks for those assets:

- *Mitigation*—Applying controls and safeguards that eliminate or reduce the remaining uncontrolled risk
- *Transference*—Shifting risks to other areas or to outside entities
- *Acceptance*—Understanding the consequences of choosing to leave an information asset's vulnerability facing the current level of risk, but only after a formal evaluation and intentional acknowledgment of this decision
- *Termination*—Removing or discontinuing the information asset from the organization's operating environment

Some methodologies use different terminology or a different number of strategies. Some approaches merge acceptance and termination or don't list termination as a strategy; they just remove the asset when it is no longer supported. Therefore, it's important to understand the organization's terminology before adapting a particular methodology.

Risk Mitigation

The **mitigation risk treatment strategy**, sometimes referred to as **risk defense** or simply **risk mitigation**, attempts to prevent the exploitation of the vulnerability. This is the preferred approach, and is accomplished by means of countering threats,

mitigation risk treatment strategy

The risk treatment strategy that attempts to eliminate or reduce any remaining uncontrolled risk through the application of additional controls and safeguards in an effort to change the likelihood of a successful attack on an information asset; also known as the *defense strategy*.

risk defense

See *mitigation risk treatment strategy*.

risk mitigation

See *mitigation risk treatment strategy*.

removing vulnerabilities in assets, limiting access to assets, and adding protective safeguards. In essence, the organization is attempting to improve the security of an information asset by reducing the likelihood or probability of a successful attack.

There are three common approaches to implement the mitigation risk treatment strategy:

- *Application of policy*—As discussed in Module 3, the application of policy allows all levels of management to mandate that certain procedures always be followed. For example, if the organization needs to control password use more tightly, it can implement a policy requiring passwords on all IT systems. However, policy alone may not be enough. Effective management always couples changes in policy with the training and education of employees, an application of technology, or both.
- *Application of security education, training, and awareness (SETA) programs*—Simply communicating new or revised policy to employees may not be adequate to assure compliance. Awareness, training, and education are essential to creating a safer and more controlled organizational environment and to achieving the necessary changes in end-user behavior.
- *Application of technology*—In the everyday world of InfoSec, technical controls and safeguards are frequently required to effectively reduce risk. For example, firewall administrators can deploy new firewall and IDPS technologies where and how policy requires them, and where administrators are both aware of the requirements and trained to implement them.

Risks can be mitigated by countering the threats facing an asset or by minimizing the exposure of a particular asset. Eliminating the risk posed by a threat is virtually impossible, but it is possible to reduce the residual risk to an acceptable level in alignment with the organization's documented *risk appetite*.

Risk Transference

The **transference risk treatment strategy**, sometimes known as **risk sharing** or simply **risk transfer**, attempts to shift risk to another entity. This goal may be accomplished by rethinking how services are offered, revising deployment models, outsourcing to other organizations, purchasing insurance, or implementing service contracts with providers.

In their best-selling book *In Search of Excellence*, management consultants Thomas Peters and Robert Waterman presented case studies of high-performing corporations. One of the eight characteristics of excellent organizations the authors describe is that they "stick to their knitting." In other words, "They stay reasonably close to the business they know."[9] What does this mean? It means that Nabisco focuses on the manufacture and distribution of snack foods, while General Motors focuses on the design and manufacture of cars and trucks. Neither company spends strategic energy on the technology for securing Web sites. They focus energy and resources on what they do best while relying on consultants or contractors for other types of expertise.

Organizations should consider this point whenever they begin to expand their operations, including information management, systems management, and even InfoSec. When an organization does not have adequate security management and administration experience, it should consider hiring individuals or organizations that provide expertise in those areas. For example, many organizations want Web services, including Web presences, domain name registration, and domain and Web hosting. Rather than implementing their own servers and hiring their own Web developers, Web systems administrators, and even specialized security experts, savvy organizations hire Web services organizations. This approach allows them to transfer the risks associated with the management of these complex systems to other organizations with more experience in dealing with those risks.

The key to an effective transference risk treatment strategy is the implementation of an effective *service level agreement (SLA)*. In some circumstances, an SLA is the only guarantee that an external organization will implement the level of security the client organization wants for valued information assets.

According to the Federal Deposit Insurance Corporation (FDIC) in their document "Tools to Manage Technology Providers' Performance Risk: Service Level Agreements," a typical SLA should contain the following elements:

- Service category (e.g., system availability or response time)
- Acceptable range of service quality

transference risk treatment strategy

The risk treatment strategy that attempts to shift risk to other assets, processes, or organizations.

risk sharing

See *transference risk treatment strategy*.

risk transfer

See *transference risk treatment strategy*.

- Definition of what is being measured
- Formula for calculating the measurement
- Relevant credits/penalties for achieving/failing performance targets
- Frequency and interval of measurement[10]

The FDIC also suggests that organizations use the following four steps to create a successful SLA. While originally written for InfoSec and IT departments within financial institutions, these recommendations are equally applicable and easily adaptable to virtually any organization:

- *Determining objectives*—Reviewing the strategic business needs of the institution includes evaluating its day-to-day operating environment, risk factors, and market conditions. Consideration should be given to how the outsourced service fits into the organization's overall strategic plan.
- *Defining requirements*—Identifying the operational objectives (for example, the need to improve operating efficiency, reduce costs, or enhance security) will help the institution define performance requirements. It will also help identify the levels of service the organization needs from the service provider to meet its strategic goals and objectives for the outsourced activity.
- *Setting measurements*—Clear and impartial measurements, or metrics, can be developed once the strategic needs and operating objectives have been defined. The metrics are used to confirm that the necessary service levels have been achieved and the objectives and strategic intent have been met.
- *Establishing accountability*—It is useful to develop and adopt a framework that ensures accountability after the metrics have been clearly defined. The service provider rarely has full accountability and responsibility for all tasks.

Establishing this accountability usually includes a clear statement of the outcome if the level of service is exceeded or if the expected service fails to meet the stated standard.[11]

Of course, outsourcing is not without its own risks. It is up to the owner of the information asset, IT management, and the InfoSec team to ensure that the requirements of the outsourcing contract are sufficient and have been met before they are needed.

Risk Acceptance

As described earlier, mitigation is a treatment approach that attempts to reduce the effects of an exploited vulnerability by preparing to react if and when it occurs. In contrast, the **acceptance risk treatment strategy**, or simply **risk acceptance**, is the decision to do nothing beyond the current level of protection to shield an information asset from risk and to accept the outcome from any resulting exploitation. While the selection of this treatment strategy may not be a conscious business decision in some organizations, the unconscious acceptance of risk is not a productive approach to risk treatment.

Acceptance is recognized as a valid strategy only when the organization has done the following:

- Determined the level of risk posed to the information asset
- Assessed the probability of attack and the likelihood of a successful exploitation of a vulnerability
- Estimated the potential impact (damage or loss) that could result from a successful attack
- Evaluated potential controls using each appropriate type of feasibility
- Performed a thorough risk assessment, including a financial analysis such as a cost-benefit analysis
- Determined that the costs to treat the risk to the function, service, collection of data, or information asset do not justify the cost of implementing and maintaining the controls

acceptance risk treatment strategy

The risk treatment strategy that indicates the organization is willing to accept the current level of residual risk and, as a result, the organization makes a conscious decision to do nothing else to protect an information asset from risk and to "live with" the outcome from any resulting exploitation.

risk acceptance

See *acceptance risk treatment strategy.*

This strategy assumes that it can be a prudent business decision to examine the alternatives and conclude that the cost of protecting an asset does not justify the security expenditure. For example, suppose an organization has an older Web server that only provides information related to legacy products. All information on the server is considered public and is only provided for the benefit of legacy users. The information has no significant value and does not contain any information the organization has a legal obligation to protect. A risk assessment and an evaluation of treatment options determine that it would cost a substantial amount of money to update the security on this server. The management team is unwilling to remove it from operation but determines it is not feasible to upgrade the existing controls or add new controls. They may choose to make a conscious business decision to accept the current level of residual risk for this information asset, in spite of any identified vulnerabilities. Under those circumstances, management may be satisfied with taking its chances and saving the money that would otherwise be spent on protecting this particular asset.

An organization that decides on acceptance as a strategy for every identified risk of loss may be unable to conduct proactive security activities and may have an apathetic approach to security in general. It is not acceptable for an organization to plead ignorance and thus abdicate its legal responsibility to protect employees' and customers' information. It is also unacceptable for management to hope that if it does not try to protect information, the opposition will believe it can gain little by an attack. In general, unless the organization has formally reviewed an information asset and determined the current residual risk is at or below the organization's risk appetite, the risks far outweigh the benefits of this approach.

Risk Termination

Like acceptance, the **termination risk treatment strategy**, also known as **risk avoidance** or simply **risk termination**, is based on the organization's intentional choice not to protect an asset. Here, however, the organization does not want the information asset to remain at risk, and removes it from the operating environment by shutting it down or disabling its connectivity to potential threats. Only the complete shutdown and sanitization of an asset provides total protection because attackers will have no access. Simply disabling program functions or disconnecting the host system from the network may not remove the data from exposure.

Sometimes, the cost of protecting an asset outweighs its value. In other words, it may be too difficult or expensive to protect an asset, compared to the value or advantage that asset offers the company. In any case, termination must be a conscious business decision, not simply the abandonment of an asset, which would technically qualify as acceptance.

Process Communications, Monitoring, and Review

As the process team works through the various RM activities, it needs to continually provide feedback to the framework team about the relative success and challenges of its RM activities. This feedback is used to improve not only the process but the framework as well. It is critical that the process team have one or more individuals designated to collect and provide this feedback, as well as a formal mechanism to submit it to the framework team. These **process communications** facilitate the actions in the **process monitoring and review**. The former involves requesting and providing information as direct feedback about issues that arise in the implementation and operation of each stage of the process. The latter involves establishing and collecting formal performance measures and assessment methods to determine the relative success of the RM program.

Mitigation and Risk

Previous editions of this text referred to a different form of mitigation that focused on planning and preparation to reduce the impact or potential consequences of an incident or disaster. This form of mitigation is part of contingency planning (CP), which you will learn about in Module 5. Not to be confused with risk mitigation, CP mitigation derives its value from the ability to detect, react to, respond to, and recover from incidents and disasters as quickly as possible, thus minimizing the damage to an information asset. Table 4-11 summarizes the four types of CP mitigation plans,

termination risk treatment strategy

The risk treatment strategy that eliminates all risk associated with an information asset by removing it from service.

risk avoidance

See *termination risk treatment strategy*.

risk termination

See *termination risk treatment strategy*.

process communications

The necessary information flow within and between the governance group, RM framework team, and RM process team during the implementation of RM.

process monitoring and review

The data collection and feedback associated with performance measures used during the conduct of the process.

Table 4-11 Summary of CP Mitigation Plans

Plan	Description	Example	When Deployed	Time Frame
Incident response (IR) plan	Actions an organization takes during incidents (attacks or accidental data loss)	• List of steps to be taken during an incident • Intelligence gathering • Information analysis	As an incident or disaster unfolds	Immediate and real-time reaction
Disaster recovery (DR) plan	• Preparations for recovery should a disaster occur • Strategies to limit losses before and during a disaster • Step-by-step instructions to regain normalcy	• Procedures for the recovery of lost data • Procedures for the reestablishment of lost technology infrastructure and services • Shutdown procedures to protect systems and data	Immediately after the incident is labeled a disaster	Short-term recovery
Business continuity (BC) plan	Steps to ensure continuation of the overall business when the scale of a disaster exceeds the DR plan's ability to quickly restore operations	• Preparation steps for activation of alternate data centers • Establishment of critical business functions in an alternate location	Immediately after the disaster is determined to affect the continued operations of the organization	Long-term organizational stability
Crisis management (CM) plan	Steps to ensure the safety and welfare of the people associated with an organization in the event of an incident or disaster that threatens their well being	• Procedures for the notification of personnel in the event of an incident or disaster • Procedures for communication with associated emergency services • Procedures for reacting to and recovering from personnel safety threats	Immediately after the incident or disaster is deemed to threaten personnel safety	Both short-term safety and long-term personnel welfare stability

including descriptions and examples of each. Regardless of which risk treatment strategy the organization selects for a particular asset, it is important to ensure that CP mitigation plans are in effect, in the event that the risk treatment approach fails to stop an attack.

Managing Risk

When vulnerabilities have been controlled to the greatest degree possible, there is often remaining risk that has not been completely removed, shifted, or planned for—in other words, residual risk. Figure 4-11 illustrates how residual risk persists even after safeguards are implemented to reduce the levels of risk associated with threats, vulnerabilities, and information assets.

Although it might seem counterintuitive, the goal of InfoSec is not to bring residual risk to zero; rather, it is to bring residual risk in line with an organization's risk appetite. If decision makers have been informed of uncontrolled risks and the proper authority groups within the communities of interest decide to leave residual risk in place, then the InfoSec program has accomplished its primary goal.

Figure 4-12 illustrates the process by which an organization chooses from among the risk treatment strategies. As shown in this diagram, after the information system is designed, the organization must determine whether the system has vulnerabilities that can be exploited. If a viable threat exists, determine what an attacker will gain from a successful attack. Next, estimate the expected loss the organization will incur if the vulnerability is successfully exploited. If this loss is within the range of losses the organization can absorb, or if the attacker's gain is less than the likely cost of executing the attack, the organization may choose to accept the risk. Otherwise, it must select one of the other treatment strategies.

Here are some rules of thumb for selecting a strategy, keeping in mind that the level of threat and the value of the asset should play major roles in treatment strategy selection:

- *When a vulnerability (flaw or weakness) exists in an important asset*—Implement security controls to reduce the likelihood of a vulnerability being exploited.
- *When a vulnerability can be exploited*—Apply layered protections, architectural designs, and administrative controls to minimize the risk or prevent the occurrence of an attack.
- *When the attacker's potential gain is greater than the costs of attack*—Apply protections to increase the attacker's cost or reduce the attacker's gain by using technical or managerial controls. Note that the attacker's potential

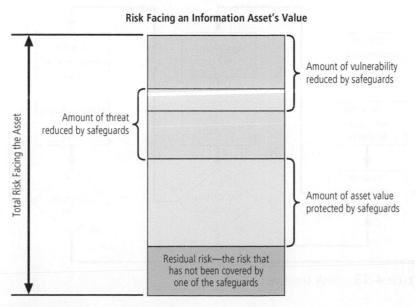

Risk Facing an Information Asset's Value

Total Risk Facing the Asset

Amount of threat reduced by safeguards

Amount of vulnerability reduced by safeguards

Amount of asset value protected by safeguards

Residual risk—the risk that has not been covered by one of the safeguards

Figure 4-11   Residual risk

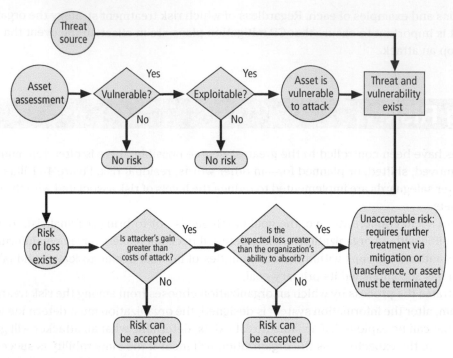

Figure 4-12 Risk-handling action points

gain is considered from his or her perspective, not the organization's, so the latter's perceived potential loss could be much smaller than the attacker's potential gain.

- *When the potential loss is substantial*—Apply design principles, architectural designs, and technical and non-technical protections to limit the extent of the attack, thereby reducing the potential for loss.[12]

Once a treatment strategy has been selected and implemented, controls should be monitored and measured on an ongoing basis to determine their effectiveness and to maintain an ongoing estimate of the remaining risk. Figure 4-13 shows how this cyclical process ensures that risks are controlled.

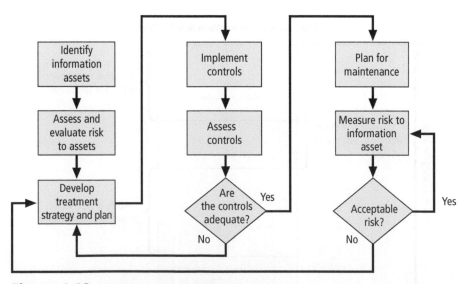

Figure 4-13 Risk treatment cycle

At a minimum, each information TVA triple that was developed in the risk assessment described earlier should have a documented treatment strategy that clearly identifies any remaining residual risk after the proposed strategy has been executed. This approach must articulate which of the fundamental risk-reducing strategies will be used and how multiple strategies might be combined. This process must justify the selection of the chosen treatment strategies by referencing feasibility studies. Organizations should document the outcome of the treatment strategy selection process for each TVA combination in an action plan. This action plan includes concrete tasks, with accountability for each task being assigned to an organizational unit or to an individual. The plan may include hardware and software requirements, budget estimates, and detailed timelines.

As shown in the Clearwater Information Risk Management application in Figure 4-14 and Figure 4-15, once the organization has decided on a risk treatment strategy, it must then re-estimate the effect of the proposed strategy on the residual risk that would be present after the proposed treatment was implemented. For situations in which the organization has decided to adopt the mitigation risk treatment strategy, the software provides recommendations for implementing general controls of all categories (policy, training and awareness, and technology) to reduce the likelihood and impact of an attack. The software then requires the RM process team to specify the estimated effectiveness and feasibility of the proposed changes and a recommendation to add new controls, enhance existing controls, or omit a proposed control if it is ineffective or infeasible. The team then specifies the level of residual risk that would exist after the proposed changes are made and any modifications to the current level of controls and safeguards are implemented. The comparison of the pre- and post-risk treatment assessments provides a foundation for the actual purchasing and implementation of proposed controls based on further assessment of feasibility and cost-benefit analysis.

Feasibility and Cost-Benefit Analysis

Before deciding on the treatment strategy for a specific TVA triple, an organization should explore all readily accessible information about the economic and noneconomic consequences of a vulnerability's exploitation when the threat causes a loss to the asset. This exploration attempts to answer the question, "What are the actual and perceived advantages of implementing a control as opposed to the actual and perceived disadvantages?" In other words, the

Figure 4-14   Clearwater IRM—risk treatment

Source: Clearwater Compliance IRM.

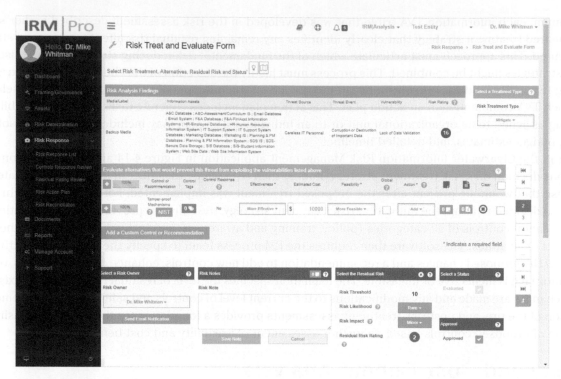

Figure 4-15 Clearwater IRM—residual risk selection

Source: Clearwater Compliance IRM.

organization is simply trying to answer the question, "Before we spend any more time, money, or resources on additional mechanisms to protect this asset, is it worth it?" The costs associated with the various risk treatment strategies may help the organization decide which option to choose. The only overriding factor may be a legal or regulatory requirement to protect certain sensitive information, regardless of the cost—such as with customer financial information under Gramm–Leach–Bliley or patient healthcare information under HIPAA, the Health Insurance Portability and Accountability Act.

While the advantages of a specific strategy can be identified in different ways, the primary method is to determine the value of the information assets it is designed to protect. There are also many ways to identify the disadvantages associated with specific risk treatment options. The following sections describe some of the more commonly used techniques for making these choices. Some of these techniques use dollar-denominated expenses and savings from economic **cost avoidance**, while others use noneconomic feasibility criteria.

The criterion most often used when evaluating a strategy to implement InfoSec controls and safeguards is economic feasibility. While any number of alternatives may solve a problem, some are more expensive than others. Most organizations can spend only a reasonable amount of time and money on InfoSec, although the definition of *reasonable* varies from organization to organization and even from manager to manager. Organizations can begin this type of economic feasibility analysis by valuing the information assets and determining the loss in value if those information assets are compromised. Common sense dictates that an organization should not spend more to protect an asset than it is worth. This decision-making process is called a **cost-benefit analysis (CBA)** or an *economic feasibility study*.

cost avoidance

The financial savings from using the mitigation risk treatment strategy to implement a control and eliminate the financial ramifications of an incident.

cost-benefit analysis (CBA)

The formal assessment and presentation of the economic expenditures needed for a particular security control, contrasted with its projected value to the organization; also known as an economic feasibility study.

Cost

Just as it is difficult to determine the value of information, it is difficult to determine the *cost* of safeguarding it. Among the items that affect the cost of a particular risk treatment strategy, including implementing new or improved controls or safeguards under the mitigation option, are the following:

- *Cost of development or acquisition*—Hardware, software, and services
- *Training fees*—Cost to train personnel
- *Cost of implementation*—Installing, configuring, and testing hardware, software, and services
- *Service costs*—Vendor fees for maintenance and upgrades or from outsourcing the information asset's protection and/or insurance
- *Cost of maintenance*—Labor expense to verify and continually test, maintain, train, and update
- *Potential cost from the loss of the asset*—Either from removal of service (termination) or compromise by attack

Benefit

Benefit is the value to the organization of using controls to prevent losses associated with a specific vulnerability. It is usually determined by valuing the information asset or assets exposed by the vulnerability and then determining how much of that value is at risk and how much risk exists for the asset. This result is expressed as the annualized loss expectancy (ALE), which is defined later in this module.

Asset Valuation

As discussed earlier, the value of information differs within organizations and between organizations. Some argue that it is virtually impossible to accurately determine the true value of information and information-bearing assets, which is perhaps one reason why insurance underwriters currently have no definitive valuation tables for information assets. **Asset valuation** can draw on the assessment of information assets performed as part of the risk identification process.

Asset valuation involves the estimation of real or perceived costs. These costs can be selected from any or all costs associated with the design, development, installation, maintenance, protection, recovery, and defense against loss or litigation. Some costs are easily determined, such as the cost of replacing a network switch or the cost of the hardware needed for a specific class of server. Other costs are almost impossible to determine, such as the dollar value of the loss in market share if information on a firm's new product offerings is released prematurely and the company loses its competitive edge. A further complication is that over time, some information assets acquire value that is beyond their essential or *intrinsic value*. This higher acquired value is the more appropriate value in most cases.

Asset valuation is a complex process. While each organization must decide for itself how it wishes to value its information assets, the more commonly used quantitative approaches include the following:

- *Value retained from the cost of creating the information asset*—Information is created or acquired at a cost, which can be calculated or estimated. Software development costs include the efforts of the many people involved in the systems development life cycle for each application and system. Although this effort draws mainly on IT personnel, it also includes the user and general management community and sometimes the InfoSec staff. In today's marketplace, with high programmer salaries and even higher contractor expenses, the average cost to complete even a moderately sized application can quickly escalate.
- *Value retained from past maintenance of the information asset*—It is estimated that between 60 and 80 percent of the total cost of acquiring (or developing) and operating an information asset is incurred in the maintenance phase. That typically means for every dollar spent on developing an application or acquiring and processing data, another $3 to $5 will be spent after the software is in use. If actual costs have not been recorded, the cost can be estimated in terms of the human resources required to continually update, support, modify, and service the applications and systems.
- *Value implied by the cost of replacing the information*—The costs associated with replacing information should include the human and technical resources needed to reconstruct, restore, or regenerate the information from backups, independent transaction logs, or even hard copies of data sources. Most organizations rely on routine media backups to protect their information. When estimating recovery costs, keep in mind that you may have to hire contractors to carry out the regular workload that employees will be unable to perform during recovery efforts. To restore this information, the various information sources may have to be reconstructed, with the data reentered into the system and validated for accuracy.
- *Value from providing the information*—Separate from the cost of developing or maintaining the information is the cost of providing the information to users who need it. Such costs include the values associated with the delivery of the information through hardware and software systems, databases, and networks.

asset valuation
The process of assigning financial value or worth to each information asset.

They also include the cost of the infrastructure necessary to provide access to and control of the information, including the personnel costs associated with it.

- *Value acquired from the cost of protecting the information*—The value of an asset is based in part on the cost of protecting it, and the amount of money spent to protect an asset is based in part on the value of the asset. While this is a seemingly unending circle, estimating the value of protecting an information asset can help you better understand the expense associated with its potential loss. The values listed previously are easy to calculate with some precision. This value and those that follow are likely to be estimates of cost.

- *Value to owners*—How much is your Social Security number worth to you? Or your bank account number? Although it may be impossible for organizations to estimate the value of their information or what portion of revenue is directly attributable to it, they must understand the overall costs that could result from its loss so they realize its true value. Here again, estimating value may be the only method possible.

- *Value of intellectual property*—The value of a new product or service to a customer may ultimately be unknowable. How much would a cancer patient pay for a cure? How much would a shopper pay for a new flavor of cheese? What is the value of a logo or advertising slogan? Related but separate are intellectual properties known as trade secrets. Intellectual information assets are the primary assets of some organizations.

- *Value to adversaries*—How much is it worth to an organization to know what the competition is doing? Many organizations have established departments tasked with the assessment and estimation of the activities of their competition. Even organizations in traditionally nonprofit industries can benefit from knowing what is going on in political, business, and competitive organizations. Stories are common of how disgruntled employees steal information and present it to competitive organizations to curry favor and get new jobs. Those who hire such applicants to gain from their larceny should consider whether benefiting from such a tactic is wise. After all, such thieves could presumably repeat their activities when they become disgruntled with their new employers.

- *Loss of productivity while the information assets are unavailable*—When a network (or Internet) outage occurs, users may be able to access local but not remote data, hindering their productivity. Although this is not an example of an attack that damages information, it is an instance in which a threat affects an organization's productivity. (This threat is known as deviations in quality of service from service providers, as shown in Table 4-4.) The hours of wasted employee time, the cost of using alternatives, and the general lack of productivity will incur costs and can severely set back a critical operation or process.

- *Loss of revenue while information assets are unavailable*—Have you ever been purchasing something at a retail store and your payment card could not be read by the card terminal? How many times did you try using the card before the clerk had to enter the numbers manually, if they could? How long did it take to enter the numbers manually in contrast to the quick swipe? What if the payment card verification process was offline? Did the organization even have a manual process to validate or process payment card transactions in the absence of the electronic approval system, or did they just assert a "cash only" policy? Most organizations have all but abandoned manual backups for automated processes, and many would be unable to conduct business if certain information was unavailable.

- *Total cost of ownership*—Ultimately, the single value that best reflects all costs associated with an information asset is known as the total cost of ownership (TCO). This is the total of the elements of the previous categories, encompassing all expenses associated with acquiring, operating, and disposing of the asset. It is critical to the economics of project management to understand that the cost to an organization of a software application or data management project includes much more than the cost of the development and implementation of the project. The true TCO may never be fully understood; what the organization must do is devise a method of estimating TCO that management can live with and that makes sense to them.

A traditional model of calculating quantitative cost-benefit analyses involves estimating the likelihood of an attack based on an annualized rate of occurrence and the impact of an attack based on loss expectancy. Once an organization has estimated the worth of various assets, it can begin to calculate the potential loss from the successful exploitation of vulnerability; this calculation yields an estimate of potential loss per risk. The questions that must be asked at this stage include the following:

- What damage could occur, and what financial impact would it have?
- What would it cost to recover from the attack, in addition to the financial impact of damage?
- What is the single loss expectancy for each risk?

A **single loss expectancy (SLE)** is the calculated value associated with the most likely loss from a single occurrence of a specific attack (impact). It takes into account both the value of the asset and the expected percentage of loss that would occur from a particular attack. In other words:

$$\text{SLE} = \text{asset value (AV)} \times \text{exposure factor (EF)}$$

where

EF = the percentage loss that would occur from a given vulnerability being exploited

For example, say a Web site has an estimated value of $1 million, as determined by asset valuation, and a sabotage or vandalism scenario shows that 10 percent of the Web site's value would be damaged or destroyed in such an attack (the EF). In this case, the SLE for the Web site would be $1,000,000 × 0.10 = $100,000.

As difficult as it is to estimate the value of information, estimating the likelihood (probability) of a threat occurrence or attack is even more difficult. Records of the frequency or probability of any given attack are not always available or reliable. In most cases, however, an organization can rely only on its internal information to calculate the security of its information assets. Even if the network, systems, and security administrators have been actively and accurately tracking these threat occurrences, the organization's information will be sketchy at best. As a result, this information is usually estimated.

Usually, the probability of a threat occurring is depicted as a table that indicates how frequently an attack from each threat type is likely to occur within a given time frame (for example, once every 10 years). This value is commonly referred to as the **annualized rate of occurrence (ARO)**. For example, if a successful act of sabotage or vandalism occurs about once every two years, then the ARO would be 50 percent (0.5). A network attack that can occur multiple times per second might be successful once per month and thus would have an ARO of 12.

Once you determine the loss from a single attack and the likely frequency of successful attacks, you can calculate the overall loss potential per risk expressed as an **annualized loss expectancy (ALE)** using the values for the ARO and SLE defined previously.

$$\text{ALE} = \text{SLE} \times \text{ARO}$$

To use our previous example, if SLE = $100,000 and ARO = 0.5, then

$$\text{ALE} = \$100,000 \times 0.5$$
$$\text{ALE} = \$50,000$$

Thus, the organization could expect to lose $50,000 per year unless it increases its Web security. Now, armed with a figure to justify its expenditures for controls and safeguards, the InfoSec design team can deliver a budgeted value for planning purposes. Sometimes, noneconomic factors are considered in this process, so even when ALE amounts are not large, control budgets can be justified.

The CBA determines whether the benefit from a control alternative is worth the associated cost of implementing and maintaining the control. Such analyses may be performed before implementing a control or safeguard, or they can be performed after controls have been in place for a while. Observation over time adds precision to the evaluation of the safeguard's benefits and the determination of whether the safeguard is functioning as intended.

Although many CBA techniques exist, the easiest way to calculate it is by using the ALE from earlier assessments:

$$\text{CBA} = \text{ALE(pre-control)} - \text{ALE(post-control)} - \text{ACS}$$

where

ALE(pre-control) = ALE of the risk before the implementation of the control

ALE(post-control) = ALE examined after the control has been in place for a period of time

ACS = annualized cost of the safeguard

---

single loss expectancy (SLE)

In a cost-benefit analysis, the calculated value associated with the most likely loss from an attack (impact); the SLE is the product of the asset's value and the exposure factor.

annualized rate of occurrence (ARO)

In a cost-benefit analysis, the expected frequency of an attack, expressed on a per-year basis.

annualized loss expectancy (ALE)

In a cost-benefit analysis, the product of the annualized rate of occurrence and single loss expectancy.

Once the controls are implemented, it is crucial to examine their benefits continuously to determine when they must be upgraded, supplemented, or replaced.

Alternative Risk Management Methodologies

Until now, this module has presented a general treatment of risk management, synthesizing methodologies and approaches from many sources to present the customary or usual approaches that organizations often employ to manage risk. The following sections present alternative approaches to risk management, including international and national standards and methodologies from industry-leading organizations.

The OCTAVE Methods

The Operationally Critical Threat, Asset, and Vulnerability Evaluation (OCTAVE) Method was an InfoSec risk evaluation methodology promoted by Carnegie Mellon University's Software Engineering Institute (SEI) that allowed organizations to balance the protection of critical information assets against the costs of providing protective and detection controls. This process, illustrated in Figure 4-16, could enable an organization to measure itself against known or accepted good security practices and then establish an organization-wide protection strategy and InfoSec risk mitigation plan. While no longer actively promoted by SEI, the methodology provides valid insight into a viable alternate RM methodology. The OCTAVE process had three variations:[13]

- The original OCTAVE Method, which formed the basis for the OCTAVE body of knowledge, was designed for large organizations (300 or more users)
- OCTAVE-S, for smaller organizations of about 100 users
- OCTAVE-Allegro, a streamlined approach for InfoSec assessment and assurance

While no longer actively promoted by SEI, the documents are still available and provide excellent references to an alternate approach to understanding RM (see *https://resources.sei.cmu.edu/library/asset-view.cfm?assetid=309051*).

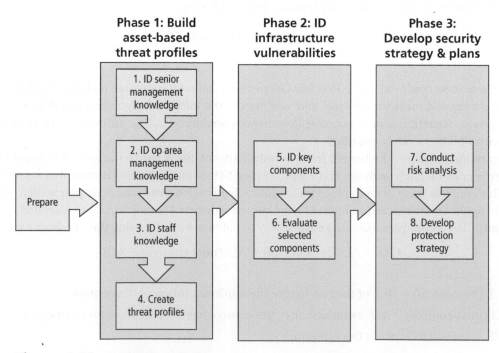

Figure 4-16 OCTAVE overview

FAIR

Factor Analysis of Information Risk (FAIR), a risk management framework developed by Jack A. Jones, can also help organizations understand, analyze, and measure information risk. The reported outcomes include more cost-effective information risk management, greater credibility for the InfoSec profession, and a foundation from which to develop a scientific approach to information risk management. The FAIR framework, as shown in Figure 4-17, includes the following:

- A taxonomy for information risk
- Standard nomenclature for information risk terms
- A framework for establishing data collection criteria
- Measurement scales for risk factors
- A computational engine for calculating risk
- A modeling construct for analyzing complex risk scenarios

Basic FAIR analysis comprises 10 steps in four stages:

Stage 1—Identify Scenario Components

1. Identify the asset at risk.
2. Identify the threat community under consideration.

Stage 2—Evaluate Loss Event Frequency (LEF)

3. Estimate the probable Threat Event Frequency (TEF).
4. Estimate the Threat Capability (TCap).
5. Estimate Control Strength (CS).
6. Derive Vulnerability (Vuln).
7. Derive Loss Event Frequency (LEF).

Stage 3—Evaluate Probable Loss Magnitude (PLM)

8. Estimate worst-case loss.
9. Estimate probable loss.

Stage 4—Derive and Articulate Risk

10. Derive and articulate risk.[14]

In 2011, FAIR became the cornerstone of a commercial consulting venture, CXOWARE, which built FAIR into an analytical software suite called RiskCalibrator. In 2014, FAIR was adopted by the Open Group as an international standard for risk management and rebranded as Open FAIR™. Shortly thereafter, the publicly viewable information on the FAIR Wiki site was taken down, and all Web links to the archival material were redirected to the FAIR Institute Web site or the Open Group Standards e-commerce site. In 2015, CXOWARE was rebranded as RiskLens, and the FAIR Institute was established.[15]

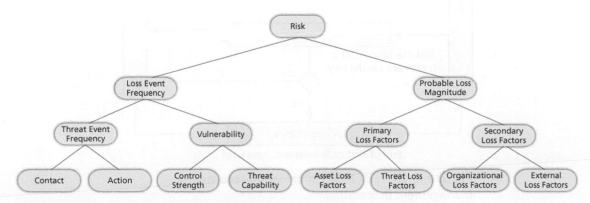

Figure 4-17   Factor Analysis of Information Risk (FAIR)

ISO Standards for InfoSec Risk Management

The International Organization for Standardization (ISO) has several standards related to information security and two that specifically focus on risk management. These standards include ISO 27005 and ISO 31000. ISO 31000 was developed using the Australian/New Zealand standard AS/NZS 4360:2004 as a foundation.[16] In 2018, both standards were updated to create a unified approach to risk management, which the methodology in this text is based upon.

Originally there was a slight difference in the 27005 and 31000 approaches, as the 31000 approaches were more general in nature and focused on all types of risk management, not just information security. With the 2018 update, the standards have a common perspective as applicable to all. However, ISO 27005 focuses on the RM process aspect of the model, as shown in Figure 4-18, while ISO 31000 includes the framework and a set of guiding principles, as illustrated in Figure 4-19.

Other related standards include ISO Guide 73: 2009 Risk management–Vocabulary and ISO/IEC 31010:2019 Risk Management–Risk Assessment Techniques.

NIST Risk Management Framework (RMF)

The National Institute of Standards and Technology (NIST) has modified its fundamental approach to systems management and certification/accreditation to one that follows the industry standard of effective risk management. Two key documents describe the RMF: SP 800-37, Rev. 2, and SP 800-39. You can find both at *https://csrc.nist.gov/publications/sp*.

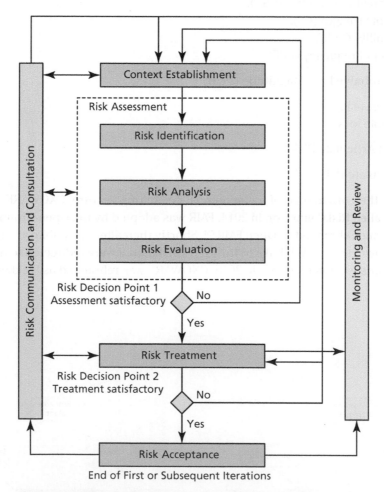

Figure 4-18   ISO 27005 information security risk management process[17]

Source: ISO 27005:2018.

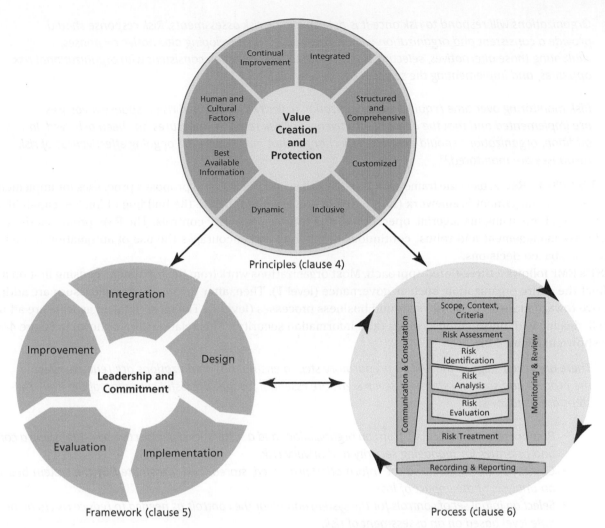

Figure 4-19   ISO 31000 risk management principles, framework, and process[18]

Source: ISO 31000:2018.

As discussed in SP 800-39:

> *This NIST document describes a process that organizations can use to frame risk decisions, assess risk, respond to risk when identified, and then monitor risk for ongoing effectiveness and continuous improvement to the risk management process. The intent is to offer a complete and organization-wide approach that integrates risk management into all operations and decisions.*

> *Framing risk establishes the organization's context for risk-based decision making with the intent of establishing documented processes for a risk management strategy that enables assessing, responding to, and monitoring risk. The risk frame identifies boundaries for risk responsibilities and delineates key assumptions about the threats and vulnerabilities found in the organization's operating environment.*

> *Assessing risk within the context of the organizational risk frame requires the identification of threats, vulnerabilities, consequences of exploitation leading to losses, and the likelihood of such losses. Risk assessment relies on a variety of tools, techniques, and underlying factors. These factors include organizational assumptions about risk, a variety of constraints within the organization and its environment, the roles and responsibilities of the organization's members, how and where risk information is collected and processed, the particular approach to risk assessment in the organization, and the frequency of periodic reassessments of risk.*

Organizations will respond to risk once it is determined by risk assessments. Risk response should provide a consistent and organization-wide process based on developing alternative responses, evaluating those alternatives, selecting appropriate courses of action consistent with organizational risk appetites, and implementing the selected course(s) of action.

Risk monitoring over time requires the organization to verify that planned risk response measures are implemented and that the ongoing effectiveness of risk response measures has been achieved. In addition, organizations should describe how changes that may impact the ongoing effectiveness of risk responses are monitored.[19]

NIST SP 800-37, Rev. 2, uses the framework level described in SP 800-39 and proposes processes for implementation called the Risk Management Framework (RMF). Those processes emphasize the building of InfoSec capabilities into information systems using managerial, operational, and technical security controls. The RMF promotes the concept of timely risk management and robust continuous monitoring and encourages the use of automation to make cost-effective, risk-based decisions.

NIST's RMF follows a three-tiered approach. Most organizations work from the top down, focusing first on aspects that affect the entire organization, such as governance (level 1). Then, after the more strategic issues are addressed, they move toward more tactical issues around business processes (level 2). The most detailed aspects are addressed in level 3, dealing with information systems (and information security). This relationship is shown in Figure 4-20.

As shown in Figure 4-21:

There are seven steps in the RMF; a preparatory step to ensure that organizations are ready to execute the process and six main steps. All seven steps are essential for the successful execution of the RMF. The steps are as follows:

- *Prepare to execute the RMF from an organization- and a system-level perspective by establishing a context and priorities for managing security and privacy risk.*
- *Categorize the system and the information processed, stored, and transmitted by the system based on an analysis of the impact of loss.*
- *Select an initial set of controls for the system and tailor the controls as needed to reduce risk to an acceptable level based on an assessment of risk.*

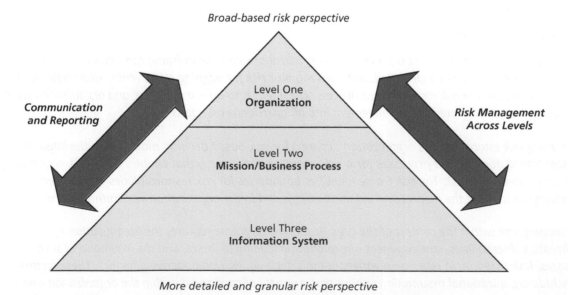

Figure 4-20   NIST organization-wide risk management approach[20]

Source: NIST SP 800-37, Revision 2, "Risk Management Framework for Information Systems and Organizations."

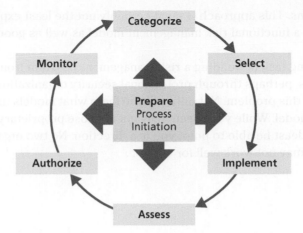

Figure 4-21 NIST RMF framework[21]

Source: NIST, SP 800-37, Revision 2, "Risk Management Framework for Information Systems and Organizations."

- *Implement the controls and describe how the controls are employed within the system and its environment of operation.*
- *Assess the controls to determine if the controls are implemented correctly, operating as intended, and producing the desired outcomes with respect to satisfying the security and privacy requirements.*
- *Authorize the system or common controls based on a determination that the risk to organizational operations and assets, individuals, other organizations, and the Nation is acceptable.*
- *Monitor the system and the associated controls on an ongoing basis to include assessing control effectiveness, documenting changes to the system and environment of operation, conducting risk assessments and impact analyses, and reporting the security and privacy posture of the system.[22]*

According to NIST SP 800-37, Rev. 2:

The RMF operates at all levels in the risk management hierarchy illustrated in Figure [4-21] ...

While the RMF steps are listed in sequential order above..., the steps following the Prepare step can be carried out in a nonsequential order. After completing the tasks in the Prepare step, organizations executing the RMF for the first time for a system or set of common controls typically carry out the remaining steps in sequential order. However, there could be many points in the risk management process where there is a need to diverge from the sequential order due to the type of system, risk decisions made by senior leadership, or to allow for iterative cycles between tasks or revisiting of tasks (e.g., during agile development). Once the organization is in the Monitor step, events may dictate a nonsequential execution of steps. For example, changes in risk or in system functionality may necessitate revisiting one or more of the steps in the RMF to address the change.[23]

Selecting the Best Risk Management Model

Most organizations already have a set of risk management practices in place. The model followed is often an adaptation of a model mentioned earlier in this module. For organizations that have no risk management process in place, starting such a process may be somewhat intimidating. A recommended approach is that the people assigned to implement a risk management program should begin by studying the models presented earlier in this module and identifying what each offers to the envisioned process. Once the organization understands what each risk management model offers, it can adapt one that is a good fit for the specific needs at hand.

Other organizations may hire a consulting firm to provide or even develop a proprietary model. Many of these firms have tried to adapt approaches based on popular risk management models and have gained expertise in customizing them to suit specific organizations. This approach is most certainly not the least expensive option, but it guarantees that the organization can obtain a functional risk management model as well as good advice and training for how to put it into use.

When faced with the daunting task of building a risk management program from scratch, it may be best to talk with other security professionals, perhaps through professional security organizations like ISSA, to find out how others in the field have approached this problem. Not only will you learn what models they prefer, you may also find out why they selected a particular model. While your peers may not disclose proprietary details about their models and how they use them, they may at least be able to point you in a direction. No two organizations are identical, so what works well for one organization may not work well for others.

Closing Scenario

As Charlie wrapped up the meeting, he ticked off a few key reminders for everyone involved in the asset identification project.

"Okay, everyone, before we finish, please remember that you should try to make your asset lists complete, but be sure to focus your attention on the more valuable assets first. Also, remember that we evaluate our assets based on business impact to profitability first, and then economic cost of replacement. Make sure you check with me about any questions that come up. We will schedule our next meeting in two weeks, so please have your draft inventories ready."

Discussion Questions

1. Did Charlie effectively organize the work plan before the meeting? Why or why not? Make a list of important issues you think should be covered by the work plan. For each issue, provide a short explanation.
2. Will the company get useful information from the team it has assembled? Why or why not?
3. Why might some attendees resist the goals of the meeting? Does it seem that each person invited was briefed on the importance of the event and the issues behind it?

Ethical Decision Making

Suppose Amy Windahl left the kickoff meeting with a list of more than 200 assets that needed to be evaluated. When she looked at the amount of effort needed to finish assessing the asset values and their risk evaluations, she decided to "fudge" the numbers so that she could attend a concert and then spend the weekend with her friends. In the hour just before the meeting in which the data was due, she made up some values without much consideration beyond filling in the blanks. Is Amy's approach to her assignment ethical?

After the kickoff meeting, suppose Charlie had said, "Amy, the assets in your department are not that big of a deal for the company, but everyone on the team has to submit something. Just put anything on the forms so we can check you off the list, and then you will get the bonus being paid to all team members. You can buy me lunch for the favor."

Is Amy now ethically justified in falsifying her data? Has Charlie acted ethically by establishing an expected payback for this arrangement?

Selected Readings

- *Against the Gods: The Remarkable Story of Risk*, by Peter L. Bernstein. 1998. John Wiley and Sons.
- *Information Security Risk Analysis*, 2nd Edition, by Thomas R. Peltier. 2005. Auerbach.
- *The Security Risk Assessment Handbook: A Complete Guide for Performing Security Risk Assessments*, by Douglas J. Landoll. 2005. CRC Press.
- "Guide for Conducting Risk Assessments," NIST SP 800-30, Rev. 1, September 2012 (*https://nvlpubs.nist.gov/nistpubs/Legacy/SP/nistspecialpublication800-30r1.pdf*).

- "Risk Management Framework for Information Systems and Organizations—A System Life Cycle Approach for Security and Privacy," NIST SP 800-37, Rev. 2, December 2018 (*https://nvlpubs.nist.gov/nistpubs/SpecialPublications/NIST.SP.800-37r2.pdf*).
- "Managing Information Security Risk: Organization, Mission, and Information System View," NIST SP 800-39, March 2011 (*https://nvlpubs.nist.gov/nistpubs/Legacy/SP/nistspecialpublication800-39.pdf*).

Module Summary

- Risk management examines and documents an organization's information assets.
- Management is responsible for identifying and controlling the risks that an organization encounters. In the modern organization, the InfoSec group often plays a leadership role in risk management.
- Risk appetite defines the quantity and nature of risk that organizations are willing to accept as they evaluate the trade-offs between perfect security and unlimited accessibility.
- Residual risk is the amount of risk unaccounted for after the application of controls.
- A key component of a risk management strategy is the identification, classification, and prioritization of the organization's information assets.
- Assessment is the identification of assets, including all the elements of an organization's system: people, procedures, data, software, hardware, and networking elements.
- The human resources, documentation, and data information assets of an organization are not as easily identified and documented as tangible assets, such as hardware and software. Less tangible assets should be identified and described using knowledge, experience, and judgment.
- You can use the answers to the following questions to develop weighting criteria for information assets:
  - Which information asset is the most critical to the success of the organization?
  - Which information asset generates the most revenue?
  - Which information asset generates the highest profitability?
  - Which information asset is the most expensive to replace?
  - Which information asset is the most expensive to protect?
  - Which information asset's loss or compromise would be the most embarrassing or cause the greatest liability?
- After an organization identifies and performs a preliminary classification of information assets, the threats facing the organization should be examined. There are 12 general categories of threats to InfoSec.
- Each threat must be examined during a threat assessment process that addresses the following questions: Which of the threats exist in the organization's environment? Which are the most dangerous to the organization's information? Which require the greatest expenditure for recovery? Which require the greatest expenditure for protection?
- Each information asset is evaluated for each threat it faces; the resulting information is used to create a list of the vulnerabilities that pose risks to the organization. This process results in an information asset and vulnerability list, which serves as the starting point for risk assessment.
- A threats-vulnerabilities-assets (TVA) worksheet lists assets in priority order along one axis and threats in priority order along the other axis. The resulting grid provides a convenient method of examining the "exposure" of assets, allowing a simple vulnerability assessment.
- The goal of risk assessment is the assignment of a risk rating or score that represents the relative risk for a specific vulnerability of a specific information asset.
- It is possible to perform risk analysis using estimates based on a qualitative assessment.
- If any specific vulnerability is completely managed by an existing control, it no longer needs to be considered for additional controls.

- The risk identification process should designate what function the resulting reports serve, who is responsible for preparing them, and who reviews them. The TVA worksheet and other risk worksheets are working documents for the next step in the risk management process: treating and controlling risk.
- Once vulnerabilities are identified and ranked, a strategy to control the risks must be chosen. Four control strategies are mitigation, transference, acceptance, and termination.
- Economic feasibility studies determine and compare costs and benefits from potential controls (often called a cost-benefit analysis or CBA). A CBA determines whether a control alternative is worth its associated cost. CBA calculations are based on costs before and after controls are implemented and the cost of the controls.
- An organization must be able to place a dollar value on each collection of information and information assets it owns. There are several methods an organization can use to calculate these values.
- Single loss expectancy (SLE) is calculated from the value of the asset and the expected percentage of loss that would occur from a single successful attack. Annualized loss expectancy (ALE) represents the potential loss per year.
- Alternative approaches to risk management include the OCTAVE Method, ISO 27005, the NIST risk management approach, and FAIR.

Review Questions

1. What is risk management?
2. According to Sun Tzu, what two things must be achieved to secure information assets successfully?
3. Which community of interest usually takes the lead in information asset risk management? Which community of interest usually provides the resources used when undertaking information asset risk management?
4. In risk management strategies, why must periodic reviews be a part of the process?
5. What value would an automated asset inventory system have for the risk identification process?
6. Which is more important to the information asset classification scheme: that it be comprehensive or that it be mutually exclusive?
7. What is the difference between an asset's ability to generate revenue and its ability to generate profit?
8. Describe the TVA worksheet. What is it used for?
9. Examine the simplest risk formula presented in this module. What are its primary elements?

10. What is competitive advantage? How has it changed in the years since the IT industry began? What is competitive disadvantage? Why has it emerged as a factor?
11. Describe the strategy of risk transfer.
12. Describe the strategy of risk mitigation.
13. Describe residual risk.
14. What are the three common approaches to implement the mitigation risk treatment strategy?
15. Describe how outsourcing can be used for risk transfer.
16. What conditions must be met to ensure that risk acceptance has been used properly?
17. What is risk appetite? Explain why risk appetite varies from organization to organization.
18. What is a cost-benefit analysis?
19. What is the difference between intrinsic value and acquired value?
20. What is single loss expectancy? What is annualized loss expectancy?
21. What is a qualitative risk assessment?

Exercises

1. If an organization must evaluate the following three information assets for risk management, which vulnerability should be evaluated first for additional controls? Which should be evaluated last?

   - Switch L47 connects a network to the Internet. It has two vulnerabilities: It is susceptible to hardware failure at a likelihood of 0.2, and it is subject to an SNMP buffer overflow attack at a likelihood of 0.1. This switch has an impact rating of 90 and has no current controls in place. You are 75 percent certain of the assumptions and data.

- Server WebSrv6 hosts a company Web site and performs e-commerce transactions. It has a Web server version that can be attacked by sending it invalid Unicode values. The likelihood of that attack is estimated at 0.1. The server has been assigned an impact value of 100, and a control has been implanted that reduces the impact of the vulnerability by 75 percent. You are 80 percent certain of the assumptions and data.
- Operators use an MGMT45 control console to monitor operations in the server room. It has no passwords and is susceptible to unlogged misuse by the operators. Estimates show the likelihood of misuse is 0.1. There are no controls in place on this asset; it has an impact rating of 5. You are 90 percent certain of the assumptions and data.

2. Using the data classification scheme in this module, identify and classify the information in your personal computer or personal digital assistant. Based on the potential for misuse or embarrassment, what information would be confidential, internal, or for public release?

XYZ Software Company (Asset value: $1,200,000 in projected revenues)		
Threat Category	Cost per Incident	Frequency of Occurrence
Programmer mistakes	$5,000	1 per week
Loss of intellectual property	$75,000	1 per year
Software piracy	$500	1 per week
Theft of information (hacker)	$2,500	1 per quarter
Theft of information (employee)	$5,000	1 per 6 months
Web defacement	$500	1 per month
Theft of equipment	$5,000	1 per year
Viruses, worms, Trojan horses	$1,500	1 per week
Denial-of-service attack	$2,500	1 per quarter
Earthquake	$250,000	1 per 20 years
Flood	$250,000	1 per 10 years
Fire	$500,000	1 per 10 years

3. Suppose XYZ Software Company has a new application development project with projected revenues of $1.2 million. Using the table shown at right, calculate the ARO and ALE for each threat category the company faces for this project.

4. How might XYZ Software Company arrive at the values in the table shown in Exercise 3? For each entry, describe the process of determining the cost per incident and frequency of occurrence.

5. Assume that a year has passed and XYZ has improved security by applying several controls. Using the information from Exercise 3 and the following table, calculate the post-control ARO and ALE for each threat category listed.

XYZ Software Company (Asset value: $1,200,000 in projected revenues)				
Threat Category	Cost per Incident	Frequency of Occurrence	Cost of Controls	Type of Control
Programmer mistakes	$5,000	1 per month	$20,000	Training
Loss of intellectual property	$75,000	1 per 2 years	$15,000	Firewall/IDS
Software piracy	$500	1 per month	$30,000	Firewall/IDS
Theft of information (hacker)	$2,500	1 per 6 months	$15,000	Firewall/IDS
Theft of information (employee)	$5,000	1 per year	$15,000	Physical security
Web defacement	$500	1 per quarter	$10,000	Firewall
Theft of equipment	$5,000	1 per 2 years	$15,000	Physical security
Viruses, worms, Trojan horses	$1,500	1 per month	$15,000	Antivirus
Denial-of-service attack	$2,500	1 per 6 months	$10,000	Firewall
Earthquake	$250,000	1 per 20 years	$5,000	Insurance/backups
Flood	$50,000	1 per 10 years	$10,000	Insurance/backups
Fire	$100,000	1 per 10 years	$10,000	Insurance/backups

Why have some values changed in the Cost per Incident and Frequency of Occurrence columns? How could a control affect one but not the other? Assume that the values in the Cost of Controls column are unique costs directly associated with protecting against the threat. In other words, don't consider overlapping costs between controls. Calculate the CBA for the planned risk control approach in each threat category. For each threat category, determine whether the proposed control is worth the costs.

References

1. Sun Tzu. *The Art of War*. 1988. Translation by Griffith, Samuel B. Oxford: Oxford University Press, 84.
2. KPMG. "Understanding and Articulating Risk Appetite." 2008. Accessed September 4, 2020, from *https://erm.ncsu.edu/library/article/articulating-risk-appetite*.
3. NIST. Special Publication 800-30, Revision 1, "Guide for Conducting Risk Assessments." National Institute of Standards and Technology (NIST). 2012. Accessed September 4, 2020, from *https://nvlpubs.nist.gov/nistpubs/Legacy/SP/nistspecialpublication800-30r1.pdf*.
4. Quaglieri, E. "The Hacking of Microsoft." SANS Institute. Accessed September 4, 2020, from *www.giac.org/paper/gsec/488/hacking-microsoft/101184*.
5. NIST. Special Publication 800-30, Revision 1, "Guide for Conducting Risk Assessments." National Institute of Standards and Technology (NIST). 2012. Accessed September 4, 2020, from *https://nvlpubs.nist.gov/nistpubs/Legacy/SP/nistspecialpublication800-30r1.pdf*.
6. Ibid.
7. Ibid.
8. Ibid.
9. Peters, Thomas, and Waterman, Robert. *In Search of Excellence: Lessons from America's Best-Run Companies*. New York: Harper and Row, 2004.
10. FDIC. "Tools to Manage Technology Providers' Performance Risk: Service Level Agreements." 2014. Accessed September 5, 2020, from *www.fdic.gov/news/financial-institution-letters/2014/tools-to-manage-technology-providers.pdf*.
11. Ibid.
12. NIST. Special Publication 800-30, Revision 1, "Guide for Conducting Risk Assessments." National Institute of Standards and Technology (NIST). September 2012. Accessed September 5, 2020, from *https://nvlpubs.nist.gov/nistpubs/Legacy/SP/nistspecialpublication800-30r1.pdf*.
13. Carnegie Mellon University Software Engineering Institute. "OCTAVE-Related Assets." Accessed September 5, 2020, from *https://resources.sei.cmu.edu/library/asset-view.cfm?assetid=309051*.
14. Freund, J., and Jones, J. *Measuring and Managing Information Risk: A FAIR Approach*. Butterworth-Heinemann Publishing, Waltham, MA.
15. RiskLens. "CXOWARE Becomes RiskLens." Accessed September 5, 2020, from *www.prnewswire.com/news-releases/cxoware-becomes-risklens-aligning-with-mission-to-empower-organizations-to-manage-cyber-risk-from-the-business-perspective-300109155.html*.
16. AS/NZS ISO 31000: 2009. "Joint Australian New Zealand International Standard Risk Management–Principles and Guidelines." ISO. Vernier, Geneva. Page 6.
17. ISO 27005:2018-07. "Information Technology—Security Techniques—Information Security Risk Management." ISO. Vernier, Geneva. Page 3.
18. ISO 31000:2018-02. "Risk Management—Guidelines." ISO. Vernier, Geneva. Page 5.
19. NIST. SP 800-39, "Managing Information Security Risk: Organization, Mission, and Information System View." National Institute of Standards and Technology (NIST). March 2011. Accessed September 5, 2020, from *https://nvlpubs.nist.gov/nistpubs/Legacy/SP/nistspecialpublication800-39.pdf*.
20. NIST. SP 800-37, Rev. 2, "Risk Management Framework for Information Systems and Organizations." National Institute of Standards and Technology (NIST). December 2018. Accessed September 5, 2020, from *https://nvlpubs.nist.gov/nistpubs/SpecialPublications/NIST.SP.800-37r2.pdf*.
21. Ibid.
22. Ibid.
23. Ibid.

The spray blowing over him from the fire hoses was icing the cars

Incident Response and Contingency Planning

Upon completion of this material, you should be able to:

1. Discuss the need for contingency planning

2. Describe the major components of incident response, disaster recovery, and business continuity

3. Identify the processes used in digital forensics investigations

4. Define the components of crisis management

5. Discuss how the organization would prepare and execute a test of contingency plans

> *A little fire is quickly trodden out; which, being suffered, rivers cannot quench.*
>
> —William Shakespeare, King Henry VI, Part III, Act IV, Scene 8

Opening Scenario

Charlie Moody flipped up his jacket collar to cover his ears. The spray blowing over him from the fire hoses was icing the cars along the street where he stood watching his office building burn. The warehouse and shipping dock were not gone but were severely damaged by smoke and water. He tried to hide his dismay by turning to speak to Fred Chin, standing beside him overlooking the smoking remains.

"Look at the bright side," said Charlie. "At least we can get the new servers that we've been putting off."

Fred shook his head. "Charlie, you must be dreaming. We don't have enough insurance for a full replacement of everything we've lost."

Charlie was stunned. The offices were gone; all the computer systems, servers, and desktops were melted slag. He would have to try to rebuild without the resources he needed. At least he had good backups, or so he hoped. He thought hard, trying to remember the last time the off-site backups had been tested.

He wondered where all the network design diagrams were. He knew he could call his Internet provider to order new connections as soon as Fred found some new office space. But where was all the vendor contact information? The only copy had been on the computer in his office, which wasn't there anymore. This was not going to be fun. He would have to call his boss, Gladys Williams, the chief information officer (CIO), at home just to get the contact information for the rest of the executive team.

Charlie heard a buzzing noise to his left. He turned to see the flashing numbers of his alarm clock. Relief flooded him as he realized it was just a nightmare; Sequential Label and Supply (SLS) had not burned down. He turned on the light and started making notes to review with his staff as soon as he got into the office. Charlie would make some changes to the company contingency plans *today*.

Introduction To Incident Response And Contingency Planning

You were introduced to planning in Module 3, when you learned about planning for the organization in general and for the information security (InfoSec) program in particular. This module focuses on another type of planning—plans that are made for unexpected adverse events—when the use of technology is disrupted and business operations can come to a standstill. Because technology drives business, planning for an unexpected adverse event usually involves managers from general business management as well as the information technology (IT) and InfoSec communities of interest. They collectively analyze and assess the entire technological infrastructure of the organization using the mission statement and current organizational objectives to drive their planning activities. But, for a plan to gain the support of all members of the organization, it must be sanctioned and actively supported by the general business community of interest. It must also be carefully monitored and coordinated with the InfoSec community of interest to ensure that information is protected during and after an adverse event, such as an incident or disaster. Information that affects the plan must be made securely available to the organization when it may not be operating under normal circumstances or in its normal locations.

The need to have a plan in place that systematically addresses how to identify, contain, and resolve any possible unexpected adverse event was identified in the earliest days of IT. Professional practice in the area of contingency planning continues to evolve, as reflected in Special Publication (SP) 800-34, Rev. 1, "Contingency Planning Guide for Federal Information Systems," published by the National Institute of Standards and Technology (NIST). NIST is a non-regulatory federal agency within the U.S. Department of Commerce that serves to enhance innovation and competitiveness in the United States by acting as a clearinghouse for standards related to technology.[1] The Applied Cybersecurity Division of NIST facilitates sharing of information about practices that can be used to secure information systems. NIST advises the following:

> Because information system resources are essential to an organization's success, it is critical that identified services provided by these systems are able to operate effectively without excessive interruption. Contingency planning supports this requirement by establishing thorough plans, procedures, and technical measures that can enable a system to be recovered as quickly and effectively as possible following a service disruption.[2]

Some organizations—particularly federal agencies for national security reasons—are charged by law, policy, or other mandate to have such plans and procedures in place at all times.

Organizations of every size and purpose should also prepare for the unexpected. In general, an organization's ability to weather losses caused by an adverse event depends on proper planning and execution of the plan. Without a workable plan, an adverse event can cause severe damage to an organization's information resources and assets from which it may never recover. The Hartford insurance company estimates that, on average, more than 40 percent of businesses that don't have a disaster plan go out of business after a major loss like a fire, a break-in, or a storm.[3]

The development of a plan for handling unexpected events should be a high priority for all managers. The plan should account for the possibility that key members of the organization will not be available to assist in the recovery process. In fact, many organizations expect that some key members of the team may not be present when an unexpected event occurs. To keep the consequences of adverse events less catastrophic, many firms limit the number of executives or other key personnel who take the same flight or attend special events. The concept of a designated survivor has become more common in government and corporate organizations—a certain number of specifically skilled personnel are kept away from group activities in case of unexpected adverse events.

There is a growing emphasis on the need for comprehensive and robust planning for adverse circumstances. In the past, organizations tended to focus on defensive preparations, using comprehensive threat assessments combined with defense in depth to harden systems and networks against all possible risks. More organizations now understand that preparations against the threat of attack remain an urgent and important activity, but that defenses will fail as attackers acquire new capabilities and systems reveal latent flaws. When—not if—defenses are compromised, prudent security managers have prepared the organization in order to minimize losses and reduce the time and effort needed to recover. Sound risk management practices dictate that organizations must be ready for anything.

Fundamentals Of Contingency Planning

The overall process of preparing for unexpected **adverse events** is called **contingency planning (CP)**. During CP, the IT and InfoSec communities of interest position their respective organizational units to prepare for, detect, react to, and recover from events that threaten the security of information resources and assets, including human, information, and capital assets. The main goal of CP is to restore normal modes of operation with minimal cost and disruption to normal business activities after an adverse event—in other words, to make sure things get back to the way they were within a reasonable period of time. Ideally, CP should ensure the continuous availability of information systems to the organization even in the face of the unexpected.

CP consists of four major components:

- Business impact analysis (BIA)
- Incident response plan (IR plan)
- Disaster recovery plan (DR plan)
- Business continuity plan (BC plan)

The BIA is a preparatory activity common to both CP and risk management, which was covered in Module 4. It helps the organization determine which business functions and information systems are the most critical to the success of the organization. The IR plan focuses on the immediate response to an incident. Any unexpected adverse event is treated as an incident unless and until a response team deems it to be a disaster. Then the DR plan, which focuses on restoring operations at the primary site, is invoked. If operations at the primary site cannot be quickly restored—for example, when the damage is major or will affect the organization's functioning over the long term—the BC plan occurs concurrently with the DR plan, enabling the business to continue at an alternate site until the organization is able to resume operations at its primary site or select a new primary location.

Depending on the organization's size and business philosophy, IT and InfoSec managers can either create and develop these four CP components as one unified plan or create the four separately in conjunction with a set of interlocking procedures that enable continuity. Typically, larger, more complex organizations create and develop the CP components separately, as the functions of each component differ in scope, applicability, and design. Smaller organizations tend to adopt a one-plan method, consisting of a straightforward set of recovery strategies.

Ideally, the chief information officer (CIO), systems administrators, the chief information security officer (CISO), and key IT and business managers should be actively involved during the creation and development of all CP components, as well as during the distribution of responsibilities among the three communities of interest. The elements required to begin the CP process are a planning methodology; a policy environment to enable the planning process; an understanding of the causes and effects of core precursor activities, known as the BIA; and access to financial and other resources, as articulated and outlined by the planning budget. Each of these is explained in the sections that follow. Once formed, the **contingency planning management team (CPMT)** begins developing a CP document, for which NIST recommends using the following steps:

1. Develop the CP policy statement. A formal policy provides the authority and guidance necessary to develop an effective contingency plan.
2. Conduct the BIA. The BIA helps identify and prioritize information systems and components critical to supporting the organization's mission/business processes. A template for developing the BIA is provided to assist the user.
3. Identify preventive controls. Measures taken to reduce the effects of system disruptions can increase system availability and reduce contingency life cycle costs.
4. Create contingency strategies. Thorough recovery strategies ensure that the system may be recovered quickly and effectively following a disruption.

adverse event

An event with negative consequences that could threaten the organization's information assets or operations; also referred to as an incident candidate.

contingency planning (CP)

The actions taken by senior management to specify the organization's efforts and actions if an adverse event becomes an incident or disaster; CP typically includes incident response, disaster recovery, and business continuity efforts, as well as preparatory business impact analysis.

contingency planning management team (CPMT)

The group of senior managers and project members organized to conduct and lead all CP efforts.

5. **Develop a contingency plan.** The contingency plan should contain detailed guidance and procedures for restoring damaged organizational facilities unique to each business unit's impact level and recovery requirements.

6. **Ensure plan testing, training, and exercises.** Testing validates recovery capabilities, whereas training prepares recovery personnel for plan activation and exercising the plan identifies planning gaps; when combined, the activities improve plan effectiveness and overall organization preparedness.

7. **Ensure plan maintenance.** The plan should be a living document that is updated regularly to remain current with system enhancements and organizational changes.[4]

Even though NIST methodologies are used extensively in this module, NIST treats incident response separately from contingency planning; the latter is focused on disaster recovery and business continuity. This module integrates the approach to contingency planning from NIST SP 800-34, Rev. 1, with the guide to incident handling from NIST SP 800-61, Rev. 2. It also incorporates material from the newly released NIST SP 800-184, "Guide for Cybersecurity Event Recovery."

Effective CP begins with effective policy. Before the CPMT can fully develop the planning document, the team must receive guidance from executive management, as described earlier, through formal CP policy. This policy defines the scope of the CP operations and establishes managerial intent in regard to timetables for response to incidents, recovery from disasters, and reestablishment of operations for continuity. It also stipulates responsibility for the development and operations of the CPMT in general and may provide specifics on the constituencies of all CP-related teams. It is recommended that the CP policy contain, at a minimum, the following sections:

- An introductory statement of philosophical perspective by senior management as to the importance of CP to the strategic, long-term operations of the organization
- A statement of the scope and purpose of the CP operations, stipulating the requirement to cover all critical business functions and activities
- A call for periodic (e.g., yearly) risk assessment and BIA by the CPMT, to include identification and prioritization of critical business functions (while the need for such studies is well understood by the CPMT, the formal inclusion in policy reinforces that need to the rest of the organization)
- A description of the major components of the CP to be designed by the CPMT, as described earlier
- A call for, and guidance in, the selection of recovery options and continuity strategies
- A requirement to test the various plans on a regular basis (e.g., annually, semiannually, or more often as needed)
- Identification of key regulations and standards that impact CP and a brief overview of their relevance
- Identification of key individuals responsible for CP operations, such as establishment of the chief operations officer (COO) as CPMT lead, the CISO as IR team lead, the manager of business operations as DR team lead, the manager of information systems and services as BC team lead, and legal counsel as crisis management team lead
- An appeal to the individual members of the organization, asking for their support and reinforcing their importance as part of the overall CP process
- Additional administrative information, including the original date of the document, revision dates, and a schedule for periodic review and maintenance

A number of individuals and teams are involved in CP operations:

The CPMT collects information about the organization and the threats it faces, conducts the BIA, and then coordinates the development of contingency plans for incident response, disaster recovery, and business continuity. The CPMT often consists of a coordinating executive, representatives from major business units, and the managers responsible for each of the other three teams. It should include the following personnel:

- *Champion*—As with any strategic function, the CP project must have a high-level manager to support, promote, and endorse the findings of the project. This champion could be the COO or (ideally) the CEO/president.
- *Project manager*—A champion provides the strategic vision and the linkage to the power structure of the organization but does not manage the project. A project manager—possibly a mid-level operations manager or even the CISO—leads the project, putting in place a sound project planning process, guiding the development of a complete and useful project, and prudently managing resources.
- *Team members*—The team members should be the managers or their representatives from the various communities of interest: business, IT, and InfoSec. Business managers supply details of their activities and

insight into functions that are critical to running the business. IT managers supply information about the at-risk systems used in the development of the BIA and the IR, DR, and BC plans. InfoSec managers oversee the security planning and provide information on threats, vulnerabilities, attacks, and recovery requirements. A representative from the legal affairs or corporate counsel's office helps keep all planning steps within legal and contractual boundaries. A member of the corporate communications department makes sure the crisis management and communications plan elements are consistent with the needs of that group. Supplemental team members also include representatives of supplemental planning teams: the **incident response planning team (IRPT)**, **disaster recovery planning team (DRPT)**, and **business continuity planning team (BCPT)**. For organizations that decide to separate crisis management from disaster recovery, there may also be representatives from the **crisis management planning team (CMPT)**.

As indicated earlier, in larger organizations these teams are distinct entities, with non-overlapping memberships, although the latter three teams have representatives on the CPMT. In smaller organizations, the four teams may include overlapping groups of people, although this is discouraged because the three planning teams (IR, DR, and BC) will most likely include members of their respective response teams—the individuals who will actually respond to an incident or disaster. The planning teams and response teams are distinctly separate groups, but representatives of the response team will most likely be included on the planning team for continuity purposes and to facilitate plan development and the communication of planning activities to the response units. *If the same individuals are on the DR and BC teams, for example, they may find themselves with different responsibilities in different locations at the same time.* It is virtually impossible to establish operations at the alternate site if team members are busy managing the recovery at the primary site, some distance away. Thus, if the organization has sufficient personnel, it is advisable to staff the two groups with separate members.

As illustrated in the opening scenario of this module, many organizations' contingency plans are woefully inadequate. CP often fails to receive the high priority necessary for the efficient and timely recovery of business operations during and after an unexpected event. The fact that many organizations do not place an adequate premium on CP does not mean that it is unimportant, however. Here is how NIST's Computer Security Resource Center (CSRC) describes the need for this type of planning:

> These procedures (contingency plans, business interruption plans, and continuity of operations plans) should be coordinated with the backup, contingency, and recovery plans of any general support systems, including networks used by the application. The contingency plans should ensure that interfacing systems are identified and contingency/disaster planning coordinated.[5]

As you learn more about CP, you may notice that it shares certain characteristics with risk management and the SDLC methodology. Many IT and InfoSec managers are already familiar with these processes and thus can readily adapt their existing knowledge to the CP process.

Components of Contingency Planning

As noted earlier, CP includes four major components: the BIA and the IR, DR, and BC policies and plans. Whether an organization adopts the one-plan method or the multiple-plan method with interlocking procedures, each of these CP components must be addressed and developed in their entirety. The following sections describe each component in detail, including when and how each should be used. They also explain how to determine which plan is best suited for the identification, containment, and resolution of any given unexpected event. Figure 5-1 depicts the major project modules performed during CP efforts. Figure 5-2 shows the overall stages of the CP process, which are derived from the NIST IR and CP methodologies presented earlier.

incident response planning team (IRPT)

The team responsible for designing and managing the IR plan by specifying the organization's preparation, reaction, and recovery from incidents.

disaster recovery planning team (DRPT)

The team responsible for designing and managing the DR plan by specifying the organization's preparation, response, and recovery from disasters, including reestablishment of business operations at the primary site after the disaster.

business continuity planning team (BCPT)

The team responsible for designing and managing the BC plan of relocating the organization and establishing primary operations at an alternate site until the disaster recovery planning team can recover the primary site or establish a new location.

crisis management planning team (CMPT)

The individuals from various functional areas of the organization assigned to develop and implement the CM plan.

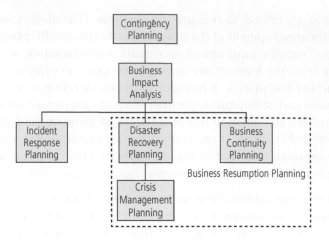

Figure 5-1 Contingency planning hierarchies

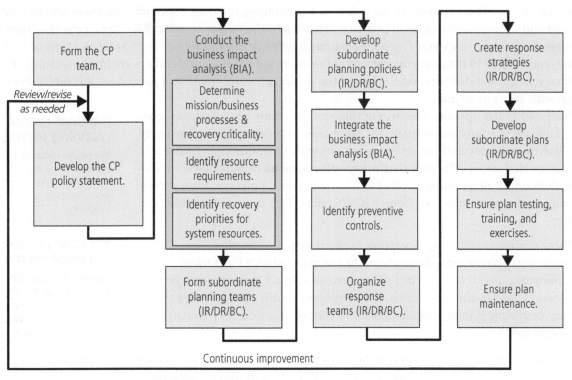

Figure 5-2 Contingency planning life cycle

Business Impact Analysis

The **business impact analysis (BIA)** is the first major component of the CP process. A crucial foundation for the initial planning stages, it serves as an investigation and assessment of the impact that various adverse events can have on the organization.

One of the fundamental differences between a BIA and the risk management processes discussed in Module 4 is that risk management focuses on identifying threats, vulnerabilities, and attacks to determine which controls can protect information. The BIA assumes that these controls have been bypassed, have failed, or have otherwise proved ineffective, that the attack succeeded, and that the adversity that was being defended against has been successful. By assuming the worst has happened, and then assessing how that adversity will impact the organization, insight is gained for how the organization must respond to the adverse event, minimize the damage, recover from the effects, and return to normal operations.

business impact analysis (BIA)

An investigation and assessment of adverse events that can affect the organization, conducted as a preliminary phase of the contingency planning process; it includes a determination of how critical a system or set of information is to the organization's core processes and its recovery priorities.

The BIA begins with the prioritized list of threats and vulnerabilities identified in the risk management process discussed in Module 4, and then the list is enhanced by adding the information needed to respond to the adversity. Obviously, the organization's security team does everything in its power to stop attacks, but as you have seen, some attacks, such as natural disasters, deviations from service providers, acts of human failure or error, and deliberate acts of sabotage and vandalism, may be unstoppable.

When undertaking the BIA, the organization should consider the following:

1. *Scope*—Carefully consider which parts of the organization to include in the BIA; determine which business units to cover, which systems to include, and the nature of the risk being evaluated.
2. *Plan*—The needed data will likely be voluminous and complex, so work from a careful plan to ensure that the proper data is collected to enable a comprehensive analysis. Getting the correct information to address the needs of decision makers is important.
3. *Balance*—Weigh the information available; some information may be objective in nature, while other information may only be available as subjective or anecdotal references. Facts should be weighted properly against opinions; however, sometimes the knowledge and experience of key personnel can be invaluable.
4. *Objective*—Identify in advance what the key decision makers require for making choices. Structure the BIA to bring them the information they need and to facilitate consideration of those choices.
5. *Follow-up*—Communicate periodically to ensure that process owners and decision makers will support the process and end result of the BIA.[6]

According to NIST's SP 800-34, Rev. 1, the CPMT conducts the BIA in three stages described in the sections that follow:[7]

1. Determine mission/business processes and recovery criticality.
2. Identify resource requirements.
3. Identify recovery priorities for system resources.

Determine Mission/Business Processes and Recovery Criticality

The first major BIA task is the analysis and prioritization of business processes within the organization, based on their relationship to the organization's mission. Each business department, unit, or division must be independently evaluated to determine how important its functions are to the organization as a whole. For example, recovery operations would probably focus on the IT department and network operation before turning to the personnel department's hiring activities. Likewise, recovering a manufacturing company's assembly line is more urgent than recovering its maintenance tracking system. This is not to say that personnel functions and assembly line maintenance are not important to the business, but unless the organization's main revenue-producing operations can be restored quickly, other functions are irrelevant.

Note that throughout this section, the term *mission/business process* is used, as some agencies that adopt this methodology are not businesses and thus do not have business processes per se. Do not let the term confuse you. Whenever you see the term, it's essentially describing a **business process**. NIST prefers *mission/business process*, although *business process* is just as accurate.

It is important to collect critical information about each business unit before beginning the process of prioritizing the business units. The key thing to remember is to avoid "turf wars" and instead focus on the selection of business functions that must be sustained to continue business operations. While one manager or executive might feel that his or her function is the most critical to the organization, that function might prove to be less critical in the event of a major incident or disaster. It is the role of senior management to arbitrate these inevitable conflicts about priority; after all, senior management has the perspective to make these types of trade-off decisions.

A weighted table analysis (WTA), or weighted factor analysis, as shown in Table 5-1, can be useful in resolving the issue of what business function is the most critical. The CPMT can use this tool by first identifying the characteristics of each business function that matter most to the organization—in other words, the criteria. The team should then allocate relative weights to each of these criteria. Each of the criteria is assessed on its influence toward overall importance in the decision-making process. Once the characteristics to be used as criteria have been identified and weighted (usually as columns in the WTA worksheet), the various

business process

A task performed by an organization or one of its units in support of the organization's overall mission and operations.

Table 5-1 Example of Weighted Table Analysis of Business Processes

#	Criterion Criterion⟶ Weight Business Process ↓	Impact on Revenue 0.25	Impact on Profitability 0.3	Impact on Product/Service Delivery 0.15	Impact on Market Share 0.2	Impact on Reputation 0.1	TOTAL	Importance (0–5; Not Important to Critically Important)
1	Customer sales	5	5	5	5	4	4.9	Critically Important
2	Production	5	5	5	3	3	4.4	Critically Important
3	Information security services	3	3	3	3	5	3.2	Very Important
4	IT services	4	3	4	2	2	3.1	Very Important
5	Customer service	2	3	2	1	4	2.3	Important
6	Research & development	1	1	2	3	3	1.75	Somewhat Important
7	Employee support services	1	1	2	1	2	1.25	Somewhat Important

business functions are listed (usually as rows on the same worksheet). Each business function is assessed a score for each of the criteria. Next, the weights can be multiplied against the scores in each of the criteria, and then the rows are summed to obtain the overall scored value of the function to the organization. The higher the value computed for a given business function, the more important that function is to the organization.

A BIA questionnaire is an instrument used to collect relevant business impact information for the required analysis. It is useful as a tool for identifying and collecting information about business functions for the analysis just described. It can also be used to allow functional managers to directly enter information about the business processes within their area of control, the impacts of these processes on the business, and dependencies that exist for the functions from specific resources and outside service providers.

recovery time objective (RTO)

The maximum amount of time that a system resource can remain unavailable before there is an unacceptable impact on other system resources, supported business processes, and the maximum tolerable downtime.

recovery point objective (RPO)

The point in time before a disruption or system outage to which business process data can be recovered after an outage, given the most recent backup copy of the data.

NIST Business Process and Recovery Criticality   NIST's SP 800-34, Rev. 1, recommends that organizations use simple qualitative categories like "low impact," "moderate impact," or "high impact" for the security objectives of confidentiality, integrity, and availability (NIST's Risk Management Framework Step 1). Note that large quantities of information are assembled, and a data collection process is essential if all meaningful and useful information collected in the BIA process is to be made available for use in overall CP development.

When organizations consider recovery criticality, key recovery measures are usually described in terms of how much of the asset they must recover and what time frame it must be recovered within. The following terms are most frequently used to describe these values:

- **Recovery time objective (RTO)**
- **Recovery point objective (RPO)**
- **Maximum tolerable downtime (MTD)**
- **Work recovery time (WRT)**

The difference between RTO and RPO is illustrated in Figure 5-3. WRT typically involves the addition of nontechnical tasks required for the organization to make the information asset usable again for its intended business function. The WRT can be added to the RTO to determine the realistic amount of elapsed time required before a business function is back in useful service, as illustrated in Figure 5-4.

NIST goes on to say that failing to determine MTD "could leave contingency planners with imprecise direction on (1) selection of an appropriate recovery method and (2) the depth of detail that will be required when developing recovery procedures, including their scope and content."[8] Determining the RTO for the information system resource, NIST adds, "is important for selecting appropriate technologies that are best suited for meeting the MTD."[9] As for reducing RTO, that requires mechanisms to shorten the start-up time or provisions to make data available online at a failover site. Unlike RTO, NIST adds, "RPO is not considered as part of MTD. Rather, it is a factor of how much data loss the mission/business process can tolerate during the recovery process."[10] Reducing RPO requires mechanisms to increase the synchronicity of data replication between production systems and the backup implementations for those systems.

maximum tolerable downtime (MTD)

The total amount of time the system owner or authorizing official is willing to accept for a business process outage or disruption. The MTD includes all impact considerations.

work recovery time (WRT)

The amount of effort (expressed as elapsed time) needed to make business functions work again after the technology element is recovered. This recovery time is identified by the RTO.

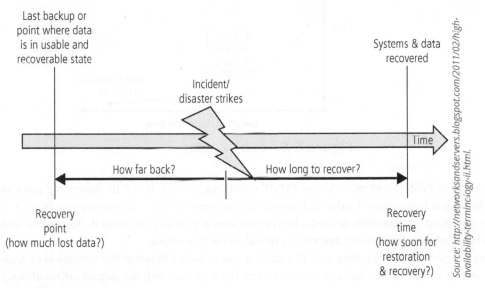

Source: http://networksandservers.blogspot.com/2011/02/high-availability-terminology-ii.html.

Figure 5-3   RTO vs. RPO

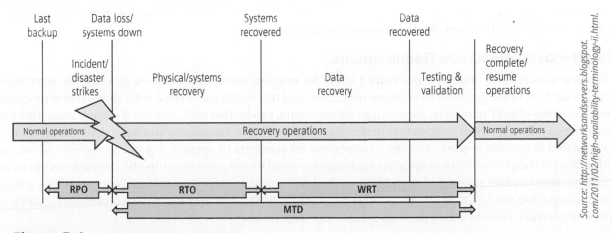

Source: http://networksandservers.blogspot.com/2011/02/high-availability-terminology-ii.html.

Figure 5-4   RTO, RPO, MTD, and WRT

Because of the critical need to recover business functionality, the total time needed to place the business function back in service must be shorter than the MTD. Planners should determine the optimal point to recover the information system in order to meet BIA-mandated recovery needs while balancing the cost of system inoperability against the cost of the resources required for restoring systems. This must be done in the context of the BIA-identified critical business processes and can be shown with a simple chart, such as the one in Figure 5-5.

The longer an interruption to system availability remains, the more impact and cost it will have for the organization and its operations. When plans require a short RTO, the solutions that will be required are usually more expensive to design and use. For example, if a system must be recovered immediately, it will have an RTO of 0.

These types of solutions will require fully redundant alternative processing sites and will therefore have much higher costs. On the other hand, a longer RTO would allow a less expensive recovery system. Plotting the cost balance points will show an optimal point between disruption and recovery costs. The intersecting point, labeled the cost balance point in Figure 5-5, will be different for every organization and system, based on the financial constraints and operating requirements.[11]

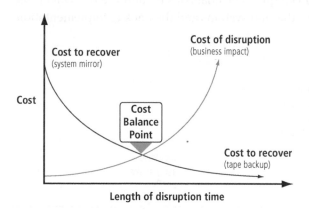

Figure 5-5   Cost balancing

Information Asset Prioritization   As the CPMT conducts the BIA, it will be assessing priorities and relative values for mission/business processes. To do so, it needs to understand the information assets used by those processes. In essence, the organization has determined which processes are most critical to its long-term viability, and now it must determine which information assets are most critical to each process.

Note that the presence of high-value information assets may influence the valuation of a particular business process. In any event, once the business processes have been prioritized, the organization should identify, classify, and prioritize the information assets both across the organization and within each business process, placing classification labels on each collection or repository of information in order to better understand its value and to prioritize its protection. Normally, this task would be performed as part of the risk assessment function within the risk management process. If the organization has not performed this task, the BIA process is the appropriate time to do so. Again, the WTA can be a useful tool to determine the information asset priorities.

Identify Recovery Resource Requirements

Once the organization has created a prioritized list of its mission/business processes, it needs to determine what resources would be required to recover those processes and the assets associated with them. Some processes are resource-intensive—like IT functions. Supporting customer data, production data, and other organizational information requires extensive quantities of information processing, storage, and transmission (through networking). Other business production processes require complex or expensive components to operate. For each process and information asset identified in the previous BIA stage, the organization should identify and describe the relevant resources needed to provide or support that process. A simplified method for organizing this information is to put it into a resource/component table, like the example shown in Table 5-2. Note in the table how one business process will typically have multiple components, each of which must be enumerated separately.

Table 5-2   Example Resource/Component Table

Mission/Business Process	Required Resource Components	Additional Resource Details	Description and Estimated Costs
Provide customer support (help desk)	Trouble ticket and resolution application	Application server built from Linux OS, Apache server, and SQL database	Each help-desk technician requires access to the organization's trouble ticket and resolution software application, hosted on a dedicated server. See current cost recovery statement for valuation.
Provide customer support (help desk)	Help-desk network segment	25 Cat5e network drops, gigabit network hub	The help-desk applications are networked and require a network segment to access. See current cost recovery statement for valuation.
Provide customer support (help desk)	Help-desk access terminals	1 laptop/PC per technician, with Web-browsing software	The help-desk applications require a Web interface on a laptop/PC to access. See current cost recovery statement for valuation.
Provide customer billing	Customized accounts receivable application	Application server with Linux OS, Apache server, and SQL database	Accounts Receivable requires access to its customized AR software and customer database to process customer billing. See current cost recovery statement for valuation.

Identify System Resource Recovery Priorities

The last stage of the BIA is prioritizing the resources associated with the mission/business processes, which provides a better understanding of what must be recovered first, even within the most critical processes. With the information from previous steps in hand, the organization can create additional weighted tables of the resources needed to support the individual processes. By assigning values to each resource, the organization will have a custom-designed "to-do" list available once the recovery phase commences. Whether it is an IR- or DR-focused recovery or the implementation of critical processes in an alternate site during business continuity, these lists will prove invaluable to those who are tasked to establish (or reestablish) critical processes quickly.

In addition to the weighted tables described earlier, a simple valuation and classification scale, such as Primary/Secondary/Tertiary or Critical/Very Important/Important/Routine, can be used to provide a quicker method of valuating the supporting resources. What is most important is not to get so bogged down in the process that you lose sight of the objective (the old "can't see the forest for the trees" problem). Teams that spend too much time developing and completing weighted tables may find a simple classification scheme more suited to their task. However, in a complex process with many resources, a more sophisticated valuation method like the weighted tables may be more appropriate. One of the jobs of the CPMT while preparing to conduct the BIA is to determine what method to use for valuating processes and their supporting resources.

Contingency Planning Policies

Prior to the development of each of the types of CP documents outlined in this module, the CP team should work to develop the policy environment that will enable the BIA process and should provide specific policy guidance toward authorizing the creation of each of the planning components (IR, DR, and BC). These policies provide guidance on the structure of the subordinate teams and the philosophy of the organization, and they assist in the structuring of the plan.

Each of the CP documents will include a policy similar in structure to all other policies used by the organization. Just as the enterprise InfoSec policy defines the InfoSec roles and responsibilities for the entire enterprise, each of the CP documents is based on a specific policy that defines the related roles and responsibilities for that element of the overall CP environment within the organization.

Incident Response

Most organizations have experience detecting, reacting to, and recovering from cyberattacks, employee errors, service outages, and small-scale natural disasters. While they may not have formally labeled such efforts, these organizations are performing **incident response (IR)**. IR must be carefully planned and coordinated because organizations heavily depend on the quick and efficient containment and resolution of incidents.

Incident response planning (IRP), therefore, is the preparation for such an effort and is performed by the IRP team (IRPT). Note that the term *incident response* could be used either to describe the entire set of activities or a specific phase in the overall reaction. However, in an effort to minimize confusion, this text will use the term *IR* to describe the overall process, and *reaction* rather than *response* to describe the organization's performance after it detects an incident.

In business, unexpected events happen. When those events represent the potential for loss, they are referred to as adverse events or **incident candidates**. When an adverse event begins to manifest as a real threat to information, it becomes an **incident**. The **incident response plan (IR plan)** is usually activated when the organization detects an incident that affects it, regardless of how minor the effect is.

Getting Started

As mentioned previously, an early task for the CPMT is to form the IRPT, which will begin work by developing policy to define the team's operations, articulate the organization's response to various types of incidents, and advise users how to contribute to the organization's effective response rather than contributing to the problem at hand. The IRPT then forms the **computer security incident response team (CSIRT)**. Some key members of the IRPT may be part of the CSIRT. You will learn more about the CSIRT's roles and composition later in this section. Figure 5-6 illustrates the NIST incident response life cycle.

As part of an increased focus on cybersecurity infrastructure protection, NIST has developed a Framework for Improving Critical Infrastructure Cybersecurity, also referred to as the NIST Cybersecurity Framework (CSF). The CSF includes, and is designed to be complementary to, the existing IR methodologies and SPs. In fact, the documents described in this module are the foundation of the new CSF. Figure 5-6 shows the phases in the CSF, including those of event recovery, which is the subject of NIST SP 800-184, "Guide for Cybersecurity Event Recovery" (2016). It is

incident response (IR)

An organization's set of planning and preparation efforts for detecting, reacting to, and recovering from an incident.

incident response planning (IRP)

The actions taken by senior management to develop and implement the IR policy, plan, and computer security incident response team.

incident candidate

See *adverse event*.

incident

An adverse event that could result in a loss of information assets but does not threaten the viability of the entire organization.

incident response plan (IR plan)

The documented product of incident response planning; a plan that shows the organization's intended efforts in the event of an incident.

computer security incident response team (CSIRT)

An IR team composed of technical IT, managerial IT, and InfoSec professionals who are prepared to detect, react to, and recover from an incident; may include members of the IRPT.

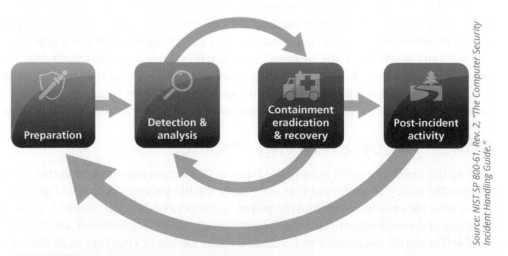

Source: NIST SP 800-61, Rev. 2, "The Computer Security Incident Handling Guide."

Figure 5-6   NIST incident response life cycle

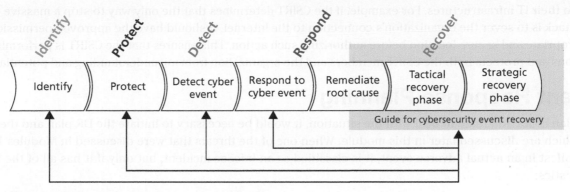

Figure 5-7   NIST Cybersecurity Framework

not difficult to map the phases shown in Figure 5-6 to those of Figure 5-7. Within the CSF, the five stages shown in Figure 5-7 include the following:

- *Identify*—Relates to risk management and governance
- *Protect*—Relates to implementation of effective security controls (policy, education, training and awareness, and technology)
- *Detect*—Relates to the identification of adverse events
- *Respond*—Relates to reacting to an incident
- *Recover*—Relates to putting things "as they were before" the incident[12]

The Detect, Respond, and Recover stages directly relate to NIST's IR strategy, as described in detail in SP 800-61, Rev. 2.

 For more information on the NIST Cybersecurity Framework, download the Framework for Improving Critical Infrastructure Cybersecurity from *www.nist.gov/sites/default/files/documents/cyberframework/cybersecurity-framework-021214.pdf.*

Incident Response Policy

An important early step for the CSIRT is to develop an **IR policy**. NIST's SP 800-61, Rev. 2, "The Computer Security Incident Handling Guide," identifies the following key components of a typical IR policy:

- *Statement of management commitment*
- *Purpose and objectives of the policy*
- *Scope of the policy (to whom and what it applies and under what circumstances)*
- *Definition of InfoSec incidents and related terms*
- *Organizational structure and definition of roles, responsibilities, and levels of authority; should include the authority of the incident response team to confiscate or disconnect equipment and to monitor suspicious activity, the requirements for reporting certain types of incidents, the requirements and guidelines for external communications and information sharing (e.g., what can be shared with whom, when, and over what channels), and the handoff and escalation points in the incident management process*
- *Prioritization or severity ratings of incidents*
- *Performance measures*
- *Reporting and contact forms*[13]

IR policy, like all policies, must gain the full support of top management and be clearly understood by all affected parties. It is especially important to gain the support of communities of interest that will be required to alter business practices or make

IR policy

The policy document that guides the development and implementation of IR plans and the formulation and performance of IR teams.

changes to their IT infrastructures. For example, if the CSIRT determines that the only way to stop a massive denial-of-service attack is to sever the organization's connection to the Internet, it should have the approved permission stored in an appropriate and secure location before authorizing such action. This ensures that the CSIRT is performing authorized actions and protects both the CSIRT members and the organization from misunderstanding and potential liability.

Incident Response Planning

If the IR plan is not adequate to deal with the situation, it would be necessary to initiate the DR plan and the BC plan, both of which are discussed later in this module. When one of the threats that were discussed in Modules 1 and 2 is made manifest in an actual adverse event, it is classified as an InfoSec incident, but only if it has all of the following characteristics:

- It is directed against information assets.
- It has a realistic chance of success.
- It threatens the confidentiality, integrity, or availability of information resources and assets.

The prevention of threats and attacks has been intentionally omitted from this discussion because guarding against such possibilities is primarily the responsibility of the InfoSec department, which works with the rest of the organization to implement sound policy, effective risk controls, and ongoing training and awareness programs. It is important to understand that IR is a reactive measure, not a preventive one, although most IR plans include preventative recommendations.

The responsibility for creating an organization's IR plan usually falls to the CIO, the CISO, or an IT manager with security responsibilities. With the aid of other managers and systems administrators on the CP team, the CISO should select members from each community of interest to form an independent IR team, which executes the IR plan. The roles and responsibilities of IR team members should be clearly documented and communicated throughout the organization. The IR plan also includes an alert roster, which lists certain critical individuals and organizations to be contacted during the course of an incident.

Using the multistep CP process discussed in the previous section as a model, the CP team can create the IR plan. According to NIST SP 800-61, Rev. 2, the IR plan should include the following elements:

- *Mission*
- *Strategies and goals*
- *Senior management approval*
- *Organizational approach to incident response*
- *How the incident response team will communicate with the rest of the organization and with other organizations*
- *Metrics for measuring incident response capability and its effectiveness*
- *Roadmap for maturing incident response capability*
- *How the program fits into the overall organization*[14]

During this planning process, the **IR procedures** take shape. For every incident scenario, the CP team creates three sets of incident handling procedures:

1. *During the incident*—The planners develop and document the procedures that must be performed during the incident. These procedures are grouped and assigned to individuals. Systems administrators' tasks differ from managerial tasks, so members of the planning committee must draft a set of function-specific procedures.
2. *After the incident*—Once the procedures for handling an incident are drafted, the planners develop and document the procedures that must be performed immediately after the incident has ceased. Again, separate functional areas may develop different procedures.
3. *Before the incident*—The planners draft a third set of procedures: those tasks that must be performed to prepare for the incident, including actions that could mitigate any damage from the incident. These procedures include details of the data backup schedules, disaster recovery preparation, training schedules, testing plans, copies of service agreements, and BC plans, if any. At this level, the BC plan could consist just of additional material about a service bureau that stores data off-site via electronic vaulting, with an agreement to provide office space and lease equipment as needed.

IR procedures

Detailed, step-by-step methods of preparing, detecting, reacting to, and recovering from an incident.

Planning for an incident and the responses to it requires a detailed understanding of the information systems and the threats they face. The BIA provides the data used to develop the IR plan. The IRPT seeks to develop a series of predefined responses that will guide the CSIRT and InfoSec staff through the IR process. Predefining incident responses enables the organization to react to a detected incident quickly and effectively, without confusion or wasted time and effort.

The execution of the IR plan typically falls to the CSIRT. As noted previously, the CSIRT is a separate group from the IRPT, although some overlap may occur; the CSIRT is composed of technical and managerial IT and InfoSec professionals who are prepared to diagnose and respond to an incident. In some organizations, the CSIRT may simply be a loose or informal association of IT and InfoSec staffers who would be called if an attack were detected on the organization's information assets. In other, more formal implementations, the CSIRT is a set of policies, procedures, technologies, people, and data put in place to prevent, detect, react to, and recover from an incident that could potentially damage the organization's information. At some level, all members of an organization are members of the CSIRT, because every action they take can cause or avert an incident.

The CSIRT should be available for contact by anyone who discovers or suspects that an incident involving the organization has occurred. One or more team members, depending on the magnitude of the incident and availability of personnel, then handle the incident. The incident handlers analyze the incident data, determine the impact of the incident, and act appropriately to limit the damage to the organization and restore normal services. Although the CSIRT may have only a few members, the team's success depends on the participation and cooperation of individuals throughout the organization.

The CSIRT consists of professionals who can handle the systems and functional areas affected by an incident. For example, imagine a firefighting team responding to an emergency call. Rather than responding to the fire as individuals, every member of the team has a specific role to perform, so that the team acts as a unified body that assesses the situation, determines the appropriate response, and coordinates the response. Similarly, each member of the IR team must know his or her specific role, work in concert with other team members, and execute the objectives of the IR plan.

Incident response actions can be organized into three basic phases:

- *Detection*—Recognition that an incident is under way
- *Reaction*—Responding to the incident in a predetermined fashion to contain and mitigate its potential damage (the new NIST CSF refers to this stage as "Respond" in its Detect, Respond, Recover approach)
- *Recovery*—Returning all systems and data to their state before the incident. Table 5-3 shows the incident handling checklist from NIST SP 800-61, Rev 2.

Data Protection in Preparation for Incidents

An organization has several options for protecting its information and getting operations up and running quickly after an incident:

- *Traditional data backups*—The organization can use a combination of on-site and off-site tape-drive, hard-drive, and cloud backup methods, in a variety of rotation schemes; because the backup point is sometime in the past, recent data is potentially lost. Most common data backup schemes involve a redundant array of independent disks (RAID) or disk-to-disk-to-cloud methods.
- *Electronic vaulting*—The organization can employ bulk batch transfer of data to an off-site facility, usually via leased lines or secure Internet connections. The receiving server archives the data as it is received. Some DR companies specialize in **electronic vaulting** services.
- *Remote journaling*—The organization can transfer live transactions to an off-site facility. **Remote journaling** differs from electronic vaulting in two ways: (1) Only transactions are transferred, not archived data, and (2) the transfer takes place online and in much closer to real time. While electronic vaulting is akin to a traditional backup, with a dump of data to the off-site storage, remote journaling involves online activities on a systems level, much like server fault tolerance, where data is written to two locations simultaneously.
- *Database shadowing*—The organization can store duplicate online transaction data, along with duplicate databases, at the remote site on a redundant server; **database shadowing** combines electronic vaulting with remote

electronic vaulting

A backup strategy that transfers data in bulk batches to an off-site facility.

remote journaling

A backup strategy that transfers only transaction data in near real time to an off-site facility.

database shadowing

A backup strategy that transfers duplicate online transaction data and duplicate databases to a remote site on a redundant server, combining electronic vaulting with remote journaling by writing multiple copies of the database simultaneously to two locations.

Table 5-3 Incident Handling Checklist from NIST SP 800-61, Rev. 2

		Action	Completed
		Detection and Analysis	
1.		Determine whether an incident has occurred	
	1.1	Analyze the precursors and indicators	
	1.2	Look for correlating information	
	1.3	Perform research (e.g., search engines, knowledge base)	
	1.4	As soon as the handler believes an incident has occurred, begin documenting the investigation and gathering evidence	
2.		Prioritize handling the incident based on the relevant factors (functional impact, information impact, recoverability effort, etc.)	
3.		Report the incident to the appropriate internal personnel and external organizations	
		Containment, Eradication, and Recovery	
4.		Acquire, preserve, secure, and document evidence	
5.		Contain the incident	
6.		Eradicate the incident	
	6.1	Identify and mitigate all vulnerabilities that were exploited	
	6.2	Remove malware, inappropriate materials, and other components	
	6.3	If more affected hosts are discovered (e.g., new malware infections), repeat the Detection and Analysis steps (1.1, 1.2) to identify all other affected hosts, then contain (5) and eradicate (6) the incident for them	
7.		Recover from the incident	
	7.1	Return affected systems to an operationally ready state	
	7.2	Confirm that the affected systems are functioning normally	
	7.3	If necessary, implement additional monitoring to look for future related activity	
		Post-Incident Activity	
8.		Create a follow-up report	
9.		Hold a lessons learned meeting (mandatory for major incidents, optional otherwise). While not explicitly noted in the NIST document, most organizations will document the findings from this activity and use it to update relevant plans, policies, and procedures.	

Source: NIST SP 800-61, Rev. 2.

journaling by writing multiple copies of the database simultaneously to two separate locations.

3-2-1 backup rule

A backup strategy that recommends the creation of at least three copies of critical data (the original and two copies) on at least two different media, with at least one copy stored off-site.

Industry recommendations for data backups include the "**3-2-1 backup rule**," which encourages maintaining three copies of important data (the original and two backup copies) on at least two different media (like local hard drives and cloud backup), with at least one copy stored off-site. Other recommendations include daily backups that are stored on-site and a weekly backup stored off-site.

Detecting Incidents

The challenge for every IR team is determining whether an event is the product of routine systems use or an actual incident. **Incident classification** involves reviewing each adverse event that has the potential to escalate into an incident and determining whether it constitutes an actual incident and thus should trigger the IR plan. Classifying an incident is the responsibility of the CSIRT, unless the organization has deployed a security operations center (SOC) with individuals trained to perform this task prior to notifying the CSIRT and activating the IR plan. Initial reports from end users, intrusion detection systems, host- and network-based virus detection software, and systems administrators are all ways to detect, track, and classify adverse events. Careful training in the reporting of an adverse event allows end users, help-desk staff, and all security personnel to relay vital information to the IR team. But, no matter how well trained the team is, event data that flows in an endless stream from hundreds or thousands of network devices and system components requires automated tools for collection and screening. Later modules describe processes for event log data collection, analysis, and event detection using intrusion detection and prevention systems as well as security information and event management systems. For now, let's say that once an actual incident is properly identified and classified, members of the IR team can effectively execute the corresponding procedures from the IR plan. This is the primary purpose of the first phase of IR: **incident detection**.

Several occurrences could signal an incident. Unfortunately, these same events can result from an overloaded network, computer, or server, and some are similar to the normal operation of these information assets. Other incidents mimic the actions of a misbehaving computing system, software package, or other less serious threat. To help make incident detection more reliable, renowned security consultant Donald Pipkin has identified three categories of incident indicators: possible, probable, and definite.[15]

Possible Indicators

The following types of incident candidates are considered possible indicators of actual incidents:

- *Presence of unfamiliar files*—Users might discover unfamiliar files in their home directories or on their office computers. Administrators might also find unexplained files that do not seem to be in a logical location or are not owned by an authorized user.
- *Presence or execution of unknown programs or processes*—Users or administrators might detect unfamiliar programs running, or processes executing, on office machines or network servers. Users should become familiar with accessing running programs and processes (usually through the Windows Task Manager shown in Figure 5-8) so they can detect rogue instances.
- *Unusual consumption of computing resources*—An example would be a sudden spike or fall in consumption of memory or hard disk space. Many computer operating systems, including Windows, Linux, and UNIX variants, allow users and administrators to monitor CPU and memory consumption. The Windows Task Manager has a Performance tab that provides this information, also shown in Figure 5-8. Most computers also have the ability to monitor hard drive space. In addition, servers maintain logs of file creation and storage.
- *Unusual system crashes*—Computer systems can crash. Older operating systems running newer programs are notorious for locking up or spontaneously rebooting whenever the operating system is unable to execute a requested process or service. You are probably familiar with system error messages such as "Unrecoverable Application Error," "General Protection Fault," and the infamous Windows "Blue Screen of Death." However, if a computer system seems to be crashing, hanging, rebooting, or freezing more frequently than usual, the cause could be an incident candidate.

Probable Indicators

The following types of incident candidates are considered probable indicators of actual incidents:

- *Activities at unexpected times*—If traffic levels on the organization's network exceed the measured baseline values, an incident candidate is probably present. If this activity surge occurs outside normal business hours, the probability becomes much higher. Similarly, if systems are accessing drives and otherwise indicating high activity when employees aren't using them, an incident may also be occurring.

---

incident classification

The process of examining an adverse event or incident candidate and determining whether it constitutes an actual incident.

incident detection

The identification and classification of an adverse event as an incident, accompanied by the notification of the CSIRT and the activation of the IR reaction phase.

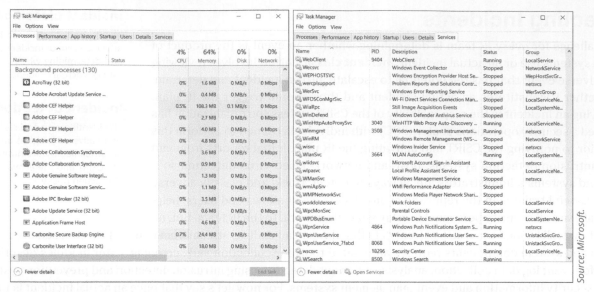

Figure 5-8 Windows Task Manager showing processes (left) and services (right)

- *Presence of new accounts*—Periodic review of user accounts can reveal accounts that the administrator does not remember creating or that are not logged in the administrator's journal. Even one unlogged new account is an incident candidate. An unlogged new account with root or other special privileges has an even higher probability of being an actual incident.
- *Reported attacks*—If users of the system report a suspected attack, there is a high probability that an incident has occurred, whether it was an attack or not. The technical sophistication of the person making the report should be considered. If systems administrators are reporting attacks, odds are that additional attacks are occurring throughout the organization.
- *Notification from an IDPS*—If the organization has installed and correctly configured a host- or network-based intrusion detection and prevention system (IDPS), then a notification from the IDPS indicates that an incident might be in progress. However, IDPSs are difficult to configure perfectly, and even when they are, they tend to issue false positives or false alarms. The administrator must then determine whether the notification is real or the result of a routine operation by a user or other administrator.

Definite Indicators

The following five types of incident candidates are definite indicators of an actual incident. That is, they clearly signal that an incident is in progress or has occurred. In these cases, the IR plan must be activated immediately, and appropriate measures must be taken by the CSIRT.

- *Use of dormant accounts*—Many network servers maintain default accounts, and there are often accounts from former employees, employees on a leave of absence or sabbatical without remote access privileges, or dummy accounts set up to support system testing. If any of these accounts activate and begin accessing system resources, querying servers, or engaging in other activities, an incident is certain to have occurred.
- *Changes to logs*—Smart systems administrators back up system logs as well as system data. As part of a routine incident scan, systems administrators can compare these logs to the online versions to determine whether they have been modified. If they have, and the systems administrator cannot determine explicitly that an authorized individual modified them, an incident has occurred.
- *Presence of hacker tools*—Network administrators sometimes use system vulnerability and network evaluation tools to scan internal computers and networks to determine what a hacker can see. These tools are also used to support research into attack profiles. All too often, however, they are used by individuals with local network access to hack into systems or just "look around." To combat this problem, many organizations explicitly prohibit the use of these tools without permission from the CISO, making any unauthorized installation a policy violation. Most organizations that engage in penetration testing require that all tools in this category be confined to specific systems and that they not be used on the general network unless active penetration testing is under way. Finding hacker tools, or even legal security tools, in places they should not be is an indicator that an incident has occurred.

- *Notifications by partner or peer*—If a business partner or another integrated organization reports an attack from your computing systems, then an incident has occurred. It's quite common for an attacker to use a third party's conscripted systems to attack another system rather than attacking directly.
- *Notification by hacker*—Some hackers enjoy taunting their victims. If an organization's Web pages are defaced, it is an incident. If an organization receives an extortion request for money in exchange for its stolen data, an incident is in progress. Note that even if an actual attack has not occurred—for example, the hacker is just making an empty threat—the reputational risk is real and should be treated as such.

Potential Incident Results

The situations described in the following list may simply be caused by the abnormal performance of a misbehaving IT system. However, because accidental and intentional incidents can lead to the following results, organizations should err on the side of caution and treat every adverse event as if it could evolve into an actual incident:

- *Loss of availability*—Information or information systems become unavailable.
- *Loss of integrity*—Users report corrupt data files, garbage where data should be, or data that just looks wrong.
- *Loss of confidentiality*—There is a notification of a sensitive information leak, or information that was thought to be protected has been disclosed.
- *Violation of policy*—There is a violation of organizational policies addressing information or InfoSec.
- *Violation of law or regulation*—The law has been broken and the organization's information assets are involved.

Reacting to Incidents

Once an actual incident has been confirmed and properly classified, the IR plan moves from the detection phase to the reaction phase. NIST SP 800-61, Rev. 2, combines the reaction and recovery phases into their "Containment, Eradication, and Recovery" phase, but the phases are treated separately as "Respond" and "Recover" under the new CSF.[16]

The steps in IR are designed to stop the incident, mitigate its effects, and provide information for recovery from the incident. In the Reaction or Response phase, several action steps taken by the CSIRT and others must occur quickly and may take place concurrently. An effective IR plan prioritizes and documents these steps to allow for efficient reference during an incident. These steps include notification of key personnel, documentation of the incident, determining containment options, and escalation of the incident if needed.

Notification of Key Personnel

As soon as the CSIRT determines that an incident is in progress, the right people must be notified in the right order. Most "reaction" organizations, such as firefighters or the military, use an **alert roster** for just such a situation. Organizations can adopt this approach to ensure that appropriate personnel are notified in the event of an incident or disaster.

There are two ways to activate an alert roster: sequentially and hierarchically. A sequential roster requires that a designated contact person initiate contact with each and every person on the roster using the identified method. A hierarchical roster requires that the first person initiate contact with a specific number of designated people on the roster, who in turn contact other designated people, and so on. Each approach has advantages and disadvantages. The hierarchical system is quicker because more people are making contacts at the same time, but the message can become distorted as it is passed from person to person. A hierarchical system can also suffer from a break in the chain if people can't reach all of the employees they're supposed to contact. In that situation, everyone "downstream" may not be notified. The sequential system is more accurate, but slower because a single contact person must contact each recipient and deliver the message. Fortunately, many automated systems are available to facilitate either approach.

alert roster

A document that contains contact information for personnel to be notified in the event of an incident or disaster.

 For more information on selecting an automated notification system, read the article by Steven Ross on TechTarget's page at *https://searchdisasterrecovery.techtarget.com/feature/Selecting-an-automated-notification-system-for-data-center-disasters*.

alert message

A description of the incident or disaster that usually contains just enough information so that each person knows what portion of the IR or DR plan to implement without slowing down the notification process.

The alert roster is used to deliver the **alert message**, which tells each team member his or her expected task and situation. It provides just enough information so that each responder, CSIRT or otherwise, knows what portion of the IR plan to implement without impeding the notification process. It is important to recognize that not everyone is on the alert roster—only individuals who must respond to an actual incident. As with any part of the IR plan, the alert roster must be regularly maintained, tested, and rehearsed if it is to remain effective.

During this phase, other key personnel not on the alert roster, such as general management, must be notified of the incident as well. This notification should occur only after the incident has been confirmed but before media or other external sources learn of it. Among those likely to be included in the notification process are members of the legal, communications, and human resources departments. In addition, some incidents are disclosed to the employees in general as a lesson in security, and some are not, as a measure of security. Furthermore, other organizations may need to be notified if it is determined that the incident is not confined to internal information resources or is part of a larger-scale assault. Distributed denial-of-service attacks are an example of this type of general assault against the cyber infrastructure. In general, the IR planners should determine in advance whom to notify and when, and should offer guidance about additional notification steps to take as needed.

Documenting an Incident

As soon as an incident has been confirmed and the notification process is under way, the team should begin to document it. The documentation should record the who, what, when, where, why, and how of each action taken while the incident is occurring. This documentation serves as a case study after the fact to determine whether the right actions were taken and if they were effective. It also proves that the organization did everything possible to prevent the spread of the incident.

Legally, the standards of due care may offer some protection to the organization if an incident adversely affects individuals inside and outside the organization, or if it affects other organizations that use the target organization's systems. Incident documentation can also be used as a simulation in future training sessions with the IR plan.

Incident Containment Strategies

One of the most critical components of IR is stopping the incident and containing its scope or impact. Incident containment strategies vary depending on the incident and on the amount of damage caused. Before an incident can be stopped or contained, however, the affected areas must be identified. Now is not the time to conduct a detailed analysis of the affected areas; that task is typically performed after the fact, in the forensics process. Instead, simple identification of what information and systems are involved determines the containment actions to be taken. Incident containment strategies focus on two tasks: stopping the incident and recovering control of the affected systems.

The CSIRT can stop the incident and attempt to recover control by means of several strategies. If the incident originates outside the organization, the simplest and most straightforward approach is to disconnect the affected communication circuits. Of course, if the organization's lifeblood runs through that circuit, this step may be too drastic; if the incident does not threaten critical functional areas, it may be more feasible to monitor the incident and contain it another way. One approach used by some organizations is to apply filtering rules dynamically to limit certain types of network access. For example, if a threat agent is attacking a network by exploiting a vulnerability in the Simple Network Management Protocol (SNMP), then applying a blocking filter on the commonly used IP ports for that vulnerability will stop the attack without compromising other services on the network. Depending on the nature of the attack and the organization's technical capabilities, using ad hoc controls can sometimes buy valuable time to devise a more permanent control strategy. Typical containment strategies include the following:

- Disabling compromised user accounts
- Reconfiguring a firewall to block the problem traffic
- Temporarily disabling compromised processes or services
- Taking down the conduit application or server—for example, the e-mail server
- Disconnecting affected networks or network segments
- Stopping (powering down) all computers and network devices

Obviously, the final strategy is used only when all system control has been lost and the only hope is to preserve the data stored on the computers so that operations can resume normally once the incident is resolved. The CSIRT, following the procedures outlined in the IR plan, determines the length of the interruption.

Consider what would happen during an incident if key personnel are on sick leave, vacation, or otherwise not at work? Think of how many people in your class or office are not there on a regular basis. Many businesses require travel, with employees going off-site to meetings, seminars, or training, and to fulfill other diverse requirements. In addition, "life happens"—employees are sometimes absent due to illness, injury, routine medical activities, and other unexpected events. In considering these possibilities, the importance of preparedness becomes clear. Everyone should know how to react to an incident, not just the CISO and security administrators.

Incident Escalation

An incident may increase in scope or severity to the point that the IR plan cannot adequately handle it. An important part of knowing how to handle an incident is knowing at what point to escalate it to a disaster, or to transfer the incident to an outside authority such as law enforcement or some other public response unit. During the BIA, each organization will have to determine the point at which an incident is deemed a disaster. These criteria must be included in the IR plan. The organization must also document when to involve outside responders, as discussed in other sections. Escalation is one of those things that, once done, cannot be undone, so it is important to know when and where it should be used.

Recovering from Incidents

Once the incident has been contained and system control has been regained, incident recovery can begin. As in the incident reaction phase, the first task is to inform the appropriate human resources. Almost simultaneously, the CSIRT must assess the full extent of the damage to determine what must be done to restore the systems. Everyone involved should begin recovery operations based on the appropriate incident recovery section of the IR plan. NIST SP 800-184, "Guide for Cybersecurity Event Recovery," contains a detailed methodology for recovering from security incidents.

The CSIRT uses a process called incident damage assessment to immediately determine the impact from a breach of confidentiality, integrity, and availability on information and information assets. Incident damage assessment can take days or weeks, depending on the extent of the damage. The damage can range from minor, such as when a curious hacker snoops around, to a more severe case in which hundreds of computer systems are infected by malware.

System logs, intrusion detection logs, configuration logs, and other documents, as well as the documentation from the incident response, provide information on the type, scope, and extent of damage. Using this information, the CSIRT assesses the current state of the data and systems and compares it to a known state. Individuals who document the damage from actual incidents must be trained to collect and preserve evidence in case the incident is part of a crime or results in a civil action.

Once the extent of the damage has been determined, the recovery process begins. According to noted security consultant and author Donald Pipkin, this process involves the following steps:[17]

- Identify the vulnerabilities that allowed the incident to occur and spread. Resolve them.
- Address the safeguards that failed to stop or limit the incident or were missing from the system in the first place. Install, replace, or upgrade them.
- Evaluate monitoring capabilities (if present). Improve detection and reporting methods or install new monitoring capabilities.
- Restore the data from backups, as needed. The IR team must understand the backup strategy used by the organization, restore the data contained in backups, and then use the appropriate recovery processes, from incremental backups or database journals, to recreate any data that was created or modified since the last backup.
- Restore the services and processes in use. Compromised services and processes must be examined, cleaned, and then restored. If services or processes were interrupted while regaining control of the systems, they need to be brought back online.
- Continuously monitor the system. If an incident happened once, it could easily happen again. Hackers frequently boast of their exploits in chat rooms and dare their peers to match their efforts. If word gets out, others may be tempted to try the same or different attacks on your systems. It is therefore important to maintain vigilance during the entire IR process.

- Restore the confidence of the organization's communities of interest. The CSIRT, following a recommendation from management, may want to issue a short memorandum outlining the incident and assuring everyone that it was handled and the damage was controlled. If the incident was minor, say so. If the incident was major or severely damaged systems or data, reassure users that they can expect operations to return to normal as soon as possible. The objective of this communication is to prevent panic or confusion from causing additional disruption to the operations of the organization.

According to NIST SP 800-184, every organization should have a recovery plan (as a subset of the IR plan) to guide specific efforts after the incident has been contained. The following is the summary of recommendations from that document:

> *Understand how to be prepared for resilience at all times, planning how to operate in a diminished capacity or restore services over time based on their relative priorities.*
>
> *Identify and document the key personnel who will be responsible for defining recovery criteria and associated plans, and ensure these personnel understand their roles and responsibilities.*
>
> *Create and maintain a list of people, process, and technology assets that enable the organization to achieve its mission (including external resources), along with all dependencies among these assets. Document and maintain categorizations for these assets based on their relative importance and interdependencies to enable prioritization of recovery efforts.*
>
> *Develop comprehensive plan(s) for recovery that support the prioritizations and recovery objectives, and use the plans as the basis of developing recovery processes and procedures that ensure timely restoration of systems and other assets affected by future cyber events. The plan(s) should ensure that underlying assumptions (e.g., availability of core services) will not undermine recovery, and that processes and procedures address both technical and non-technical activity affecting people, processes, and technologies.*
>
> *Develop, implement, and practice the defined recovery processes, based upon the organization's recovery requirements, to ensure timely recovery team coordination and restoration of capabilities or services affected by cyber events.*
>
> *Formally define and document the conditions under which the recovery plan is to be invoked, who has the authority to invoke the plan, and how recovery personnel will be notified of the need for recovery activities to be performed.*
>
> *Define key milestones for meeting intermediate recovery goals and terminating active recovery efforts.*
>
> *Adjust incident detection and response policies, processes, and procedures to ensure that recovery does not hinder effective response (e.g., by alerting an adversary or by erroneously destroying forensic evidence).*
>
> *Develop a comprehensive recovery communications plan, and fully integrate communications considerations into recovery policies, plans, processes, and procedures.*
>
> *Clearly define recovery communication goals, objectives, and scope, including information sharing rules and methods. Based upon this communications plan, consider sharing actionable information about cyber threats with relevant organizations, such as those described in NIST SP 800-150.*[18]

Before returning to its routine duties, the CSIRT should conduct an **after-action review (AAR)**. The AAR is an opportunity for everyone who was involved in an incident or disaster to sit down and discuss what happened. In an AAR, a designated person acts as a moderator and allows everyone to share what happened from his or her own perspective, while ensuring there is no blame or finger-pointing. All team members review their actions during the incident and identify areas where the IR plan worked, did not work, or could be improved. Once completed, the AAR is written up and shared.

All key players review their notes and the AAR and verify that the IR documentation is accurate and precise. The AAR allows the team to update the plan and brings the reaction team's actions to a close. The AAR can serve as a training case for future staff.

after-action review (AAR)

A detailed examination and discussion of the events that occurred during an incident or disaster, from first detection to final recovery.

According to McAfee, there are 10 common mistakes that an organization's CSIRTs make in IR:

1. Failure to appoint a clear chain of command with a specified individual in charge
2. Failure to establish a central operations center
3. Failure to "know their enemy," as described in Modules 2 and 4

4. Failure to develop a comprehensive IR plan with containment strategies
5. Failure to record IR activities at all phases, especially help-desk tickets to detect incidents
6. Failure to document the events as they occur in a timeline
7. Failure to distinguish incident containment from incident remediation (as part of reaction)
8. Failure to secure and monitor networks and network devices
9. Failure to establish and manage system and network logging
10. Failure to establish and support effective antivirus and antimalware solutions[19]

NIST SP 800-61, Rev. 2, makes the following recommendations for handling incidents:

- *Acquire tools and resources that may be of value during incident handling*—The team will be more efficient at handling incidents if various tools and resources are already available to them. Examples include contact lists, encryption software, network diagrams, backup devices, digital forensic software, and port lists.
- *Prevent incidents from occurring by ensuring that networks, systems, and applications are sufficiently secure*— Preventing incidents is beneficial to the organization and reduces the workload of the incident response team. Performing periodic risk assessments and reducing the identified risks to an acceptable level are effective in reducing the number of incidents. Awareness of security policies and procedures by users, IT staff, and management is also very important.
- *Identify precursors and indicators through alerts generated by several types of security software*—Intrusion detection and prevention systems, antivirus software, and file integrity checking software are valuable for detecting signs of incidents. Each type of software may detect incidents that the other types cannot, so the use of several types of computer security software is highly recommended. Third-party monitoring services can also be helpful.
- *Establish mechanisms for outside parties to report incidents*—Outside parties may want to report incidents to the organization—for example, they may believe that one of the organization's users is attacking them. Organizations should publish a phone number and e-mail address that outside parties can use to report such incidents.
- *Require a baseline level of logging and auditing on all systems and a higher baseline level on all critical systems*— Logs from operating systems, services, and applications frequently provide value during incident analysis, particularly if auditing was enabled. The logs can provide information such as which accounts were accessed and what actions were performed.
- *Profile networks and systems*—Profiling measures the characteristics of expected activity levels so that changes in patterns can be more easily identified. If the profiling process is automated, deviations from expected activity levels can be detected and reported to administrators quickly, leading to faster detection of incidents and operational issues.
- *Understand the normal behaviors of networks, systems, and applications*—Team members who understand normal behavior should be able to recognize abnormal behavior more easily. This knowledge can best be gained by reviewing log entries and security alerts; the handlers should become familiar with typical data and can investigate unusual entries to gain more knowledge.
- *Create a log retention policy*—Information about an incident may be recorded in several places. Creating and implementing a log retention policy that specifies how long log data should be maintained may be extremely helpful in analysis because older log entries may show reconnaissance activity or previous instances of similar attacks.
- *Perform event correlation*—Evidence of an incident may be captured in several logs. Correlating events among multiple sources can be invaluable in collecting all the available information for an incident and validating whether the incident occurred.
- *Keep all host clocks synchronized*—If the devices that report events have inconsistent clock settings, event correlation will be more complicated. Clock discrepancies may also cause problems from an evidentiary standpoint.
- *Maintain and use a knowledge base of information*—Handlers need to reference information quickly during incident analysis; a centralized knowledge base provides a consistent, maintainable source of information. The knowledge base should include general information such as data on precursors and indicators of previous incidents.

- *Start recording all information as soon as the team suspects that an incident has occurred*—Every step taken, from the time the incident was detected to its final resolution, should be documented and time-stamped. Information of this nature can serve as evidence in a court of law if legal prosecution is pursued. Recording the steps performed can also lead to a more efficient, more systematic, and less error-prone handling of the problem.

- *Safeguard incident data*—This data often contains sensitive information about vulnerabilities, security breaches, and users who may have performed inappropriate actions. The team should ensure that access to incident data is properly restricted, both logically and physically.

- *Prioritize handling of incidents based on relevant factors*—Because of resource limitations, incidents should not be handled on a first-come, first-served basis. Instead, organizations should establish written guidelines that outline how quickly the team must respond to the incident and what actions should be performed, based on relevant factors such as the functional and information impact of the incident and the likely recoverability from the incident. This saves time for the incident handlers and provides a justification to management and system owners for their actions. Organizations should also establish an escalation process for instances when the team does not respond to an incident within the designated time.

- *Include provisions for incident reporting in the organization's incident response policy*—Organizations should specify which incidents must be reported, when they must be reported, and to whom. The parties most commonly notified are the CIO, the head of information security, the local information security officer, other incident response teams within the organization, and system owners.

- *Establish strategies and procedures for containing incidents*—It is important to contain incidents quickly and effectively limit their business impact. Organizations should define acceptable risks in containing incidents and develop strategies and procedures accordingly. Containment strategies should vary based on the type of incident.

- *Follow established procedures for evidence gathering and handling*—The team should clearly document how all evidence has been preserved. Evidence should be accounted for at all times. The team should meet with legal staff and law enforcement agencies to discuss evidence handling and then develop procedures based on those discussions.

- *Capture volatile data from systems as evidence*—This data includes lists of network connections, processes, login sessions, open files, network interface configurations, and the contents of memory. Running carefully chosen commands from trusted media can collect the necessary information without damaging the system's evidence.

- *Obtain system snapshots through full forensic disk images, not file system backups*—Disk images should be made to sanitized write-protectable or write-once media. This process is superior to a file system backup for investigatory and evidentiary purposes. Imaging is also valuable in that it is much safer to analyze an image than it is to perform analysis on the original system because the analysis may inadvertently alter the original.

- *Hold lessons-learned meetings after major incidents*—Lessons-learned meetings are extremely helpful in improving security measures and the incident handling process itself.[20]

Note that some of these recommendations were covered earlier in this section. CSIRT members should be very familiar with these tools and techniques prior to an incident. Trying to use unfamiliar procedures in the middle of an incident could prove very costly to the organization and cause more harm than good.

 For more information on incident handling, read the *Incident Handlers Handbook* by Patrick Kral, which is available from the SANS reading room at *www.sans.org/reading-room/whitepapers/incident/incident-handlers-handbook-33901*. You can search for other incident handling papers at *www.sans.org/reading-room/whitepapers/incident/*.

Organizational Philosophy on Incident and Disaster Handling

Eventually, the organization will encounter incidents and disasters that stem from an intentional attack on its information assets by an individual or group, as opposed to an incident from an unintentional source, such as a service outage, employee mistake, or natural disaster. At that point, the organization must choose one of two philosophies that will affect its approach to IR and DR as well as subsequent involvement of digital forensics and law enforcement:

- ***Protect and forget***—This approach, also known as "patch and proceed," focuses on the defense of data and the systems that house, use, and transmit it. An investigation that takes this approach focuses on the detection and analysis of events to determine how they happened and to prevent reoccurrence. Once the current event is over, the questions of who caused it and why are almost immaterial.

- *Apprehend and prosecute*—This approach, also known as "pursue and punish," focuses on the identification and apprehension of responsible individuals, with additional attention paid to the collection and preservation of potential evidentiary material that might support administrative or criminal prosecution. This approach requires much more attention to detail to prevent contamination of evidence that might hinder prosecution.

An organization might find it impossible to retain enough data to successfully handle even administrative penalties, but it should certainly adopt the apprehend-and-prosecute approach if it wants to pursue formal punishment, especially if the employee is likely to challenge that punishment. The use of digital forensics to aid in IR and DR when dealing with intentional attacks will be discussed later in this module, along with information for when or if to involve law enforcement agencies.

What is shocking is how few organizations notify individuals that their personal data has been breached. Should it ever be exposed to the public, those organizations could find themselves confronted with criminal charges or corporate negligence suits. Laws like the Sarbanes–Oxley Act of 2002 specifically implement personal ethical liability requirements for organizational management. Failure to report loss of personal data can run directly afoul of these laws.

protect and forget

The organizational CP philosophy that focuses on the defense of information assets and preventing reoccurrence rather than the attacker's identification and prosecution; also known as "patch and proceed."

apprehend and prosecute

The organizational CP philosophy that focuses on an attacker's identification and prosecution, the defense of information assets, and preventing reoccurrence; also known as "pursue and punish."

Viewpoint on the Causes of Incidents and Disasters

By Karen Scarfone, Principal Consultant, Scarfone Cybersecurity

The term *incident* has somewhat different meanings in the contexts of incident response and disaster recovery. People in the incident response community generally think of an incident as being caused by a malicious attack and a disaster as being caused by natural causes (fire, floods, earthquakes, etc.). Meanwhile, people in the disaster recovery community tend to use the term *incident* in a cause-free manner, with the cause of the incident or disaster generally being irrelevant and the difference between the two being based solely on the scope of the event's impact. An incident is a milder event, and a disaster is a more serious event.

The result is that people who are deeply embedded in the incident response community often think of incident response as being largely unrelated to disaster recovery, because they think of a disaster as being caused by a natural event, not an attack. Incident responders also often think of operational problems, such as major service failures, as being neither incidents nor disasters. Meanwhile, people who are deeply embedded in the disaster recovery community see incident response and disaster recovery as being much more similar and covering a much more comprehensive range of problems.

So where does the truth lie? Well, it depends on the organization. Some organizations take a more integrated approach to business continuity and have their incident response, disaster recovery, and other business continuity components closely integrated with one another so that they work together fairly seamlessly. Other organizations treat these business continuity components as more discrete elements and focus on making each element strong rather than establishing strong commonalities and linkages among the components. There are pluses and minuses to each of these approaches.

Personally, I find that the most important thing is to avoid turf wars between the business continuity component teams. There is nothing more frustrating than delaying the response to an incident or disaster because people disagree on its cause. The security folks say it is an operational problem, the operational folks say it is a disaster, and the disaster folks say it is a security incident. So, like a hot potato, the event gets passed from team to team while people argue about its cause. In reality, for some problems the cause is not immediately apparent.

What is important to any organization is that each adverse event, regardless of the cause, be assessed and prioritized as quickly as possible. That means teams need to be willing to step up and address adverse events, regardless of whether the event is clearly their responsibility. The impact of the incident is largely unrelated to the cause. If later information shows that a particular cause better fits a different team, the handling of the event can be transferred to the other team. Teams should be prepared to transfer events to other teams and to receive transferred events from other teams at any time.

Responding as quickly as possible to incidents has become even more important with the increasing integration between the cyber world and the physical world. Operational technology (OT), cyber-physical systems (CPS), and the Internet of Things (IoT) are all driving this integration. Now an attacker can exploit cyber vulnerabilities to cause physical impacts, including overriding a building's card readers and other physical security systems to gain unauthorized access and feeding crafted malicious data into a factory's power system in order to start a fire or cause an explosion. Delaying the response to an incident may put human lives at unnecessary risk and ultimately lead to deaths that should have been prevented.

Digital Forensics

Whether due to a character flaw, a need for vengeance, a profit motive, or simple curiosity, an employee or outsider may attack a physical asset or information asset. When the asset is the responsibility of the CISO, he or she is expected to understand how policies and laws require the matter to be managed and protected. To protect the organization and possibly assist law enforcement in an investigation, the CISO must determine what happened and how an incident occurred. This process is called **digital forensics**.

Digital forensics is based on the field of traditional **forensics**. Made popular by scientific detective shows that focus on crime scene investigations, forensics involves the use of science to investigate events. Not all events involve crimes; some involve natural events, accidents, or system malfunctions. Forensics allows investigators to determine what happened by examining the results of an event. It also allows them to determine how the event happened by examining activities, individual actions, physical evidence, and testimony related to the event. However, forensics might not figure out the "why" of the event; that's the focus of psychological, sociological, and criminal justice studies. Here, the focus is on the application of forensics techniques in the digital arena.

Digital forensics involves the preservation, identification, extraction, documentation, and interpretation of digital media, including computer media, for evidentiary and root cause analysis. Like traditional forensics, it follows clear, well-defined methodologies, but it still tends to be as much an art as a science. In other words, the natural curiosity and personal skill of the investigator play a key role in discovering potential **evidentiary material (EM)**. An item does not become evidence until it is formally admitted by a judge or other ruling official.

Digital forensics investigators use a variety of tools to support their work, as you will learn later in this module. However, the tools and methods used by attackers can be equally sophisticated. Digital forensics can be used for two key purposes:

- To investigate allegations of **digital malfeasance**. Such an investigation requires digital forensics to gather, analyze, and report the findings. This is the primary mission of law enforcement in investigating crimes that involve computer technologies or online information.
- To perform **root cause analysis**. If an incident occurs and the organization suspects an attack was successful, digital forensics can be used to examine the path and methodology for gaining unauthorized access, and to determine how pervasive and successful the attack was. This type of analysis is used primarily by incident response teams to examine their equipment after an incident.

Some investigations are undertaken by an organization's own personnel, while others require the immediate involvement of law enforcement. In general, whenever investigators discover evidence of a crime, they should immediately notify management and recommend contacting law enforcement. Failure to do so could result in unfavorable action against the investigator or organization.

digital forensics

Investigations that involve the preservation, identification, extraction, documentation, and interpretation of computer media for evidentiary and root cause analysis, following clear, well-defined methodologies.

forensics

The coherent application of methodical investigatory techniques to present evidence of crimes in a court or similar setting.

evidentiary material (EM)

Any information that could potentially support an organization's legal or policy-based case against a suspect; also known as items of potential evidentiary value.

digital malfeasance

A crime involving digital media, computer technology, or related components.

root cause analysis

The determination of the source or origin of an event, problem, or issue like an incident.

For more information on digital forensics, visit the American Society of Digital Forensics and eDiscovery at *www.asdfed.com.*

The Digital Forensics Team

Most organizations cannot sustain a permanent digital forensics team; such expertise is so rarely called upon that it may be better to collect the data and then outsource the analysis component to a regional expert. The organization can then maintain an arm's-length distance from the case and have additional expertise to call upon if the process ends in court. Even so, the information security group should contain members who are trained to understand and manage the forensics process. If the group receives a report of suspected misuse, either internally or externally, a group member must be familiar with digital forensics procedures to avoid contaminating potential EM.

This expertise can be obtained by sending staff members to a regional or national information security conference with a digital forensics track or to dedicated digital forensics training. The organization should use caution in selecting training for the team or a specialist, as many forensics training programs begin with the analysis process and promote a specific tool rather than teaching management of the process.

Affidavits and Search Warrants

Most investigations begin with an allegation or an indication of an incident. Whether via the help desk, the organization's sexual harassment reporting channels, or a direct report, someone alleges that a worker is performing actions explicitly prohibited by the organization or that make another worker uncomfortable in the workplace. In the InfoSec department, a security analyst notes unusual system or network behavior, as described earlier in this module.

The organization's forensics team or other authorized entity must then obtain permission to examine digital media for potential EM. In law enforcement, the investigating agent would create an **affidavit** requesting permission to search for and confiscate related EM. The affidavit summarizes the facts of the case, items relevant to the investigation, and the location of the event. When an approving authority signs the affidavit or creates a synopsis form based on the document, it becomes a **search warrant**. In corporate environments, the names of these documents may change, and in many cases written authorization may not be needed, but the process should be the same. Formal permission is obtained before an investigation occurs.

Digital Forensics Methodology

In digital forensics, all investigations follow the same basic methodology once permission for search and seizure has been obtained:

1. Identify relevant EM.
2. Acquire (seize) the evidence without alteration or damage.
3. Take steps to ensure that the evidence is verifiably authentic at every step and is unchanged from the time it was seized.
4. Analyze the data without risking modification or unauthorized access.
5. Report the findings to the proper authority.

This process is illustrated in Figure 5-9.

To support the selection and implementation of a methodology for forensics, the organization may want to seek legal advice or consult with local or state law enforcement. Other references that should become part of the organization's library include the following:

- Electronic Crime Scene Investigation: A Guide for First Responders, 2nd Edition, April 2008 (*https://www.ncjrs.gov/pdffiles1/nij/219941.pdf*)
- Searching and Seizing Computers and Obtaining Electronic Evidence in Criminal Investigations (*www.justice.gov/criminal/cybercrime/docs/ssmanual2009.pdf*)

affidavit

Sworn testimony that certain facts are in the possession of an investigating officer and that they warrant the examination of specific items located at a specific place; the affidavit specifies the facts, the items, and the place.

search warrant

Permission to search for evidentiary material at a specified location or to seize items to return to an investigator's lab for examination.

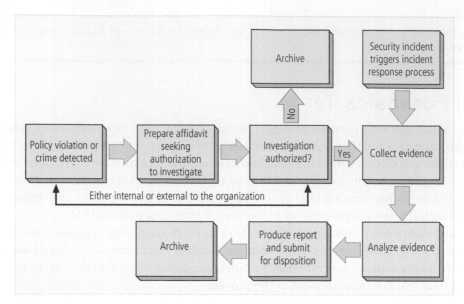

Figure 5-9   The digital forensics process

- Scientific Working Group on Digital Evidence: Published Guidelines and Best Practices (*https://www.swgde.org/documents/published*)
- First Responders Guide to Computer Forensics (*https://resources.sei.cmu.edu/asset_files/Handbook/2005_002_001_14429.pdf*)
- First Responders Guide to Computer Forensics: Advanced Topics (*http://resources.sei.cmu.edu/asset_files/handbook/2005_002_001_14432.pdf*)

Identifying Relevant Items

The affidavit or warrant that authorizes a search must identify what items of evidence can be seized and where they are located. Only EM that fits the description on the authorization can be seized. These seizures often occur under stressful circumstances and strict time constraints, so thorough item descriptions help the process function smoothly and ensure that critical evidence is not overlooked. Thorough descriptions also ensure that items are not wrongly included as EM, which could jeopardize the investigation.

Because users have access to many online server locations via free e-mail archives, FTP servers, and video archives, and could have terabytes of information stored in off-site locations across the Web or on their local systems, investigators must have an idea of what to look for or they may never find it.

Acquiring the Evidence

The principal responsibility of the response team is to acquire the information without altering it. Computers and users modify data constantly. Every time someone opens, modifies, or saves a file, or even opens a directory index to view the available files, the state of the system is changed. Normal system file changes may be difficult to explain to a layperson—for example, a jury member with little or no technical knowledge. A normal system consequence of the search for EM could be portrayed by a defense attorney as harmful to the EM's authenticity or integrity, which could lead a jury to suspect it was planted or is otherwise suspect.

Online Versus Offline Data Acquisition   There are generally two methods of acquiring evidence from a system. The first is the offline model, in which the investigator removes the power source and then uses a utility or special device to make a bit-stream, sector-by-sector copy of the hard drives on the system. By copying the drives at the sector level, you can ensure that any hidden or erased files are also captured. The copied drive then becomes the image that can be used for analysis, and the original drive is stored for safekeeping as true EM or possibly returned to service. For the purposes of this discussion, the term *copy* refers to a drive duplication technique, whereas an *image* is the file that contains all the information from the source drive.

This approach requires the use of sound processes and techniques or read-only hardware known as write-blockers to prevent the accidental overwriting of data on the source drive. The use of these tools also allows investigators to assert that the EM was not modified during acquisition. In another offline approach, the investigator can reboot the system with an alternate operating system or a specialty boot disk like Helix or Knoppix. Still another approach involves specialty hardware that connects directly to a powered-down hard drive and provides direct power and data connections to copy data to an internal drive.

In online or live data acquisition, investigators use network-based tools to acquire a protected copy of the information. The only real difference between the two methods is that the source system cannot be taken offline, and the tools must be sophisticated enough to avoid altering the system during data acquisition. Furthermore, live data acquisition techniques may acquire data that is in movement and in an inconsistent state with some transactions that are only partially recorded. Table 5-4 lists common methods of acquiring data.

The creation of a copy or image can take a substantial amount of time. Users who have made USB copies of their data know how much time it takes to back up several gigabytes of data. When dealing with networked server drives, the data acquisition phase can take many hours to complete, which is one reason investigators prefer to seize drives and take them back to the lab to be imaged or copied.

Other Potential EM   Not all EM is on a suspect's computer hard drive. A technically savvy attacker is more likely to store incriminating evidence on other digital media, such as smartphones, removable drives, CDs, DVDs, flash drives, memory chips or sticks, or other computers accessed across the organization's networks or via the Internet. EM located outside the organization is particularly problematic because the organization cannot legally search systems it doesn't own. However, the simple act of viewing EM on a system leaves clues about the location of the source material, and a skilled investigator can at least provide some assistance to law enforcement when conducting a preliminary investigation. Log files are another source of information about the access and location of EM, as well as what happened and when.

Table 5-4   Summary of Methods Employed to Acquire Forensic Data

Method	Advantages	Disadvantages
Use a dedicated forensic workstation to examine a write-protected hard drive or image of the suspect hard drive.	No concern about the validity of software or hardware on the suspect host. Produces evidence most easily defended in court.	Inconvenient, time-consuming. May result in loss of volatile information.
Boot the system using a verified, write-protected CD or other media with kernel and tools.	Convenient, quick. Evidence is defensible if suspect drives are mounted as read-only.	Assumes that hardware has not been compromised because it is much less likely than compromised software. May result in loss of volatile information.
Build a new system that contains an image of the suspect system and examine it.	Completely replicates operating environment of suspect computer without running the risk of changing its information.	Requires availability of hardware that is identical to that on the suspect computer. May result in los of volatile information.
Examine the system using external media with verified software.	Convenient, quick. Allows examination of volatile information.	If a kernel is compromised, results may be misleading. External media may not contain every necessary utility.
Verify the software on the suspect system, and then use the verified local software to conduct the examination.	Requires minimal preparation. Allows examination of volatile information. Can be performed remotely.	Lack of write protection for suspect drives makes evidence difficult to defend in court. Finding sources for hash values and verifying the local software requires at least several hours, unless Tripwire was used ahead of time.
Examine the suspect system using the software on it, without verifying the software.	Requires least amount of preparation. Allows examination of volatile information. Can be performed remotely.	Least reliable method. This is exactly what cyberattackers are hoping you will do. Often a complete waste of time.

Some evidence isn't electronic or digital. Many suspects have been further incriminated when passwords to their digital media were discovered in the margins of user manuals, in calendars and day planners, and even on notes attached to their systems.

EM Handling   Once the evidence is acquired, both the copy image and the original drive should be handled properly to avoid legal challenges based on authenticity and preservation of integrity. If the organization or law enforcement cannot demonstrate that no one had access to the evidence, they cannot provide strong assurances that it has not been altered. Such access can be physical or logical if the device is connected to a network. Once the evidence is in the possession of investigators, they must track its movement, storage, and access until the resolution of the event or case. This is typically accomplished through **chain of evidence** (also known as **chain of custody**) procedures. The evidence is then tracked wherever it is located. When the evidence changes hands or is stored, the documentation is updated.

Not all evidence-handling requirements are met through the chain of custody process. Digital media must be stored in a specially designed environment that can be secured to prevent unauthorized access. For example, individual items might need to be stored in containers or bags that protect them from electrostatic discharge or magnetic fields. Additional details are provided in the nearby feature on search-and-seizure procedures.

Authenticating the Recovered Evidence   The copy or image is typically transferred to the laboratory for the next stage of authentication. Using cryptographic hash tools, the team must be able to demonstrate that any analyzed copy or image is a true and accurate replica of the source EM. As you will learn in Module 10, the hash tool takes a variable-length file and creates a single numerical value, usually represented in hexadecimal notation, that functions like a digital fingerprint. By hashing the source file and the copy, the investigator can assert that the copy is a true and accurate duplicate of the source.

Analyzing the Data   The most complex part of an investigation is analyzing the copy or image for potential EM. While the process can be performed manually using simple utilities, three industry-leading applications dominate the market for digital forensics:

chain of evidence

The detailed documentation of the collection, storage, transfer, and ownership of evidentiary material from the crime scene through its presentation in court and its eventual disposition.

chain of custody

See *chain of evidence.*

- Guidance Software's EnCase (*www.guidancesoftware.com*)
- AccessData Forensics Tool Kit (FTK, at *www.accessdata.com*)
- OSForensics (*www.osforensics.com*)

Open-source alternatives to these rather expensive tools include Autopsy and The Sleuth Kit, which are available from *www.sleuthkit.org.* Autopsy, shown in Figure 5-10, is a stand-alone GUI interface for The Sleuth Kit, which natively uses a command-line interface. Each tool is designed to support an investigation and assist in the management of the entire case.

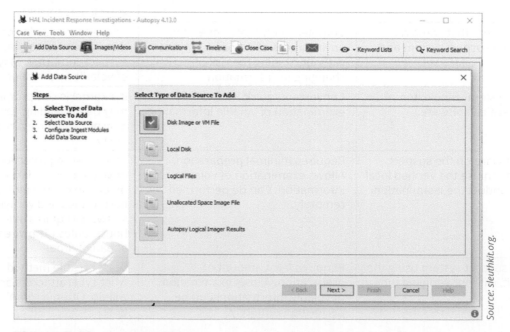

Source: sleuthkit.org.

Figure 5-10   Autopsy software

General Procedures for Evidence Search and Seizure

At the crime scene, a fully qualified and authorized forensics team should be supervised as it completes the following tasks:

1. Secure the crime scene by clearing all unauthorized personnel, delimit the scene with tape or other markers, and post a guard or other person at the entrance.
2. Log in to the crime scene by signing the entry/exit log.
3. Photograph the scene beginning at the doorway and covering the entire room in 360 degrees. Include specific photos of potential evidentiary material.
4. Sketch the layout of the room, including furniture and equipment.
5. Following proper procedure, begin searching for physical, documentary evidence to support your case, including papers, media such as CDs or flash memory devices, or other artifacts. Identify the location of each piece of evidence with a marker or other designator, and cross-reference it on the sketch. Photograph the item in situ to establish its location and state.
6. For each computer, first check for the presence of a screensaver by moving the mouse. Do not click the mouse or use the keyboard. If the screen is active, photograph the screen. Turn off the power on permitted systems. Document each computer by taking a photograph and providing a detailed written description of the manufacturer, model number, serial number, and other details. Using sound processes, remove each disk drive and image it using the appropriate process and equipment. Document each source drive by photographing it and providing a detailed description of the manufacturer, serial number, and other details. Package and secure the image.
7. For each object found, complete the necessary evidence or chain of custody labels.
8. Log out of the crime scene by signing the entry/exit log.
9. Transfer all evidence to the lab for investigation or to a suitable evidence locker for storage. Store and transport all evidence, documentation, and photographic materials in a locked field evidence locker.

Analyze the image:

1. Build the case file by entering background information, including the investigator, suspect, date, time, and system analyzed.
2. Load the image file into the case file. Typical image files have .img, .e01, or .001 extensions.
3. Index the image. Note that some systems use a database of known files to filter out files that are applications, system files, or utilities. The use of this filter improves the quality and effectiveness of the indexing process.
4. Identify, export, and bookmark related text files by searching the index.
5. Identify, export, and bookmark related graphics by reviewing the images folder. If the suspect is accused of viewing child pornography, do not directly view the images. Some things you can't "unsee." Use the database of known images to compare hash values and tag them as suspect.
6. Identify, export, and bookmark other evidence files.
7. Integrate all exported and bookmarked material into the case report.

The first component of the analysis phase is indexing. During indexing, many investigatory tools create an index of all text found on the drive, including data found in deleted files and in file slack space. This indexing is similar to that performed by Google Desktop or Windows Desktop Search tools. The index can then be used by the investigator to locate specific documents or document fragments. While indexing, the tools typically organize files into categories, such as documents, images, and executables. Unfortunately, like imaging, indexing is a time- and processor-consuming operation, and it could take days on images that are larger than 20 gigabytes.

In some cases, the investigator may find password-protected files that the suspect used to protect the data. Several commercial password-cracking tools can assist the investigator. Some are sold in conjunction with forensics tools, like the AccessData Password Recovery Tool Kit.

Reporting the Findings   As investigators examine the analyzed copies or images and identify potential EM, they can tag it and add it to their case files. Once they have found a suitable amount of information, they can summarize their findings with a synopsis of their investigatory procedures in a report and submit it to the appropriate authority. This authority could be law enforcement or management. The suitable amount of EM is a flexible determination made by the investigator. In certain cases, like child pornography, one file is sufficient to warrant turning over the entire investigation to law enforcement. On the other hand, dismissing an employee for the unauthorized sale of intellectual property may require a substantial amount of information to support the organization's assertion. Reporting methods and formats vary among organizations and should be specified in the digital forensics policy. A general guideline is that the report should be sufficiently detailed to allow a similarly trained person to repeat the analysis and achieve similar results.

Evidentiary Procedures

In information security, most operations focus on policies—documents that provide managerial guidance for ongoing implementation and operations. In digital forensics, however, the focus is on procedures. When investigating digital malfeasance or performing root cause analysis, keep in mind that the results and methods of the investigation may end up in criminal or civil court. For example, during a routine systems update, suppose that a technician finds objectionable material on an employee's computer. The employee is fired and promptly sues the organization for wrongful termination, so the investigation of the objectionable material comes under scrutiny by the plaintiff's attorney, who will attempt to cast doubt on the ability of the investigator. While technically not illegal, the presence of the material may have been a clear violation of policy, prompting the dismissal of the employee. However, if an attorney can convince a jury or judge that someone else could have placed the material on the plaintiff's system, the employee could win the case and potentially a large financial settlement.

When the scenario involves criminal issues in which an employee discovers evidence of a crime, the situation changes somewhat. The investigation, analysis, and report are typically performed by law enforcement personnel. However, if the defense attorney can cast reasonable doubt on whether the organization's information security professionals compromised the digital evidentiary material, the employee might win the case. How do you avoid these legal pitfalls? Strong procedures for handling potential evidentiary material can minimize the probability that an organization will lose a legal challenge.

Organizations should develop specific procedures, along with guidance for their effective use. The policy document should specify the following:

- Who may conduct an investigation
- Who may authorize an investigation
- What affidavits and related documents are required
- What search warrants and related documents are required
- What digital media may be seized or taken offline
- What methodology should be followed
- What methods are required for chain of custody or chain of evidence
- What format the final report should take and to whom it should be given

disaster recovery (DR)

An organization's set of planning and preparation efforts for detecting, reacting to, and recovering from a disaster.

disaster recovery planning (DRP)

The actions taken by senior management to develop and implement the DR policy, plan, and recovery teams.

disaster recovery plan (DR plan)

The documented product of disaster recovery planning; a plan that shows the organization's intended efforts in the event of a disaster.

The policy document should be supported by a procedures manual and developed based on the documents discussed earlier, along with guidance from law enforcement or consultants. By creating and using these policies and procedures, an organization can best protect itself from challenges by employees who have been subject to unfavorable action from an investigation.

Disaster Recovery

The next vital part of CP focuses on **disaster recovery (DR)**. **Disaster recovery planning (DRP)** entails the preparation for and recovery from a disaster, whether natural or human-made. In some cases, incidents detected by the IR team may escalate to the level of disaster, and the IR plan may no longer be able to handle the effective and efficient recovery from the loss. For example, if a malicious program evades containment actions and infects and disables many or most of an organization's systems and their ability to function, the **disaster recovery plan (DR plan)** is activated. Sometimes, events are by their nature immediately classified as disasters, such as an extensive fire, flood, damaging storm, or earthquake.

As you learned earlier in this module, the CP team creates the DR planning team (DRPT). The DRPT in turn organizes and prepares the DR response teams (DRRTs) to implement the DR plan in the event of a disaster. In reality, there may be many different DRRTs, each tasked with a different aspect of recovery. InfoSec staff most likely will not lead these teams but will support their efforts, ensuring that no new vulnerabilities arise during the recovery process. The various DRRTs will have multiple responsibilities in the recovery of the primary site and the reestablishment of operations:

- Recover information assets that are salvageable from the primary facility after the disaster.
- Purchase or otherwise acquire replacement information assets from appropriate sources.
- Reestablish functional information assets at the primary site if possible or at a new primary site, if necessary.

Some common DRRTs include the following:

- *DR management team*—Coordinates the on-site efforts of all other DRRTs.
- *Communications team*—With representatives from the public relations and legal departments, provides feedback to anyone who wants additional information about the organization's efforts in recovering from the disaster.
- *Computer recovery (hardware) team*—Works to recover any physical computing assets that might be usable after the disaster and acquire replacement assets for resumption of operations.
- *Systems recovery (OS) team*—Works to recover operating systems and may contain one or more specialists on each operating system that the organization employs; may be combined with the applications recovery team as a "software recovery team" or with the hardware team as a "systems recovery team" or "computer recovery team."
- *Network recovery team*—Works to determine the extent of damage to the network wiring and hardware (hubs, switches, and routers) as well as to Internet and intranet connectivity.
- *Storage recovery team*—Works with the other teams to recover storage-related information assets; may be subsumed into other hardware and software teams.
- *Applications recovery team*—Works to recover critical applications.
- *Data management team*—Works on data restoration and recovery, whether from on-site, off-site, or online transactional data.
- *Vendor contact team*—Works with suppliers and vendors to replace damaged or destroyed materials, equipment, or services, as determined by the other teams.
- *Damage assessment and salvage team*—Specialized individuals who provide initial assessments of the extent of damage to materials, inventory, equipment, and systems on-site.
- *Business interface team*—Works with the remainder of the organization to assist in the recovery of nontechnology functions.
- *Logistics team*—Responsible for providing any needed supplies, space, materials, food, services, or facilities at the primary site; may be combined with the vendor contact team.
- *Other teams as needed.*

The Disaster Recovery Process

In general, a disaster has occurred when either of two criteria is met: (1) The organization is unable to contain or control the impact of an incident, or (2) the level of damage or destruction from an incident is so severe that the organization cannot quickly recover from it. The distinction between an incident and a disaster may be subtle. The DRPT must document in the DR plan whether a particular event is classified as an incident or a disaster. This determination is critical because it determines which plan is activated. The key role of the DR plan is to prepare to reestablish operations at the organization's primary location after a disaster or to establish operations at a new location if the primary site is no longer viable.

You learned earlier in this module about the CP process recommended by NIST, which uses seven steps. In the broader context of organizational CP, these steps form the overall CP process. These steps are adapted and applied here within the narrower context of the DRP process, resulting in an eight-step DR process.

1. *Organize the DR team*—The initial assignments to the DR team, including the team lead, will most likely be performed by the CPMT; however, additional personnel may need to be assigned to the team as the specifics of the DR policy and plan are developed, and as individual roles and responsibilities are defined and assigned.
2. *Develop the DR planning policy statement*—A formal department or agency policy provides the authority and guidance necessary to develop an effective contingency plan.
3. *Review the BIA*—The BIA was prepared to help identify and prioritize critical information and its host systems. A review of what was discovered is an important step in the process.
4. *Identify preventive controls*—Measures taken to reduce the effects of business and system disruptions can increase information availability and reduce contingency life cycle costs.
5. *Create DR strategies*—Thorough recovery strategies ensure that the system can be recovered quickly and effectively following a disruption.
6. *Develop the DR plan document*—The plan should contain detailed guidance and procedures for restoring a damaged system.
7. *Ensure DR plan testing, training, and exercises*—Testing the plan identifies planning gaps, whereas training prepares recovery personnel for plan activation; both activities improve plan effectiveness and overall agency preparedness.
8. *Ensure DR plan maintenance*—The plan should be a living document that is updated regularly to remain current with system enhancements.

Disaster Recovery Policy

As noted in step 2 of the preceding list, the DR team, led by the manager designated as the DR team leader, begins with the development of the **DR policy** soon after the team is formed. The policy presents an overview of the organization's philosophy on the conduct of DR operations and serves as the guide for the development of the DR plan. The DR policy itself may have been created by the organization's CP team and handed down to the DR team leader. Alternatively, the DR team may be assigned the role of developing the DR policy. In either case, the DR policy contains the following key elements:

- *Purpose*—The purpose of the DR program is to provide direction and guidance for all DR operations. In addition, the program provides for the development and support of the DR plan. In everyday practice, those responsible for the program must also work to emphasize the importance of creating and maintaining effective DR functions. As with any major enterprise-wide policy effort, it is important for the DR program to begin with a clear statement of executive vision.
- *Scope*—This section of the policy identifies the organizational units and groups of employees to which the policy applies. This clarification is important if the organization is geographically dispersed or is creating different policies for different organizational units.
- *Roles and responsibilities*—This section of the policy identifies the roles and responsibilities of the key players in the DR operation. It can include a delineation of the responsibilities of executive management down to individual employees. Some sections of the DR policy may be duplicated from the organization's overall CP policy. In smaller organizations, this redundancy can be eliminated, as many of the functions are performed by the same group.
- *Resource requirements*—An organization can allocate specific resources to the development of DR plans here. While this may include directives for individuals, it can be separated from the previous section for emphasis and clarity.
- *Training requirements*—This section defines and highlights training requirements for units within the organization and the various categories of employees.
- *Exercise and testing schedules*—This section stipulates the testing intervals of the DR plan as well as the type of testing and the individuals involved.
- *Plan maintenance schedule*—This section states the required review and update intervals of the plan and identifies who is involved in the review. It is not necessary for the entire DR team to be involved, but the review can be combined with a periodic test of the DR plan as long as the resulting discussion includes areas for improving the plan.
- *Special considerations*—This section includes such items as information storage and maintenance.

DR policy

The policy document that guides the development and implementation of DR plans and the formulation and performance of DR teams.

Disaster Classification

A DR plan can classify disasters in a number of ways. The most common method of **disaster classification** is to evaluate the amount of damage that could potentially be caused by the disaster—usually on a scale of Moderate, Severe, or Critical, for example. Disasters could also be classified by their origin, such as natural or human-made. Most incidents fall into the human-made category (like hacker intrusions or malware), but some could be tied to natural origins, such as fires or floods. Many disasters begin as incidents, and only when they reach a specified threshold are they escalated from incident to disaster. A denial-of-service attack that affects a single system for a short time may be an incident, but when it escalates to affect an entire organization for a much longer period of time, it may be reclassified as a disaster. Who makes this classification? It is most commonly done by a senior IT or InfoSec manager working closely with the CSIRT and DR team leads. When the CSIRT reports that an incident or collection of incidents has begun to exceed their capability to respond, they may request that the incident(s) be reclassified as a disaster in order for the organization to better handle the expected damage or loss.

Disasters may also be classified by their rate of occurrence. **Slow-onset disasters** build up gradually over time before they can degrade the operations of the organization to withstand their effect. Hazards that cause these disaster conditions typically include natural causes such as droughts, famines, environmental degradation, desertification, deforestation, and pest infestation, as well as human-made causes such as malware, hackers, disgruntled employees, and service provider issues. The series of U.S. hurricanes during the fall of 2017 were an example of slow-onset disasters—effective weather predictions enabled much of the southeast United States to prepare for the hurricanes' potential impacts days before the storms made landfall. Similarly, the COVID-19 pandemic of 2020 was an example of a slow-onset disaster, as its progression was tracked by global media from the start.

Usually, disasters that strike quickly are instantly classified as disasters. These disasters are commonly referred to as **rapid-onset disasters**, as they occur suddenly with little warning, taking people's lives and destroying the means of production. Rapid-onset disasters may be caused by natural effects like earthquakes, floods, storm winds, tornadoes, and mud flows, or by human-made effects like massively distributed denial-of-service attacks; acts of terrorism, including cyberterrorism or hacktivism; and acts of war. Interestingly, fire is an example of an incident that can either escalate to disaster or begin as one (in the event of an explosion, for example). Fire can be categorized as a natural disaster when caused by a lightning strike or as human-made when it is the result of arson or an accident.

Table 5-5 presents a list of natural disasters, their effects, and recommendations for mitigation.

Disaster Classification (sidebar)

disaster classification

The process of examining an adverse event or incident and determining whether it constitutes an actual disaster.

slow-onset disasters

Disasters that occur over time and gradually degrade the capacity of an organization to withstand their effects.

rapid-onset disasters

Disasters that occur suddenly, with little warning, taking people's lives and destroying the means of production.

Planning to Recover

To plan for disasters, the CPMT engages in scenario development and impact analysis, along the way categorizing the level of threat that each potential disaster poses. When generating a DR scenario, start with the most important asset: people. Do you have the human resources with the appropriate organizational knowledge to restore business operations? Organizations must cross-train their employees to ensure that operations and a sense of normalcy can be restored. In addition, the DR plan must be tested regularly so that the DR team can lead the recovery effort quickly and efficiently. Key elements that the CPMT must build into the DR plan include the following:

1. *Clear delegation of roles and responsibilities*—Everyone assigned to the DR team should be aware of his or her duties during a disaster. Some team members may be responsible for coordinating with local services, such as fire, police, and medical personnel. Some may be responsible for the evacuation of company personnel, if required. Others may be assigned to simply pack up and leave.

2. *Execution of the alert roster and notification of key personnel*—These notifications may extend outside the organization to include the fire, police, or medical services mentioned earlier, as well as insurance agencies, disaster teams such as those of the Red Cross, and management teams.

Table 5-5   Natural Disasters and Their Effects on Information Systems

Natural Disaster	Effects and Mitigation
Fire	Damages the building housing the computing equipment that constitutes all or part of the information system. Also encompasses smoke damage from the fire and water damage from sprinkler systems or firefighters. Can usually be mitigated with fire casualty insurance or business interruption insurance.
Flood	Can cause direct damage to all or part of the information system or to the building that houses all or part of the information system. May also disrupt operations by interrupting access to the buildings that house all or part of the information system. Can sometimes be mitigated with flood insurance or business interruption insurance.
Earthquake	Can cause direct damage to all or part of the information system or, more often, to the building that houses it. May also disrupt operations by interrupting access to the buildings that house all or part of the information system. Can sometimes be mitigated with specific casualty insurance or business interruption insurance, but is usually a specific and separate policy.
Lightning	Can directly damage all or part of the information system or its power distribution components. Can also cause fires or other damage to the building that houses all or part of the information system. May also disrupt operations by interrupting access to the buildings that house all or part of the information system as well as the routine delivery of electrical power. Can usually be mitigated with multipurpose casualty insurance or business interruption insurance.
Landslide or mudslide	Can damage all or part of the information system or, more likely, the building that houses it. May also disrupt operations by interrupting access to the buildings that house all or part of the information system as well as the routine delivery of electrical power. Can sometimes be mitigated with casualty insurance or business interruption insurance.
Tornado or severe windstorm	Can directly damage all or part of the information system or, more likely, the building that houses it. May also disrupt operations by interrupting access to the buildings that house all or part of the information system as well as the routine delivery of electrical power. Can sometimes be mitigated with casualty insurance or business interruption insurance.
Hurricane or typhoon	Can directly damage all or part of the information system or, more likely, the building that houses it. Organizations located in coastal or low-lying areas may experience flooding. May also disrupt operations by interrupting access to the buildings that house all or part of the information system as well as the routine delivery of electrical power. Can sometimes be mitigated with casualty insurance or business interruption insurance.
Tsunami	Can directly damage all or part of the information system or, more likely, the building that houses it. Organizations located in coastal areas may experience tsunamis. May also cause disruption to operations by interrupting access or electrical power to the buildings that house all or part of the information system. Can sometimes be mitigated with casualty insurance or business interruption insurance.
Electrostatic discharge (ESD)	Can be costly or dangerous when it ignites flammable mixtures and damages costly electronic components. Static electricity can draw dust into clean-room environments or cause products to stick together. The cost of servicing ESD-damaged electronic devices and interruptions can range from a few cents to millions of dollars for critical systems. Loss of production time in information processing due to the effects of ESD is significant. While not usually viewed as a threat, ESD can disrupt information systems and is not usually an insurable loss unless covered by business interruption insurance. ESD can be mitigated with special static discharge equipment and by managing HVAC temperature and humidity levels.
Dust contamination	Can shorten the life of information systems or cause unplanned downtime. Can usually be mitigated with an effective HVAC filtration system and simple procedures, such as efficient housekeeping, placing tacky floor mats at entrances, and prohibiting the use of paper and cardboard in the data center.

3. *Clear establishment of priorities*—During a disaster response, the first priority is always the preservation of human life. Data and systems protection is subordinate when the disaster threatens the lives, health, or welfare of the employees or members of the community. Only after all employees and neighbors have been safeguarded can the DR team attend to protecting other organizational assets.

4. *Procedures for documentation of the disaster*—Just as in an incident response, the disaster must be carefully recorded from the onset. This documentation is used later to determine how and why the disaster occurred.

5. *Action steps to mitigate the impact of the disaster on the operations of the organization*—The DR plan should specify the responsibilities of each DR team member, such as the evacuation of physical assets or making sure that all systems are securely shut down to prevent further loss of data.

6. *Alternative implementations for the various system components, should primary versions be unavailable*— These components include standby equipment that is either purchased, leased, or under contract with a DR service agency. Developing systems with excess capacity, fault tolerance, autorecovery, and fail-safe features facilitates a quick recovery. Something as simple as using Dynamic Host Control Protocol (DHCP) to assign network addresses instead of using static addresses can allow systems to regain connectivity quickly and easily without technical support. Networks should support dynamic reconfiguration; restoration of network connectivity should be planned. Data recovery requires effective backup strategies as well as flexible hardware configurations. System management should be a top priority. All solutions should be tightly integrated and developed in a strategic plan to provide continuity. Piecemeal construction can result in a disaster after the disaster, as incompatible systems are unexpectedly thrust together.

As part of DR plan readiness, each employee should have two sets of emergency information in his or her possession at all times. The first is personal emergency information—the person to notify in case of an emergency (next of kin), medical conditions, and a form of identification. The second is a set of instructions on what to do in the event of an emergency. This snapshot of the DR plan should contain a contact number or hotline for calling the organization during an emergency, emergency services numbers (fire, police, medical), evacuation and assembly locations (e.g., storm shelters), the name and number of the DR coordinator, and any other needed information. An example of an emergency ID card is shown in Figure 5-11.

Responding to the Disaster

When a disaster strikes, actual events can at times overwhelm even the best of DR plans. To be prepared, the CPMT should incorporate a degree of flexibility into the plan. If the physical facilities are intact, the DR team should begin the restoration of systems and data to work toward full operational capability. If the organization's facilities are destroyed, alternative actions must be taken until new facilities can be acquired. When a disaster threatens the viability of an organization at the primary site, the DR process becomes a business continuity process, which is described next.

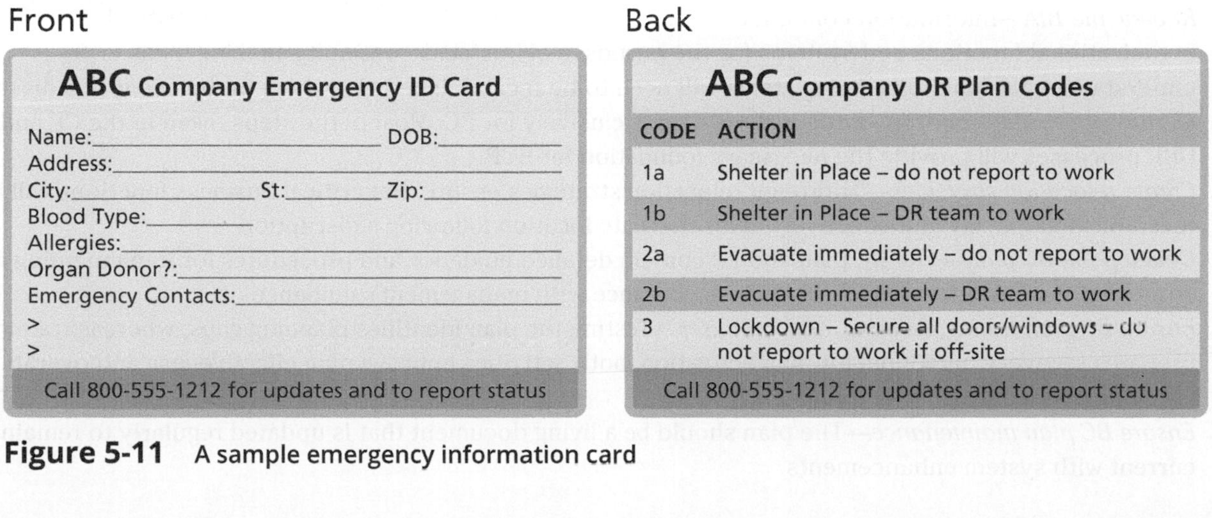

Front

ABC Company Emergency ID Card

Name:_____ DOB:_____
Address:_____
City:_____ St:_____ Zip:_____
Blood Type:_____
Allergies:_____
Organ Donor?:_____
Emergency Contacts:_____
 >
 >

Call 800-555-1212 for updates and to report status

Back

ABC Company DR Plan Codes

CODE	ACTION
1a	Shelter in Place – do not report to work
1b	Shelter in Place – DR team to work
2a	Evacuate immediately – do not report to work
2b	Evacuate immediately – DR team to work
3	Lockdown – Secure all doors/windows – do not report to work if off-site

Call 800-555-1212 for updates and to report status

Figure 5-11   A sample emergency information card

business continuity (BC)

An organization's set of efforts to ensure its long-term viability when a disaster precludes normal operations at the primary site; typically includes temporarily establishing critical operations at an alternate site until operations can be resumed at the primary site or a new permanent site.

business continuity planning (BCP)

The actions taken by senior management to develop and implement the BC policy, plan, and continuity teams.

BC plan

The documented product of business continuity planning; a plan that shows the organization's intended efforts to continue critical functions when operations at the primary site are not feasible.

Business Continuity

Sometimes, disasters have such a profound effect on the organization that it cannot continue operations at its primary site until it fully completes all DR efforts. To deal with such events, the organization implements its **business continuity (BC)** strategies.

Business continuity planning (BCP) ensures that critical business functions can continue if a disaster occurs. Like the DR plan, the BC plan involves teams from across the organization, including IT and business operations, and is supported by InfoSec. The **BC plan** is usually managed by the CEO or COO of the organization, and is activated and executed concurrently with the DR plan when the disaster is major or long-term and requires fuller and more complex restoration of information and IT resources. If a disaster renders the current business location unusable, there must be a plan to allow the business to continue to function. While the BC plan reestablishes critical business functions at an alternate site, the DR plan focuses on reestablishment of the technical infrastructure and business operations at the primary site. Not every business needs a BC plan or BC facilities. Some small companies or fiscally sound organizations may be able simply to cease operations until the primary facilities are restored. Manufacturing and retail organizations, however, depend on continued operations for revenue. Thus, these entities must have a BC plan in place if they need to relocate operations quickly with minimal loss of revenue.

BC is an element of CP, and it is best accomplished using a repeatable process or methodology. NIST's SP 800-34, Rev. 1, "Contingency Planning Guide for Federal Information Systems,"[21] includes guidance for planning for incidents, disasters, and situations that call for BC. The approach used in that document has been adapted for BC use here.

The first step in all contingency efforts is the development of policy; the next step is planning. In some organizations, these steps are considered concurrent operations in which development of policy is a function of planning; in other organizations, policy comes before planning and is a separate process. In this text, the BC policy is developed prior to the BC plan, and both are developed as part of BC planning. The same seven-step approach that NIST recommends for CP can be adapted to an eight-step model that can be used to develop and maintain a viable BC program. Those steps are as follows:

1. *Form the BC team*—As was done with the DR planning process, the initial assignments to the BC team, including the team lead, will most likely be performed by the CPMT; however, additional personnel may need to be assigned to the team as the specifics of the BC policy and plan are developed, and their individual roles and responsibilities will have to be defined and assigned.
2. *Develop the BC planning policy statement*—A formal organizational policy provides the authority and guidance necessary to develop an effective continuity plan. As with any enterprise-wide policy process, it is important to begin with the executive vision.
3. *Review the BIA*—Information contained within the BIA can help identify and prioritize critical organizational functions and systems for the purposes of business continuity, making it easier to understand what functions and systems will need to be reestablished elsewhere in the event of a disaster.
4. *Identify preventive controls*—Little is done here exclusively for BC. Most of the steps taken in the CP and DRP processes will provide the necessary foundation for BCP.
5. *Create relocation strategies*—Thorough relocation strategies ensure that critical business functions will be reestablished quickly and effectively at an alternate location following a disruption.
6. *Develop the BC plan*—The BC plan should contain detailed guidance and procedures for implementing BC strategies at predetermined locations in accordance with management's guidance.
7. *Ensure BC plan testing, training, and exercises*—Testing the plan identifies planning gaps, whereas training prepares recovery personnel for plan activation; both activities improve plan effectiveness and overall agency preparedness.
8. *Ensure BC plan maintenance*—The plan should be a living document that is updated regularly to remain current with system enhancements.

Business Continuity Policy

BCP begins with the development of the **BC policy**, which reflects the organization's philosophy on the conduct of BC operations and serves as the guiding document for the development of BCP. The BC team leader might receive the BC policy from the CP team or might guide the BC team in developing one. The BC policy contains the following key sections:

- *Purpose*—The purpose of the BC program is to provide the necessary planning and coordination to help relocate critical business functions should a disaster prohibit continued operations at the primary site.
- *Scope*—This section identifies the organizational units and groups of employees to which the policy applies. This is especially useful in organizations that are geographically dispersed or that are creating different policies for different organizational units.
- *Roles and responsibilities*—This section identifies the roles and responsibilities of key players in the BC operation, from executive management down to individual employees. In some cases, sections may be duplicated from the organization's overall CP policy. In smaller organizations, this redundancy can be eliminated because many of the functions are performed by the same group of individuals.
- *Resource requirements*—Organizations can allocate specific resources to the development of BC plans. Although this section may include directives for individual team members, it can be separated from the roles and responsibilities section for emphasis and clarity.
- *Training requirements*—This section specifies the training requirements for the various employee groups.
- *Exercise and testing schedules*—This section stipulates the frequency of BC plan testing and can include both the type of exercise or testing and the individuals involved.
- *Plan maintenance schedule*—This section specifies the procedures and frequency of BC plan reviews and identifies the personnel who will be involved in the review. It is not necessary for the entire BC team to be involved; the review can be combined with a periodic test of the BC plan (as in a talk-through) as long as the resulting discussion includes areas for plan improvement.
- *Special considerations*—In extreme situations, the DR and BC plans overlap, as described earlier. Thus, this section provides an overview of the organization's information storage and retrieval plans. While the specifics do not have to be elaborated on in this document, the plan should at least identify where more detailed documentation is kept, which individuals are responsible, and any other information needed to implement the strategy.

You may have noticed that this structure is virtually identical to that of the disaster recovery policy and plans. The processes are generally the same, with minor differences in focus and implementation.

The identification of critical business functions and the resources to support them is the cornerstone of the BC plan. When a disaster strikes, these functions are the first to be reestablished at the alternate site. The CP team needs to appoint a group of individuals to evaluate and compare the various alternatives and to recommend which strategy should be selected and implemented. The strategy selected usually involves an off-site facility, which should be inspected, configured, secured, and tested on a periodic basis. The selection should be reviewed periodically to determine whether a better alternative has emerged or whether the organization needs a different solution.

Many organizations with operations in New York City had their BC efforts (or lack thereof) tested critically on September 11, 2001. Similarly, organizations on the U.S. Gulf Coast had their BC plan effectiveness tested during the aftermath of Hurricane Katrina in 2005 and by the series of hurricanes that affected Texas and Florida in 2017.

Business Resumption

Because the DR and BC plans are closely related, most organizations merge the two functions into a single function called **business resumption planning (BRP)**. Such a comprehensive plan must be able to support the reestablishment of operations at two different locations—one immediately at an alternate site and one eventually back at the primary site. Therefore, although a single planning team can develop the BR plan, execution of the plan requires separate execution teams.

The planning process for the BR plan should be tied to, but distinct from, the IR plan. As noted earlier in the module, an incident may escalate into a disaster when it grows dramatically in scope and intensity. It is important that the three planning development processes be so tightly integrated that the reaction teams can easily make the transition from incident response to disaster recovery and BCP.

Continuity Strategies

The CPMT can choose from several strategies in its BC planning. The determining factor is usually cost. Note that these strategies are chosen from a spectrum of options rather than from the absolute specifications that follow. Also, many organizations now use cloud-based production systems that would supplement, if not preclude, the following approaches.

In general, two categories of strategies are used in BC: exclusive use and shared use. Exclusive-use facilities are reserved for the sole use of the leasing organization, and shared-use facilities represent contractual agreements between parties to share or support each other during a BC event. Three general exclusive-use strategies are available:

- *Hot site*—A hot site is a fully configured computing facility that includes all services, communications links, and physical plant operations. It duplicates computing resources, peripherals, phone systems, applications, and workstations. Essentially, this duplicate facility needs only the latest data backups and the personnel to function. If the organization uses an adequate data service, a hot site can be fully functional within minutes. Not surprisingly, a hot site is the most expensive alternative. Disadvantages include the need to provide maintenance for all the systems and equipment at the hot site, as well as physical and information security. However, if the organization requires a 24/7 capability for near real-time recovery, the hot site is the optimal strategy.
- *Warm site*—A warm site provides many of the same services and options as the hot site, but typically software applications are not included or are not installed and configured. A warm site frequently includes computing equipment and peripherals with servers but not client workstations. Overall, it offers many of the advantages of a hot site at a lower cost. The disadvantage is that several hours of preparation—perhaps days—are required to make a warm site fully functional.

hot site

A fully configured BC facility that includes all computing services, communications links, and physical plant operations.

warm site

A BC facility that provides many of the same services and options as a hot site, but typically without installed and configured software applications.

cold site

A BC facility that provides only rudimentary services, with no computer hardware or peripherals.

timeshare

A continuity strategy in which an organization co-leases facilities with a business partner or sister organization, which allows the organization to have a BC option while reducing its overall costs.

service bureau

A BC strategy in which an organization contracts with a service agency to provide a facility for a fee.

- *Cold site*—A cold site provides only rudimentary services and facilities. No computer hardware or peripherals are provided. All communications services must be installed after the site is occupied. A cold site is an empty room with standard heating, air conditioning, and electrical service. Everything else is an added-cost option. Despite these disadvantages, a cold site may be better than nothing. Its primary advantage is its low cost. The most useful feature of this approach is that it ensures an organization has floor space if a widespread disaster strikes, but some organizations are prepared to struggle to lease new space rather than pay maintenance fees on a cold site.

Likewise, there are three strategies in which an organization can gain shared use of a facility when needed for contingency options:

- *Timeshare*—A timeshare operates like one of the three sites described previously but is leased in conjunction with a business partner or sister organization. It allows the organization to provide a DR/BC option while reducing its overall costs. The primary disadvantage is the possibility that more than one timeshare participant will need the facility simultaneously. Other disadvantages include the need to stock the facility with equipment and data from all organizations involved, the complexity of negotiating the timeshare with sharing organizations, and the possibility that one or more parties might exit the agreement or sublease their options. Operating under a timeshare is much like agreeing to co-lease an apartment with a group of friends. One can only hope that the organizations remain on amicable terms, as they all could potentially gain physical access to each other's data.
- *Service bureau*—A service bureau is an agency that provides a service for a fee. In the case of DR/BC planning, this service is the provision of physical facilities in the event of a disaster. Such agencies also frequently provide off-site data storage

for a fee. Contracts with service bureaus can specify exactly what the organization needs under what circumstances. A service agreement usually guarantees space when needed; the service bureau must acquire additional space in the event of a widespread disaster. In this sense, it resembles the rental-car provision in a car insurance policy. The disadvantage is that service contracts must be renegotiated periodically and rates can change. The contracts can also be quite expensive.

- *Mutual agreement*—A mutual agreement is a contract between two organizations in which each party agrees to assist the other in the event of a disaster. It stipulates that an organization is obligated to provide necessary facilities, resources, and services until the receiving organization is able to recover from the disaster. This arrangement can be a lot like moving in with relatives or friends—it does not take long for an organization to wear out its welcome.

Many organizations balk at the idea of having to fund duplicate services and resources, even in the short term. Still, mutual agreements between divisions of the same parent company, between subordinate and senior organizations, or between business partners may be a cost-effective solution when both parties to the agreement have a mutual interest in the other's continued operations and both have similar capabilities and capacities.

In addition to the preceding basic strategies, there are specialized alternatives, such as the following:

- A **rolling mobile site** is configured in the payload area of a tractor-trailer.
- Externally stored resources, such as a rental storage area that contains duplicate or older equipment, can be positioned to provide backup systems. These alternatives are similar to the Prepositioning of Material Configured to Unit Sets (POMCUS) sites of the Cold War era, in which caches of materials to be used in the event of an emergency or war were stored outside normal operations areas.
- An organization might arrange with a prefabricated building contractor to provide immediate, temporary facilities (mobile offices) on-site in the event of a disaster.
- In recent years, the option to use cloud-based provisioning has emerged. These types of services can be both a potential continuity option for production systems and a mechanism to manage recovery from disrupted operations.

Timing and Sequence of CP Elements

As indicated earlier, the IR plan focuses on immediate response, but if the incident escalates into a disaster, the IR plan may give way to the DR plan and BC plan, as illustrated in Figure 5-12. The DR plan typically focuses on restoring systems after disasters occur and is therefore closely associated with the BC plan. The BC plan occurs concurrently with the DR plan when the damage is major or long-term, and when the plan requires more than simple restoration of information and information resources, as illustrated in Figure 5-13.

mutual agreement

A BC strategy in which two organizations sign a contract to assist the other in a disaster by providing BC facilities, resources, and services until the organization in need can recover from the disaster.

rolling mobile site

A BC strategy that involves contracting with an organization to provide specialized facilities configured in the payload area of a tractor-trailer.

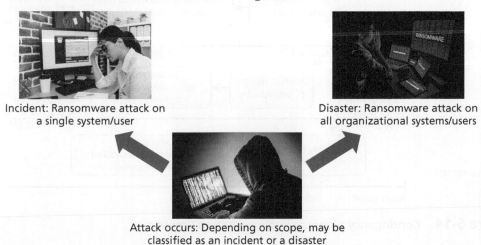

Incident: Ransomware attack on a single system/user

Disaster: Ransomware attack on all organizational systems/users

Attack occurs: Depending on scope, may be classified as an incident or a disaster

Source: This figure has multiple sources. Top left: PR Image Factory/Shutterstock.com. Top right: Zephyr_p/ Shutterstock.com. Bottom center: poylock19/Shutterstock. com.

Figure 5-12   Incident response and disaster recovery

Organizational disaster occurs

Staff implements DR/BC plans;
BC plan relocates organization to...

DR plan works to
reestablish
operations at

Primary site (or new permanent site)

Alternate site

Source: This figure has multiple sources. Top left: sandyman/Shutterstock. com. Bottom left: Konstantin L/Shutterstock.com. Top right: Monkey Business Images/Shutterstock.com. Bottom right: Sylvie Bouchard/Shutterstock.com.

Figure 5-13   Disaster recovery and business continuity planning

Some experts argue that the three planning components (IR, DR, and BC) of CP are so closely linked that they are indistinguishable. Actually, each has a distinct place, role, and planning requirement. Furthermore, each component comes into play at a specific time in the life of an incident. Figure 5-14 illustrates this sequence and shows the overlap that may occur.

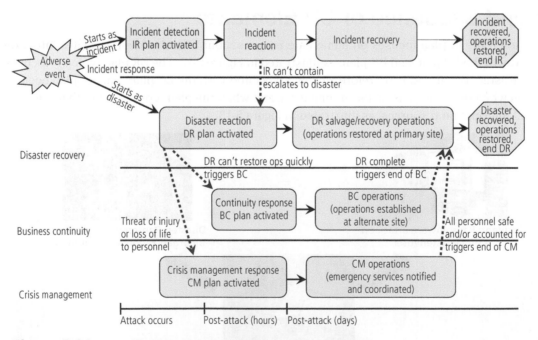

Figure 5-14   Contingency planning implementation timeline

Crisis Management

Another process that many organizations plan for separately is **crisis management (CM)**, which focuses more on the effects that a disaster has on people than its effects on other assets. While some organizations include crisis management as a subset of the DR plan, the protection of human life and the organization's image are such high priorities that crisis management may deserve its own committee, policy, and plan. Thus, the organization should form a crisis management planning team (CMPT), which then organizes a crisis management response team (CMRT). The appropriate DRRT works closely with the CMRT to ensure complete and timely communication during a disaster. According to Gartner Research, the crisis management team is responsible for managing the event from an enterprise perspective and performs the following roles:

- Supporting personnel and their loved ones during the crisis
- Keeping the public informed about the event and the actions being taken to ensure the recovery of personnel and the enterprise
- Communicating with major customers, suppliers, partners, regulatory agencies, industry organizations, the media, and other interested parties[22]

The CMPT should establish a base of operations or command center near the site of the disaster as soon as possible. The CMPT should include individuals from all functional areas of the organization in order to facilitate communications and cooperation. The CMPT is charged with three primary responsibilities:

1. *Verifying personnel status*—Everyone must be accounted for, including individuals who are on vacations, leaves of absence, and business trips.
2. *Activating the alert roster*—Alert rosters and general personnel phone lists are used to notify individuals whose assistance may be needed or simply to tell employees not to report to work until the disaster is over.
3. *Coordinating with emergency services*—If someone is injured or killed during a disaster, the CM response team will work closely with fire officials, police, medical response units, and the Red Cross to provide appropriate services to all affected parties as quickly as possible.

The CMPT should plan an approach for releasing information in the event of a disaster and should perhaps even have boilerplate scripts prepared for press releases. Advice from Lanny Davis, former counselor to President Bill Clinton, is relevant here. When beset by damaging events, heed the subtitle to Davis's memoir: *Truth to Tell: Tell It Early, Tell It All, Tell It Yourself.*[23]

As with IR, DR, and BC, if CM is organized and conducted as a separate entity, it should have a **CM policy** and a **CM plan**. The methodologies for CM policies and **CM planning (CMP)** can follow the same basic models as DR policies and plans, but they should include additional content focused on personnel safety (such as shelter areas), evacuation plans, contact information for emergency services, and the like.

crisis management (CM)

An organization's set of planning and preparation efforts for dealing with potential human injury, emotional trauma, or loss of life as a result of a disaster.

crisis management policy (CM policy)

The policy document that guides the development and implementation of CM plans and the formulation and performance of CM teams.

crisis management plan (CM plan)

The documented product of crisis management planning; a plan that shows the organization's intended efforts to protect its personnel and respond to safety threats.

crisis management planning (CMP)

The actions taken by senior management to develop and implement the CM policy, plan, and response teams.

desk check

The CP testing strategy in which copies of the appropriate plans are distributed to all individuals who will be assigned roles during an actual incident or disaster; each individual reviews the plan and validates its components.

Testing Contingency Plans

Very few plans are executable as initially written; instead, they must be tested to identify vulnerabilities, faults, and inefficient processes. Once problems are identified during the testing process, improvements can be made, and the resulting plan can be relied on in times of need. The following strategies can be used to test contingency plans:

- *Desk check*—The simplest kind of validation involves distributing copies of the appropriate plans to all individuals who will be assigned roles during an actual incident or disaster. Each of these individuals performs a desk check by reviewing the plan and creating a list of correct and incorrect components. While not a true

structured walk-through

The CP testing strategy in which all involved individuals walk through a site and discuss the steps they would take during an actual CP event; can also be conducted as a conference room talk-through.

talk-through

A form of structured walk-through in which individuals meet in a conference room and discuss a CP plan rather than walking around the organization.

simulation

The CP testing strategy in which the organization conducts a role-playing exercise as if an actual incident or disaster had occurred. The CP team is presented with a scenario in which all members must specify how they would react and communicate their efforts.

full-interruption testing

The CP testing strategy in which all team members follow each IR/DR/BC procedure, including those for interruption of service, restoration of data from backups, and notification of appropriate individuals.

test, this strategy is a good way to review the perceived feasibility and effectiveness of the plan and ensure at least a nominal update of the policies and plans.

- *Structured walk-through*—In a structured walk-through, all involved individuals walk through the steps they would take during an actual incident or disaster. This exercise can consist of an on-site walk-through, in which everyone discusses his or her actions at each particular location and juncture, or it may be more of a **talk-through**, in which all involved individuals sit around a conference table and discuss their responsibilities as the incident unfolds.

- *Simulation*—In a simulation, the organization creates a role-playing exercise in which the CP team is presented with a scenario of an actual incident or disaster and expected to react as if it had occurred. The simulation usually involves performing the communications that should occur and specifying the required physical tasks, but it stops short of performing the actual tasks required, such as installing the backup data or disconnecting a communications circuit. The major difference between a walk-through and a simulation is that in simulations, the discussion is driven by a scenario, whereas walk-throughs focus on simply discussing the plan in the absence of any particular incident or disaster. Simulations tend to be much more structured, with time limits, planned AARs, and moderators to manage the scenarios.

- *Full-interruption testing*—In full-interruption testing, individuals follow each and every IR/DR/BC procedure, including the interruption of service, restoration of data from backups, and notification of appropriate individuals. This exercise is often performed after normal business hours in organizations that cannot afford to disrupt or simulate the disruption of business functions. Although full-interruption testing is the most rigorous testing strategy, it is unfortunately too risky for most businesses.

At a minimum, organizations should conduct periodic walk-throughs (or talk-throughs) of each of the CP component plans. Failure to update these plans as the business and its information resources change can erode the team's ability to respond to an incident, or possibly cause greater damage than the incident itself. If this sounds like a major training effort, note what the author Richard Marcinko, a former Navy SEAL, has to say about motivating a team:[24]

- The more you sweat to train, the less you bleed in combat.
- Training and preparation can hurt.
- Lead from the front, not the rear.
- You don't have to like it; you just have to do it.
- Keep it simple.
- Never assume.
- You are paid for results, not methods.

One often-neglected aspect of training is cross-training. In a real incident or disaster, the people assigned to particular roles are often not available. In some cases, alternate people must perform the duties of personnel who have been incapacitated by the disastrous event that triggered the activation of the plan. The testing process should train people to take over in the event that a team leader or integral member of the execution team is unavailable.

Final Thoughts on CP

As in all organizational efforts, iteration results in improvement. A critical component of the NIST-based methodologies presented in this module is continuous process improvement (CPI). Each time the organization rehearses its plans, it should learn from the process, improve the plans, and then rehearse again. Each time an incident or disaster occurs, the organization should review what went right and what went wrong. The actual results should be so thoroughly analyzed that any changes to the plans that could have improved the outcome will be implemented into a revised set of plans. Through ongoing evaluation and improvement, the organization continues to move forward and continually improves upon the process so that it can strive for an even better outcome.

Closing Scenario

Charlie sat at his desk the morning after his nightmare. He had answered the most pressing e-mails in his inbox and had a piping hot cup of coffee at his elbow. He looked down at a blank legal pad, ready to make notes about what to do in case his nightmare became reality.

Discussion Questions

1. What would be the first note you wrote down if you were Charlie?
2. What else should be on Charlie's list?
3. Suppose Charlie encountered resistance to his plans to improve contingency planning. What appeals could he use to sway opinions toward improved business contingency planning?

Ethical Decision Making

Suppose Charlie's manager, Gladys, tells him that everything is just fine the way it is. Charlie is firmly convinced that the company is not prepared for any significant adverse events that may occur. Should Charlie's professional responsibilities include escalating this matter to higher levels of the organization?

Selected Readings

- A complete treatment of the contingency planning process is presented in *Principles of Incident Response and Disaster Recovery*, 3rd Edition, by Michael Whitman and Herbert Mattord, published by Cengage Learning.
- A book that focuses on the incident response elements of contingency planning is *Intelligence-Driven Incident Response: Outwitting the Adversary* by Scott J. Roberts and Rebekah Brown, published by O'Reilly.

Module Summary

- Planning for unexpected events is usually the responsibility of general business managers and the information technology and information security communities of interest.
- For a plan to be seen as valid by all members of the organization, it must be sanctioned and actively supported by the general business community of interest.
- Some organizations are required by law or other mandate to have contingency planning procedures in place at all times, but all business organizations should prepare for the unexpected.
- Contingency planning (CP) is the process by which the information technology and information security communities of interest position their organizations to prepare for, detect, react to, and recover from events that threaten the security of information resources and assets.
- CP is made up of four major components: the data collection and documentation process known as the business impact analysis (BIA), the incident response (IR) plan, the disaster recovery (DR) plan, and the business continuity (BC) plan.
- Organizations can either create and develop the four planning elements of the CP process as one unified plan, or they can create these elements separately in conjunction with a set of interlocking procedures that enable continuity.

- To ensure continuity during the creation of the CP components, a seven-step CP process is used:
  1. Develop the contingency planning policy statement.
  2. Conduct the BIA.
  3. Identify preventive controls.
  4. Create contingency strategies.
  5. Develop a contingency plan.
  6. Ensure plan testing, training, and exercises.
  7. Ensure plan maintenance.
- Four teams are involved in contingency planning and contingency operations: the CP team, the IR team, the DR team, and the BC team. The IR team ensures that the CSIRT is formed.
- The IR plan is a detailed set of processes and procedures that plan for, detect, and resolve the effects of an unexpected event on information resources and assets.
- For every scenario identified, the CP team creates three sets of procedures—for before, during, and after the incident—to detect, contain, and resolve the incident.
- Incident classification is the process by which the IR team examines an incident candidate and determines whether it constitutes an actual incident.
- Three categories of incident indicators are used: possible, probable, and definite.
- When any one of the following happens, an actual incident is in progress: loss of availability of information, loss of integrity of information, loss of confidentiality of information, violation of policy, or violation of law.
- Digital forensics is the investigation of wrongdoing in the arena of information security. Digital forensics requires the preservation, identification, extraction, documentation, and interpretation of computer media for evidentiary and root cause analysis.
- DR planning encompasses preparation for handling and recovering from a disaster, whether natural or human-made.
- BC planning ensures that critical business functions continue if a catastrophic incident or disaster occurs. BC plans can include provisions for hot sites, warm sites, cold sites, timeshares, service bureaus, and mutual agreements.
- Because the DR and BC plans are closely related, most organizations prepare the two at the same time and may combine them into a single planning document called the business resumption (BR) plan.
- The DR plan should include crisis management, the action steps taken during and after a disaster. In some cases, the protection of human life and the organization's image are such high priorities that crisis management may deserve its own policy and plan.
- All plans must be tested to identify vulnerabilities, faults, and inefficient processes. Several strategies can be used to test contingency plans: desk checks, structured walk-throughs, simulations, and full interruption.

Review Questions

1. What is the name for the broad process of planning for the unexpected? What are its primary components?
2. Which two communities of interest are usually associated with contingency planning? Which community must give authority to ensure broad support for the plans?
3. According to some reports, what percentage of businesses that do not have a disaster plan go out of business after a major loss?
4. List the seven-step CP process recommended by NIST.
5. List and describe the teams that perform the planning and execution of the CP plans and processes. What is the primary role of each?

6. Define the term *incident* as used in the context of IRP. How is it related to the concept of incident response?
7. List and describe the criteria used to determine whether an actual incident is occurring.
8. List and describe the sets of procedures used to detect, contain, and resolve an incident.
9. What is incident classification?
10. List and describe the actions that should be taken during the reaction to an incident.
11. What is an alert roster? What is an alert message? Describe the two ways they can be used.
12. List and describe several containment strategies given in the text. On which tasks do they focus?

13. What is a disaster recovery plan, and why is it important to the organization?

14. What is a business continuity plan, and why is it important?

15. What is a business impact analysis, and what is it used for?

16. Why should contingency plans be tested and rehearsed?

17. Which types of organizations might use a unified continuity plan? Which types of organizations might use the various contingency planning components as separate plans? Why?

18. What strategies can be used to test contingency plans?

19. List and describe two specialized alternatives not often used as a continuity strategy.

20. What is digital forensics, and when is it used in a business setting?

Exercises

1. Using a Web search engine, search for the terms *disaster recovery* and *business continuity*. How many responses do you get for each term? Note the names of some of the companies in the response. Now perform the search again, adding the name of your metropolitan area or community.

2. Go to *http://csrc.nist.gov*. Under "Publications," select Special Publications, and then locate SP 800-34, Rev. 1, "Contingency Planning Guide for Federal Information Systems." Download and review this document. Outline and summarize the key points for an in-class discussion.

3. Use your library or the Web to find a reported natural disaster that occurred at least six months ago. From the news accounts, determine whether local or national officials had prepared disaster plans and if the plans were used. See if you can determine how the plans helped officials improve disaster response. How do the plans help the recovery?

4. Using the format provided in the text, design an incident response plan for your home computer. Include actions to be taken if each of the following events occur:
   a. Virus attack
   b. Power failure
   c. Fire
   d. Burst water pipe
   e. ISP failure

   What other scenarios do you think are important to plan for?

5. Classify each of the following occurrences as an incident or disaster. If an occurrence is a disaster, determine whether business continuity plans would be called into play.
   a. A hacker breaks into the company network and deletes files from a server.
   b. A fire breaks out in the storeroom and sets off sprinklers on that floor. Some computers are damaged, but the fire is contained.
   c. A tornado hits a local power station, and the company will be without power for three to five days.
   d. Employees go on strike, and the company could be without critical workers for weeks.
   e. A disgruntled employee takes a critical server home, sneaking it out after hours.

   For each of the scenarios (a–e), describe the steps necessary to restore operations. Indicate whether law enforcement would be involved.

References

1. "NIST General Information." National Institute of Standards and Technology. Accessed September 1, 2020, from *www.nist.gov/director/pao/nist-general-information*.

2. Swanson, M., Bowen, P., Phillips, A., Gallup, D., and Lynes, D. Special Publication 800-34, Rev. 1: "Contingency Planning Guide for Federal Information Systems." National Institute of Standards and Technology. Accessed September 1, 2020, from *https://csrc.nist.gov/publications/detail/sp/800-34/rev-1/final*.

3. "Disaster Recovery Guide." The Hartford. Accessed September 1, 2020, from *www.thehartford.com/higrd16/claims/business-disaster-recovery-guide*.

4. Swanson, M., Bowen, P., Phillips, A., Gallup, D., and Lynes, D. Special Publication 800-34, Rev. 1: "Contingency Planning Guide for Federal Information Systems." National Institute of Standards and Technology. Accessed September 1, 2020, from *https://csrc.nist.gov/publications/detail/sp/800-34/rev-1/final*.

5. Swanson, M., Hash, J., and Bowen, P. Special Publication 800-18, Rev 1: "Guide for Developing Security Plans for Information Systems." National Institute of Standards and Technology. February 2006. Page 31. Accessed December 6, 2017, from *csrc.nist.gov/publications/nistpubs/800-18-Rev1/sp800-18-Rev1-final.pdf*.

6. Zawada, B., and Evans, L. "Creating a More Rigorous BIA." CPM Group. November/December 2002. Accessed May 12, 2005, from *www.contingencyplanning.com/archives/2002/novdec/4.aspx*.

7. Swanson, M., Bowen, P., Phillips, A., Gallup, D., and Lynes, D. Special Publication 800-34, Rev. 1: "Contingency Planning Guide for Federal Information Systems." National Institute of Standards and Technology. Accessed September 1, 2020, from *https://csrc.nist.gov/publications/detail/sp/800-34/rev-1/final*.

8. Ibid.

9. Ibid.

10. Ibid.

11. Ibid.

12. Bartock, M., Cichonski, J., Souppaya, M., Smith, M., Witte, G., and Scarfone, K. Special Publication 800-184, "Guide for Cybersecurity Event Recovery." National Institute of Standards and Technology. Accessed September 1, 2020, from *https://csrc.nist.gov/publications/detail/sp/800-184/final*.

13. Cichonski, P., Millar, T., Grance, T., and Scarfone, K. Special Publication 800-61, Rev. 2: "Computer Security Incident Handling Guide." National Institute of Standards and Technology. Accessed September 1, 2020, from *https://csrc.nist.gov/publications/detail/sp/800-61/rev-2/final*.

14. Ibid.

15. Pipkin, D. *Information Security: Protecting the Global Enterprise*. Upper Saddle River, NJ: Prentice Hall PTR, 2000:285.

16. Cichonski, P., Millar, T., Grance, T., and Scarfone, K. Special Publication 800-61, Rev. 2: "Computer Security Incident Handling Guide." National Institute of Standards and Technology. Accessed September 1, 2020, from *https://csrc.nist.gov/publications/detail/sp/800-61/rev-2/final*.

17. Pipkin, D. *Information Security: Protecting the Global Enterprise*. Upper Saddle River, NJ: Prentice Hall PTR, 2000:285.

18. Bartock, M., Cichonski, J., Souppaya, M., Smith, M., Witte, G., and Scarfone, K. Special Publication 800-184, "Guide for Cybersecurity Event Recovery." Pages 13–14. National Institute of Standards and Technology. Accessed September 1, 2020, from *https://csrc.nist.gov/publications/detail/sp/800-184/final*.

19. McAfee. "Emergency Incident Response: 10 Common Mistakes of Incident Responders." Accessed September 1, 2020, from *www.techwire.net/uploads/2012/09/wp-10-common-mistakes-incident-responders.pdf*.

20. Cichonski, P., Millar, T., Grance, T., and Scarfone, K. Special Publication 800-61, Rev. 2: "Computer Security Incident Handling Guide." National Institute of Standards and Technology. Accessed September 1, 2020, from *https://csrc.nist.gov/publications/detail/sp/800-61/rev-2/final*.

21. Swanson, M., Bowen, P., Phillips, A., Gallup, D., and Lynes, D. Special Publication 800-34, Rev. 1: "Contingency Planning Guide for Federal Information Systems." National Institute of Standards and Technology. Accessed September 1, 2020, from *https://csrc.nist.gov/publications/detail/sp/800-34/rev-1/final*.

22. Witty, R. "What is Crisis Management?" Gartner Online. September 19, 2001. Accessed December 6, 2017, from *www.gartner.com/doc/340971*.

23. Davis, L. *Truth to Tell: Tell It Early, Tell It All, Tell It Yourself: Notes from My White House Education*. New York: Free Press, May 1999.

24. Marcinko, R., and Weisman, J. *Designation Gold*. New York: Pocket Books, 1998.

Legal, Ethical, and Professional Issues in Information Security

Upon completion of this material, you should be able to:

1 Explain the differences between laws and ethics

2 Describe the relevant laws, regulations, and professional organizations of importance to information security

3 Identify major national and international laws that affect the practice of information security

4 Discuss the role of privacy as it applies to law and ethics in information security

5 Explain the roles of some U.S. law enforcement agencies with an interest in information security

> *In civilized life, law floats in a sea of ethics.*
>
> —Earl Warren, Chief Justice of the United States

Opening Scenario

Henry Magruder made a mistake—he left a flash drive at the coffee station. Later, when Iris Majwubu was topping off her mug with fresh tea while taking a breather from her current project, she saw the unlabeled drive on the counter. Being the helpful sort, she picked it up, intending to return it to the person who had left it behind.

Expecting to find a program from someone on the development team or a project management schedule, Iris slotted the drive in her computer. The system automatically ran a virus scan before opening the file explorer program. She had been correct in assuming the drive contained SLS company data files. There were lots of them. She opened a file at random: Names, addresses, and Social Security numbers appeared on her screen. These were not the test records she expected; they looked more like confidential payroll data. The next file she picked to review was full of what seemed to be customers' credit card numbers. Concerned, she found a readme.txt file and opened it. It read:

> *Jill, see files on this drive. Hope they meet your expectations. Wire money to account as arranged. Rest of data sent on payment.*

Iris realized that someone was selling sensitive company data. She looked back at the directory listing and saw that the files spanned the range of every department at Sequential Label and Supply—everything from customer financial records to shipping invoices. She opened another file and saw that it contained only a sampling of the relevant data. Whoever did this had split the data into two parts. That made sense: just a sample to see the type of data and then payment on delivery.

Now, who did the drive belong to? She opened the file properties option of the readme.txt file. The file owner was listed as "hmagruder." That must be Henry Magruder, the developer two cubicles over in the next aisle. Iris pondered her next action.

Introduction To Law And Ethics In Information Security

As a future information security professional or IT professional with security responsibilities, you must understand the scope of an organization's legal and ethical responsibilities. The information security professional plays an important role in an organization's approach to managing responsibility and liability for privacy and security risks. In modern litigious societies around the world, laws are sometimes enforced in civil courts, where large damages can be awarded to plaintiffs who bring suits against organizations. Sometimes these damages are punitive—a punishment assessed as a deterrent to future transgressions. To minimize liability and reduce risks from electronic and physical threats, and to reduce all losses from legal action, information security practitioners must thoroughly understand the current legal environment, stay current with laws and regulations, and watch for new and emerging issues. By educating the management and employees of an organization on their legal and ethical obligations and the proper use of information technology and information security, security professionals can help keep an organization focused on its primary business objectives.

In the first part of this module, you will learn about the legislation and regulations that affect the management of information in an organization. In the second part, you will learn about the ethical issues related to information security and about several professional organizations with established codes of ethics. Use this module both as a reference to the legal aspects of information security and as an aid in planning your professional career.

laws

Rules that mandate or prohibit certain behavior and are enforced by the state.

ethics

The branch of philosophy that considers nature, criteria, sources, logic, and the validity of moral judgment.

cultural mores

The fixed moral attitudes or customs of a particular group.

In general, people elect to trade some aspects of personal freedom for social order. It is often a necessary but somewhat ironic proposition, as Benjamin Franklin asserted: "Those who would give up essential Liberty, to purchase a little temporary Safety, deserve neither Liberty nor Safety."[1] As Jean-Jacques Rousseau explained in *The Social Contract, or Principles of Political Right*, the rules that members of a society create to balance the individual rights to self-determination against the needs of the society as a whole are called **laws**.[2] The key difference between laws and **ethics** is that laws carry the authority of a governing body and ethics do not. Ethics, in turn, are based on **cultural mores**. Some ethical standards are universal. For example, murder, theft, assault, and arson are generally prohibited in ethical and legal standards throughout the world.

Organizational Liability and the Need for Counsel

liability

An entity's legal obligation or responsibility.

restitution

A legal requirement to make compensation or payment resulting from a loss or injury.

What if an organization does not demand or even encourage strong ethical behavior from its employees? What if an organization does not behave ethically? Even if there is no breach of criminal law in a case, there can still be **liability**—legal and financial responsibility. Liability includes the legal obligation to make **restitution**—to pay penalties or fines for wrongs committed. The bottom line is that if an employee performs an illegal or unethical act that causes some degree of harm, the employer may be held financially liable for that action, regardless of whether the employer authorized the act. An organization increases its liability if it refuses to take measures known as **due care** (or a *standard of due care*). Similarly, **due diligence** requires that an organization make a valid attempt to *continually maintain* this level of effort. Whereas due care means the organization *acts* legally and ethically, due diligence means it *ensures compliance* with this level of expected behavior, essentially the management of due care. Given the Internet's global reach, those who could be injured or wronged by an organization's employees might live anywhere in the world. Under the U.S. legal system, any court can assert its authority over an individual or organization if it can establish **jurisdiction**. This is sometimes referred to as **long-arm jurisdiction** when laws are stretched to apply to parties in distant locations. Trying a case in the injured party's home area is usually favorable to the injured party.[3]

Policy Versus Law

Within an organization, information security professionals help maintain security via the establishment and enforcement of *policy*. As discussed in greater detail in Module 3, "Information Security Management," policies function as laws within the operational boundaries of an organization. These policies come complete with penalties, judicial practices, and sanctions to require compliance. Because policies function as laws, they must be crafted and implemented with the same care to ensure that they are complete, appropriate, and fairly applied to everyone in the workplace. The difference between a policy and a law, however, is that ignorance of a policy is an acceptable defense, whereas ignorance of the law is not.

As discussed in Module 3, policies must be able to stand up in court if challenged, because if an employee is punished or fired based on a policy violation, they may challenge the action, and most likely in court. Thus, for a policy to be enforceable, it must meet the following five criteria:

- *Dissemination (distribution)*—The organization must be able to demonstrate that the relevant policy has been made readily available for review by the employee. Common dissemination techniques include hard copy and electronic distribution.
- *Review (reading)*—The organization must be able to demonstrate that it disseminated the document in an intelligible form, including versions for employees who are illiterate, reading impaired, and unable to read English. Common techniques include recordings of the policy in English and alternate languages.
- *Comprehension (understanding)*—The organization must be able to demonstrate that the employee understands the requirements and content of the policy. Common techniques include quizzes and other assessments.
- *Compliance (agreement)*—The organization must be able to demonstrate that the employee agreed to comply with the policy through act or affirmation. Common techniques include login banners, which require a specific action (mouse click or keystroke) to acknowledge agreement, or a signed document clearly indicating the employee has read, understood, and agreed to comply with the policy.
- *Uniform enforcement*—The organization must be able to demonstrate that the policy has been uniformly enforced, regardless of employee status or assignment.

Only when all of these conditions are met can an organization penalize employees who violate a policy without fear of successful legal retribution.

Types of Law

There are several ways to categorize laws within the United States. In addition to the hierarchical perspective of local, state, federal, and international laws, most U.S. laws can be categorized based on their origins:

- *Constitutional law*—Originates with the U.S. Constitution, a state constitution, or local constitution, bylaws, or charter.

---

due care

Reasonable and prudent measures that an organization takes to ensure it is in compliance with a law, regulation, or requirement.

due diligence

Measures taken to ensure that an organization *continues* to meet the obligations imposed by laws, regulations, and requirements; the management of due care.

jurisdiction

The power to make legal decisions and judgments; also, the domain or area within which an entity such as a court or law enforcement agency is empowered to make legal decisions and perform legal actions.

long-arm jurisdiction

The ability of a legal entity to exercise its influence beyond its normal boundaries by asserting a connection between an out-of-jurisdiction entity and a local legal case.

- *Statutory law*—Originates from a legislative branch specifically tasked with the creation and publication of laws and statutes.
- *Regulatory or administrative law*—Originates from an executive branch or authorized regulatory agency and includes executive orders and regulations.
- *Common law, case law, and precedent*—Originates from a judicial branch or oversight board and involves the interpretation of law based on the actions of a previous and/or higher court or board.

Within statutory law, one can further divide laws into their association with individuals, groups, and the "state":

- *Civil law* embodies a wide variety of laws pertaining to relationships among individuals and organizations. Civil law includes contract law, employment law, family law, and tort law. *Tort law* is the subset of civil law that allows individuals to seek redress in the event of personal, physical, or financial injury. Perceived damages within civil law are pursued in civil court and are not prosecuted by the state.
- *Criminal law* addresses violations harmful to society and is actively enforced and prosecuted by the state. Criminal law addresses statutes associated with traffic law, public order, property damage, and personal damage, where the state takes on the responsibility of seeking retribution on behalf of the plaintiff or injured party.

Yet another distinction addresses how legislation affects individuals in society and is categorized as private law or public law. *Private law* is considered a subset of civil law and regulates the relationships among individuals as well as relationships between individuals and organizations. It encompasses family law, commercial law, and labor law. *Public law* regulates the structure and administration of government agencies and their relationships with citizens, employees, and other governments. Public law includes criminal law, administrative law, and constitutional law.

Regardless of how you categorize laws, it is important to understand which laws and regulations are relevant to your organization and what the organization needs to do to comply.

Relevant U.S. Laws

Historically, the United States has been a leader in the development and implementation of information security legislation to prevent misuse and exploitation of information and information technology. Information security legislation contributes to a more reliable business environment, which in turn enables a stable economy. In its global leadership capacity, the United States has demonstrated a clear understanding of the importance of securing information and has specified penalties for people and organizations that breach U.S. civil statutes. The sections that follow present the most important U.S. laws that apply to information security.

General Computer Crime Laws

Several key laws are relevant to the field of information security and are of particular interest to those who live or work in the United States. The *Computer Fraud and Abuse Act of 1986 (CFA Act or CFAA)* is the cornerstone of many computer-related federal laws and enforcement efforts. It was originally written as an extension and clarification to the *Comprehensive Crime Control Act of 1984*. The CFAA was amended by the *National Information Infrastructure Protection Act of 1996*, which modified several sections of the previous act and increased the penalties for selected crimes. The punishment for offenses prosecuted under this statute includes fines, imprisonment of up to 20 years, or both. The severity of the penalty depends on the value of the information obtained and whether the offense is judged to have been committed for the following reasons:

- For purposes of commercial advantage
- For private financial gain
- In furtherance of a criminal act

The preceding law and many others were further modified by the *USA PATRIOT Act of 2001*, which provides law enforcement agencies with broader latitude to combat terrorism-related activities. The full title of this act is the Uniting and Strengthening America by Providing Appropriate Tools Required to Intercept and Obstruct Terrorism Act of 2001. In 2006, this act was amended by the *USA PATRIOT Improvement and Reauthorization Act*, which made permanent 14 of the 16 expanded powers of the Department of Homeland Security and the FBI in investigating terrorist activity. The act also reset an expiration date written into the law as a so-called sunset clause for certain wiretaps under the Foreign Intelligence Surveillance Act of 1978 (FISA) and revised many of the criminal penalties and procedures associated with criminal and terrorist activities.[4]

In 2011, President Obama signed the *PATRIOT Sunset Extension Act*, which provided yet another extension of certain provisions of the USA PATRIOT Act, specifically those related to wiretaps, searching of business records, and the surveillance of people with suspected ties to terrorism. Some of the laws modified by the USA PATRIOT Act are among the earliest laws created to deal with electronic technology. Certain portions of the USA PATRIOT Act were extended in 2006, 2010, and 2011.

In May 2015, the U.S. Senate failed to extend the act, resulting in its expiration on June 1, 2015. The controversy over Section 215, which allowed the National Security Agency (NSA) to collect metadata (for example, the to: and from: information from phone records), initially resulted in an attempt to transfer the responsibility for collecting and reporting this information to the telecommunications companies involved as part of the *USA FREEDOM Act*. The act's name is an abbreviation of "Uniting and Strengthening America by Fulfilling Rights and Ending Eavesdropping, Dragnet-collection and Online Monitoring Act." However, this act met with similar resistance until the stalemate in Congress resulted in the sunset of key components of the USA PATRIOT Act. The complex political issues of this legislation were eventually resolved, and the USA FREEDOM Act was signed into law by President Obama in June 2015.

After much controversy over the past several years, the USA PATRIOT Act is currently expired, after an amended version of the act was threatened with a veto by President Trump and then was indefinitely postponed by Congress in June 2020.

Another key law, the *Computer Security Act of 1987*, was one of the first attempts to protect federal computer systems by establishing minimum acceptable security practices. The National Institute of Standards and Technology (NIST)—known as the National Bureau of Standards prior to 1988—is responsible for developing these security standards and guidelines in cooperation with the National Security Agency.

In 2002, Congress passed the *Federal Information Security Management Act (FISMA)*, which mandates that all federal agencies establish information security programs to protect their information assets. The act effectively brought the federal government into alignment with the private sector. FISMA extended NIST's responsibilities, along with those of the Office of Management and Budget. The document also provided many of the definitions used today in information security.

FISMA requires federal agencies to implement information security management programs for systems that support their mission. The program must include periodic risk assessment of the potential problems that could result from security failures and implementation of policies and procedures based on the assessment. Additional planning is also expected for network security, incident response, disaster recovery, and continuity of operations. Agency management is expected to implement ongoing evaluations of their security program's effectiveness and provide security education, training, and awareness for all people who interact with agency systems.[5]

FISMA was updated by the *Federal Information Security Modernization Act of 2014* (a.k.a. FISMA Reform), which specifically focused on enhancing the federal government's ability to respond to security attacks on government agencies and departments.

 For more information on FISMA, visit NIST's FISMA Implementation Project at *https://csrc.nist.gov/topics/laws-and-regulations/laws/fisma*.

Privacy

Privacy has become one of the hottest topics in information security at the beginning of the 21st century. Many organizations collect, swap, and sell personal information as a commodity, and as a result, many people are looking to governments to protect their privacy from such organizations. The ability to collect information, combine facts from separate sources, and merge it all with other information has resulted in databases that were previously impossible to create. One technology that was proposed to monitor private communications responsibly, known as the Clipper chip

privacy

In the context of information security, the right of individuals or groups to protect themselves and their information from unauthorized access, providing confidentiality.

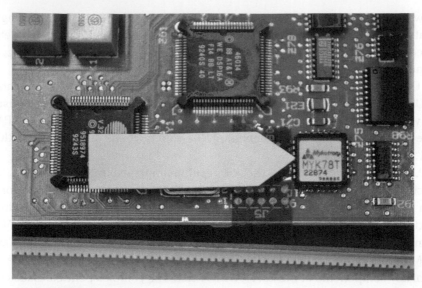

Figure 6-1 The Clipper chip

(see Figure 6-1), used an algorithm with a two-part key that was to be managed by two separate government agencies. The chip was reportedly designed to protect individual communications while allowing the government to decrypt suspect transmissions.[6] This technology was the focus of intense discussion between advocates for personal privacy and people who believed the chip would enable more effective law enforcement. Ultimately, the technology was not implemented by the U.S. government. In response to the pressure for privacy protection, the number of statutes that address individual rights to privacy has grown. To help you better understand this rapidly evolving issue, some of the more relevant privacy laws are presented here.

aggregate information

Collective data that relates to a group or category of people and that has been altered to remove characteristics or components that make it possible to identify individuals within the group. Not to be confused with *information aggregation*.

information aggregation

Pieces of nonprivate data that, when combined, may create information that violates privacy. Not to be confused with *aggregate information*.

Some regulations in the U.S. legal code stipulate responsibilities of common carriers (organizations that process or move data for hire) to protect the confidentiality of customer information. The *Privacy of Customer Information* section of the common carrier regulation states that any proprietary information shall be used explicitly for providing services and not for marketing purposes. Carriers cannot disclose this information except when it is necessary to provide their services. The only other exception is applied when a customer requests the disclosure of information, in which case the disclosure is restricted to that customer's information only. This law does allow for the use of **aggregate information** if the same information is provided to all common carriers and all of them engage in fair competitive business practices. Note that aggregate information— the "blinding" of data collected for the purposes of managing networks or systems—is different from **information aggregation**, which is the development of individual profiles by combining information collected from multiple sources (see Figure 6-2).

While common carrier regulation oversees public carriers to protect individual privacy, the *Federal Privacy Act of 1974* regulates government agencies and holds them accountable if they release private information about individuals or businesses without permission. The following agencies, regulated businesses, and individuals are exempt from some of the regulations so they can perform their duties:

- Bureau of the Census
- National Archives and Records Administration
- Congress
- Comptroller General
- Federal courts with regard to specific issues using appropriate court orders
- Credit reporting agencies
- Individuals or organizations that demonstrate information is necessary to protect the health or safety of an individual party

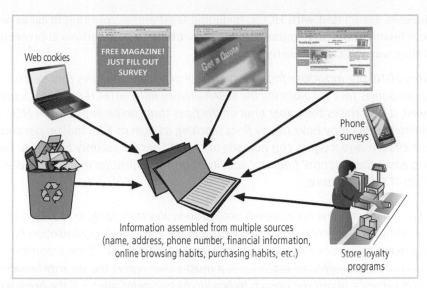

Figure 6-2   Information aggregation

The *Electronic Communications Privacy Act (ECPA) of 1986*, informally referred to as the wiretapping act, is a collection of statutes that regulates the interception of wire, electronic, and oral communications. These statutes work in conjunction with the *Fourth Amendment to the U.S. Constitution*, which protects individual citizens from unlawful search and seizure.

The *Health Insurance Portability and Accountability Act of 1996 (HIPAA)*, also known as the *Kennedy–Kassebaum Act*, protects the confidentiality and security of healthcare data by establishing and enforcing standards and by standardizing electronic data interchange. HIPAA affects all healthcare organizations, including doctors' practices, health clinics, life insurers, and universities, as well as some organizations that have self-insured employee health programs. HIPAA specifies stiff penalties for organizations that fail to comply with the law, with fines of up to $250,000 and 10 years imprisonment for knowingly misusing client information.

How does HIPAA affect the field of information security? Beyond the basic privacy guidelines, the act requires organizations to use information security mechanisms as well as policies and procedures to protect healthcare information. It also requires a comprehensive assessment of information security systems, policies, and procedures in which healthcare information is handled or maintained. Electronic signatures have become more common, and HIPAA provides guidelines for the use of these signatures based on security standards that ensure message integrity, user authentication, and nonrepudiation. There is no specification of particular security technologies for each of the security requirements, except that security must be implemented to ensure the privacy of the healthcare information.

The privacy standards of HIPAA severely restrict the dissemination and distribution of private health information without documented consent. The standards provide patients with the right to know who has access to their information and who has accessed it. The standards also restrict the use of health information to the minimum necessary for the healthcare services required.

HIPAA has five fundamental principles:

1. Consumer control of medical information
2. Boundaries on the use of medical information
3. Accountability to maintain the privacy of specified types of information
4. Balance of public responsibility for the use of medical information for the greater good measured against its impact to the individual patient
5. Security of health information

In 2009, an act that attempted to stimulate the American economy, *the American Recovery and Reinvestment Act of 2009 (ARRA)*, updated and broadened the scope of HIPAA in a section referred to as the *Health Information Technology for Economic and Clinical Health Act (HITECH)*. The update also provided "bounties" for investigators—financial monetary incentives to pursue violators. HIPAA only covered healthcare organizations (HCOs), but HITECH expanded

HIPAA to include businesses associated with HCOs, including legal and accounting firms as well as IT firms or any business partners. These business partners must now comply with HIPAA regulations in protecting patient healthcare information (PHI) as if they were HCOs themselves.[7]

> *Effective February 2010, organizations face the same civil and legal penalties that doctors, hospitals, and insurance companies face for violating the HIPAA Privacy Rule. HITECH not only changes how fines will be levied, it also raises the upper limit on the fines that can be imposed. An HCO or business partner who violates HIPAA may have to pay fines reaching as high as $1.5 million per calendar year. In addition, private citizens and lawyers can now sue to collect fines for security breaches. Overall, HITECH considerably increases the potential financial liability of any organization that mishandles the PHI that passes through its IT infrastructure.*
>
> *The HITECH Act also includes new data breach notification rules that apply to HCOs and business partners. If an employee discovers a PHI security breach, the employee's organization has only 60 days in which to notify each individual whose privacy has been compromised. If the organization is unable to contact ten or more of the affected individuals, it must either report the security breach on its Web site or issue a press release about the breach to broadcast and print media. If the breach affects 500 or more individuals, the organization must additionally notify the Secretary of the HHS, along with major media outlets. The HHS will then report the breach on its own Web site.[8]*

HIPAA was again updated in 2013 with a Department of Health and Human Services Regulatory Action intended to strengthen the act's privacy and security protections. The changes increased liability for the protection of patient information, strengthened penalties for noncompliance, increased requirements for notifying patients about breaches of confidentiality of their information, and implemented other related PHI protection practices.[9]

The *Financial Services Modernization Act* or *Gramm–Leach–Bliley Act of 1999* contains many provisions that focus on facilitating affiliations among banks, securities firms, and insurance companies. Specifically, this act requires all financial institutions to disclose their privacy policies on the sharing of nonpublic personal information. It also requires due notice to customers so they can request that their information not be shared with third parties. In addition, the act ensures that an organization's privacy policies are fully disclosed when a customer initiates a business relationship and then distributed at least annually for the duration of the professional association.

 For more information on federal privacy laws, visit the Center for Democracy and Technology at *https://cdt.org/insights/existing-federal-privacy-laws/*.

See Table 6-1 for a summary of information security–related laws.

Table 6-1 Key U.S. Laws of Interest to Information Security Professionals

Area	Act	Date	Description
Online commerce and information protection	Federal Trade Commission Act (FTCA)	1914	Recently used to challenge organizations with deceptive claims regarding the privacy and security of customers' personal information
Telecommunications	Communications Act (47 USC 151 et seq.)	1934	Includes amendments found in the Telecommunications Deregulation and Competition Act of 1996; this law regulates interstate and foreign telecommunications (amended 1996 and 2001)

(continues)

Table 6-1   Key U.S. Laws of Interest to Information Security Professionals (*Continued*)

Area	Act	Date	Description
Freedom of information	Freedom of Information Act (FOIA)	1966	Allows for the disclosure of previously unreleased information and documents controlled by the U.S. government
Protection of credit information	Fair Credit Reporting Act (FCRA)	1970	Regulates the collection and use of consumer credit information
Privacy	Federal Privacy Act	1974	Governs federal agency use of personal information
Privacy of student information	Family Educational Rights and Privacy Act (FERPA) (20 U.S.C. § 1232g; 34 CFR Part 99)	1974	Also known as the Buckley Amendment; protects the privacy of student education records
Copyright	Copyright Act (update to U.S. Copyright Law (17 USC))	1976	Protects intellectual property, including publications and software
Cryptography	Electronic Communications Privacy Act (update to 18 USC)	1986	Regulates interception and disclosure of electronic information; also referred to as the Federal Wiretapping Act
Access to stored communications	Unlawful Access to Stored Communications (18 USC 2701)	1986	Provides penalties for illegally accessing communications (such as e-mail and voice mail) stored by a service provider
Threats to computers	Computer Fraud and Abuse (CFA) Act (also known as Fraud and Related Activity in Connection with Computers) (18 USC 1030)	1986	Defines and formalizes laws to counter threats from computer-related acts and offenses (amended 1996, 2001, and 2006)
Federal agency information security	Computer Security Act (CSA)	1987	Requires all federal computer systems that contain classified information to have security plans in place, and requires periodic security training for all individuals who operate, design, or manage such systems
Trap and trace restrictions	General prohibition on wiretap intercept equipment and trap-and-trace device use; exception (18 USC 3121 et seq.)	1993	Prohibits the use of electronic wiretap intercept equipment and trap-and-trace devices without a court order
Criminal intent	National Information Infrastructure Protection Act (update to 18 USC 1030)	1996	Categorizes crimes based on defendant's authority to access a protected computer system and criminal intent
Trade secrets	Economic Espionage Act	1996	Prevents abuse of information gained while employed elsewhere
Personal health information protection	Health Insurance Portability and Accountability Act (HIPAA)	1996	Requires medical practices to ensure the privacy of personal medical information
Encryption and digital signatures	Security and Freedom Through Encryption Act	1997	Affirms the rights of people in the United States to use and sell products that include encryption and to relax export controls on such products

(continues)

Table 6-1   Key U.S. Laws of Interest to Information Security Professionals (*Continued*)

Area	Act	Date	Description
Intellectual property	No Electronic Theft Act amends 17 USC 506(a)—copyright infringement, and 18 USC 2319—criminal infringement of copyright (Public Law 105-147)	1997	These parts of the U.S. Code amend copyright and criminal statutes to provide greater copyright protection and penalties for electronic copyright infringement
Copy protection	Digital Millennium Copyright Act (DMCA) (update to 17 USC 101)	1998	Provides specific penalties for removing copyright protection from media
Identity theft	Identity Theft and Assumption Deterrence Act (18 USC 1028)	1998	Attempts to instigate specific penalties for identity theft by identifying the individual who loses their identity as the true victim, not just those commercial and financial credit entities who suffered losses
Child privacy protection	Children's Online Privacy Protection Act (COPPA)	1998	Provides requirements for online service and Web site providers to ensure the privacy of children under 13 is protected
Banking	Gramm-Leach-Bliley (GLB) Act (also known as the Financial Services Modernization Act)	1999	Repeals the restrictions on banks affiliating with insurance and securities firms; has significant impact on the privacy of personal information used by these industries
Accountability	Sarbanes-Oxley (SOX) Act (also known as the Public Company Accounting Reform and Investor Protection Act)	2002	Enforces accountability for executives at publicly traded companies; is having ripple effects throughout the accounting, IT, and related units of many organizations
General InfoSec	Federal Information Security Management Act, or FISMA (44 USC § 3541, et seq.)	2002	Requires each federal agency to develop, document, and implement an agency-wide program to provide InfoSec for the information and information systems that support the operations and assets of the agency, including those provided or managed by another agency, contractor, or other source
Spam	Controlling the Assault of Non-Solicited Pornography and Marketing (CAN-SPAM) Act (15 USC 7701 et seq.)	2003	Sets the first national standards for regulating the distribution of commercial e-mail, including mobile phone spam
Fraud with access devices	Fraud and Related Activity in Connection with Access Devices (18 USC 1029)	2004	Defines and formalizes law to counter threats from counterfeit access devices like ID cards, credit cards, telecom equipment, mobile or electronic serial numbers, and the equipment that creates them
Terrorism and extreme drug trafficking	USA PATRIOT Improvement and Reauthorization Act (update to 18 USC 1030)	2006	Renews critical sections of the USA PATRIOT Act

(continues)

Table 6-1   Key U.S. Laws of Interest to Information Security Professionals (*Continued*)

Area	Act	Date	Description
Privacy of PHI	American Recovery and Reinvestment Act	2009	In the privacy and security area, requires new reporting requirements and penalties for breach of Protected Health Information (PHI)
Privacy of PHI	Health Information Technology for Economic and Clinical Health (HITECH) Act (part of ARRA-2009)	2009	Addresses privacy and security concerns associated with the electronic transmission of PHI, in part, through several provisions that strengthen HIPAA rules for civil and criminal enforcement
Defense information protection	International Traffic in Arms Regulations (ITAR) Act	2012	Restricts the exportation of technology and information related to defense and military-related services and materiel, including research and development information
National cyber infrastructure protection	National Cybersecurity Protection Act	2014	Updates the Homeland Security Act of 2002, which established the Department of Homeland Security, to include a national cybersecurity and communications integration center to share information and facilitate coordination between agencies, and perform analysis of cybersecurity incidents and risks
Federal information security updates	Federal Information Security Modernization Act	2014	Updates many outdated federal information security practices, updating FISMA, providing a framework for ensuring effectiveness in information security controls over federal information systems, and centralizing cybersecurity management within DHS
National information security employee assessment	Cybersecurity Workforce Assessment Act	2014	Tasks DHS to perform an evaluation of the national cybersecurity employee workforce at least every three years, and to develop a plan to improve recruiting and training of cybersecurity employees
Terrorist tracking	USA FREEDOM Act	2015	Updates the Foreign Intelligence Surveillance Act (FISA); transfers the requirement to collect and report communications to/from known terrorist phone numbers to communications carriers, to be provided to select federal agencies upon request, among other updates to surveillance activities

To learn more about laws that are not specifically discussed in this module, visit *CSO Magazine*'s directory of security laws, regulations, and guidelines at *www.csoonline.com/article/2126072/compliance-the-security-laws-regulations-and-guidelines-directory.html*.

identity theft

The unauthorized taking of personally identifiable information with the intent of committing fraud and abuse of a person's financial and personal reputation, purchasing goods and services without authorization, and generally impersonating the victim for illegal or unethical purposes.

personally identifiable information (PII)

Information about a person's history, background, and attributes that can be used to commit identity theft. This information typically includes a person's name, address, Social Security number, family information, employment history, and financial information.

Identity Theft

Related to privacy legislation is the growing body of law on **identity theft**. Identity theft can occur when someone steals a victim's **personally identifiable information (PII)** and uses it to purchase goods and services or conduct other actions while posing as the victim. According to the most recent report from the U.S. Department of Justice, "An estimated 10% of persons age 16 or older reported that they had been victims of identity theft during the prior 12 months."[10] As shown in Table 6-2, some of this theft occurred with bank accounts and credit card accounts. Organizations can also be victims of identity theft by means of URL manipulation or DNS redirection, as described in Module 2.

As shown in Table 6-3, the most common way victims discovered they were the victims of identity theft was by notification from a financial institution regarding suspicious activity.

In May 2006, President Bush signed an executive order creating the Identity Theft Task Force. On April 27, 2007, it issued a strategic plan to improve efforts by the government, private organizations, and individuals in combating identity theft. The U.S.

Table 6-2 Prevalence of Identity Theft, 2014 and 2016[11]

Type of identity theft	Continuing National Crime Victimization Survey for sample counties		Full National Crime Victimization Survey sample	
	2014*	2016	2014**	2016
Total	7.4%	9.7%†	7.0%	10.2%†
Existing account				
Credit card	3.3%	4.1%†	3.4%	5.3%†
Bank	3.7	5.3†	3.2	4.7†
Other	0.6	0.7†	0.6	0.8†
Opened new account	0.5%	0.6%†	0.4%	0.6%†
Misused personal information	0.3%	0.4%†	0.3%	0.5%†

Note: Details do not sum to totals because people could experience more than one type of identity theft.

*Comparison year. Continuing sample counties for 2014 are compared to continuing sample counties for 2016.

**Comparison year. Full sample for 2014 is compared to full sample for 2016.

†Significant difference from comparison year at 95% confidence level.

Source: Bureau of Justice Statistics, National Crime Victimization Survey, Identity Theft Supplement, 2014 and 2016.

Table 6-3   The Most Common Ways Victims Discovered Identity Theft, 2016[12]

How victims discovered identity theft	Any identity theft	Misuse of existing account*a	Other identity theftb
Total	100%	100%	100%
Contacted by financial institution about suspicious activity	47.6	50.8	15.4†
Noticed fraudulent charges on account	18.7	20.0	6.1†
Noticed money missing from account	8.0	8.6	2.0†
Contacted financial institution to report a theft	6.1	6.5	1.8†
Credit card declined, check bounced, or account closed due to insufficient funds	4.7	5.0	1.8†
Notified by company or agency	4.6	3.0	21.2†
Received a bill or contacted about an unpaid bill	2.9	2.0	12.6†
Problems with applying for a loan, government benefits, or with income taxes	1.6	0.4	13.8†
Discovered through credit report or credit monitoring service	1.4	0.8	7.3†
Received merchandise or card that victim did not order or did not receive product ordered	0.6	0.4	2.4†
Notified by police	0.5	0.1	4.3†
Notified by family member	0.4	0.4	0.7!
Another wayc	2.9	2.1	10.7†

Note: Estimates are based on the most recent incident of identity theft.

*Comparison group.

†Significant difference from comparison group at 95% confidence level.

!Interpret with caution. Estimate is based on 10 or fewer sample cases, or coefficient of variation is greater than 50%.

ªincludes identity-theft incidents involving only the misuse of one type of existing account or the misuse of multiple types of existing accounts.

bIncludes the following identity-theft incidents: the misuse of at least one type of existing account and the misuse of personal information to open a new account or for another fraudulent purpose; and the misuse of personal information to open a new account or for another fraudulent purpose.

cIncludes someone other than a family member notified the victim; victim noticed account information was missing or stolen; victim noticed from suspicious computer activity, including hacked e-mail; victim noticed from suspicious contact, including phishing; and discovery in other ways.

Source: Bureau of Justice Statistics, National Crime Victimization Survey, Identity Theft Supplement, 2016.

Federal Trade Commission (FTC) now oversees efforts to foster coordination among groups, more effective prosecution of criminals engaged in identify theft, and methods to increase restitution made to victims.[13]

While numerous states have passed identity theft laws, the legislation at the federal level primarily began with the passing of the Identity Theft and Assumption Deterrence Act of 1998 (Public Law 105-318). This law was later revised by the *Fraud and Related Activity in Connection with Identification Documents, Authentication Features, and Information*

Act (Title 18, U.S.C. § 1028), which criminalizes the creation, reproduction, transfer, possession, or use of unauthorized or false identification documents or document-making equipment. The penalties for such offenses range from one to 25 years in prison and fines as determined by the courts.

The FTC recommends that people take the following four steps when they suspect they are victims of identity theft:

1. *Place an initial fraud alert*—Report to one of the three national credit reporting companies and ask for an initial fraud alert on your credit report. This makes it harder for an identity thief to open more accounts in your name.
2. *Order your credit reports*—Filing an initial fraud alert entitles you to a free credit report from *each* of the three credit reporting companies. Examine the reports for fraud activity and contact the fraud department in the organization that holds the suspect account.
3. *Create an identity theft report*—Filing a complaint with the FTC will generate an identity theft affidavit, which can be used to file a police report and create an identity theft report. This report helps when dealing with credit reporting companies, debt collectors, and any businesses with whom the identity thief has interacted.
4. *Monitor your progress*—Document all calls, letters, and communications during the process.[14]

In 2008, Congress passed another update to the CFAA titled the *Identity Theft Enforcement and Restitution Act*, which specifically addressed the malicious use of spyware or keyloggers to steal PII. This act also created a new designation of a level of identity theft that provided much stronger penalties for violators who used 10 or more computers to commit theft. The new law also created a mechanism by which victims of identity theft may receive restitution from criminals convicted under the act. The penalties that may be levied under this act include substantial fines, from which the restitution is paid, and prison terms of up to 10 or 20 years, depending on the severity of the crime.[15] Increasingly, consumers who recognize the increased threat of identity theft elect to buy credit protection insurance products that offset the expenses associated with such theft.

 For more information on privacy and identity theft, visit the FTC's Web site at *www.consumer.ftc.gov/topics/privacy-identity* and the U.S. Department of Justice Web site at *www.justice.gov/criminal-fraud/identity-theft*.

Export and Espionage Laws

To meet national security needs and to protect trade secrets and other state and private assets, several laws restrict which information, information management resources, and security resources may be exported from the United States. These laws attempt to stem the theft of information by establishing strong penalties for such crimes. The laws have limited effectiveness in many cases because the theft is initiated from offshore, and the ability to apply the law is reduced when perpetrators are from another jurisdiction.

To protect American ingenuity, intellectual property, and competitive advantage, Congress passed the *Economic Espionage Act* in 1996. This law attempts to prevent trade secrets from being illegally shared.

The *Security and Freedom Through Encryption Act of 1999* provides guidance for the use of encryption and provides protection from government intervention. The acts include provisions that:

- Reinforce a person's right to use or sell encryption algorithms without concern for regulations requiring some form of key registration. Key registration is the storage of a cryptographic key (or its text equivalent) with another party for breaking the encryption of data. This is often called "key escrow."
- Prohibit the federal government from requiring the use of encryption for contracts, grants, and other official documents and correspondence.
- State that the use of encryption is not probable cause to suspect criminal activity.
- Relax export restrictions by amending the Export Administration Act of 1979.
- Provide additional penalties for the use of encryption in the commission of a criminal act.

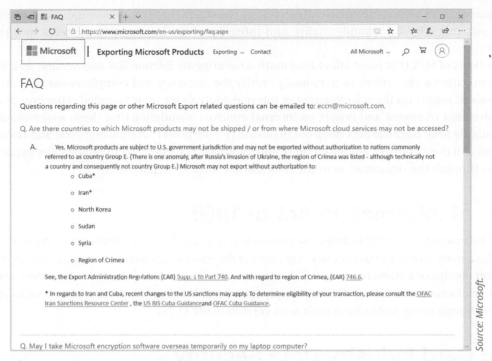

Figure 6-3   Exporting Microsoft products

As illustrated in Figure 6-3, which shows restrictions on the shipment of Microsoft products, the distribution of many software packages is restricted to approved organizations, governments, and countries.

U.S. Copyright Law

Intellectual property is a protected asset in the United States. The *U.S. Copyright Law* extends this privilege to published works, including those in electronic formats. Fair use allows copyrighted materials to be used to support news reporting, teaching, scholarship, and similar activities, if the use is for educational or library purposes, is not for profit, and is not excessive. As long as proper acknowledgment is provided to the original author of such works, including a proper citation of the location of source materials, and the work is not represented as one's own, it is entirely permissible to include portions of someone else's work as reference. It is *illegal*, however, to post a complete or substantial portion of someone else's work online—such as scanning and posting books like this one—without the expressed permission of the copyright holder (in this case, Cengage Learning).

 For more information on the U.S. Copyright Law, visit the U.S. Copyright Office's Web site at *www.copyright.gov/.* You can view the law in its entirety at *www.copyright.gov/title17/.*

Financial Reporting

The *Sarbanes–Oxley Act of 2002*, also known as SOX or the *Corporate and Auditing Accountability and Responsibility Act of 2002*, is a critical piece of legislation that affects the executive management of publicly traded corporations and public accounting firms. The law seeks to improve the reliability and accuracy of financial reporting, as well as increase the accountability of corporate governance, in publicly traded companies. Penalties for noncompliance range from fines to jail terms. Executives in firms covered by this law seek assurance for the reliability and quality of information systems from senior information technology managers. In turn, IT managers will likely ask information security managers to verify the confidentiality and integrity of the information systems in a process known as subcertification.

The two sections of SOX that most affect information security are Section 302 and Section 404. Section 302 of SOX requires an organization's executives to personally certify the accuracy and completeness of their financial reports as well as assess and report on the effectiveness of internal controls for their financial reporting. Section 404 complements the requirement to assess and report on internal controls, mandating that these assessment reports must be audited by an outside firm. Because SOX does not delineate IT from non-IT internal controls, and because most modern financial systems and their controls are based on IT and information security technologies, the expectation of effective controls trickles through the organization to the Information Security department.

Freedom of Information Act of 1966

The *Freedom of Information Act (FOIA)* allows any person to request access to federal agency records or information not determined to be a matter of national security. Agencies of the federal government are required to disclose requested information upon receipt of a written request. This requirement is enforceable in court. However, some information is protected from disclosure, and the act does not apply to state or local government agencies or to private businesses or individuals, although many states have their own version of the FOIA.

Payment Card Industry Data Security Standards (PCI DSS)

For organizations that process payment cards, such as credit cards, debit cards, ATM cards, store-value cards, gift cards, or other related items, the Payment Card Industry (PCI) Security Standards Council offers a standard of performance to which participating organizations must comply. While not a law, per se, this standard has proven to be very effective in improving industry practices. The PCI Security Standards Council was founded in 2006 by a group of industry businesses that include American Express, Visa, Discover Financial Services, JCB, and MasterCard Worldwide. The Security Standards Council established a set of regulatory mandates with which organizations must comply to be certified by the PCI Council. These regulations, the *Payment Card Industry Data Security Standards (PCI DSS)*, are designed to enhance the security of customers' account data. The regulations include requirements for information security policies, procedures, and management, as well as technical software and networking specifications.

> *PCI DSS was developed to encourage and enhance cardholder data security and facilitate the broad adoption of consistent data security measures globally. PCI DSS provides a baseline of technical and operational requirements designed to protect account data. PCI DSS applies to all entities involved in payment card processing, including merchants, processors, acquirers, issuers, and service providers. PCI DSS also applies to all other entities that store, process, or transmit cardholder data (CHD) and/or sensitive authentication data (SAD).*[16]

PCI DSS addresses six key areas with 12 requirements, as shown in Table 6-4.

The Council has also issued requirements called the Payment Application Data Security Standard (PA DSS) and PCI Pin Transaction Security (PCI PTS), which provide additional specifications for components of payment card processing.

 For more information on PCI DSS, visit *www.pcisecuritystandards.org/*.

Table 6-4   PCI DSS Requirements[17]

PCI DSS Area	PCI DSS Requirement
Build and maintain a secure network and systems	Install and maintain a firewall configuration to protect cardholder data.
	Do not use vendor-supplied defaults for system passwords and other security parameters.
Protect cardholder data	Protect stored cardholder data.
	Encrypt transmission of cardholder data across open, public networks.
Maintain a vulnerability management program	Protect all systems against malware and regularly update antivirus software or programs.
	Develop and maintain secure systems and applications.
Implement strong access control measures	Restrict access to cardholder data by a business need to know.
	Identify and authenticate access to system components.
	Restrict physical access to cardholder data.
Regularly monitor and test networks	Track and monitor all access to network resources and cardholder data.
	Regularly test security systems and processes.
Maintain an information security policy	Maintain a policy that addresses information security for all personnel.

State and Local Regulations

A critical fact to keep in mind when reading federal computer laws is that most of them are written specifically to protect federal information systems. Those laws have little applicability to private organizations, so an organization first must determine which federal laws apply to it and when. Security practitioners in all organizations must also be cognizant of the state and local laws that protect and apply to them. Information security professionals must understand state laws and regulations and ensure that their organizations' security policies and procedures are in compliance. Most U.S. states have their own breach notification laws and regulations that apply to residents; practitioners are expected to be aware of nuanced differences from state to state.

For example, in 1991, the state of Georgia passed the *Georgia Computer Systems Protection Act*, which protects information and established penalties for the use of information technology to attack or exploit information systems. In 1998, Georgia passed its *Identity Fraud Act* (updated in 2002 and 2010), which established strong penalties for identity theft and the inappropriate disposal of customer confidential information.

 For more information on state security laws, visit the National Conference of State Legislatures Web site at *www.ncsl.org*. Use the search box to find your state's security breach notification laws, data disposal laws, and identity theft statutes.

International Laws And Legal Bodies

IT professionals and information security practitioners must realize that when their organizations do business on the Internet, they do business globally. As a result, these professionals must be sensitive to the laws and ethical values of many different cultures, societies, and countries. When it comes to certain ethical values, you may be unable to please all of the people all of the time, but the laws of other nations is one area in which it is certainly *not* easier to ask for forgiveness than for permission.

Several security bodies and laws are described in this section. Because of the political complexities of relationships among nations and differences in culture, few current international laws cover privacy and information security. The laws discussed in this section are important, but they are limited in their enforceability. The American Society of International Law is one example of an American institution that deals with international law (see *www.asil.org*).

U.K. Computer Security Laws

The following laws are in force in the United Kingdom and are similar to those described earlier for the United States:

- *Computer Misuse Act, 1990*—Defines three "computer misuse offenses": unauthorized access to computer material, unauthorized access with intent to commit or facilitate commission of further offenses, and unauthorized acts with intent to impair, or with recklessness as to impairing, operation of computers, etc.[18]
- *Privacy and Electronic Communications (EC Directive) Regulations, 2003*—Revoked the Data Protection and Privacy Regulations of 1999 and focuses on protection against unwanted or harassing phone, e-mail, and SMS messages.
- *Police and Justice Act, 2006*—Updated the Computer Misuse Act, modified the penalties, and created new crimes defined as "unauthorized acts with intent to impair operation of computers, etc.,"[19] and the manufacture or provision of materials used in computer misuse offenses.
- *Personal Internet Safety, 2007*—A report published by the House of Lords Science and Technology Committee provided a public service and criticized the U.K. government's lack of action in protecting personal Internet safety.

Australian Computer Security Laws

The following laws are in force in Australia and its territories, and are like those described earlier for the United States:

- *Privacy Act, 1988*—Regulates the collection, storage, use, and disclosure of personal information. Applies both to private and public sectors. Contains 11 information privacy principles for handling personal information by most public-sector agencies, and 10 national privacy principles for handling of personal information by nongovernment agencies.[20]
- *Telecommunications Act, 1997*—Updated as of October 2013; contains regulation related to the collection and storage of privacy data held by telecommunications service providers.
- *Corporations Act, 2001*—Updated by the Corporations Regulations of 2001 and 2002; focuses on business relationships but, like SOX, contains provisions related to financial reporting and audits.
- *Spam Act, 2003*—Legislation designed to regulate the amount of unwanted commercial marketing materials, especially via e-mail. Requires businesses to obtain *consent* of recipients, ensure that businesses accurately *identify* the recipients, and provide a mechanism by which the recipients may *unsubscribe* from commercial messages.
- *Cybercrime Legislation Amendment Bill, 2011*—Designed to align Australian laws with the European Convention on Cybercrime (see next section); the bill specifies information that communications carriers and Internet service providers must retain and surrender when requested by law enforcement.

Council of Europe Convention on Cybercrime

In 2001, the Council of Europe drafted the European Council Cybercrime Convention, which empowers an international task force to oversee a range of Internet security functions and to standardize technology laws across international borders. It also attempts to improve the effectiveness of international investigations into breaches of technology law. This convention is well received by advocates of intellectual property rights because it provides for copyright infringement prosecution.

As with any complex international legislation, the Cybercrime Convention lacks any realistic provisions for enforcement. The goal of the convention is to simplify the acquisition of information by law enforcement agents in certain types of international crimes and during the extradition process. The convention has more than its share of skeptics, who see it as an attempt by the European community to exert undue influence to control a complex problem. Critics of the convention say that it could create more problems than it resolves. As the product of a number of governments, the convention tends to favor the interests of national agencies over the rights of businesses, organizations, and individuals.

Until October 2015, many U.S. organizations that worked internationally with European Union (EU) countries and organizations had to comply with the U.S.–EU Safe Harbor Framework, a set of guidelines implemented between 1998 and 2000 and designed to facilitate data transfers between EU- and U.S.-regulated organizations. Differences in regulations between these two groups had created difficulties in transferring customer data, especially because of the EU's stricter privacy regulations.

In October 2015, the European Court of Justice (ECJ) overturned the Safe Harbor Framework, claiming the self-certification provisions were inadequate to protect customer privacy data. In 2016, a replacement framework known as the EU–U.S. Privacy Shield was developed to allow for the transfer of personal data between the EU and the United States. A similar framework has been developed for U.S. and Swiss business commerce.

The set of laws known as the General Data Protection Regulation (GDPR) has specific requirements regarding the transfer of data from the EU. One of these requirements is that transfers can occur only to countries deemed to have adequate data protection laws. The Privacy Shield is designed to implement a program in which participating companies are deemed as having adequate protection, which will facilitate the transfer of information.

 For more information on the Privacy Shield framework, visit the International Trade Commission's (ITC) privacy shield Web page at *www.privacyshield.gov/welcome*.

World Trade Organization and the Agreement on Trade-Related Aspects of Intellectual Property Rights

The *Agreement on Trade-Related Aspects of Intellectual Property Rights (TRIPS)*, created by the World Trade Organization (WTO) and negotiated from 1986 to 1994, introduced intellectual property rules into the multilateral trade system. It is the first significant international effort to protect intellectual property rights. It outlines requirements for governmental oversight and legislation of WTO member countries to provide minimum levels of protection for intellectual property. The WTO TRIPS agreement covers five issues:

- How basic principles of the trading system and other international intellectual property agreements should be applied
- How to give adequate protection to intellectual property rights
- How countries should enforce those rights adequately within their own borders
- How to settle disputes on intellectual property between members of the WTO
- Special transitional arrangements during the period when the new system was being introduced[21]

Digital Millennium Copyright Act

The *Digital Millennium Copyright Act (DMCA)* is the American contribution to an international effort by the World Intellectual Properties Organization (WIPO) to reduce the impact of copyright, trademark, and privacy infringement, especially when accomplished via the removal of technological copyright protection measures. This law was created in response to the 1995 adoption of *Directive 95/46/EC* by the European Union, which added protection for individual citizens with regard to the processing of personal data and its use and movement. The United Kingdom has implemented a version of this law called the *Database Right* to comply with Directive 95/46/EC.

The DMCA includes the following provisions:

- Prohibits the circumvention of protections and countermeasures implemented by copyright owners to control access to protected content
- Prohibits the manufacture of devices to circumvent protections and countermeasures that control access to protected content
- Bans trafficking in devices manufactured to circumvent protections and countermeasures that control access to protected content
- Prohibits the altering of information attached or embedded into copyrighted material
- Excludes Internet service providers from certain forms of contributory copyright infringement

In June 2016, the United States and the EU signed an agreement that superseded the Safe Harbor guidelines discussed earlier. The replacement agreement serves as a data privacy umbrella for EU citizens and allows cooperation between American and European law enforcement agencies in criminal investigations. It is the latest attempt to implement a solution for the issues that emerged when the Safe Harbor data-sharing agreement was ruled invalid by a Court of Justice of the European Union in October 2015. Industry observers had warned of economic consequences that the lack of certainty involving data-sharing agreements could create. Even the 2016 agreement may not have the desired effect. Some organizations have responded to this uncertainty by avoiding simple compliance with specific government policies and moving to use more stringent standards. Some companies are considering the adoption of Binding Corporate Rules (BCRs) accreditation. That standard enables companies that obtain BCR accreditation to transfer personal data outside of the EU in a secure manner and in accordance with local laws and regulations. Security practitioners are closely monitoring this policy difference between the United States and the EU to find ways to meet important policy compliance demands.

Ethics And Information Security

Many professionally regulated disciplines have explicit rules that govern the ethical behavior of their members. For example, doctors and lawyers who commit egregious violations of their professions' canons of conduct can have their legal ability to practice revoked. Unlike the medical and legal fields, however, the information technology and information security fields do not have binding codes of ethics. Instead, professional associations such as the ACM and ISSA, and certification agencies such as (ISC)² and ISACA, work to maintain ethical codes of conduct for their respective memberships. While these professional organizations can prescribe ethical conduct, they do not have the authority to banish violators from practicing their trade. To begin exploring some of the ethical issues of information security, review the Ten Commandments of Computer Ethics in the nearby feature.

The Ten Commandments of Computer Ethics from the Computer Ethics Institute[22]

1. Thou shalt not use a computer to harm other people.
2. Thou shalt not interfere with other people's computer work.
3. Thou shalt not snoop around in other people's computer files.
4. Thou shalt not use a computer to steal.
5. Thou shalt not use a computer to bear false witness.
6. Thou shalt not copy or use proprietary software for which you have not paid.
7. Thou shalt not use other people's computer resources without authorization or proper compensation.
8. Thou shalt not appropriate other people's intellectual output.
9. Thou shalt think about the social consequences of the program you are writing or the system you are designing.
10. Thou shalt always use a computer in ways that ensure consideration and respect for your fellow humans.

Ethical Differences Across Cultures

Cultural differences can make it difficult to determine what is ethical and what is not—especially when it comes to the use of computers. Studies on ethics and computer use reveal that people of different nationalities have different perspectives; difficulties arise when one nationality's ethical behavior violates the ethics of another national group. For example, to Western cultures, many of the ways in which Asian cultures use computer technology amount to software piracy. This ethical conflict arises out of Asian traditions of collective ownership, which clash with the protection of intellectual property.

Approximately 90 percent of all packaged software used by firms in the United States is created within the country. The Business Software Alliance's 2018 global software study found that in 2017, 37 percent of software installed on computers globally was not properly licensed. Table 6-5 shows the results from the global BSA software study of the rates and commercial values of unlicensed PC software installations biennially between 2011 and 2017, both by world region and within G20 countries.

Some countries are more relaxed than others when dealing with intellectual property copy restrictions. A study published in 1999 examined the computer-use ethics in several nations, including Singapore, Hong Kong, the United States, England, Australia, Sweden, Wales, and the Netherlands.[23] This study selected various computer-use vignettes (see the feature titled "The Use of Scenarios in Computer Ethics Studies") and presented them to university students in the various nations. The study did not categorize or classify the responses as ethical or unethical. Instead, the responses only indicated a degree of ethical sensitivity or knowledge about the performance of the characters in the short case studies. The scenarios were grouped into three categories of ethical computer use: software license infringement, illicit use, and misuse of corporate resources.[24]

Table 6-5   Rates and Commercial Value of Unlicensed PC Software Installations, 2011–2017[25]

	Rates and Commercial Values of Unlicensed PC Software Installations							
	Rates of Unlicensed Software Installation				Commercial Value of Unlicensed Software ($M)			
	2017	2015	2013	2011	2017	2015	2013	2011
Asia Pacific	57%	61%	62%	60%	$16,439	$19,064	$21,041	$20,998
Central and Eastern Europe	57%	58%	61%	62%	$2,910	$3,136	$5,318	$6,133
Latin America	52%	55%	59%	61%	$4,957	$5,787	$8,422	$7,459
Middle East and Africa	56%	57%	59%	58%	$3,077	$3,696	$4,309	$4,159
North America	16%	17%	19%	19%	$9,458	$10,016	$10,853	$10,958
Western Europe	26%	28%	29%	32%	$9,461	$10,543	$12,766	$13,749
Worldwide	37%	39%	43%	42%	$46,302	$52,242	$62,709	$63,456
Top 5 Countries								
United States	15%	17%	18%	19%	$8,612	$9,095	$9,737	$9,773
New Zealand	16%	18%	20%	22%	$62	$66	$78	$99
Japan	16%	18%	19%	21%	$982	$994	$1,349	$1,875
Australia	18%	20%	21%	23%	$540	$579	$743	$763
Austria	19%	21%	22%	23%	$121	$131	$173	$22
Bottom 5 Countries								
Libya	90%	90%	89%	90%	$66	$65	$50	$60
Venezuela	89%	88%	88%	88%	$317	$402	$1,030	$668
Zimbabwe	89%	90%	91%	92%	$7	$7	$4	$4
Yemen	88%	87%	87%	89%	$10	$11	$9	$15
Armenia	85%	86%	86%	88%	$17	$18	$26	$26

Software License Infringement

The topic of software license infringement, or piracy, is routinely covered by the popular press. Among study participants, attitudes toward piracy were generally similar; however, participants from the United States and the Netherlands showed statistically significant differences in attitudes from those of the overall group. Participants from the United States were significantly less tolerant of piracy, while those from the Netherlands were significantly more permissive. Although other studies have reported that the Pacific Rim countries of Singapore and Hong Kong are hotbeds of software piracy, this study found tolerance for copyright infringement in those countries to be moderate, as were attitudes in England, Wales, Australia, and Sweden. This could mean that the people surveyed understood what software license infringement was but felt either that certain use was not piracy or that their society permitted this piracy in some way. Peer pressure, the lack of legal disincentives, the lack of punitive measures, and other reasons could explain why users in these alleged piracy centers disregarded intellectual property laws despite their professed attitudes toward them. Even though participants from the Netherlands displayed a more permissive attitude toward piracy, that country only ranked third in piracy rates of the nations surveyed in the study.

Illicit Use

The study respondents unilaterally condemned viruses, hacking, and other forms of system abuse. There were, however, different degrees of tolerance for such activities among the groups. Students from Singapore and Hong Kong proved to be significantly more tolerant than those from the United States, Wales, England, and Australia. Students from Sweden and the Netherlands were also significantly more tolerant than those from Wales and Australia, but significantly less tolerant than those from Hong Kong. The low overall degree of tolerance for illicit system use may be a function of the easy correspondence between the common crimes of breaking and entering, trespassing, theft, destruction of property, and their computer-related counterparts.

Misuse of Corporate Resources

The scenarios examined levels of tolerance for misuse of corporate resources, and each presented a different situation in which corporate assets were used for nonbusiness purposes without specifying the company's policy on personal use of its resources. In general, participants displayed a rather lenient view of personal use of company equipment. Only students from Singapore and Hong Kong viewed this personal use as unethical. There were several substantial differences in this category, with students from the Netherlands revealing the most lenient views. With the exceptions of students from Singapore and Hong Kong, many people from many cultural backgrounds indicated that unless an organization explicitly forbids personal use of its computing resources, such use is acceptable.[26]

Larger organizations, especially those that operate in international markets, are faced with cultural differences in ethical perceptions and decision making. For example, the Boeing Company has a clear and well-developed Ethics and Business Conduct program. It seeks to communicate company standards of ethical business conduct to all employees, inform all stakeholders of the policy and procedure that governs ethical conduct, identify company processes that help stakeholders comply with corporate standards of conduct, and promote an ongoing awareness of ethical conduct within the company. Like other large organizations, Boeing takes its business values and corporate conduct program very seriously. The approach is best summarized as "Communicate, Educate, and Execute," in which Boeing seeks to inform all corporate stakeholders about ethically motivated actions and then implement programs to achieve its stated values in practice.

In a nutshell, Boeing promotes the goal that all stakeholders will conduct business dealings fairly, impartially, and in an ethical and proper manner consistent with its code of conduct.

 To learn more about the Boeing ethics program, visit the Boeing Web site at *www.boeing.com/principles/ethics-and-compliance.page*.

Ethics and Education

Attitudes toward the ethics of computer use are affected by many factors other than nationality. Differences are found among people within the same country, within the same social class, and within the same company. Key studies reveal that education is the overriding factor in leveling ethical perceptions within a small population. Employees must be trained and kept aware of many topics related to information security, not the least of which is the expected behavior of an ethical employee. This education is especially important in information security, as many employees may not have the formal technical training to understand that their behavior is unethical or even illegal. Proper ethical and legal training is vital to creating an informed and well-prepared system user.

The Use of Scenarios in Computer Ethics Studies[27]

The following vignettes can be used in an open and frank discussion of computer ethics. Review each scenario carefully and respond to each question using a form of the following statement, choosing the description you consider most appropriate: *I feel the actions of this person were (very ethical/ethical/neither ethical nor unethical/unethical/very unethical).* Then, justify your response.

1. A scientist developed a theory that required proof through the construction of a computer model. He hired a computer programmer to build the model, and the theory was shown to be correct. The scientist won several awards for the development of the theory, but he never acknowledged the contribution of the computer programmer.

   The scientist's failure to acknowledge the computer programmer was:

2. The owner of a small business needed a computer-based accounting system. He identified the various inputs and outputs he felt were required to satisfy his needs. Then he showed his design to a computer programmer and asked if she could implement such a system. The programmer knew she could because she had developed much more sophisticated systems in the past. In fact, she thought the design was rather crude and would soon need several major revisions. But she didn't voice her thoughts because the business owner didn't ask, and she wanted to be hired to implement the needed revisions.

   The programmer's decision not to point out the design flaws was:

3. A student found a loophole in his university's computer system that allowed him access to other students' records. He told the system administrator about the loophole, but continued to access student records until the problem was corrected two weeks later.

   The student's action in searching for the loophole was:

   The student's action in continuing to access others' records for two weeks was:

   The system administrator's failure to correct the problem sooner was:

4. A computer user ordered an accounting system from a popular software vendor's Web site. When he received his order, he found that the store had accidentally sent him a very expensive word-processing program as well as the accounting package he had ordered. The invoice listed only the accounting package. The user decided to keep the word-processing program.

   The customer's decision to keep the word-processing program was:

5. A programmer at a bank realized that she had accidentally overdrawn her checking account. She made a small adjustment in the bank's accounting system so that her account would not incur a service charge. As soon as she deposited funds that made her balance positive again, she corrected the bank's accounting system.

   The programmer's modification of the accounting system was:

6. A computer programmer built and sold small computer applications to supplement his income. He worked for a moderately sized computer vendor, and would frequently go to his office on Saturdays when no one was working and use his employer's computer to develop the applications. He did not hide the fact that he was entering the building; he had to sign a register at a security desk each time he entered.

   The programmer's weekend use of the company computer was:

7. A student in a computer class was also employed at a local business part-time. Frequently her class homework required using popular word-processing and spreadsheet packages. Occasionally she did her homework on the office computer at her part-time job during coffee or meal breaks.

   The student's use of the company computer was:

   If the student had done her homework during "company time" (not during a break), her use of the company computer would have been:

8. A university student learned to use an expensive accounting program in her accounting class. The student would go to the university computer lab and use the software to complete her assignments. Signs were posted in the lab indicating that copying software was forbidden. One day, she decided to copy the software anyway to complete her work assignments at home.

   If the student destroyed her copy of the software at the end of the term, her action in copying the software was:

   If the student forgot to destroy her copy of the software at the end of the term, her action in copying the software was:

   If the student never intended to destroy her copy of the software at the end of the term, her action in copying the software was:

9. A university student found out that a fellow student's personal Web site contained a "pirate" section of illegally copied software programs. He accessed the Web site and proceeded to download several games and professional programs, which he then distributed to several of his friends.

   The student's actions in downloading the games were:

   The student's actions in downloading the programs were:

   The student's actions in sharing the programs and games with his friends were:

10. An engineer needed a program to perform a series of complicated calculations. He found a computer programmer who was capable of writing the program, but would only hire the programmer if he agreed to share any liability that may result from an error in the engineer's calculations. The programmer was willing to assume any liability due to a program malfunction, but was unwilling to share liability due to an error in the engineer's calculations.

   The programmer's position in this situation is:

   The engineer's position in this situation is:

11. A manager of a company that sells Web hosting services bought similar services from a competitor. She used her access to the competitor's computer to try to break the security system, identify other customers, and cause the system to crash. She used the service for a year and always paid her bills promptly.

   The manager's actions were:

12. A student programmer decided to write a virus program. Such programs usually spread automatically by making copies of themselves onto other users' media (like flash drives). The student wrote a program that caused the computer to ignore every fifth command entered by a user. The student took his program to the university computing lab and installed it on one of the computers. Before long, the virus had spread to hundreds of users.

   The student's action of infecting hundreds of users' flash drives was:

   If the virus program output the message "Have a nice day," then the student's action of infecting hundreds of users' flash drives would have been:

   If the virus erased files, then the student's action of infecting hundreds of users' flash drives would have been:

Deterring Unethical and Illegal Behavior

There are three general causes of unethical and illegal behavior:

- *Ignorance*—Ignorance of the law is no excuse; however, ignorance of policy and procedures is. The first method of deterrence is education, which is accomplished by designing, publishing, and disseminating an organization's policies and relevant laws, and by obtaining agreement to comply with these policies and laws from all members of the organization. Reminders, training, and awareness programs keep policy information in front of employees to support retention and compliance.
- *Accident*—People who have authorization and privileges to manage information within the organization are most likely to cause harm or damage by accident. Careful planning and control help prevent accidental modification to systems and data.
- *Intent*—Criminal or unethical intent goes to the state of mind of the person performing the act; it is often necessary to establish criminal intent to successfully prosecute offenders. Protecting a system against those with intent to cause harm or damage is best accomplished by means of technical controls, and vigorous litigation or prosecution if these controls fail.

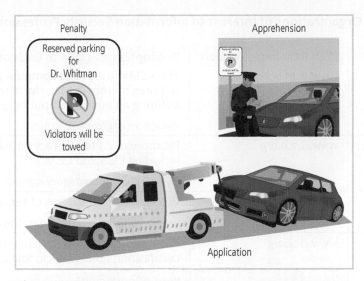

Figure 6-4   Deterrents to illegal or unethical behavior

Whatever the cause of illegal, immoral, or unethical behavior, one thing is certain: Information security personnel must do everything in their power to deter these acts and to use policy, education and training, and technology to protect information and systems. Many security professionals understand the technology aspect of protection but underestimate the value of policy. However, laws, policies, and their associated penalties only provide deterrence if three conditions are present, as illustrated in Figure 6-4:

- *Fear of penalty*—Potential offenders must fear the penalty. Threats of informal reprimand or verbal warnings do not have the same impact as the threat of imprisonment or forfeiture of pay.
- *Probability of being apprehended*—Potential offenders must believe there is a strong possibility of being caught.
- *Probability of penalty being applied*—Potential offenders must believe that the penalty will be administered.

Codes Of Ethics Of Professional Organizations

Many professional organizations have established codes of conduct or codes of ethics that members are expected to follow. Codes of ethics can have a positive effect on people's judgment regarding computer use.[28] Unfortunately, many employers do not encourage their employees to join these professional organizations. However, employees who have earned some level of certification or professional accreditation can be deterred from ethical lapses if they fear losing that accreditation or certification by violating a code of conduct. Loss of certification or accreditation can dramatically reduce their marketability and earning power.

Security professionals have a responsibility to act ethically and according to the policies and procedures of their employers, their professional organizations, and the laws of society. Likewise, it is the organization's responsibility to develop, disseminate, and enforce its policies. The following discussion explains where professional organizations fit into the ethical landscape. Table 6-6 provides an overview of these organizations. Many of them offer certification programs that require applicants to subscribe formally to the ethical codes. Professional certification is discussed in Module 7.

Major IT and InfoSec Professional Organizations

Many of the major IT and information security professional organizations maintain their own codes of ethics.

Table 6-6 Professional Organizations of Interest to Information Security Professionals

Professional Organization	Web Resource Location	Description and Link to Code of Ethics
ACM	www.acm.org	The ACM is the oldest computing society; its code of ethics requires members to perform their duties in a manner befitting an ethical computing professional. www.acm.org/code-of-ethics
ISACA	www.isaca.org	Promotes a code of ethics for its certification holders, including CISA and CISM. www.isaca.org/credentialing/code-of-professional-ethics
ISSA	www.issa.org	Professional association of security professionals. www.members.issa.org/page/CodeofEthics
(ISC)²	www.isc2.org	Promotes a code of ethics based on four canons for its certification holders, including CISSP and SSCP. www.isc2.org/Ethics
SANS GIAC	www.giac.org	Promotes a code of ethics based on respect for the public, the certification, and its certification holders, including GIAC and GSE. www.giac.org/about/ethics
EC-Council	www.eccouncil.org	Promotes a code of ethics for its certification holders, including CCISO and CEH. www.eccouncil.org/code-of-ethics/

Association for Computing Machinery (ACM)

The ACM is a respected professional society that was established in 1947. Today it is "the world's largest educational and scientific computing society."[29] It is one of the few organizations that strongly promotes education and provides discounts for student members. The ACM's code of ethics requires its more than 100,000 members to perform their duties in a manner befitting an ethical computing professional. The code contains specific references to protecting the confidentiality of information, causing no harm (with specific references to viruses), protecting the privacy of others, and respecting the intellectual property and copyrights of others. The ACM (www.acm.org) also hosts more than 170 conferences annually and publishes a wide variety of professional computing publications, including the highly regarded Communications of the ACM.

International Information Systems Security Certification Consortium, Inc. (ISC)²

(ISC)² is a nonprofit organization that focuses on the development and implementation of information security certifications and credentials. The organization manages a body of knowledge on information security and administers and evaluates examinations for information security certifications. The code of ethics put forth by (ISC)² is primarily designed for the more than 167,000 information security professionals who have earned an (ISC)² certification, and has four mandatory canons: "Protect society, the commonwealth, and the infrastructure; act honorably, honestly, justly, responsibly, and legally; provide diligent and competent service to principals; and advance and protect the profession."[30] This code enables (ISC)² to promote reliance on the ethicality and trustworthiness of information security professionals as the guardians of information and systems. For more information, visit www.isc2.org.

SANS

Formerly known as the System Administration, Networking, and Security Institute, SANS was founded in 1989 as a professional research and education cooperative organization and has awarded certifications to more than 153,000 information security professionals since 1999. SANS offers a set of certifications through its Global Information Assurance Certification (GIAC) certification group. All GIAC-certified professionals are required to acknowledge that certification, and its privileges carry a corresponding obligation to uphold the GIAC code of ethics. Certificate holders who do not conform to this code face censure and may lose GIAC certification. For more information, visit *www.sans.org* and *www.giac.org*.

ISACA

Originally known as the Information Systems Audit and Control Association, ISACA is a professional association that focuses on auditing, control, and security. The membership comprises both technical and managerial professionals. ISACA (*www.isaca.org*) provides IT control practices and standards and includes many information security components within its areas of concentration, although it does not focus exclusively on information security. ISACA also has a code of ethics for its 145,000 constituents, and it requires many of the same high standards for ethical performance as the other organizations and certifications.

Information Systems Security Association (ISSA)

ISSA is a nonprofit society of more than 10,000 information security professionals in more than 100 countries. As a professional association, its primary mission is to bring together qualified information security practitioners for information exchange and educational development. ISSA (*www.issa.org*) provides regional chapters, scheduled conferences, meetings, publications, and information resources to promote information security awareness and education. ISSA also promotes a code of ethics, similar in content to those of (ISC)^2, ISACA, and the ACM, whose focus is "promoting management practices that will ensure the confidentiality, integrity, and availability of organizational information resources."[31]

EC-Council

EC-Council is another security certification organization, founded by CEO and Chairman of the Board Jay Bavisi. EC-Council (*www.eccouncil.org*) boasts more than 220,000 certified professionals in more than 145 countries. It offers a variety of security technical and managerial certifications, building on its renowned Certified Ethical Hacker (CEH) and CCISO certifications. EC-Council promotes a 19-point code of ethics for its certificate holder, available at *www.eccouncil.org/code-of-ethics/*.

Key U.S. Federal Agencies

Several key U.S. federal agencies are charged with the protection of American information resources and the investigation of threats or attacks against these resources. These organizations include the Department of Homeland Security (DHS) and its subordinate agencies—the U.S. Secret Service (USSS) and US-CERT—the National Security Agency, the Federal Bureau of Investigation (FBI), and the FBI's InfraGard program.

Department of Homeland Security

The *Department of Homeland Security (DHS*, at *www.dhs.gov*) was created in 2003 by the Homeland Security Act of 2002, which was passed in response to the events of September 11, 2001. DHS is made up of several directorates and offices through which it carries out its mission of protecting American citizens as well as the physical and information assets of the United States. The Cybersecurity and Infrastructure Security Agency (CISA) coordinates and leads efforts to discover and respond to attacks on national information systems and critical infrastructure. The Science and Technology Directorate is responsible for research and development activities in support of domestic defense. This effort is guided by an ongoing examination of vulnerabilities throughout the national infrastructure; the directorate sponsors the emerging best practices developed to counter threats and weaknesses in the system.

Table 6-7 describes the DHS departments and their functions.

DHS works with academic institutions nationally, focusing on resilience, recruitment, internationalization, growing academic maturity, and academic research. Resilience calls for academic institutions to improve their own preparedness for unexpected events. Recruitment refers to the roles of academic organizations in preparing students and recent graduates to fill the increasing demand for workers and managers in the preparedness industry. Internationalization recognizes that students around the world can help meet the increased demand. Recently, information security/cybersecurity and infrastructure protection have become more recognized as a discrete area of academic study. Academic organizations conduct ongoing research to help develop solutions in the areas of information security and crisis preparedness.[32]

Table 6-7 DHS Departments and Functions[33]

DHS Department	Function
Countering Weapons of Mass Destruction Office (CWMD)	CWMD is focused on preventing WMD attacks against the United States.
Cybersecurity and Infrastructure Security Agency (CISA)	CISA focuses on protecting the national critical infrastructure against cyber and physical threats, coordinating efforts of government agencies and private organizations.
Federal Emergency Management Agency (FEMA)	Supports citizens and first responders by providing preparation for, protection against, response to, and recovery from national and regional emergency events
Federal Law Enforcement Training Center (FLETC)	Provides training for all levels of law enforcement professionals
Management Directorate	Responsible for DHS budgets and appropriations, expenditure of funds, accounting and finance, procurement, human resources, information technology systems, facilities and equipment, and the identification and tracking of performance measurements
Office of Intelligence and Analysis	Uses information and intelligence from multiple sources to identify and assess current and future threats to the United States
Office of Operations Coordination	Monitors national security on a daily basis and coordinates activities within DHS and with governors, Homeland Security advisors, law enforcement partners, and critical infrastructure operators in all 50 states and more than 50 major urban areas nationwide
Science and Technology Directorate	The primary research and development arm of the DHS; it provides federal, state, and local officials with the technology and capabilities to protect the country
Transportation Security Agency (TSA)	Protects the nation's transportation systems
United States Citizenship and Immigration Services (USCIS)	Secures America's promise as a nation of immigrants by providing accurate and useful information to customers, granting immigration and citizenship benefits, promoting an awareness and understanding of citizenship, and ensuring the integrity of the immigration system
United States Coast Guard (USCG)	One of the five armed forces of the United States and the only military organization within DHS; the Coast Guard protects the maritime economy and the environment and defends maritime borders
United States Customs and Border Protection (CBP)	One of DHS's largest and most complex components, with the mission of keeping terrorists and their weapons out of the United States; it also helps secure and facilitate trade and travel while enforcing hundreds of U.S. regulations, including immigration and drug laws
United States Immigration and Customs Enforcement (ICE)	Promotes security and public safety through the criminal and civil enforcement of federal laws governing border control, customs, trade, and immigration
United States Secret Service (USSS)	Safeguards the nation's financial infrastructure and payment systems to preserve the integrity of the economy, and protects national leaders, visiting heads of state and government, designated sites, and national special security events

Source: Department of Homeland Security.

DHS's cybersecurity role extends from its Cybersecurity and Infrastructure Security Agency (CISA), which offers a variety of services to government, industry and the private sector, academia, nonprofit/NGO organizations, and the general public through their services portal, as illustrated in their services catalog (see Figure 6-5).

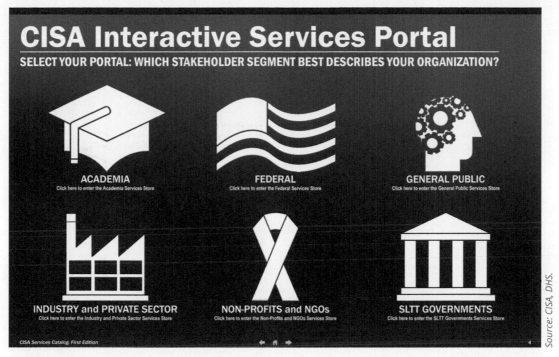

Figure 6-5   CISA interactive services portal[34]

The CISA services portal has components tailored to its constituent sectors, as illustrated in Figure 6-6.

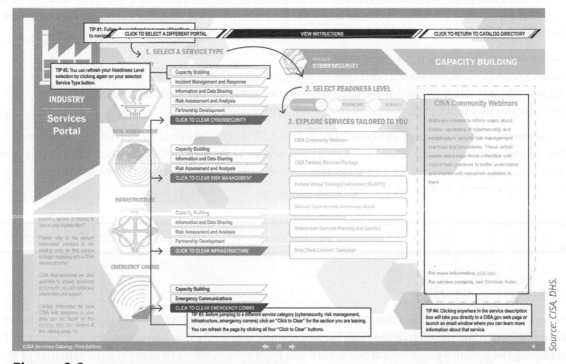

Figure 6-6   CISA services portal for industry[35]

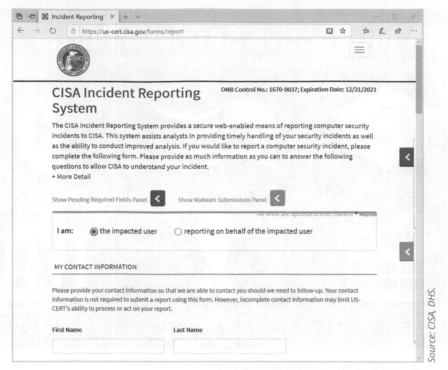

Figure 6-7 CISA incident reporting system

US-CERT

The U.S. Computer Emergency Readiness Team (US-CERT) is a division of DHS's CISA, which is focused on information security and response. CISA provides mechanisms to report the following attacks, including incidents, as illustrated in Figure 6-7:

- Phishing (*https://us-cert.cisa.gov/report-phishing*)
- Malware (*https://www.malware.us-cert.gov/MalwareSubmission/pages/submission.jsf*)
- Software vulnerabilities (*https://www.cisa.gov/coordinated-vulnerability-disclosure-process*)
- Other types of incidents (*https://us-cert.cisa.gov/forms/report*)

A cybersecurity career support program under US-CERT is the National Initiative for Cybersecurity Careers and Studies. "The National Initiative for Cybersecurity Careers & Studies (NICCS) is the nation's one-stop shop for cybersecurity careers and studies. It connects the public with information on cybersecurity awareness, degree programs, training, careers, and talent management."[36]

 For more information on NICCS and careers in cybersecurity, visit its Web site at *https://niccs.us-cert.gov/*.

U.S. Secret Service

The U.S. Secret Service was relocated from the Department of the Treasury to the DHS in 2002. In addition to its well-known mission of providing protective services for key members of the U.S. government, the Secret Service is charged with safeguarding the nation's financial infrastructure and payments systems to preserve the integrity of the economy. This charge is an extension of the agency's original mission to protect U.S. currency—a logical extension, given that the communications networks of the United States carry more funds than all the armored cars in the world combined. By protecting the networks and their data, the Secret Service protects money, stocks, and other financial transactions.

The Secret Service has a strategic mission to address cybersecurity-related activity:

Over the past several decades, the U.S. Secret Service has successfully identified, located, and arrested cybercriminals responsible for some of the most significant and widely publicized public and private industry data breaches. The U.S. Secret Service cybercrime mission has expanded the scope of its investigative efforts beyond its traditional limits.

As part of its mandate to combat financially motivated cybercrime, the U.S. Secret Service complements its investigative efforts with educational outreach programs. These programs are aimed at strengthening the ability of private and public sector entities to protect themselves against an array of cybercrime. The U.S. Secret Service conducts in-depth analyses of the activities, tools, and methodologies used by cybercriminals to better assess the evolving threats they pose to the financial infrastructure. The U.S. Secret Service then shares the results of these reviews with its network of public and private partners through its outreach programs.[37]

The USSS is active in fighting cybercrime, as illustrated in its 2019 annual report:

Secret Service investigations brought numerous high-profile cyber-criminals to justice in FY 2019. With a sustained investigative focus by dedicated special agents and analysts, our investigators closed cases amounting to $3.5 billion in victim losses. By arresting individuals before they could fully realize the gains from their crimes, Secret Service investigations also prevented a further $7.1 billion in potential fraud loss. The types of cases investigated in FY 2019 provide a window into the cyber threat environment. Examples include business e-mail compromises, card skimmers, network intrusions, and ATM unlimited cash out schemes.[38]

In 2004, Operation Firewall, a joint task force of the USSS, the Department of Justice, domestic and foreign law enforcement, and financial industry investigators, led to 28 arrests across the United States and six other countries; "the suspects … were involved in a global cyber organized crime network. Charges against the suspects included identity theft, computer fraud, credit card fraud and conspiracy."[39]

Federal Bureau of Investigation (FBI)

The FBI is the primary U.S. law enforcement agency. As such, it investigates both traditional crimes and cybercrimes, and works with the U.S. Attorney's Office to prosecute suspects under federal law (the U.S. Code). The FBI's mission changed dramatically after the terrorist attacks of September 11, 2001. Robert Mueller, the FBI's new director at the time, reorganized the agency to restructure its focus and priorities:

- *Protect the United States from terrorist attack*
- *Protect the United States against foreign intelligence operations and espionage*
- *Protect the United States against cyber-based attacks and high-technology crimes*
- *Combat public corruption at all levels*
- *Protect civil rights*
- *Combat transnational/national criminal organizations and enterprises*
- *Combat major white-collar crime*[40]

As part of the FBI's cybercrime mission, its key divisions include the Cyber Crime Division (*www.fbi.gov/investigate/cyber*) and Violent Crimes, including crimes against children by online predators (*www.fbi.gov/investigate/violent-crime*).

The Internet Crime Complaint Center (IC3; *www.ic3.gov*) is a partnership between the FBI and the National White-Collar Crime Center (NW3C). The IC3 serves as a clearinghouse for cybercrime complaints. People may submit claims through the IC3 Web site, as shown in Figure 6-8.

The FBI Cyber's Most Wanted list of its top 80 wanted cybercriminals (*https://www.fbi.gov/wanted/cyber*) is shown in Figure 6-9.

Source: FBI.

Figure 6-8   FBI Internet crime complaint reporting Web site

Source: FBI.

Figure 6-9   FBI Cyber's Most Wanted list

National InfraGard Program

Established in January 2001, the national InfraGard program (*www.infragard.org/*) began as a cooperative effort between the FBI's Cleveland field office and local technology professionals. The FBI sought assistance in determining a more effective method of protecting critical national information resources. The resulting cooperative, the first InfraGard chapter, was a formal effort to combat both cyber and physical threats. Since then, every FBI field office has established an InfraGard chapter to collaborate with public and private organizations and the academic community, and to share information about attacks, vulnerabilities, and threats. The national InfraGard program serves its members in four basic ways:

- Maintains an intrusion alert network using encrypted e-mail
- Maintains a secure Web site for communication about suspicious activity or intrusions
- Sponsors local chapter activities
- Operates a help desk for questions

InfraGard's most significant contribution is the free exchange of information with the private sector in the areas of threats and attacks on information resources. InfraGard has more than 60 regional chapters (such as *http://infragardatlanta.org/*), which provide numerous opportunities for individuals and organizations to interact with the agency.

National Security Agency (NSA)

Another key federal agency in the world of cybersecurity is the *National Security Agency (NSA)*:

> *The National Security Agency/Central Security Service (NSA/CSS) leads the U.S. government in cryptology that encompasses both signals intelligence (SIGINT) and information assurance (now referred to as cybersecurity) products and services, and enables computer network operations (CNO) in order to gain a decision advantage for the Nation and our allies under all circumstances.*[41]

The director of the NSA is also the chief of the Central Security Service, which is tasked with providing "timely and accurate cryptologic support, knowledge, and assistance to the military cryptologic community."[42]

The NSA is responsible for signals intelligence and **cybersecurity**—formerly referred to by the federal government as **information assurance**—both of which are synonymous with information security. The NSA's Cybersecurity Directorate provides advisories and technical guidance, threat intelligence and assessments, recommendations on cybersecurity products and services, and information on cybersecurity careers and education, as well as partnership opportunities.[43] The NSA is responsible for the protection of systems that store, process, and transmit classified information or information deemed to be of high national military or intelligence value.

The NSA's academic outreach program, called the National IA Education and Training Program (NIETP; *https://www.iad.gov/nietp/*), supports cybersecurity education and training. As part of the NIETP, the NSA works with DHS to recognize universities that offer information security education and that have integrated information security philosophies and efforts into their internal operations. These recognized "Centers of Excellence in Cyber Defense" for research or education receive the honor of displaying the recognition as well as being acknowledged by the NSA. Graduates of these programs receive certificates that indicate their accomplishment.

---

cybersecurity

The affirmation or guarantee of the confidentiality, integrity, and availability of information in storage, processing, and transmission; often used synonymously with "information security."

information assurance

See *cybersecurity*.

 For more information on the NSA's Cybersecurity Directorate, visit the Web site at *www.nsa.gov/what-we-do/cybersecurity/*.

Closing Scenario

Iris called the company's security hotline. The hotline is an anonymous way to report suspicious activity or abuse of company policy, although Iris chose to identify herself. The next morning, she was called to a meeting with an investigator from corporate security, which led to more meetings with others from corporate security and then with the director of human resources and Gladys Williams, the CIO of SLS.

Discussion Questions

1. Should Iris have approached Henry directly, or was the hotline the most effective way to take action? Why do you think so?
2. Should Gladys call the legal authorities? If so, which agency should she call?
3. Do you think this matter needs to be communicated elsewhere inside the company? Who should be informed and how? How about outside the company?

Ethical Decision Making

It seems obvious that Henry is doing something wrong. Do you think Henry acted in an ethical manner? Did Iris act in an ethical manner by determining the owner of the flash drive? Assuming that this incident took place in the United States, what law or laws has Henry violated? Suppose Iris had placed the flash drive back at the coffee station and forgotten the whole thing. Explain why her action would have been ethical or unethical.

Selected Readings

- *The Digital Person: Technology and Privacy in the Information Age*, by Daniel Solove. 2004. New York University Press.
- *The Practical Guide to HIPAA Privacy and Security Compliance*, by Kevin Beaver and Rebecca Herold. 2003. Auerbach.
- *When Good Companies Do Bad Things*, by Peter Schwartz. 1999. John Wiley and Sons.

Module Summary

- Laws are formally adopted rules for acceptable behavior in modern society. Ethics are socially acceptable behavior. The key difference between laws and ethics is that laws carry the authority of a governing body and ethics do not.
- Organizations formalize desired behavior in documents called policies. Policies must be read and agreed to before they are binding.
- Civil law comprises a wide variety of laws that govern a nation or state. Criminal law addresses violations that harm society and is enforced by agents of the state or nation.
- Private law focuses on individual relationships, and public law governs regulatory agencies. Key U.S. laws to protect privacy include the Federal Privacy Act of 1974, the Electronic Communications Privacy Act of 1986, and the Health Insurance Portability and Accountability Act of 1996.
- The desire to protect national security, trade secrets, and a variety of other state and private assets has led to the passage of several laws that restrict what information, information management resources, and security resources may be exported from the United States.
- Intellectual property is recognized as a protected asset in this country. U.S. copyright law extends this privilege to published works, including electronic media.
- Studies have determined that people of differing nationalities have varying perspectives on ethical practices with the use of computer technology.

- Deterrence can prevent an illegal or unethical activity from occurring. Deterrence requires significant penalties, a high probability of apprehension, and an expectation that penalties will be enforced.
- As part of an effort to encourage ethical behavior, many professional organizations have established codes of conduct or codes of ethics that their members are expected to follow.
- Several U.S. federal agencies are responsible for protecting American information resources and investigating threats against them.

Review Questions

1. What is the difference between law and ethics?
2. What is civil law, and what does it accomplish?
3. What are the primary examples of public law?
4. Which law amended the Computer Fraud and Abuse Act of 1986, and what did it change?
5. Which law was created specifically to deal with encryption policy in the United States?
6. What is privacy in an information security context?
7. What is another name for the Kennedy–Kassebaum Act (1996), and why is it important to organizations that are not in the healthcare industry?
8. If you work for a financial services organization such as a bank or credit union, which 1999 law affects your use of customer data? What other effects does it have?
9. What is the primary purpose of the USA PATRIOT Act, and how has it been revised since its original passage?
10. What is PCI DSS, and why is it important for information security?
11. What is intellectual property (IP)? What laws currently protect IP in the United States and Europe?
12. How does the Sarbanes–Oxley Act of 2002 affect information security managers?
13. What is due care? Why should an organization make sure to exercise due care in its usual course of operations?
14. How is due diligence different from due care? Why are both important?
15. What is a policy? How is it different from a law?
16. What are the three general categories of unethical computer use?
17. What are the three general causes of illegal or unethical activity?
18. Of the information security organizations listed in this module that have codes of ethics, which has been established for the longest time? When was it founded?
19. Of the organizations listed in this module that have codes of ethics, which is focused on auditing and control?
20. How do people from varying ethnic backgrounds differ in their views of computer ethics?

Exercises

1. What does CISSP stand for? Use the Internet to identify the ethical rules CISSP holders have agreed to follow.
2. For what kind of information security jobs does the NSA recruit? Use the Internet to visit the NSA's Web page and find out.
3. Using the resources in your library, find out what laws your state has passed to prosecute computer crime.
4. Go to *www.eff.org*. What are the current top concerns of this organization?
5. Using the ethical scenarios presented earlier in this module in the feature called "The Use of Scenarios in Computer Ethics Studies," finish each of the incomplete statements and bring your answers to class to compare them with those of your peers.

References

1. Franklin, Benjamin. "Pennsylvania Assembly: Reply to the Governor." National Archives. Accessed August 14, 2020, from *https://founders.archives.gov/documents/Franklin/01-06-02-0107*.

2. Noone, John B. *Rousseau's Social Contract: A Conceptual Analysis*. 1981. Athens: University of Georgia Press.

3. Aalberts, Robert J., Townsend, Anthony M., and Whitman, Michael E. "The Threat of Long-Arm Jurisdiction to Electronic Commerce." *Communications of the ACM* 41, no. 12 (December 1998): 15–20.

4. Doyle, Charles. "The USA PATRIOT Act: A Legal Analysis." April 15, 2002. Accessed August 14, 2020, from *www.fas.org/irp/crs/RL31377.pdf*.

5. Federal Information Security Management Act of 2002. Accessed August 14, 2020, from *https://csrc.nist.gov/topics/laws-and-regulations/laws/fisma*.

6. EPIC. "The Clipper Chip." March 6, 2004. Accessed August 14, 2020, from *http://epic.org/crypto/clipper/*.

7. Proofpoint. "Healthcare Email Security Regulations: HIPAA and Beyond." Accessed August 14, 2020, from *www.findwhitepapers.com/whitepaper8558*.

8. Ibid.

9. U.S. Government Federal Register. "Rules and Regulations." Vol. 78, No 17. January 25, 2013. Accessed August 14, 2020, from *www.govinfo.gov/content/pkg/FR-2013-01-25/pdf/2013-01073.pdf*.

10. Harrell, E. "Victims of Identity Theft, 2016." Report prepared for the Department of Justice Bureau of Justice Statistics. January 8, 2019. NCJ 251147. Accessed August 14, 2020, from *www.bjs.gov/content/pub/pdf/vit16.pdf*.

11. Ibid.

12. Ibid.

13. Federal Trade Commission. "The President's Identity Theft Task Force Releases Comprehensive Strategic Plan to Combat Identity Theft." Accessed June 6, 2016, from *www.ftc.gov/news-events/press-releases/2007/04/presidents-identity-theft-task-force-releases-comprehensive*.

14. Federal Trade Commission. "Immediate Steps to Repair Identity Theft." Accessed August 14, 2020, from *www.identitytheft.gov/Steps*.

15. Krebs, Brian. "New Federal Law Targets ID Theft, Cybercrime." October 1, 2008. Accessed August 14, 2020, from *http://voices.washingtonpost.com/securityfix/2008/10/new_federal_law_targets_id_the.html*.

16. PCI Security Standards Council. "Payment Card Industry (PCI) Data Security Standard: Requirements and Security Assessment Procedures, V. 3.2.1." Accessed August 14, 2020, from *www.pcisecuritystandards.org/document_library?category=pcidss&document=pci_dss*.

17. Ibid.

18. Computer Misuse Act of 1990. Accessed August 14, 2020, from *www.legislation.gov.uk/ukpga/1990/18/contents*.

19. Police and Justice Act of 2006. Accessed August 14, 2020, from *www.legislation.gov.uk/ukpga/2006/48/pdfs/ukpga_20060048_en.pdf*.

20. Australian Privacy Act of 1988. Accessed August 14, 2020, from *www.oaic.gov.au/privacy/the-privacy-act/*.

21. World Trade Organization. "Understanding the WTO: The Agreements—Intellectual Property: Protection and Enforcement." Accessed August 14, 2020, from *www.wto.org/english/thewto_e/whatis_e/tif_e/agrm7_e.htm*.

22. The Computer Ethics Institute. "The 10 Commandments of Computer Ethics." Accessed August 14, 2020, from *http://cpsr.org/issues/ethics/cei/*.

23. Whitman, Michael E., Townsend, Anthony M., and Hendrickson, Anthony R. "Cross-National Differences in Computer-Use Ethics: A Nine Country Study." *The Journal of International Business Studies* 30, no. 4 (1999): 673–687.

24. Ibid.

25. Business Software Alliance. "Seizing Opportunity through License Compliance: The BSA Global Software Survey 2018." Accessed August 14, 2020, from *https://gss.bsa.org/wp-content/uploads/2018/05/2018_BSA_GSS_Report_en.pdf*.

26. Whitman, Michael E., Townsend, Anthony M., and Hendrickson, Anthony R. "Cross-National Differences in Computer-Use Ethics: A Nine Country Study." *The Journal of International Business Studies* 30, no. 4 (1999): 673–687.

27. Ibid.

28. Harrington, Susan J. "The Effects of Codes of Ethics and Personal Denial of Responsibility on Computer Abuse Judgment and Intentions." *MIS Quarterly* 20, no. 3 (September 1996): 257–278.

29. ACM. "About ACM." Accessed August 14, 2020 from *www.acm.org/about-acm*.

30. International Information Systems Security Certification Consortium, Inc. "(ISC)[2] Code of Ethics." Accessed August 14, 2020, from *www.isc2.org/Ethics*.

31. Information Systems Security Association (ISSA). "ISSA Code of Ethics." ISSA Online. Accessed August 14, 2020, from *www.issa.org/issa-code-of-ethics*.

32. Department of Homeland Security. "Academic Engagement Overview." Accessed August 15, 2020, from *www.dhs.gov/topic/academic-engagement*.

33. Department of Homeland Security Department Components. Accessed August 15, 2020, from *www.dhs.gov/operational-and-support-components*.

34. CISA. CISA Services Catalog, Summer 2020. Accessed August 15, 2020, from *www.cisa.gov/sites/default/files/publications/FINAL%20FINAL_CISA%20Services%20Catalog_20200723_508.pdf*.

35. Ibid.

36. National Initiative for Cybersecurity Careers and Studies (NICCS). "About NICCS." Accessed August 15, 2020, from *http://niccs.us-cert.gov/home/about-niccs*.

37. United States Secret Service Cyber Investigations. Accessed August 15, 2020, from *www.secretservice.gov/investigation/#cyber*.

38. U.S. Secret Service. *Annual Report* 2019. Accessed August 15, 2020, from *www.secretservice.gov/data/press/reports/FY-2019-Annual-Report.pdf*.

39. U.S. Secret Service Operation Firewall Nets 28 Arrests. Accessed August 15, 2020, from *https://legacy.secretservice.gov/press/pub2304.pdf*.

40. FBI. Mission & Priorities. Accessed August 15, 2020, from *www.fbi.gov/about/mission*.

41. National Security Agency. Accessed August 15, 2020, from *www.nsa.gov/about/mission-strategy*.

42. Central Security Service (CSS). Accessed August 15, 2020, from *www.nsa.gov/about/central-security-service/*.

43. National Security Agency. "Cybersecurity." Accessed August 15, 2020, from *www.nsa.gov/What-We-Do/Cybersecurity/*.

Security and Personnel

I think we need to be paranoid optimists.

—Robert J. Eaton, Chairman
of the Board of Management,
DaimlerChrysler AG (Retired)

Upon completion of this material, you should be able to:

1. Describe where and how the information security function should be positioned within organizations

2. Explain the issues and concerns related to staffing the information security function

3. List and describe the credentials that information security professionals can earn to gain recognition in the field

4. Discuss how an organization's employment policies and practices can support the information security effort

5. Identify special security controls and privacy considerations for personnel management

Opening Scenario

Among Iris Majwubu's morning e-mails was a message from Charlie Moody. As she read the subject line and opened the message, Iris wondered why on earth the company CISO needed to see her. The e-mail read:

```
From: Charles Moody [cmoody@slsco.com]
To: Iris Majwubu [imajwubu@slsco.com]
Subject: I need to see you
Iris,
Since you were a material witness in the investigation, I wanted to advise you of
the status of the Magruder case. We completed all of the personnel actions on this
matter yesterday, and it is now behind us.
I wanted to thank you for the key role you played in helping the Corporate
Security Department resolve this security matter in its early stages so no company
assets were compromised.
Please set up an appointment with me in the next few days to discuss a few things.
—Charlie
```

Two days later, Iris entered Charlie Moody's office. He rose from his desk as she entered. "Come in, Iris," Charlie said. "Have a seat."

Nervously, she chose a chair closest to the door, not anticipating that Charlie would come around his desk and sit next to her. As he took his seat, Iris noticed that the folder in his hand looked like her personnel file. She took a deep breath, unsure exactly why Charlie had her file.

"I'm sure you're wondering why I asked you to meet with me," said Charlie. "The company really appreciates your efforts in the Magruder case. Because you followed policy and acted so quickly, we avoided a significant loss. You were right to bring that issue to your manager's attention rather than confronting Magruder directly. You not only made the right choice, but you acted quickly and showed a positive attitude throughout the whole situation—basically, I think you demonstrated an information security mindset. And that's why I'd like to offer you a transfer to Kelvin Urich's security projects team. I think they would really benefit from having someone like you on board."

"I'm glad I was able to help," Iris said, "but I'm not sure what to say. I've been a database administrator with the company for almost three years. I really don't know much about information security other than what I learned from the company training and awareness sessions."

"That's not a problem," Charlie said. "What you don't know you can learn." He smiled. "So how about it, are you interested in the job?"

Iris said, "It does sound interesting, but to be honest I hadn't been considering a career change." She paused for a moment, then added, "I am willing to think about it. But I have a few questions . . . ."

Introduction To Security And Personnel

When implementing information security, an organization must first address how to position and label the security function. Second, the information security community of interest must plan for the function's proper staffing or for adjustments to the staffing plan. Third, the IT community of interest must assess the impact of information security on every IT function and adjust job descriptions and documented practices accordingly. Finally, the general management community of interest must work with information security professionals to integrate solid information security concepts into the organization's personnel management practices.

To assess the effect that changes will have on the organization's personnel management practices, the organization should conduct a behavioral feasibility study *before* the program is implemented—that is, during the planning phase. The study should include an investigation into the levels of employee acceptance of change and resistance to it. Employees often feel threatened when an organization is creating or enhancing an information security program. They may perceive the program to be a manifestation of a "Big Brother" attitude and have questions such as the following:

- Will management be monitoring my work or my e-mail?
- Will information security staff go through my hard drive looking for evidence to fire me?
- Will the information security changes affect how efficient and effective I am in my job?

As you have learned in other modules, resolving these sorts of doubts and reassuring employees about the role of information security programs are fundamental objectives of implementation. Thus, it is important to gather employee feedback early and respond to it quickly. This module explores the issues involved in positioning the information security unit within the organization and in staffing the information security function. The module also discusses how to manage the many personnel challenges that arise across the organization and demonstrates why these challenges should be considered part of the organization's overall information security program.

Positioning The Security Function

There are several valid choices for positioning the information security department within an organization. The model commonly used by large organizations places information security within the information technology department and usually designates a CISO (chief information security officer) or CSO (chief security officer) to lead the function. The CISO most commonly reports directly to the company's top computing executive: the CIO (chief information officer) or vice president for IT. Such a structure implies that the goals and objectives of the CISO and CIO are aligned, but this is not always the case. By its very nature, an information security program can sometimes work at odds with the goals and objectives of the information technology department as a whole. The CIO, as the executive in charge of the organization's technology, strives for *efficiency* in the availability, processing, and accessing of company information. Thus, anything that limits access or slows information processing can impede the CIO's mission.

The 2019 (ISC)[2] Cybersecurity Workforce Study found that only 62 percent of organizations with 500 or more employees were led by a CISO, while 27 percent were led by a senior IT executive. The numbers drop to 50 percent and 30 percent, respectively, in organizations with fewer than 500 employees.[1]

The CISO's function is more like that of an internal auditor in that the CISO must direct the information security department to examine data in transmission and storage to detect suspicious traffic, and examine systems to discover information security faults and flaws in technology, software, and employees' activities and processes. These examinations can affect the speed at which the organization's information is processed and accessed. Because the addition of multiple layers of security inevitably slows users' access to information, information security may be viewed by some employees as a hindrance to the organization's operations. A good information security program maintains a careful balance between access and security, and works to educate all employees about the need for necessary delays to ensure the protection of critical information.

Because the goals and objectives of CIOs and CISOs tend to contradict each other, the trend among many organizations has been to separate the information security function from the IT division. An article in the IT industry magazine *InformationWeek* summarized the reasoning behind this trend quite succinctly: "The people who do and the people who watch shouldn't report to a common manager."[2] This sentiment was echoed in an ISO 27001 posting: "One of the most important things in information security is to avoid conflict of interest; that is, to separate the operations from control and audit."[3]

A survey conducted by the consulting firm Meta Group found that while only 3 percent of its clients position the information security department outside IT, these clients regarded such positioning as the mark of a forward-thinking organization. Another group, Forrester Research, concludes that the traditional structure of the CISO or CSO reporting to the CIO will be prevalent for years to come, but that it will begin to involve numerous variations in which different IT sections report information to the CSO, and thereby provide IS departments the critical input and control they need to protect the organization's IT assets.[4] In general, the data seems to suggest that while many organizations believe the CISO or CSO should function as an independent, executive-level decision maker, information security and IT are currently too closely aligned to separate into two departments.

In his book *Information Security Roles and Responsibilities Made Easy*, Charles Cresson Wood compiles the best practices from many industry groups regarding the positioning of information security programs. According to Wood, information security can be placed within any of the following organizational functions:[5]

- IT, as a peer of other subfunctions such as networks, applications development, and the help desk
- Physical security, as a peer of physical security or protective services
- Administrative services, as a peer of human resources or purchasing
- Insurance and risk management
- The legal department

According to the 2015 SEC/CISE Threats to Information Protection Report, which included a snapshot of the state of the industry:

> *Of those reporting they were the senior-most executive/manager responsible for security, exactly half (50.0 percent) indicated they reported to a top IT executive (CIO, CTO, VP-IT, etc.), 9.7 percent reported to a senior finance or accounting executive, and 5.6 percent reported to a senior operations*

executive (COO, CBO, etc.). Interestingly, 5.6 percent reported to some form of legal or regulatory executive (general counsel, VP of regulatory compliance, etc.) and 20.8 percent reported to an undisclosed general executive (VP, director). Of particular note were the 6.9 percent who indicated they reported to a specialized risk management executive (chief risk officer or executive director for risk management).

Only 15.5 percent of survey respondents reported directly to their company's top executive. Also, 45.1 percent had one executive between themselves and the top executive, while approximately 40 percent reported through three or more levels. The distance between these individuals and strategic decision makers is unsettling.[6]

Once the proper position of information security has been determined, the challenge is to design a reporting structure that balances the competing needs of each community of interest. The placement of information security in the reporting structure often reflects the fact that no one actually wants to manage it; thus, the unit is moved from place to place within the organization without regard for the impact on its effectiveness. Organizations should find a rational compromise by placing information security where it can best balance its duty to monitor compliance with its ability to provide the education, training, awareness, and customer service needed to make information security an integral part of the organization's culture. Also, the need to have the top security officer report directly to the executive management group instead of just the CIO becomes critical, especially if the security department is positioned in the IT function.

Staffing The Information Security Function

The selection of information security personnel is based on several criteria, some of which are not within the control of the organization. Consider the fundamental concept of supply and demand. When the demand for any commodity—for example, a critical technical skill—increases too quickly, supply initially fails to meet demand. Many future IS professionals seek to enter the security market by gaining the skills, experience, and credentials they need to meet this demand. In other words, they enter high-demand markets by changing jobs, going to school, or becoming trained. Until the new supply reaches the demand level, organizations must pay the higher costs associated with limited supply. Once the supply meets or exceeds the demand, organizations can become more selective, and the amount they are willing to pay drops. Hiring trends swing back and forth like a pendulum, from high demand and low supply to the other extreme of low demand and high supply, because the economy is seldom in a state of equilibrium. In 2002, the information security industry enjoyed a period of high demand, with relatively few qualified and experienced applicants available for organizations seeking their services. The economic realities of 2003 through 2006—a climate of lower demand for all IT professionals—led to more limited job growth for information security practitioners. From 2008 to 2014, the lackluster performance of the U.S. economy stifled jobs across IT, not just in information security. Since 2015, the demand has begun to skyrocket.

The latest forecasts for IT hiring in general and information security in particular project more openings than in many previous years. According to the Bureau of Labor Statistics (BLS), employment of information security analysts is projected to grow 31 percent from 2019 to 2029, which is much faster than the 4 percent average for all occupations.[7]

The BLS data shown in Figure 7-1 only examines one set of security positions that it terms as "information security analyst." It does not consider the positions of a security manager or executive, or those of an IT administrator or manager with information security responsibilities.

According to CyberSeek (*cyberseek.org*), there were more than a half million open cybersecurity and information security jobs in the United States at the end of 2020. The cybersecurity supply/demand "heat map" shown in Figure 7-2 illustrates the demand on a per-state basis and provides a national summary.

 For more information on job openings in information security, visit *www.cyberseek.org* and click on the Interactive map.

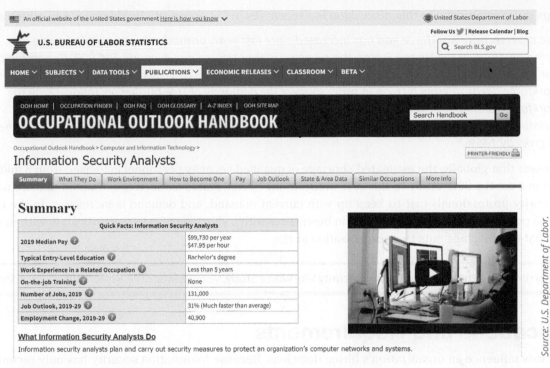

Figure 7-1   BLS information for information security analysts

Figure 7-2   *Cyberseek.org* supply/demand heat map

Perhaps more meaningful to this discussion is a recent (ISC)² Cybersecurity Workforce Study, which states:

> *The cybersecurity workforce gap has increased since last year, primarily due to a global surge in hiring demand. In the United States, the cybersecurity workforce gap is nearly 500,000. By combining our U.S. cybersecurity workforce estimates and this gap data, we can calculate that the cybersecurity workforce needs to grow by 62% in order to meet the demands of U.S. businesses today. Using the workforce estimate of 2.8 million based on the 11 economies for which we provided a workforce estimate and the global gap estimate of 4.07 million, we can estimate that the global workforce needs to grow by 145%.*[8]

This means that globally, the estimated shortage of qualified security personnel increased from 3 million to more than 4 million from the 2018 study to the 2019 study. In the United States alone, it is estimated that we need another 310,000 security professionals just to keep up with current demand, and demand is increasing. In the (ISC)² study, more than 65 percent of respondents worked in businesses with a shortage of cybersecurity staff, with more than half indicating that the shortage puts their organization at risk.[9]

 To download the 2020 (ISC)² Cybersecurity Workforce Study, visit *www.isc2.org/Research/Workforce-Study*.

Qualifications and Requirements

Several factors influence an organization's hiring decisions. Because information security has only recently emerged as a separate discipline, hiring in this field is complicated by a lack of understanding among organizations about what qualifications an information security professional should possess. In many organizations, information security teams currently lack established roles and responsibilities. Establishing better hiring practices in an organization requires the following:

- The general management community of interest should learn more about the skills and qualifications for information security positions and IT positions that affect information security.
- Upper management should learn more about the budgetary needs of information security and its positions. This knowledge will enable management to make sound fiscal decisions for information security and the IT functions that carry out many information security initiatives.
- The IT and general management communities should grant appropriate levels of influence and prestige to information security, especially to the role of CISO.

In most cases, organizations look for a technically qualified information security generalist who has a solid understanding of how an organization operates. In many fields, the more specialized professionals are more marketable. In information security, however, overspecialization can be risky. It is important, therefore, to balance technical skills with general knowledge about information security.

When hiring information security professionals, organizations frequently look for candidates who understand the following:

- How an organization operates at all levels
- That information security is usually a management problem and is seldom an exclusively technical problem
- How to work with people and collaborate with end users, and the importance of strong communications and writing skills
- The role of policy in guiding security efforts, and the role of education and training in making employees and other authorized users part of the solution rather than part of the problem
- Most mainstream IT technologies at a general level, not necessarily as an expert
- The terminology of IT and information security
- The threats facing an organization and how they can become attacks
- How to protect an organization's information assets from attacks
- How business solutions, including technology-based solutions, can be applied to solve specific information security problems

Entry into the Information Security Profession

Traditionally, information security professionals entered the field through one of two career paths. Some came from law enforcement or the military, where they were involved in national security or cybersecurity. Others were technical professionals—networking experts, programmers, database administrators, and systems administrators—who found themselves working on information security applications and processes more often than traditional IT assignments.

Today there are an increasing number of security professionals who actually start their careers in security, beginning as college students who select and tailor their degree programs to prepare for work in the field of information security. According to the most recent data from the (ISC)² Cybersecurity Workforce Study, 42 percent of respondents started their careers with a job in security, with 56 percent selecting security as a career during their education and 65 percent intending to work in security throughout their career.[10] Figure 7-3 illustrates the most common career path options.

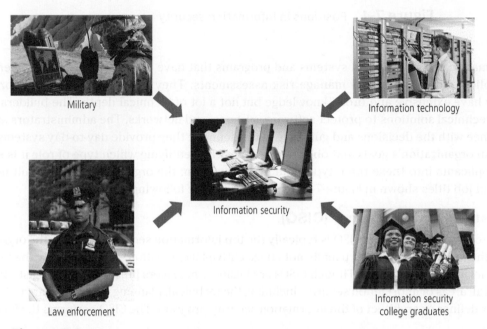

Figure 7-3   Career paths to information security positions

Source: This figure has multiple sources. Bottom left: © pio3/Shutterstock.com. Bottom right: © michaeljung/Shutterstock.com. Top right: © dotshock/Shutterstock.com. Center: © IM_photo/Shutterstock.com. Top left: Gorodenkoff/Shutterstock.com.

Many hiring managers in information security prefer to recruit security professionals who have proven IT skills and professional experience in another IT field. IT professionals who move into information security, however, tend to focus on technology, sometimes in place of general information security issues. Organizations can foster greater professionalism in the discipline by expanding beyond the hiring of proven IT professionals and instead filling positions by matching qualified candidates to clearly defined roles in information security.

Information Security Positions

The use of standard job descriptions can increase the degree of professionalism in the information security field and improve the consistency of roles and responsibilities among organizations. Organizations that expect to revise these roles and responsibilities can consult Charles Cresson Wood's book, *Information Security Roles and Responsibilities Made Easy,* which offers a set of model job descriptions for information security positions. The book also identifies the responsibilities and duties of IT staff members whose work involves information security.[11] Figure 7-4 illustrates a standard reporting structure for information security positions.

In an Information Security Roundtable interview with Andy Briney, Eddie Schwartz, then VP of Strategy at Guardent, described security positions as being classified into one of three areas: those that *define* information security programs, those that *build* the systems and create the programs to implement information security controls, and those that

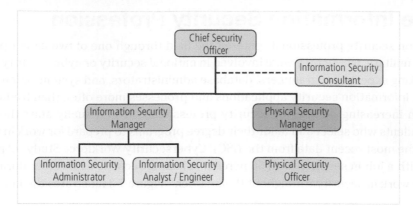

Figure 7-4 Positions in information security

administer information security control systems and programs that have been created. The "definers" are managers who provide policy and planning and manage risk assessments. They are typically senior information security managers—they have extensive and broad knowledge but not a lot of technical depth. The builders are techies who create security technical solutions to protect software, systems, and networks. The administrators apply the techies' tools in accordance with the decisions and guidance of the definers; they provide day-to-day systems monitoring and use to support an organization's goals and objectives. By clearly identifying which type of role it is seeking and then classifying all applicants into these three types and matching them, the organization can recruit more effectively.[12] Some examples of job titles shown in Figure 7-4 are discussed in the following sections.

Chief Information Security Officer (CISO)

Although the exact title may vary, the CISO is typically the top information security officer in the organization. As indicated earlier in the module, the CISO is usually not an executive-level position, and frequently the person in this role reports to the chief information officer. Though CISOs are business managers first and technologists second, they must be conversant in all areas of information security, including the technical, planning, and policy areas. In many cases, the CISO is the major definer or architect of the information security program. The CISO performs the following functions:

- Manages the overall information security program for the organization
- Drafts or approves information security policies
- Works with the CIO on strategic plans, develops tactical plans, and works with security managers on operational plans
- Develops information security budgets based on available funding
- Sets priorities for the purchase and implementation of information security projects and technology
- Makes decisions or recommendations for the recruiting, hiring, and firing of security staff
- Acts as the spokesperson for the information security team

The most common certification for this type of position is the Certified Information Security Manager (CISM), which is described later in this module. A bachelor's degree is almost always required, and in some cases a graduate degree is also preferred, although it may be from a number of possible disciplines, including information systems, computer science, another information technology field, criminal justice, military science, business, or other fields related to the broader topic of security.

A typical example of a CISO's job description is shown here. The example has been edited for length and is from a state government job posting, but it is very similar to postings in general industry.

Position: *Chief Information Security Officer*

Job duties: *The Chief Information Security Officer reports to the state's deputy division administrator (DET) and is responsible for the statewide security program.*

The CISO's role is to provide vision and leadership for developing and supporting security initiatives. The CISO directs the planning and implementation of enterprise IT system, business operation, and facility defenses against security breaches and vulnerability issues. This individual is also responsible for auditing existing systems while directing the administration of security policies, activities, and standards.

The CISO is responsible for providing regulatory oversight for information security. This oversight includes the development of enterprise-wide policy, procedures, and guidance for compliance with federal laws, regulations, and guidelines, and sound security and privacy practices. Additionally, the CISO is responsible for reviewing security program documentation developed to ensure compliance and further enhance security practices across all component agencies.

The CISO is responsible for deployed security across the enterprise, including platforms, networks, and security tools. The CISO is also responsible for identifying and assessing internal and external threats, vulnerabilities, and risks, as well as ensuring that robust monitoring, timely detection, containment, and incident response are in place to mitigate the exposure caused by a breach. The CISO provides leadership, guidance, direction, and authority for technology security across all corporate technology departments, including measurements applicable to services provided.

The CISO is responsible for ensuring that workflow within the division runs smoothly so that new technology projects are appropriately monitored for security risks and appropriate risk mitigation requirements are efficiently set forth and appropriately designed and delivered with the newly developed production system. Policies, procedures, technical standards, and architecture will need to be regularly reviewed and updated to prevent unauthorized access of State of Wisconsin technology systems.

Special notes:

Due to the nature of the position, the Department of Administration will conduct a thorough background check on applicant prior to selection.

Job knowledge, skills, and abilities:

General:

- *Strong oral and written communication skills, including the ability to communicate business and technical concepts and information effectively to a wide range of audiences, including the public*
- *Strong interpersonal skills, including the ability to work independently with high-level government officials, with business and IS managers and staff in federal, state, and local agencies, and with division and department managers in a decentralized environment*
- *Strong project management skills*
- *Demonstrated ability to effectively interface with technical staff, senior management, and external parties*
- *Proven ability to plan and organize work, requiring an in-depth understanding of security issues and ability to integrate into the work of others*
- *Ability to defend and explain difficult issues with respect to key decisions and positions to staff and senior officials*
- *Experience in analyzing enterprise business and technology issues in a large corporation or government organization*
- *Ability to establish credibility so decisions and recommendations are adopted*
- *Ability to identify appropriate members and develop effective teams with specific knowledge and skills needed to develop solutions and make recommendations*
- *Resourcefulness in identifying and obtaining information sources needed to perform responsibilities effectively*

Technological/specific:

- *Must be an intelligent, articulate, and persuasive leader who can serve as an effective member of the senior management team and who is able to communicate security-related concepts to a broad range of technical and nontechnical staff*
- *Security background, experience in business management, and professional expertise in security and law*
- *Strong technical background in information technology security*

- *Knowledge of secure software development*
- *Computer/network investigation skills and forensics knowledge*
- *Extensive knowledge of networks as well as system, database, and applications security*
- *Demonstrated ability to work with management and staff at various levels of the organization to implement sound security practices*
- *Ability to provide technical direction to security architects and project consultants to ensure appropriate security requirements are set forth on new development efforts*
- *Knowledge of standards-based architectures, with an understanding of how to get there, including compliance monitoring and enforceability*
- *Experience with business continuity planning, auditing, and risk management, as well as contract and vendor negotiation*
- *Strong working knowledge of security principles (such as authentication, vulnerability testing, penetration testing, auditing, crime scene preservation, and risk management) and security elements (such as locking systems, evacuation methods, perimeter controls, VPNs, and firewalls)*
- *Certifications such as Certified Protection Professional (CPP), Certified Information Systems Manager (CISM), or Certified Information Systems Security Professional (CISSP) preferred*[13]

Chief Security Officer (CSO)

In some organizations, the CISO's position may be combined with physical security responsibilities or may even report to a security manager who is responsible for both logical (information) security and physical security. Such a position is generally referred to as a CSO. The CSO must be capable and knowledgeable in both information security requirements and the "guards, gates, and guns" approach to protecting the physical infrastructure, buildings, and grounds of a business.

To qualify for this position, the candidate must demonstrate experience as a security manager and with planning, policy, and budgets. As mentioned earlier, some organizations prefer to hire people with law enforcement experience. The following is a typical example of a CSO's job description:

Position: *Director of Security*

Responsibilities: *Reporting to the Senior Vice President of Administration, the Director of Corporate Security will be responsible for all issues related to the security and protection of the company's employees, executives, facilities, proprietary data, and information. Accountable for the planning and design of the company's security programs and procedures, this individual will facilitate protection from and resolution of theft, threats, and other situations that may endanger the well-being of the organization. Working through a small staff, the Director will be responsible for executive protection, travel advisories, employee background checks, and a myriad of other activities throughout the corporation on a case-by-case basis. The Director will serve as the company's chief liaison with law enforcement agencies and, most importantly, will serve as a security consultant to all of the company's autonomously run divisions. Travel requirements will be extensive.*

Qualifications: *The ideal candidate will have a successful background with a federal law enforcement agency, or other applicable experience, that will afford this individual an established network of contacts throughout the country. Additional private industry experience with a sizeable corporation—or as a consultant to same—is preferable. A proactive attitude with regard to security and protection is a must. The successful candidate must be capable of strategically assessing ... client security needs and have a track record in areas such as crisis management, investigation, facility security, and executive protection. Finally, the candidate should have a basic understanding of the access and use of electronic information services as they apply to security issues. We seek candidates who are flexible enough to deal with varied business cultures and who possess the superior interpersonal skills to perform well in a consulting role where recommendations and advice are sought and valued, but perhaps not always acted upon. A college degree is required.*[14]

Security Manager

Security managers are accountable for the day-to-day operation of the information security program. They accomplish objectives identified by the CISO and resolve issues identified by technicians. Management of technology requires a general understanding of that technology, but it does not necessarily require proficiency in the technology's configuration, operation, and fault resolution. Note that several positions have titles that contain the word *manager* or suggest management responsibilities, but only people who are responsible for management functions, such as scheduling, setting relative priorities, or administering budgetary control, should be considered true managers.

A candidate for this position often has a bachelor's degree in technology, business, or a security-related field, as well as a CISSP certification. Traditionally, managers earn the CISSP or CISM, and technical professionals earn the Global Information Assurance Certification (GIAC). You will learn more about these certifications later in the module.

Security managers must have the ability to draft middle- and lower-level policies as well as standards and guidelines. They must have experience in traditional business matters, such as budgeting, project management, and personnel management. They must also be able to manage technicians, both in the assignment of tasks and in the monitoring of activities. Experience with business continuity planning is usually a plus.

The following is a typical example of a security manager's job description. Note that there are several types of security managers, as the position is much more specialized than that of a CISO's. Thus, when applying for a job as a security manager, you should read the job description carefully to determine exactly what the employer wants.

Position: *Information Security Manager*

Job description: *This management position reports to the Chief Information Security Officer. The successful candidate will manage the development of information security programs and control systems in conformance with organizational policy and standards across the organization. This is a high-visibility role that involves the day-to-day management of IT Security staff and their career development. The principal accountabilities for this role are as follows:*

- *Develop and manage information security programs and control systems under the supervision of the CISO in conjunction with the evolving information security architecture of the organization.*
- *Monitor performance of information security programs and control systems to maintain alignment with organizational policy and common industry practices for emerging threats and technologies.*
- *Prepare and communicate risk assessments for business risk in software developments as well as ongoing systems events (to include merger, acquisition, and divestiture) and ensure effective risk management across the organization's IT systems.*
- *Represent the information security organization in the organization's change management process.*
- *Perform assigned duties in the area of incident response management and disaster recovery response.*
- *Supervise assigned staff and perform other general management tasks as assigned, including budgeting, staffing, and employee performance reviews.*

Compare the preceding general job description with the following more specific job description found in a recent advertisement:

Position: *IT Security Compliance Manager*

Job description: *A job has arisen for an IT Security Compliance Manager reporting to the IT Security Manager. In this role you will manage the development of the client's IT security standards and operate a compliance program to ensure conformance at all stages of the systems life cycle. This is a key, hands-on role with the job holder taking an active part in the delivery of the compliance program. The role will also involve the day-to-day management of IT security staff and their career development. The principal accountabilities for this role are as follows:*

- *Develop and manage an IT security compliance program.*
- *Develop the client's security standards in line with industry standards and emerging threats and technologies.*

- *Identify IT-related business risk in new software development and ensure that effective risk management solutions are identified and complied with.*
- *Manage and conduct IT security compliance reviews in conjunction with operational and IT audit staff.*
- *Conduct investigations into security breaches or vulnerabilities.*

Candidate profile: *The ideal candidate should have five years' experience of managing the implementation of technical security controls and related operational procedures and must have sound business risk management skills. You must have a flexible approach to working and must be able and willing to work unsociable hours to meet the demands of the role.*[15]

The second example illustrates the confusion in the information security field regarding job titles and reporting relationships. The first job description identifies responsibilities for the position and describes points where information security interacts with other business functions, but the second spreads responsibilities among several business functions and does not seem to reflect a clearly defined role for the position or the information security unit within the organization. Until some similarity in job titles and expected roles and responsibilities emerges, information security job candidates should carefully research open positions instead of relying solely on the job title.

Security Analyst

Security analysts, also commonly referred to as security technicians, security architects, or security engineers, are technically qualified employees who are tasked to configure firewalls, deploy IDPSs, implement security software, diagnose and troubleshoot problems, and coordinate with systems and network administrators to ensure that an organization's security technology is properly implemented. A security analyst is often an entry-level position, but to be hired for this role, candidates must possess some technical skills. This often poses a dilemma for applicants, as many find it difficult to get a job in a new field without experience—they can only attain such experience by getting a job. As in the networking arena, security analysts tend to specialize in one major security technology group (such as firewalls, IDPSs, servers, routers, or software) and in one particular software or hardware package (such as Check Point firewalls, Palo Alto firewalls, or Tripwire IDPSs). These areas are sufficiently complex to warrant a high level of specialization, but to move up in the corporate hierarchy, security analysts must expand their knowledge horizontally—that is, they must gain an understanding of general organizational issues related to information security and its technical areas. Many of these tasks rely on the ability to work with security information and event management (SIEM) systems in widespread use.

The technical qualifications and position requirements vary for a security analyst. Organizations prefer an expert, certified, proficient technician. Regardless of the area of needed expertise, the job description covers some level of experience with a particular hardware and software package. Sometimes, familiarity with a technology secures an applicant an interview; however, actual experience in using the technology is usually required. The following is a typical job announcement for a security analyst:

Position: *Firewall Engineering Consultant*

Job Description: *Working for an exciting customer-focused security group within one of the largest managed network providers in the country. You will have the opportunity to expand your experience and gain all the technical and professional support to achieve within the group. Must have experience with third-line technical support of firewall technologies. Check Point certified. Experienced in Nokia systems.*

Package: *Possible company car, discretionary bonus, private health care, on-call pay, and overtime pay.*[16]

Because overtime and on-call pay are listed, this job is probably an hourly position rather than a salaried one, which is not uncommon for security analysts.

Credentials For Information Security Professionals

As mentioned earlier, many organizations seek industry-recognized certifications to screen candidates for the required level of technical proficiency. Unfortunately, however, most existing certifications are relatively new and not fully understood by hiring organizations. The certifying bodies are working hard to educate employers and professionals on the value and qualifications of their certificate programs. In the meantime, employers are trying to understand the match between certifications and position requirements, and hopeful professionals are trying to gain meaningful employment based on their new certifications.

There are many certifications available to a security professional. Some of the more prominent are covered here. Beyond these are a variety of certifications in related areas, such as digital forensics, networking, and other computing domains. Note that the requirements for these certifications are constantly evolving and may differ from what is shown here. Those interested in certification should always verify the current requirements from the vendor before attempting the exam.

(ISC)² Certifications

The International Information Systems Security Certification Consortium, known as (ISC)², offers security certifications such as the Certified Information Systems Security Professional (CISSP), the Systems Security Certified Practitioner (SSCP), and the Certified Secure Software Lifecycle Professional (CSSLP). You can visit the Web site at *www.isc2.org*.

CISSP

The CISSP certification is considered the most prestigious for security managers and CISOs. It recognizes mastery of an internationally identified Common Body of Knowledge (CBK) in information security. To sit for the CISSP exam, the candidate must have at least five years of direct, full-time experience as a security professional working in at least two of the eight domains of information security knowledge, or four years of direct security work experience in two or more domains. The candidate must also have a four-year college degree.

The CISSP exam consists of 100 to 150 multiple-choice questions and must be completed within six hours. It tests candidates on their knowledge of the following eight domains:

- Security and risk management
- Asset security
- Security architecture and engineering
- Communication and network security
- Identity and access management
- Security assessment and testing
- Security operations
- Software development security

CISSP certification requires successful completion of the exam and an endorsement. Once candidates successfully complete the exam, they have nine months to submit an endorsement by an actively credentialed CISSP or by their employer as validation of their professional experience. After earning the certification, the CISSP holder must earn 120 hours of continuing professional education (CPE) every three years, with a minimum of 20 hours per year. The breadth and depth of each of the eight domains makes CISSP certification one of the most challenging to obtain in information security.[17]

CISSP Concentrations   In addition to the major certifications that (ISC)² offers, a number of concentrations are available for CISSPs to demonstrate advanced knowledge beyond the CISSP CBK. Each concentration requires that the applicant be a CISSP in good standing, pass a separate examination, and maintain the certification through continuing professional education. These concentrations and their respective areas of knowledge are shown in the following list and presented on the (ISC)² Web site:

CISSP-ISSAP®: Information Systems Security Architecture Professional

- *Architect for Governance, Compliance and Risk Management*
- *Security Architecture Modeling*
- *Infrastructure Security Architecture*

- *Identity and Access Management (IAM) Architecture*
- *Architect for Application Security*
- *Security Operations Architecture*

CISSP-ISSEP: Information Systems Security Engineering Professional

- *Security Engineering Principles*
- *Risk Management*
- *Security Planning, Design, and Implementation*
- *Secure Operations, Maintenance, and Disposal*
- *Systems Engineering Technical Management*

CISSP-ISSMP: Information Systems Security Management Professional

- *Leadership and Business Management*
- *Systems Lifecycle Management*
- *Risk Management*
- *Threat Intelligence and Incident Management*
- *Contingency Management*
- *Law, Ethics, and Security Compliance Management*[18]

SSCP

Because it is difficult to master the broad array of knowledge encompassed in the eight domains covered by the flagship CISSP exam, many security professionals seek less rigorous certifications, such as (ISC)²'s SSCP certification. The SSCP also has lower professional experience requirements than the CISSP and focuses on practices, roles, and responsibilities as defined by experts from major information security industries.[19] The SSCP certification is more applicable to a security administrator than to a technician, as the bulk of its questions focus on the operational nature of security. Nevertheless, information security analysts who seek advancement may find that achieving some certifications can help them move up.

The SSCP exam consists of 125 multiple-choice questions and must be completed within three hours. The exam covers seven domains:

- Access controls
- Security operations and administration
- Risk identification, monitoring, and analysis
- Incident response and recovery
- Cryptography
- Network and communications security
- Systems and application security[20]

Many consider the SSCP to be a scaled-down version of the CISSP. The seven domains are not a subset of the CISSP domains; they contain slightly more technical content. As with the CISSP, SSCP holders must either earn continuing education credits to retain the certification or retake the exam.

CSSLP

The Certified Secure Software Lifecycle Professional (CSSLP) is another (ISC)² certification focused on the development of secure applications. To qualify for the CSSLP, you must have at least four years of recent experience in one or more of the following eight domains:

- Secure software concepts
- Secure software requirements
- Secure software architecture and design
- Secure software implementation
- Secure software testing

- Secure software lifecycle management
- Secure software deployment, operations, and maintenance
- Secure software supply chain[21]

You must compose an essay in each of your four areas of expertise and submit it as your exam. This test is radically different from the multiple-choice exams (ISC)² normally administers. Once your experience has been verified and you successfully complete the essay exam, you can be certified. If necessary, you can qualify as an (ISC)² Associate until you obtain the requisite experience to qualify for the CSSLP.

CAP

For people who work with the NIST Risk Management Framework, the Certified Authorization Professional is a certification that focuses on the deployment of the RMF, mainly in the government and the Department of Defense, but also in other public or private sectors. The CAP certification covers seven domains:

- Information security risk management program
- Categorization of information systems (IS)
- Selection of security controls
- Implementation of security controls
- Assessment of security controls
- Authorization of information systems (IS)
- Continuous monitoring[22]

To qualify for this certification, candidates must have at least two years of work experience in one or more of the domains and pass the certification exam.

HCISPP

A new and relevant certification for information security professionals working in the healthcare field is the HealthCare Information Security and Privacy Practitioner (HCISPP). Similar to the CISSP but focused on security management topics and healthcare, this certification requires the candidate to demonstrate knowledge in six domains:

- Healthcare industry
- Information governance in healthcare
- Information technologies in healthcare
- Regulatory and standards environment
- Privacy and security in healthcare
- Risk management and risk assessment[23]

Candidates must have two or more years of experience in at least one of these domains and at least one year of experience in the top three domains (healthcare industry, regulatory environment, or privacy and security in healthcare). The other year can be in any of the other domains and does not have to be experience in the healthcare field.

CCSP

Completing the list of new (ISC)² certifications is the Certified Cloud Security Professional. This certification, cosponsored by the Cloud Security Alliance, is aimed at professionals who are primarily responsible for specifying, acquiring, securing, and managing cloud-based services for their organization. The CCSP covers six domains:

- Architectural concepts and design requirements
- Cloud data security
- Cloud platform and infrastructure security
- Cloud application security
- Operations
- Legal and compliance

There are endorsement, experience, and continuing education requirements for this certification, as with all previously mentioned (ISC)² certifications.

Associate of (ISC)²

(ISC)² has an innovative approach to the experience requirement in its certification program. Its Associate of (ISC)² program is geared toward people who want to earn a certification but don't have the requisite experience. Candidates who pass any of the described (ISC)² exams, agree to subscribe to the (ISC)² code of ethics, maintain continuing professional education (CPE) credits, and pay the appropriate fees can maintain their status as an associate until they have logged the required years of experience. They then receive the certification they've passed the exam for.

 For more information on any of the (ISC)² certifications, visit *www.isc2.org*.

ISACA Certifications

ISACA (*www.isaca.org*) also offers several reputable security certifications, including the Certified Information Security Manager (CISM), Certified Information Systems Auditor (CISA), Certified in Risk and Information Systems Control (CRISC), Certified in the Governance of Enterprise IT (CGEIT), and the Certified Data Privacy Solutions Engineer (CDPSE).

CISM

The CISM credential is geared toward experienced information security managers and others who may have similar management responsibilities. The CISM can assure executive management that a candidate has the required background knowledge needed for effective security management and consulting. This exam is offered annually. The CISM examination covers the following practice domains:

- Information security governance (24 percent)
- Information risk management (30 percent)
- Information security program development and management (27 percent)
- Information security incident management (19 percent)[24]

To be certified, the applicant must do the following:

- Pass the examination.
- Adhere to a code of ethics promulgated by ISACA.
- Pursue continuing education as specified.
- Document five years of information security work experience with at least three years in information security management in three of the four defined areas of practice.

CISA

The CISA credential is not specifically a security certification, but it does include many information security components. ISACA touts the certification as being appropriate for auditing, networking, and security professionals. CISA requirements are as follows:

- Successful completion of the CISA examination
- Experience as an information security auditor, with a minimum of five years' professional experience in information systems auditing, control, or security
- Agreement to the Code of Professional Ethics
- Payment of maintenance fees, a minimum of 20 contact hours of continuing education annually, and a minimum of 120 contact hours during a fixed three-year period
- Adherence to the Information Systems Auditing Standards

The exam covers the following areas of information systems auditing:

- Information systems auditing process (21 percent)
- Governance and management of IT (17 percent)
- Information systems acquisition, development, and implementation (12 percent)
- Information systems operations and business resilience (23 percent)
- Protection of information assets (27 percent)[25]

CRISC

Another valuable ISACA certification is the Certified in Risk and Information Systems Control (CRISC). The certification is targeted at managers and employees with knowledge and experience in risk management. The CRISC areas of knowledge include risk management components, making it an interesting certification for upper-level information security managers. The exam covers the following areas, as described in ISACA's 2020 Exam Candidate Information Guide:

- IT risk identification (27 percent)
- IT risk assessment (28 percent)
- Risk response and mitigation (23 percent)
- Risk and control monitoring and reporting (22 percent)[26]

The certification requires the candidate to have a minimum of three years' experience in risk management and information systems control in at least two of the stated domains, and at least one year of that experience must be in one of the first two domains, although the candidate may elect to take the exam before fulfilling the experience requirement. This practice is accepted and encouraged by ISACA, but the candidate will not receive the certification until the experience requirement is met.

CGEIT

Also available from ISACA is the Certified in the Governance of Enterprise IT (CGEIT) certification. The exam is targeted at upper-level executives, including CISOs and CIOs, directors, and consultants with knowledge and experience in IT governance. The CGEIT areas of knowledge include risk management components, which make it an interesting certification for upper-level information security managers. The exam covers the following areas:

- Governance of enterprise IT (40 percent)
- Benefits realization (26 percent)
- Risk optimization (19 percent)
- IT resources (15 percent)[27]

The certification requirements are similar to those for other ISACA certifications. Candidates must have at least one year of experience in IT governance and additional experience in at least two of the domains listed.

CDPSE

One of the newest certifications available from ISACA is the Certified Data Privacy Solutions Engineer (CDPSE), which focuses on protecting customers' personal information. The certification also addresses data life cycles, privacy compliance, and best data practices from a data scientist or data analyst's perspective. The CDPSE exam covers the following areas:

- Privacy governance (34 percent)
- Privacy architecture (36 percent)
- Data life cycle (30 percent)[28]

The certification is so new that ISACA is offering early adopters the opportunity to receive the certification without taking the exam if they document at least five years' experience and expertise in two or more of the domain areas. Current holders of other ISACA certifications can reduce this requirement to three years' experience.

 For more information on any of the ISACA certifications, visit *www.isaca.org*.

SANS Certifications

In 1999, the SANS Institute—formerly known as the SysAdmin, Audit, Network, and Security Institute (*www.sans.org*)—developed a series of technical cybersecurity certifications currently offered under the Global Information Assurance Certification (GIAC; *www.giac.org*). GIAC certifications not only test for knowledge, they require candidates to demonstrate application of that knowledge. With the introduction of the GIAC Information Security Professional (GISP), the GIAC Security Leadership Certification (GSLC), and several new managerial certifications, SANS now offers more than just technical certifications. The GIAC family of certifications includes more than 40 certifications in six focus areas: offensive security, cyber defense, cloud security, industrial control systems, digital forensics and incident response and management, and legal and audit. Unlike other certifications, some GIAC certifications require applicants to complete a written practical assignment that tests their ability to apply skills and knowledge. These assignments are submitted to the SANS Information Security Reading Room for review by security practitioners, potential certificate applicants, and others with an interest in information security. Only when the practical assignment is complete is the candidate allowed to take the online exam.

The GIAC certifications as of 2020 are shown in Table 7-1.

Table 7-1 Roadmap of GIAC Certifications[29]

GIAC Certification	Level
Cyber Defense Focus Area	
GISF: GIAC Information Security Fundamentals	Introductory
GSEC: GIAC Security Essentials	Intermediate
GOSI: GIAC Open Source Intelligence	Advanced
GCED: GIAC Certified Enterprise Defender	Advanced
GPPA: GIAC Certified Perimeter Protection Analyst	Advanced
GCIA: GIAC Certified Intrusion Analyst	Advanced
GCWN: GIAC Certified Windows Security Administrator	Advanced
GCUX: GIAC Certified UNIX Security Administrator	Advanced
GMON: GIAC Continuous Monitoring Certification	Advanced
GDSA: GIAC Defensible Security Architecture	Advanced
GCDA: GIAC Certified Detection Analyst	Advanced
GCCC: GIAC Critical Controls Certification	Advanced
GDAT: GIAC Defending Advanced Threats	Advanced
Industry Control Systems Focus Area	
GICSP: Global Industrial Cyber Security Professional	Intermediate
GRID: GIAC Response and Industrial Defense	Advanced
GCIP: GIAC Critical Infrastructure Protection	Advanced
Offensive Security Focus Area	
GCIH: GIAC Certified Incident Handler	Intermediate
GEVA: GIAC Enterprise Vulnerability Assessor	Advanced
GPEN: GIAC Certified Penetration Tester	Advanced
GWAPT: GIAC Web Application Penetration Tester	Advanced
GPYC: GIAC Python Coder	Advanced
GMOB: GIAC Mobile Device Security Analyst	Advanced
GAWN: GIAC Assessing Wireless Networks	Advanced
GXPN: GIAC Exploit Researcher and Advanced Penetration Tester	Advanced
Digital Forensics & Incident Response Focus Area	
GCFE: GIAC Certified Forensics Examiner	Intermediate
GBFA: GIAC Battlefield Forensics and Acquisition	Intermediate
GCFA: GIAC Certified Forensic Analyst	Advanced
GNFA: GIAC Network Forensic Analyst	Advanced
GCTI: GIAC Cyber Threat Intelligence	Advanced
GASF: GIAC Advanced Smartphone Forensics	Advanced
GREM: GIAC Reverse Engineering Malware	Advanced

(continues)

Table 7-1   Roadmap of GIAC Certifications (*Continued*)

GIAC Certification	Level
Cloud Security Focus Area	
GWEB: GIAC Certified Web Application Defender	Advanced
GCSA: GIAC Cloud Security Automation	Advanced
Management & Leadership Focus Area	
GISP: GIAC Information Security Professional	Intermediate
GSLC: GIAC Security Leadership Certification	Advanced
GSTRT: GIAC Strategic Planning, Policy, and Leadership	Advanced
GCPM: GIAC Certified Project Manager Certification	Advanced
GLEG: GIAC Law of Data Security & Investigations	Advanced
GSNA: GIAC Systems and Network Auditor	Advanced
GIAC Security Expert	
GSE: GIAC Security Expert	Expert

Most GIAC certifications are offered in conjunction with SANS training.

 For more information on the GIAC security-related certification requirements, visit *www.giac.org/certifications/*.

EC-Council Certifications

Another competitor in certifications for security management, EC-Council (*www.eccouncil.org*), now offers a variety of certifications across both technical and managerial topics. These certifications are organized into six domains: Security Awareness, Fundamentals, Core, Specialist, Advanced, and Management. The certifications offered are listed here; many are accompanied by training.

Security Awareness
- Secure Computer User

Fundamentals
- Encryption Specialist
- Security Specialist

Core
- Certified Network Defender
- Certified Ethical Hacker
- CEH (Master)
- Network Defense Architect

Specialist
- Certified Threat Intelligence Analyst
- Incident Handler
- Forensic Investigator
- Application Security Engineer—Java
- Application Security Engineer—.NET
- Disaster Recovery Professional

Advanced
- Certified Penetration Testing Professional
- Advanced Penetration Testing

- Licensed Penetration Tester
- Advanced Network Defense
- Certified SOC Analyst

Management
- EC-Council Information Security Manager
- Certified Chief Information Security Officer

The Certified CISO (CCISO) certification is designed to be a unique recognition for those at the peak of their professional careers. The CCISO tests security domain knowledge and knowledge of executive business management. The CCISO includes the following domains:

- Governance and risk management
- Information security controls, compliance, and auditing management
- Security program management and operations
- Information security core competencies
- Strategic planning, finance, procurement, and vendor management[30]

Before you can take the CCISO exam, EC-Council requires five years' experience in at least three of the domains. Those not meeting the experience requirements can take the EISM exam, which is described as a "light version of the CCISO exam,"[31] and then receive a discount on the CCISO exam when they've earned the necessary experience.

CompTIA Certifications

CompTIA (*www.comptia.com*)—the organization that offered the first vendor-neutral professional IT certifications, the A+ series—also offers security-related programs: the Security+, Cybersecurity Analyst+, PenTest+, and the CompTIA Advanced Security Professional+ Certifications.

Security+

The CompTIA Security+ certification tests for entry-level security knowledge. Candidates should have two years of on-the-job networking experience. CompTIA Security+ curricula are taught at colleges, universities, and commercial training centers around the globe. CompTIA Security+ is used as an elective or prerequisite to advanced vendor-specific and vendor-neutral security certifications.

> The CompTIA Security+ certification exam will verify that the successful candidate has the knowledge and skills required to assess the security posture of an enterprise environment and recommend and implement appropriate security solutions; monitor and secure hybrid environments, including cloud, mobile, and IoT; operate with an awareness of applicable laws and policies, including principles of governance, risk, and compliance; identify, analyze, and respond to security events and incidents.[32]

CySA+

The Cybersecurity Analyst+ certification from CompTIA is an intermediate certification with both knowledge-based and performance-based assessment. This certification focuses on incident response activities, including networking security, security operations, and vulnerability assessment and remediation. CompTIA recommends that candidates have a Security+ or Network+ level of knowledge and four years of related experience.

> The CompTIA Cybersecurity Analyst (CySA+) certification verifies that successful candidates have the knowledge and skills required to leverage intelligence and threat detection techniques, analyze and interpret data, identify and address vulnerabilities, suggest preventative measures, and effectively respond to and recover from incidents.[33]

PenTest+

One of the newer certifications from CompTIA is the Penetration Tester Plus certification, which includes both the managerial and technical skills needed to investigate and examine systems for potential vulnerabilities and susceptibility to successful attacks. The certification includes both traditional knowledge-based questions and hands-on performance assessments as it evaluates the candidate's ability to exploit systems and manage the vulnerabilities identified. Like the CySA+, CompTIA recommends that the candidate possess a Security+ certification level of knowledge and at least three to four years of experience.

> *The CompTIA PenTest+ certification verifies that successful candidates have the knowledge and skills required to plan and scope an assessment, understand legal and compliance requirements, perform vulnerability scanning and penetration testing, analyze data, and effectively report and communicate results.*[34]

CASP+

CompTIA's Advanced Security Professional+ certification is designed to build upon the knowledge of the Security+ and CySA+ certifications and to assess an advanced understanding of risk, security controls, cryptography, cloud security, virtualization, and the enterprise security domain. CompTIA recommends that candidates possess at least 10 years of experience in the field before attempting the exam, which contains both knowledge- and performance-based assessments.

> *CASP+ covers the technical knowledge and skills required to conceptualize, engineer, integrate, and implement secure solutions across complex environments to support a resilient enterprise.*[35]

Cloud Security Certifications

A rapidly emerging area of certification among companies and organizations involves the deployment of cloud-based information systems. For example, Amazon offers a foundational certificate, three associate-level certificates, two professional-level certificates, and three specialty certificates. You can learn more at the AWS Certification Web site (*https://aws.amazon.com/certification/*), where you can "validate technical skills and cloud expertise to grow your career and business." Other cloud service companies offer similar certification programs. In addition, vendor-neutral cloud security certifications are available, as previously discussed.

Certification Costs

Certifications cost money, and the more preferred certifications can be expensive. Individual certification exams can cost $750 or more, and certifications that require multiple exams can cost thousands of dollars. In addition, the cost of formal training to prepare for the exams can be significant. While you should not rely completely on certification preparation courses as groundwork for a real-world position, they can help you round out your knowledge and fill in gaps. Some certification exams, such as the CISSP, are very broad; others, such as GIAC specializations, are very technical. Given the nature of the knowledge needed to pass the examinations, most experienced professionals find the tests difficult without at least some review. Many prospective certificate holders engage in individual or group study sessions and purchase one of the many excellent exam review books on the subject.

Certifications are designed to recognize experts in their respective fields, but the cost of certification serves to deter those who might take the exam just to see if they can pass. Most examinations require years of work experience, with some programs requiring that candidates document such experience before they are permitted to sit for the exams or receive the certification.

Before attempting a certification exam, do your homework. Look into the exam's stated body of knowledge as well as its purpose and requirements to ensure that the time and energy spent pursuing the certification are worthwhile. Figure 7-5 shows several approaches to preparing for security certification.

On the topic of professional certification for information security practitioners, Charles Cresson Wood reports the following:

> *With résumé fraud on the rise, one of the sure-fire methods for employers to be sure that the people they hire are indeed familiar with the essentials of the field is to insist that they have certain certifications. The certifications can then be checked with the issuing organizations to make sure that they have indeed been conferred on the applicant for employment. . . . Professional certifications are relevant primarily to centralized information security positions. They are not generally relevant*

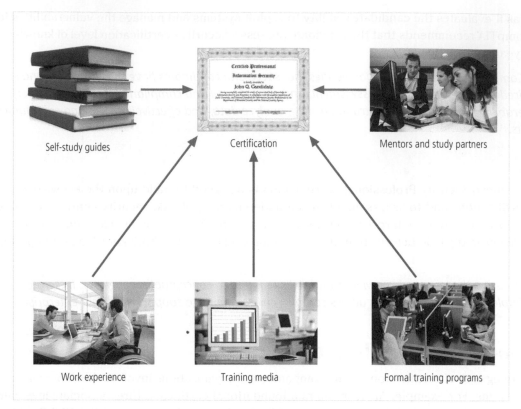

Figure 7-5   Preparing for security certification

Source: This figure has multiple sources. Top left: © Hong Vo/Shutterstock.com. Bottom left: © Phovoir/Shutterstock.com. Bottom center: © Petinov Sergey Mihilovich/Shutterstock.com. Bottom right: © ESB Professional/Shutterstock.com. Top right: © Goodluz/Shutterstock.com.

to staff working in decentralized information security positions, unless these individuals intend to become information security specialists. You may also look for these certifications on the résumés of consultants and contractors working in the information security field. You may wish to list these designations in help-wanted advertisements, look for them on résumés, and ask about them during interviews. Automatic résumé scanning software can also be set up to search for these strings of characters.[36]

Advice for Information Security Professionals

As a future information security professional, you may benefit from the following suggestions:

- Always remember: business before technology. Technology solutions are tools for solving business problems. Information security professionals are sometimes guilty of looking for ways to apply the newest technology to problems that do not require technology-based solutions.
- When evaluating a problem, look at the source of the problem first, determine what factors affect the problem, and see where organizational policy can lead you in designing a solution that is independent of technology. Then use technology to deploy the controls necessary for implementing the solution. Technology can provide elegant solutions to some problems, but it only exacerbates others.
- Your job is to protect the organization's information and information system resources. Never lose sight of the goal: protecting the organization's information assets from losses. Some people get so wrapped up in the technology or implementation details that they lose track of the primary mission.
- Be heard and not seen. Information security should be transparent to users. With minor exceptions, the actions taken to protect information should not interfere with users' actions. Information security supports the work of end users, not the other way around. The only routine communications from the security team to users should be periodic awareness messages, training announcements, newsletters, and e-mails.

- Know more than you say, and be more skillful than you let on. Don't try to impress users, managers, and other nontechnical people with your level of knowledge and experience. One day you just might run into a Jedi master of information security who puts you in your place.
- Speak to users, not at them. Use their language, not yours. Users aren't impressed with technobabble and jargon. They may not comprehend all the TLAs (three-letter acronyms), technical components, software, and hardware necessary to protect their systems, but they do know how to short-circuit your next budget request or pick out the flaws in your business report.
- Your education is never complete. As sensitive as you are to the fact that information technology is ever-evolving, you must be equally sensitive to the fact that information security education is never complete. Just when you think you have mastered the latest skills, you will encounter changes in threats, protection technology, your business environment, or the regulatory environment. As a security professional, you must expect to continue the learning process throughout your career. This is best accomplished by seeking out periodic seminars, training programs, and formal education. Even if the organization or your pocketbook cannot afford the more extensive and expensive training programs and conferences, you can keep abreast of the market by reading trade magazines, textbooks, and news articles about security. You can also subscribe to the many mailing lists for information security professionals. Join at least one professional information security association, such as the Information Systems Security Association (*www.issa.org*). Whatever approach you take, keep on top of the reading, never stop learning, and make yourself the best-informed security professional possible. It can only enhance your worth to the organization and your career.

Employment Policies And Practices

To create an environment in which information security is taken seriously, an organization should make it a documented part of every employee's job description. In other words, the general management community of interest should integrate solid concepts for information security into the organization's employment policies and practices. This section examines important information security issues associated with recruiting, hiring, firing, and managing human resources in an organization.

From an information security perspective, the hiring of employees is a responsibility laden with potential security pitfalls. Therefore, the CISO and information security manager should work with the human resources department to incorporate information security into the guidelines used for hiring all personnel. Figure 7-6 and several of the following sections highlight some of the hiring issues.

Figure 7-6   Hiring issues

Source: This figure has multiple sources. Top left: The Federal Bureau of Investigation.
Bottom center: © Andrey_Popov/www.shutterstock.com.

Job Descriptions

Integrating information security into the hiring process begins with reviewing and updating all job descriptions. To prevent people from applying for positions based solely on access to sensitive information, the organization should avoid revealing access privileges to prospective employees when it advertises open positions.

Interviews

Some interviews with job candidates are conducted with members of the human resources (HR) staff, while others include members of the department for which the position is being offered. An opening within the information security department creates a unique opportunity for the security manager to educate HR on various certifications and the specific experience each certification requires, as well as the qualifications of a good candidate. In all other areas of the organization, information security staff should advise HR to limit information provided to the candidate about responsibilities and access rights of the new hire. For organizations that include on-site visits as part of their initial or follow-up interviews, it is important to exercise caution when showing a candidate around the facility. Avoid tours through secure and restricted sites. Candidates who receive tours may be able to retain enough information about operations or information security functions to become a threat.

Background Checks

A background check should be conducted before an organization extends an offer to a job candidate. A background check is an investigation into the candidate's past that looks for criminal behavior or other types of behavior that could indicate potential for future misconduct. Several government regulations specify what the organization can investigate and how much of the information uncovered can be allowed to influence the hiring decision. The security manager and HR manager should discuss these matters with legal counsel to determine what state, federal, and perhaps international regulations affect the hiring process.

Background checks differ in the level of detail and depth with which they examine a candidate. In the military, background checks determine the candidate's level of security classification, a requirement for many positions. In the business world, a background check can determine the level of trust the business places in the candidate. People being considered for security positions should expect to be subjected to a moderately high-level background check. Those considering careers in law enforcement or high-security positions may even be required to submit to polygraph tests. The following list summarizes various types of background checks and the information checked for each:

- *Identity checks*—Validation of identity and Social Security number
- *Education and credential checks*—Validation of institutions attended, degrees and certifications earned, and certification status
- *Previous employment verification*—Validation of where candidates worked, why they left, what they did, and for how long
- *Reference checks*—Validation of references and integrity of reference sources
- *Social media review*—Possible review of social media activity for evidence of inappropriate or unprofessional actions
- *Worker's compensation history*—Investigation of claims from worker's compensation
- *Motor vehicle records*—Investigation of driving records, suspensions, and DUIs
- *Drug history*—Screening for drugs and drug usage, past and present
- *Credit history*—Investigation of credit problems, financial problems, and bankruptcy
- *Civil court history*—Investigation of the candidate's involvement as a plaintiff or defendant in civil suits
- *Criminal court history*—Investigation of criminal background, arrests, convictions, and time served

As mentioned, there are federal regulations for the use of personal information in employment practices, including the Fair Credit Reporting Act (FCRA), which governs the activities of consumer credit reporting agencies and the uses of information procured from them.[37] These credit reports generally contain information about a job candidate's credit history, employment history, and other personal data.

Among other things, the FCRA prohibits employers from obtaining credit reports unless the candidate is informed in writing that such a report will be requested as part of the employment process. The FCRA also allows the candidate to request information about the nature and type of reporting used in making the employment decision, and subsequently enables the candidate to learn the content of these reports. The FCRA also restricts the periods of time these reports can address. If the candidate earns less than $75,000 per year, the report can contain only seven years of negative credit information. If the candidate earns $75,000 or more per year, there is no time limitation. Note that "any person who knowingly and willfully obtains information on a consumer from a consumer reporting agency under false pretenses shall be fined under Title 18, United States Code, imprisoned for not more than two years, or both."[38]

Employment Contracts

Once a candidate has accepted a job offer, the employment contract becomes an important security instrument. Many of the policies discussed in Module 3—specifically, the fair and responsible use policies—require an employee to agree in writing to monitoring and nondisclosure agreements. If existing employees refuse to sign these agreements, security personnel are placed in a difficult situation. They may not be able to force employees to sign or to deny employees access to the systems necessary to perform their duties. With new employees, however, security personnel are in a different situation because the procedural step of policy acknowledgment can be made a requirement of employment. Policies that govern employee behavior and are applied to all employees may be classified as "employment contingent upon agreement." This classification means the potential employee must agree in a written affidavit to conform with binding organizational policies before being hired. Some organizations choose to execute the remainder of the employment contract *after* the candidate has signed the security agreements. Although this may seem harsh, it is a necessary component of the security process. Employment contracts may also contain restrictive clauses regarding the creation and ownership of intellectual property while the candidate is employed by the organization. These provisions may require the employee to actively protect the organization's information assets—especially assets that are critical to security.

 Most of us are not attorneys, but we should know some basic business law. If you want to know more about employment contracts, you can visit *Monster.com* to read the article "What to Know Before Signing an Employment Contract" at *www.monster.com/career-advice/article/employment-contract-guide*.

New Hire Orientation

When new employees are introduced into the organization's culture and workflow, they should receive an extensive information security briefing as part of their employee orientation. All major policies should be explained, along with procedures for performing necessary security operations and the new position's other information security requirements. In addition, the levels of authorized access should be outlined for new employees, and training should be provided regarding the secure use of information systems. By the time new employees are ready to report to their positions, they should be thoroughly briefed on the security components of their particular jobs and on the rights and responsibilities of all personnel in the organization.

On-the-Job Security Training

The organization should integrate the security awareness education described in Module 3 into a new hire's job orientation and make it a part of every employee's on-the-job security training. Keeping security at the forefront of employees' minds helps minimize their mistakes and is therefore an important part of the information security team's mission. Formal external and informal internal seminars should also be used to increase the security awareness of employees, especially that of security employees. An example of the importance of proper security training awareness for employees can be found in *The 9/11 Commission Report,* a U.S. congressional examination published three years after the terrorist attacks of September 11, 2001. As the following excerpt shows, security investigators reviewed videotapes from security checkpoints in airports as the terrorists were passing through and found the security process inadequate not from a technological standpoint but from human shortcomings:

> When the local civil aviation security office of the Federal Aviation Administration (FAA) later investigated these security screening operations, the screeners recalled nothing out of the ordinary. They could not recall that any of the passengers they screened were CAPPS (computer-assisted passenger prescreening system) selectees. We asked a screening expert to review the videotape of the

hand-wanding, and he found the quality of the screener's work to have been "marginal at best." The screener should have "resolved" what set off the alarm, and in the case of both Moqed and Hazmi, it was clear that he did not.[39]

This excerpt illustrates how physical security depends on the human element. The maintenance of information security depends heavily on the consistent vigilance of people. In many information security breaches, the hardware and software usually accomplished what they were designed to do, but people failed to make the correct decisions and follow-up choices. Education and regular training of employees and authorized users are important elements of information security and therefore cannot be ignored.

Evaluating Performance

To heighten information security awareness and minimize risky workplace behavior, organizations should incorporate information security into employee performance evaluations. For example, if employees have been observed keeping system passwords on notes stuck to their monitors, they should be warned. If such behavior continues, they should be reminded of their failure to comply with the organization's information security regulations during their annual performance review. In general, employees pay close attention to job performance evaluations and are more likely to take information security seriously if violations are documented in them.

Termination

Leaving the organization may or may not be a decision made by the employee. Organizations may downsize, be bought out or taken over, shut down, or go out of business. They may be forced to lay off, fire, or relocate their workforce. In any event, when an employee leaves an organization, several security issues arise. Key among these is the continuity of protection of all information to which the employee had access. Therefore, when an employee prepares to leave an organization, the following tasks must be performed:

- Access to the organization's systems must be disabled.
- Removable media must be returned.
- Hard drives must be secured.
- File cabinet locks must be changed.
- Office door locks must be changed.
- Keycard access must be revoked.
- Personal effects must be removed from the organization's premises.

After the employee has delivered keys, keycards, and other business property, he or she should be escorted from the premises.

exit interview

A meeting with an employee who is leaving the organization to remind the employee of contractual obligations, such as nondisclosure agreements, and to obtain feedback about the employee's tenure.

In addition to the tasks just listed, many organizations use an **exit interview** to remind the employee of contractual obligations, such as nondisclosure agreements, and to obtain feedback about the employee's tenure in the organization. At the interview, the employee should be reminded that failure to comply with contractual obligations could lead to civil or criminal action.

In reality, most employees are allowed to clean out their own offices and collect their personal belongings, and are simply asked to return their keys. From a security standpoint, these procedures are risky and lax because they expose the organization's information to disclosure and theft. To minimize such risks, an organization should have security-minded termination procedures that are followed consistently. In other words, the procedures should be followed regardless of the level of trust the organization had for the employee. However, a universally consistent approach is difficult and sometimes awkward to implement, which is why it's not often applied. Given the realities of workplaces, the simplest and best method for handling a departing employee may be to select one of the following scenarios, based on the employee's reasons for leaving.

Hostile Departures

Hostile departures include termination for cause, permanent downsizing, temporary layoffs, and quitting in some instances. While the employee may not seem overly hostile, the unexpected termination of employment can prompt the person to lash out against the organization.

Before employees know they are leaving, or as soon as the hostile resignation is tendered, the security staff should terminate all logical and keycard access. In the case of involuntary terminations, the employee should be escorted into the supervisor's office for the bad news. Upon receiving the termination notice or tendering a hostile resignation, the employee should be escorted to his office or cubicle and allowed to collect personal effects. No organizational property can be taken from the premises, including pens, papers, and books, as well as portable digital media like CDs, DVDs, and memory devices. Regardless of the claim the employee makes on organizational property, he should not be allowed to take it from the premises. If the employee has property he strongly wants to retain, he should be informed that he can submit a written list of the items and the reasons he should be allowed to retain them. After the employee's personal property has been gathered, he should be asked to surrender all company property, such as keys, keycards, other organizational identification, physical access devices, PDAs, pagers, cell phones, and portable computers. The employee should then be escorted out of the building.

Friendly Departures

Friendly departures include resignation, retirement, promotion, or relocation. In such cases, the employee may have tendered notice well in advance of the actual departure date. This scenario actually makes it more difficult for the security team to maintain positive control over the employee's access and information usage. Employee accounts are usually allowed to continue to exist, though an expiration date can be set for the employee's declared date of departure. Another complication associated with friendly departures is that the employees can come and go at will until their departure date, which means they will probably collect their own belongings and leave under their own recognizance. As with hostile departures, employees should be asked to drop off all organizational property on their way out for the final time.

For either type of departure, hostile or friendly, the offices and information used by the employee must be inventoried, files must be stored or destroyed, and all property must be returned to organizational stores. In either scenario, employees might foresee their departure well in advance and start taking home organizational information such as files, reports, and data from databases, perhaps thinking such items could be valuable in their future employment. This may be impossible to prevent. Only by scrutinizing systems logs after the employee has departed and sorting out authorized actions from systems misuse or information theft can the organization determine if a breach of policy or loss of information has occurred. If information is illegally copied or stolen, the action should be declared an incident and the appropriate policy followed.

Personnel Control Strategies

Among internal control strategies, separation of duties is a cornerstone in the protection of information assets and the prevention of financial loss. **Separation of duties** is used to reduce the chance that an employee will violate information security and breach the confidentiality, integrity, or availability of information. The control stipulates that the completion of a significant task involving sensitive information requires at least two people. The idea behind this separation is that if only one person has authorization to access a particular set of information, there may be nothing the organization can do to prevent the person from copying the information and removing it from the premises. Separation of duties is especially important, and thus commonly implemented, when financial information must be protected. For example, consider that two people are required to issue a cashier's check at a bank. The first is authorized to prepare the check, acquire the numbered financial document, and ready the check for signature. The process then requires a second person, usually a supervisor, to sign the check. Only then can the check be issued. If one person had the authority to perform both functions, he could write a number of checks, sign them, and steal large sums from the bank.

separation of duties

The principle that requires significant tasks to be split up so that more than one employee is required to complete them.

The same level of control should be applied to critical data. One programmer updates the system, and a supervisor or coworker accesses the file location in which the updates are stored. Or, one employee can be authorized to run backups to the system, and another can install and remove the physical media.

A similar concept is known as **two-person control**, in which two employees review and approve each other's work. This concept is distinct from separation of duties, in which the two people work in sequence. In two-person control, each person

two-person control

The organization of a task or process so that at least two employees must work together to complete it. Also known as dual control.

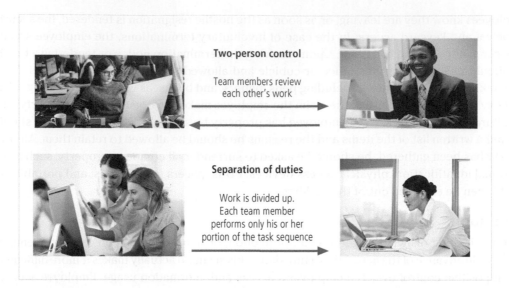

Figure 7-7   Internal control strategies

Source: This figure has multiple sources. Top left: © Rawpixel.com/Shutterstock.com. Bottom left: © Goodluz/ Shutterstock.com. Top right: © imtmphoto/Shutterstock.com. Bottom right: © EdBockStock/Shutterstock.com.

completely finishes the necessary work and then submits it to the other coworker. Each coworker then examines the work performed, double-checking to make sure no errors or inconsistencies exist. Figure 7-7 illustrates these operations.

job rotation

The requirement that every employee be able to perform the work of another employee.

task rotation

The requirement that all critical tasks can be performed by multiple employees.

Another control used to prevent personnel from misusing information assets is **job rotation** (or **task rotation**). If one employee cannot feasibly learn the entire job of another, the organization should at least try to ensure that multiple employees on staff can perform each critical task. Such job or task rotations can greatly increase the chance that an employee's misuse of the system or abuse of information will be detected by another. They also ensure that no one employee performs actions that cannot be physically audited by another employee. In general, this method makes good business sense. One threat to information is the organization's inability to have multiple employees who can perform the same task in case one employee is unable to perform his or her normal duties. If everyone knows at least part of another worker's job, the organization can survive the loss of any one employee.

This leads to a control measure that may seem surprising: mandatory vacations. Why should a company *require* its employees to take vacations? A mandatory vacation of at least one week gives the organization the ability to audit the work of an employee. People who are stealing from the organization or otherwise misusing information or systems are generally reluctant to take vacations, for fear that their actions will be detected. Therefore, all employees should be required to take a vacation so their jobs can be audited. This is not meant to imply that employees are untrustworthy but to show how organizations must be creative with the control measures they apply and even consider the security situation as a potential attacker would. The mandatory vacation policy is effective because it makes employees consider that they might be caught if they abuse the system. Information security professionals who think this practice impugns the character of their coworkers should note that some bonding authorities, auditing agencies, and oversight boards require mandatory vacations for all employees.

A related concept, *garden leave,* is used by some companies to restrict the flow of proprietary information when an employee leaves to join a competitor. When this procedure is invoked, an employee is paid salary and benefits after departure for a period of time, often 15 or 30 days; is not allowed access to the former place of employment; and is not allowed to report to the new employer yet. The intent is to have employees lose the immediate value of any current knowledge about tactical intelligence at the former firm and ensure that the employee's recollections of specific details fade. Technically, such employees remain on the payroll of the former company, but they cannot go to work at their new company yet. The term *garden leave* comes from the fact that the employee can do little more than stay home and tend a garden for a while. In some organizations, employees are required to sign a covenant not to compete

(CNC) or a noncompete clause (NCC), which prevents them from working for a direct competitor within a specified time frame—usually a few months to several years. This clause is designed to minimize the loss of intellectual property when employees change jobs.

 You can learn more about the intricacies of garden leave from an article called *The Law and Practice of Garden Leave: Rights, Duties, Enforcement, and Resistance*, which is available from Law Gazette at *https://lawgazette.com.sg/feature/the-law-and-practice-of-garden-leave-rights-duties-enforcement-and-resistance/*.

One final control measure is that employees should have access to the minimum amount of information necessary for them to perform their duties, and only as long as needed. In other words, there is no need for everyone in the organization to have access to all information. This principle is called **need to know**. A similar concept is **least privilege**, in which employees are restricted in their access and use of information based on their need to know. For example, an HR employee may have the need to access all employees' HR files, but may have the least privilege of only being allowed to edit (update) the retirement benefits sections of those files. The whole purpose of information security is to allow people who need to use system information to do so without being concerned about its confidentiality, integrity, and availability. Organizations should keep in mind that everyone who can access data probably will, with potentially serious consequences for the organization's information security.

need to know

The principle of limiting users' access privileges to the specific information required to perform their assigned tasks.

least privilege

The data access principle that ensures no unnecessary access to data exists by regulating members so they can perform only the minimum data manipulation needed; least privilege implies a need to know.

Privacy and the Security of Personnel Data

Organizations are required by law to protect employee information that is sensitive or personal, as you learned in Module 6. This information includes employee addresses, phone numbers, Social Security numbers, medical conditions, and even names and addresses of family members.

In principle, personnel data is no different from other data that an organization's information security group must protect, but a great deal more regulation covers its protection. As a result, information security groups should ensure that this data receives at least the same level of protection as other important data in the organization, including intellectual property, strategic planning data, and other business-critical information.

Security Considerations for Temporary Employees, Consultants, and Other Workers

Temporary employees, contract employees, and other types of workers are not subject to rigorous screening, contractual obligations, or eventual secured termination, but they often have access to sensitive organizational information. As outlined in the sections that follow, relationships with workers in these categories should be carefully managed to prevent a possible information leak or theft.

Temporary Employees

Some employees are hired to serve in a temporary position or to supplement the existing workforce. These employees do not work for the organization where they perform their duties, but instead are usually paid employees of a temp agency or organization that provides qualified workers at the paid request of another company. Temps typically provide secretarial or administrative support and thus may be exposed to a wide range of information. Because they are not employed by the host organization, they are often not subject to the contractual obligations or general policies that govern other employees. If temps violate a policy or cause a problem, the strongest action the host organization can take is to terminate the relationships and request that the temps be censured. The employing agency is under no contractual obligation to comply, although it may censure the employee to appease an important client.

From a security standpoint, temporary employees' access to information should be limited to that necessary for them to perform their duties. The organization can attempt to have temporary employees sign nondisclosure agreements and fair use policies, but the temp agency may refuse, forcing the host organization to find a new temp agency, go without the assistance of the temp worker, or allow the temp to work without the agreement. This can create a potentially awkward and dangerous situation, as temporary workers may inadvertently gain access to information that does not directly relate to their responsibilities. The only way to combat this threat is to ensure that the supervisor restricts the information to which the temp has access and makes sure all employees follow good security practices, especially clean desk policies and those for the security of classified data. Temps can provide great benefits to the host organization, but they should not be employed at the cost of sacrificing information security.

Contract Employees

Contract employees are typically hired to perform specific services for the organization. In such cases, the host company often makes a contract with a parent organization rather than with an individual employee for a particular task. Typical contract employees include groundskeepers, maintenance workers, electrical contractors, mechanical service contractors, and other service and repair workers. Although some contract workers may require access to virtually all areas of the organization to do their jobs, they seldom need access to information or information resources, except when the organization has leased computing equipment or contracted with a disaster recovery service. Contract employees may also need access to various facilities, but this does not mean they should be allowed to wander freely in and out of buildings. For the organization to maintain a secure facility, all contract employees should be escorted from room to room, as well as into and out of the facility. When contract employees report for maintenance or repair services, security personnel should first verify that these services are actually scheduled or approved. As indicated in earlier modules, attackers have been known to dress up as telephone repairmen, maintenance technicians, or janitors to gain physical access to a building. Therefore, direct supervision of contract employees is a necessity.

Another necessary aspect of hiring contract employees is making certain that restrictions or requirements are negotiated into the contract agreements before they are activated. For example, regulations like the following should be negotiated well in advance: The facility requires 24 to 48 hours' notice of a maintenance visit, the facility requires all on-site personnel to undergo background checks, and the facility requires advance notice for cancellation or rescheduling of a maintenance visit.

Consultants

Sometimes, on-site contracted workers are self-employed or are employees of an organization hired for a specific, one-time purpose. These workers are typically referred to as consultants, and they have their own security requirements and contractual obligations. Contracts for consultants should specify all requirements for information or facility access before the consultants are allowed into the workplace. Security and technology consultants in particular must be prescreened, escorted through work areas, and subjected to nondisclosure agreements to protect the organization from possible breaches of confidentiality. It is human nature (and a trait often found among consultants) to brag about the complexity of a particular job or an outstanding service provided to another client. If the organization does not want the consultant to mention their working relationship or to disclose any details about a particular system configuration, the organization must write these restrictions into the contract. Consultants typically request permission to present work samples to other companies as part of their résumés, but a client organization is not obligated to grant this permission and can even explicitly deny permission in writing. Organizations should also remember that just because they are paying an information security consultant, the protection of their information doesn't become the consultant's top priority.

Business Partners

On occasion, businesses create strategic alliances with other organizations that want to exchange information, integrate systems, or simply discuss operations for mutual advantage. In these situations, a prior business agreement is needed to specify the level of exposure both organizations are willing to tolerate. Sometimes, one division of a company enters a strategic partnership with an organization that directly competes with another of the company's own divisions. If the strategic partnership evolves into an integration of both companies' systems, competing groups might exchange information that neither parent organization expected to share. As a result, both organizations must make a meticulous, deliberate determination of what information is to be exchanged, in what format, and with whom. Nondisclosure agreements must be in place. Also, the security levels of both systems must be examined before any physical integration takes place—once systems are connected, the vulnerability of one system becomes the vulnerability of all.

Closing Scenario

After her meeting with Charlie, Iris returned to her office. When she had completed her daily assignments, she began to make some notes about the information security position Charlie had offered her.

Discussion Questions

1. What questions should Iris ask Charlie about the future of the information security unit at the company?
2. What questions should Iris ask Kelvin about the job for which she is being considered?

Ethical Decision Making

Suppose that Iris and Kelvin are involved in a romantic relationship, unknown to anyone else in the company. Romantic relationships between employees are not against company policy, but married employees are specifically prohibited from being in a direct reporting relationship with each other.

1. Should Iris inform Charlie about her relationship with Kelvin if she does not plan to apply for the transfer?
2. If Iris does apply for the job but has no current plans for marriage, should she inform Charlie of her relationship?

Selected Readings

There are many excellent sources of additional information in the area of information security. A few that can add to your understanding of this module are listed here:

- *Information Security Roles and Responsibilities Made Easy, Version 3,* by Charles Cresson Wood. 2012. Information Shield.
- *Management of Information Security,* 6th Edition, by Michael E. Whitman and Herbert J. Mattord. 2019. Cengage Learning.

Module Summary

- Where to place the information security function within the organization is a key decision. The most popular options involve placing information security within IT or the physical security function. Organizations searching for a rational compromise should place the information security function where it can balance its need to enforce company policy with its need to deliver service to the entire organization.
- The selection of information security personnel is based on several criteria, not all of which are within the control of the organization. In most cases, organizations look for a technically qualified information security generalist with a solid understanding of how an organization operates. The following attributes are also desirable:
  - An attitude that information security is usually a management problem, not an exclusively technical problem
  - Good people skills, communication skills, writing skills, and a tolerance for users
  - An understanding of the role of policy in guiding security efforts
  - An understanding of the role of education and training in making users part of the solution
  - An understanding of the threats facing an organization, how they can become attacks, and how to protect the organization from information security attacks
  - A working knowledge of many common technologies and a general familiarity with most mainstream IT technologies
- Many information security professionals enter the field through one of two career paths: via law enforcement or the military, or from other professions related to technical information systems. In recent years, college students have been able to take courses that prepare them to enter the information security workforce directly.

- During the hiring process for an information security position, an organization should use standard job descriptions to increase the degree of professionalism among applicants and to make sure the position's roles and responsibilities are consistent with those of similar positions in other organizations. Studies of information security positions have found that they can be classified into one of three areas: those that define, those that build, and those that administer.
- When filling information security positions, many organizations indicate the level of proficiency required for the job by specifying that candidates have recognizable certifications. Some of the more popular certifications are the following:
  - The (ISC)² family of certifications, including the Certified Information Systems Security Professional (CISSP), a number of specialized CISSP certifications, the Systems Security Certified Practitioner (SSCP), the Associate of (ISC)², and several other specialized certifications
  - The ISACA family of certifications, including the Certified Information Security Manager (CISM), the Certified Information Systems Auditor (CISA), and several other specialized certifications
  - The Global Information Assurance Certification (GIAC) family of certifications, including the GIAC Information Security Professional and the GIAC Security Leadership Certification
  - CompTIA's Security+ and EC-Council's CCISO
- The general management community of interest should integrate information security concepts into the organization's employment policies and practices. Areas in which information security should be a consideration include employment contracts, new hire orientation, performance evaluation, termination, and hiring. The hiring process includes job descriptions, interviews, and background checks.
- Separation of duties is a control used to reduce the chance of any person violating information security and breaching the confidentiality, integrity, or availability of information. According to the principle behind this control, any major task that involves sensitive information should require two people to complete.
- Organizations may need the special services of temporary employees, contract employees, consultants, and business partners, but these relationships should be carefully managed to prevent information leaks or theft.

Review Questions

1. What member of an organization should decide where the information security function belongs within the organizational structure? Why?

2. List and describe the options for placing information security within the organization.

3. For each major information security job title covered in the module, list and describe the key qualifications and requirements for the position.

4. What factors influence an organization's decisions to hire information security professionals?

5. Prioritize the list of general attributes that organizations seek when hiring information security professionals. In other words, list the most important attributes first. Use the list you developed to answer the previous review question.

6. What are critical considerations when dismissing an employee? Do they change according to whether the departure is friendly or hostile, or according to which position the employee is leaving?

7. How do security considerations for temporary or contract employees differ from those for regular full-time employees?

8. What career paths do most experienced professionals take when moving into information security? Are other pathways available? If so, describe them.

9. Why is it important to use specific and clearly defined job descriptions for hiring information security professionals?

10. What functions does the CISO perform?

11. What functions does the security manager perform?

12. What functions does the security analyst perform?

13. What rationale should an aspiring information security professional use in acquiring professional credentials?

14. List some of the information security certifications mentioned in this module.

15. Discuss the financial costs of certification. How expensive is the process?

16. List and describe the standard personnel policies and practices that are part of the information security function.

17. Why shouldn't an organization give a job candidate a tour of secure areas during an interview?

18. List and describe the typical relationships that organizations have with temporary employees, contract employees, consultants, and business partners. What special security precautions must an organization consider for such workers, and why are they significant?

19. What is separation of duties? How can it be used to improve an organization's information security practices?

20. What is job rotation, and what benefits does it offer an organization?

Exercises

1. Search your library's database and the Web for an article about people who violate their organization's policy and are terminated. Did you find many? Why or why not?

2. Go to the (ISC)² Web site at *www.isc2.org*. Research the knowledge areas included in the tests for the CISSP and SSCP certifications. What areas must you study that are *not* included in this book?

3. Using the Web, identify some certifications with an information security component that were not discussed in this module.

4. Search the Web for at least five job postings for a security analyst. What qualifications do the listings have in common?

5. Search the Web for three different employee hiring and termination policies. Review each and look carefully for inconsistencies. Do each of the policies have sections that address information security requirements? What clauses should a termination policy contain to prevent disclosure of an organization's information? Create your own version of either a hiring policy or a termination policy.

References

1. (ISC)². Strategies for Building and Growing Strong Cybersecurity Teams. (ISC)² Cybersecurity Workforce Study. 2019. Accessed November 4, 2020, from *www.isc2.org/-/media/ISC2/Research/2019-Cybersecurity-Workforce-Study/ISC2-Cybersecurity-Workforce-Study-2019.ashx*.

2. Hayes, M. "Where the Chief Security Officer Belongs." *InformationWeek*. February 22, 2002. Accessed November 1, 2020, from *www.informationweek.com/where-the-chief-securityofficer-belongs/d/d-id/1013832?*.

3. Kosutic, D. "Chief Information Security Officer (CISO)—Where Does He Belong in an Org Chart?" Accessed November 1, 2020, from *http://blog.iso27001standard.com/2012/09/11/chief-information-security-officer-ciso-where-does-he-belong-in-an-org-chart/*.

4. Hunt, Steve. "The CISO in 2010 Still Touches Technology." *CSO Magazine*. July 2004.

5. Wood, Charles Cresson. *Information Security Roles and Responsibilities Made Easy*. Version 3. Accessed November 1, 2020, from *https://informationshield.com/products/information-security-roles-and-responsibilities-made-easy/*.

6. Kennesaw State University Center for Information Security Education (CISE) and Security Executive Council (SEC). 2015 SEC/CISE Threats to Information Protection Report. Accessed November 1, 2020, from *www.securityexecutivecouncil.com/spotlight/?sid=29185*.

7. Bureau of Labor Statistics. BLS Occupational Outlook Handbook for Information Security Analysts. Accessed November 1, 2020, from *www.bls.gov/ooh/computer-and-information-technology/information-security-analysts.htm*.

8. (ISC)². Strategies for Building and Growing Strong Cybersecurity Teams. (ISC)² Cybersecurity Workforce Study, 2019. Accessed November 4, 2020, from *www.isc2.org/-/media/ISC2/Research/2019-Cybersecurity-Workforce-Study/ISC2-Cybersecurity-Workforce-Study-2019.ashx*.

9. Ibid.

10. Ibid.

11. Wood, Charles Cresson. *Information Security Roles and Responsibilities Made Easy*. Version 3. Accessed November 1, 2020, from *https://informationshield.com/products/information-security-roles-and-responsibilities-made-easy/*.

12. Schwartz, E., Erwin, D., Toner, A., Weafer, V., and Briney, A. "Roundtable: Info-Sec Staffing Help Wanted!" *Information Security Magazine*. April 2001.

13. "Wisconsin Jobs: Chief Information Security Officer." Accessed October 10, 2016, from *http://wiscjobs .state.wi.us/PUBLIC/print_view.asp?jobid=64037&annoid=64522*. Note that this link was disabled after the job was filled.

14. Security Jobs Network, Inc. "Sample Job Descriptions: Director of Security." Security Jobs Network, Inc. Online. Accessed October 10, 2016, from *securityjobs.net/documents/Director%20of%20Security%20 Position,%20Cox.html*. Note that this link was disabled after the job was filled.

15. IT Security Jobs. "IT Security Vacancies." SSR Personnel Online. July 22, 2002. Accessed July 5, 2007, from *www.ssr-personnel.com/ucs/vacancies/IT%20Security.htm*. Note that this link was disabled after the job was filled.

16. IT Security Jobs. "623873—Firewall Engineering Consultant." SSR Personnel Online. July 16, 2002. Accessed July 5, 2007, from *www.itsecurityjobs.com/vacancies.htm*. Note that this link was disabled after the job was filled.

17. (ISC)². "CISSP Information." Accessed November 4, 2020, from *www.isc2.org/Certifications/CISSP*.

18. (ISC)². "CISSP Concentrations." Accessed November 4, 2020, from *www.isc2.org/Certifications/ CISSP-Concentrations*.

19. (ISC)². "SSCP." Accessed November 4, 2020, from *www.isc2.org/Certifications/SSCP*.

20. Ibid.

21. (ISC)². "CSSLP." Accessed November 4, 2020, from *www.isc2.org/Certifications/CSSLP*.

22. (ISC)². "CAP." Accessed November 4, 2020, from *www.isc2.org/Certifications/CAP*.

23. (ISC)². "HCISPP." Accessed November 4, 2020, from *www.isc2.org/Certifications/HCISPP*.

24. ISACA. "CISM." Accessed November 5, 2020, from *www.isaca.org/credentialing/cism/cism-job-practice-areas*.

25. ISACA. "CISA." Accessed November 5, 2020, from *www.isaca.org/credentialing/cisa/cisa-job-practice-areas*.

26. ISACA. "CRISC." Accessed November 5, 2020, from *www.isaca.org/credentialing/crisc/ crisc-job-practice-areas*.

27. ISACA. "CGEIT." Accessed November 5, 2020, from *www.isaca.org/credentialing/cgeit/ cgeit-exam-content-outline*.

28. ISACA. "CDPSE." Accessed November 5, 2020, from *www.isaca.org/credentialing/ certified-data-privacy-solutions-engineer/cdpse-exam-content-outline*.

29. GIAC. "Get Certified: Roadmap." Accessed November 5, 2020, from *www.giac.org/certifications/ get-certified/roadmap*.

30. EC-Council. "Certified Chief Information Security Officer." Accessed November 5, 2020, from *https://ciso.eccouncil.org/wp-content/uploads/2020/01/CCISO-v3-Courseware-Table-of-Contents-1.pdf*.

31. EC-Council. "About the EISM Program." Accessed November 5, 2020, from *https://ciso.eccouncil.org/ cciso-certification/eism-program/*.

32. CompTIA. Security+ "Exam Details." Accessed November 7, 2020, from *www.comptia.org/certifications/ security#examdetails*.

33. CompTIA. CySA+ "Exam Details." Accessed November 7, 2020, from *www.comptia.org/certifications/ cybersecurity-analyst#examdetails*.

34. CompTIA. PenTest+ "Exam Details." Accessed November 7, 2020, from *www.comptia.org/certifications/ pentest#examdetails*.

35. CompTIA. CASP+ "Exam Details." Accessed November 7, 2020, from *www.comptia.org/certifications/ comptia-advanced-security-practitioner#examdetails*.

36. Wood, Charles Cresson. *Information Security Roles and Responsibilities Made Easy*. 2012. Houston, TX: Information Shield Corporation, 577.

37. Background Check International, LLC. "BCI." BCI Online. Accessed November 7, 2020, from *www.bcint.com*.

38. Federal Trade Commission. Fair Credit Reporting Act. 2002. 15 U.S.C., S. 1681 et seq. Accessed November 7, 2020, from *www.ftc.gov/enforcement/statutes/fair-credit-reporting-act*.

39. U.S. Congress. September 11th Commission Final Report. July 2004.

Security Technology: Access Controls, Firewalls, and VPNs

Upon completion of this material, you should be able to:

1. Discuss the role of access control in information systems, and identify and discuss the four fundamental functions of access control systems

2. Define authentication and explain the three commonly used authentication factors

3. Describe firewall technologies and the various categories of firewalls

4. Explain the various approaches to firewall implementation

5. Identify the various approaches to control remote and dial-up access by authenticating and authorizing users

6. Describe virtual private networks (VPNs) and discuss the technology that enables them

> *If you think technology can solve your security problems, then you don't understand the problems and you don't understand the technology.*
>
> —Bruce Schneier, American Cryptographer, Computer Security Specialist, and Writer

Opening Scenario

Kelvin Urich came into the meeting room a few minutes late. He took the empty chair at the head of the conference table, flipped open his notepad, and went straight to the point. "Okay, folks, I'm scheduled to present a plan to Charlie Moody and the IT planning staff in two weeks. I saw in the last project status report that you still don't have a consensus for the DMZ architecture. Without that, we can't specify the needed hardware or software, so we haven't even started costing the project and planning for deployment. We cannot make acquisition and operating budgets, and I will look very silly at the presentation. What seems to be the problem?"

Laverne Nguyen replied, "Well, we seem to have a difference of opinion among the members of the architecture team. Some of us want to set up bastion hosts, which are simpler and cheaper to implement, and others want to use a screened subnet with proxy servers—much more complex, more difficult to design but higher overall security. That decision will affect the way we implement application and Web servers."

Miller Harrison, a contractor brought in to help with the project, picked up where Laverne had left off. "We can't seem to move beyond this impasse, but we have done all the planning up to that point."

Kelvin asked, "Laverne, what does the consultant's report say?"

Laverne said, "Well, there is a little confusion about that. The consultant is from Costly & Firehouse, one of the big consulting firms. She proposed two alternative designs: one that seems like an adequate, if modest, design and another that might be a little more than we need. The written report indicates we have to make the decision about which way to go, but when we talked, she really built up the expensive plan and kind of put down the more economical plan."

Miller looked sour.

Kelvin said, "Sounds like we need to make a decision, and soon. Get a conference room reserved for tomorrow, ask the consultant if she can come in for a few hours first thing, and let everyone on the architecture team know we will meet from 8 to 11 on this matter. Now, here is how I think we should prepare for the meeting."

access control

The selective method by which systems specify who may use a particular resource and how they may use it.

discretionary access controls (DACs)

Access controls that are implemented at the judgment or option of the data user.

nondiscretionary access controls (NDACs)

Access controls that are implemented by a central authority.

lattice-based access control (LBAC)

A variation on mandatory access controls that assigns users a matrix of authorizations for particular areas of access, incorporating the information assets of subjects such as users and objects.

Introduction To Access Controls

Technical controls are essential to a well-planned information security program, particularly to enforce policy for the many IT functions that are not under direct human control. Network and computer systems make millions of decisions every second, and they operate in ways and at speeds that people cannot control in real time. Technical control solutions, when properly implemented, can improve an organization's ability to balance the often conflicting objectives of making information readily and widely available and of preserving the information's confidentiality and integrity. This module describes the function of many common technical controls and explains how they fit into the physical design of an information security program. Students who want to acquire expertise on the configuration and maintenance of technology-based control systems will require additional education and usually specialized training.

Access control is the method by which systems determine whether and how to admit a user into a trusted area of the organization—that is, information systems, restricted areas such as computer rooms, and the entire physical location. Access control is achieved through a combination of policies, programs, and technologies. To understand access controls, you must first understand they are focused on the permissions or privileges that a subject (user or system) has on an object (resource), including *if*, *when*, and from *where* a subject may access an object and especially *how* the subject may use that object.

In the early days of access controls during the 1960s and 1970s, the government defined only mandatory access controls (MACs) and discretionary access controls. These definitions were later codified in the Trusted Computer System Evaluation Criteria (TCSEC) documents from the U.S. Department of Defense (DoD). As the definitions and applications evolved, MACs became further refined as a specific type of lattice-based, nondiscretionary access control, as described in the following sections.

In general, access controls can be discretionary or nondiscretionary (see Figure 8-1).

Discretionary access controls (DACs) provide the ability to share resources in a peer-to-peer configuration, which allows users to control and possibly provide access to information or resources at their disposal. The users can allow general, unrestricted access, or they can allow specific people or groups to access these resources, usually with controls on other users' ability to read, edit, or delete. For example, a user might have a hard drive that contains information to be shared with office coworkers. This user can elect to allow access to specific coworkers by providing access by name in the share control function. Figure 8-2 shows an example of a discretionary access control from Microsoft Windows 10.

Nondiscretionary access controls (NDACs) are managed by a central authority in the organization. A form of nondiscretionary access controls is called **lattice-based access control (LBAC)**, in which users are assigned a matrix of authorizations for particular areas of access. The authorization may vary between levels, depending on the classification of authorizations that users possess for each group of information or resources. The lattice structure contains subjects and objects, and the boundaries associated with each pair are demarcated. Lattice-based control specifies

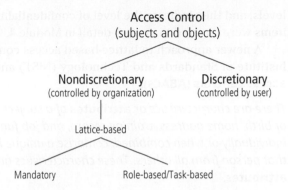

Figure 8-1   Access control approaches

the level of access each subject has to each object, as implemented in *access control lists (ACLs)* and *capabilities tables*. Both were defined in Module 3.

Some lattice-based controls are tied to a person's duties and responsibilities; such controls include **role-based access controls (RBACs)** and **task-based access controls (TBACs)**. Role-based controls are associated with the duties a user performs in an organization, such as a position or temporary assignment like project manager, while task-based controls are tied to a particular chore or responsibility, such as a department's printer administrator. Some consider TBACs a sub-role access control and a method of providing more detailed control over the steps or stages associated with a role or project. These controls make it easier to maintain the restrictions associated with a particular role or task, especially if different people perform the role or task. Instead of constantly assigning and revoking the privileges of employees who come and go, the administrator simply assigns access rights to the role or task. Then, when users are associated with that role or task, they automatically receive the corresponding access. When their turns are over, they are removed from the role or task and access is revoked. Roles tend to last for a longer term and be related to a position, whereas tasks are much more granular and short-term. In some organizations, the terms are used synonymously.

Mandatory access controls (MACs) are also a form of lattice-based, nondiscretionary access controls that use data classification schemes; they give users and data owners limited control over access to information resources. In a data classification scheme, each collection of information is rated, and all users are rated to specify the level of information they may access. These ratings are often referred to as sensitivity

role-based access control (RBAC)

A nondiscretionary control where privileges are tied to the role or job a user performs in an organization and are inherited when a user is assigned to that role.

task-based access control (TBAC)

A nondiscretionary control where privileges are tied to a task or temporary assignment a user performs in an organization and are inherited when a user is assigned to that task.

mandatory access control (MAC)

A required, structured data classification scheme that assigns a sensitivity or classification rating to each collection of information as well as each user.

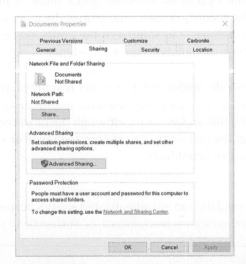
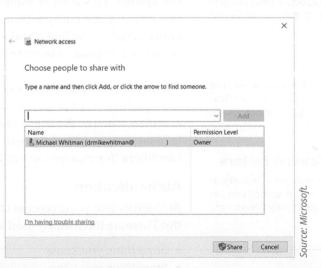

Source: Microsoft.

Figure 8-2   Example of Windows 10 discretionary access controls

attribute-based access control (ABAC)

An access control approach whereby the organization specifies the use of objects based on some attribute of the user or system.

attribute

A characteristic of a subject (user or system) that can be used to restrict access to an object; also known as a *subject attribute*.

subject attribute

See *attribute*.

levels, and they indicate the level of confidentiality the information requires. These items were covered in greater detail in Module 4.

A newer approach to lattice-based access controls is promoted by the National Institute of Standards and Technology (NIST) and referred to as **attribute-based access controls (ABACs)**.

There are characteristics or **attributes** *of a subject such as name, date of birth, home address, training record, and job function that may, either individually or when combined, comprise a unique identity that distinguishes that person from all others. These characteristics are often called* **subject attributes**.[1]

An ABAC system simply uses one of these attributes to regulate access to a particular set of data. This system is similar in concept to looking up movie times on a Web site that requires you to enter your zip code to select a particular theatre, or a home supply or electronics store that asks for your zip code to determine if a particular discount is available at your nearest store. According to NIST, ABAC is the parent approach to lattice-based, MAC, and RBAC controls, as they all are based on attributes.

 For more information on ABAC and access controls in general, read NIST SP 800-162 at *https://csrc.nist.gov/publications/sp800* and NISTIR 7316 at *https://csrc.nist.gov/publications/nistir*.

Access Control Mechanisms

In general, all access control approaches rely on the following four mechanisms, which represent the four fundamental functions of access control systems:

- *Identification*—I am a user of the system.
- *Authentication*—I can prove I'm a user of the system.
- *Authorization*—Here's what I am allowed to do with the system.
- *Accountability*—You can track and monitor my use of the system.

identification

The access control mechanism whereby unverified or unauthenticated entities who seek access to a resource provide a label or username by which they are known to the system.

authentication

The access control mechanism that requires the validation and verification of an entity's unsubstantiated identity.

authentication factors

Mechanisms that provide authentication based on something an unauthenticated entity knows, has, and is.

Identification

Identification (ID) is a mechanism whereby unverified or unauthenticated entities who seek access to a resource provide a unique label by which they are known to the system. This label is sometimes called an identifier, and it must be mapped to one and only one entity within the security domain. Sometimes the unauthenticated entity supplies the label, and sometimes it is applied to the entity. Some organizations use composite identifiers by concatenating elements—department codes, random numbers, or special characters—to make unique identifiers within the security domain. Other organizations generate random IDs to protect resources from potential attackers. Most organizations use a single piece of unique information, such as a complete name or the user's first initial and surname, although the most recent trend is to add one or more numbers at the end—either a random sequence or sequential identifiers (for example, msmith01 or msmith02).

Authentication

Authentication is the process of validating an unauthenticated entity's purported identity. There are three widely used authentication mechanisms, or **authentication factors**:

- Something you know
- Something you have
- Something you are

Something You Know   This factor of authentication relies on what the unverified user or system knows and can recall—for example, a password, passphrase, or other unique authentication code, such as a personal identification number (PIN). One of the biggest debates in the information security industry concerns the complexity of **passwords**. On one hand, a password should be difficult to guess, which means it cannot be a series of letters or a word that is easily associated with the user, such as the name of the user's spouse, child, or pet. By the same token, a password should not be a series of numbers easily associated with the user, such as a phone number, Social Security number, or birth date. On the other hand, the password must be easy for the user to remember, which means it should be short or easily associated with something the user can remember.

A **passphrase** is typically longer than a password and can be used to derive a **virtual password**. By using the words of the passphrase as cues to create a stream of unique characters, you can create a longer, stronger password that is easy to remember. For example, while a typical password might be "23skedoo," a typical passphrase might be "MayTheForceBeWithYouAlways," represented as the virtual password "MTFBWYA."

Users increasingly employ longer passwords or passphrases to provide effective security, as discussed in Module 2 and illustrated in Table 2-6. As a result, it is becoming increasingly difficult for users to keep track of the multitude of system usernames and passwords needed to access information for business or personal transactions. Recent studies have found that average users have between 70 and 80 passwords they must track.[2] A common method of keeping up with so many passwords is to write them down, which is a cardinal sin in information security. A better solution is automated password-tracking storage, like the eWallet application shown in Figure 8-3. This example shows a mobile application that uses encryption and can be synchronized across multiple platforms, including Apple iOS, Android, Windows, Macintosh, and Linux, to manage access control information in all its forms.

Something You Have   This authentication factor relies on something an unverified user or system has and can produce when necessary. One example is **dumb cards**, such as ID cards or ATM cards with magnetic stripes that contain

password

A secret word or combination of characters that only the user should know; it is used to authenticate the user.

passphrase

A plain-language phrase, typically longer than a password, from which a virtual password is derived.

virtual password

A stream of characters generated by taking elements from an easily remembered phrase.

dumb card

An authentication card that contains digital user data, such as a personal identification number, against which user input is compared.

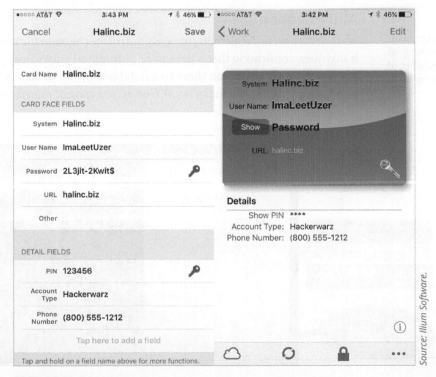

Source: Ilium Software.

Figure 8-3   eWallet

smart card

An authentication component similar to a *dumb card* that contains a computer chip to verify and validate several pieces of information instead of just a personal identification number.

synchronous token

An authentication component in the form of a card or fob that contains a computer chip and a display that shows a computer-generated number used to support remote login authentication; the token must be calibrated with the corresponding software on a central authentication server.

asynchronous token

An authentication component in the form of a card or fob that contains a computer chip and a display that shows a computer-generated number used to support remote login authentication; the token does not require calibration of the central authentication server but uses a challenge/response system instead.

strong authentication

In access control, the use of at least two different authentication mechanisms drawn from two or more different factors of authentication; this is sometimes called multifactor or dual-factor authentication.

authorization

The access control mechanism that represents the matching of an authenticated entity to a list of information assets and corresponding access levels.

a digital (and often encrypted) user PIN, which is compared against the number the user enters. The **smart card** contains a computer chip that can verify and validate several pieces of information instead of just a PIN. Another common device is a token—a card or key fob with a computer chip and a liquid crystal display that shows a computer-generated number used to support remote login authentication.

Tokens are synchronous or asynchronous. Once **synchronous tokens** are synchronized with a server, both the server and token use the same time setting or a time-based database to generate a number that must be entered during the user login phase. **Asynchronous tokens** don't require that the server and tokens maintain the same time setting. Instead, they use a challenge/response system, in which the server challenges the unauthenticated entity during login with a numerical sequence. The unauthenticated entity places this sequence into the token and receives a response. The prospective user then enters the response into the system to gain access. Some examples of synchronous and asynchronous tokens are presented in Figure 8-4.

Something You Are or Can Produce This authentication factor relies on individual characteristics, such as fingerprints, palm prints, hand topography, hand geometry, or retina and iris scans, or something an unverified user can produce on demand, such as voice patterns, signatures, or keyboard kinetic measurements. Some of these characteristics are known collectively as biometrics, which is covered later in this module.

Note that certain critical logical or physical areas may require the use of **strong authentication**—at least two authentication mechanisms drawn from two different factors of authentication, which are most often something you have and something you know. For example, access to a bank's ATM services requires a banking card plus a PIN. Such systems are called two-factor or multifactor authentication because at least two separate mechanisms are used. The DUO and Google Authenticator apps shown in Figure 8-4 are examples of such systems. Strong authentication requires that at least one of the mechanisms be something other than what you know.

Authorization

Authorization is the defining access control mechanism for information asset access. It involves confirming that a person or automated entity is approved to use an information asset by matching them to a database or list of assets they have permission to access. This list is usually an *ACL* or *access control matrix*, as defined in Module 3.

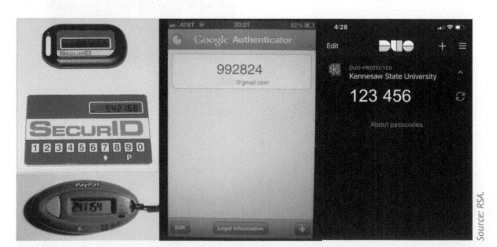

Source: RSA.

Figure 8-4 Access control authenticators

In general, authorization can be handled in one of three ways:

- Authorization for each authenticated user, in which the system performs an authentication process to verify each entity and then grants access to resources for only that entity. This process quickly becomes complex and resource-intensive in a computer system.
- Authorization for members of a group, in which the system matches authenticated entities to a list of group memberships and then grants access to resources based on the group's access rights. This is the most common authorization method.
- Authorization across multiple systems, in which a central authentication and authorization system verifies an entity's identity and grants it a set of credentials.

Authorization credentials, which are also called authorization tickets, are issued by an authenticator and are honored by many or all systems within the authentication domain. Sometimes called single sign-on (SSO) or reduced sign-on, authorization credentials are becoming more common and are frequently enabled using a shared directory structure such as the Lightweight Directory Access Protocol (LDAP).

Accountability

Accountability, also known as **auditability**, ensures that every action performed on a computer system or using an information asset can be associated with an authorized user or system. Accountability is most often accomplished by means of system logs, database journals, and the auditing of these records.

System logs record specific information, such as failed access attempts and system modifications. Logs have many uses, such as intrusion detection, determining the root cause of a system failure, or simply tracking the use of a particular resource.

Biometrics

Biometric access control relies on recognition—the same thing you rely on to identify friends, family, and other people you know. The use of biometric-based authentication is expected to have a significant impact in the future as technical and ethical issues are resolved with the technology.

Biometric authentication technologies include the following:

- Fingerprint comparison of the unauthenticated person's fingerprint to a stored fingerprint
- Palm print comparison of the unauthenticated person's palm print to a stored palm print
- Hand geometry comparison of the unauthenticated person's hand to a stored measurement
- Facial recognition using a photographic ID card, in which a human security guard compares the unauthenticated person's face to a photo
- Facial recognition using a digital camera, in which an unauthenticated person's face is compared to a stored image
- Retinal print comparison of the unauthenticated person's retina to a stored image
- Iris pattern comparison of the unauthenticated person's iris to a stored image
- DNA (deoxyribonucleic acid) comparison of the unique polymer combinations of adenine, guanine, cytosine, and thymine, which are abbreviated as A, G, C, and T, respectively, in the human genome.

Among all possible biometrics, only four human characteristics are usually considered truly unique:

- Fingerprints
- Retina of the eye (blood vessel pattern)
- Iris of the eye (random pattern of features found in the iris, including freckles, pits, striations, vasculature, coronas, and crypts)
- DNA

Figure 8-5 depicts some of these human recognition characteristics.

Most of the technologies that scan human characteristics convert these images to some form of **minutiae**. Each subsequent access attempt results in a measurement that is compared with an encoded value to verify the user's

---

accountability

The access control mechanism that ensures all actions on a system—authorized or unauthorized—can be attributed to an authenticated identity; also known as *auditability*.

auditability

See *accountability*.

biometric access control

The use of physiological characteristics to provide authentication for a provided identification; also referred to as *biometrics*.

minutiae

In biometric access controls, unique points of reference that are digitized and stored in an encrypted format when the user's system access credentials are created, and are then used in subsequent requests for access to authenticate the user's identity.

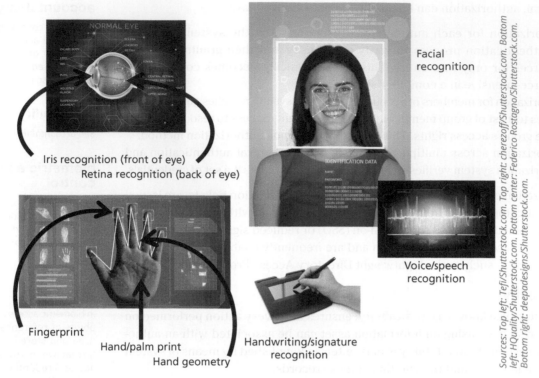

Iris recognition (front of eye)
Retina recognition (back of eye)

Fingerprint
Hand/palm print
Hand geometry

Handwriting/signature
recognition

Facial
recognition

Voice/speech
recognition

Sources: Top left: Tefi/Shutterstock.com. Top right: cherezoff/Shutterstock.com. Bottom left: HQuality/Shutterstock.com. Bottom center: Federico Rostagno/Shutterstock.com. Bottom right: deepadesigns/Shutterstock.com.

Figure 8-5   Biometric recognition characteristics

false reject rate

The rate at which authentic users are denied or prevented access to authorized areas as a result of a failure in the biometric device; also known as a Type I error or a false negative.

identity. A problem with this method is that some human characteristics can change over time due to normal development, injury, or illness, which means that system designers must create fallback or failsafe authentication mechanisms.

Signature and voice recognition technologies are also considered to be biometric access control measures. Signature recognition has become commonplace; retail stores use it, or at least signature captures, for authentication during a purchase. The customer signs a digital pad with a special stylus that captures the signature. The signature is digitized and either saved for future reference or compared with a signature in a database for validation. Currently, the technology for signature capturing is much more widely accepted than that for signature comparison because signatures change due to several factors, including age, fatigue, and the speed with which the signature is written.

Voice recognition works in a similar fashion; the system captures and stores a voiceprint of the user reciting a phrase. Later, when the user attempts to access the system, the authentication process requires the user to speak the same phrase so that the technology can compare the current voiceprint against the stored value.

Effectiveness of Biometrics

Biometric technologies are evaluated on three basic criteria: the false reject rate, which is the percentage of authorized users who are denied access; the false accept rate, which is the percentage of unauthorized users who are granted access; and the crossover error rate, the level at which the number of false rejections equals the false acceptances.

The **false reject rate** describes the number of legitimate users who are denied access because of a failure in the biometric device. This failure is known as a Type I error. While it is a nuisance to unauthenticated people who are authorized users, this error rate is probably of little concern to security professionals because rejection of an authorized user represents no threat to security. Therefore, the false reject rate is often ignored unless it reaches a level high enough to generate complaints from irritated unauthenticated users. For example, most people have experienced the frustration of having a credit card or ATM card fail to perform because of problems with the magnetic strip. In the field of biometrics, similar problems can occur when a system fails to pick up the various information points it uses to authenticate a prospective user properly.

The **false accept rate** conversely describes the number of unauthorized users who somehow are granted access to a restricted system or area, usually because of a failure in the biometric device. This failure is known as a Type II error and is unacceptable to security professionals.

The **crossover error rate (CER)**, the point at which false reject and false accept rates intersect, is possibly the most common and important overall measure of accuracy for a biometric system. Most biometric systems can be adjusted to compensate both for false positive and false negative errors. Adjustment to one extreme creates a system that requires perfect matches and results in a high rate of false rejects, but almost no false accepts. Adjustment to the other extreme produces a low rate of false rejects but excessive false accepts. The trick is to find the balance between providing the requisite level of security and minimizing the frustrations of authentic users. Thus, the optimal setting is somewhere near the point at which the two error rates are equal—the CER. CERs are used to compare various biometrics and may vary by manufacturer. If a biometric device provides a CER of 1 percent, its failure rates for false rejections and false acceptance are both 1 percent. A device with a CER of 1 percent is considered superior to a device with a CER of 5 percent.

false accept rate

The rate at which fraudulent users or nonusers are allowed access to systems or areas as a result of a failure in the biometric device; also known as a Type II error or a false positive.

crossover error rate (CER)

The point at which the rate of false rejections equals the rate of false acceptances; also called the *equal error rate*.

Acceptability of Biometrics

As you've learned, a balance must be struck between a security system's acceptability to users and how effective it is in maintaining security. Many biometric systems that are highly reliable and effective are considered intrusive by users. As a result, many information security professionals don't implement these systems to avoid confrontation and possible user boycott of the biometric controls. Table 8-1 shows how certain biometrics rank in terms of effectiveness and acceptance. (Note that in the table, H equals a high ranking, M is for medium, and L is low.) Interestingly, the orders of effectiveness and acceptance are almost exactly opposite.

 For more information on using biometrics for identification and authentication, read NIST SP 800-76-1 and SP 800-76-2 at *https://csrc.nist.gov/publications/sp800*.

Table 8-1   Ranking of Biometric Effectiveness and Acceptance[3]

Biometrics	Universality	Uniqueness	Permanence	Collectability	Performance	Acceptability	Circumvention
Face	H	L	M	H	L	H	L
Face Thermogram	H	H	L	H	M	H	H
Fingerprint	M	H	H	M	H	M	H
Hand Geometry	M	M	M	H	M	M	M
Hand Vein	M	M	M	M	M	M	H
Eye: Iris	H	H	H	M	H	H	H
Eye: Retina	H	H	M	L	H	L	H
DNA	H	H	H	L	H	L	L
Odor & Scent	H	H	H	L	L	M	L
Voice	M	L	L	M	L	H	L
Signature	L	L	L	H	L	H	L
Keystroke	L	L	L	M	L	M	M
Gait	M	L	L	H	L	H	M

Access Control Architecture Models

trusted computing base (TCB)

Under the Trusted Computer System Evaluation Criteria (TCSEC), the combination of all hardware, firmware, and software responsible for enforcing the security policy.

Security access control architecture models, which are often referred to simply as architecture models, illustrate access control implementations and can help organizations quickly make improvements through adaptation. Formal models do not usually find their way directly into usable implementations; instead, they form the theoretical foundation that an implementation uses. These formal models are discussed here so you can become familiar with them and see how they are used in various access control approaches. When a specific implementation is put into place, noting that it is based on a formal model may lend credibility, improve its reliability, and lead to improved results. Some models are implemented in computer hardware and software, some are implemented as policies and practices, and some are implemented in both. Some models focus on the confidentiality of information, while others focus on the information's integrity as it is being processed.

The first models discussed here—specifically, the trusted computing base, the Information Technology System Evaluation Criteria, and the set of standards known as the Common Criteria—are used as evaluation models and to demonstrate the evolution of trusted system assessment, which include evaluations of access controls. The later models—Bell–LaPadula, Biba, and others—demonstrate implementations in some computer security systems to ensure that the confidentiality, integrity, and availability of information is protected by controlling the access of one part of a system on another. The final model to be discussed is the zero trust architecture or ZTA, an approach to access control that, while not yet dominant, is rapidly becoming part of the mainstream.

TCSEC's Trusted Computing Base

The Trusted Computer System Evaluation Criteria (TCSEC) is an older Department of Defense (DoD) standard that defines the criteria for assessing the access controls in a computer system. This standard is part of a larger series of standards collectively referred to as the Rainbow Series because of the color coding used to uniquely identify each document (see Figure 8-6). TCSEC is also known as the "Orange Book" and is considered the cornerstone of the series. As described later in this module, this series was replaced in 2005 with the Common Criteria, but information security professionals should be familiar with the terminology and concepts of this legacy approach. For example, TCSEC uses the concept of the **trusted computing base (TCB)** to enforce security policy. In this context, "security policy" refers to the rules of configuration for a system rather than a managerial guidance document. TCB is only as effective as its internal control mechanisms and the administration of the systems being configured. TCB is made up of the hardware

Figure 8-6 The DoD Rainbow series[4]

Source: Wikimedia Commons.

and software that has been implemented to provide security for a particular information system. This usually includes the operating system kernel and a specified set of security utilities, such as the user login subsystem.

The term "trusted" can be misleading—in this context, it means that a component is part of TCB's security system, but not that it is necessarily trustworthy. The frequent discovery of flaws and delivery of patches by software vendors to remedy security vulnerabilities attest to the relative level of trust you can place in current generations of software.

Within TCB is an object known as the **reference monitor**, which is the piece of the system that manages access controls. Systems administrators must be able to audit or periodically review the reference monitor to ensure it is functioning effectively, without unauthorized modification.

One of the biggest challenges in TCB is the existence of **covert channels**. Covert channels could be used by attackers who seek to exfiltrate sensitive data without being detected. Data loss prevention technologies monitor standard and covert channels to attempt to reduce an attacker's ability to accomplish exfiltration. For example, the cryptographic technique known as steganography allows the embedding of data bits in the digital version of graphical images, which enables a user to hide a message in a picture. TCSEC defines two kinds of covert channels:

reference monitor

Within the trusted computing base, a conceptual piece of the system that manages access controls.

covert channels

Unauthorized or unintended methods of communications hidden inside a computer system.

storage channels

TCSEC-defined covert channels that communicate by modifying a stored object, as in steganography.

timing channels

TCSEC-defined covert channels that communicate by managing the relative timing of events.

- **Storage channels**, which are used in steganography, as described before, and in the embedding of data in TCP or IP header fields. For more details on steganography, see Module 10.
- **Timing channels**, which are used in a system that places a long pause between packets to signify a 1 and a short pause between packets to signify a 0.

 For more information on the Rainbow Series, visit *https://csrc.nist.gov/publications/detail/white-paper/1985/12/26/dod-rainbow-series/final or www.fas.org/irp/nsa/rainbow.htm*.

ITSEC

The Information Technology System Evaluation Criteria (ITSEC), an international set of criteria for evaluating computer systems, is very similar to TCSEC. Under ITSEC, Targets of Evaluation (ToE) are compared to detailed security function specifications, resulting in an assessment of systems functionality and comprehensive penetration testing. Like TCSEC, ITSEC was functionally replaced for the most part by the Common Criteria, which are described in the following section. ITSEC rates products on a scale of E1 to the highest level of E6, much like the ratings of TCSEC and the Common Criteria. E1 is roughly equivalent to the EAL2 evaluation of the Common Criteria, and E6 is roughly equivalent to EAL7.

The Common Criteria

The Common Criteria for Information Technology Security Evaluation, often called the Common Criteria or just CC, is an international standard (ISO/IEC 15408) for computer security certification. It is widely considered the successor to both TCSEC and ITSEC in that it reconciles some differences between the various other standards. Most governments have discontinued their use of the other standards. CC is a combined effort of contributors from Australia, New Zealand, Canada, France, Germany, Japan, the Netherlands, Spain, the United Kingdom, and the United States. In the United States, the National Security Agency (NSA) and NIST were the primary contributors. CC and its companion, the Common Methodology for Information Technology Security Evaluation, are the technical basis for an international agreement called the Common Criteria Recognition Agreement (CCRA), which ensures that products can be evaluated to determine their particular security properties. CC seeks the widest possible mutual recognition of secure IT products.[5] The CC process ensures that the specification, implementation, and evaluation of computer security products are performed in a rigorous and standard manner.[6]

CC terminology includes the following:

- *Target of Evaluation (ToE)*—The system being evaluated
- *Protection Profile (PP)*—User-generated specification for security requirements
- *Security Target (ST)*—Document describing the ToE's security properties

- *Security Functional Requirements (SFRs)*—Catalog of a product's security functions
- *Evaluation Assurance Levels (EALs)*—The rating or grading of a ToE after evaluation

EAL is typically rated on the following scale:

- *EAL1*—Functionally Tested: Confidence in operation against nonserious threats
- *EAL2*—Structurally Tested: More confidence required but comparable with good business practices
- *EAL3*—Methodically Tested and Checked: Moderate level of security assurance
- *EAL4*—Methodically Designed, Tested, and Reviewed: Rigorous level of security assurance but still economically feasible without specialized development
- *EAL5*—Semiformally Designed and Tested: Certification requires specialized development above standard commercial products
- *EAL6*—Semiformally Verified Design and Tested: Specifically designed security ToE
- *EAL7*—Formally Verified Design and Tested: Developed for extremely high-risk situations or high-value systems.[7]

 For more information on the Common Criteria, visit *www.common criteriaportal.org*.

Bell–LaPadula Confidentiality Model

The Bell–LaPadula (BLP) confidentiality model is a "state machine reference model"—in other words, a model of an automated system that can manipulate its state or status over time. BLP ensures the confidentiality of the modeled system by using MACs, data classification, and security clearances. The intent of any state machine model is to devise a conceptual approach in which the system being modeled can always be in a known secure condition; in other words, this kind of model is provably secure. A system that serves as a reference monitor compares the level of data classification with the clearance of the entity requesting access; it allows access only if the clearance is equal to or higher than the classification. BLP security rules prevent information from being moved from a level of higher security to a lower level. Access modes can be one of two types: *simple security* and the * *(star)* property.

Simple security (also called the read property) prohibits a subject of lower clearance from reading an object of higher clearance, but it allows a subject with a higher clearance level to read an object at a lower level (read down).

The * property (the write property), on the other hand, prohibits a high-level subject from sending messages to a lower-level object. In short, subjects can read down, and objects can write or append up. BLP uses access permission matrices and a security lattice for access control.[8]

This model can be explained by imagining a fictional interaction between General Bell, whose thoughts and actions are classified at the highest possible level, and Private LaPadula, who has the lowest security clearance in the military. It is prohibited for Private LaPadula to read anything written by General Bell and for General Bell to write in any document that Private LaPadula could read. In short, the principle is "no read up, no write down."

Biba Integrity Model

The Biba integrity model is like BLP. It is based on the premise that higher levels of integrity are more worthy of trust than lower ones. The intent is to provide access controls to ensure that objects or subjects cannot have less integrity because of read/write operations. The Biba model assigns integrity levels to subjects and objects using two properties: the *simple integrity (read)* property and the *integrity * (write)* property.

The simple integrity property permits a subject to have read access to an object only if the subject's security level is lower than or equal to the level of the object. The integrity * property permits a subject to have write access to an object only if the subject's security level is equal to or higher than that of the object.

The Biba model ensures that no information from a subject can be passed on to an object at a higher security level. This prevents contaminating data of higher integrity with data of lower integrity.[9]

This model can be illustrated by imagining fictional interactions among some priests, a monk named Biba, and parishioners in the Middle Ages. Priests are considered holier (of greater integrity) than monks, who are in turn holier than parishioners. A priest cannot read (or offer) Masses or prayers written by Biba the Monk, who in turn cannot read items written by his parishioners. Biba the Monk is also prohibited from writing in a priest's sermon books, just as parishioners are prohibited from writing in Biba's book. These properties prevent the lower integrity of the lower level from corrupting the "holiness" or higher integrity of the upper level. On the other hand, higher-level entities can share their writings with the lower levels without compromising the integrity of the information. This example illustrates the "no write up, no read down" principle behind the Biba model.

Clark–Wilson Integrity Model

The Clark–Wilson integrity model, which is built upon principles of change control rather than integrity levels, was designed for the commercial environment. The model's change control principles are as follows:

- No changes by unauthorized subjects
- No unauthorized changes by authorized subjects
- The maintenance of internal and external consistency

Internal consistency means that the system does what it is expected to do every time, without exception. External consistency means that the data in the system is consistent with similar data in the outside world.

This model establishes a system of subject-program-object relationships so that the subject has no direct access to the object. Instead, the subject is required to access the object using a well-formed transaction via a validated program. The intent is to provide an environment where security can be proven using separated activities, each of which is also provably secure. The following controls are part of the Clark–Wilson model:

- Subject authentication and identification
- Access to objects by means of well-formed transactions
- Execution by subjects on a restricted set of programs

The following elements make up the Clark–Wilson model:

- Constrained data item (CDI): A data item with protected integrity
- Unconstrained data item: Data not controlled by Clark–Wilson; nonvalidated input or any output
- Integrity verification procedure (IVP): A procedure that scans data and confirms its integrity
- Transformation procedure (TP): A procedure that only allows changes to a constrained data item

All subjects and objects are labeled with TPs. The TPs operate as the intermediate layer between subjects and objects. Each data item has a set of access operations that can be performed on it. Each subject is assigned a set of access operations that it can perform. The system then compares these two parameters and either permits or denies access by the subject to the object.[10] As an example, consider a database management system (DBMS) that sits between a database user and the actual data. The DBMS requires the user to be authenticated before accessing the data, only accepts specific inputs (such as SQL queries), and only provides a restricted set of operations, in accordance with its design.

Graham–Denning Access Control Model

The Graham–Denning access control model has three parts: a set of objects, a set of subjects, and a set of rights. The subjects are composed of two things: a process and a domain. The domain is the set of constraints that control how subjects may access objects. The set of rights governs how subjects may manipulate the passive objects. This model describes eight primitive protection rights, called commands, which subjects can execute to influence other subjects or objects. Note that these commands are like the rights a user can assign to an entity in modern operating systems.[11]

The eight primitive protection rights are as follows:

1. Create object
2. Create subject
3. Delete object
4. Delete subject
5. Read access right
6. Grant access right
7. Delete access right
8. Transfer access right

Harrison–Ruzzo–Ullman Model

The Harrison–Ruzzo–Ullman (HRU) model defines a method to allow changes to access rights and the addition and removal of subjects and objects, a process that the Bell–LaPadula model does not allow. Because systems change over time, their protective states need to change. HRU is built on an access control matrix and includes a set of generic rights and a specific set of commands. These include the following:

- Create subject/create object
- Enter specific command or generic right into a subject or object
- Delete specific command or generic right from a subject or object
- Destroy subject/destroy object

By implementing this set of rights and commands and restricting the commands to a single operation each, it is possible to determine if and when a specific subject can obtain a particular right to an object.[12]

Brewer–Nash Model

The Brewer–Nash model, commonly known as a Chinese Wall, is designed to prevent a conflict of interest between two parties. Imagine that a law firm represents two people who are involved in a car accident. One sues the other, and the firm has to represent both. To prevent a conflict of interest, the individual attorneys should not be able to access the private information of these two litigants. The Brewer–Nash model requires users to select one of two conflicting sets of data, after which they cannot access the conflicting data.[13]

zero trust architecture (ZTA)

An approach to access control in IT networks that does not rely on trusting devices or network connections; rather, it relies on mutual authentication to verify the identity and integrity of devices, regardless of their location.

firewall

In information security, a combination of hardware and software that filters or prevents specific information from moving between the outside network and the inside network.

untrusted network

The system of networks outside the organization over which the organization has no control, such as the Internet.

trusted network

The system of networks inside the organization that contains its information assets and is under the organization's control.

Zero Trust Architecture

Zero trust is an approach to access control that moves defenses from static, network-based perimeters to focus on authentication of users, assets, and resources and then dynamically allow access based on access control rules. A **zero trust architecture (ZTA)** assumes there is no implicit trust granted to assets or user accounts based on physical location or network connectivity. Authentication and authorization become discrete functions repeated before each access is granted. Zero trust is meant to address environments that include remote users, bring your own device (BYOD), and cloud-based infrastructures. Zero trust focuses on protecting resources such as assets, services, workflows, and network accounts, not network segments. In a ZTA, physical location and network connectivity are no longer seen as the prime components of a resource's security posture.

 For more on the NIST zero trust architecture, read about Special Publication 800-207 at *www.nist.gov/publications/zero-trust-architecture*.

Firewall Technologies

In building construction, firewalls are concrete or masonry walls that run from the basement through the roof to prevent a fire from spreading from one section of the building to another. In aircraft and automobiles, a firewall is an insulated metal barrier that keeps the hot and dangerous moving parts of the motor separate from the flammable interior where the passengers sit. A **firewall** in an information security program is similar to physical firewalls in that it prevents specific types of information from moving between two different levels of networks, such as an **untrusted network** like the Internet and a **trusted network** like the organization's internal network. Some organizations place firewalls that have different levels of trust between portions of their network environment to add extra security for their most important applications and data. The firewall may be a separate computer system, a software service running on an existing router or server, or a separate network that contains several supporting devices. Firewalls can be categorized by processing mode, development era, or structure. Each of these will be examined in turn.

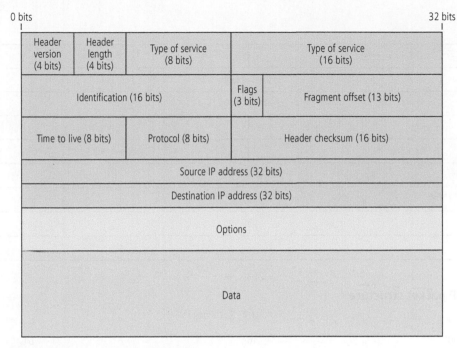

Figure 8-7   IP packet structure

Firewall Processing Modes

Firewalls fall into several major categories of processing modes: packet-filtering firewalls, application layer proxy firewalls, media access control layer firewalls, and hybrids. Hybrid firewalls use a combination of the other modes; in practice, most firewalls fall into this category because most implementations use multiple approaches.

Packet-Filtering Firewalls

The **packet-filtering firewall** examines the header information of data packets that come into a network. A packet-filtering firewall installed on a TCP/IP-based network typically functions at the IP layer and determines whether to deny (drop) a packet or allow (forward) it to the next network connection, based on the rules programmed into the firewall. Packet-filtering firewalls examine every incoming packet header and can selectively filter packets based on header information such as destination address, source address, packet type, and other key information. Figure 8-7 shows the structure of an IPv4 packet.

Packet-filtering firewalls scan network data packets looking for compliance with the rules of the firewall's database or violations of those rules. Filtering firewalls inspect packets at the network layer, or Layer 3, of the Open Systems Interconnect (OSI) model, which represents the seven layers of networking processes. The OSI model is illustrated later in this module in Figure 8-11. If the device finds a packet that matches a restriction, it stops the packet from traveling from one network to another. The restrictions most implemented in packet-filtering firewalls are based on a combination of the following:

- IP source and destination address
- Direction (inbound or outbound)
- Protocol, for firewalls capable of examining the IP protocol layer
- Transmission Control Protocol (TCP) or User Datagram Protocol (UDP) source and destination port requests, for firewalls capable of examining the TCP/UDP layer

Packet structure varies depending on the nature of the packet. The two primary service types are TCP and UDP, as noted before. Figures 8-8 and 8-9 show the structures of these two major elements of the combined protocol known as TCP/IP.

Simple firewall models examine two aspects of the packet header: the destination and source address. They enforce address restrictions through ACLs, which are created and modified by the firewall administrators. Figure 8-10 shows

> **packet-filtering firewall**
>
> A networking device that examines the header information of data packets that come into a network and determines whether to drop them (deny) or forward them to the next network connection (allow), based on its configuration rules.

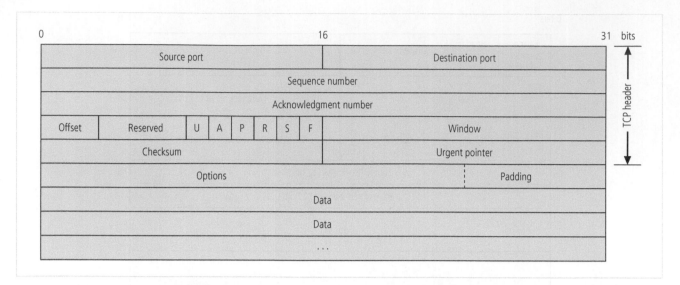

Figure 8-8   TCP packet structure

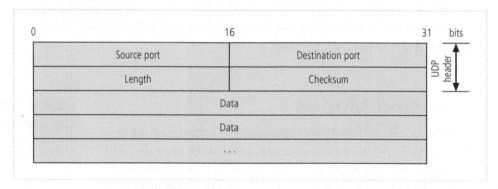

Figure 8-9   UDP packet structure

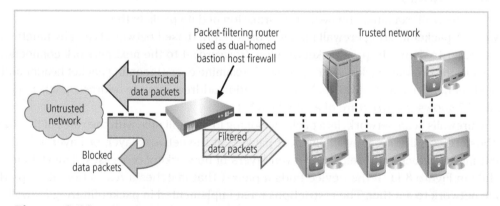

Figure 8-10   Packet-filtering router

how a packet-filtering router can be used as a firewall to filter data packets from inbound connections and allow outbound connections unrestricted access to the public network. Dual-homed bastion host firewalls are discussed later in this module.

To better understand an address restriction scheme, consider an example. If an administrator configured a simple rule based on the content of Table 8-2, any connection attempt made by an external computer or network device in the 192.168.x.x address range (192.168.0.0–192.168.255.255) to the Web server at 10.10.10.25 would be allowed. The ability to restrict a specific service rather than just a range of IP addresses is available in a more advanced version of this first-generation firewall. Additional details on firewall rules and configuration are presented later in this module.

Table 8-2   Sample Firewall Rules and Format

Source Address	Destination Address	Service (e.g., HTTP, SMTP, FTP)	Action (Allow or Deny)
172.16.x.x	10.10.x.x	Any	Deny
192.168.x.x	10.10.10.25	HTTP	Allow
192.168.0.1	10.10.10.10	FTP	Allow

The ability to restrict a specific service is now considered standard in most routers and is invisible to the user. Unfortunately, such systems are unable to detect whether packet headers have been modified, which is an advanced technique used in IP spoofing attacks and other attacks.

The three subsets of packet-filtering firewalls are **static packet filtering**, **dynamic packet filtering**, and **stateful packet inspection (SPI)**. They enforce **address restrictions**, which are rules designed to prohibit packets with certain addresses or partial addresses from passing through the device. Static packet filtering requires that the filtering rules be developed and installed with the firewall. The rules are created and sequenced by a person who either directly edits the rule set or uses a programmable interface to specify the rules and the sequence. Any changes to the rules require human intervention. This type of filtering is common in network routers and gateways.

A dynamic packet-filtering firewall can react to an emergent event and update or create rules to deal with that event. This reaction could be positive, as in allowing an internal user to engage in a specific activity upon request, or it could be negative, as in dropping all packets from a particular address when the system detects an increased presence of a particular type of malformed packet. While static packet-filtering firewalls allow entire sets of one type of packet to enter in response to authorized requests, dynamic packet filtering allows only a particular packet with a particular source, destination, and port address to enter. This filtering works by opening and closing "doors" in the firewall based on the information contained in the packet header, which makes dynamic packet filters an intermediate form between traditional static packet filters and application proxies. These proxies are described in the next section.

SPI firewalls, also called stateful inspection firewalls, keep track of each network connection between internal and external systems using a **state table**. A state table tracks the state and context of each packet in the conversation by recording which station sent what packet and when. Like first-generation firewalls, stateful inspection firewalls perform packet filtering, but they take it a step further. Whereas simple packet-filtering firewalls only allow or deny certain packets based on their address, a stateful firewall can expedite incoming packets that are responses to internal requests. If the stateful firewall receives an incoming packet that it cannot match in its state table, it refers to its ACL to determine whether to allow the packet to pass.

The primary disadvantage of this type of firewall is the additional processing required to manage and verify packets against the state table. Without this processing, the system is vulnerable to a DoS or DDoS attack. In such an attack, the system receives a very large number of external packets, which slows the firewall because it attempts to compare all of the incoming packets first to the state table and then to the ACL. On the positive side, these firewalls can track connectionless packet traffic, such as UDP and remote procedure calls (RPC) traffic. Dynamic SPI firewalls keep a dynamic state table to make changes to the filtering rules within predefined limits, based on events as they happen.

A state table looks like a firewall rule set but has additional information, as shown in Table 8-3. The state table contains the familiar columns for source IP address, source port, destination IP address, and destination port, but it adds information for the protocol used (UDP or TCP), total time in seconds, and time remaining in seconds. Many state table implementations allow a connection to remain in place for up to 60 minutes without any activity before the state entry is deleted. The example in Table 8-3 shows this value in the Total Time column. The Time Remaining column shows a countdown of the time left until the entry is deleted.

static packet filtering

A firewall type that requires the configuration rules to be manually created, sequenced, and modified within the firewall.

dynamic packet filtering

A firewall type that can react to network traffic and create or modify its configuration rules to adapt.

stateful packet inspection (SPI)

A firewall type that keeps track of each network connection between internal and external systems using a state table and that expedites the filtering of those communications; also known as a stateful inspection firewall.

address restrictions

Firewall rules designed to prohibit packets with certain addresses or partial addresses from passing through the device.

state table

A tabular record of the state and context of each packet in a conversation between an internal and external user or system; used to expedite traffic filtering.

Table 8-3 State Table Entries

Source Address	Source Port	Destination Address	Destination Port	Time Remaining (in Seconds)	Total Time (in Seconds)	Protocol
192.168.2.5	1028	10.10.10.7	80	2725	3600	TCP

Application Layer Proxy Firewalls

The **application layer proxy firewall**, also known as an **application firewall**, is frequently installed on a dedicated computer separate from the filtering router, but it is commonly used in conjunction with a filtering router. The application firewall is also known as a **proxy server** (or **reverse proxy**) because it can be configured to run special software that acts as a proxy for a service request. For example, an organization that runs a Web server can avoid exposing it to direct user traffic by installing a proxy server configured with the registered domain's URL. This proxy server receives requests for Web pages, accesses the Web server on behalf of the external client, and returns the requested pages to users. These servers can store the most recently accessed pages in their internal cache and are thus also called *cache servers*. The benefits from this type of implementation are significant. For one, the proxy server is placed in an unsecured area of the network or in the **demilitarized zone (DMZ)** so that it is exposed to the higher levels of risk from less trusted networks, rather than exposing the Web server to such risks. Additional filtering routers can be implemented behind the proxy server, limiting access to the more secure internal system and providing further protection.

The primary disadvantage of application layer proxy firewalls is that they are designed for one or a few specific protocols and cannot easily be reconfigured to protect against attacks on other protocols. Because these firewalls work at the application layer, they are typically restricted to a single application, such as File Transfer Protocol (FTP), Telnet, Hypertext Transfer Protocol (HTTP), Simple Mail Transfer Protocol (SMTP), or Simple Network Management Protocol (SNMP). The processing time and resources necessary to read each packet down to the application layer diminishes the ability of these firewalls to handle multiple types of applications.

Media Access Control Layer Firewalls

While not as well known or widely referenced as the firewall approaches described in the previous sections, **media access control layer firewalls** make filtering decisions based on the specific host computer's identity, as represented by its media access control (MAC) address or network interface card (NIC) address, which operates at the data link layer of the OSI model or the subnet layer of the TCP/IP model. Thus, media access control layer firewalls link the addresses of specific host computers to ACL entries that identify the specific types of packets that can be sent to each host and block all other traffic. While media access control layer firewalls are also referred to as MAC layer firewalls, we don't do so here to avoid confusion with mandatory access controls (MACs).

Figure 8-11 shows where each of the firewall processing modes inspects data in the OSI model.

Hybrid Firewalls

Hybrid firewalls combine the elements of other types of firewalls—that is, the elements of packet-filtering, application layer proxy, and media access control layer firewalls. A hybrid firewall system may consist of two separate firewall devices; each is a separate firewall system, but they are connected so that they work in tandem. For example, a hybrid firewall system might include a packet-filtering firewall that is set up to screen all acceptable requests and then pass the requests to a proxy server, which in turn requests services from a Web server deep inside the organization's

application layer proxy firewall

A device capable of functioning both as a firewall and an application layer proxy server.

application firewall

See *application layer proxy firewall.*

proxy server

A server that exists to intercept requests for information from external users and provide the requested information by retrieving it from an internal server, thus protecting and minimizing the demand on internal servers; some are also cache servers.

reverse proxy

A proxy server that most commonly retrieves information from inside an organization and provides it to a requesting user or system outside the organization.

demilitarized zone (DMZ)

An intermediate area designed to provide servers and firewall filtering between a trusted internal network and the outside, untrusted network.

media access control layer firewall

A firewall designed to operate at the media access control sublayer of the network's data link layer (Layer 2).

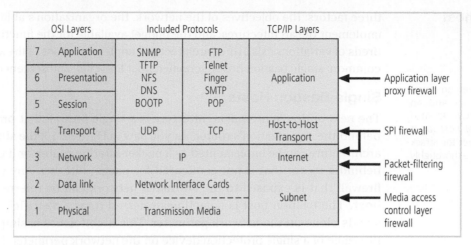

Figure 8-11 Firewall types and protocol levels

networks. An added advantage to the hybrid firewall approach is that it enables an organization to improve security without completely replacing its existing firewalls.

The most recent generations of firewalls aren't really new; they are hybrids built from capabilities of modern networking equipment that can perform a variety of tasks according to the organization's needs. The first type of hybrid firewall is known as **Unified Threat Management (UTM)**. These devices are categorized by their ability to perform the work of an SPI firewall, network IDPS, content filter, spam filter, and malware scanner and filter. UTM systems take advantage of increasing memory capacity and processor capability and can reduce the complexity associated with deploying, configuring, and integrating multiple networking devices. With the proper configuration, these devices are even able to "drill down" into the protocol layers and examine application-specific data, encrypted data, compressed data, and encoded data. The primary disadvantage of UTM systems is the creation of a single point of failure if the device has technical problems.

The second type of hybrid firewall is known as the **Next Generation Firewall** (**NextGen** or **NGFW**). Like UTM devices, NextGen firewalls combine traditional firewall functions with other network security functions, such as deep packet inspection, IDPSs, and the ability to decrypt encrypted traffic. The functions are so similar to those of UTM devices that the only difference may lie in the vendor's description. According to Kevin Beaver of Principle Logic, LLC, the only difference may be one of scope: "Unified Threat Management systems do a good job at a lot of things, while Next Generation Firewalls do an excellent job at just a handful of things."[14] Careful review of the solution's capabilities against the organization's needs will facilitate selection of the best equipment. Organizations with tight budgets may benefit from "all-in-one" devices, while larger organizations with more staff and funding may prefer separate devices that can be managed independently and function more efficiently on their own platforms.

Firewall Architectures

The value of a firewall comes from its ability to filter out unwanted or dangerous traffic as it enters the network perimeter of an organization. A challenge to the value proposition offered by firewalls is the changing nature of the way networks are used. As organizations implement cloud-based IT solutions, bring-your-own-device (BYOD) options for employees, and other emerging network solutions, the network perimeter may be dissolving for them. One reaction is the use of a software-defined perimeter that employs secure VPN technology to deliver network connectivity only to verified devices, regardless of location. No matter what approach companies take to meet these challenges, they will often make use of expertise from other companies that offer managed security services (MSS). These companies assist their clients with highly available monitoring services from secure network operations centers (NOCs). Many companies still rely on the defined network perimeter as their first line of network security defense.

All firewall devices can be configured in several network connection architectures. These approaches are sometimes mutually exclusive, but sometimes they can be combined. The configuration that works best for a particular organization depends on

Unified Threat Management (UTM)

Networking devices categorized by their ability to perform the work of multiple devices, such as stateful packet inspection firewalls, network intrusion detection and prevention systems (IDPSs), content filters, spam filters, and malware scanners and filters.

Next Generation Firewall (NextGen or NGFW)

A security appliance that delivers Unified Threat Management capabilities in a single integrated device.

single bastion host

See *bastion host.*

bastion host

A device placed between an external, untrusted network and an internal, trusted network; also known as a *sacrificial host*, as it serves as the sole target for attack and should therefore be thoroughly secured.

sacrificial host

See *bastion host.*

Network Address Translation (NAT)

A networking scheme in which multiple real, routable external IP addresses are converted to special ranges of internal IP addresses, usually on a one-to-one basis; that is, one external valid address directly maps to one assigned internal address.

three factors: the objectives of the network, the organization's ability to develop and implement the architectures, and the budget available for the function. Although hundreds of variations exist, three architectural implementations of firewalls are especially common: single bastion hosts, screened host firewalls, and screened subnet firewalls.

Single Bastion Hosts

The next option in firewall architecture is a single firewall that provides protection behind the organization's router. As you saw in Figure 8-10, the **single bastion host** architecture can be implemented as a packet-filtering router, or it could be a firewall behind a router that is not configured for packet filtering. Any system, router, or firewall that is exposed to the untrusted network can be referred to as a **bastion host**. The bastion host is sometimes referred to as a **sacrificial host** because it stands alone on the network perimeter. This architecture is simply defined as the presence of a single protection device on the network perimeter. It is commonplace in residential small office/home office (SOHO) environments. Larger organizations typically look to implement architectures with more defense in depth and with additional security devices designed to provide a more robust defense strategy.

The bastion host is usually implemented as a *dual-homed host* because it contains two network interfaces: one that is connected to the external network and one that is connected to the internal network. All traffic must go through the device to move between the internal and external networks. Such an architecture lacks defense in depth, and the complexity of the ACLs used to filter the packets can grow and degrade network performance. An attacker who infiltrates the bastion host can discover the configuration of internal networks and possibly provide external sources with internal information.

Each protocol and protocol element used by the Internet to perform network operations is defined by documentation known as an RFC. The name comes from "request for comments"—the format used to propose ideas for consideration by the Internet community. As protocols evolve from the discussion generated by the RFCs, the details are documented in each successive RFC until a critical mass of the Internet community agrees to implement the ideas. Every protocol used by the Internet can be understood by reading the relevant RFCs. You can find most of them on the Internet Engineering Task Force's Web site at *www.ietf.org/standards/rfcs/.*

 You can see a numerically ordered index of RFC documentation at *www.rfc-editor.org/rfc-index.html.*

Implementation of the bastion host architecture often makes use of **Network Address Translation (NAT)**. RFC 2663 uses the term *network address and port translation (NAPT)* to describe both NAT and Port Address Translation (PAT), which is covered later in this section. NAT is a method of mapping valid, external IP addresses to special ranges of nonroutable internal IP addresses, known as private IPv4 addresses, to create another barrier to intrusion from external attackers. In IPv6 addressing, these addresses are referred to as *Unique Local Addresses (ULA)*, as defined by RFC 4193. The internal addresses used by NAT consist of three different ranges. Organizations that need a large group of addresses for internal use will use the private IP address ranges reserved for nonpublic networks, as shown in Table 8-4. Messages sent with internal addresses within these three reserved ranges cannot be routed externally, so if a computer with one of these internal-use addresses is directly connected to the external network and avoids the NAT server, its traffic cannot be routed on the public network. Taking advantage of this, NAT prevents external attacks from reaching internal machines with addresses in specified ranges. If the NAT server is a multi-homed bastion host, it translates between the true, external IP addresses assigned to the organization by public network naming authorities and the internally assigned, non-routable IP addresses. NAT translates by dynamically assigning addresses to internal communications and tracking the conversations with sessions to determine which incoming message is a response to which outgoing traffic.

A variation on NAT is **Port Address Translation (PAT)**. Where NAT performs a one-to-one mapping between assigned external IP addresses and internal private addresses, PAT performs a one-to-many assignment that allows the mapping of many internal hosts to a single assigned external IP address. The system is able to maintain the integrity of each communication by assigning a unique port number to the external IP address and mapping the address and port combination

Table 8-4   Reserved Non-Routable Address Ranges

Classful Description	Usable Addresses	From	To	CIDR Mask	Decimal Mask
Class A or 24 Bit	~16.5 million	10.0.0.0	10.255.255.255	/8	255.0.0.0
Class B or 20 Bit	~1.05 million	172.16.0.0	172.31.255.255	/12 or /16	255.240.0.0 or 255.255.0.0
Class C or 16 Bit	~65,500	192.168.0.0	192.168.255.255	/16 or /24	255.255.0.0 or 255.255.255.0
IPv6 Space	~65,500 sets of 18.45 quintillion (18.45 × 10^{18})	fc00::/7, where the first 7 digits are fixed (1111 110x), followed by a 10-digit organization ID, then 4 digits of subnet ID and 16 digits of host ID. ([F][C or D]xx:xxxx:xxxx:yyyy:zzzz:zzzz:zzzz:zzzz).			

Note that CIDR stands for classless inter-domain routing.

Source: Internet Engineering Task Force, RFC 6761.[15]

(known as a socket) to the internal IP address. Multiple communications from a single internal address would have a unique matching of the internal IP address and port to the external IP address and port, with unique port addresses for each communication. Figure 8-12 shows an example configuration of a dual-homed firewall that uses NAT to protect the internal network.

Screened Host Architecture

A **screened host architecture** combines the packet-filtering router with a separate, dedicated firewall, such as an application proxy server, which retrieves information on behalf of other system users and often caches copies of Web pages and other needed information on its internal drives to speed up access. This approach allows the router to prescreen packets to minimize the network traffic and load on the internal proxy. The application proxy examines an application layer protocol, such as HTTP, and performs the proxy services. Because an application proxy may retain working copies of some Web documents to improve performance, unanticipated losses can result if it is compromised and the documents were not designed for general access. The screened host firewall may present a promising target because compromise of the bastion host can lead to attacks on the proxy server that could disclose the configuration of internal networks and possibly provide attackers with

Port Address Translation (PAT)

A networking scheme in which multiple real, routable external IP addresses are converted to special ranges of internal IP addresses, usually on a one-to-many basis; that is, one external valid address is mapped dynamically to a range of internal addresses by adding a unique port number to the address when traffic leaves the private network and is placed on the public network.

screened host architecture

A firewall architectural model that combines the packet-filtering router with a second, dedicated device such as a proxy server or proxy firewall.

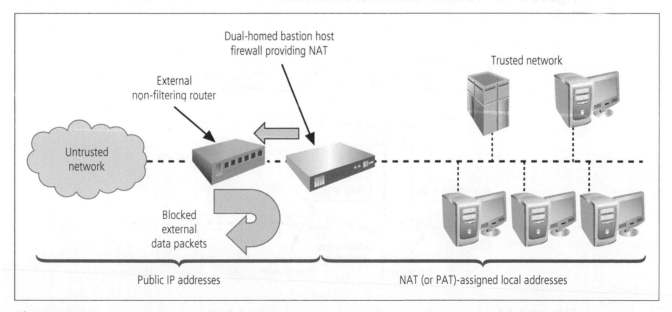

Figure 8-12   Dual-homed bastion host firewall architecture

internal information. To its advantage, this configuration requires the external attack to compromise two separate systems before the attack can access internal data. In this way, the bastion host protects the data more fully than the router alone. Figure 8-13 shows a typical configuration of a screened host architecture.

Screened Subnet Architecture (with DMZ)

The dominant architecture today is the screened subnet used with a DMZ. The DMZ can be a dedicated port on the firewall device linking a single bastion host, or it can be connected to a screened subnet, as shown in Figure 8-14. Until recently, servers that provided services through an untrusted network were commonly placed in the DMZ. Examples include Web servers, FTP servers, and certain database servers. More recent strategies using proxy servers have provided much more secure solutions.

A common arrangement is a subnet firewall that consists of two or more internal bastion hosts behind a packet-filtering router, with each host protecting the trusted network. There are many variants of the screened subnet architecture. The first general model consists of two filtering routers, with one or more dual-homed bastion hosts between them. In the second general model, as illustrated in Figure 8-15, the connections are routed as follows:

- Connections from the outside or untrusted network are routed through an external filtering router.

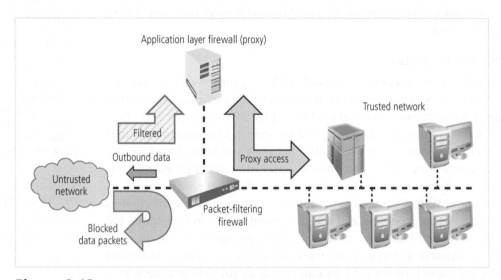

Figure 8-13   Screened host firewall architecture

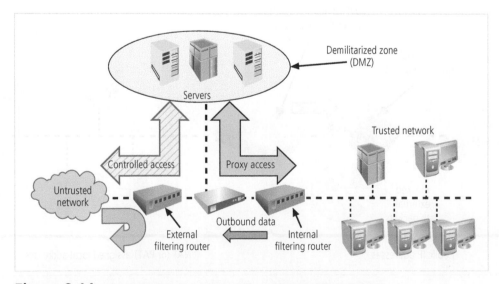

Figure 8-14   Screened subnet firewall architecture with DMZ

- Connections from the outside or untrusted network are routed into—and then out of—a routing firewall to the separate network segment known as the DMZ.
- Connections into the trusted internal network are allowed only from the DMZ bastion host servers.

The **screened subnet architecture** is an entire network segment that performs two functions. First, it protects the DMZ systems and information from outside threats by providing a level of intermediate security, which means the network is more secure than public networks but less secure than the internal network. Second, the screened subnet protects the internal networks by limiting how external connections can gain access to them. Although extremely secure, the screened subnet can be expensive to implement and complex to configure and manage. The value of the information it protects must justify the cost.

Another facet of the DMZ is the creation of an area known as an extranet. An **extranet** is a segment of the DMZ where additional authentication and authorization controls are put into place to provide services that are not available to the public. An example is an online retailer that allows anyone to browse the product catalog and place items into a shopping cart but requires extra authentication and authorization when the customer is ready to check out and place an order.

Selecting the Right Firewall

When trying to determine the best firewall for an organization, you should consider the following questions:

1. Which type of firewall technology offers the right balance between protection and cost for the needs of the organization?
2. What features are included in the base price? What features are available at extra cost? Are all cost factors known?
3. How easy is it to set up and configure the firewall? Does the organization have staff members on hand who are trained to configure the firewall, or would the hiring of additional employees (or contractors or managed service providers) be required?
4. Can the firewall adapt to the organization's growing network?

The most important factor, of course, is the extent to which the firewall design provides the required protection. The next important factor is cost, which may keep a certain make, model, or type of firewall out of reach. As with all security decisions, certain compromises may be necessary to provide a viable solution under the budgetary constraints stipulated by management.

screened subnet architecture

A firewall architectural model that consists of one or more internal bastion hosts located behind a packet-filtering router on a dedicated network segment, with each host performing a role in protecting the trusted network.

extranet

A segment of the DMZ where additional authentication and authorization controls are put into place to provide services that are not available to the general public.

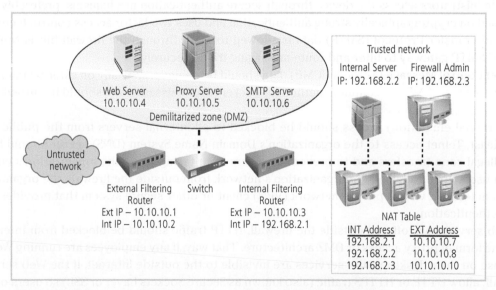

Figure 8-15   Second example of screened subnet with DMZ

configuration rules

The instructions a system administrator codes into a server, networking device, or security device to specify how it operates.

Configuring and Managing Firewalls

Once the firewall architecture and technology have been selected, the organization must provide for the initial configuration and ongoing management of the firewall(s). Good policy and practice dictate that each firewall device—whether a filtering router, bastion host, or other implementation—must have its own set of **configuration rules**. In theory, packet-filtering firewalls examine each incoming packet using a rule set to determine whether to allow or deny the packet. That set of rules is made up of simple statements that identify source and destination addresses and the type of requests a packet contains based on the ports specified in the packet. In fact, the configuration of firewall policies can be complex and difficult. IT professionals who are familiar with application programming can appreciate the difficulty of debugging both syntax errors and logic errors. Syntax errors in firewall policies are usually easy to identify, as the systems alert the administrator to incorrectly configured policies. However, logic errors, such as allowing instead of denying, specifying the wrong port or service type, and using the wrong switch, are another story. A myriad of simple mistakes can take a device designed to protect users' communications and turn it into one giant choke point. A choke point that restricts all communications or an incorrectly configured rule can cause other unexpected results. For example, novice firewall administrators often improperly configure a virus-screening e-mail gateway to operate as a type of e-mail firewall. Instead of screening e-mail for malicious code, it blocks all incoming e-mail and causes a great deal of frustration among users.

Configuring firewall policies is as much an art as it is a science. Each configuration rule must be carefully crafted, debugged, tested, and placed into the firewall's rule base in the proper sequence. Good, correctly sequenced firewall rules ensure that the actions taken comply with the organization's policy. In a well-designed, efficient firewall rule set, rules that can be evaluated quickly and govern broad access are performed before rules that may take longer to evaluate and affect fewer cases. The most important thing to remember when configuring firewalls is that when security rules conflict with the performance of business, security often loses. If users can't work because of a security restriction, the security administration is usually told in no uncertain terms to remove the safeguard. In other words, organizations are much more willing to live with potential risk than certain failure.

Best Practices for Firewalls

This section outlines some of the best practices for firewall use. Note that these rules are not presented in any particular sequence. For sequencing of rules, refer to the next section.

- All traffic from the trusted network is allowed out. This rule allows members of the organization to access the services they need. Filtering and logging of outbound traffic can be implemented when required by specific organizational policies.
- The firewall device is never directly accessible from the public network for configuration or management purposes. Almost all administrative access to the firewall device is denied to internal users as well. Only authorized firewall administrators access the device through secure authentication mechanisms, preferably via a method that is based on cryptographically strong authentication and uses two-factor access control techniques.
- Simple Mail Transfer Protocol (SMTP) data is allowed to enter through the firewall but is routed to a well-configured SMTP gateway to filter and route messaging traffic securely.
- All Internet Control Message Protocol (ICMP) data should be denied, especially on external interfaces. Known as the ping service, ICMP is a common method for hacker reconnaissance and should be turned off to prevent snooping.
- Telnet (terminal emulation) access should be blocked to all internal servers from the public networks. At the very least, Telnet access to the organization's Domain Name System (DNS) server should be blocked to prevent illegal zone transfers and to prevent attackers from taking down the organization's entire network. If internal users need to access an organization's network from outside the firewall, the organization should enable them to use a virtual private network (VPN) client or other secure system that provides a reasonable level of authentication.
- When Web services are offered outside the firewall, HTTP traffic should be blocked from internal networks using some form of proxy access or DMZ architecture. That way, if any employees are running Web servers for internal use on their desktops, the services are invisible to the outside Internet. If the Web server is behind the firewall, allow HTTP or HTTPS traffic (also known as Secure Sockets Layer or SSL) so users on the Internet at large can view it. The best solution is to place the Web servers that contain critical data inside the network

and use proxy services from a DMZ (screened network segment), and to restrict Web traffic bound for internal network addresses to allow only the requests that originated from internal addresses. This restriction can be accomplished using NAT or other stateful inspection or proxy server firewalls. All other incoming HTTP traffic should be blocked. If the Web servers only contain advertising, they should be placed in the DMZ and rebuilt on a timed schedule or when—not *if*, but *when*—they are compromised.

- All data that is not verifiably authentic should be denied. When attempting to convince packet-filtering firewalls to permit malicious traffic, attackers frequently put an internal address in the *source* field. To avoid this problem, set rules so that the external firewall blocks all inbound traffic with an organizational source address.

Firewall Rules

As you learned earlier in this module, firewalls operate by examining a data packet and performing a comparison with some predetermined logical rules. The logic is based on a set of guidelines programmed by a firewall administrator or created dynamically based on outgoing requests for information. This logical set is commonly referred to as firewall rules, a rule base, or firewall logic. Most firewalls use packet header information to determine whether a specific packet should be allowed to pass through or be dropped. Firewall rules operate on the principle of "that which is not permitted is prohibited," also known as expressly permitted rules. In other words, unless a rule explicitly permits an action, it is denied.

When your organization (or even your home network) uses certain cloud services, like backup providers or Application as a Service providers, or implements some types of device automation, such as those for the Internet of Things, you may have to make firewall rule adjustments. This may include allowing remote servers access to specific on-premises systems or requiring firewall controls to block undesirable outbound traffic. When these special circumstances occur, you will need to understand how firewall rules are implemented.

To better understand more complex rules, you must be able to create simple rules and understand how they interact. In the exercise that follows, many of the rules are based on the best practices outlined earlier. Note that some of the example rules may be implemented automatically by certain brands of firewalls. Therefore, it is imperative to become well trained on a particular brand of firewall before attempting to implement one in any setting outside of a lab. For the purposes of this discussion, assume a network configuration as illustrated in Figure 8-15, with an internal and external filtering firewall.

The exercise discusses the rules for both firewalls and provides a recap at the end that shows the complete rule sets for each filtering firewall. Note that separate access control lists are created for each interface on a firewall and are *bound* to that interface. This creates a set of unidirectional flow checks for dual-homed hosts, for example, which means that some of the rules shown here are designed for *inbound* traffic from the untrusted side of the firewall to the trusted side, and some rules are designed for *outbound* traffic from the trusted side to the untrusted side. It is important to ensure that the appropriate rule is used, as permitting certain traffic on the wrong side of the device can have unintended consequences. These examples assume that the firewall can process information beyond the IP level (TCP/UDP) and thus can access source and destination port addresses. If it could not, you could substitute the IP "Protocol" field for the source and destination port fields.

Some firewalls can filter packets by protocol name as opposed to protocol port number. For instance, Telnet protocol packets usually go to TCP port 23, but they can sometimes be redirected to another much higher port number in an attempt to conceal the activity. The system (or well-known) port numbers are 0 through 1023, user (or registered) port numbers are 1024 through 49151, and dynamic (or private) port numbers are 49152 through 65535. See *https://www.iana.org/assignments/service-names-port-numbers/service-names-port-numbers.xhtml* for more information.

The example shown in Table 8-5 uses the port numbers associated with several well-known protocols to build a rule base.

Rule Set 1   Responses to internal requests are allowed. In most firewall implementations, it is desirable to allow a response to an internal request for information. In stateful firewalls, this response is most easily accomplished by matching the incoming traffic to an outgoing request in a state table. In simple packet filtering, this response can be accomplished by setting the following rule for the external filtering router. (Note that the network address for the destination ends with .0; some firewalls use a notation of .x instead.) Use extreme caution in deploying this rule, as some attacks use port assignments greater than 1023. However, most modern firewalls use stateful inspection filtering and make this concern obsolete.

The rule is shown in Table 8-6. It states that *any* inbound packet destined for the internal network and for a destination port greater than 1023 is allowed to enter. The inbound packets can have any source address and be from any source port. The destination address of the internal network is 10.10.10.0, and the destination port is any port beyond the range of well-known ports.

Table 8-5 Well-Known Port Numbers

Port Number	Protocol
7	Echo
20	File Transfer [Default Data] (FTP)
21	File Transfer [Control] (FTP)
23	Telnet
25	Simple Mail Transfer Protocol (SMTP)
53	Domain Name System (DNS)
80	Hypertext Transfer Protocol (HTTP)
110	Post Office Protocol version 3 (POP3)
123	Network Time Protocol (NTP)
161	Simple Network Management Protocol (SNMP)
443	Hypertext Transfer Protocol Secure (HTTPS)

Table 8-6 Rule Set 1

Source Address	Source Port	Destination Address	Destination Port	Action
Any	Any	10.10.10.0	>1023	Allow

Why allow all such packets? While outbound communications request information from a specific port (for example, a port 80 request for a Web page), the response is assigned a number outside the well-known port range. If multiple browser windows are open at the same time, each window can request a packet from a Web site, and the response is directed to a specific destination port, allowing the browser and Web server to keep each conversation separate. While this rule is sufficient for the external firewall, it is dangerous to allow any traffic in just because it is destined to a high port range. A better solution is to have the internal firewall use state tables that track connections and thus prevent dangerous packets from entering this upper port range. Again, this practice is known as stateful packet inspection. This is one of the rules allowed by default by most modern firewall systems.

Rule Set 2 The firewall device is never accessible directly from the public network. If attackers can directly access the firewall, they may be able to modify or delete rules and allow unwanted traffic through. For the same reason, the firewall itself should never be allowed to access other network devices directly. If hackers compromise the firewall and then use its permissions to access other servers or clients, they may cause additional damage or mischief. The rules shown in Table 8-7 prohibit anyone from directly accessing the firewall and prohibit the firewall from directly accessing any other devices. Note that this example is for the external filtering router and firewall only. Similar rules should be crafted for the internal router. Why are there separate rules for each IP address? The 10.10.10.1 address regulates external access to and by the firewall, while the 10.10.10.2 address regulates internal access. Not all attackers are outside the firewall!

Note that if the firewall administrator needs direct access to the firewall from inside or outside the network, a permission rule allowing access from his or her IP address should preface this rule. The interface can also be accessed on the opposite side of the device, as traffic would be routed through the firewall and "boomerang" back when it hits the first router on the far side. Thus, the rule protects the interfaces in both the inbound and outbound rule set.

Table 8-7 Rule Set 2

Source Address	Source Port	Destination Address	Destination Port	Action
Any	Any	10.10.10.1	Any	Deny
Any	Any	10.10.10.2	Any	Deny
10.10.10.1	Any	Any	Any	Deny
10.10.10.2	Any	Any	Any	Deny

Rule Set 3 All traffic from the trusted network is allowed out. As a general rule, it is wise not to restrict outbound traffic unless separate routers and firewalls are configured to handle it, to avoid overloading the firewall. If an organization wants control over outbound traffic, it should use a separate filtering device. The rule shown in Table 8-8 allows internal communications out, so it would be used on the outbound interface.

Why should rule set 3 come after rule sets 1 and 2? It makes sense to allow rules that unambiguously affect the most traffic to be placed earlier in the list. The more rules a firewall must process to find one that applies to the current packet, the slower the firewall will run. Therefore, most widely applicable rules should come first because the firewall employs the first rule that applies to any given packet.

Rule Set 4 The rule set for SMTP data is shown in Table 8-9. As shown, the packets governed by this rule are allowed to pass through the firewall but are all routed to a well-configured SMTP gateway. It is important that e-mail traffic reach your e-mail server and *only* your e-mail server. Some attackers try to disguise dangerous packets as e-mail traffic to fool a firewall. If such packets can reach only the e-mail server and it has been properly configured, the rest of the network ought to be safe. Note that if the organization allows home access to an internal e-mail server, then it may want to implement a second, separate server to handle the POP3 protocol that retrieves mail for e-mail clients like Outlook and Thunderbird. This is usually a low-risk operation, especially if e-mail encryption is in place. More challenging is the transmission of e-mail using the SMTP protocol, a service that is attractive to spammers who may seek to hijack an outbound mail server.

Rule Set 5 All ICMP data should be denied. Pings, formally known as ICMP Echo requests, are used by internal systems administrators to ensure that clients and servers can communicate. There is virtually no legitimate use for ICMP outside the network, except to test the perimeter routers. ICMP may be the first indicator of a malicious attack. It's best to make all directly connected networking devices "black holes" to external probes. A common networking diagnostic command in most operating systems is traceroute; it uses a variation of the ICMP Echo requests, so restricting this port provides protection against multiple types of probes. Allowing internal users to use ICMP requires configuring two rules, as shown in Table 8-10.

The first of these two rules allows internal administrators and users to use ping. Note that this rule is unnecessary if the firewall uses internal permissions rules like those in rule set 2. The second rule in Table 8-10 does not allow anyone else to use ping. Remember that rules are processed in order. If an internal user needs to ping an internal or external address, the firewall allows the packet and stops processing the rules. If the request does not come from an internal source, then it bypasses the first rule and moves to the second.

Rule Set 6 Telnet (terminal emulation) access should be blocked to all internal servers from the public networks. Though it is not used much in Windows environments, Telnet is still useful to systems administrators on UNIX and Linux systems. However, the presence of external requests for Telnet services can indicate an attack. Allowing internal use of Telnet requires the same type of initial permission rule you use with ping. See Table 8-11. Again, this rule is unnecessary if the firewall uses internal permissions rules like those in rule set 2.

Table 8-8   Rule Set 3

Source Address	Source Port	Destination Address	Destination Port	Action
10.10.10.0	Any	Any	Any	Allow

Table 8-9   Rule Set 4

Source Address	Source Port	Destination Address	Destination Port	Action
Any	Any	10.10.10.0	25	Allow

Table 8-10   Rule Set 5

Source Address	Source Port	Destination Address	Destination Port	Action
10.10.10.0	Any	Any	7	Allow
Any	Any	10.10.10.0	7	Deny

Table 8-11 Rule Set 6

Source Address	Source Port	Destination Address	Destination Port	Action
10.10.10.0	Any	10.10.10.0	23	Allow
Any	Any	10.10.10.0	23	Deny

Rule Set 7 When Web services are offered outside the firewall, HTTP and HTTPS traffic should be blocked from the internal networks via the use of some form of proxy access or DMZ architecture. With a Web server in the DMZ, you simply allow HTTP to access the Web server and then use the cleanup rule described later in rule set 8 to prevent any other access. To keep the Web server inside the internal network, direct all HTTP requests to the proxy server and configure the internal filtering router/firewall only to allow the proxy server to access the internal Web server. The rule shown in Table 8-12 illustrates the first example.

This rule accomplishes two things: It allows HTTP traffic to reach the Web server, and it uses the cleanup rule (Rule 8) to prevent non-HTTP traffic from reaching the Web server. If someone tries to access the Web server with non-HTTP traffic (other than port 80), then the firewall skips this rule and goes to the next one.

Proxy server rules allow an organization to restrict all access to a device. The external firewall would be configured as shown in Table 8-13.

The effective use of a proxy server requires that the DNS entries be configured as if the proxy server were the Web server. The proxy server is then configured to repackage any HTTP request packets into a new packet and retransmit to the Web server inside the firewall. The retransmission of the repackaged request requires that the rule shown in Table 8-14 enables the proxy server at 10.10.10.5 to send to the internal router, assuming the IP address for the internal Web server is 10.10.10.8. Note that when an internal NAT server is used, the rule for the inbound interface uses the externally routable address because the device performs rule filtering *before* it performs address translation. For the outbound interface, however, the address is in the native 192.168.x.x format.

The restriction on the source address then prevents anyone else from accessing the Web server from outside the internal filtering router/firewall.

Rule Set 8 Now it's time for the cleanup rule. As a general practice in firewall rule construction, if a request for a service is not explicitly allowed by policy, that request should be denied by a rule. The rule shown in Table 8-15

Table 8-12 Rule Set 7a

Source Address	Source Port	Destination Address	Destination Port	Action
Any	Any	10.10.10.4	80	Allow

Table 8-13 Rule Set 7b

Source Address	Source Port	Destination Address	Destination Port	Action
Any	Any	10.10.10.5	80	Allow

Table 8-14 Rule Set 7c

Source Address	Source Port	Destination Address	Destination Port	Action
10.10.10.5	Any	10.10.10.8	80	Allow

Table 8-15 Rule Set 8

Source Address	Source Port	Destination Address	Destination Port	Action
Any	Any	Any	Any	Deny

implements this practice and blocks any requests that aren't explicitly allowed by other rules. This is another rule that is usually allowed by default by most modern firewall devices. It is included here for discussion purposes.

Additional rules that restrict access to specific servers or devices can be added, but they must be put into the sequence before the cleanup rule. The specific sequence of the rules becomes crucial because once a rule is selected to be acted upon, that action is taken, and the firewall stops processing the rest of the rules in the list. Misplacement of a particular rule can result in unintended consequences and unforeseen results. One organization installed an expensive new firewall only to discover that the security it provided was too perfect—nothing was allowed in and nothing was allowed out! Not until the firewall administrators realized that the rules were out of sequence was the problem resolved.

Tables 8-16 through 8-19 show the rule sets in their proper sequences for both the external and internal firewalls.

Note that the first rule prevents spoofing of internal IP addresses. The rule that allows responses to internal communications (rule 6 in Table 8-16) comes after the four rules prohibiting direct communications to or from the firewall (rules 2–5 in Table 8-16). In reality, rules 4 and 5 are redundant—rule 1 covers their actions. They are listed here for illustrative purposes. Next come the rules that govern access to the SMTP server, denial of ping and Telnet access, and access to the HTTP server. If heavy traffic to the HTTP server is expected, move the HTTP server rule closer to the top (for example, into the position of rule 2), which would expedite rule processing for external communications. Rules 8 and 9 are actually unnecessary because the cleanup rule would take care of their tasks. The final rule in Table 8-16 denies any other types of communications.

In the outbound rule set (see Table 8-17), the first rule allows the firewall, system, or network administrator to access any device, including the firewall. Because this rule is on the outbound side, you do not need to worry about external attackers. The next four rules prohibit access to and by the firewall itself, and the remaining rules allow outbound communications and deny all else.

Note the similarities and differences in the two firewalls' rule sets. The rule sets for the internal filtering router/firewall, shown in Tables 8-18 and 8-19, must both protect against traffic to the internal network (192.168.2.0) and

Table 8-16 External Filtering Firewall Inbound Interface Rule Set

Rule #	Source Address	Source Port	Destination Address	Destination Port	Action
1	10.10.10.0	Any	Any	Any	Deny
2	Any	Any	10.10.10.1	Any	Deny
3	Any	Any	10.10.10.2	Any	Deny
4	10.10.10.1	Any	Any	Any	Deny
5	10.10.10.2	Any	Any	Any	Deny
6	Any	Any	10.10.10.0	>1023	Allow
7	Any	Any	10.10.10.6	25	Allow
8	Any	Any	10.10.10.0	7	Deny
9	Any	Any	10.10.10.0	23	Deny
10	Any	Any	10.10.10.4	80	Allow
11	Any	Any	Any	Any	Deny

Table 8-17 External Filtering Firewall Outbound Interface Rule Set

Rule #	Source Address	Source Port	Destination Address	Destination Port	Action
1	10.10.10.12	Any	10.10.10.0	Any	Allow
2	Any	Any	10.10.10.1	Any	Deny
3	Any	Any	10.10.10.2	Any	Deny
4	10.10.10.1	Any	Any	Any	Deny
5	10.10.10.2	Any	Any	Any	Deny
6	10.10.10.0	Any	Any	Any	Allow
7	Any	Any	Any	Any	Deny

content filter

A software program or hardware/software appliance that allows administrators to restrict content that comes into or leaves a network.

reverse firewall

See *content filter*.

allow traffic from it. Most of the rules in Tables 8-18 and 8-19 are similar to those in Tables 8-16 and 8-17: They allow responses to internal communications, deny communications to and from the firewall itself, and allow all outbound internal traffic.

Because the 192.168.2.x network is an non-routable network, external communications are handled by the NAT server, which maps internal (192.168.2.0) addresses to external (10.10.10.0) addresses. This prevents an attacker from compromising one of the internal firewalls and accessing the internal network with it. The exception is the proxy server, which is covered by rule 6 in Table 8-18 on the internal router's inbound interface. This proxy server should be very carefully configured. If the organization does not need it, as in cases where all externally accessible services are provided from machines in the DMZ, then rule 6 is not needed. Note that Tables 8-18 and 8-19 have no rules set to allow ping and Telnet because the external firewall filters out these external requests. The last rule in Table 8-19, rule 7, provides cleanup and may not be needed, depending on the firewall.

The development and maintenance of an organization's firewall rules is a major effort, and these rule sets can become a valuable asset. The rules and management of firewall configuration must be treated as a critical function within a company. The rules must be backed up regularly, and duplicate copies of each version must be maintained as the rule sets evolve through carefully controlled changes.

Content Filters

Besides firewalls, a **content filter** is another utility that can help protect an organization's systems from misuse and unintentional denial-of-service problems. A content filter is a software filter—technically not a firewall—that allows administrators to restrict access to content within a network. A content filter is essentially a set of scripts or programs that restricts user access to certain networking protocols and Internet locations, or that restricts users from receiving general types or specific examples of Internet content. Some content filters are combined with reverse proxy servers, which is why many are referred to as **reverse firewalls**, as their primary purpose is to restrict internal access to external material. In most common implementation models, the content filter has two components: rating and filtering. The rating is like a set of firewall rules

Table 8-18   Internal Filtering Firewall Inbound Interface Rule Set

Rule #	Source Address	Source Port	Destination Address	Destination Port	Action
1	Any	Any	10.10.10.3	Any	Deny
2	Any	Any	10.10.10.7	Any	Deny
3	10.10.10.3	Any	Any	Any	Deny
4	10.10.10.7	Any	Any	Any	Deny
5	Any	Any	10.10.10.0	>1023	Allow
6	10.10.10.5	Any	10.10.10.8	Any	Allow
7	Any	Any	Any	Any	Deny

Table 8-19   Internal Filtering Firewall Outbound Interface Rule Set

Rule #	Source Address	Source Port	Destination Address	Destination Port	Action
1	Any	Any	10.10.10.3	Any	Deny
2	Any	Any	192.168.2.1	Any	Deny
3	10.10.10.3	Any	Any	Any	Deny
4	192.168.2.1	Any	Any	Any	Deny
5	Any	Any	192.168.2.0	>1023	Allow
6	192.168.2.0	Any	Any	Any	Allow
7	Any	Any	Any	Any	Deny

for Web sites and is common in residential content filters. The rating can be complex, with multiple access control settings for different levels of the organization, or it can be simple, with a basic allow/deny scheme like that of a firewall. The filtering is a method used to restrict specific access requests to identified resources, which may be Web sites, servers, or other resources the content filter administrator configures. The result is like a reverse ACL (technically speaking, a capabilities table); an ACL normally records a set of users who have access to resources, but the control list records resources that the user cannot access.

> **data loss prevention**
>
> A strategy to ensure that the users of a network do not send high-value information or other critical information outside the network without authorization.

The first content filters were systems designed to restrict access to specific Web sites and were stand-alone software applications. These could be configured in either an exclusive or inclusive manner. In an exclusive mode, certain sites are specifically excluded, but the problem with this approach is that an organization might want to exclude thousands of Web sites, and more might be added every hour. The inclusive mode works from a list of sites that are specifically permitted. To have a site added to the list, the user must submit a request to the content filter manager, which could be time-consuming and restrict business operations. Newer models of content filters are protocol-based, examining content as it is dynamically displayed and restricting or permitting access based on a logical interpretation of content.

The most common content filters restrict users from accessing Web sites that are obviously not related to business, such as pornography sites, or they deny incoming spam e-mail. Content filters can be small add-on software programs for the home or office, such as NetNanny, CleanBrowsing, DansGuardian, OpenDNS, or Yandex. Content filters can also be built into corporate firewall applications, cloud services such as Microsoft's Azure Content Moderator, or the end-user client with Microsoft Defender Advanced Threat Protection. The primary benefit of implementing content filters is the assurance that employees are not distracted by nonbusiness material and cannot waste the organization's time and resources. The downside is that these systems require extensive configuration and ongoing maintenance to update the list of unacceptable destinations or the source addresses for incoming restricted e-mail. Some newer content filtering applications, like newer antivirus programs, come with a service of downloadable files that update the database of restrictions. These applications work by matching either a list of disapproved or approved Web sites and by matching key content words, such as "nude," "naked," and "sex." Of course, creators of restricted content have realized this and work to bypass the restrictions by suppressing such words, creating additional problems for networking and security professionals.

One use of content filtering technology is to implement **data loss prevention**. When implemented, network traffic is monitored and analyzed. If patterns of use and keyword analysis reveal that high-value information is being transferred, an alert may be invoked or the network connection may be interrupted.

 For a list of reviewed small business content filters, visit *www.toptenreviews.com* and search for "Small Business Content Filter Reviews."

Protecting Remote Connections

As became painfully clear during the COVID-19 pandemic, the networks that organizations create are seldom used only by people at one location. When connections are made between networks, the connections are arranged and managed carefully. Installing such network connections requires using leased lines or other data channels provided by common carriers; therefore, these connections are usually permanent and secured under the requirements of a formal service agreement. However, a more flexible option for network access must be provided for employees working in their homes, contract workers hired for specific assignments, or other workers who are traveling. In the past, organizations provided these remote connections exclusively through dial-up services like Remote Authentication Service (RAS). As high-speed Internet connections have become mainstream, other options such as virtual private networks (VPNs) have become more popular. As more and more employees work from home, these connections have become critical to supporting remote work.

Remote Access

Before the Internet emerged, organizations created their own private networks and allowed individual users and other organizations to connect to them using dial-up or leased line connections. In the current networking environment, where high-speed Internet connections are commonplace, dial-up access and leased lines from customer networks are

war dialer

An automatic phone-dialing program that dials every number in a configured range and checks whether a person, voicemail, or modem picks up.

Remote Authentication Dial-In User Service (RADIUS)

A computer connection system that centralizes the management of user authentication by placing the responsibility for authenticating each user on a central authentication server.

almost nonexistent. The connections between company networks and the Internet use firewalls to safeguard that interface. Although connections via dial-up and leased lines have become less popular, they are still common in older systems. A widely held view is that unsecured, dial-up connection points represent a substantial exposure to attack. An attacker who suspects that an organization has dial-up lines can use a device called a war dialer to locate the connection points. A **war dialer** dials every number in a configured range, such as 555–1000 to 555–2000, and checks to see if a person, answering machine, or modem picks up. If a modem answers, the war dialer program makes a note of the number and then moves to the next target number. The attacker then attempts to hack into the network via the identified modem connection using a variety of techniques. Dial-up network connectivity is usually less sophisticated than that deployed with Internet connections. For the most part, simple username and password schemes are the only means of authentication. However, some technologies, such as RADIUS systems, TACACS, and CHAP password systems, have improved the authentication process, and some systems now use strong encryption.

RADIUS, Diameter, and TACACS

RADIUS and TACACS are systems that authenticate the credentials of users who are trying to access an organization's network via a dial-up connection. Typical dial-up systems place the responsibility for user authentication on the system directly connected to the modems. If there are multiple points of entry into the dial-up system, the authentication system can become difficult to manage. The **Remote Authentication Dial-In User Service (RADIUS)** system centralizes the responsibility for authenticating each user on the RADIUS server. RADIUS was initially described in RFCs 2058 and 2059, and is currently described in RFCs 6929 and 8044, among others.

When a network access server (NAS) receives a request for a network connection from a dial-up client, it passes the request and the user's credentials to the RADIUS server. RADIUS then validates the credentials and passes the resulting decision (accept or deny) back to the accepting remote access server. Figure 8-16 shows the typical configuration of a RADIUS-hosted NAS system. While RADIUS was originally developed for dial-in services, it is still implemented in some modern VPN configurations.

An emerging alternative that is derived from RADIUS is the Diameter protocol. The *Diameter protocol* defines the minimum requirements for a system that provides authentication, authorization, and accounting (AAA) services and that can go beyond these basics and add commands and/or object attributes. Diameter security uses respected encryption standards

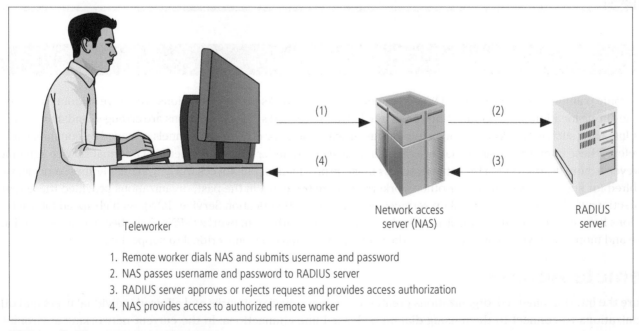

Teleworker   Network access server (NAS)   RADIUS server

1. Remote worker dials NAS and submits username and password
2. NAS passes username and password to RADIUS server
3. RADIUS server approves or rejects request and provides access authorization
4. NAS provides access to authorized remote worker

Figure 8-16   RADIUS configuration

such as Internet Protocol Security (IPSec) or Transport Layer Security (TLS); its cryptographic capabilities are extensible and will be able to use future encryption protocols as they are implemented. Diameter-capable devices are emerging into the marketplace, and this protocol is expected to become the dominant form of AAA services.

The *Terminal Access Controller Access Control System (TACACS)*, defined in RFC 1492, is another remote access authorization system that is based on a client/server configuration. Like RADIUS, it contains a centralized database, and it validates the user's credentials at the TACACS server. The three versions of TACACS are the original version, Extended TACACS, and TACACS+. Of these, only TACACS+ is still in use. The original version combines authentication and authorization services. The extended version separates the steps needed to authenticate individual user or system access attempts from the steps needed to verify that the authenticated individual or system is allowed to make a given type of connection. The extended version keeps records for accountability and to ensure that the access attempt is linked to a specific individual or system. The TACACS+ version uses dynamic passwords and incorporates two-factor authentication.

Kerberos

> **Kerberos**
>
> An authentication system that uses symmetric key encryption to validate an individual user's access to various network resources by keeping a database containing the private keys of clients and servers that are in the authentication domain it supervises.

Two authentication systems can provide secure third-party authentication: Kerberos and SESAME. **Kerberos**—named after the three-headed dog of Greek mythology that guards the gates to the underworld—uses symmetric key encryption to validate an individual user to various network resources. As described in RFC 4120, Kerberos keeps a database containing the private keys of clients and servers; in the case of a client, this key is simply the client's encrypted password. Network services running on servers in the network register with Kerberos, as do the clients that use those services. The Kerberos system knows the private keys and can authenticate one network node (client or server) to another. For example, Kerberos can authenticate a user once—at the time the user logs in to a client computer—and then, later during that session, it can authorize the user to have access to a printer without requiring the user to take any additional action. Kerberos also generates temporary session keys, which are private keys given to the two parties in a conversation. The session key is used to encrypt all communications between these two parties. Typically, a user logs in to the network, is authenticated to the Kerberos system, and is then authenticated to other resources on the network by the Kerberos system itself.

Kerberos consists of three interacting services, all of which use a database library:

1. *Authentication server (AS), which is a Kerberos server that authenticates clients and servers.*
2. *Key Distribution Center (KDC), which generates and issues session keys.*
3. *Kerberos ticket granting service (TGS), which provides tickets to clients who request services. In Kerberos, a ticket is an identification card for a particular client that verifies to the server that the client is requesting services and that the client is a valid member of the Kerberos system and therefore authorized to receive services. The ticket consists of the client's name and network address, a ticket validation starting and ending time, and the session key, all encrypted in the private key of the server from which the client is requesting services.*

Kerberos is based on the following principles:

- *The KDC knows the secret keys of all clients and servers on the network.*
- *The KDC initially exchanges information with the client and server by using these secret keys.*
- *Kerberos authenticates a client to a requested service on a server through TGS and by issuing temporary session keys for communications between the client and KDC, the server and KDC, and the client and server.*
- *Communications then take place between the client and server using these temporary session keys.*[16]

Figures 8-17 and 8-18 illustrate this process.

If the Kerberos servers are subjected to denial-of-service attacks, no client can request services. If the Kerberos servers, service providers, or clients' machines are compromised, their private key information may also be compromised.

 For more information on Kerberos, including available downloads, visit the MIT Kerberos page at *http://web.mit.edu/Kerberos/*.

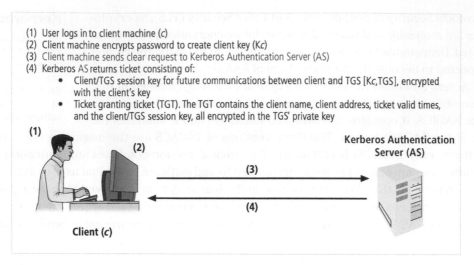

(1) User logs in to client machine (c)
(2) Client machine encrypts password to create client key (Kc)
(3) Client machine sends clear request to Kerberos Authentication Server (AS)
(4) Kerberos AS returns ticket consisting of:
   • Client/TGS session key for future communications between client and TGS [Kc,TGS], encrypted with the client's key
   • Ticket granting ticket (TGT). The TGT contains the client name, client address, ticket valid times, and the client/TGS session key, all encrypted in the TGS' private key

Figure 8-17 Kerberos login

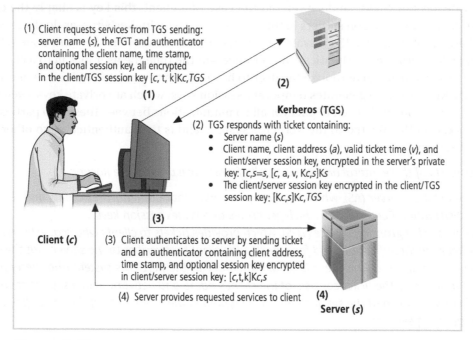

(1) Client requests services from TGS sending: server name (s), the TGT and authenticator containing the client name, time stamp, and optional session key, all encrypted in the client/TGS session key [c, t, k]Kc,TGS

(2) TGS responds with ticket containing:
   • Server name (s)
   • Client name, client address (a), valid ticket time (v), and client/server session key, encrypted in the server's private key: Tc,s=s, [c, a, v, Kc,s]Ks
   • The client/server session key encrypted in the client/TGS session key: [Kc,s]Kc,TGS

(3) Client authenticates to server by sending ticket and an authenticator containing client address, time stamp, and optional session key encrypted in client/server session key: [c,t,k]Kc,s

(4) Server provides requested services to client

Figure 8-18 Kerberos request for services

SESAME

The Secure European System for Applications in a Multivendor Environment (SESAME), defined in RFC 1510, is the result of a European research and development project partly funded by the European Commission. SESAME is similar to Kerberos in that the user is first authenticated to an authentication server and receives a token. The token is then presented to a privilege attribute server, instead of a ticket-granting service as in Kerberos, as proof of identity to gain a privilege attribute certificate (PAC). The PAC is like the ticket in Kerberos; however, a PAC conforms to the standards of the European Computer Manufacturers Association (ECMA) and the International Organization for Standardization/International Telecommunications Union (ISO/ITU-T). The remaining differences lie in the security protocols and distribution methods. SESAME uses public key encryption to distribute secret keys. SESAME also builds on the Kerberos model by adding sophisticated access control features, more scalable encryption systems, improved manageability, auditing features, and the option to delegate responsibility for allowing access.

Virtual Private Networks (VPNs)

Virtual private networks (VPNs) are implementations of cryptographic technology. (You will learn more about cryptography in Module 10.) A VPN is a private data network that uses the public telecommunications infrastructure to create a means for private communication via a tunneling protocol coupled with security procedures. VPNs are commonly used to securely extend an organization's internal network connections to remote locations. The international trade association for manufacturers in the VPN market, the Virtual Private Network Consortium, has defined three VPN technologies: trusted VPNs, secure VPNs, and hybrid VPNs. A **trusted VPN**, also known as a legacy VPN, uses leased circuits from a service provider and conducts packet switching over these leased circuits. The organization must trust the service provider, who gives contractual assurance that no one else is allowed to use these circuits and that they are properly maintained and protected—hence the name *trusted* VPN. **Secure VPNs** use security protocols like IPSec to encrypt traffic transmitted across unsecured public networks like the Internet. A **hybrid VPN** combines the trusted and secure technologies, providing encrypted transmissions (as in secure VPN) over some or all of a trusted VPN network.

A VPN that proposes to offer a secure and reliable capability while relying on public networks must accomplish the following, regardless of the specific technologies and protocols being used:

- *Encapsulation* of incoming and outgoing data, in which the native protocol of the client is embedded within the frames of a protocol that can be routed over the public network and be usable by the server network environment.
- *Encryption* of incoming and outgoing data to keep the data contents private while in transit over the public network, but usable by the client and server computers and/or the local networks on both ends of the VPN connection.
- *Authentication* of the remote computer and perhaps the remote user as well. Authentication and subsequent user authorization to perform specific actions are predicated on accurate and reliable identification of the remote system and user.

In the most common implementation, a VPN allows a user to turn the Internet into a private network. As you know, the Internet is anything but private. However, an individual user or organization can set up tunneling points across the Internet and send encrypted data back and forth, using the IP packet-within-an-IP packet method to transmit data safely and securely. VPNs are simple to set up and maintain, and they usually require only that the tunneling points be dual-homed—that is, connecting a private network to the Internet or to another outside connection point. VPN support is built into most Microsoft server software, and client support for VPN services is built into most Windows clients. While connections for true private network services can cost hundreds of thousands of dollars to lease, configure, and maintain, an Internet VPN can cost very little. A VPN can be implemented in several ways. IPSec, the dominant protocol used in VPNs, uses either transport mode or tunnel mode. IPSec can be used as a stand-alone protocol or coupled with the Layer Two Tunneling Protocol (L2TP).

Transport Mode

In *transport mode*, the data within an IP packet is encrypted, but the header information is not. This allows the user to establish a secure link directly with the remote host, encrypting only the data contents of the packet. The downside of this implementation is that packet eavesdroppers can still identify the destination system. Once attackers know the destination, they may be able to compromise one of the end nodes and acquire the packet information from it. On the other hand, transport mode eliminates the need for special servers and tunneling software, and allows end users to transmit traffic from anywhere, which is especially useful for traveling or telecommuting employees. Figure 8-19 illustrates the transport mode methods of implementing VPNs.

Transport mode VPNs have two popular uses. The first is the end-to-end transport of encrypted data. In this model, two end users can communicate directly, encrypting and decrypting their communications as needed. Each machine acts as the end-node VPN server and client. In the second approach, a remote access worker or teleworker connects

virtual private network (VPN)

A private, secure network operated over a public and insecure network; it uses encryption to protect the data between endpoints.

trusted VPN

Also known as a legacy VPN, a VPN implementation that uses leased circuits from a service provider who gives contractual assurance that no one else is allowed to use these circuits and that they are properly maintained and protected.

secure VPN

A VPN implementation that uses security protocols to encrypt traffic transmitted across unsecured public networks.

hybrid VPN

A combination of trusted and secure VPN implementations.

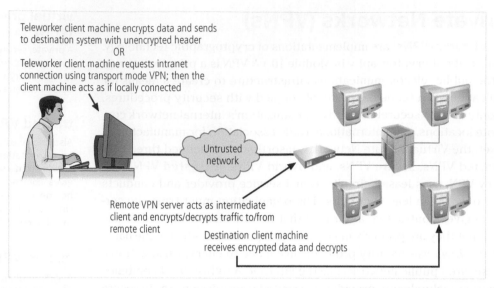

Figure 8-19 Transport mode VPN

to an office network over the Internet by connecting to a VPN server on the perimeter. This allows the teleworker's system to work as if it were part of the local area network. The VPN server in this example acts as an intermediate node, encrypting traffic from the secure intranet and transmitting it to the remote client, and decrypting traffic from the remote client and transmitting it to its final destination. This model frequently allows the remote system to act as its own VPN server, which is a weakness, because most work-at-home employees do not have the same level of physical and logical security they would have in an office.

Tunnel Mode

Tunnel mode establishes two perimeter tunnel servers to encrypt all traffic that will traverse an unsecured network. In tunnel mode, the entire client packet is encrypted and added as the data portion of a packet addressed from one tunneling server to another. The receiving server decrypts the packet and sends it to the final address. The primary benefit of this model is that an intercepted packet reveals nothing about the true destination system.

An example of a tunnel mode VPN is provided with Microsoft's Internet Security and Acceleration (ISA) Server. With ISA Server, an organization can establish a gateway-to-gateway tunnel, encapsulating data within the tunnel. ISA can use the Point-to-Point Tunneling Protocol (PPTP), L2TP, or IPSec technologies. Additional information about IPSec is provided in Module 10. Figure 8-20 shows an example of tunnel mode VPN implementation. On the client end, a Windows user can establish a VPN by configuring his or her system to connect to a VPN server. The process is straightforward. First, the user connects to the Internet through an ISP or direct network connection. Second, the user establishes the link with the remote VPN server. Figure 8-21 shows the connection screens used to configure the VPN link.

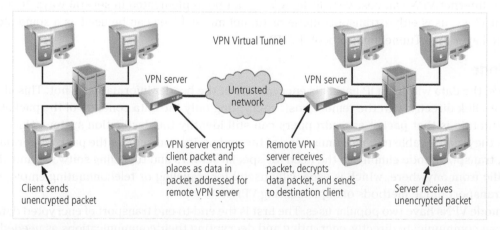

Figure 8-20 Tunnel mode VPN

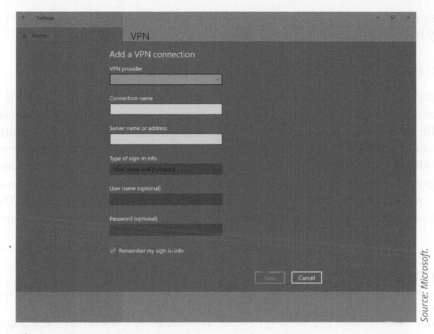

Figure 8-21   Adding a Windows VPN connection

Source: Microsoft.

 For more information on VPNs, read the reviews of the best VPN services at PC Magazine's Web site (*www.pcmag.com*) and search for "Best VPN Services."

Final Thoughts On Remote Access And Access Controls

deperimeterization

The recognition that there is no clear information security boundary between an organization and the outside world, meaning that the organization must be prepared to protect its information both inside and outside its digital walls.

Two topics warrant additional discussion at the end of this module: deperimeterization and remote access in the age of COVID-19.

Deperimeterization

Deperimeterization is a buzzword that was coined 20 years ago to describe the expansion of an organization beyond a traditional security boundary. However, the concept has recently begun to be considered when implementing security systems, as computing services and data management continue to be migrated to the cloud and remote work locations. Throughout most of this module, an imaginary boundary has been defined around the organization; the boundary is guarded by the organization's firewall architecture and is just behind its gateway connection to the Internet. This imaginary boundary represents a traditional security perspective that has existed for decades. Over the last few years, though, a concept known as the "death of the perimeter" has emerged in the information security trade press. With the extensive push toward cloud-based computing and data storage as well as massive deployment of mobile applications running smartphones and tablets, security authors have asked, "Is the perimeter dead?"[17] If much of an organization's information transmission, storage, and processing is in the cloud and not behind the organization's firewall, does the perimeter even exist?

These questions led the UK Royal Mail's Jon Measham to create the term *deperimeterization* as far back as 2001.[18] In a white paper for the JERiCHO forums, he stated, "Many (and in some cases most) network security perimeters will disappear. Like it or not, de-perimeterisation will happen; the business drivers already exist within your organization. It's already started and it's only a matter of how fast, how soon, and whether you decide to control it."[19]

In reality, the network perimeter is whatever an organization defines it to be. Wherever it exists, it is the boundary between the information inside trusted technical systems and the many untrusted environments that may be interconnected to it. Whether data is in the cloud, on an employee's laptop, or in the office data center, it has to be protected. The technology discussed in this module can help do just that. Whether the organization defines a perimeter as the area around its firewall or ignores the concept of the perimeter entirely, it still has a responsibility to protect the transmission, processing, and storage of its information. Firewalls will not be obsolete anytime soon, and VPNs are currently the best way to ensure that users can remotely access information securely.

Remote Access in the Age of COVID-19

During the COVID-19 pandemic, the need to remotely access information and the corresponding need to secure both information and connections took on a new significance. Organizations that never thought about allowing employees to work remotely found themselves forced to revisit their entire approach to the issue. Many organizations succeeded in implementing remote access, using VPNs or other mechanisms to enable employees to access needed information and keep their businesses afloat. At the time of this writing, the pandemic is still under way. Many businesses may yet fail as they struggle to engage customers, employ their workers, and earn a profit. Some organizations were well prepared, but others scrambled, overloading vendors that support remote access and remote meetings. The organizations that remain after the pandemic has subsided will have learned a painful but valuable lesson about enabling remote work.

Closing Scenario

The next morning at 8 a.m., Kelvin called the meeting to order. The first person to address the group was Susan Hamir, the network design consultant from Costly & Firehouse. She reviewed the critical points from the design report, going over its options and outlining the trade-offs in the design choices.

When she finished, she sat down and Kelvin addressed the group again: "We need to break the logjam on this design issue. We have all the right people in this room to make the right choice for the company. Now here are the questions I want us to consider over the next three hours." Kelvin pressed a key on his PC to show a slide with a list of discussion questions on the projector screen.

Discussion Questions

1. What questions do you think Kelvin should have included on his slide to start the discussion?
2. If the questions were broken down into two categories, they would be cost versus maintaining high security while keeping flexibility. Which is more important for SLS?

Ethical Decision Making

Suppose that Susan stacked the deck with her design proposal. In other words, she purposefully under-designed the less expensive solution and produced an estimate for the higher-end version that she knew would come in over budget if it were chosen. She also knew that SLS had a tendency to hire design consultants to build projects. Is it unethical to produce a consulting report that steers a client toward a specific outcome?

Suppose instead that Susan had prepared a report that truthfully recommended the more expensive option as the better choice for SLS, in her professional opinion. Further suppose that SLS management chose the less expensive option solely to reduce costs, without regard for the project's security outcomes. Would it be ethical of Susan to urge reconsideration of such a decision?

Selected Readings

Many excellent sources of additional information are available in the area of information security. The following can add to your understanding of this module's content:

- *Guide to Firewalls and VPNs*, by Michael E. Whitman, Herbert J. Mattord, and Andrew Green. 2012. Cengage Learning.
- SP 800-41, Rev. 1, "Guidelines on Firewalls and Firewall Policy." National Institute of Standards and Technology. September 2009.
- SP 800-77, "Guide to IPSec VPNs." National Institute of Standards and Technology. December 2005.

Module Summary

- Access control is a process by which systems determine if and how to admit a user into a trusted area of the organization.
- Mandatory access controls offer users and data owners little or no control over access to information resources. MACs are often associated with a data classification scheme in which each collection of information is rated with a sensitivity level. This type of control is sometimes called lattice-based access control.
- Nondiscretionary access controls are strictly enforced versions of MACs that are managed by a central authority, whereas discretionary access controls are implemented at the discretion or option of the data user.
- All access control approaches rely on identification, authentication, authorization, and accountability.
- Authentication is the process of validating an unauthenticated entity's purported identity. The three widely used types of authentication factors are something a person knows, something a person has, and something a person is or can produce.
- Strong authentication requires a minimum of two authentication mechanisms drawn from two different authentication factors.
- Biometrics is the use of a person's physiological characteristics to provide authentication for system access.
- Security access control architecture models illustrate access control implementations and can help organizations quickly make improvements through adaptation. Some models, like the trusted computing base, ITSEC, and the Common Criteria, are evaluation models used to demonstrate the evolution of trusted system assessment. Models such as Bell–LaPadula and Biba ensure that information is protected by controlling the access of one part of a system on another.
- A firewall is any device that prevents a specific type of information from moving between the outside network, known as the untrusted network, and the inside network, known as the trusted network.
- Firewalls can be categorized into four groups: packet filtering, MAC layers, application gateways, and hybrid firewalls.
- Packet-filtering firewalls can be implemented as static filtering, dynamic filtering, and stateful packet inspection firewalls.
- The three common architectural implementations of firewalls are single bastion hosts, screened hosts, and screened subnets.
- Firewalls operate by evaluating data packet contents against logical rules. This logical set is most commonly referred to as firewall rules, a rule base, or firewall logic.
- Content filtering can improve security and assist organizations in improving the manageability of their technology.
- Dial-up protection mechanisms help secure organizations that use modems for remote connectivity. Kerberos and SESAME are authentication systems that add security to this technology.
- Virtual private networks enable remote offices and users to connect to private networks securely over public networks.

Review Questions

1. What is the typical relationship among the untrusted network, the firewall, and the trusted network?
2. What are the two primary types of network data packets? Describe their packet structures.
3. List some authentication technologies for biometrics.
4. How is static filtering different from dynamic filtering of packets? Which is perceived to offer improved security?
5. What is stateful packet inspection? How is state information maintained during a network connection or transaction?
6. Explain the conceptual approach that should guide the creation of firewall rule sets.
7. List some common architectural models for access control.
8. What is the main difference between discretionary and nondiscretionary access controls?
9. What is a hybrid firewall?

10. Describe Unified Threat Management (UTM). How does UTM differ from Next Generation Firewalls?
11. What is a Next Generation Firewall (NextGen or NGFW)?
12. What is the primary value of a firewall?
13. What is Port Address Translation (PAT), and how does it work?
14. What are the main differences between a password and a passphrase?
15. What is a sacrificial host? What is a bastion host?
16. What is a DMZ?
17. What questions must be addressed when selecting a firewall for a specific organization?
18. What is RADIUS?
19. What is a content filter? Where is it placed in the network to gain the best result for the organization?
20. What is a VPN? Why is it becoming more widely used?

Exercises

1. Using the Web, search for "Personal VPN." Examine the various alternatives available and compare their functionality, cost, features, and type of protection. Create a weighted ranking according to your own evaluation of the features and specifications of each software package.
2. Look at the network devices used in Figure 8-14, and create one or more rules necessary for both the internal and external firewalls to allow a remote user to access an internal machine from the Internet using the Timbuktu software. Your answer requires researching the ports used by this type of data packet and the software.
3. Suppose management wants to create a "server farm" for the configuration in Figure 8-14 that allows a proxy firewall in the DMZ to access an internal Web server (rather than a Web server in the DMZ). Do you foresee any technical difficulties in deploying this architecture? What are the advantages and disadvantages of this implementation?
4. Using the Internet, determine what applications are commercially available to enable secure remote access to a PC.
5. Using a Microsoft Windows system, open the Edge browser. Click the Settings and More button in the upper-right corner, or press Alt+F. Select the Settings option. From the menu on the left side of the window, choose "Privacy, search, and services." Examine the contents of the section. How can these options be configured to provide content filtering and protection from unwanted items like trackers?

References

1. Hu, V., Ferraiolo, D., Kuhn, R., Schnitzer, A., Sandlin, K., Miller, R., and Scarfone, K. Special Publication 800-162, "Guide to Attribute Based Access Control (ABAC) Definition and Considerations." National Institute of Standards and Technology. January 2014 (with updates from August 2019). Accessed September 21, 2020, from *https://csrc.nist.gov/publications/sp800*.
2. NordPass. "Press Area." Accessed September 21, 2020, from *https://nordpass.com/press-area/*.
3. From multiple sources, including Jain, A., Ross, A., and Prabhakar, S. "An Introduction to Biometric Recognition." *IEEE Transactions on Circuits and Systems for Video Technology* 14, no. 8. January 2004; Yun, W. "The '123' of Biometric Technology." 2003. Accessed September 21, 2020, from *www.newworldencyclopedia.org/entry/Biometrics*; DJW. "Analysis of Biometric Technology and Its Effectiveness for Identification Security." Yahoo Voices. May 2011. Accessed August 12, 2016, from *http://voices.yahoo.com/analysis-biometric-technology-its-effectiveness-7607914.html*.
4. The TCSEC Rainbow Series. Used under published permissions. Accessed September 21, 2020, from *http://commons.wikimedia.org/wiki/File:Rainbow_series_documents.jpg*.
5. "The Common Criteria." Accessed September 22, 2020, from *www.commoncriteriaportal.org*.
6. Ibid.
7. Ibid.

8. McIntyre, G., and Krause, M. "Security Architecture and Design." *Official (ISC)² Guide to the CISSP CBK*, 2nd Edition. Edited by Tipton, H., and Henry, K. Boca Raton, FL: Auerbach Publishers, 2010.

9. Ibid.

10. Ibid.

11. Ibid.

12. Ibid.

13. Ibid.

14. Beaver, Kevin. "Finding Clarity: Unified Threat Management Systems vs. Next-Gen Firewalls." Accessed September 22, 2020, from *http://searchsecurity.techtarget.com/tip/Finding-clarity-Unified-threat-management-systems-vs-next-gen-firewalls*.

15. Cheshire, S., and Krochmal, M. "Special-Use Domain Names." RFC 6761. Internet Engineering Task Force. 2013. Accessed September 22, 2020, from *https://tools.ietf.org/html/rfc6761*.

16. Krutz, Ronald L., and Vines, Russell Dean. *The CISSP Prep Guide: Mastering the Ten Domains of Computer Security*. 2001. New York: John Wiley and Sons Inc., 40.

17. Chickowski, E. "Is the Perimeter Really Dead?" DARKReading. 2013. Accessed September 22, 2020, from *www.darkreading.com/attacks-breaches/is-the-perimeter-really-dead/d/d-id/1140482*.

18. Measham, J. "Business Rationale for De-perimeterisation." JERiCHO forum. Accessed September 22, 2020, from *https://collaboration.opengroup.org/jericho/Business_Case_for_DP_v1.0.pdf*.

19. Ibid.

Security Technology: Intrusion Detection and Prevention Systems and Other Security Tools

Upon completion of this material, you should be able to:

1 Identify and describe the categories and models of intrusion detection and prevention systems

2 Describe the detection approaches employed by modern intrusion detection and prevention systems

3 Define and describe honeypots, honeynets, and padded cell systems

4 List and define the major categories of scanning and analysis tools and describe the specific tools used within each category

Do not wait; the time will never be just right. Start where you stand, and work with whatever tools you may have at your command, and better tools will be found as you go along.

—Napoleon Hill (1883–1970),
Founder of *The Science of Success*

Opening Scenario

Miller Harrison was going to make them sorry and make them pay. Earlier today, his contract with SLS had been terminated, and he'd been sent home. Oh, sure, the big-shot manager, Charlie Moody, had said Miller would still get paid for the two weeks remaining in his contract and that the decision was based on "changes in the project and evolving needs as project work continued," but Miller knew better. He knew he'd been let go because of that know-nothing Kelvin and his simpering lapdog Laverne Nguyen. And now he was going to show them and everyone else at SLS who knew more about security.

Miller knew that the secret to hacking into a network successfully was to apply the same patience, attention to detail, and dogged determination that defending a network required. He also knew that the first step in a typical hacking protocol was footprinting—that is, getting a fully annotated diagram of the network. Miller already had one—in a violation of company policy, he had brought a copy home last week when Laverne first started trying to tell him how to do his job.

When they terminated his contract today, Miller's supervisors made him turn in his company laptop and then actually had the nerve to search his briefcase. By then, however, Miller had already stashed all the files and access codes he needed to attack SLS's systems.

To begin, he thought about activating his VPN client to connect to the SLS network from his free Wi-Fi connection at his favorite coffee shop. But then he remembered that Charlie Moody had confiscated the authentication token that enabled him to use the VPN for remote access, and it would also be obvious who had attacked the system. No problem, Miller thought. Let's see how good SLS is at protecting its antiquated dial-up lines. He connected his laptop to its wireless cellular modem and entered the number for SLS's legacy modem bank; he had gotten the number from the network administrator's desk. "Silly man," he thought, "writing passwords on sticky notes." After the connection was established, Miller positioned his hands on the keyboard and then read the prompt on his screen:

> *SLS Inc. Company Use Only. Unauthorized use is prohibited and subject to prosecution.*
> *Enter Username:*
> *Enter Password:*
> *Enter Dynamic Authentication Code:*

Miller muttered under his breath. Apparently, the SLS security team had rerouted all dial-up connections to the same RADIUS authentication server that the VPN used. So, he was locked out of the back door, but no worries. Miller moved on to his next option, which was to use a back door of his very own. It consisted of a zombie program he had installed on the company's extranet quality assurance server. No one at SLS worried about securing the QA server because it did not store any production data. In fact, the server wasn't even subject to the change control procedures that were applied to other systems on the extranet.

Miller's action was risky, as there was a slight chance that SLS had added the server to the host intrusion detection and prevention system it deployed last quarter. If so, Miller would be detected before he got too far. He activated the program he used to remotely control the zombie program and typed in the IP address of the computer running the zombie. No response. He opened a command window and pinged the zombie. The computer at that address answered each ping promptly, which meant it was alive and well. Miller checked the zombie's UDP port number and ran an Nmap scan against the port on that system. No response. He cursed the firewall, the policy that controlled it, and the technicians who kept it up to date.

With all of his planned payback cut off at the edge of SLS's network, he decided to continue his hack by going back to the first step—specifically, to perform a detailed fingerprinting of all SLS Internet addresses. Because the front door and both back doors were locked, it was time to get a new floor plan. He launched a simple network port scanner from his Linux laptop and configured it to scan the entire IP address range for SLS's extranet. With a single keystroke, he unleashed the port scanner on the SLS network.

Introduction To Intrusion Detection And Prevention Systems

The protection of an organization's information assets relies at least as much on managerial controls as on technical safeguards, but properly implemented technical solutions guided by policy are an essential component of an information security program. Module 8 introduced the subject of security technology and covered some specific technologies, including firewalls, VPNs, and other remote access protection mechanisms. This module builds on that discussion by describing additional, more advanced technologies that organizations can use to enhance the security of their information assets. These technologies include intrusion detection and prevention systems, honeypots, honeynets, padded cell systems, and scanning and analysis tools.

intrusion

An adverse event in which an attacker attempts to gain entry into an information system or disrupt its normal operations, almost always with the intent to do harm.

An **intrusion** occurs when an attacker attempts to gain entry into an organization's information systems or disrupt their normal operations. Even when such attacks are self-propagating, as with viruses and distributed denial-of-service (DDoS) attacks, they are almost always instigated by someone whose purpose is to harm an organization. Often, the differences among intrusion types lie with the attacker— some intruders don't care which organizations they harm and prefer to remain anonymous, while others crave notoriety. While every intrusion is an incident, not every incident is an intrusion; examples include service outages and natural disasters.

As you learned in Module 3, "Information Security Management," intrusion *prevention* consists of activities that deter or even stop an intrusion. Some important intrusion prevention activities are writing and implementing good enterprise information security policy; planning and executing effective information security programs; installing and testing technology-based information security countermeasures, such as firewalls and intrusion detection and prevention systems; and conducting and measuring the effectiveness of employee training and awareness activities.

Intrusion *detection* consists of procedures and systems that identify system intrusions. Intrusion *reaction* encompasses the actions an organization takes when an intrusion is detected. These actions seek to limit the loss from an intrusion and return operations to a normal state as rapidly as possible. Intrusion *correction* activities complete the restoration of operations to a normal state and seek to identify the source and method of the intrusion to ensure that the same type of attack cannot occur again—thus reinitiating intrusion prevention.

Information security **intrusion detection systems (IDSs)** became commercially available in the late 1990s. An IDS works like a burglar alarm in that it detects a violation and activates an alarm. This alarm can be a sound, a light or other visual signal, or a silent warning, such as an e-mail message or text alert. With almost all IDSs, system administrators can choose the configuration of various alerts and the alarm levels associated with each type of alert. Many IDSs enable administrators to configure the systems to notify them directly of trouble via their e-mail or smartphones. The systems can also be configured—again like a burglar alarm—to notify an external security service of a "break-in." The configurations that enable IDSs to provide customized levels of detection and response are quite complex. A current extension of IDS technology is the incorporation of *intrusion prevention* technology, which can prevent an intrusion from successfully attacking the organization by means of an active response. Because you seldom find a prevention system that does not also have detection capabilities, the term **intrusion detection and prevention system (IDPS)** is commonly used.

> **intrusion detection system (IDS)**
>
> A system capable of automatically detecting an intrusion into an organization's networks or host systems and notifying a designated authority.

> **intrusion detection and prevention system (IDPS)**
>
> The general term for a system that can both detect and modify its configuration and environment to prevent intrusions. An IDPS encompasses the functions of both intrusion detection systems and intrusion prevention technology.

According to NIST Special Publication (SP) 800-94, Rev. 1, IDPSs use several response techniques, which can be divided into the following groups:

- An IDPS is capable of interdicting the attack by itself, without human intervention. This could be accomplished by the following:
  - Terminating the user session or network connection over which the attack is being conducted
  - Blocking access to the target system or systems from the source of the attack, such as a compromised user account, inbound IP address, or other attack characteristic
  - Blocking all access to the targeted information asset
- The IDPS can dynamically modify its environment by changing the configuration of other security controls to disrupt an attack. This could include modifying a firewall's rule set or configuring another network device to shut down the communications channel to filter the offending packets.
- Some IDPSs are capable of changing an attack's components by replacing malicious content with benign material or by quarantining a network packet's contents.[1]

IDPS Terminology

To understand how an IDPS works, you must first become familiar with some IDPS terminology.

- **Alarm** or **alert**—An indication or notification that a system has just been attacked or is under attack. IDPS alerts and alarms take the form of audible signals, e-mail messages, pager notifications, or pop-up windows.
- **Alarm clustering and compaction**—A process of grouping almost identical alarms that occur nearly at the same time into a single higher-level alarm. This consolidation reduces the number of alarms, which reduces administrative overhead and identifies a relationship among multiple alarms. Clustering may be based on combinations of frequency, similarity in attack signature, similarity in attack target, or other criteria that are defined by system administrators.

- **Alarm filtering**—The process of classifying IDPS alerts so they can be more effectively managed. An IDPS administrator can set up alarm filtering by running the system for a while to track the types of false positives it generates and then adjusting the alarm classifications. For example, the administrator may set the IDPS to discard alarms produced by false attack stimuli or normal network operations. Alarm filters are similar to packet filters in that they can filter items by their source or destination IP addresses, but they can also filter by operating systems, confidence values, alarm type, or alarm severity.
- **Confidence value**—The measure of an IDPS's ability to correctly detect and identify certain types of attacks. The confidence value an organization places in the IDPS is based on experience and past performance measurements. The confidence value, which is based on *fuzzy logic*, helps an administrator determine the likelihood that an IDPS alert or alarm indicates an actual attack in progress. For example, if a system deemed 90 percent capable of accurately reporting a denial-of-service (DoS) attack sends a DoS alert, there is a high probability that an actual attack is occurring.
- **Evasion**—The process by which attackers change the format or timing of their activities to avoid being detected by an IDPS.
- **False attack stimulus**—An event that triggers an alarm when no actual attack is in progress. Scenarios that test the configuration of IDPSs may use false attack stimuli to determine if the IDPSs can distinguish between these stimuli and real attacks.
- **False negative**—The failure of a technical control (such as an IDPS) to react to an actual attack event. This is the most grievous IDPS failure, given that its purpose is to detect and respond to attacks.
- **False positive**—An alert or alarm that occurs in the absence of an actual attack. A false positive can sometimes be produced when an IDPS mistakes normal system activity for an attack. False positives tend to make users insensitive to alarms and thus reduce their reactions to actual intrusion events.
- **Noise**—In incident response, alarm events that are accurate and noteworthy but do not pose significant threats to information security. Unsuccessful attacks are the most common source of IDPS noise, although some noise might be triggered by scanning and enumeration tools run by network users without harmful intent.
- **Site policy**—The rules and configuration guidelines governing the implementation and operation of IDPSs within the organization.
- **Site policy awareness**—An IDPS's ability to dynamically modify its configuration in response to environmental activity. A so-called dynamic IDPS can adapt its reactions in response to administrator guidance over time and the local environment. A dynamic IDPS logs events that fit a specific profile instead of minor events, such as file modifications or failed user logins. A smart IDPS knows when it does *not* need to alert the administrator—for example, when an attack is using a known and documented exploit from which the system is protected.
- **True attack stimulus**—An event that triggers an alarm and causes an IDPS to react as if a real attack is in progress. The event may be an actual attack, in which an attacker is attempting a system compromise, or it may be a drill, in which security personnel are using hacker tools or performing port scanning to test a network segment.
- **Tuning**—The process of adjusting an IDPS to maximize its efficiency in detecting true positives while minimizing false positives and false negatives.

Why Use an IDPS?

There are several compelling reasons to acquire and use an IDPS, beginning with its primary function of intrusion detection. These reasons include documentation, deterrence, and other benefits, as described in the following sections.[2]

Intrusion Detection

The primary purpose of an IDPS is to identify and report an intrusion. By detecting the early signs of an intrusion, the organization can quickly contain the attack and prevent or at least substantially mitigate loss or damage to information assets. The notification process is critical; if the organization is not notified that an intrusion is under way, the IDPS serves no real purpose. Once notified, the organization's IR team can activate the IR plan and contain the intrusion. Notification is described later in this module.

IDPSs can also help administrators detect the preambles to attacks; this is known as *attack reconnaissance*. Most attacks begin with an organized and thorough probing of the organization's network environment and its defenses. This initial probing is called *doorknob rattling* and is accomplished through two general activities. *Footprinting* refers to activities that gather information about the organization, its network activities, and its assets, while *fingerprinting* refers to activities that scan network locales for active systems and then identify the network services offered by the host systems. A system that can detect the early warning signs of footprinting and fingerprinting functions like a neighborhood watch that spots would-be burglars as they case the community. This early detection enables administrators to prepare for a potential attack or to minimize potential losses from an attack.

IDPSs can also help the organization protect its assets when its networks and systems are still exposed to **known vulnerabilities** or are unable to respond to a rapidly changing threat environment. Many factors can delay or undermine an organization's ability to secure its systems from attack and subsequent loss. For example, even though popular information security technologies such as scanning tools allow security administrators to evaluate the readiness of their systems, they may still fail to detect or correct a known deficiency or check for vulnerabilities frequently enough. In addition, even when a vulnerability is detected in a timely manner, it cannot always be corrected quickly. Because such corrective measures usually require administrators to install patches and upgrades, they are subject to fluctuations in the administrator's workload.

> **known vulnerability**
>
> A published weakness or fault in an information asset or its protective systems that may be exploited and result in loss.

Note that vulnerabilities might be known to vulnerability-tracking groups without being known to the general public. The number and complexity of reported vulnerabilities continue to increase, so it is extremely difficult to stay on top of them. Instead, organizations rely on developers to identify problems and patch systems, yet there is inevitably a delay between detection and distribution of a patch or update to resolve the vulnerability. Similarly, substantial delays are common between the detection of a new virus or worm and the distribution of a signature that allows antimalware applications to detect and contain the threat.

To further complicate the matter, services that are known to be vulnerable sometimes cannot be disabled or otherwise protected because they are essential to ongoing operations. When a system has a known vulnerability or deficiency, an IDPS can be set up to detect attacks or attempts to exploit existing weaknesses, an important part of the strategy of defense in depth.

While a diligent organization may be well prepared against known vulnerabilities, it's the unknown that still causes the organization concern. **Zero-day vulnerabilities** (or zero-day attacks) are unknown or undisclosed vulnerabilities that can't be predicted or prepared for. They are called *zero-day* (or *zero-hour*) because once they are discovered, the technology owners have zero days to identify, mitigate, and resolve the vulnerability. Unfortunately, most of these vulnerabilities become "known" only when they are used in an attack. Therefore, it is critical for the organization to diligently monitor online trade press and industry user groups to stay abreast of such issues.

> **zero-day vulnerability**
>
> An unknown or undisclosed vulnerability in an information asset or its protection systems that may be exploited and result in loss; once it is discovered, there are zero days to identify, mitigate, and resolve the vulnerability.

Organizations continue to expand the number of items on networks they manage and where those items are operated. The Internet of Things requires different types of devices to be connected, while cloud service use results in valuable assets housed in places where defenses are established with software-defined perimeters instead of the old-school hardware perimeter. These changes in how networks are used and what can be found on them make the need for IDPS technologies even more pronounced.

Data Collection

In the process of analyzing data and network activity, IDPSs can be configured to log data for later analysis. This logging function allows the organization to examine *what* happened after an intrusion occurred and *why*. As an accountability function, logging may even provide the *who* if the individual responsible for the intrusion works within the organization. Even when intruders are not internal, some information may be available, such as where they are connecting from (IP address) and how they connected (browser details). Logging also allows improvement in incident response; evaluation by specialized log monitors, as described later in this module; and assessment of the effectiveness of the IDPS itself.

Even if an IDPS fails to prevent an intrusion, it can still contribute to the after-attack review by assisting investigators in determining how the attack occurred, what the intruder accomplished, and which methods the attacker employed. This information can be used to remedy deficiencies and to prepare the organization's network environment for future attacks. The IDPS can also provide forensic information that may be useful if the attacker is caught and then prosecuted or sued.

Examining this information to understand attack frequencies and attributes can help identify insufficient, inappropriate, or compromised security measures. This process can also provide insight for management into threats the organization faces and can help justify current and future expenditures to support and improve incident detection controls. When asked for funding to implement additional security technology, upper management usually requires documentation of the threat from which the organization must be protected.

Attack Deterrence

Another reason to install an IDPS is that it serves as a deterrent by increasing the fear of detection among would-be attackers. If internal and external users know that an organization has deployed an IDPS, they are less likely to probe the system or attempt to compromise it, just as criminals are much less likely to break into a house that appears to have a burglar alarm.

Other Reasons to Deploy an IDPS

Data collected by an IDPS can help management with quality assurance and continuous improvement activities. IDPSs consistently pick up information about attacks that have successfully compromised the outer layers of information security controls, such as a firewall. This information can be used to identify and repair flaws in the security and network architectures, which helps the organization expedite its incident response and make other continuous improvements.

An IDPS can provide a level of quality control for security policy implementation. This can be accomplished when the IDPS is used to detect incomplete firewall configuration where inappropriate network traffic is allowed that should have been filtered at the firewall. This detection could alert administrators to a poorly configured or compromised firewall. IDPSs may also be used to identify security policy violations.

Certain IDPSs can monitor network traffic and systems data in an effort to flag suspicious data transfers and detect unusual activities that could indicate data theft. If the organization's employees have no reason to copy data files over a certain size, an IDPS may be able to detect large file transfers, either from a host-based or network-based IDPS. Similarly, certain protected files may be specified to flag or notify administrators if they are accessed, copied, or modified. This is one of the primary functions of a host-based IDPS, which is described later in this module.

Another use of the intrusion awareness that an IDPS provides, even when alerts are given after the actual intrusion, is part of the process known as the *kill chain.* This concept, an adaptation of combat tactics brought to the world of information security by Lockheed Martin, is that the success of an attack can be disrupted at several points in the sequence. By disrupting the attack at any point up to the final exfiltration of its proceeds, potential losses can be stopped. Figure 9-1 shows the various steps in the attack sequence and the associated opportunities to interrupt it using the kill chain.

Types of IDPSs

IDPSs generally operate as network- or host-based systems. A network-based IDPS is focused on protecting network information assets by examining network communications traffic. Two specialized types of network-based IDPSs are the wireless IDPS and the network behavior analysis (NBA) IDPS. The wireless IDPS focuses on wireless networks, as the name indicates, while the NBA IDPS examines traffic flow on a network in an attempt to recognize abnormal patterns like DDoS, malware, and policy violations.

A host-based IDPS protects a server or host's information assets, usually by monitoring the files stored on the system or by monitoring the actions of connected users; the example shown in Figure 9-2 monitors both network connection activity and current information states on host servers. The application-based model works on one or more host systems that support a single application and defends that application from special forms of attack.

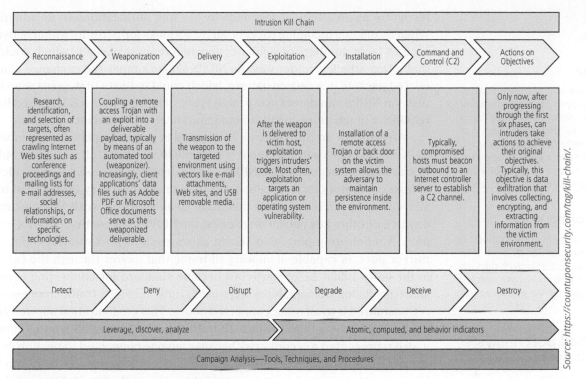

Figure 9-1   The cyberattack kill chain

Source: https://countuponsecurity.com/tag/kill-chain/.

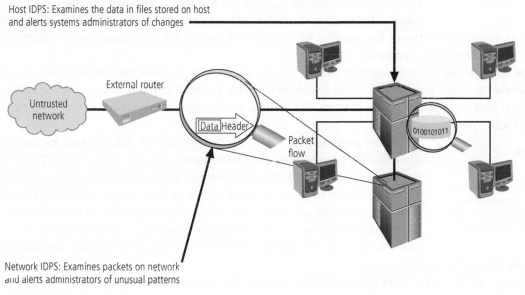

Host IDPS: Examines the data in files stored on host and alerts systems administrators of changes

Network IDPS: Examines packets on network and alerts administrators of unusual patterns

Figure 9-2   Intrusion detection and prevention systems

Network-Based IDPS

A **network-based IDPS (NIDPS)** consists of a specialized hardware appliance and software designed to monitor network traffic. The NIDPS may include separate management software, referred to as a console, and a number of specialized hardware and software components, referred to as **agents** or **sensors**. These agents can be installed on other network segments and network technologies to remotely monitor traffic at multiple locations for a potential intrusion, reporting back to the central NIDPS application. When the NIDPS identifies activity that it is programmed to

network-based IDPS (NIDPS)

An IDPS that resides on a computer or appliance connected to a segment of an organization's network and monitors traffic on that segment, looking for indications of ongoing or successful attacks.

agent

See *sensor*.

sensor

A hardware and software component deployed on a remote computer or network segment and designed to monitor network or system traffic for suspicious activities and report back to the host application. For example, IDPS sensors report to an IDPS application.

monitoring port

A specially configured connection on a network device that can view all the traffic that moves through the device; also known as a *switched port analysis (SPAN) port* or *mirror port*.

switched port analysis (SPAN) port

See *monitoring port*.

mirror port

See *monitoring port*.

recognize as an attack, it responds by sending notifications to its administrators. When examining incoming packets, an NIDPS looks for patterns within network traffic such as large numbers of similar connection request packets, which could indicate that a DoS attack is under way. An NIDPS also examines the exchange of a series of related packets in a certain pattern, which could indicate that a port scan is in progress. An NIDPS can detect many more types of attacks than a host-based IDPS, but it requires a much more complex configuration and maintenance program.

An NIDPS or an NIDPS sensor is installed at a specific place in the network, such as inside an edge router, where it is possible to monitor traffic into and out of a particular network segment. The NIDPS can be deployed to monitor a specific grouping of host computers on a specific network segment, or it may be installed to monitor all traffic between the systems that make up an entire network. When placed next to a switch or other key networking device, the NIDPS may use that device's **monitoring port**. A monitoring port, also known as a **switched port analysis (SPAN) port** or **mirror port**, is capable of viewing all traffic that moves through the entire device. In the early 1990s, before switches became standard for connecting networks in a shared-collision domain, hubs were used. Hubs received traffic from one node and retransmitted it to all other connected nodes. This configuration allowed any device connected to the hub to monitor all traffic passing through the hub. Unfortunately, it also represented a security risk because anyone connected to the hub could monitor all the traffic that moved through the network segment. Switches, on the other hand, create dedicated point-to-point links between their ports. These links create a higher level of transmission security and privacy to effectively prevent anyone from capturing traffic and thus eavesdropping on it as it passes through the switch. Unfortunately, the ability to capture the traffic is necessary for the use of an IDPS. Thus, monitoring ports are required. These connections enable network administrators to collect traffic from across the network for analysis by the IDPS, as well as for occasional use in diagnosing network faults and measuring network performance.

To determine whether an attack has occurred or is under way, NIDPSs compare measured activity to known signatures in their knowledge base. The comparisons are made through a special implementation of the TCP/IP stack that reassembles the packets and applies protocol stack verification, application protocol verification, or other verification and comparison techniques.

protocol stack verification

The process of examining and verifying network traffic for invalid data packets—that is, packets that are malformed under the rules of the TCP/IP protocol.

In the process of **protocol stack verification**, NIDPSs look for invalid data packets—that is, packets that are malformed under the rules of the TCP/IP protocol. A data packet is verified when its configuration matches one that is defined by the various Internet protocols. The elements of these protocols (IP, TCP, UDP, and application layers such as HTTP) are combined in a complete set called the *protocol stack* when the software is implemented in an operating system or application. Many types of intrusions, especially DoS and DDoS attacks, rely on the creation of improperly formed packets to take advantage of weaknesses in the protocol stack in certain operating systems or applications.

Figure 9-3 shows data from the Snort Network IDPS Engine. In this case, the display is a sample screen from Snorby, a GUI client that can manage Snort as well as display generated alerts.

 For more information on the Snort Network IDPS Engine, visit *www.snort.org*. For more information on the Snorby front end for Snort and other IDPSs, visit *https://github.com/Snorby/snorby*.

application protocol verification

The process of examining and verifying the higher-order protocols (HTTP, FTP, and Telnet) in network traffic for unexpected packet behavior or improper use.

In **application protocol verification**, the higher-order protocols (HTTP, SMTP, and FTP) are examined for unexpected packet behavior or improper use. Sometimes an attack uses valid protocol packets but in excessive quantities; in the case of the tiny fragment attack, the packets are also excessively fragmented. While protocol stack verification looks for violations in the protocol packet *structure*, application protocol verification looks for violations in the protocol packet's *use*. One example

Figure 9-3 Snorby demo

is DNS cache poisoning, in which valid packets exploit poorly configured DNS servers to inject false information and corrupt the servers' answers to routine DNS queries from other systems on the network. Unfortunately, this higher-order examination of traffic can have the same effect on an IDPS as it can on a firewall—that is, it slows the throughput of the system. It may be necessary to have more than one NIDPS installed, with one of them performing protocol stack verification and one performing application protocol verification.

The advantages of NIDPSs include the following:

- Good network design and placement of NIDPS devices can enable an organization to monitor a large network using only a few devices.
- NIDPSs are usually passive devices and can be deployed into existing networks with little or no disruption to normal network operations.
- NIDPSs are not usually susceptible to direct attack and may not be detectable by attackers.[3]

The disadvantages of NIDPSs include the following:

- An NIDPS can become overwhelmed by network volume and fail to recognize attacks it might otherwise have detected. Some IDPS vendors are accommodating the need for ever-faster network performance by improving the processing of detection algorithms in dedicated hardware circuits. Additional efforts to optimize rule set processing may also reduce the overall effectiveness of detecting attacks.
- NIDPSs require access to all traffic to be monitored. As mentioned earlier, switches have replaced hubs. Because some switches have limited or no monitoring port capability, some networks are not capable of providing aggregate data for analysis by an NIDPS. Even when switches do provide monitoring ports, they may not be able to mirror all activity with a consistent and reliable time sequence.
- NIDPSs cannot analyze encrypted packets, making some network traffic invisible to the process. The increasing use of encryption that hides the contents of some or all packets by some network services (such as SSL, SSH, and VPN) limits the effectiveness of NIDPSs.
- NIDPSs cannot reliably ascertain whether an attack was successful, which requires ongoing effort by the network administrator to evaluate logs of suspicious network activity.
- Some forms of attack are not easily discerned by NIDPSs, specifically those involving fragmented packets. In fact, some NIDPSs are so vulnerable to malformed packets that they may become unstable and stop functioning.[4]

Wireless NIDPS   A wireless IDPS monitors and analyzes wireless network traffic, looking for potential problems with the wireless protocols (Layers 2 and 3 of the OSI model). Unfortunately, wireless IDPSs cannot evaluate and diagnose issues with higher-layer protocols like TCP and UDP. Wireless IDPS capability can be built into a device that provides a wireless access point (AP).

Sensors for wireless networks can be located at the access points, on specialized sensor components, or in selected mobile stations. Centralized management stations collect information from these sensors, much as other network-based IDPSs do, and aggregate the information into a comprehensive assessment of wireless network intrusions. The implementation of wireless IDPSs includes the following issues:

- *Physical security*—Unlike wired network sensors, which can be physically secured, many wireless sensors are located in public areas like conference rooms, lobbies, galleries, and hallways to obtain the widest possible network range. Some of these locations may even be outdoors; more and more organizations are deploying networks in external locations to provide seamless connectivity across the organization. Thus, the physical security of these devices may require additional configuration and monitoring.
- *Sensor range*—A wireless device's range can be affected by atmospheric conditions, building construction, and the quality of the wireless network card and access point. Some IDPS tools allow an organization to identify the optimal location for sensors by modeling the wireless footprint based on signal strength. Sensors are most effective when their footprints overlap.
- *Access point and wireless switch locations*—Wireless components with bundled IDPS capabilities must be carefully deployed to optimize the IDPS sensor detection grid. The minimum range is just that; you must guard against the possibility of an attacker connecting to a wireless access point from a range far beyond the minimum.
- *Wired network connections*—Wireless network components work independently of the wired network when sending and receiving traffic between stations and access points. However, a network connection eventually integrates wireless traffic with the organization's wired network. In places where no wired network connection is available, it may be impossible to deploy a sensor.
- *Cost*—The more sensors you deploy, the more expensive the configuration. Wireless components typically cost more than their wired counterparts, so the total cost of ownership of IDPSs for both wired and wireless varieties should be carefully considered.
- *AP and wireless switch locations*—The locations of APs and wireless switches are important for organizations buying bundled solutions (APs with preinstalled IDPS applications).[5]

In addition to the traditional types of intrusions detected by other IDPSs, the wireless IDPS can detect existing WLANs and WLAN devices for inventory purposes as well as detect the following:

- Unauthorized WLANs and WLAN devices
- Poorly secured WLAN devices
- Unusual usage patterns
- The use of wireless network scanners
- DoS attacks and conditions
- Impersonation and man-in-the-middle attacks[6]

Wireless IDPSs are generally more accurate than other types of IDPSs, mainly because of the reduced set of protocols and packets they have to examine. However, they are unable to detect certain passive wireless protocol attacks, in which the attacker monitors network traffic without active scanning and probing. Wireless IDPSs are also susceptible to evasion techniques. By simply looking at wireless devices, which are often visible in public areas, attackers can design customized evasion methods to exploit the system's channel scanning scheme. Wireless IDPSs can protect their associated WLANs, but they may be susceptible to logical and physical attacks on the wireless access point or the IDPS devices themselves. Always keep in mind the physical vulnerabilities of security technologies: "The best-configured security technology in the world cannot withstand an attack using a well-placed brick."[7]

Network Behavior Analysis System   NBA systems identify problems related to the flow of network traffic. They use a version of the anomaly detection method described later in this section to identify excessive packet flows that might occur in the case of equipment malfunction, DoS attacks, virus and worm attacks, and some forms of network policy violations. NBA IDPSs typically monitor internal networks but occasionally monitor connections between internal and external networks. Intrusion detection and prevention typically includes the following relevant flow data:

- Source and destination IP addresses
- Source and destination TCP or UDP ports or ICMP types and codes
- Number of packets and bytes transmitted in the session
- Starting and ending timestamps for the session[8]

Most NBA sensors can be deployed in **passive mode** *only, using the same connection methods (e.g., network tap, switch spanning port) as network-based IDPSs. Passive sensors that are performing direct network monitoring should be placed so that they can monitor key network locations, such as the divisions between networks, and key network segments, such as demilitarized zone (DMZ) subnets.* **Inline sensors** *are typically intended for network perimeter use, so they would be deployed in close proximity to the perimeter firewalls, often between the firewall and the Internet border router to limit incoming attacks that could overwhelm the firewall.*[9]

passive mode

An IDPS sensor setting in which the device simply monitors and analyzes observed network or system traffic.

inline sensor

An IDPS sensor intended for network perimeter use and deployed in close proximity to a perimeter firewall to detect incoming attacks that could overwhelm the firewall.

Figures 9-4 and 9-5 illustrate examples of inline and passive NIDPS sensor architecture, respectively.

NBA sensors can most commonly detect the following:

- DoS attacks (including DDoS attacks)
- Scanning
- Worms
- Unexpected application services, such as tunneled protocols, back doors, and use of forbidden application protocols
- Policy violations

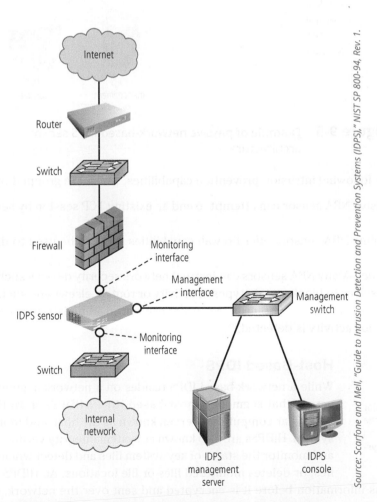

Source: Scarfone and Mell, "Guide to Intrusion Detection and Prevention Systems (IDPS)," NIST SP 800-94, Rev. 1.

Figure 9-4   Example of inline network-based IDPS sensor architecture

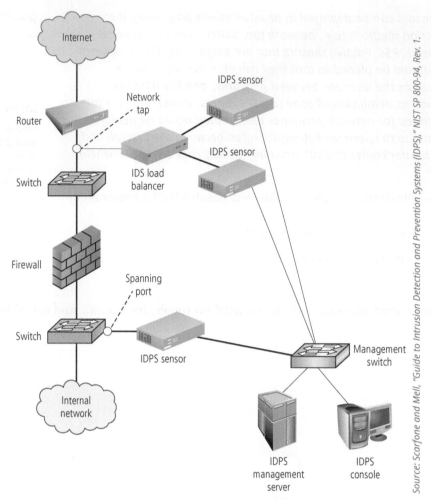

Source: Scarfone and Mell, "Guide to Intrusion Detection and Prevention Systems (IDPS)," NIST SP 800-94, Rev. 1.

Figure 9-5 Example of passive network-based IDPS sensor architecture

NBA sensors offer the following intrusion prevention capabilities, which are grouped by sensor type:

- *Passive only*—A passive NBA sensor can attempt to end an existing TCP session by sending TCP reset packets to both endpoints.
- *Inline only*—Most inline NBA sensors offer firewall capabilities that can be used to drop or reject suspicious network activity.
- *Both passive and inline*—Many NBA sensors can instruct network security devices such as firewalls and routers to reconfigure themselves to block certain types of activity or route it elsewhere, such as to a quarantined virtual local area network (VLAN). Also, some NBA sensors can run an administrator-specified script or program when certain malicious activity is detected.[10]

Host-Based IDPS

host-based IDPS (HIDPS)

An IDPS that resides on a particular computer or server, known as the host, and monitors activity only on that system; also known as a system integrity verifier.

While a network-based IDPS resides on a network segment and monitors activities across that segment, a **host-based IDPS (HIDPS)** or an HIDPS sensor resides on a particular computer or server, known as the host, and monitors activity only on that system. HIDPSs are also known as system integrity verifiers because they benchmark and monitor the status of key system files and detect when an intruder creates, modifies, or deletes monitored files or file locations. An HIDPS has an advantage over an NIDPS in that it can access information before it is encrypted and sent over the network, or after it is received and decrypted, and use it to make decisions about potential or actual attacks. Also, because the HIDPS works on only one computer system, all the traffic it examines exists within that system.

An HIDPS is also capable of monitoring system configuration databases, such as Windows registries, in addition to stored configuration files like .ini, .cfg, and .dat files. Most HIDPSs work on the principle of configuration management, which means that they record the sizes, locations, and other attributes of system files. The HIDPS triggers an alert when file attributes change, new files are created, or existing files are deleted. An HIDPS can also monitor systems logs for predefined events. The HIDPS examines these files and logs to determine if an attack is under way or has occurred; it also examines whether the attack is succeeding or was successful. The HIDPS maintains its own log file so that an audit trail is available even when hackers modify files on the target system to cover their tracks.

Once properly configured, an HIDPS is very reliable. The only time an HIDPS produces a false positive alert is when an authorized change occurs for a monitored file. This action can be quickly reviewed by an administrator, who may choose to disregard subsequent changes to the same set of files. If properly configured, an HIDPS can also detect when users attempt to modify or exceed their access authorization level.

An HIDPS classifies files into various categories and then sends notifications when changes occur. Most HIDPSs provide only a few general levels of alert notification. For example, an administrator can configure an HIDPS to report changes in a system folder, such as C:\Program Files\Windows NT, and configure changes to a security-related application, such as C:\TripWire. The configuration rules may classify changes to a specific application folder (for example, C:\Program Files\Microsoft Office) as normal and hence unreportable. Administrators can configure the system to log all activity but to send them a page or e-mail only if a reportable security event occurs. Because data files and internal application files such as dictionaries and configuration files are frequently modified, a poorly configured HIDPS can generate a large volume of false alarms.

Managed HIDPSs can monitor multiple computers simultaneously by creating a configuration file on each monitored host and by making each HIDPS report back to a master console system, which is usually located on the system administrator's computer. This master console monitors the information provided by the managed hosts and notifies the administrator when it senses recognizable attack conditions.

One of the most common methods of categorizing folders and files is by color coding. Critical system components are coded red and usually include the system registry, any folders containing the OS kernel, and critical system drivers. Critically important data could also be included in the red category. Support components, such as device drivers and other relatively important files, are generally coded yellow. User data is usually coded green, not because it is unimportant, but because monitoring changes to user data is practically difficult and strategically less urgent. User data files are frequently modified, but system kernel files, for example, should only be modified during upgrades or installations. If the preceding three-color system is too simplistic, an organization can use a scale of 0–10, as long as the scale doesn't become excessively granular. For example, an organization could easily create confusion for itself by using a 100-point scale and then trying to classify level 67 and 68 intrusions. Sometimes simpler is better.

The advantages of HIDPSs include the following:

- An HIDPS or one of its sensors can detect local events on host systems and can detect attacks that may elude a network-based IDPS.
- An HIDPS functions on the host system, where encrypted traffic will have been decrypted and is available for processing.
- The use of switched network protocols does not affect an HIDPS.
- An HIDPS can detect inconsistencies in how applications and system programs were used by examining the records stored in audit logs. This can enable the HIDPS to detect some types of attacks, including Trojan horse programs.[11]

The disadvantages of HIDPSs include the following:

- HIDPSs pose more management issues because they are configured and managed on each monitored host. An HIDPS requires more management effort to install, configure, and operate than a comparably sized NIDPS solution.
- An HIDPS is vulnerable both to direct attacks and to attacks against the host operating system. Either attack can result in the compromise or loss of HIDPS functionality.
- An HIDPS is not optimized to detect multihost scanning, nor is it able to detect scanning from network devices that are not hosts, such as routers or switches. Unless complex correlation analysis is provided, the HIDPS will not be aware of attacks that span multiple devices in the network.
- An HIDPS is susceptible to some DoS attacks.

- An HIDPS can use large amounts of disk space to retain the host OS audit logs; for the HIDPS to function properly, it may be necessary to add disk capacity to the system.
- An HIDPS can inflict a performance overhead on its host systems and may sometimes reduce system performance below acceptable levels.[12]

Note that many of these shortcomings can be mitigated by using distributed HIDPSs that aggregate data from HIDPSs running on multiple hosts into a centralized management console, allowing comparison of findings across multiple systems.

IDPS Detection Methods

IDPSs use a variety of detection methods to monitor and evaluate network traffic. Three methods dominate: signature-based detection, anomaly-based detection, and stateful protocol analysis.

signature-based detection

The examination of system or network data in search of patterns that match known attack signatures; also known as *knowledge-based detection* or *misuse detection*.

knowledge-based detection

See *signature-based detection*.

misuse detection

See *signature-based detection*.

signatures

Patterns that correspond to a known attack.

anomaly-based detection

An IDPS detection method that compares current data and traffic patterns to an established baseline of normalcy; also known as *behavior-based detection*.

behavior-based detection

See *anomaly-based detection*.

clipping level

A predefined assessment level that triggers a predetermined response when surpassed. Typically, the response is to write the event to a log file, notify an administrator, or both.

Signature-Based Detection

An IDPS that uses **signature-based detection** (sometimes called **knowledge-based detection** or **misuse detection**) examines network traffic in search of patterns that match known **signatures**—that is, preconfigured, predetermined attack patterns. Signature-based technology is widely used because many attacks have clear and distinct signatures:

- Footprinting and fingerprinting activities use ICMP, DNS querying, and e-mail routing analysis.
- Exploits use a specific attack sequence designed to take advantage of a vulnerability to gain access to a system.
- DoS and DDoS attacks, during which the attacker tries to prevent the normal usage of a system, overload the system with requests so that its ability to process them efficiently is compromised or disrupted.[13]

A potential problem with the signature-based approach is that new attack patterns must continually be added to the IDPS's database of signatures; otherwise, attacks that use new strategies will not be recognized and might succeed. Another weakness of the signature-based method is that a slow, methodical attack involving multiple events might escape detection. The only way signature-based detection can resolve this vulnerability is to collect and analyze data over longer periods of time, a process that requires substantially greater data storage capability and additional processing capacity. However, detection in real time becomes extremely unlikely.

Similarly, using signature-based detection to compare observed events with known patterns is relatively simplistic; the technologies that deploy it typically cannot analyze some application or network protocols, nor can they understand complex communications.

Anomaly-Based Detection

Anomaly-based detection (or **behavior-based detection**) collects statistical summaries by observing traffic that is known to be normal. This normal period of evaluation establishes a performance baseline over a period of time known as the *training period*. Once the baseline is established, the IDPS periodically samples network activity and uses statistical methods to compare the sampled activity to the baseline. When the measured activity is outside the baseline parameters—exceeding the **clipping level**—the IDPS sends an alert to the administrator. The baseline data can include variables such as host memory or CPU usage, network packet types, and packet quantities.

The profiles compiled by an anomaly-based detection IDPS are generally either static or dynamic. Static profiles do not change until modified or recalibrated by an administrator. Dynamic profiles continually collect additional observations on data and traffic patterns and then use that information to update their baselines. This can prove to be a vulnerability if the attacker uses a very slow attack, because the system using the dynamic detection method interprets attack activity as normal traffic and updates its profile accordingly.

The advantage of anomaly-based detection is that the IDPS can detect new types of attacks because it looks for abnormal activity of any type. Unfortunately, these systems require much more overhead and processing capacity than signature-based IDPSs because they must constantly compare patterns of activity against the baseline. Another drawback is that these systems may not detect minor changes to system variables and may generate many false positives. If the actions of network users or systems vary widely, with periods of low activity interspersed with periods of heavy packet traffic, this type of IDPS may not be suitable because the dramatic swings will almost certainly generate false alarms. Because of the complexity of anomaly-based detection, its impact on the overhead computing load of the host computer, and the number of false positives it can generate, this type of IDPS is less commonly used than the signature-based type.

Stateful Protocol Analysis

As you learned in Module 8, stateful inspection firewalls track each network connection between internal and external systems using a state table to record which station sent which packet and when. An IDPS extension of this concept is **stateful protocol analysis (SPA)**. SPA uses the opposite of a signature approach. Instead of comparing known attack patterns against observed traffic or data, the system compares known normal or benign protocol profiles against observed traffic. These profiles are developed and provided by the protocol vendors. Essentially, the IDPS knows how a protocol such as FTP is supposed to work, and therefore can detect anomalous behavior. By storing relevant data detected in a session and then using it to identify intrusions that involve multiple requests and responses, the IDPS can better detect specialized, multisession attacks. This process is sometimes called *deep packet inspection* because SPA closely examines packets at the application layer for information that indicates a possible intrusion. SPA can examine authentication sessions for suspicious activity as well as for attacks that incorporate unusual commands, such as commands that are out of sequence or submitted repeatedly. SPA can also detect intentionally malformed commands or commands that are outside the expected length parameters.[14]

> **stateful protocol analysis (SPA)**
>
> The comparison of vendor-supplied profiles of protocol use and behavior against observed data and network patterns to detect misuse and attacks; sometimes referred to as deep packet inspection.

The models used for SPA are similar to signatures in that they are provided by vendors. These models are based on industry protocol standards established by such entities as the Internet Engineering Task Force, but they vary along with the protocol implementations in such documents. Also, proprietary protocols are not published in sufficient detail to enable an IDPS to provide accurate and comprehensive assessments.

Unfortunately, the analytical complexity of session-based assessments is the principal drawback to this type of IDPS method. It also requires heavy processing overhead to track multiple simultaneous connections. Additionally, unless a protocol violates its fundamental behavior, this IDPS method may completely fail to detect an intrusion. One final concern is that the IDPS may actually interfere with the normal operations of the protocol it is examining.[15]

Log File Monitors

A **log file monitor (LFM)** IDPS is similar to an NIDPS. An LFM reviews the log files generated by servers, network devices, and even other IDPSs, looking for patterns and signatures that may indicate an attack or intrusion is in process or has already occurred. This attack detection is enhanced by the fact that the LFM can look at multiple log files from different systems, even if they use different operating systems or log formats. The patterns that signify an attack can be subtle and difficult to distinguish when one system is examined in isolation, but they may be more identifiable

> **log file monitor (LFM)**
>
> An attack detection method that reviews log files generated by computer systems looking for patterns and signatures that may indicate an attack or intrusion is in process or has already occurred.

when the events recorded for the entire network and each of its component systems can be viewed as a whole. Of course, this holistic approach requires considerable resources because it involves the collection, movement, storage, and analysis of very large quantities of log data.

Security Information and Event Management (SIEM)

Many organizations have come to rely on **security information and event management (SIEM)** as a central element to empower a security operations center (SOC) to identify and react to the many events, incidents, and attacks against the organization's information systems. SIEM's roots are in the UNIX syslog approach to log file aggregation; for

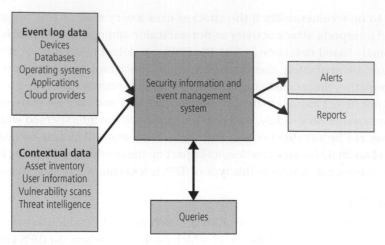

Figure 9-6   SIEM data flows

security information and event management (SIEM)

An information management system specifically tasked to collect and correlate events and other log data from a number of servers or other network devices for the purpose of interpreting, filtering, correlating, analyzing, storing, reporting, and acting on the resulting information.

threat intelligence

A process used to develop knowledge that allows an organization to understand the actions and intentions of threat actors and develop methods to prevent or mitigate cyberattacks.

years, organizations and security professionals have sought ways to leverage existing systems and have them work together to maintain situation awareness, identify noteworthy issues, and enable response to adverse events.

A SIEM system supports threat detection and informs many aspects of **threat intelligence**. It is also instrumental in managing aspects of compliance vulnerability management. It often plays a pivotal role in an organization's security incident management through data collection and analysis by enabling near real-time and historical analysis of security events. It integrates data from multiple sources, including local events and contextual data sources. SIEM systems are derived from legacy log file monitoring systems and procedures. The basics of SIEM data flows are shown in Figure 9-6.

The core capabilities of SIEM systems leverage the broad scope of log event collection and management from point sources across the organization, including firewalls, endpoint defenses, and IDPS systems. They give the organization the ability to analyze log events and other data from varied sources. The correlated results derived from advanced data analysis techniques enable several operational capabilities, including dashboards for situational awareness, reporting of trends, and incident management.

SIEM systems have been a mainstay in larger organizations for many years, evolving from locally developed LFM systems whose capabilities have been integrated into commercially developed platforms. This has allowed organizations with large numbers of devices used in information systems to collect and act on events from these devices, including servers and networking equipment, endpoint defense systems, desktop computing systems, and laptops. The reliance on cloud-based computing solutions has added significant complexity to larger information technology systems, and current-generation SIEM platforms have evolved to include those environments as well.

As the volume and complexity of data flowing into the SIEM system have multiplied, analysis of that data using data analytics techniques has been included in SIEM solutions. This has enabled organizations using SIEM solutions to keep pace as they monitor for intrusions and attacks against a mixed environment of on-premises systems, cloud hosted services, and hybrid system models that include both enabling technologies. The current level of capability is made possible by the analytics-driven SIEM system.

Larger organizations are faced with several needs that SIEM platforms can address:

- Aggregation of security-related events from across the organization regardless of the source technology
- Correlation of events with context from external sources, including vendor-specific updates and cooperative industry associations
- Integration of events from devices, systems, and technologies from disparate sources deployed throughout the organization

- Detection of known threats when patterns of attack behavior are known
- Possible detection of emerging threats when analysis is coupled with threat analysis techniques designed into the SIEM system
- Enablement of ad hoc searches and reporting from recorded events to enable advanced breach analysis during and after incident response and provide support for forensic investigation into breach events
- Tracking the actions of attackers and allowing sequencing of events to provide an understanding of what happened and when it occurred

The essential capabilities that an analytics-driven SIEM system should provide include the following:

- *Real-time monitoring*—Enable flexible and timely reaction to attacks.
- *Incident response*—Information about the incident response process improves the ability of the organization to detect and respond to attacks to reduce the degree of damage and enable more rapid containment and recovery.
- *User monitoring*—The monitoring of user activity can identify breaches and reveal insider misuse, which is often a requirement for compliance to external regulators.
- *Threat intelligence*—The development of threat intelligence can enable the recognition of abnormal events and prioritize the response process.
- *Analytics and threat detection*—Advanced query and reporting tools enable analysis of past events and make it possible to detect threats and vulnerabilities that are not otherwise apparent.

These capabilities give the organization the ability to identify and respond to a wide variety of situations.

Real-Time Monitoring

Many successful attacks remain undetected for significant periods of time. Mandiant reports that in 2019, an attack's median dwell time—the duration between the start of a cyber intrusion and the time it is detected—was 56 days.[16] While this is an improvement over recent years, it is still a significant delay. The longer the dwell times are, the more likely it is that attackers can be successful in the exfiltration of data and causing other damage. The SolarWinds attack in 2020 was massive in scope and had a dwell time of months; the attackers showed extraordinary skill in remaining undetected after compromising systems.

Improvement in an organization's capability to detect intrusions can reduce the dwell time and allow containment and recovery to be implemented more quickly. Reducing the time that attackers operate undetected inside the organization reduces the potential for data loss. A SIEM system that can integrate contextual data and ongoing events may be able to reduce the time attackers can operate and reduce losses. An example of a real-time monitoring capability from AT&T Security's Unified Security Management Anywhere demonstration is shown in Figure 9-7.

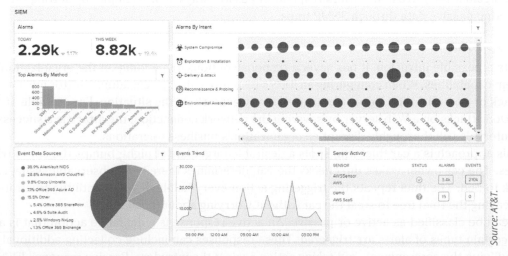

Figure 9-7   Example of a SIEM system real-time display

Incident Response

A properly implemented SIEM platform can enable the ability to identify incidents and enable a process to track and respond to them. SIEM systems enable responders to track and document ongoing incidents and perform record keeping and reporting on the incident response activities. In addition, the system can automatically or manually aggregate multiple events, interact with other systems, and assist in the collection of evidentiary materials. Some SIEM platforms can integrate response playbooks that guide staff on how to respond to specific incident categories. In some circumstances, a SIEM system can initiate predefined defensive scripts to automatically disrupt ongoing cyberattacks. An effective SIEM system can be a central service to coordinate the response workflow, combining predefined automatic response with notifications to enable a coordinated defensive reaction with a unified flow of information to the CSIRT and the SOC staff.

User Monitoring

An effective SIEM system can analyze user access and authentication activities and provide alerts for suspicious behaviors and violation of policy. This is of particular importance for privileged user accounts and is often a requirement for many compliance reporting functions. To be effective, these functions must be implemented to provide alerts of reporting and alerts in near real time.

Threat Intelligence

To enable the threat intelligence function of the organization, the SIEM system must be able to integrate threat intelligence services that provide current information on compromise indicators and adversary tactics, techniques, and procedures (TTP) with knowledge of organizational asset criticality and usage behaviors. These will enable analysts to recognize abnormal behaviors and assess the risks and impact of various forms of attack. Threat intelligence information can then be integrated with data from the IT infrastructure to create watch lists and enable correlation of event data with the nature of the infrastructure to identify and prioritize threats to organizational assets.

Analytics and Advanced Threat Detection

SIEM systems should have capabilities to analyze event data to detect anomalies and track the interactions between users and data repositories. The SIEM system should be able to correlate and visualize events to support incident investigations. By using machine learning, the SIEM system can learn to distinguish normal behavior from abnormal user behaviors. As the threat landscape evolves, a SIEM system should have the capacity to identify and respond to new and more advanced threats.

IDPS Response Behavior

Each IDPS responds to external stimulation in a different way, depending on its configuration and function. Some respond in active ways, collecting additional information about the intrusion, modifying the network environment, or even taking action against the intrusion. Others respond in passive ways—for example, by setting off alarms or notifications or collecting passive data through SNMP traps.

IDPS Response Options

When an IDPS detects a possible intrusion, it has several response options, depending on the organization's policy, objectives, and system capabilities. When configuring an IDPS's responses, the system administrator must ensure that a response to an attack or potential attack does not inadvertently exacerbate the situation. For example, if an NIDPS reacts to suspected DoS attacks on a Web server by severing the network connection, the attack is a success. Similar attacks repeated at intervals will thoroughly disrupt an organization's business operations.

An analogy to this approach is a car thief who spots a desirable target late at night, bumps the car to trigger the alarm, and then hides. The car owner wakes up, checks the car, determines there is no observable issue, resets the alarm, and goes back to bed. The thief repeats the triggering action every half-hour or so until the frustrated owner disables the alarm, leaving the thief free to steal the car without worrying about the alarm.

IDPS responses can be classified as active or passive. An active response is a definitive action that is automatically initiated when certain types of alerts are triggered. These responses can include collecting additional information, changing or modifying the environment, and taking action against the intruders. Passive-response IDPSs simply report the information they have collected and wait for the administrator to act. Generally, the administrator chooses a course of action after analyzing the collected data. A passive IDPS is the more common implementation, although most systems include some active options that are disabled by default.

The following list describes some of the responses an IDPS can be configured to produce. Note that some of these responses apply only to a network-based or host-based IDPS, while others are applicable to both.[17]

- *Audible/visual alarm*—The IDPS can trigger a sound file, beep, whistle, siren, or other audible or visual notification to alert the administrator of an attack. The most common type of notification is the computer pop-up, which can be configured with color indicators and specific messages. The pop-up can also contain specifics about the suspected attack, the tools used in the attack, the system's level of confidence in its own determination, and the addresses and locations of the systems involved.

- *SNMP traps and plug-ins*—The Simple Network Management Protocol contains trap functions, which allow a device to send a message to the SNMP management console indicating that a certain threshold has been crossed, either positively or negatively. The IDPS can execute this trap to inform the SNMP console that an event has occurred. Some advantages of this operation include the relatively standard implementation of SNMP in networking devices; the ability to configure the network system to use SNMP traps in this manner; the ability to use systems specifically to handle SNMP traffic, including IDPS traps; and the ability to use standard communications networks.

- *E-mail message*—The IDPS can send e-mail to notify network administrators of an event. Many administrators use smartphones and other e-mail devices to check for alerts and other notifications frequently. Organizations should use caution in relying on e-mail systems as the primary means of communication from an IDPS because attacks or even routine performance issues can disrupt, delay, or block such messages.

- *Phone or SMS message*—The IDPS can be configured to dial a phone number and deliver a recorded message or send a preconfigured SMS text message.

- *Log entry*—The IDPS can enter information about the event into an IDPS system log file or operating system log file. This information includes addresses, times, involved systems, and protocol information. The log files can be stored on separate servers to prevent skilled attackers from deleting entries about their intrusions.

- *Evidentiary packet dump*—Organizations that require an audit trail of IDPS data may choose to record all log data in a special way. This method allows the organization to perform further analysis on the data and to submit the data as evidence in a civil or criminal case. Once the data has been written using a cryptographic hashing algorithm (see Module 10), it becomes evidentiary documentation—that is, suitable for criminal or civil court use, as described in Module 5. However, this packet logging can be resource-intensive, especially during DoS attacks.

- *Taking action against the intruder*—Although it is not advisable, organizations could—with authorization—take action against an intruder using trap-and-trace, back-hacking, or trace-back methods. Such responses involve configuring IDPSs to trace the data from the target system back to the attacking system to initiate a counterattack. While this response may sound tempting, it may not be legal. An organization only owns a network to its perimeter, so conducting traces or back-hacking to systems beyond that point may make the organization just as criminally liable as the original attackers. Also, the attacking system is sometimes a compromised intermediary system; in other cases, attackers use address spoofing. In either situation, a counterattack would actually harm an innocent third party. Any organization that plans to configure retaliation efforts into an automated IDPS is strongly encouraged to seek legal counsel.

- *Launching a program*—An IDPS can be configured to execute a specific program when it detects specific types of attacks. Several vendors have specialized tracking, tracing, and response software that can be part of an organization's intrusion response strategy.

- *Reconfiguring a firewall*—An IDPS can send a command to the firewall to filter out suspected packets by IP address, port, or protocol. (Unfortunately, it is still possible for a skilled attacker to break into a network simply by spoofing a different address, shifting to a different port, or changing the protocols used in the attack.) While it may not be easy, an IDPS can block or deter intrusions via one of the following methods:
  - Establishing a block for all traffic from the suspected attacker's IP address or even from the entire source network the attacker appears to be using. This blocking can be set for a specific period of time and reset to normal rules after that period has expired.
  - Establishing a block for specific TCP or UDP port traffic from the suspected attacker's address or source network. Only services that seem to be under attack are blocked.

○ Blocking all traffic to or from the organization's Internet connection or other network interface if the severity of the suspected attack warrants such a response.

- *Terminating the session*—Terminating the session by using the TCP/IP protocol packet *TCP close* is a simple process. Some attacks would be deterred or blocked by session termination, but others would simply continue when the attacker issues a new session request.
- *Terminating the connection*—The last resort for an IDPS under attack is to terminate the organization's internal or external connections. Smart switches can cut traffic to or from a specific port if the connection is linked to a system that is malfunctioning or otherwise interfering with efficient network operations. As indicated earlier, this response should be the last attempt to protect information, as termination may actually be the goal of the attacker.

Note: The following sections have been adapted from NIST SP 800-94 and SP 800-94, Rev. 1, "Guide to Intrusion Detection and Prevention Systems," and their predecessor, NIST SP 800-31, "Intrusion Detection Systems."

Reporting and Archiving Capabilities

Many, if not all, commercial IDPSs can generate routine reports and other detailed documents, such as reports of system events and intrusions detected over a particular reporting period. Some systems provide statistics or logs in formats that are suitable for inclusion in database systems or for use in report-generating packages.

Fail-Safe Considerations for IDPS Responses

Fail-safe features protect an IDPS from being circumvented or defeated by an attacker. Several functions require fail-safe measures; for instance, IDPSs need to provide silent, reliable monitoring of attackers. If the response function of an IDPS breaks this silence by broadcasting alarms and alerts in plaintext over the monitored network, attackers can detect the IDPS and directly target it in the attack. Encrypted tunnels or other cryptographic measures that hide and authenticate communications are excellent ways to ensure the reliability of the IDPS.

Selecting IDPS Approaches and Products

The wide array of available intrusion detection products addresses a broad range of security goals and considerations; selecting products that represent the best fit for a particular organization is challenging. The following considerations and questions can help you prepare a specification for acquiring and deploying an intrusion detection product.

Technical and Policy Considerations

To determine which IDPS best meets an organization's needs, first consider its environment in technical, physical, and political terms.

What Is Your System Environment?   The first requirement for a potential IDPS is that it functions in your system environment. This is important; if an IDPS is not designed to accommodate the information sources on your systems, it will not be able to see anything— neither normal activity nor an attack—on those systems.

- What are the technical specifications of your system environment? First, specify the technical attributes of your system environment, including network diagrams and maps that specify the number and locations of hosts; operating systems for each host; the number and types of network devices, such as routers, bridges, and switches; the number and types of terminal servers and dial-up connections; and descriptions of any network servers, including their types, configurations, and the application software and versions running on each. If you run an enterprise network management system, specify it here.
- What are the technical specifications of your current security protections? Describe the security protections you already have in place. Specify numbers, types, and locations of network firewalls, identification and authentication servers, data and link encryptors, antivirus/antimalware packages, access control products, specialized security hardware (such as crypto accelerators for Web servers), virtual private networks, and any other security mechanisms on your systems.

- What are the goals of your enterprise? Some IDPSs are designed to accommodate the special needs of certain industries or market niches, such as electronic commerce, healthcare, or financial services. Define the functional goals of your enterprise that are supported by your systems. Several goals can be associated with a single organization.
- How formal is the system environment and management culture in your organization? Organizational styles vary depending on their function and traditional culture. For instance, the military and other organizations that deal with national security tend to operate with a high degree of formality, especially when contrasted with universities or other academic environments. Some IDPSs support enforcement of formal use policies, with built-in configuration options that can enforce common issue-specific or system-specific security policies. Some IDPSs also provide a library of reports for typical policy violations or routine matters.

What Are Your Security Goals and Objectives?   The next step is to articulate the goals and objectives of using an IDPS.

- Is your organization primarily concerned with protecting itself from outside threats? Perhaps the easiest way to identify security goals is by categorizing your organization's threat concerns. Identify its concerns regarding external threats.
- Is your organization concerned about insider attacks? Address concerns about threats that originate within your organization. For example, a shipping clerk might attempt to access and alter the payroll system, or an authorized user might exceed his privileges and violate your organization's security policy or laws. As another example, a customer service agent might be driven by curiosity to access earnings and payroll records for company executives.
- Does your organization want to use the output of your IDPS to determine new needs? System usage monitoring is sometimes a generic system management tool used to determine when system assets require upgrading or replacement.
- Does your organization want to use an IDPS to maintain managerial control over network usage rather than security controls? Some organizations implement system use policies that may be classified as personnel management rather than system security. For example, they might prohibit access to pornographic Web sites or other sites, or prohibit the use of organizational systems to send harassing e-mail or other messages. Some IDPSs provide features that detect such violations of management controls.

What Is Your Existing Security Policy?   You should review your organization's existing security policy because it is the template against which your IDPS will be configured. You may find that you need to augment the policy or derive the following items from it.

- How is it structured? It is helpful to articulate the goals outlined in the security policy. These goals include standard security goals, such as integrity, confidentiality, and availability, as well as more generic management goals, such as privacy, protection from liability, and manageability.
- What are the general job descriptions of your system users? List the general job functions of system users as well as the data and network access that each function requires. Several functions are often applied to a single user.
- Does the policy include reasonable use policies or other management provisions? As mentioned previously, the security policies of many organizations include system use policies.
- Has your organization defined processes for dealing with specific policy violations? It is helpful to know what the organization plans to do when the IDPS detects that a policy has been violated. If the organization doesn't intend to react to such violations, it may not make sense to configure the IDPS to detect them. On the other hand, if the organization wants to respond to such violations, IDPS administrators should be informed so they can deal with alarms in an appropriate manner.

Organizational Requirements and Constraints

Your organization's goals, constraints, and culture will affect the selection of the IDPS and other security tools and technologies to protect your systems. Consider the following requirements and limitations.

What Requirements Are Levied from Outside the Organization?

- Is your organization subject to oversight or review by another organization?
- If so, does that oversight authority require IDPSs or other specific system security resources?
- Are there requirements for public access to information on your organization's systems? Do regulations or statutes require that information be accessible by the public during certain hours of the day or during certain intervals?
- Are any other security-specific requirements levied by law? Are there legal requirements for protection of personal information stored on your systems? Such information can include earnings or medical records. Are there legal requirements for investigating security violations that divulge or endanger personal information?
- Are there internal audit requirements for security best practices or due diligence? Do any of these audit requirements specify functions that the IDPSs must provide or support?
- Is the system subject to accreditation? If so, what is the accreditation authority's requirement for IDPSs or other security protection?
- Are there requirements for law enforcement investigation and resolution of security incidents?
- Do they require any IDPS functions, especially those that involve collection and protection of IDPS logs as evidence?

What Are Your Organization's Resource Constraints?   IDPSs can protect the systems of an organization, but at a price. It makes little sense to incur additional expenses for IDPS features if your organization does not have sufficient systems or personnel to handle the alerts they will generate.

- What is the budget for acquisition and life cycle support of intrusion detection hardware, software, and infrastructure? Remember that the IDPS software is not the only element of the total cost of ownership; you may also have to acquire a system for running the software, obtain specialized assistance to install and configure the system, and train your personnel. Ongoing operations may also require additional staff or outside contractors.
- Is there sufficient staff to monitor an IDPS full time? Some IDPSs require around-the-clock attendance by systems personnel. If your organization cannot meet this requirement, you may want to explore systems that accommodate part-time attendance or unattended use.
- Does your organization provide authority to instigate changes based on the findings of an IDPS? The organization must be clear about how to address problems uncovered by an IDPS. If you are not empowered to handle incidents that arise as a result of monitoring, you should coordinate your selection and configuration of the IDPS with the person who is empowered.

IDPS Product Features and Quality

It's important to evaluate any IDPS product by carefully considering the following questions.

Is the Product Sufficiently Scalable for Your Environment?   Many IDPSs cannot function within large or widely distributed enterprise network environments.

How Has the Product Been Tested?   Simply asserting that an IDPS has certain capabilities does not demonstrate they are real. You should request demonstrations of an IDPS to evaluate its suitability for your environment and goals.

- Has the product been tested against functional requirements? Ask the vendor about any assumptions made for the goals and constraints of customer environments.
- Has the product been tested for performance against anticipated load? Ask vendors for details about their products' ability to perform critical functions with high reliability under load conditions similar to those expected in the production environment.
- Has the product been tested to reliably detect attacks? Ask vendors for details about their products' ability to respond to attacks reliably.

- Has the product been tested against attack? Ask vendors for details about their products' security testing. If the product includes network-based vulnerability assessment, ask whether test routines that produce system crashes or other denials of service have been identified and flagged in system documentation and interfaces.

What User Level of Expertise Is Targeted by the Product? Different IDPS vendors target users with different levels of technical and security expertise. Ask vendors to describe their assumptions about users and administrators of their products.

Is the Product Designed to Evolve as the Organization Grows? An important goal of product design is the ability to adapt to your needs over time.

- Can the product adapt to growth in user expertise? Ask whether the IDPS's interface can be configured on the fly to accommodate shortcut keys, customizable alarm features, and custom signatures. Ask also whether these features are documented and supported.
- Can the product adapt to growth and change of the organization's system infrastructure? This question addresses the ability of the IDPS to scale to an expanding and increasingly diverse network. Most vendors have experience in adapting their products as target networks grow. Ask also about commitments to support new protocol standards and platform types.
- Can the product adapt to growth and change in the security threat environment? This question is especially critical given the current Internet threat environment, in which hundreds of new malware variants are posted to the Web every day.

What Are the Support Provisions for the Product? Like other systems, IDPSs require maintenance and support over time. These needs should be identified in a written report.

- What are the commitments for product installation and configuration support? Many vendors provide expert assistance to customers when installing and configuring IDPSs. Other vendors expect your own staff to handle such functions and provide only telephone or e-mail support.
- What are the commitments for ongoing product support? Ask about the vendor's commitment to supporting your use of its IDPS product.
- Are subscriptions to signature updates included? Most IDPSs are misuse detectors, so their value is only as good as the signature database against which events are analyzed. Most vendors provide subscriptions to signature updates for a year or other specified period of time.
- How often are subscriptions updated? In today's threat environment, in which 30 to 40 new attacks are published every month, this is a critical question.
- After a new attack is made public, how quickly will the vendor ship a new signature? If you are using IDPSs to protect highly visible or heavily traveled Internet sites, it is critical that you receive the signatures for new attacks as soon as possible.
- Are software updates included? Most IDPSs are software products and therefore subject to bugs and revisions. Ask the vendor about its support for software updates and bug patches, especially for the product you purchase.
- How quickly will software updates and patches be issued after a problem is reported to the vendor? Software bugs in IDPSs can allow attackers to nullify their protective effect, so any problems must be fixed reliably and quickly.
- Are technical support services included? What is the cost? In this category, technical support services mean vendor assistance in tuning or adapting your IDPS to accommodate special needs. These needs might include monitoring a custom or legacy system within your enterprise or reporting IDPS results in a custom protocol or format. This also includes support in resolving installation or configuration issues.
- What are the provisions for contacting technical support via e-mail, telephone, online chats, or Web-based reporting? The contact provisions will probably tell you whether technical support services are accessible enough to support incident handling or other time-sensitive needs.

- Are any guarantees associated with the IDPS? As with other software products, IDPSs traditionally come with few guarantees; however, in an attempt to gain market share, some vendors are initiating guarantee programs.
- What training resources does the vendor provide? Once an IDPS is selected, installed, and configured, your personnel can operate it, but they need to be trained in its use. Some vendors provide this training as part of the product package.
- What additional training resources are available from the vendor and at what cost? If the vendor does not provide training as part of the IDPS package, you should budget appropriately to train your personnel.

Strengths and Limitations of IDPSs

Although IDPSs are a valuable addition to an organization's security infrastructure, they have strengths and weaknesses, like any technology. As you plan the security strategy for your organization's systems, you need to understand what IDPSs can be trusted to do and what goals might be better served by other security mechanisms.

Strengths of IDPSs

Intrusion detection and prevention systems perform the following functions well:

- Monitoring and analysis of system events and user behaviors
- Testing the security states of system configurations
- Baselining the security state of a system and then tracking any changes to that baseline
- Recognizing patterns of system events that correspond to known attacks
- Recognizing patterns of activity that vary statistically from normal activity
- Managing operating system audit and logging mechanisms and the data they generate
- Alerting appropriate staff by appropriate means when attacks are detected
- Measuring enforcement of security policies encoded in the analysis engine
- Providing default information security policies
- Allowing people who are not security experts to perform important security monitoring functions

Limitations of IDPSs

IDPSs cannot perform the following functions:

- Compensating for weak or missing security mechanisms in the protection infrastructure, such as firewalls, identification and authentication systems, link encryption systems, access control mechanisms, and virus detection and eradication software
- Instantaneously detecting, reporting, and responding to an attack when there is a heavy network or processing load
- Detecting newly published attacks or variants of existing attacks
- Effectively responding to attacks launched by sophisticated attackers
- Automatically investigating attacks without human intervention
- Resisting all attacks that are intended to defeat or circumvent them
- Compensating for problems with the fidelity of information sources
- Dealing effectively with switched networks

There is also the considerable challenge of configuring an IDPS to respond accurately to a perceived threat. Once a device is empowered to react to an intrusion by filtering or even severing a communication session or by severing a communication circuit, the impact from a false positive becomes significant. It's one thing to fill an administrator's e-mail box or compile a large log file with suspected attacks; it's quite another to shut down critical communications. Some forms of attacks, conducted by attackers called *IDPS terrorists*, are designed to trip the organization's IDPS, essentially causing the organization to conduct its own DoS attack by overreacting to an actual but insignificant attack.

Note: The preceding sections were developed and adapted from NIST SP 800-94 and SP 800-94, Rev. 1, "Guide to Intrusion Detection and Prevention Systems," and their predecessor, NIST SP 800-31, "Intrusion Detection Systems."

Deployment and Implementation of an IDPS

Deploying and implementing an IDPS is not always a straightforward task. The strategy for deploying an IDPS should account for several factors, the foremost being how the IDPS will be managed and where it should be placed. These factors determine the number of administrators needed to install, configure, and monitor the IDPS, as well as the number of management workstations, the size of the storage needed for data generated by the systems, and the ability of the organization to detect and respond to remote threats.

NIST SP 800-94, Rev. 1, provides the following recommendations for implementation:

- Organizations should ensure that all IDPS components are secured appropriately, as IDPSs are a prime target for attackers. If they can compromise the IDPS, they are then free to conduct unobserved attacks on other systems.
- Organizations should consider using multiple types of IDPS technologies to achieve more comprehensive and accurate detection and prevention of malicious activity. Defense in depth, even within IDPS technologies, is key to detecting the wide and varied attack strategies the organization faces.
- Organizations that plan to use multiple types of IDPS technologies or multiple products of the same IDPS technology type should consider whether the IDPSs should be integrated. Using integrated technologies provides much easier configuration and administration. Using a common management platform provides multidevice cross-assessments and reporting.
- Before evaluating IDPS products, organizations should define the requirements that the products should meet. Knowing what you need in an IDPS can prevent purchasing a product that does not solve the organization's problems, and can save time and money in the long haul.
- When evaluating IDPS products, organizations should consider using a combination of data sources to evaluate the products' characteristics and capabilities. Vendors have been known to "influence" reviews by using friendly reviewers or just writing their own and posting them to review sites. Finding multiple reviews from different sources should provide more accurate insight into the strengths and weaknesses of any technology.[18]

IDPS Control Strategies

A *control strategy* determines how an organization supervises and maintains the configuration of an IDPS. It also determines how the input and output of the IDPS are managed. The three common control strategies for an IDPS are *centralized, partially distributed*, and *fully distributed*. The IT industry has been exploring technologies and practices to enable the distribution of computer processing cycles and data storage for many years. These explorations have long considered the advantages and disadvantages of the centralized strategy versus strategies with varying degrees of distribution. In the early days of computing, all systems were fully centralized, resulting in a control strategy that provided high levels of security and control as well as efficiencies in resource allocation and management. During the 1980s and 1990s, with the rapid growth in networking and computing capabilities, the trend was to implement a fully distributed strategy. In the mid-1990s, however, the high costs of a fully distributed architecture became apparent, and the IT industry shifted toward a mixed strategy of partially distributed control. A strategy of partial distribution, in which some features and components are distributed and others are centrally controlled, has emerged as the recommended practice for IT systems in general and for IDPS control systems in particular.

Centralized Control Strategy   In a **centralized IDPS control strategy**, all IDPS control functions are implemented and managed in a central location, as represented in Figure 9-8 by the large square symbol labeled "IDS Console." The IDPS console includes the management software, which collects information from the remote sensors (the triangular symbols in the figure), analyzes the systems or networks, and

centralized IDPS control strategy

An IDPS implementation approach in which all control functions are managed in a central location.

determines whether the current situation has deviated from the preconfigured baseline. All reporting features are implemented and managed from this central location.

The primary advantages of this strategy are cost and control. With one central implementation, there is one management system, one place to monitor the status of the systems or networks, one location for reports, and one staff to perform needed administrative tasks. This centralization of IDPS management supports task specialization because all managers either are located near the IDPS management console or can acquire an authenticated remote connection to it, and technicians are located near the remote sensors. This means that each person can focus on an assigned task. In addition, the central control group can evaluate the systems and networks as a whole, and because it can compare pieces of information from all sensors, the group is better positioned to recognize a large-scale attack.

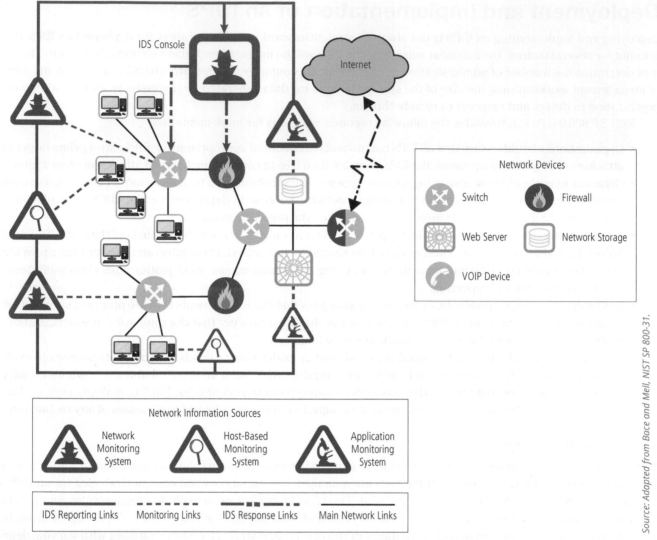

Figure 9-8   Centralized IDPS control[19]

Source: Adapted from Bace and Mell, NIST SP 800-31.

fully distributed IDPS control strategy

An IDPS implementation approach in which all control functions are applied at the physical location of each IDPS component.

partially distributed IDPS control strategy

An IDPS implementation approach that combines the best aspects of the centralized and fully distributed strategies.

Fully Distributed Control Strategy   A **fully distributed IDPS control strategy**, illustrated in Figure 9-9, is the opposite of the centralized strategy. All control functions are applied at the physical location of each IDPS component; in the figure, these functions are represented as small square symbols enclosing a computer icon. Each monitoring site uses its own paired sensors to perform its own control functions and achieve the necessary detection, reaction, and response. Thus, each sensor/ agent is best configured to deal with its own environment. Because the IDPSs do not have to wait for a response from a centralized control facility, their response time to individual attacks is greatly enhanced.

Partially Distributed Control Strategy   A **partially distributed IDPS control strategy**, depicted in Figure 9-10, combines the best aspects of the other two strategies. While the individual agents can still analyze and respond to local threats, their reporting to a hierarchical central facility enables the organization to detect widespread attacks. This blended approach to reporting is one of the more effective methods of detecting intelligent attackers, especially those who probe an organization at multiple points of entry, trying to identify the systems' configurations and weaknesses before launching a concerted attack. The partially distributed control strategy also allows the organization to optimize for economy of scale in the implementation of key management software and personnel, especially in the reporting areas. When the organization can create a pool of security managers to evaluate reports from multiple distributed IDPS systems, it becomes more capable of detecting distributed attacks before they become unmanageable.

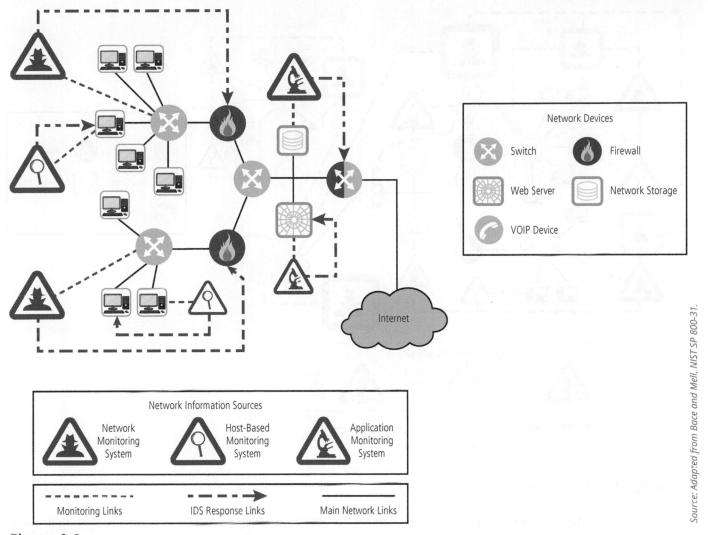

Source: Adapted from Bace and Mell, NIST SP 800-31.

Figure 9-9   Fully distributed IDPS control[20]

IDPS Deployment

Given the highly technical skills required to implement and configure IDPSs and the imperfection of the technology, great care must be taken when deciding where to locate the components, both in their physical connection to the network and host devices and in how they are logically connected to each other. Because IDPSs are designed to detect, report, and even react to anomalous stimuli, placing IDPSs in an area where such traffic is common can result in excessive reporting. Moreover, locating the administrators' monitoring systems in such areas can desensitize them to the information flow and cause them to miss actual attacks in progress.

As an organization selects an IDPS and prepares for implementation, planners must select a deployment strategy that is based on a careful analysis of the organization's information security requirements and that integrates with the existing IT infrastructure while causing minimal impact. After all, the purpose of the IDPS is to detect anomalous situations, not create them. One consideration is the skill level of the personnel who install, configure, and maintain the systems. An IDPS is a complex system in that it involves numerous remote monitoring agents both on individual systems and networks, which require proper configuration to gain the needed authentication and authorization. As the IDPS is deployed, each component should be installed, configured, fine-tuned, tested, and monitored. A mistake in any step of the deployment process may produce a range of problems—from a minor inconvenience to a network-wide disaster. Thus, the people who install the IDPS and the people who use and manage the system require proper training.

NIDPSs and HIDPSs can be used in tandem to cover the individual systems that connect to an organization's networks and the networks themselves. It is important to use a phased implementation strategy so the entire organization isn't affected at once. A phased implementation strategy also allows security technicians to resolve problems that arise without compromising the very information security the IDPS is installed to protect. When sequencing the

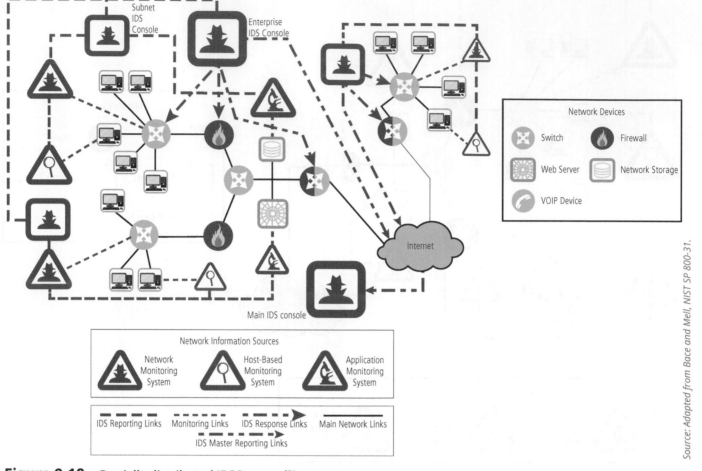

Source: Adapted from Bace and Mell, NIST SP 800-31.

Figure 9-10 Partially distributed IDPS control[21]

implementation, the organization should first implement the NIDPSs, as they are easier to configure than their host-based counterparts. After the NIDPSs are configured and running without problems, the HIDPSs can be installed to protect the critical systems on the host server. Once the NIDPSs and HIDPSs are working, administrators should scan the network with a vulnerability scanner like Nmap or Nessus to determine if it picks up anything new or unusual and to see if the IDPS can detect the scans.

Deploying Network-Based IDPSs   The placement of the sensor agents is critical to the operation of all IDPSs, but especially for NIDPSs. NIST recommends the following four locations for NIDPS sensors, as illustrated in Figure 9-11.

Location 1 is behind each external firewall, in the network DMZ. This location has the following characteristics:

- The IDPS sees attacks that originate from the outside and may penetrate the network's perimeter defenses.
- The IDPS can identify problems with the network firewall's policy or performance.
- The IDPS sees attacks that might target the Web server or FTP server, both of which commonly reside in this DMZ.
- Even if the incoming attack is not detected, the IDPS can sometimes recognize patterns in the outgoing traffic that suggest the server has been compromised.

Location 2 is outside an external firewall. This location has the following characteristics:

- The IDPS documents the number of attacks originating on the Internet that target the network.
- The IDPS documents the types of attacks originating on the Internet that target the network.

Location 3 is on major network backbones. This location has the following characteristics:

- The IDPS monitors a large amount of a network's traffic, thus increasing its chances of spotting attacks.
- The IDPS detects unauthorized activity by authorized users within the organization's security perimeter.

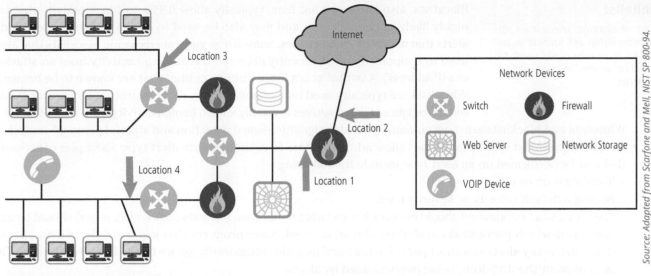

Figure 9-11   Network IDPS sensor locations[22]

Location 4 is on critical subnets. This location has the following characteristics:

- The IDPS detects attacks that target critical systems and resources.
- This location allows organizations with limited resources to focus on the most valuable network assets.[23]

Deploying Host-Based IDPSs   The proper implementation of HIDPSs can be a painstaking and time-consuming task, as each HIDPS must be customized to its host systems. Deployment begins with implementing the most critical systems first. This poses a dilemma for the deployment team because the first systems to be implemented are mission-critical, and any problems with the installation could be catastrophic to the organization. Thus, it may be beneficial to practice an implementation on one or more test servers configured on a network segment that resembles the mission-critical systems. Practice helps the installation team gain experience and helps determine if the installation might trigger any unusual events. Gaining an edge on the learning curve by training on nonproduction systems benefits the overall deployment process by reducing the risk of unforeseen complications.

Installation continues until all systems are installed or the organization reaches the planned degree of coverage it will accept, in terms of the number of systems or percentage of network traffic. To provide ease of management, control, and reporting, each HIDPS should be configured to interact with a central management console.

Just as technicians can install the HIDPS in offline systems to develop expertise and identify potential problems, users and managers can learn about the operation of the HIDPS by using a test facility. This facility could use the offline systems configured by technicians and be connected to the organization's backbone to allow the HIDPS to process actual network traffic. This setup will also enable technicians to create a baseline of normal traffic for the organization. During system testing, training scenarios can be developed that enable users to recognize and respond to common attacks. To ensure effective and efficient operation, the management team can establish policy for the operation and monitoring of the HIDPS.

Measuring the Effectiveness of IDPSs

When selecting an IDPS, an organization typically examines the following four measures of comparative effectiveness:

- *Thresholds*—A **threshold** is a value that usually specifies a maximum acceptable level, such as *x* failed connection attempts in 60 seconds or *x* characters for a filename length. Thresholds are most often used for anomaly-based detection and stateful protocol analysis.
- *Blacklists and whitelists*—A **blacklist** is used to document hosts, TCP or UDP port numbers, ICMP types and codes, applications, usernames, URLs, filenames, or file extensions that have been associated with malicious activity.

threshold

A value that sets the limit between normal and abnormal behavior. See also *clipping level*.

blacklist

A list of systems, users, files, or addresses that have been associated with malicious activity; it is commonly used to block those entities from systems or network access.

Source: Adapted from Scarfone and Mell, NIST SP 800-94.

whitelist

A list of systems, users, files, or addresses that are known to be benign; it is commonly used to expedite access to systems or networks.

Blacklists, also known as hot lists, typically allow IDPSs to block activity that is highly likely to be malicious, and may also be used to assign a higher priority to alerts that match blacklist entries. Some IDPSs generate dynamic blacklists that are used to temporarily block recently detected threats (e.g., activity from an attacker's IP address). A **whitelist** is a list of discrete entities that are known to be benign. Whitelists are typically used on a granular basis, such as protocol by protocol, to reduce or ignore false positives involving known benign activity from trusted hosts.

Whitelists and blacklists are most commonly used in signature-based detection and stateful protocol analysis.

- *Alert settings*—Most IDPS technologies allow administrators to customize each alert type. Examples of actions that can be performed on an alert type include the following:
  - Toggling it on or off
  - Setting a default priority or severity level
  - Specifying what information should be recorded and what notification methods (e.g., e-mail, pager) should be used
  - Specifying which prevention capabilities should be used. Some products also suppress alerts if an attacker generates many alerts in a short period of time and may also temporarily ignore traffic from the attacker. This is to prevent the IDPS from being overwhelmed by alerts.
- *Code viewing and editing*—Some IDPS technologies permit administrators to see some or all of the detection-related code. This is usually limited to signatures, but some technologies allow administrators to see additional code, such as programs used to perform stateful protocol analysis.[24]

Once implemented, IDPSs are evaluated using two dominant metrics. First, administrators evaluate the number of attacks detected in a known collection of probes. Second, the administrators examine the level of use at which the IDPSs fail; this level is commonly measured in megabits per second of network traffic. An evaluation of an IDPS might read something like this: *At 1 Gbps, the IDPS was able to detect 99.84 percent of directed attacks.* This is a dramatic change from the previous method used for assessing IDPS effectiveness, which was based on the total number of signatures the system was currently running—somewhat of a "more is better" approach. This evaluation method was flawed for several reasons. Not all IDPSs use simple signature-based detection, and some systems use the almost infinite combination of network performance characteristics in anomaly-based detection to identify a potential attack. Also, some sophisticated signature-based systems actually use *fewer* signatures or rules than older, simpler versions—in direct contrast to traditional signature-based assessments, these systems suggest that less may actually be more. Recognizing that the size of the signature base is an insufficient measure of an IDPS's effectiveness led to the development of stress test measurements for evaluating its performance. These measurements only work, however, if the administrator has a collection of known negative and positive actions that can be proven to elicit a desired response. Because developing this collection can be tedious, most IDPS vendors provide testing mechanisms to verify that their systems are performing as expected. Some of these testing processes enable the administrator to do the following:

- Record and retransmit packets from a real virus or worm scan.
- Record and retransmit packets from a real virus or worm scan with incomplete TCP/IP session connections (missing SYN packets).
- Conduct a real virus or worm attack against a hardened or sacrificial system.

This last measure is important because future IDPSs will probably include much more detailed information about the overall site configuration. According to an expert in the field, "It may be necessary for the IDPSs to be able to actively probe a potentially vulnerable machine, in order to either preload its configuration with correct information or perform a retroactive assessment. An IDPS that performed some kind of actual system assessment would be a complete failure in today's generic testing labs, which focus on replaying attacks and scans against nonexistent machines."[25]

With the rapid growth in technology, each new generation of IDPSs will require new testing methodologies. However, the measured values that continue to hold interest for IDPS administrators and managers will most certainly include some assessment of how much traffic the IDPS can handle, the numbers of false positives and false negatives it generates, and a measure of the IDPS's ability to detect actual attacks. Vendors of IDPS systems could also include a report of alarms sent and the relative accuracy of the system in correctly matching the alarm level to the true seriousness of the threat. Some planned metrics for IDPSs include the flexibility of signatures and detection policy customization.

IDPS administrators may soon be able to purchase tools that test IDPS effectiveness. Until these tools are available from a neutral third party, however, the diagnostics from IDPS vendors will always be suspect. No vendor, no matter how reliable, would provide a test that its system would fail.

One note of caution: There is a strong tendency among IDPS administrators to use common vulnerability assessment tools, such as Nmap or Nessus, to evaluate the capabilities of an IDPS. While this may seem like a good idea, the tools will not work as expected because most IDPS systems are equipped to recognize the differences between a locally implemented vulnerability assessment tool and a true attack.

To accurately assess the effectiveness of IDPS systems, the testing process should be as realistic as possible in its simulation of an actual event. This means coupling realistic traffic loads with realistic levels of attacks. You cannot expect an IDPS to respond to a few packet probes as if they represent a DoS attack. In one reported example, a program was used to create a synthetic load of network traffic made up of many TCP sessions, with each session consisting of a SYN (synchronization) packet, a series of data, and ACK (acknowledgment) packets, but no FIN or connection termination packets. Of the several IDPS systems tested, one of them crashed due to lack of resources while it waited for the sessions to be closed. Another IDPS passed the test with flying colors because it did not perform state tracking on the connections. Neither of the tested IDPS systems worked as expected, but the one that didn't perform state tracking was able to remain working and therefore received a better score on the test.[26]

Honeypots, Honeynets, And Padded Cell Systems

A class of powerful security tools that go beyond routine intrusion detection are known as honeypots or padded cell systems. To understand why these tools are not yet widely used, you must first understand how they differ from a traditional IDPS.

Honeypots are decoy systems designed to lure potential attackers away from critical systems. In the industry, these systems are also known as decoys, lures, and flytraps. When several honeypot systems are connected together on a network segment, they may be called a **honeypot farm** or **honeynet**. A honeypot system or honeynet subnetwork contains pseudo-services that emulate well-known services, but it is configured in ways that make it look vulnerable to attacks. This combination is meant to lure attackers into revealing themselves—the idea is that once organizations have detected these attackers, they can better defend their networks against future attacks that target real assets. In sum, honeypots are designed to do the following:

- Divert an attacker from critical systems.
- Collect information about the attacker's activity.
- Encourage the attacker to stay on the system long enough for administrators to document the event and perhaps respond.

Because the information in a honeypot appears to be valuable, any unauthorized access to it constitutes suspicious activity. Honeypots are outfitted with sensitive monitors and event loggers that detect attempts to access the system and collect information about the potential attacker's activities. A simple IDPS that specializes in honeypot techniques is called Deception Toolkit; Figure 9-12 shows the configuration of this honeypot as it waits for an attack.

Even smaller than the honeypot is the **honeytoken**, which is a single service, record, or file placed in a production system. If a honeytoken attracts attention, it is from unauthorized access and will trigger a notification or response. An example would be a bogus record placed in a database and monitored by the system. If the record is accessed, it is an indicator of unwanted activity. Another example is the small antitheft tag that bookstores put into many of their books. If someone takes a book and leaves the shop without paying (and the antitheft tag resets), an alarm sounds.

A hardened honeypot, or **padded cell system**, operates in tandem with a traditional IDPS. After attracting attackers with tempting data, the IDPS detects the attackers, and then the padded cell system seamlessly transfers them to a special simulated environment where they can cause no harm—hence the name *padded cell*. As in honeypots, this environment can be filled with interesting data, which can convince an intruder that the attack is going according to plan. Like honeypots, padded cells are well instrumented and offer unique opportunities for a target organization

honeypot

An application that entices people who are illegally perusing the internal areas of a network by providing simulated rich content while the software notifies the administrator of the intrusion.

honeypot farm

See *honeynet*.

honeynet

A monitored network or network segment that contains multiple honeypot systems.

honeytoken

Any system resource that is placed in a functional system but has no normal use in the system, and that instead serves as a decoy and alarm, similar to a honeypot.

padded cell system

A protected honeypot that cannot be easily compromised.

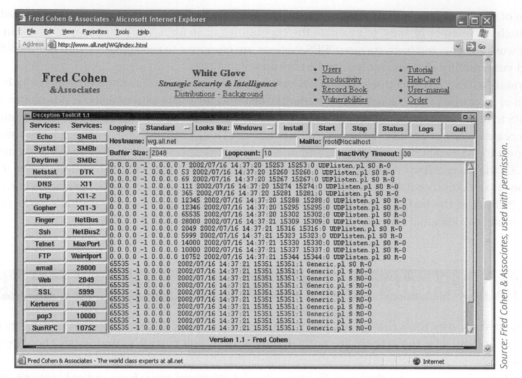

Source: Fred Cohen & Associates, used with permission.

Figure 9-12 Deception Toolkit

to monitor the actions of an attacker. IDPS researchers have used padded cell and honeypot systems since the late 1980s, but until recently, no commercial versions of these products were available. It is important to seek guidance from legal counsel before using either of these systems in your operating environment—using an attractant and then launching a back hack or counterstrike might be illegal in some areas, and could make the organization vulnerable to a lawsuit or criminal complaint.

The advantages and disadvantages of using honeypots or the padded cell approach are summarized in Table 9-1.

Trap-and-Trace Systems

trap-and-trace application

An application that combines the function of honeypots or honeynets with the capability to track the attacker back through the network.

Trap-and-trace applications, which are an extension of the attractant technologies discussed in the previous section, are still in use. These systems use a combination of techniques to detect an intrusion and then trace it back to its source. The trap usually consists of a honeypot or padded cell and an alarm. While the intruders are distracted (or trapped) by what they perceive to be successful intrusions, the system notifies the administrator of their presence. The trace feature is an extension of the

Table 9-1 Advantages and disadvantages of using honeypots or padded cell systems[27]

Advantages	Disadvantages
Attackers can be diverted to targets that they cannot damage.	The legal implications of using such devices are not well understood.
Administrators have time to decide how to respond to an attacker.	Honeypots and padded cells have not yet been shown to be generally useful security technologies.
Attackers' actions can be easily and more extensively monitored, and the records can be used to refine threat models and improve system protections.	An expert attacker, once diverted into a decoy system, may become angry and launch a more aggressive attack against an organization's systems.
Honeypots may be effective at catching insiders who are snooping around a network.	Administrators and security managers need a high level of expertise to use these systems.

honeypot or padded cell approach. The trace—which is similar to caller ID—is a process by which the organization attempts to identify an entity discovered in unauthorized areas of the network or systems. If the intruder is someone inside the organization, administrators are completely within their power to track the person and turn the case over to internal or external authorities. If the intruder is outside the organization's security perimeter, numerous legal issues arise. Products in this genre were initially popular in the early 2000s but quickly ran into legal issues when used outside the boundaries of the organization. No commercial products have taken their place due to the drawbacks and complications of using these technologies. However, similar applications are used by common carriers in conjunction with law enforcement to allow legal tracing of computer communications as part of investigations.

Trap-and-trace systems are similar to **pen registers**, earlier versions of which recorded numbers that were dialed in voice communications. Older pen registers were much like key loggers for phones, but more current models and trap-and-trace systems are used in data networks as well as voice communications networks. According to the Electronic Frontier Foundation, trap-and-trace systems record attributes of inbound communications such as phone numbers or IP addresses, while pen registers are used frequently in law enforcement and antiterrorism operations to record attributes of outbound communications.[28]

> **pen register**
>
> An application that records information about outbound communications.

On the surface, trap-and-trace systems seem like an ideal solution. Security is no longer limited to defense; security administrators can now go on the offensive to track down perpetrators and turn them over to the appropriate authorities. Under the guise of justice, less scrupulous administrators may even be tempted to **back hack**, or break into a hacker's system to find out as much as possible about the hacker. Vigilante justice would be an appropriate term for these activities, which are deemed unethical by most codes of professional conduct. In tracking the hacker, administrators may end up wandering through other organizations' systems, especially if a more wily hacker has used IP spoofing, compromised systems, or other techniques to throw trackers off the trail. In other words, the back-hacking administrator becomes the hacker.

> **back hack**
>
> The process of illegally attempting to determine the source of an intrusion by tracing it and trying to gain access to the originating system.

Trap-and-trace systems and pen registers are covered under Title 18, U.S. Code Module 206, §3121, which essentially states that you can't use them unless you're a service provider attempting to prevent misuse and (1) they are used for systems maintenance and testing, (2) they are used to track connections, or (3) you have permission from the user of the service.[29]

There are more legal drawbacks to trap and trace. The trap portion frequently involves honeypots or honeynets; when using them, administrators should be careful not to cross the line between **enticement** and **entrapment**. Enticement is legal and ethical, but entrapment is not. It is difficult to gauge the effect of such a system on average users, especially if they have been nudged into looking at the information in the system. Administrators should also be wary of the *wasp trap syndrome*, which describes a homeowner who installs a wasp trap in his backyard to trap the insects he sees flying about. Because these traps use scented bait, however, they wind up attracting far more wasps than were originally present. Security administrators should keep the wasp trap syndrome in mind before implementing honeypots, honeynets, padded cells, or trap-and-trace systems.

> **enticement**
>
> The act of attracting attention to a system by placing tantalizing information in key locations.

> **entrapment**
>
> The act of luring a person into committing a crime in order to get a conviction.

Active Intrusion Prevention

Some organizations want to do more than simply wait for the next attack, so they implement active countermeasures. One tool that provides active intrusion prevention is known as LaBrea. This "sticky" honeypot and IDPS works by taking up the unused IP address space within a network. When LaBrea notes an address resolution protocol (ARP) request, it checks to see if the requested IP address is valid on the network. If the address is not being used by a real computer or network device, LaBrea pretends to be a computer at that IP address and allows the attacker to complete the TCP/IP connection request, known as the three-way handshake. Once the handshake is complete, LaBrea changes the TCP sliding window size to a low number to hold open the attacker's TCP connection for hours or even days. Holding the connection open but inactive greatly slows down network-based worms and other attacks. It also gives LaBrea time to notify system and network administrators about anomalous behavior on the network.

For more information on LaBrea, visit its Web page at *https://labrea.sourceforge.io/labrea-info.html*.

Scanning And Analysis Tools

To secure a network, someone in the organization must know exactly where the network needs to be secured. Although this step may sound simple and obvious, many companies skip it. They install a perimeter firewall and then relax, lulled into a sense of security by this single layer of defense. To truly assess the risks within a computing environment, you must deploy technical controls using a strategy of defense in depth, which is likely to include IDPSs, active vulnerability scanners, passive vulnerability scanners, automated log analyzers, and protocol analyzers (commonly referred to as sniffers). As you've learned, an IDPS helps to secure networks by detecting intrusions; the remaining items in the preceding list help administrators identify where the network needs securing. More specifically, scanner and analysis tools can find vulnerabilities in systems, holes in security components, and unsecured aspects of the network.

Although some information security experts may not perceive them as defensive tools, scanners, sniffers, and other vulnerability analysis applications can be invaluable because they enable administrators to see what the attacker sees. Some of these tools are extremely complex, and others are rather simple. Some tools are expensive commercial products, but many of the best scanning and analysis tools are developed by the hacker community or open-source project teams and are available for free on the Web. Good administrators should have several hacking Web sites bookmarked and should try to keep up with chat room discussions on new vulnerabilities, recent conquests, and favorite assault techniques. Security administrators are well within their rights to use tools that potential attackers use in order to examine network defenses and find areas that require additional attention.

In the military, there is a long and distinguished history of generals inspecting the troops under their command before battle. In a similar way, security administrators can use vulnerability analysis tools to inspect the computers and network devices under their supervision. A word of caution, though: Many of these scanning and analysis tools have distinct signatures, and some Internet service providers (ISPs) scan for these signatures. If the ISP discovers someone using hacker tools, it can revoke that user's access privileges. Therefore, organizational administrators are advised to establish a working relationship with their ISPs and notify them of any plans that could lead to misunderstandings. Amateur users are advised not to use these tools on the Internet.

attack protocol

A logical sequence of steps or processes used by an attacker to launch an attack against a target system or network.

footprinting

The organized research and investigation of Internet addresses owned or controlled by a target organization.

Scanning tools are typically used as part of an **attack protocol** to collect information that an attacker needs to launch a successful attack. The process of collecting publicly available information about a potential target is known as **footprinting**. The attacker uses public Internet data sources to perform keyword searches that identify the network addresses of an organization. This research is augmented by browsing the organization's Web pages. Web pages usually contain information about internal systems, the people who develop the Web pages, and other tidbits that can be used for social engineering attacks. For example, the *view source* option on most popular Web browsers allows users to see the source code behind the graphics. Details in the source code of the Web page can provide clues to potential attackers and give them insight into the configuration of an internal network, such as the locations and directories for Common Gateway Interface (CGI) script bins and the names or addresses of computers and servers.

In addition, public business Web sites such as those for Forbes or Yahoo! Business often reveal information about their company structure, commonly used company names, and other details that attackers find useful. Furthermore, common search engines allow attackers to query for any site that links to their proposed target. By doing a bit of initial Internet research, an attacker can often find additional Internet locations that are not commonly associated with the company—that is, business-to-business (B2B) partners and subsidiaries. Armed with this information, the attacker can find the "weakest link" into the target network.

For example, consider a company that has a large data center in Atlanta. The data center has been secured, so an attacker will have a difficult time breaking into it via the Internet. However, the attacker has run a "link" query on a search engine and found a small Web server that links to the company's main Web server. After further investigation, the attacker learns that the server was set up by an administrator at a remote facility that has an

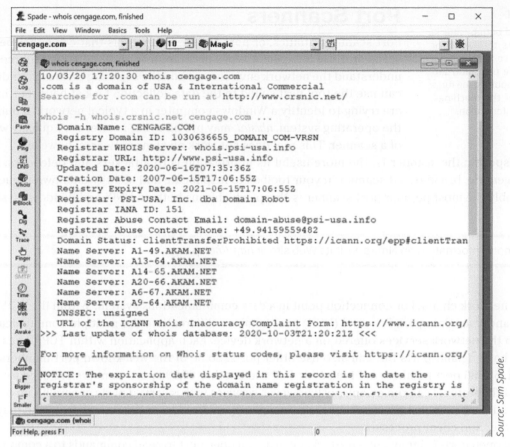

Source: Sam Spade.

Figure 9-13   Sam Spade

unrestricted internal link into the company's corporate data center. The attacker can attack the weaker site at the remote facility and use the compromised internal network to attack the true target. While it may seem trite or cliché, the old saying that "a chain is only as strong as its weakest link" is very relevant to network and computer security. If a company has a trusted network connection with 15 business partners, one weak business partner can compromise all 16 networks.

To assist in footprint intelligence collection, you can use an enhanced Web scanner that examines entire Web sites for valuable pieces of information, such as server names and e-mail addresses. One such scanner is called Sam Spade (see Figure 9-13), which you can obtain by searching the Web for a copy of the last version (1.14). Although antiquated, Sam Spade can perform a host of scans and probes, such as sending multiple ICMP information requests (pings), attempting to retrieve multiple and cross-zoned DNS queries, and performing network analysis queries known as traceroutes from the commonly used UNIX command. All of these scans are powerful diagnostic and hacking activities, but Sam Spade is not considered *hackerware* (hacker-oriented software). Rather, it is a utility that is useful to network administrators and miscreants alike.

For Linux or BSD systems, a tool called GNU Wget allows a remote user to "mirror" entire Web sites. With this tool, attackers can copy an entire Web site and then go through the source HTML, JavaScript, and Web-based forms at their leisure, collecting and collating all of the data from the source code that will help them mount an attack.

The next phase of the attack protocol is a data-gathering process called **fingerprinting**. Fingerprinting deploys various tools that are described in the following sections to reveal useful information about the internal structure and nature of the target system or network to be attacked. These tools were created to find vulnerabilities in systems and networks quickly and with a minimum of effort. They are valuable to the network defender because they can quickly pinpoint parts of the systems or network that need prompt repair to close vulnerabilities.

fingerprinting

The systematic survey of a targeted organization's Internet addresses collected during the footprinting phase to identify the network services offered by the hosts in that range.

port scanner

A type of tool used both by attackers and defenders to identify or fingerprint active computers on a network, the active ports and services on those computers, the functions and roles of the machines, and other useful information.

Port Scanners

Port scanning utilities, or **port scanners**, are tools that can either perform generic scans or those for specific types of computers, protocols, or resources. You need to understand the network environment and the scanning tools at your disposal so you can use the tool best suited to the data collection task at hand. For instance, if you are trying to identify a Windows computer in a typical network, a built-in feature of the operating system, *nbtstat*, may provide your answer very quickly without the use of a scanner. This tool does not work on some networks, however.

The more specific the scanner is, the more useful its information is to attackers and defenders. However, you should keep a generic, broad-based scanner in your toolbox to help locate and identify unknown rogue nodes on the network. Probably the most popular port scanner is Nmap, which runs both on UNIX and Windows systems.

 For more information on Nmap, visit its Web site at *http://nmap.org*.

A port is a network channel or connection point in a data communications system. Within the TCP/IP networking protocol, TCP and User Datagram Protocol (UDP) port numbers differentiate the multiple communication channels that connect to the network services offered on a network device. Each application within TCP/IP has a unique port number. Some have default ports but can also use other ports. Some of the well-known port numbers are shown in Table 9-2. In all, 65,536 port numbers are in use for TCP and another 65,536 port numbers are used for UDP. Services that use the TCP/IP protocol can run on any port; however, services with reserved ports generally run on ports 1–1023. Port 0 is not used. Port numbers greater than 1023 are typically referred to as ephemeral ports and may be randomly allocated to server and client processes.

Why secure open ports? Simply put, an attacker can use an open port to send commands to a computer, potentially gain access to a server, and possibly exert control over a networking device. As a rule of thumb, any port that is not absolutely necessary for conducting business should be secured or removed from service. For example, if a business doesn't host Web services, there is no need for port 80 to be available on its servers.

attack surface

The functions and features that a system exposes to unauthenticated users.

The number and nature of the open ports on a system are an important part of its **attack surface**. As a general design goal, security practitioners seek to reduce the attack surface of each system to minimize the potential for latent defects and unintended consequences to cause losses.

At this point, we must caution that some activities performed routinely by security professionals—specifically, port scanning—may cause problems for casual system users. Even the use of the network ping command can cause issues at some organizations. Some organizations have strong policy prohibitions for activities that test network security. Many endpoint protection products trigger

Table 9-2   Commonly Used Port Numbers

Port Number	Protocol
7	Echo
20	File Transfer [Default Data] (FTP)
21	File Transfer [Control] (FTP)
23	Telnet
25	Simple Mail Transfer Protocol (SMTP)
53	Domain Name System (DNS)
80	Hypertext Transfer Protocol (HTTP)
110	Post Office Protocol version 3 (POP3)
161	Simple Network Management Protocol (SNMP)

alarms when these activities are detected. Always ask permission from the organization's security office before "testing" network security.

Firewall Analysis Tools

Understanding exactly where an organization's firewall is located and the functions of its existing rule sets are very important steps for any security administrator. Several tools automate the remote discovery of firewall rules and assist the administrator (or attacker) in analyzing the rules to determine what they allow and reject.

The Nmap tool mentioned earlier has some advanced options that are useful for firewall analysis. For example, the option called *idle scanning*, which is run with the -I switch, allows the Nmap user to bounce a scan across a firewall by using one of the idle DMZ hosts as the initiator of the scan. More specifically, most operating systems do not use truly random IP packet identification numbers (IP IDs), so if the DMZ has multiple hosts and one of them uses nonrandom IP IDs, the attacker can query the server and obtain the currently used IP ID as well as the known algorithm for incrementing IP IDs. The attacker can then spoof a packet that is allegedly from the queried server and destined for an internal IP address behind the firewall. If the port is open on the internal machine, the machine replies to the server with a SYN-ACK packet, which forces the server to respond with a TCP RESET packet. In its response, the server increments its IP ID number. The attacker can now query the server again to see if the IP ID has incremented. If it has, the attacker knows that the internal machine is alive and has the queried service port open. In a nutshell, running the Nmap idle scan allows attackers to scan an internal network as if they were on a trusted machine inside the DMZ.

Firewalk is another tool that can be used to analyze firewalls. Written by noted network security experts Mike Schiffman and David Goldsmith, Firewalk uses incrementing Time-To-Live (TTL) packets to determine the path into a network as well as the default firewall policy. Running Firewalk against a target machine reveals where routers and firewalls are filtering traffic to the target host.

We must again caution that many tools used by security professionals may cause problems for casual system users. Some organizations have strong policy prohibitions against any form of hackerware, and even possessing the files needed to install it or having results from its use may be a violation that carries grave consequences. Many endpoint protection products trigger alarms for these types of tools. Always ask permission from the organization's security office before using any tools of this nature.

 For more information on Firewall, read Goldsmith and Schiffman's article at *http://packetfactory.openwall.net/projects/firewalk/firewalk-final.pdf*. Firewalk can be obtained from *https://packetstormsecurity.com/UNIX/audit/firewalk*.

A final firewall analysis tool worth consideration is HPING (*www.hping.org*), which is a modified ping client. It supports multiple protocols and has a command-line method of specifying nearly any ping parameter. For instance, you can use HPING with modified TTL values to determine the infrastructure of a DMZ. You can use HPING with specific ICMP flags to bypass poorly configured firewalls that allow all ICMP traffic to pass through and find internal systems.

Administrators who are wary of using the same tools that attackers use should remember two important points. Regardless of the tool that is used to validate or analyze a firewall's configuration, user intent dictates how the gathered information is used. To defend a computer or network well, administrators must understand the ways it can be attacked. Thus, a tool that can help close an open or poorly configured firewall will help the network defender minimize the risk from attack.

Operating System Detection Tools

The ability to detect a target computer's operating system is very valuable to an attacker. Once the OS is known, the attacker can easily determine all of the vulnerabilities to which it is susceptible. Many tools use networking protocols to determine a remote computer's OS.

One such tool is XProbe, which uses ICMP to determine the remote OS. When run, XProbe sends many different ICMP queries to the target host. As reply packets are received, XProbe matches these responses from the target's TCP/

IP stack with its own internal database of known responses. Because most OSs have a unique way of responding to ICMP requests, XProbe is very reliable in finding matches and thus detecting the operating systems of remote computers. Therefore, system and network administrators should restrict the use of ICMP through their organization's firewalls and, when possible, within their internal networks.

 For more information on XProbe, visit its Web site at *www.sourceforge.net/projects/xprobe*.

active vulnerability scanner

An application that scans networks to identify exposed usernames and groups, open network shares, configuration problems, and other vulnerabilities in servers.

Vulnerability Scanners

Active vulnerability scanners examine networks for highly detailed information. An active scanner is one that initiates traffic on the network to determine security holes. An example of a vulnerability scanner is Nessus, a professional freeware utility that uses IP packets to identify hosts available on the network, the services (ports) they offer, their operating system and OS version, the type of packet filters and firewalls in use, and dozens of other network characteristics. Figures 9-14 and 9-15 show sample screens from Nessus.

Vulnerability scanners should be proficient at finding known, documented holes, but what happens if a Web server is from a new vendor or a new application was created by an internal development team? In such cases, you should consider using a class of vulnerability scanners called *black-box scanners* or *fuzzers*. Fuzz testing is a straightforward technique that looks for vulnerabilities in a program or protocol by feeding random input to the program or a network running the protocol. Vulnerabilities can be detected by measuring the outcome of the random inputs. One example of a fuzz scanner is Spike, which has two primary components. The first is the Spike Proxy (*www.spikeproxy.com*), which is a full-blown proxy server. As Web site visitors use the proxy, Spike builds a database of each traversed page, form, and other Web-specific asset. When the Web site owner determines that enough history has been collected to completely characterize the full site, Spike can be used to check for bugs. In other words, administrators can use the usage history collected by Spike to traverse all known pages, forms, and active programs such as asp and cgibin, and then can test the system by attempting overflows, SQL injection, cross-site scripting, and many other classes of Web attacks.

Source: Nessus.

Figure 9-14   Tenable's Nessus: summary

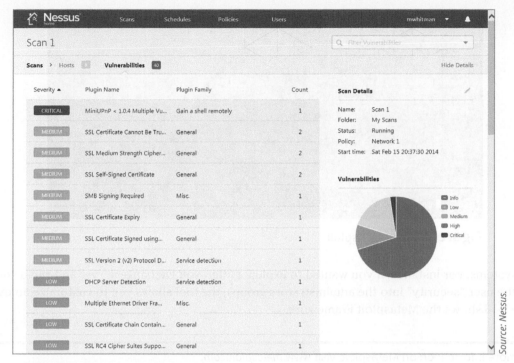

Figure 9-15   Tenable's Nessus: detail

A list of the top commercial and residential vulnerability scanners includes the following products:[30]

- Nessus
- OpenVAS
- Core Impact
- Nexpose
- GFI LanGuard
- QualysGuard
- Microsoft Baseline Security Analyzer (MBSA)
- Retina
- Secunia PSI
- Nipper
- Security Administrator's Integrated Network Tool (SAINT)

The Nessus scanner features a class of attacks called *destructive* attacks. If enabled, Nessus attempts common overflow techniques against a target host. Fuzzers or black-box scanners and Nessus in destructive mode can be very dangerous tools, so they should be used only in a lab environment. In fact, these tools are so powerful that even experienced system defenders are not likely to use them in the most aggressive modes on their production networks. At the time of this writing, the most popular scanners seem to be Nessus, OpenVAS, and Nexpose. The Nessus scanner was originally open source, but it is now strictly commercial. OpenVAS was created as a variant from the last free version of Nessus and is therefore a good open-source alternative. Nexpose offers free and commercial versions.

Members of an organization often require proof that a system is vulnerable to a certain attack. They may require such proof to avoid having system administrators attempt to repair systems that are actually not broken or because they have not yet built a satisfactory relationship with the vulnerability assessment team. In these instances, a class of scanners is available that actually exploits the remote machine and allows the vulnerability analyst (sometimes called a penetration tester) to create an account, modify a Web page, or view data. These tools can be very dangerous and should be used only when absolutely necessary. Three such tools are Core Impact, Immunity's CANVAS, and the Metasploit Framework.

Of these three tools, only the Metasploit Framework is available without a license fee. The Metasploit Framework is a collection of exploits coupled with an interface that allows penetration testers to automate the custom exploitation

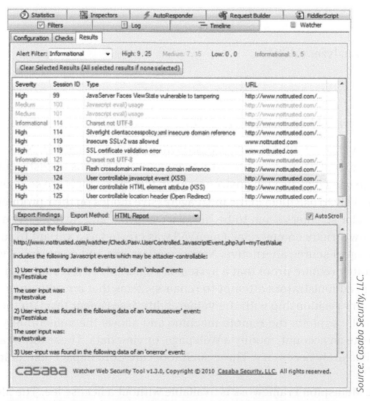

Figure 9-16   Metasploit

Source: Metasploit Framework.

of vulnerable systems. For instance, if you wanted to exploit a Microsoft Exchange server and run a single command (perhaps add the user "security" into the administrators group), the tool allows you to customize an overflow in this manner. Figure 9-16 shows the Metasploit Framework.

 For more information on Metasploit, visit *www.metasploit.com*.

passive vulnerability scanner

A scanner that listens in on a network and identifies vulnerable versions of both server and client software.

A **passive vulnerability scanner** listens in on the network and identifies vulnerable versions of both server and client software. At the time of this writing, two primary vendors offer this type of scanning solution: Tenable Network Security, with its Passive Vulnerability Scanner (PVS), and Watcher Web Security Scanner from Casaba (see Figure 9-17). The advantage of using passive scanners is that they do not require

Figure 9-17   Watcher Web Security Scanner

Source: Casaba Security, LLC.

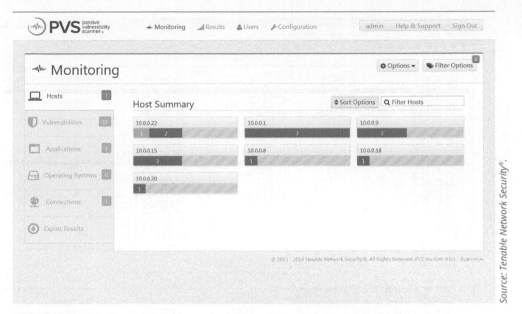

Figure 9-18   Tenable's PVS: host summary

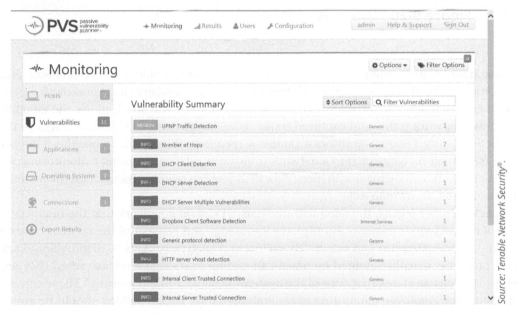

Figure 9-19   Tenable's PVS: vulnerability summary

vulnerability analysts to obtain approval prior to testing. These tools simply monitor the network connections to and from a server to obtain a list of vulnerable applications. Furthermore, passive vulnerability scanners can find client-side vulnerabilities that are typically not found by active scanners. For instance, an active scanner operating without domain admin rights would be unable to determine the version of Internet Explorer running on a desktop machine, but a passive scanner could make that determination by observing traffic to and from the client.

Figures 9-18 and 9-19 show Tenable's PVS.

Packet Sniffers

A **packet sniffer** or network protocol analyzer can provide a network administrator with valuable information for diagnosing and resolving networking issues. In the wrong hands, however, a sniffer can be used to eavesdrop on network traffic.

packet sniffer

A software program or hardware appliance that can intercept, copy, and interpret network traffic.

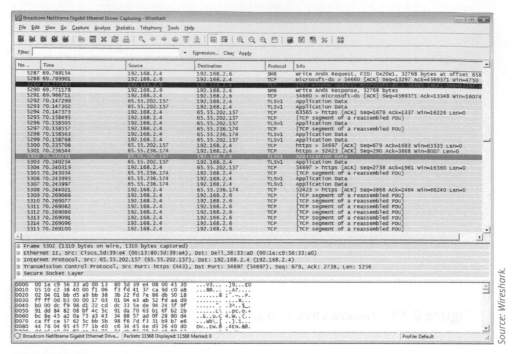

Figure 9-20   Wireshark

Commercial and open-source sniffers are both available—for example, Sniffer is a commercial product and Snort is open-source software. The dominant network protocol analyzer is Wireshark (*www.wireshark.org*), formerly known as Ethereal, which is available in open-source and commercial versions. Wireshark allows the administrator to examine data both from live network traffic and captured traffic. Wireshark's features include a language filter and a TCP session reconstruction utility. Figure 9-20 shows a sample screen from Wireshark. To use these types of programs most effectively, the user must be connected to a network from a central location using a monitoring port. Simply tapping into an Internet connection floods you with more data than you can readily process, and the action technically constitutes a violation of the U.S. Wiretap Act.

To use a packet sniffer legally, the administrator must (1) be on a network that the organization owns, (2) have authorization of the network's owners, and (3) have knowledge and consent of the content creators. If all three conditions are met, the administrator can selectively collect and analyze packets to identify and diagnose problems on the network. Consent is usually obtained by having all system users sign a release when they are issued a user ID and passwords; the release states that "use of the systems is subject to monitoring." These three conditions are the same requirements for employee monitoring in general; therefore, packet sniffing should be construed as a form of employee monitoring.

Many administrators feel safe from sniffer attacks when their computing environment is primarily a switched network, but they couldn't be more wrong. Several open-source sniffers support alternate networking approaches and can enable packet sniffing in a switched network environment. Two of these approaches are ARP spoofing and session hijacking, which use tools like Ettercap (*www.ettercap-project.org/*). To secure data in transit across any network, organizations must use a carefully designed and implemented encryption solution to ensure uncompromised content privacy.

Wireless Security Tools

802.11 wireless networks have sprung up as subnets on nearly all large networks. A wireless connection is convenient, but it has many potential security holes. An organization that spends all of its time securing the wired network while ignoring wireless networks is exposing itself to a security breach. As a security professional, you must assess the risk of wireless networks. A wireless security toolkit should include the ability to sniff wireless traffic, scan wireless hosts, and assess the level of privacy or confidentiality afforded on the wireless network. *Sectools.org* identified the top wireless tools in current use:

- Aircrack, a wireless network protocol cracking tool
- Kismet, a powerful wireless network protocol sniffer, network detector, and IDPS, which works by passively sniffing networks
- NetStumbler, a freeware Windows file parser available at *www.netstumbler.org*
- inSSIDer, an enhanced scanner for Windows, OS X, and Android
- KisMAC, a GUI passive wireless stumbler for Mac OS X (a variation of Kismet)[31]

Another wireless tool, AirSnare (*https://airsnare.en.softonic.com/*), is freeware that can be run on a low-end wireless workstation. AirSnare monitors the airwaves for any new devices or access points. When it finds one, AirSnare sounds an alarm to alert administrators that a new and potentially dangerous wireless apparatus is attempting access on a closed wireless network.

The tools discussed in this module help the attacker and the defender prepare themselves to complete the next steps in the attack protocol: attack, compromise, and exploit. These steps are beyond the scope of this text and are usually covered in more advanced classes on computer and network attack and defense.

 For more information on these and other security tools, visit *Insecure.org*'s security Web site at *sectools.org*. For more information on the site's owner and the author of the Nmap tool, visit Fyodor's page at *insecure.org/fyodor/*.

Closing Scenario

Miller Harrison was still working his way through his attack protocol.

Nmap started as it usually did, by giving the program identification and version number. Then it started reporting back on the first host in the SLS network. It reported all of the open ports on this server. The program moved on to a second host and began reporting back the open ports on that system, too. Once it reached the third host, however, it suddenly stopped.

Miller restarted Nmap, using the last host IP address as the starting point for the next scan. No response. He opened another command window and tried to ping the first host he had just port-scanned. No luck. He tried to ping the SLS firewall. Nothing. He happened to know the IP address for the SLS edge router. He pinged that and got the same result. He had been "blackholed," meaning his IP address had been put on a list of addresses from which the SLS edge router would no longer accept packets. Ironically, the list was his own doing. The IDPS he had been helping SLS configure seemed to be working fine at the moment. His attempt to hack the SLS network was shut down cold.

Discussion Questions

1. Do you think Miller is out of options as he pursues his vendetta? If you think he could take additional actions in his effort to damage the SLS network, what are they?
2. Suppose that a system administrator at SLS read the details of this case. What steps should he or she take to improve the company's information security program?
3. Consider Miller's hacking attempt in light of the intrusion kill chain described earlier and shown in Figure 9-1. At which phase in the kill chain has SLS countered his vendetta?

Ethical Decision Making

It seems obvious that Miller is breaking at least a few laws in his attempt at revenge. Suppose that when his scanning efforts were detected, SLS not only added his IP address to the list of sites banned from connecting to the SLS network, but the system also triggered a response to seek out his computer and delete key files on it to disable his operating system.

1. Would such an action by SLS be ethical? Do you think its action would be legal?
2. Suppose instead that Miller had written a routine to constantly change his assigned IP address to other addresses used by his ISP. If the SLS intrusion system determined what Miller was doing and then added the entire range of ISP addresses to the banned list, thus stopping any user of the ISP from connecting to the SLS network, would SLS's action be ethical?
3. What if SLS were part of an industry consortium that shared IP addresses flagged by its IDPSs, and all companies in the group blocked all of the ISP's users for 10 minutes? These users would be blocked from accessing perhaps hundreds of company networks. Would that be an ethical response by members of the consortium? What if these users were blocked for 24 hours?

Selected Readings

- *Intrusion Detection and Prevention*, by Carl Endorf, Gene Schultz, and Jim Mellander. 2003. McGraw-Hill Osborne Media.
- "Intrusion Detection Systems," by Rebecca Bace and Peter Mell. National Institute of Standards and Technology (NIST) Special Publication 800-31. Available from the archive section of the NIST Computer Security Resource Center at *http://csrc.nist.gov*.
- "Guide to Intrusion Detection and Prevention Systems," by Karen Scarfone and Peter Mell. NIST Special Publication 800-94. Available from the NIST Computer Security Resource Center at *http://csrc.nist.gov*.

Module Summary

- Intrusion detection systems (IDSs) identify potential intrusions and sound an alarm. The more recently developed intrusion detection and prevention systems (IDPSs) also detect intrusions and can take action to defend the network.
- An IDPS works like a burglar alarm by detecting network traffic that violates the system's configured rules and activating an alarm.
- A network-based IDPS (NIDPS) monitors network traffic and then notifies the appropriate administrator when a predefined event occurs. A host-based IDPS (HIDPS) resides on a particular computer or server and monitors activity on that system.
- Signature-based IDPSs, also known as knowledge-based IDPSs, examine data traffic for patterns that match signatures—preconfigured, predetermined attack patterns. Anomaly-based IDPSs, also known as behavior-based IDPSs, collect data from normal traffic and establish a baseline. When an activity is found to be outside the baseline parameters (or clipping level), these IDPSs activate an alarm to notify the administrator.
- Selecting IDPS products that best fit an organization's needs is a challenging and complex process. A wide array of products and vendors are available, each with different approaches and capabilities.
- Deploying and implementing IDPS technology is a complex undertaking that requires knowledge and experience. After deployment, each organization should measure the effectiveness of its IDPS and then continue with periodic assessments over time.
- Honeypots are decoy systems designed to lure potential attackers away from critical systems. In the security industry, these systems are also known as decoys, lures, or flytraps. Two variations on this technology are known as honeynets and padded cell systems.
- Trap-and-trace applications are designed to react to an intrusion event by tracing it back to its source. This process is fraught with professional and ethical issues—some people in the security field believe that the back hack in the trace process is as significant a violation as the initial attack.
- Active intrusion prevention seeks to limit the damage that attackers can perpetrate by making the local network resistant to inappropriate use.
- Scanning and analysis tools are used to pinpoint vulnerabilities in systems, holes in security components, and unsecured aspects of the network. Although these tools are used by attackers, they can also be used by administrators to learn more about their own systems and to identify and repair system weaknesses before they result in losses.

Review Questions

1. What common security system is an IDPS most like? In what ways are these systems similar?
2. How does a false positive alarm differ from a false negative alarm? From a security perspective, which is less desirable?
3. How does a network-based IDPS differ from a host-based IDPS?
4. How does a signature-based IDPS differ from a behavior-based IDPS?
5. What is a monitoring (or SPAN) port? What is it used for?
6. List and describe the three control strategies proposed for IDPSs.
7. What is a honeypot? How is it different from a honeynet?
8. How does a padded cell system differ from a honeypot?
9. What is network footprinting?
10. What is network fingerprinting?
11. How are network footprinting and network fingerprinting related?
12. Why do many organizations ban port scanning activities or the use of hacker tools on their internal networks?
13. Why would ISPs ban outbound port scanning by their customers?
14. What is an open port? Why is it important to limit the number of open ports to those that are absolutely essential?
15. What is a system's attack surface? Why should it be minimized when possible?
16. What is a vulnerability scanner? How is it used to improve security?
17. What is the difference between active and passive vulnerability scanners?
18. What is Metasploit Framework? Why is it considered riskier to use than other vulnerability scanning tools?
19. What kind of data and information can be found using a packet sniffer?
20. What capabilities should a wireless security toolkit include?

Exercises

1. A key feature of hybrid IDPS systems is event correlation. After researching event correlation online, define the following terms as they are used in the process: compression, suppression, and generalization.
2. ZoneAlarm is a PC-based firewall and IDPS tool. Visit the product manufacturer at *www.zonelabs.com* and find the product specification for the IDPS features of ZoneAlarm. Which ZoneAlarm products offer these features?
3. Using the Internet, search for commercial IDPS systems. What classification systems and descriptions are used, and how can they be used to compare the features and components of each IDPS? Create a comparison spreadsheet to identify the classification systems you find.
4. Use the Internet to search for "live DVD security toolkit." Read a few Web sites to learn about this class of tools and their capabilities. Write a brief description of a live DVD security toolkit.
5. Shodan is the world's first search engine for Internet-connected devices. Visit the Shodan Web site at *http://shodan.io* and register for a free account. When you have the account, use the Explore option to look around the site. Find the Webcam category, which is usually the top-rated category, and click it. What do you see on this page? What kind of information is shown for the webcam listed there? Continue to explore the site.

References

1. Scarfone, K., and Mell, P. Special Publication (SP) 800-94, Rev. 1 (Draft), "Guide to Intrusion Detection and Prevention Systems (IDPS)." National Institute of Standards and Technology. 2012. Accessed October 2, 2020, from *https://csrc.nist.gov/publications/detail/sp/800-94/rev-1/draft*.
2. Ibid.
3. Scarfone, K., and Mell, P. SP 800-94, "Guide to Intrusion Detection and Prevention Systems (IDPS)." National Institute of Standards and Technology. 2007. Accessed October 2, 2020, from *https://csrc.nist.gov/publications/detail/sp/800-94/final*.
4. Ibid.

5. Scarfone, K., and Mell, P. SP 800-94, Rev. 1 (Draft), "Guide to Intrusion Detection and Prevention Systems (IDPS)." National Institute of Standards and Technology. 2012. Accessed October 2, 2020, from *https://csrc.nist.gov/publications/detail/sp/800-94/rev-1/draft*.

6. Ibid.

7. Ibid.

8. Ibid.

9. Ibid.

10. Ibid.

11. Scarfone, K., and Mell, P. SP 800-94, "Guide to Intrusion Detection and Prevention Systems (IDPS)." National Institute of Standards and Technology. 2007. Accessed October 2, 2020, from *https://csrc.nist.gov/publications/detail/sp/800-94/final*.

12. Ibid.

13. Scarfone, K., and Mell, P. SP 800-94, Rev. 1 (Draft), "Guide to Intrusion Detection and Prevention Systems (IDPS)." National Institute of Standards and Technology. 2012. Accessed October 2, 2020, from *https://csrc.nist.gov/publications/detail/sp/800-94/rev-1/draft*.

14. Ibid.

15. Ibid.

16. "FireEye Mandiant M-Trends 2020 Report Reveals Cyber Criminals Are Increasingly Turning to Ransomware as a Secondary Source of Income." FireEye. Accessed April 27, 2020, at *www.fireeye.com/company/press-releases/2020/fireeye-mandiant-m-trends-2020-report-reveals-cyber-criminals-are-increasingly-turning-to-ransomware.html*.

17. Scarfone, K., and Mell, P. SP 800-94, Rev. 1 (Draft), "Guide to Intrusion Detection and Prevention Systems (IDPS)." National Institute of Standards and Technology. 2012. Accessed October 2, 2020, from *https://csrc.nist.gov/publications/detail/sp/800-94/rev-1/draft*.

18. Ibid.

19. Bace, R., and Mell, P. SP 800-31, "Intrusion Detection Systems (IDS)." National Institute of Standards and Technology. 2001. Accessed October 2, 2020, from *https://nvlpubs.nist.gov/nistpubs/Legacy/SP/nistspecial-publication800-31.pdf*.

20. Ibid.

21. Ibid.

22. Scarfone, K., and Mell, P. SP 800-94, "Guide to Intrusion Detection and Prevention Systems (IDPS)." National Institute of Standards and Technology. 2007. Accessed October 2, 2020, from *https://csrc.nist.gov/publications/detail/sp/800-94/final*.

23. Scarfone, K., and Mell, P. SP 800-94, Rev. 1 (Draft), "Guide to Intrusion Detection and Prevention Systems (IDPS)." National Institute of Standards and Technology. 2012. Accessed October 2, 2020, from *https://csrc.nist.gov/publications/detail/sp/800-94/rev-1/draft*.

24. Ibid.

25. Scarfone, K., and Mell, P. SP 800-94, "Guide to Intrusion Detection and Prevention Systems (IDPS)." National Institute of Standards and Technology. 2007. Accessed October 2, 2020, from *https://csrc.nist.gov/publications/detail/sp/800-94/final*.

26. Scarfone, K., and Mell, P. SP 800-94, Rev. 1 (Draft), "Guide to Intrusion Detection and Prevention Systems (IDPS)." National Institute of Standards and Technology. 2012. Accessed October 2, 2020, from *https://csrc.nist.gov/publications/detail/sp/800-94/rev-1/draft*.

27. "Acquiring and Deploying Intrusion Detection Systems." ITL Bulletin. National Institute of Standards and Technology. Accessed October 2, 2020, from *https://csrc.nist.gov/csrc/media/publications/shared/documents/itl-bulletin/itlbul1999-11.pdf*.

28. EFF. "Pen Registers." Accessed August 20, 2016, from *www.eff.org/cases/pen-registers*.

29. 18 U.S. Code Module 206. "Pen Registers and Trap-and-Trace Devices." Accessed October 2, 2020, from *https://uscode.house.gov/view.xhtml?path=/prelim@title18/part2/Module206&edition=prelim*.

30. "SecTools.Org: Top 125 Network Security Tools—Vulnerability Scanners." Accessed October 2, 2020, from *https://sectools.org/tag/vuln-scanners/*.

31. "SecTools.Org: Top 125 Network Security Tools—Wireless Scanners." Accessed October 10, 2020, from *https://sectools.org/tag/wireless/*.

Cryptography

Upon completion of this material, you should be able to:

1. Chronicle the most significant events and discoveries in the history of cryptology
2. Explain the basic principles of cryptography
3. Describe the operating principles of the most popular cryptographic tools
4. List and explain the major protocols used for secure communications

Yet it may roundly be asserted that human ingenuity cannot concoct a cipher which human ingenuity cannot resolve.

—Edgar Allan Poe, *The Gold Bug*

Opening Scenario

Peter Hayes, CFO of Sequential Label and Supply, was working late. He opened an e-mail from the manager of the accounting department. The e-mail had an attachment—probably a spreadsheet or a report of some kind—and from the file icon he could tell it was encrypted. He saved the file to his computer's hard drive and then double-clicked the icon to open it.

His computer operating system recognized that the file was encrypted and started the decryption program, which prompted Peter for his passphrase. Peter's mind went blank. He couldn't remember the passphrase. "Oh, good grief!" he said to himself, reaching for his phone. "Charlie, good, you're still here. I'm having trouble with a file in my e-mail program. My computer is prompting me for my passphrase, and I think I forgot it."

"Uh-oh," said Charlie.

"What do you mean 'Uh-oh'?"

"I mean you're S.O.L." Charlie replied. "Simply outta luck."

"Out of luck?" said Peter. "Why? Can't you do something? I have quite a few files that are encrypted with this PGP program. I need my files."

Charlie let him finish, then said, "Peter, remember how I told you it was important to remember your passphrase?" Charlie heard a sigh on the other end of the line but decided to ignore it. "And do you remember I said that PGP is only free for individuals and that you weren't to use it for company files since we didn't buy a license for the company? I only set that program up on your personal laptop for your home e-mail—for when your sister wanted to send you some financial records. When did you start using it on SLS systems for company business?"

"Well," Peter answered, "the manager of my accounting department had some financials that were going to be ready a few weeks ago while I was traveling. I sort of told him that you set me up on this PGP crypto thing and he googled it and set up his own account. Then I swapped public keys with him before I left, and he sent the files to me securely by e-mail while I was in Dubai. It worked out great. So the next week, I encrypted quite a few files. Now I can't get to any of them because I can't seem to remember my passphrase." There was a long pause, and then he asked, "Can you hack it for me?"

Charlie chuckled and then said, "Sure, Peter, no problem. Send me the files and I'll put the biggest server we have to work on it. Since we set you up in PGP with 256-bit AES, I should be able to apply a little brute force and crack the key to get the plaintext in a hundred trillion years or so."

Introduction To Cryptography

The science of cryptology is not as enigmatic as you might think. A variety of cryptographic techniques are used regularly in everyday life. For example, open your newspaper to the entertainment section and you'll find the daily cryptogram, a word puzzle that involves unscrambling letters to find a hidden message. Also, although it is a dying art, many secretaries still use shorthand, or stenography, an abbreviated, symbolic writing method, to take rapid dictation. A form of cryptography is used even in knitting patterns, where directions are written in coded patterns such as K1P1 (knit 1, purl 1) that only an initiate can understand. While these techniques are not intended to prevent others from understanding the message, it isn't a huge leap from the use of codes for efficiency to their use in obfuscating the underlying meaning of the message.

cryptology

The field of science that encompasses cryptography and cryptanalysis.

cryptography

The process of making and using codes to secure information.

cryptanalysis

The process of obtaining the plaintext message from a ciphertext message without knowing the keys used to perform the encryption.

The science of encryption, known as **cryptology**, encompasses cryptography and cryptanalysis. **Cryptography** comes from the Greek words *kryptos,* meaning "hidden," and *graphein,* meaning "to write," and involves making and using codes to secure messages. Originally, cryptography was used to conceal military and political secrets while the information was in transport. **Cryptanalysis** involves cracking or breaking encrypted messages back into their unencrypted origins. Cryptography uses mathematical algorithms that are usually known to all. After all, it's not the knowledge of the algorithm that protects the encrypted message; it's the knowledge of the *key*—a series of characters or bits injected into the algorithm along with the original message to create the encrypted message. An individual or system usually encrypts a plaintext message into ciphertext, making it unreadable to unauthorized people—those without the key needed to decrypt the message back into plaintext, where it can be read and understood.

The field of cryptology is so vast that it can fill many volumes. This textbook provides only a general overview of cryptology and some specific information about a few cryptographic tools. In the early sections of this module, you will learn the background of cryptology as well as key concepts in cryptography and common tools. In later sections, you will learn about common cryptographic protocols and some of the attack methods used against cryptosystems.

The History of Cryptology

Cryptology has an extensive, multicultural history. People have been making, using, and breaking codes for thousands of years, and they will not stop any time soon. Table 10-1 provides some highlights from the history of cryptology.

Today, many common IT tools use embedded encryption technologies to protect sensitive information within applications. For example, all the popular Web browsers use built-in encryption features to enable secure online banking, Web shopping, and other e-commerce.

Since World War II, there have been restrictions on the export of cryptosystems, and they continue today. In 1992, encryption tools were officially listed as Auxiliary Military Technology under the Code of Federal Regulations: International Traffic in Arms Regulations.[1] These restrictions are due in part to the role cryptography played in

Table 10-1   History of Cryptology

Date	Event
1900 B.C.	Egyptian scribes used nonstandard hieroglyphs while inscribing clay tablets; this is the first documented use of written cryptography.
487 B.C.	The Spartans of Greece developed the *skytale,* a system consisting of a strip of papyrus wrapped around a wooden staff. Messages were written down the length of the staff, and the papyrus was unwrapped. The decryption process involved wrapping the papyrus around a shaft of similar diameter.
50 B.C.	Julius Caesar used a simple substitution cipher to secure military and government communications. To form an encrypted text, Caesar shifted the letters of the alphabet three places. In addition to this monoalphabetic substitution cipher, Caesar strengthened his encryption by substituting Greek letters for Latin letters.
1466	Leon Battista Alberti, the father of Western cryptography, worked with polyalphabetic substitution and designed a cipher disk.
1914–17	Throughout World War I, the Germans, British, and French used a series of transposition and substitution ciphers in radio communications. All sides expended considerable effort to try to intercept and decode communications, and thereby created the science of cryptanalysis. British cryptographers broke the Zimmerman Telegram, in which the Germans offered Mexico U.S. territory in return for Mexico's support. This decryption helped to bring the United States into the war.
1917	Gilbert S. Vernam, an AT&T employee, invented a polyalphabetic cipher machine that used a nonrepeating random key.
1919	Hugo Alexander Koch filed a patent in the Netherlands for a rotor-based cipher machine; in 1927, Koch assigned the patent rights to Arthur Scherbius, the inventor of the Enigma machine.
1939–42	The Allies secretly broke the Enigma cipher, undoubtedly shortening World War II.
1976	Whitfield Diffie and Martin Hellman introduced the idea of public-key cryptography.
1977	Ronald Rivest, Adi Shamir, and Leonard Adleman developed a practical public-key cipher both for confidentiality and digital signatures; the RSA family of computer encryption algorithms was born.

 For more information on the history of cryptology, visit the National Cryptologic Museum's Web site at *www.nsa .gov/about/cryptologic-heritage/museum/* or visit the online Crypto Museum at *www.cryptomuseum.com*.

World War II and the belief of the American and British governments that the cryptographic tools they developed were far superior to those in less developed countries. As a result, both governments believe such countries should be prevented from using cryptosystems to communicate potential terroristic activities or gain an economic advantage.

Key Cryptology Terms

To understand the fundamentals of cryptography, you must know the meanings of the following terms:

- **Algorithm**—The mathematical formula or method used to convert an unencrypted message into an encrypted message; sometimes refers to the programs that enable the cryptographic processes.
- **Bit stream cipher**—An encryption method that involves converting plaintext to ciphertext one bit at a time.
- **Block cipher**—An encryption method that involves dividing the plaintext into blocks or sets of bits and then converting the plaintext to ciphertext one block at a time.

- **Cipher**—When used as a verb, the transformation of the individual components (characters, bytes, or bits) of an unencrypted message into encrypted components or vice versa (see *Decryption* and *Encryption*); when used as a noun, the process of encryption or the algorithm used in encryption, and a term synonymous with *cryptosystem*.
- **Ciphertext** or **cryptogram**—The unintelligible encrypted or encoded message resulting from an encryption.
- **Code**—The process of converting components (words or phrases) of an unencrypted message into encrypted components.
- **Decipher**—*See Decryption.*
- **Decryption**—The process of converting an encoded or enciphered message (ciphertext) back to its original readable form (plaintext); also referred to as *deciphering*.
- **Encipher**—*See Encryption.*
- **Encryption**—The process of converting an original message (plaintext) into a form that cannot be used by unauthorized individuals (ciphertext); also referred to as *enciphering*.
- **Key** or **cryptovariable**—The information used in conjunction with the algorithm to create the ciphertext from the plaintext; it can be a series of bits used in an algorithm or the knowledge of how to manipulate the plaintext. Sometimes called a cryptovariable.
- **Keyspace**—The entire range of values that can be used to construct an individual key.
- **Link encryption**—A series of encryptions and decryptions between a number of systems, wherein each system in a network decrypts the message sent to it, re-encrypts the message using different keys, and sends it to the next neighbor. This process continues until the message reaches the final destination.
- **Plaintext** or **cleartext**—The original unencrypted message that is encrypted and the message that results from successful decryption.
- **Steganography**—The process of hiding messages; for example, hiding a message within the digital encoding of a picture or graphic so that it is almost impossible to detect that the hidden message even exists.
- **Work factor**—The amount of effort (usually expressed in units of time) required to perform cryptanalysis on an encoded message.

Encryption Methods

There are two methods of encrypting plaintext: the *bit stream* method and the *block cipher* method, as defined in the previous section. In the bit stream method, each bit in the plaintext is transformed into a cipher bit one bit at a time. In the block cipher method, the message is divided into blocks—for example, sets of 8-, 16-, 32-, or 64-bit blocks—and then each block of plaintext bits is transformed into an encrypted block of cipher bits using an algorithm and a key. Bit stream methods commonly use algorithm functions like the exclusive OR operation (XOR), whereas block methods can use substitution, transposition, XOR, or some combination of these operations, as described in the following sections. Note that most computer-based encryption methods operate on data at the level of its binary digits (bits), while others operate at the byte or character level.

You may wonder if you need to know all of the technical details about cipher methods that follow in this section. Although most security professionals will not get involved in designing cryptographic algorithms (or cipher methods) or even wind up using them directly, you probably use many of them indirectly when you browse the Web, and it is certainly helpful to understand how the tools work. At some point, you may need to know these fundamental building blocks of cryptography so you can understand your options when evaluating commercial or open-source cipher methods. It is also useful to understand the cryptographic notation methods shown in the nearby feature.

Cryptographic Notation

The notation used to represent the encryption process varies depending on its source. The notation in this text uses the letter M to represent the original message, C to represent the ending ciphertext, E to represent the enciphering or encryption process, D to represent the decryption or deciphering process, and K to represent the key. This notation can be used as follows:

- E(M) = C. Encryption (E) is applied to a message (M) to create ciphertext (C).
- D[C] = D[E(M)] = M. By decrypting (D) an encrypted message [E(M)], you get the original message (M).
- E(M,K) = C. Encrypting (E) the message (M) with the key (K) results in the ciphertext (C). If more than one key (K) is used in a multiple-round encryption, the keys are numbered K1, K2, and so on.
- D(C,K) = D[E(M,K),K] = M. That is, decrypting the ciphertext with key K results in the original plaintext message.

To encrypt a plaintext set of data, you can use one of two methods: bit stream or block cipher, as described at the beginning of this section.

Substitution Cipher

A **substitution cipher** exchanges one value for another—for example, it might exchange a letter in the alphabet with the letter three values to the right, or it might substitute one bit for another bit four places to its left. A three-character substitution to the right results in the following transformation of the standard English alphabet.

Initial alphabet:	ABCDEFGHIJKLMNOPQRSTUVWXYZ yields
Encryption alphabet:	DEFGHIJKLMNOPQRSTUVWXYZABC

Within this substitution scheme, the plaintext MOM would be encrypted into the ciphertext PRP.

This is a simple enough method by itself, but it becomes very powerful if combined with other operations. The previous example of substitution is based on a single alphabet and thus is known as a **monoalphabetic substitution**. More advanced substitution ciphers use two or more alphabets, and are referred to as **polyalphabetic substitutions**.

To extend the previous example, consider the following block of text:

Plaintext:	ABCDEFGHIJKLMNOPQRSTUVWXYZ
Substitution cipher 1	DEFGHIJKLMNOPQRSTUVWXYZABC
Substitution cipher 2	GHIJKLMNOPQRSTUVWXYZABCDEF
Substitution cipher 3	JKLMNOPQRSTUVWXYZABCDEFGHI
Substitution cipher 4	MNOPQRSTUVWXYZABCDEFGHIJKL

The first row here is the plaintext, and the next four rows are four sets of substitution ciphers, which when taken together constitute a single polyalphabetic substitution cipher. To encode the word TEXT with this cipher, you substitute a letter from the second row for the first letter in TEXT, a letter from the third row for the second letter, and so on—a process that yields the ciphertext WKGF. Note how the plaintext letter T is transformed into a W or an F, depending on its order of appearance in the plaintext. Complexities like these make this type of encryption substantially more difficult to decipher when one doesn't have the algorithm (in this case, the rows of ciphers) and the key, which is the substitution method. A logical extension to this process is to randomize the cipher rows completely in order to create a more complex operation.

---

substitution cipher

An encryption method in which one value is substituted for another.

monoalphabetic substitution

A substitution cipher that incorporates a single alphabet in the encryption process.

polyalphabetic substitution

A substitution cipher that incorporates two or more alphabets in the encryption process.

One example of a monoalphabetic substitution cipher is the cryptogram in the daily newspaper (see Figure 10-1). Another example is the once famous Radio Orphan Annie decoder pin (shown in Figure 10-2), which consisted of two alphabetic rings that could be rotated to a predetermined pairing to form a simple substitution cipher. The device was made to be worn as a pin so one could always be at the ready. As mentioned in Table 10-1, Julius Caesar reportedly used a three-position shift to the right to encrypt his messages (A became D, B became E, and so on), so this substitution cipher was given his name—the *Caesar Cipher.*

An advanced type of substitution cipher that uses a simple polyalphabetic code is the **Vigenère cipher**. The cipher is implemented using the Vigenère square (or table), also known as a *tabula recta*—a term invented by Johannes Trithemius in the 1500s. Table 10-2 illustrates the setup of the Vigenère square, which is made up of 26 distinct cipher alphabets. In the header row and column, the alphabet is written in its normal order. In each subsequent row, the alphabet is shifted one letter to the right until a 26 × 26 block of letters is formed.

Vigenère cipher

An advanced type of substitution cipher that uses a simple polyalphabetic code.

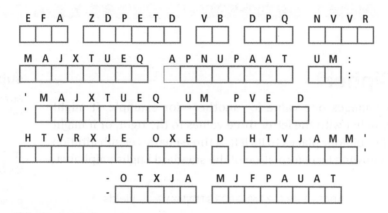

Figure 10-1   Daily cryptogram

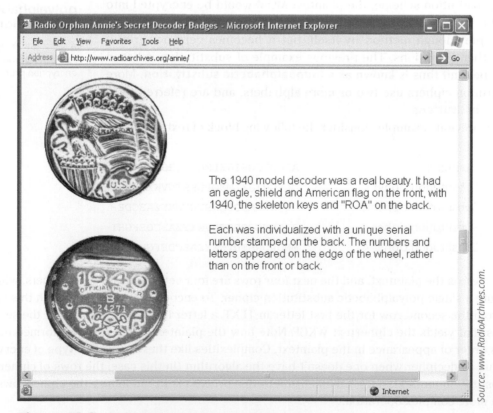

Figure 10-2   Radio Orphan Annie's decoder pin

	A	B	C	D	E	F	G	H	I	J	K	L	M	N	O	P	Q	R	S	T	U	V	W	X	Y	Z
A	A	B	C	D	E	F	G	H	I	J	K	L	M	N	O	P	Q	R	S	T	U	V	W	X	Y	Z
B	B	C	D	E	F	G	H	I	J	K	L	M	N	O	P	Q	R	S	T	U	V	W	X	Y	Z	A
C	C	D	E	F	G	H	I	J	K	L	M	N	O	P	Q	R	S	T	U	V	W	X	Y	Z	A	B
D	D	E	F	G	H	I	J	K	L	M	N	O	P	Q	R	S	T	U	V	W	X	Y	Z	A	B	C
E	E	F	G	H	I	J	K	L	M	N	O	P	Q	R	S	T	U	V	W	X	Y	Z	A	B	C	D
F	F	G	H	I	J	K	L	M	N	O	P	Q	R	S	T	U	V	W	X	Y	Z	A	B	C	D	E
G	G	H	I	J	K	L	M	N	O	P	Q	R	S	T	U	V	W	X	Y	Z	A	B	C	D	E	F
H	H	I	J	K	L	M	N	O	P	Q	R	S	T	U	V	W	X	Y	Z	A	B	C	D	E	F	G
I	I	J	K	L	M	N	O	P	Q	R	S	T	U	V	W	X	Y	Z	A	B	C	D	E	F	G	H
J	J	K	L	M	N	O	P	Q	R	S	T	U	V	W	X	Y	Z	A	B	C	D	E	F	G	H	I
K	K	L	M	N	O	P	Q	R	S	T	U	V	W	X	Y	Z	A	B	C	D	E	F	G	H	I	J
L	L	M	N	O	P	Q	R	S	T	U	V	W	X	Y	Z	A	B	C	D	E	F	G	H	I	J	K
M	M	N	O	P	Q	R	S	T	U	V	W	X	Y	Z	A	B	C	D	E	F	G	H	I	J	K	L
N	N	O	P	Q	R	S	T	U	V	W	X	Y	Z	A	B	C	D	E	F	G	H	I	J	K	L	M
O	O	P	Q	R	S	T	U	V	W	X	Y	Z	A	B	C	D	E	F	G	H	I	J	K	L	M	N
P	P	Q	R	S	T	U	V	W	X	Y	Z	A	B	C	D	E	F	G	H	I	J	K	L	M	N	O
Q	Q	R	S	T	U	V	W	X	Y	Z	A	B	C	D	E	F	G	H	I	J	K	L	M	N	O	P
R	R	S	T	U	V	W	X	Y	Z	A	B	C	D	E	F	G	H	I	J	K	L	M	N	O	P	Q
S	S	T	U	V	W	X	Y	Z	A	B	C	D	E	F	G	H	I	J	K	L	M	N	O	P	Q	R
T	T	U	V	W	X	Y	Z	A	B	C	D	E	F	G	H	I	J	K	L	M	N	O	P	Q	R	S
U	U	V	W	X	Y	Z	A	B	C	D	E	F	G	H	I	J	K	L	M	N	O	P	Q	R	S	T
V	V	W	X	Y	Z	A	B	C	D	E	F	G	H	I	J	K	L	M	N	O	P	Q	R	S	T	U
W	W	X	Y	Z	A	B	C	D	E	F	G	H	I	J	K	L	M	N	O	P	Q	R	S	T	U	V
X	X	Y	Z	A	B	C	D	E	F	G	H	I	J	K	L	M	N	O	P	Q	R	S	T	U	V	W
Y	Y	Z	A	B	C	D	E	F	G	H	I	J	K	L	M	N	O	P	Q	R	S	T	U	V	W	X
Z	Z	A	B	C	D	E	F	G	H	I	J	K	L	M	N	O	P	Q	R	S	T	U	V	W	X	Y

Table 10-2   The Vigenère Square

You can use the Vigenère square in several ways. For example, you could perform an encryption by simply starting in the first row, finding a substitute for the first letter of plaintext, and then moving down the rows for each subsequent letter of plaintext. With this method, the word SECURITY in plaintext becomes TGFYWOAG in ciphertext.

A much more sophisticated way to use the Vigenère square is to use a keyword to represent the shift. To accomplish this, you begin by writing a keyword above the plaintext message. For example, suppose the plaintext message is "SACK GAUL SPARE NO ONE" and the keyword is ITALY. We thus end up with the following:

```
ITALYITALYITALYITA
SACKGAULSPARENOOONE
```

Now you use the keyword letter and the message (plaintext) letter below it in combination. Returning to the Vigenère square, notice how the first column of text, like the first row, forms the normal alphabet. To perform the substitution, start with the first combination of keyword and message letters, "IS." Use the keyword letter to locate the column and the message letter to find the row, and then look for the letter at their intersection. Thus, for column I and row S, you will find the ciphertext letter "A." After you follow this procedure for each letter in the message, you will produce the encrypted ciphertext "ATCVEINLDNIKEYMWGE." One weakness of this method is that any keyword-message letter combination containing an "A" row or column reproduces the plaintext message letter. For example, the third letter in the plaintext message, the "C" (of "SACK"), has a combination of AC, and thus is unchanged in the ciphertext. To minimize the effects of this weakness, you should avoid choosing a keyword that contains the letter "A."

transposition cipher

A cryptographic operation that involves simply rearranging the values within a block based on an established pattern; also known as a *permutation cipher*.

permutation cipher

See *transposition cipher*.

Transposition Cipher

Like the substitution operation, the transposition cipher is simple to understand, but if properly used, it can produce ciphertext that is difficult to decipher. In contrast to the substitution cipher, however, the **transposition cipher** or **permutation cipher** simply rearranges the bits or bytes (characters) within a block to create the ciphertext. For an example, consider the following transposition key pattern.

Key pattern: $8 \rightarrow 3, 7 \rightarrow 6, 6 \rightarrow 2, 5 \rightarrow 7, 4 \rightarrow 5, 3 \rightarrow 1, 2 \rightarrow 8, 1 \rightarrow 4$

In this key, the bit or byte (character) in position 1 moves to position 4. When operating on binary data, position 1 is at the far right of the data string, and counting proceeds from right to left. Next, the bit or byte in position 2 moves to position 8, and so on. This cipher is similar to another newspaper puzzle favorite: the word jumble, as illustrated in Figure 10-3. In the jumble, words are scrambled, albeit with no defined pattern. Upon unscrambling, the words provide key characters used to decode a separate message.

The following rows show the numbering of bit locations for this key; the plaintext message 001001010110101110 01010101010100, which is broken into eight-bit blocks for clarity; and the ciphertext that is produced when the previously depicted transposition key is applied to the plaintext.

Bit locations:	87654321	87654321	87654321	87654321
Plaintext 8-bit blocks:	00100101	01101011	10010101	01010100
Ciphertext:	00001011	10111010	01001101	01100001

Reading from right to left in this example, the first bit of plaintext (position 1 of the first byte) becomes the fourth bit (in position 4) of the first byte of the ciphertext. Similarly, the second bit of the plaintext (position 2) becomes the eighth bit (position 8) of the ciphertext, and so on.

To examine further how this transposition key works, look at its effects on a plaintext message comprised of letters instead of bits. Replacing the eight-bit block of plaintext with the example plaintext message presented earlier, "SACK_GAUL_SPARE_NO_ONE," yields the following.

Letter locations:	87654321	87654321	87654321
Plaintext:	__ENO_ON	_ERAPS_L	UAG_KCAS
Key:	Same key as previously, but characters transposed, not bits		
Ciphertext:	ON_ON_E_	_AEPL_RS	A_AKSUGC

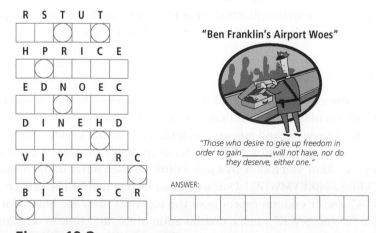

```
R  S  T  U  T
H  P  R  I  C  E
E  D  N  O  E  C
D  I  N  E  H  D
V  I  Y  P  A  R  C
B  I  E  S  S  C  R
```

"Ben Franklin's Airport Woes"

"Those who desire to give up freedom in order to gain _____ will not have, nor do they deserve, either one."

ANSWER:

Figure 10-3 Word jumble

Here, you read from right to left to match the order in which characters would be transmitted from a sender on the left to a receiver on the right. The letter in position 1 of the first block of plaintext, "S," moves to position 4 in the ciphertext. The process is continued until the letter "U," the eighth letter of the first block of plaintext, moves to the third position of the ciphertext. This process continues with subsequent blocks using the same specified pattern. Obviously, the use of different-sized blocks or multiple transposition patterns would enhance the strength of the cipher.

In addition to being credited with inventing a substitution cipher, Julius Caesar was associated with an early version of the transposition cipher. In the Caesar block cipher, the recipient of the coded message knows to fit the text to a prime number square. In practice, this means that if there are fewer than 25 characters, the recipient uses a 5 × 5 square. For example, if you received the Caesar ciphertext shown next, you would make a square of five columns and five rows and then write the letters of the message into the square, filling the slots from left to right and top to bottom. You would then read the message from the opposite direction—that is, from top to bottom, left to right.

Ciphertext: SGS_NAAPNE CUAO_KLR _ _ _EO

```
S G S _ N
A A P N E
C U A O _
K L R _ _
_ _ E O _
```

Reading from top to bottom and left to right reveals the plaintext "SACK_GAUL_SPARE_NO_ONE."

When mechanical and electronic cryptosystems became more widely used, transposition ciphers and substitution ciphers were combined to produce highly secure encryption processes. To make the encryption even stronger and more difficult to cryptanalyze, the keys and block sizes can be increased to 128 bits or more, which produces substantially more complex substitutions or transpositions. These systems use a *block padding method* to fill the last block of the plaintext with random characters to facilitate the algorithm.

Exclusive OR

The **exclusive OR operation (XOR)** is a function of Boolean algebra in which two bits are compared and a binary result is generated. XOR encryption is a very simple symmetric cipher that is used in many applications where security is not a defined requirement. Table 10-3 shows an XOR table with the results of all possible combinations of two bits.

Table 10-3 XOR Table

First Bit	Second Bit	Result
0	0	0
0	1	1
1	0	1
1	1	0

To see how XOR works, consider an example in which the plaintext is the word "CAT." The ASCII binary representation of the plaintext is 01000011 01000001 01010100.

In order to encrypt the plaintext, a key value should be selected. In this case, the bit pattern for the letter "V" (01010110) is used, and is repeated as many times as necessary for each of the characters that need to be encrypted, written from left to right. Performing the XOR operation on the two bit streams (the plaintext and the key) produces the result shown in Table 10-4.

exclusive OR operation (XOR)

A function within Boolean algebra used as an encryption function in which two bits are compared; identical bits result in a binary 0 while different bits result in a binary 1.

Table 10-4 Example of XOR Encryption

Text Value	Binary Value
CAT as bits	010000110100000101010100
V repeated three times as a key	010101100101011001010110
Cipher	000101010001011100000010

The bottom row of Table 10-4, "Cipher," is read from left to right and contains the bit stream that will be transmitted. When this cipher is received, it can be decrypted using the key value "V." Note that the XOR encryption method is very simple to implement and equally simple to break. The XOR encryption method should not be used by itself when an organization is transmitting or storing sensitive data. Actual encryption algorithms used to protect data typically use the XOR operator as part of a more complex encryption process.

You can combine XOR with a block cipher to produce a simple but powerful operation. In the example that follows (again read from left to right), the first row shows a character message "5E5+•" requiring encryption. The second row shows this message in binary notation. In order to apply an eight-bit block cipher method, the binary message is broken into eight-bit blocks in the row labeled "Message blocks." The fourth row shows the eight-bit key (01010101) chosen for the encryption. To encrypt the message, you must perform the XOR operation on each eight-bit block by using the XOR function on the message bit and the key bit to determine the bits of the ciphertext. The result is shown in the row labeled "Ciphertext." This ciphertext can now be sent to a receiver, who will be able to decipher the message simply by knowing the algorithm (XOR) and the key (01010101).

Message (text):	"5E5+•"				
Message (binary):	00110101	01000101	00110101	00101011	10010101
Message blocks:	00110101	01000101	00110101	00101011	10010101
Key:	01010101	01010101	01010101	01010101	01010101
Ciphertext:	01100000	00010000	01100000	01111110	11000000

If the receiver cannot apply the key to the ciphertext and derive the original message, either the cipher was applied with an incorrect key or the cryptosystem was not used correctly.

Vernam Cipher

Also known as the one-time pad, the **Vernam cipher**, developed by Gilbert Vernam in 1917 while working at AT&T Bell Labs, uses a set of characters only one time for each encryption process (hence the name *one-time pad*). The *pad* in the name comes from the days of manual encryption and decryption when the key values for each ciphering session were prepared by hand and bound into an easy-to-use form—a pad of paper. To perform the Vernam cipher encryption, the pad values are added to numeric values representing the plaintext that needs to be encrypted. Each character of the plaintext is turned into a number and a pad value for that position is added to it. The resulting sum for that character is then converted back to a ciphertext letter for transmission. If the sum of the two values exceeds 26, then 26 is subtracted from the total. The process of keeping a computed number within a specific range is called a *modulo;* thus, requiring that all numbers be in the range of 1–26 is referred to as

Vernam cipher

A cryptographic technique developed at AT&T and known as the "one-time pad," this cipher uses a set of characters for encryption operations only once and then discards it.

modulo 26. In this process, a number larger than 26 has 26 sequentially subtracted from it until the number is in the proper range.

To examine the Vernam cipher and its use of modulo, consider the following example, which uses "SACK GAUL SPARE NO ONE" as plaintext. In the first step of this encryption process, the letter "S" is converted into the number 19 because it is the 19th letter of the alphabet. The same conversion is applied to the rest of the letters of the plaintext message, as shown here.

Plaintext:	S	A	C	K	G	A	U	L	S	P	A	R	E	N	O	O	N	E
Plaintext value:	19	01	03	11	07	01	21	12	19	16	01	18	05	14	15	15	14	05
One-time pad text:	F	P	Q	R	N	S	B	I	E	H	T	Z	L	A	C	D	G	J
One-time pad value:	06	16	17	18	14	19	02	09	05	08	20	26	12	01	03	04	07	10
Sum of plaintext & pad:	25	17	20	29	21	20	23	21	24	24	21	44	17	15	18	19	21	15
After modulo subtraction:				03								18						
Ciphertext:	Y	Q	T	C	U	T	W	U	X	X	U	R	Q	O	R	S	U	O

Rows three and four in this example show the one-time pad text that was chosen for this encryption and the one-time pad value, respectively. As you can see, the pad value, like the plaintext value, is derived from the position of each pad text letter in the alphabet. Thus, the pad text letter "F" is assigned the position number 06. This conversion process is repeated for the entire one-time pad text. Next, the plaintext value and the one-time pad value are added together—the first sum is 25. Because 25 is in the range of 1 to 26, no modulo 26 subtraction is required. The sum remains 25, and yields the ciphertext "Y," as shown above. Skipping ahead to the fourth character of the plaintext, "K," you find that its plaintext value is 11. The pad text is "R" and the pad value is 18. The sum of 11 and 18 is 29. Because 29 is larger than 26, 26 is subtracted from it, which yields the value 3. The ciphertext for this plaintext character is then the third letter of the alphabet, "C."

Decryption of any ciphertext generated from a one-time pad requires either knowledge of the pad values or the use of elaborate and very difficult cryptanalysis (or so the encrypting party hopes). Using the pad values and the ciphertext, the decryption process works as follows: "Y" becomes the number 25, from which you subtract the pad value for the first letter of the message, 06. This yields a value of 19, or the letter "S." This pattern continues until the fourth letter of the ciphertext, where the ciphertext letter is "C" and the pad value is 18. Subtracting 18 from 3 yields negative 15. Because of modulo 26, which requires that all numbers are in the range of 1–26, you must *add* 26 to the negative 15. This operation yields a sum of 11, which means the fourth letter of the message is "K."

 For more information about Gilbert Vernam and his cryptography work, view the video "Encryption, Episode 2: The Vernam Cipher" by visiting *http://techchannel.att.com/* and using the search box.

Book-Based Ciphers

Two related encryption methods made popular by spy movies involve using the text in a book as the key to decrypt a message. These methods are the book cipher and the running key cipher. A third method, the template cipher, is not really a cipher but is related to this discussion.

Book Cipher

In a *book cipher*, the ciphertext consists of a list of codes representing the page number, line number, and word number of the plaintext word. The algorithm is the mechanical process of looking up the references from the ciphertext and converting each reference to a word by using the ciphertext's value and the key (the book). For example, from a copy of a particular popular novel, one may send the message 259,19,8; 22,3,8; 375,7,4; 394,17,2. Although almost any book can be used, dictionaries and thesauruses are typically the most popular sources, as they are likely to contain almost any word that might be needed. The recipient of a running key cipher must first know which book is used—in this case, suppose it is the science fiction novel *A Fire Upon the Deep,* the 1992 TOR edition. To decrypt the ciphertext, the receiver acquires the book, turns to page 259, finds line 19, and selects the eighth word in that line (which is "sack"). Then the receiver turns to page 22, line 3, selects the eighth word again, and so forth. In this example, the resulting message is "SACK ISLAND SHARP PATH." If a dictionary is used, the message consists only of the page number and the number of the word on the page. An even more sophisticated version might use multiple books, perhaps even in a particular sequence for each word or phrase.

Running Key Cipher

Similar in concept to the book cipher is the *running key cipher*, which uses a book for passing the key to a cipher that is similar to the Vigenère cipher. The sender provides an encrypted message with a short sequence of numbers that indicate the page, line, and word number from a predetermined book to be used as the key or *indicator block.* Unlike the Vigenère cipher, if the key needs to be extended in a running key cipher, you don't repeat the key. Instead, you continue the text from the indicator block. From this point, you follow the same basic method as the Vigenère cipher, using the tabula recta to find the column based on the plaintext, and the row based on the key-indicator block letter.

Reversing the processes deciphers the ciphertext, using the ciphertext letter and key. You simply use the row or column corresponding to the key letter, find the ciphertext in the row or column of text, and then identify the letter on the opposing axis. The mirrored layout of the table simplifies the selection of rows or columns during encryption and decryption.

Template Cipher

The *template cipher* or *perforated page cipher* is not strictly an encryption cipher, but more of an example of steganography. The template cipher involves the use of a hidden message in a book, letter, or other message. The receiver must use a page with a specific number of holes cut into it and place it over the book page or letter to extract the hidden message. Commonly shown in movies where an inmate sends coded messages from prison, this cipher is both difficult to execute and easy to detect, provided either party is physically searched. The presence of the perforated page is a clear indicator that some form of hidden message communication is occurring. A much simpler method would be to employ a variation of *acrostics,* where the first letter of each line of a message (or every *n*th letter) would spell out a hidden message.

Hash Functions

In addition to ciphers, another important encryption technique that is often incorporated into cryptosystems is the hash function. **Hash functions** are mathematical algorithms used to confirm the identity of a specific message and confirm that the content has not been changed. While they do not create ciphertext, hash functions confirm the message's identity and integrity, both of which are critical functions in e-commerce.

Hash algorithms are used to create a **hash value**, also known as a message digest, by converting variable-length messages into a single fixed-length value. The **message digest** is a fingerprint of the author's message that is compared with the recipient's locally calculated hash of the same message. If both hashes are identical after transmission, the message has arrived without modification. Hash functions are considered one-way operations in that the same message always provides the same hash value, but the hash value itself cannot be used to determine the contents of the message.

Hashing functions do not require the use of keys, but it is possible to attach a **message authentication code (MAC)** to allow only specific recipients to access the message digest. Because hash functions are one-way, they are used in password verification systems to confirm the identity of the user. In such systems, the hash value, or message digest, is calculated based on the originally issued password, and this message digest is stored for later comparison. When the user logs in for the next session, the system calculates a hash value based on the user's password input, and this value is compared against the stored value to confirm identity.

The **Secure Hash Standard (SHS)** is issued by the National Institute of Standards and Technology (NIST). Standard document FIPS 180-4 specifies SHA-1 (Secure Hash Algorithm 1) as a secure algorithm for computing a condensed representation of a message or data file. SHA-1 produces a 160-bit message digest, which can be used as an input to a digital signature algorithm. SHA-1 is based on principles modeled after MD4, which is part of the MD family of hash algorithms created by Ronald Rivest. The SHA-2 family of hash algorithms includes SHA-256, SHA-384, SHA-512, and related

---

hash functions

Mathematical algorithms that generate a message summary or digest (sometimes called a fingerprint) to confirm the message's identity and integrity.

hash algorithms

Public functions that create a *hash value,* also known as a message digest, by converting variable-length messages into a single fixed-length value.

hash value

See *message digest.*

message digest

A value representing the application of a hash algorithm on a message that is transmitted with the message so it can be compared with the recipient's locally calculated hash of the same message; also known as a *hash value.*

message authentication code (MAC)

A key-dependent, one-way hash function that allows only specific recipients (symmetric key holders) to access the message digest.

Secure Hash Standard (SHS)

A standard issued by the National Institute of Standards and Technology (NIST) that specifies secure algorithms, such as SHA-1, for computing a condensed representation of a message or data file.

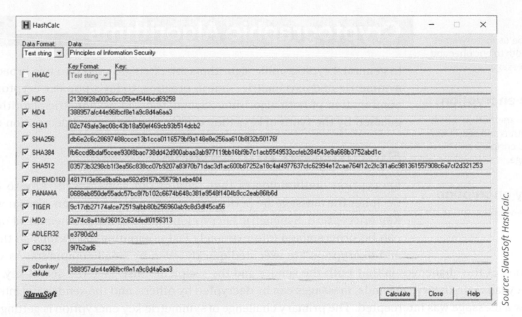

Figure 10-4   Various hash values

Source: SlavaSoft HashCalc.

variants. The number of bits used in the hash algorithm is a measurement of the algorithm's strength against *collision attacks*, where two different messages can result in an identical hash value. SHA-256 is essentially a 256-bit block cipher algorithm that creates a key by encrypting the intermediate hash value, with the message block functioning as the key. The compression function operates on each 512-bit message block and a 256-bit intermediate message digest.[2]

As shown in Figure 10-4, free tools are available that can calculate hash values using a number of popular algorithms.

 For more information on the Secure Hash Standard, read FIPS 180-4 at *http://csrc.nist.gov/publications/PubsFIPS .html.*

An attack method called *rainbow cracking* has generated concern about the strength of the processes used for password hashing. In general, if attackers gain access to a file of hashed passwords, they can use an application like RainbowCrack with its combination of brute force and dictionary attacks to reveal user passwords. Databases of hashed passwords and their plaintext equivalents are stored in *rainbow tables* and are easily used to do a reverse lookup on a hash value rather than trying to use a brute force approach.

Passwords that are short, contain dictionary words, or are poorly constructed can be easily cracked. The current industry standard is the 10.4 password standard—a password should include at least 10 characters, with at least one uppercase letter, one lowercase letter, one number, and one special character. Well-constructed passwords that are of sufficient length can take a long time to crack even using the fastest computers, but by using a rainbow table—a database of precomputed hashes from sequentially calculated passwords—the rainbow cracker simply looks up the hashed password and reads out the text version. No brute force is required. This type of attack is more properly classified as a *time-memory trade-off attack*.

To defend against such an attack, you must first protect the file of hashed passwords and implement strict limits on the number of attempts allowed per login session. You can also use an approach called *password hash salting*. Salting is the process of providing a random piece of data to the hashing function when the hash is first calculated. The use of the salt value creates a different hash; when a large set of salt values are used, rainbow cracking fails because the time-memory trade-off is no longer in the attacker's favor. The salt value is not kept a secret: It is stored along with the account identifier so that the hash value can be re-created during authentication.[3] Additional techniques include *key stretching* and *key strengthening*. Key stretching involves repeating the hashing algorithm up to several thousand times to continuously inject the password, salt value, and interim hash results back into the process. Key strengthening extends the key with the salt value but then deletes the salt value.

secret key

A key that can be used in symmetric encryption both to encipher and decipher the message.

symmetric encryption

A cryptographic method in which the same algorithm and secret key are used both to encipher and decipher the message.

private-key encryption

See symmetric encryption.

Cryptographic Algorithms

In general, cryptographic algorithms are often grouped into two broad categories—symmetric and asymmetric—but in practice, today's popular cryptosystems use a combination of both algorithms. Symmetric and asymmetric algorithms are distinguished by the types of keys they use for encryption and decryption operations.

Symmetric Encryption

Encryption methodologies that require the same **secret key** to encipher and decipher the message are performing **symmetric encryption**, also known as **private-key encryption**. Symmetric encryption methods use mathematical operations that can be programmed into extremely fast computing algorithms so that encryption and decryption are executed quickly, even by small computers. As you can see in Figure 10-5, one of the challenges is that both the sender and the recipient must have the secret key. Also, if either copy of the key falls into the wrong hands, messages can be decrypted by others, and the sender and intended receiver may not know a message was intercepted. The primary challenge of symmetric key encryption is getting the key to the receiver, a process that must be conducted *out of band* to avoid interception. In other words, the process must use a channel or band other than the one carrying the ciphertext.

There are a number of popular symmetric encryption cryptosystems. One of the most widely known is the *Data Encryption Standard (DES);* it was developed by IBM and is based on the company's Lucifer algorithm, which uses a key length of 128 bits. As implemented, DES uses a 64-bit block size and a 56-bit key. DES was adopted by NIST in 1976 as a federal standard for encryption of non-classified information, after which it became widely employed in commercial applications. DES enjoyed increasing popularity for almost 20 years until 1997, when users realized that a 56-bit key size did not provide acceptable levels of security. In 1998, a group called the Electronic Frontier Foundation (*www.eff.org*) used a specially designed computer to break a DES key in slightly more than 56 hours. Since then, it has been theorized that a dedicated attack supported by the proper hardware (not necessarily a specialized computer) could break a DES key in less than a day.[4]

Triple DES (3DES) was created to provide a level of security far beyond that of DES. 3DES was an advanced application of DES, and while it did deliver on its promise of encryption strength beyond DES, it soon proved too weak to survive indefinitely—especially as computing power continued to double every 18 months. Within just a few years, 3DES needed to be replaced.

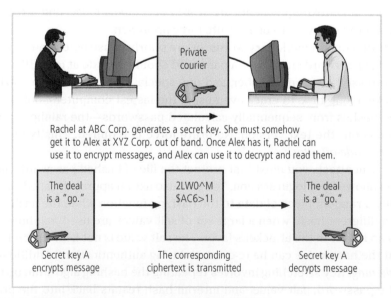

Rachel at ABC Corp. generates a secret key. She must somehow get it to Alex at XYZ Corp. out of band. Once Alex has it, Rachel can use it to encrypt messages, and Alex can use it to decrypt and read them.

The deal is a "go."	2LW0^M $AC6>1!	The deal is a "go."
Secret key A encrypts message	The corresponding ciphertext is transmitted	Secret key A decrypts message

Figure 10-5 Example of symmetric encryption

The successor to 3DES is the **Advanced Encryption Standard (AES)**. AES is a federal information processing standard (FIPS) that specifies a cryptographic algorithm used within the U.S. government to protect information in federal agencies that are not part of the national defense infrastructure. (Agencies that are considered a part of national defense use more secure methods of encryption, which are provided by the National Security Agency.) The requirements for AES stipulate that the algorithm should be unclassified, publicly disclosed, and available royalty-free worldwide. AES was developed to replace both DES and 3DES. While 3DES remains an approved algorithm for some uses, its expected useful life is limited. Historically, cryptographic standards approved by FIPS have been adopted on a voluntary basis by organizations outside government entities. The AES selection process involved cooperation among the U.S. government, private industry, and academia from around the world. AES was approved by the U.S. Secretary of Commerce as the official federal governmental standard on May 26, 2002.

> **Advanced Encryption Standard (AES)**
>
> The current federal standard for the encryption of data, as specified by NIST; based on the Rijndael algorithm.

AES implements a block cipher called the Rijndael Block Cipher with a variable block length and a key length of 128, 192, or 256 bits. Experts estimate that the special computer used by the Electronic Frontier Foundation to crack DES within a couple of days would require approximately 4,698,864 quintillion years (4,698,864,000,000,000,000,000) to crack AES.

 For more information on the Advanced Encryption Standard, read FIPS 197 at *https://csrc.nist.gov/publications/fips*.

Asymmetric Encryption

While symmetric encryption systems use a single key both to encrypt and decrypt a message, **asymmetric encryption** uses two different but related keys. Either key can be used to encrypt or decrypt the message. However, if key A is used to encrypt the message, only key B can decrypt it; if key B is used to encrypt a message, only key A can decrypt it. Asymmetric encryption can be used to provide elegant solutions to problems of secrecy and verification. This technique has its greatest value when one key is used as a private key, which means it is kept secret (much like the key in symmetric encryption) and is known only to the owner of the key pair. The other key serves as a public key, which means it is stored in a public location where anyone can use it. For this reason, the more common name for asymmetric encryption is **public-key encryption**.

Consider the following example, as illustrated in Figure 10-6. Alex at XYZ Corporation wants to send an encrypted message to Rachel at ABC Corporation. Alex

> **asymmetric encryption**
>
> A cryptographic method that incorporates mathematical operations involving both a public key and a private key to encipher or decipher a message; either key can be used to encrypt a message, but the other key is required to decrypt it.
>
> **public-key encryption**
>
> See *asymmetric encryption*.

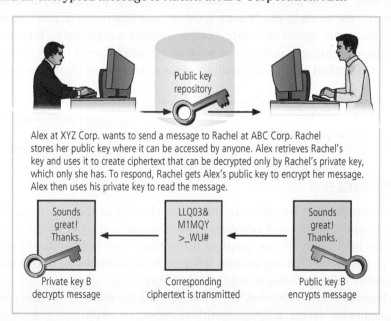

Alex at XYZ Corp. wants to send a message to Rachel at ABC Corp. Rachel stores her public key where it can be accessed by anyone. Alex retrieves Rachel's key and uses it to create ciphertext that can be decrypted only by Rachel's private key, which only she has. To respond, Rachel gets Alex's public key to encrypt her message. Alex then uses his private key to read the message.

Sounds great! Thanks.	LLQ03& M1MQY >_WU#	Sounds great! Thanks.
Private key B decrypts message	Corresponding ciphertext is transmitted	Public key B encrypts message

Figure 10-6   Example of asymmetric encryption

goes to a public-key registry and obtains Rachel's public key. Remember that the foundation of asymmetric encryption is that the same key cannot be used both to encrypt and decrypt the same message. So, when Rachel's public key is used to encrypt the message, only her private key can be used to decrypt the message; that private key is held by Rachel alone. Similarly, if Rachel wants to respond to Alex's message, she goes to the registry where Alex's public key is held and uses it to encrypt her message, which of course can only be read by Alex's private key. This approach, which keeps private keys secret and encourages the sharing of public keys in reliable directories, is an elegant solution to the key management problems of symmetric key applications.

Asymmetric algorithms are one-way functions, meaning they are simple to compute in one direction but complex to compute in the opposite direction. Again, this is the foundation of public-key encryption. It is based on a hash value, which is calculated from an input number using a hashing algorithm, as you learned earlier in this module. This hash value is essentially a summary of the original input values. It is virtually impossible to derive the original values without knowing how they were used to create the hash value. For example, if you multiply 45 by 235, you get 10,575. This is simple enough, but if you are only given the number 10,575, can you determine which two numbers were multiplied to produce it?

Now assume that each multiplier is 200 digits long and prime. The resulting multiplicative product could be up to 400 digits long. Imagine the time you'd need to factor out those numbers. There is a shortcut, however. In mathematics, it is known as a trapdoor (which is different from a software trapdoor). A mathematical trapdoor is a secret mechanism that enables you to easily accomplish the reverse function in a one-way function. With a trapdoor, you can use a key to encrypt or decrypt the ciphertext, but not both, thus requiring two keys. The public key becomes the true key, and the private key is derived from the public key using the trapdoor.

One of the most popular public-key cryptosystems is RSA, whose name is derived from Rivest, Shamir, and Adleman, the algorithm's developers. The *RSA algorithm* was the first public-key encryption algorithm developed (in 1977) and published for commercial use. It is very popular and has been embedded in essentially all widely available Web browsers to provide security for e-commerce applications. The patented RSA algorithm has become the de facto standard for public-use encryption applications.

 For more information on how the RSA algorithm works, read RFC (Request for Comments) 3447, "Public-Key Cryptography Standards (PKCS) #1: RSA Cryptography Specifications," Version 2.1, which is available from *www.rfc-editor.org/rfc/rfc3447.txt*.

The problem with asymmetric encryption, as shown in Figure 10-6, is that holding a single conversation between two parties requires four keys—two public keys and two related private keys. Moreover, if four organizations want to exchange communications, each party must manage its private key and four public keys. In such scenarios, determining which public key is needed to encrypt a particular message can become a rather confusing problem, and with more organizations in the loop, the problem expands. This is why asymmetric encryption is sometimes regarded by experts as inefficient. Compared with symmetric encryption, asymmetric encryption is also not as efficient in terms of CPU computations. Consequently, hybrid systems, such as those described later in this module, are more commonly used than pure asymmetric systems.

 RSA is now a division of Dell EMC Infrastructure Solutions Group. For information about the annual RSA security conference, see *www.rsaconference.com*.

Encryption Key Size

When deploying ciphers, it is important for users to decide on the size of the cryptovariable or key, because the strength of many encryption applications and cryptosystems is measured by key size. How exactly does key size affect the strength of an algorithm? Typically, the length of the key increases the number of random guesses that have to be made in order to break the code. Creating a larger universe of possibilities increases the time required to make guesses, so a longer key directly influences the strength of the encryption.

It may surprise you to learn that when it comes to cryptosystems, the security of encrypted data is *not* dependent on keeping the encrypting algorithm secret. In fact, algorithms should be published and often are, to enable research to uncover their weaknesses. The security of any cryptosystem depends on keeping some or all elements of the cryptovariable(s) or key(s) secret; effective security is maintained by manipulating the size (bit length) of the keys and following proper procedures and policies for key management.

For a simple example of how key size is related to encryption strength, suppose you have an algorithm that uses a three-bit key. You may recall from earlier in the module that *keyspace* is the range from which the key can be drawn. Also, you may recall that in binary notation, three bits can be used to represent values from 000 to 111, which correspond to the numbers 0 to 7 in decimal notation and thus provide a keyspace of eight keys. This means an algorithm that uses a three-bit key has eight possible keys; the numbers 0 to 7 in binary are 000, 001, 010, 011, 100, 101, 110, and 111. If you know how many keys you have to choose from, you can program a computer to try all the keys in an attempt to crack the encrypted message.

The preceding statement makes a few assumptions: (1) you know the algorithm, (2) you have the encrypted message, and (3) you have time on your hands. It is easy to satisfy the first criterion. The encryption tools that use DES can be purchased over the counter. Many of these tools are based on encryption algorithms that are standards, as is DES itself, so it is relatively easy to get a cryptosystem based on DES that enables you to decrypt an encrypted message if you possess the key. The second criterion requires the interception of an encrypted message, which is illegal but not impossible. As for the third criterion, the task required is a brute force attack, in which a computer randomly or sequentially selects possible keys of the known size and applies them to the encrypted text or a piece of the encrypted text. If the result is plaintext—bingo! But, as indicated earlier in this module, it can take quite a long time to exert brute force on more advanced cryptosystems. In fact, the strength of an algorithm is determined by how long it takes to guess the key.

When it comes to keys, how big is big? At the beginning of this section, you learned that a three-bit system has eight possible keys. An eight-bit system has 256 possible keys. If you use a 24-bit key, which is puny by modern standards, you have almost 16.8 million possible keys. Even so, a modern PC, such as the one described in Table 10-5, could discover this key in mere seconds. But, as the table shows, the amount of time needed to crack a cipher by guessing its key grows exponentially with each additional bit.

Table 10-5   Encryption Key Power

It is estimated that to crack an encryption key using a brute force attack, a computer needs to perform a maximum of 2^k operations (2^k guesses), where k is the number of bits in the key. The average estimated time to crack is approximately half that time.

Key Length (Bits)	Maximum Number of Operations (Guesses)	Maximum Time to Crack	Estimated Average Time to Crack
16	65,536	0.000000112 seconds	0.000000056 seconds
24	16,777,216	0.0000287 seconds	0.0000143 seconds
32	4,294,967,296	0.00734 seconds	0.00367 seconds
56	72,057,594,037,927,900	34.2 hours	17.1 hours
64	18,446,744,073,709,600,000	364.7 days	182.35 days
128	3.40E+38	18,431,695,314,143,700,000 years	9,215,847,657,071,860,000 years
256	1.16E+77	6,271,980,907,862,400,000, 000,000,000,000,000,000,000, 000,000,000,000,000,000 years	3,135,990,453,931,200,000, 000,000,000,000,000,000,000, 000,000,000,000,000,000,000 years
512	1.34E+154	7.26E+134 years	3.63E+134 years

Note: Estimated Time to Crack is based on a 2020-era Intel i9-10900X 10 Core CPU performing 585 Dhrystone GFLOPS (giga/billion floating point operations per second) at 5.2 GHz (overclocked). Modern workstations are capable of using multiple CPUs, further decreasing time to crack, or simply splitting the workload among multiple systems.

Note: The authors acknowledge that this benchmark is based on a very specific application test and that the results are not generalizable. However, these calculations are shown to illustrate the relative difference between key length and resulting strength rather than to accurately depict time to crack.

One thing to keep in mind is that even though the estimated time to crack grows rapidly with respect to the number of bits in the encryption key and the odds of cracking seem insurmountable at first glance, Table 10-5 doesn't account for the fact that high-end computing power has increased and continues to be more accessible. Another challenge is the use of graphics processing units (GPUs) found in video cards, as well as the emergence of quantum computing processors. These powerful approaches to computation can be used to perform cryptanalysis calculations, usually at a faster rate than a typical computer's primary CPU. Therefore, even the once-standard 56-bit encryption can't stand up anymore to brute force attacks by personal computers, especially if multiple computers are used together to crack the keys. Each additional computer reduces the amount of time needed. Two computers can divide the keyspace—the entire set of possible combinations of bits that can be the cryptovariable or key—and crack the key in approximately half the time, and so on. This means people who have access to multiple systems, grid computing environments, GPU computation clusters, or future quantum computers could radically speed up brute force key-breaking efforts. However, an even greater concern is the ease with which you can read messages encrypted by what appear to be uncrackable algorithms if you have the key. Key management (and password management) is the most critical aspect of any cryptosystem in protecting encrypted information, and is even more important in many cases than key strength.

Why, then, do encryption systems such as DES incorporate multiple elements or operations? Consider this: If a cryptosystem uses the same operation (XOR, substitution, or transposition) multiple consecutive times, it gains no additional benefit. For example, using a substitution cipher and substituting B for A, then R for B, and then Q for R has the same effect as substituting Q for A. Similarly, instead of transposing a character in position 1, then position 4, and then position 3, a cryptosystem could more easily have transposed the character from position 1 to position 3. There is no net advantage for sequential operations unless each subsequent operation is different. Therefore, to substitute, then transpose, then run an XOR operation, and then substitute again, the cryptosystem will have dramatically scrambled, substituted, and recoded the original plaintext with ciphertext, all in the hopes of making information unbreakable without the key.

Cryptographic Tools

The ability to conceal the contents of sensitive messages and to verify the contents of messages and the identities of their senders can be important in all areas of business. To be useful, these cryptographic capabilities must be embodied in tools that allow IT and information security practitioners to apply the elements of cryptography in the everyday world of computing. This section covers some of the widely used tools that bring the functions of cryptography to the world of information systems.

Public Key Infrastructure (PKI)

Public key infrastructure (PKI) systems are based on public-key cryptosystems and include digital certificates and certificate authorities (CAs). **Digital certificates** allow the PKI components and their users to validate keys and identify key owners. (Digital certificates are explained in more detail later in this module.) PKI systems and their digital certificate registries enable the protection of information assets by making verifiable digital certificates readily available to business applications. This, in turn, allows the applications to implement several key characteristics of information security and integrate these characteristics into the following business processes across an organization:

public key infrastructure (PKI)

An integrated system of software, encryption methodologies, protocols, legal agreements, and third-party services that enables users to communicate securely through the use of digital certificates.

digital certificates

Public-key container files that allow PKI system components and end users to validate a public key and identify its owner.

- *Authentication*—Individuals, organizations, and Web servers can validate the identity of each party in an Internet transaction.
- *Integrity*—Content signed by the certificate is known not to have been altered while in transit from host to host or server to client.
- *Privacy*—Information is protected from being intercepted during transmission.
- *Authorization*—The validated identity of users and programs can enable authorization rules that remain in place for the duration of a transaction; this reduces overhead and allows for more control of access privileges for specific transactions.
- *Nonrepudiation*—Customers or partners can be held accountable for transactions, such as online purchases, which they cannot later dispute.

A typical PKI solution protects the transmission and reception of secure information by integrating the following components:

- A **certificate authority (CA)**, which issues, manages, authenticates, signs, and revokes users' digital certificates. These certificates typically contain the user's name, public key, and other identifying information.
- A **registration authority (RA)**, which handles certification functions such as verifying registration information, generating end-user keys, revoking certificates, and validating user certificates, in collaboration with the CA.
- Certificate directories, which are central locations for certificate storage that provide a single access point for administration and distribution.
- Management protocols, which organize and manage communications among CAs, RAs, and end users. This includes the functions and procedures for setting up new users, issuing keys, recovering keys, updating keys, revoking keys, and enabling the transfer of certificates and status information among the parties involved in the PKI's area of authority.
- Policies and procedures, which assist an organization in the application and management of certificates, in the formalization of legal liabilities and limitations, and in actual business use.

Common implementations of PKI include systems that issue digital certificates to users and servers, directory enrollment, key issuing systems, tools for managing key issuance, and verification and return of certificates. These systems enable organizations to apply an enterprise-wide solution that allows users within the PKI's area of authority to engage in authenticated and secure communications and transactions.

The CA performs many housekeeping activities for keys and certificates that are issued and used in its zone of authority. Each user authenticates himself or herself with the CA. The CA can issue new or replacement keys, track issued keys, provide a directory of public-key values for all known users, and perform other management activities. When a private key is compromised or the user loses the privilege of using keys in the area of authority, the CA can revoke the user's keys. The CA periodically distributes a **certificate revocation list (CRL)** to all users. When important events occur, specific applications can make a real-time request to the CA to verify any user against the current CRL.

The issuance of certificates and their keys by the CA enables secure, encrypted, nonrepudiable e-business transactions. Some applications allow users to generate their own certificates and keys, but a key pair generated by the end user can only provide nonrepudiation, not reliable encryption. A central system operated by a CA or RA can generate cryptographically strong keys that are considered independently trustworthy by all users, and can provide services for users such as private-key backup, key recovery, and key revocation.

The strength of a cryptosystem relies on both the raw strength of its key's complexity and the overall quality of its key management security. PKI solutions can provide several mechanisms for limiting access and possible exposure of the private keys. These mechanisms include password protection, smart cards, hardware tokens, and other hardware-based key storage devices that are memory-capable, like flash memory or PC memory cards. PKI users should select the key security mechanisms that provide an appropriate level of key protection for their needs. Managing the security and integrity of the private keys used for nonrepudiation or the encryption of data files is critical to successfully using the encryption and nonrepudiation services within the PKI's area of trust.[5]

> ### certificate authority (CA)
> In PKI, a third party that manages users' digital certificates.
>
> ### registration authority (RA)
> In PKI, a third party that operates under the trusted collaboration of the certificate authority and handles day-to-day certification functions.
>
> ### certificate revocation list (CRL)
> In PKI, a published list of revoked or terminated digital certificates.

 For more information on public-key cryptography, read FIPS *191*, "Entity Authentication Using Public Key Cryptography," at *https://csrc.nist.gov/publications/fips*.

Digital Signatures

Digital signatures were created in response to the rising need to verify information transferred via electronic systems. Asymmetric encryption processes are used to create digital signatures. When asymmetric cryptography is used on a sender's private key to encrypt a message, the sender's public key must be used to decrypt the message. When the decryption is successful, the process verifies that the message was sent by the user and thus cannot be refuted.

nonrepudiation

The process of reversing public-key encryption to verify that a message was sent by the user and thus cannot be refuted.

digital signatures

Encrypted message components that can be mathematically proven as authentic.

Digital Signature Standard (DSS)

The NIST standard for digital signature algorithm usage by federal information systems; based on a variant of the ElGamal signature scheme.

This process is known as **nonrepudiation** and is the principle of cryptography that underpins the authentication mechanism collectively known as a digital signature. **Digital signatures**, therefore, are encrypted messages that can be mathematically proven as authentic. The management of digital signatures is built into most Web browsers. In general, digital signatures should be created using processes and products that are based on the **Digital Signature Standard (DSS).** When processes and products are certified as DSS compliant, they have been approved and endorsed by U.S. federal and state governments, as well as by many foreign governments, as a means of authenticating the author of an electronic document.

DSS algorithms can be used in conjunction with the sender's public and private keys, the receiver's public key, and the Secure Hash Standard to quickly create messages that are both encrypted and nonrepudiable. This process first creates a message digest using the hash algorithm, which is then input into the digital signature algorithm along with a random number to generate the digital signature. The digital signature function also depends on the sender's private key and other information provided by the CA. The resulting encrypted message contains the digital signature, which can be verified by the recipient using the sender's public key.

 For more information on the Digital Signature Standard, read FIPS 186-4 at *https://csrc.nist.gov/publications/fips.*

Digital Certificates

As you learned earlier in this module, a *digital certificate* is an electronic document or container file that contains a key value and identifying information about the entity that controls the key. The certificate is often issued and certified by a third party, usually a certificate authority. A digital signature attached to the certificate's container file certifies the file's origin and integrity. This verification process often occurs when you download or update software via the Internet. For example, the window tabs in Figure 10-7 show that the downloaded files come from the purported originating agency, *Amazon.com*, and thus can be trusted.

Unlike digital signatures, which help authenticate the origin of a message, digital certificates authenticate the cryptographic key that is embedded in the certificate. When used properly, these certificates enable diligent users to verify the authenticity of any organization's certificates. This process is much like what happens when the Federal Deposit Insurance Corporation (FDIC) issues its logo to assure customers that a bank is authentic. Different client-server applications use different types of digital certificates to accomplish their assigned functions, as follows:

- The CA application suite issues and uses certificates (keys) that identify and establish a trust relationship with a CA to determine what additional certificates can be authenticated.

Source: Microsoft.

Figure 10-7   Example digital certificate

Secure/Multipurpose Internet Mail Extensions (S/MIME) builds on the encoding format of the Multipurpose Internet Mail Extensions (MIME) protocol and uses digital signatures based on public-key cryptosystems to secure e-mail. In 1993, the IETF proposed the **Privacy-Enhanced Mail (PEM)** standard to use 3DES symmetric key encryption and RSA for key exchanges and digital signatures; however, it was never widely deployed. *Pretty Good Privacy (PGP)* was developed by Phil Zimmermann and uses the IDEA cipher for message encoding. PGP also uses RSA for symmetric key exchange and digital signatures. PGP is discussed in more detail later in this module.

The first commonly used Internet e-mail standard was SMTP/RFC 822, also called SMTP, but this standard has problems and limitations, such as an inability to transmit executable files or binary objects and an inability to handle character sets other than seven-bit ASCII. These limitations make SMTP unwieldy for organizations that need greater security and support for international character sets. MIME was developed to address the problems associated with SMTP. MIME's message header fields were designed to identify and describe the e-mail message and to handle a variety of e-mail content. In addition to the message header fields, the MIME specification includes predefined content types and conversion transfer encodings, such as seven-bit, eight-bit, binary, and radix-64, which it uses to deliver e-mail messages reliably across a wide range of systems.

S/MIME, an extension to MIME, is the second generation of enhancements to the SMTP standard. MIME and S/MIME have the same message header fields, except for those added to support new functionality. Like MIME, S/MIME uses a canonical form format, which allows it to standardize message content types among systems, but it has the additional ability to sign, encrypt, and decrypt messages. Table 10-8 summarizes the functions and algorithms used by S/MIME as an extension to those used by MIME. It should be mentioned that PGP is functionally similar to S/MIME, incorporates some of the same algorithms, and can interoperate with S/MIME to some degree.

 For more information on securing MIME, visit *www.rfc-editor.org* and search on "S/MIME" and "MIME" to see the numerous standards on the subject.

Secure/Multipurpose Internet Mail Extensions (S/MIME)

A security protocol that builds on the encoding format of the Multipurpose Internet Mail Extensions (MIME) protocol and uses digital signatures based on public-key cryptosystems to secure e-mail.

Privacy-Enhanced Mail (PEM)

A standard proposed by the IETF that uses 3DES symmetric key encryption and RSA for key exchanges and digital signatures.

Securing Web Transactions with SET, SSL, and HTTPS

Just as PGP, PEM, and S/MIME work to secure e-mail operations, a number of related protocols work to secure Web browsers, especially at e-commerce sites. Among these protocols are SET, SSL, HTTPS, Secure Shell (SSH-2), and IP Security (IPSec). You learned about SSL and HTTPS earlier in this module.

Secure Electronic Transactions (SET) was developed by MasterCard and Visa in 1997 to protect against electronic payment fraud. SET uses DES to encrypt credit card information transfers and uses RSA for key exchange. SET provides security for both Internet-based credit card transactions and credit card swipe systems in retail stores. SSL also provides secure online e-commerce transactions. SSL uses a number of algorithms but mainly relies on RSA for key transfer and uses IDEA, DES, or 3DES for encrypted symmetric key-based data transfer. Figure 10-7, shown earlier, illustrates the kind of certificate and SSL information that appears when you check out of an e-commerce site. If your Web connection does not automatically display such certificates, you can click the lock in your browser's URL field window to view the connection encryption and certificate properties.

Secure Electronic Transactions (SET)

A protocol developed by credit card companies to protect against electronic payment fraud.

Table 10-8 S/MIME Functions and Algorithms

Function	Algorithm
Hash code for digital signatures	Secure Hash Algorithm 1 (SHA-1)
Digital signatures	DSS
Encryption session keys	ElGamal (variant of Diffie–Hellman)
Digital signatures and session keys	RSA
Message encryption	3DES, RC2

Securing Wireless Networks with WPA and RSN

Wireless local area networks (WLANs, also known by the brand name Wi-Fi, or wireless fidelity networks) are thought by many in the IT industry to be inherently insecure. The communication channel between the wireless network interface of any computing device and the access point that provides its services uses radio transmissions. Without protection, these radio signals can be intercepted by anyone with a wireless packet sniffer. To prevent interception of these communications, wireless networks must use some form of cryptographic security control. Two sets of protocols are widely used to help secure wireless transmissions: Wired Equivalent Privacy and Wi-Fi Protected Access. Both are designed for use with the IEEE 802.11 wireless networks.

Wired Equivalent Privacy (WEP)

WEP was an early attempt to provide security with the 802.11 network protocol. It is now considered too cryptographically weak to provide any meaningful protection from eavesdropping, but for a time it did provide some measure of security for low-sensitivity networks. WEP uses the RC4 cipher stream to encrypt each packet using a 64-bit key. This key is created using a 24-bit initialization vector and a 40-bit key value. The packets are formed with an XOR function to use the RC4 key value stream to encrypt the data packet. A four-byte integrity check value (ICV) is calculated for each packet and then appended.[9] According to many experts, WEP is too weak for use in most network settings for the following reasons:[10]

- Key management is not effective because most networks use a single shared secret key value for each node. Synchronizing key changes is a tedious process, and no key management is defined in the protocol, so keys are seldom changed.
- The initialization vector (IV) is too small, resulting in the recycling of IVs. An attacker can reverse-engineer the RC4 cipher stream and decrypt subsequent packets, or the attacker can forge future packets. In 2007, a brute force decryption was accomplished in less than one minute.[11]

In summary, an intruder who collects enough data can threaten a WEP network in just a few minutes by decrypting or altering the data being transmitted, or by forging the WEP key to gain unauthorized access to the network. WEP also lacks a means of validating user credentials to ensure that only authorized network users are allowed to access it.

Wi-Fi Protected Access (WPA and WPA2)

WPA was created to resolve the issues with WEP. WPA has a key size of 128 bits; instead of static, seldom-changed keys, it uses dynamic keys created and shared by an authentication server. WPA accomplishes this through the use of the Temporal Key Integrity Protocol (TKIP). TKIP is a suite of algorithms that attempts to deliver the best security possible given the constraints of the wireless network environment. The algorithms are designed to work with legacy networking devices. TKIP adds four new algorithms in addition to those that were used in WEP:

- A cryptographic message integrity code, or MIC, called Michael, to defeat forgeries
- A new IV sequencing discipline to remove replay attacks from the attacker's arsenal
- A per-packet key mixing function to decorrelate public IVs from weak keys
- A rekeying mechanism to provide fresh encryption and integrity keys, undoing the threat of attacks stemming from key reuse.[12]

While it offered dramatically improved security over WEP, WPA was not the most secure wireless protocol design. Some compromises were made in the security design to allow compatibility with existing wireless network components. Protocols to replace TKIP are currently under development. Table 10-9 provides a summary of the differences between WEP and WPA.

In 2004, WPA2 was made available as a replacement for WPA. WPA2 provided many of the elements missing from WPA, most notably AES-based encryption. Beginning in 2006, WPA2 became mandatory for all new Wi-Fi devices. WPA2 is backward-compatible with WPA, although some older network cards have difficulty using it.

The latest version, WPA3, was deployed in 2018; it uses 192-bit keys and eliminates the Pre-Shared key by using *Simultaneous Authentication of Equals*. This is expected to improve the overall security of wireless communications and implement options for IoT devices without user display interfaces.

Closing Scenario

Charlie was getting ready to head home when the phone rang. Caller ID showed it was Peter.

"Hi, Peter," Charlie said into the receiver. "Want me to start the file cracker on your spreadsheet?"

"No, thanks," Peter answered, taking the joke well. "I remembered my passphrase. But I want to get your advice on what we need to do to make the use of encryption more effective and to get it properly licensed for the whole company. I see the value in using it for certain kinds of information, but I'm worried about forgetting a passphrase again, or even worse, that someone else forgets a passphrase or leaves the company. How would we get their files back?"

"Well, to do that we would need to use a feature called key recovery, which is usually part of PKI software," said Charlie. "Actually, if we invest in PKI software, we could solve that problem as well as several others."

"OK," said Peter. "Can you see me tomorrow at 10 o'clock to talk about this PKI solution and how we can make better use of encryption?"

Discussion Questions

1. Was Charlie exaggerating in the opening scenario when he gave Peter an estimate for the time required to crack the encryption key using a brute force attack?

Ethical Decision Making

Suppose Charlie had installed software to record all keystrokes entered on all company computer systems (known as a keylogger) and had made a copy of Peter's encryption key, but without policy authority and without anyone's knowledge, including Peter's.

1. Would the use of such a tool be an ethical violation on Charlie's part? Is it illegal?

2. Suppose that Charlie had implemented the keylogger with the knowledge and approval of senior company executives, and that every employee had signed a release acknowledging that the company can record all information entered on company systems. Two days after Peter's original call, Charlie calls back to give Peter his key: "We got lucky and cracked it early." If Charlie says this to preserve Peter's illusion of privacy, is such a "little white lie" an ethical action on Charlie's part?

Selected Readings

- *Applied Cryptography*, 2nd Edition, by Bruce Schneier. 1996. John Wiley & Sons.
- *Public Key Infrastructure: Building Trusted Applications and Web Services*, by John R. Vacca. 2004. Auerbach.

Module Summary

- Encryption is the process of converting a message into a form that is unreadable to unauthorized people.
- The science of encryption, known as cryptology, encompasses cryptography (making and using encryption codes) and cryptanalysis (breaking encryption codes).
- Cryptology has a long history and continues to change and improve.
- Two basic processing methods are used to convert plaintext data into encrypted data—bit stream and block ciphering. The other major methods used for scrambling data include substitution ciphers, transposition ciphers, the XOR function, the Vigenère cipher, and the Vernam cipher.
- Hash functions are mathematical algorithms that generate a message summary, or digest, that can be used to confirm the identity of a specific message and confirm that the message has not been altered.

- Most cryptographic algorithms can be grouped into two broad categories: symmetric and asymmetric. In practice, most popular cryptosystems are hybrids that combine symmetric and asymmetric algorithms.
- The strength of many encryption applications and cryptosystems is determined by key size. All other things being equal, the length of the key directly affects the strength of the encryption.
- Public key infrastructure (PKI) is an integrated system of software, encryption methodologies, protocols, legal agreements, and third-party services that enables users to communicate securely. PKI includes digital certificates and certificate authorities.
- Digital signatures are encrypted messages that are independently verified by a central facility and provide nonrepudiation. A digital certificate is an electronic document, similar to a digital signature, which is attached to a file to certify it came from the organization that claims to have sent it and was not modified from its original format.
- Steganography is the hiding of information. It is not technically a form of cryptography, but is similar in that it protects confidential information while in transit.
- Secure Hypertext Transfer Protocol (HTTPS), Secure Electronic Transactions (SET), and Secure Sockets Layer (SSL) are protocols designed to enable secure communications across the Internet. IPSec is the protocol used to secure communications across any IP-based network, such as LANs, WANs, and the Internet. Secure/ Multipurpose Internet Mail Extensions (S/MIME), Privacy-Enhanced Mail (PEM), and Pretty Good Privacy (PGP) are protocols that are used to secure electronic mail. PGP is a hybrid cryptosystem that combines some of the best available cryptographic algorithms; it has become the open-source de facto standard for encryption and authentication of e-mail and file storage applications.
- Wireless networks require their own cryptographic protection. Originally protected with WEP and WPA, most modern Wi-Fi networks are now protected with WPA2. Bluetooth—a short-range wireless protocol used predominantly for wireless phones and PDAs—can be exploited by anyone within its 30-foot range.

Review Questions

1. What are cryptography and cryptanalysis?
2. What was the earliest reason for the use of cryptography?
3. What is a cryptographic key, and what is it used for? What is a more formal name for a cryptographic key?
4. What are the cryptographic tools discussed in this module, and what does each accomplish?
5. What is a hash function, and what can it be used for?
6. What does it mean to be "out of band"? Why is it important to exchange keys out of band in symmetric encryption?
7. What is the fundamental difference between symmetric and asymmetric encryption?
8. How does public key infrastructure add value to an organization seeking to use cryptography to protect information assets?
9. What are the components of PKI?
10. What is the difference between a digital signature and a digital certificate?
11. What critical issue in symmetric and asymmetric encryption is resolved by using a hybrid method like Diffie–Hellman?
12. What is steganography, and what can it be used for?
13. Which security protocols are predominantly used in Web-based electronic commerce?
14. Which security protocols are used to protect e-mail?
15. IPSec can be implemented using two modes of operation. What are they?
16. Which kind of attack on cryptosystems involves sequential guessing of all possible key combinations?
17. Consider the earlier module discussion about encryption key power and key strength, and then review Table 10-5. If you were setting up an encryption-based network, what key size would you choose and why?
18. What are the strongest key sizes used in encryption systems today?
19. What encryption standard is currently recommended by NIST?
20. What are the most popular protocols used to secure Internet communication?

Exercises

1. Go to a popular online electronic commerce site like *Amazon.com*. Place several items in your shopping cart, and then go to check out. When you reach the screen that asks for your credit card number, right-click on the Web browser and select Properties. You may need to use the help feature of your browser to find the security protocols in use and the certificates used to secure your transactions. What did you find out about the cryptosystems and protocols in use to protect the transaction?

2. Repeat Exercise 1 on a different Web site, perhaps *ebay.com*. Does this site use the same protocols or different ones? Compare and contrast the protocols and certificates being used.

3. Perform a Web search for "Proton mail." Create the free trial account. Use the tool to compose and send a secure e-mail to your personal e-mail account. This will require you to use the "encryption" option in the Compose dialog box, which looks like a padlock. Set a message password. When you receive the message in your e-mail account, what looks different in the e-mail, compared with your other e-mails?

4. Perform a Web search for "Announcing the Advanced Encryption Standard (AES)." Read this document, which is a FIPS 197 standard. Write a short overview of the development and implementation of this cryptosystem.

5. Search the Web for "steganographic tools." What do you find? Download and install a trial version of one of the tools. Embed a short text file within an image. In a side-by-side comparison, can you tell the difference between the original image and the image with the embedded file?

References

1. Epic.org. "International Traffic in Arms Regulations: Code of Federal Regulations [EXCERPTS]." Title 22—Foreign Relations; Chapter I—Department of State; Subchapter M. April 1, 1992. Accessed October 23, 2020, from *https://epic.org/crypto/export_controls/itar.html*.
2. FIPS PUB 180-4, "Secure Hash Standard (SHS)." National Institute of Standards and Technology. Accessed October 23, 2020, from *https://csrc.nist.gov/publications/detail/fips/180/4/final*.
3. Paladion. "Sending Salted Hashes Just Got More Tricky." Paladion High Speed Cyber Defense. Accessed October 23, 2020, from *www.paladion.net/blogs/sending-salted-hashes-just-got*.
4. Electronic Frontier Foundation. "Eff Des Cracker Machine Brings Honesty to Crypto Debate." Accessed October 23, 2020, from *www.eff.org/press/releases/eff-des-cracker-machine-brings-honesty-crypto-debate*.
5. Kuhn, D., Hu, V., Polk, W., and Chang, S. NIST SP 800-32, "Introduction to Public Key Technology and the Federal PKI Infrastructure." National Institute of Standards and Technology. February 2001. Accessed October 23, 2020, from *https://csrc.nist.gov/publications/detail/sp/800-32/final*.
6. Stallings, W. *Cryptography and Network Security, Principles and Practice*. 1999. New Jersey: Prentice Hall.
7. Conway, M. "Code Wars: Steganography, Signals Intelligence, and Terrorism." *Knowledge, Technology & Policy* 16, 45-62 (2003). Accessed October 23, 2020.
8. McCullagh, D. "Bin Laden: Steganography Master?" Accessed October 23, 2020, from *http://archive.wired.com/politics/law/news/2001/02/41658?currentPage=all*.
9. Scarfone, K., Dicio, D., Sexton, M., and Tibbs, C. SP 800-48, Rev. 1, "Guide to Securing Legacy IEEE 802.11 Wireless Networks." National Institute of Standards and Technology. July 2008. Accessed October 23, 2020, from *https://csrc.nist.gov/publications/detail/sp/800-48/rev-1/archive/2008-07-25*.
10. Interop Net Labs. "What's Wrong with WEP?" September 9, 2002. Accessed October 23, 2020, from *www.opus1.com/www/whitepapers/whatswrongwithwep.pdf*.
11. Leyden, J. "WEP Key Wireless Cracking Made Easy." *The Register*. April 4, 2007. Accessed October 23, 2020, from *www.theregister.co.uk/2007/04/04/wireless_code_cracking*.
12. CISCO. "Security: Encryption Manager." Accessed October 23, 2020, from *www.cisco.com/web/techdoc/wireless/access_points/online_help/eag/123-02.JA/1400BR/h_ap_sec_ap-key-security.html*.

13. "What Is RSN (Robust Secure Network)?" Tech FAQ Online. Accessed October 23, 2020, from *www.tech-faq .com/rsn-robust-secure-network.html*.

14. Bialoglowy, M. "Bluetooth Security Review, Part I: Introduction to Bluetooth." Created April 24, 2005, and updated October 23, 2020. Accessed August 28, 2016, from *https://community .broadcom.com/symantecenterprise/communities/community-home/librarydocuments/ viewdocument?DocumentKey=4ac4d5c6-3bf1-4e66-acf0-6f07482cfae1&CommunityKey=1ec f5f55-9545-44d6-b0f4-4e4a7f5f5e68&tab=librarydocuments*.

15. Leyden, J. "Cabir Mobile Worm Gives Track Fans the Run Around." *The Register*. August 12, 2005. Accessed October 23, 2020, from *www.theregister.co.uk/2005/08/12/cabir_stadium_outbreak/*.

16. ITL Bulletin. National Institute of Standards and Technology. March 2001. Accessed October 23, 2020, from *https://csrc.nist.gov/csrc/media/publications/shared/documents/itl-bulletin/itlbul2001-03.pdf*.

17. The OpenPGP Home Page. Accessed October 23, 2020, from *www.openpgp.org/*.

Implementing Information Security

Upon completion of this material, you should be able to:

1. Explain how an organization's information security blueprint becomes a project plan
2. Explain the significance of the project manager's role in the success of an information security project
3. Discuss the many organizational considerations that a project plan must address
4. Describe the need for professional project management for complex projects
5. Discuss technical strategies and models for implementing a project plan
6. List and discuss the nontechnical problems that organizations face in times of rapid change

> *Change is good. You go first!*
>
> —Dilbert (by Scott Adams)

Opening Scenario

Kelvin Urich was preparing for the change control meeting that was about to start. His screen showed the slides he planned to use with his detailed notes. He scanned through the slides one final time. During the meeting last week, the technical review committee had approved his ideas, and now he was confident that the project plan he'd developed was complete, tight, and well-ordered.

The series of change requests resulting from this project would keep the company's technical analysts busy for months to come, but he hoped that the scope and scale of the project, and the vast improvements it was sure to bring to the SLS information security program, would inspire his colleagues. To help the project proceed smoothly, he had loaded his slides and supporting documents with columns of tasks, subtasks, and action items, and he had assigned dates to every action step and personnel to each required task. Everything was under control.

Kelvin started the online meeting software, activated his microphone and camera, and braced himself to start the virtual meeting.

Naomi Jackson, the change control supervisor, connected a few minutes early. She greeted Kelvin with a wave. Everyone attending had received the detailed report of planned changes the previous day; Naomi opened the list of planned change items and shared them with the meeting. Charlie Moody connected next, also nodding to Kelvin on the screen.

Once the virtual room filled, Naomi said, "Time to get started." The slide showing the planned changes highlighted the first change control item for discussion. She said, "Item 742."

One of the members of the UNIX support team responded, "As planned," meaning that the item, a routine maintenance procedure for the corporate servers, would occur as scheduled.

Naomi continued down the list in numeric order. Most items received the response "As planned" from the sponsoring team member. Occasionally, someone answered "Cancelled" or "Will be rescheduled," but for the most part, the review of the change items proceeded as usual until it came to the section with Kelvin's information security change requests.

Naomi said, "Items 761 through 767. Kelvin Urich from the security team is present to discuss these items with the change control group." Naomi passed control of the shared screen to Kelvin.

Kelvin shared his opening slide with the meeting. He waited, a little nervously, until he felt everyone had registered the material on the screen, and then began speaking: "I'm sure most of you are already aware of the information security upgrades we've been working on for the past few months. We've created an overall strategy based on the revised policies that were published last month and a detailed analysis of the threats to our systems. As the project manager, I've created what I think is a very workable plan. The seven change requests on the list today are all network changes, and each is a top priority. In the coming weeks, I'll be sending each department head a complete list of all planned changes and the expected dates. Of course, detailed change requests will be filed in advance for change control meetings, but each department can find out when any item is planned by checking the master list. As I said, there are more changes coming, and I hope we can all work together to make this a success."

"Comments or questions?" asked Naomi. "Please use our standard virtual meeting protocols."

Instantly, six virtual hands shot up on the participant list. All of them belonged to senior technical analysts. Kelvin realized belatedly that none of these analysts were on the technical review committee that had approved his plan.

As he was running the session now, Kelvin said, "OK, Davey Martinez, I think you were first. Go ahead."

Davey replied, "We should have been warned if we are going to have all this work dumped on us all at once."

Kelvin replied, "Well, Davey, I guess this is the first chance we have had to tell you about it." He continued, "Amy, you're next." She replied, "We can't make this happen on this schedule."

Meanwhile, the chat window had erupted with several threads of comments. It seemed like everyone in the meeting had started typing messages and replies at once. Amid the sudden chaos that had broken out during an otherwise orderly meeting, it occurred to Kelvin that his plan might not be as simple as he'd thought. He braced himself—it was going to be a very long afternoon.

Introduction To Information Security Implementation

Information security should be implemented into every major system in an organization. It should also be designed into every system from inception and through all phases of development and deployment. As organizations continue to make the transition to cloud-based services and application delivery, the need for information security that is designed into systems from inception becomes even more important. One approach for implementing information security into an organization's information systems is to ensure that security is a fundamental part of the organization's **systems development life cycle (SDLC)**. To understand how *security* is integrated into the systems development life cycle, you must first understand the foundations of systems development.

Each organization has a unique set of needs when it comes to developing information (and security) systems. The organization's culture will dictate the nature and types of systems development activities that will be used. Many organizations do not develop a significant proprietary system, choosing instead to use off-the-shelf applications or work with other approaches that specialize in the development and deployment of information systems. When organizations need to develop systems in-house, they can choose from a variety of approaches that have emerged over time. The traditional approach to software development (discussed in the next section) has given rise to several variations, including RAD, JAD, Agile, and one of the newest approaches, DevOps.

An early innovation in systems development was the inclusion of a broader cross section of the organization in the development process. Whereas in early development projects, systems owners and software developers would collaborate to define

systems development life cycle (SDLC)

A methodology for the design and implementation of an information system, which may contain different phases depending on the methodology deployed, but generally addresses the investigation, analysis, design, implementation, and maintenance of an information system.

specifications and create systems, an approach known as *joint application development (JAD)* added members of the management team from the supported business unit. In some cases, future users of the systems were also added. Another innovation that often occurred with the JAD approach was to increase the speed at which requirements were collected and software was prototyped, thus allowing more iterations in the design process—an approach called *rapid application development (RAD)*. This type of development later evolved into a combined approach known as the spiral method, in which each stage of development was completed in smaller increments, with delivery of working software components occurring more frequently and the software under development coming closer to its intended finished state with each pass through the development process.

Taking the objectives of JAD and RAD even further is the collective approach to systems development known as *agile programming (AP)* or *extreme programming (XP)*, including aspects of systems development known as Kanban and Scrum. As the need to reduce the time taken in the systems development cycle from gathering requirements to testing software continued to evolve, even faster feedback cycles were required to reduce time to market and shorten feature rollout times. When coupled with a need to better integrate the effort of the development team and the operations team to improve the functionality and security of applications, another model known as *Development Operations (DevOps)* has begun to emerge.

DevOps focuses on integrating the need for the development team to provide iterative and rapid improvements to system functionality and the need for the operations team to improve security and minimize the disruption from software release cycles. By collaborating across the entire software/service life cycle, DevOps uses a continuous development model that relies on systems thinking, short feedback loops, and continuous experimentation and learning.

Each of these approaches has its advantages and disadvantages, and each can be effective under the right circumstances. People who work in software development and some specialty areas of information security that support the software assurance process must be conversant with each of these methodologies.

An emerging development has been called *SecDevOps*, which is short for *security development operations* and is also known as *DevSecOps*. This is a process of using the DevOps methodologies noted earlier to bring an integrated development and operations approach that is applied to the specification, creation, and implementation of security control systems. SecDevOps is a set of best practices designed to allow organizations to build a culture of secure coding within their development approach that will bring the impact of DevOps development and deployment processes to enable the secure deployment of application functionality. The planned outcome is to embed *security* inside the development process as deeply as DevOps has enabled an operations mindset into program development.

 You can learn more about DevSecOps in general and Microsoft's support for that approach in the Azure development environment at *https://azure.microsoft.com/en-us/solutions/devsecops/*.

The Systems Development Life Cycle

An SDLC is a **methodology** for the design and implementation of an information system. Using a methodology ensures a rigorous process with a clearly defined goal and increases the probability of success. Once a methodology has been adopted, the key milestones are established, and a team is selected and made accountable for accomplishing the project goals.

Traditional Development Methods

The traditional SDLC approach consists of six general phases. If you have taken a system analysis and design course, you may have been exposed to a model consisting of a different number of phases. SDLC models range from three to 12 phases, all of which have been mapped into the six presented here. The **waterfall model** pictured in Figure 11-1 illustrates that each phase begins with the results and information gained from the previous phase.

At the end of each phase of the traditional SDLC comes a structured review or reality check, during which the team determines if the project should be continued,

methodology

A formal approach to solving a problem based on a structured sequence of procedures.

waterfall model

A type of SDLC in which each phase of the process "flows from" the information gained in the previous phase, with multiple opportunities to return to previous phases and make adjustments.

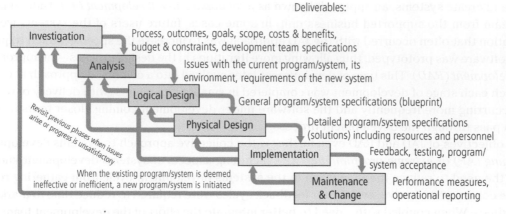

Figure 11-1 SDLC waterfall methodology

discontinued, outsourced, postponed, or returned to an earlier phase. This determination depends on whether the project is proceeding as expected and whether it needs additional expertise, organizational knowledge, or other resources.

Once the system is implemented, it is maintained and modified over the remainder of its working life. Any information systems implementation may have multiple iterations as the cycle is repeated over time. Only by constant examination and renewal can any system, especially an information security program, perform up to expectations in a constantly changing environment.

The following sections describe each phase of a traditional SDLC.[1]

Investigation

The first phase, investigation, is the most important. What problem is the system being developed to solve? The investigation phase begins by examining the event or plan that initiates the process. During this phase, the objectives, constraints, and scope of the project are specified. A preliminary cost-benefit analysis evaluates the perceived benefits and their appropriate levels of cost. At the conclusion of this phase and at every phase afterward, a process will be undertaken to assess economic, technical, and behavioral feasibilities and ensure that implementation is worth the organization's time and effort.

Analysis

The analysis phase begins with the information gained during the investigation phase. This phase consists primarily of assessments of the organization, its current systems, and its capability to support the proposed systems. Analysts begin by determining what the new system is expected to do and how it will interact with existing systems. This phase ends with documentation of the findings and an update of the feasibility analysis.

Logical Design

In the logical design phase, the information gained from the analysis phase is used to begin creating a systems solution for a business problem. In any systems solution, the first and driving factor must be the business need. Based on the business need, applications are selected to provide needed services, and then the team chooses data support and structures capable of providing the needed inputs. Finally, based on all of this, specific technologies are delineated to implement the physical solution. The logical design, therefore, is the blueprint for the desired solution. The logical design is implementation-independent, meaning that it contains no reference to specific technologies, vendors, or products. Instead, it addresses how the proposed system will solve the problem at hand. In this stage, analysts generate estimates of costs and benefits to allow for a general comparison of available options. At the end of this phase, another feasibility analysis is performed.

Physical Design

During the physical design phase, specific technologies are selected to support the alternatives identified and evaluated in the logical design. The selected components are evaluated based on a make-or-buy decision—the option to develop components in-house or purchase them from a vendor. Final designs integrate various components and technologies. After yet another feasibility analysis, the entire solution is presented to the organization's management for approval.

Implementation

In the implementation phase, any needed software is created. Components are ordered, received, and tested. Afterward, users are trained and supporting documentation created. Once all components are tested individually, they are installed and tested as a system. A feasibility analysis is again prepared, and the sponsors are then presented with the system for a performance review and acceptance test.

Maintenance and Change

The maintenance and change phase is the longest and most expensive of the process. This phase consists of the tasks necessary to support and modify the system for the remainder of its useful life cycle. Even though formal development may conclude during this phase, the life cycle of the project continues until the team determines that the process should begin again from the investigation phase. At periodic points, the system is tested for compliance, and the feasibility of continuance versus discontinuance is evaluated. Upgrades, updates, and patches are managed. As the needs of the organization change, the systems that support the organization must also change. The people who manage and support the systems must continually monitor their effectiveness in relation to the organization's environment. When a current system can no longer support the evolving mission of the organization, the system is retired from use and ongoing maintenance stops. If the services provided by the retired system are still needed, a new project is planned and implemented.

For more information on SDLCs, see Appendix E of Special Publication 800-64, Rev. 2, from the National Institute of Standards and Technology (NIST). The Web address is *http://nvlpubs.nist.gov/nistpubs/Legacy/SP/nistspecialpublication800-64r2.pdf*. Although this is a "withdrawn" document that has been superseded, it is still useful to your understanding of the methodologies used in the security of software development.

Software Assurance

Many of the information security issues facing modern information systems have their root cause in the software elements of the system. Secure systems require secure or at least securable software. The development of systems and the software they use is often accomplished using a methodology, such as the SDLC described earlier. Many organizations recognize the need to include planning for security objectives in the SDLC they use to create systems, and have established procedures to create software that is more capable of being deployed in a secure fashion. This approach to software development is known as **software assurance**, or SA. SA attempts to intentionally create software free of vulnerabilities and provide effective, efficient software that users can deploy with confidence.

Organizations are increasingly working to build security into the SDLC to prevent security problems before they begin. A national effort is under way to create a common body of knowledge focused on secure software development. The U.S. Department of Defense launched a Software Assurance Initiative in 2003. This initial process was led by Joe Jarzombek and was endorsed and supported by the Department of Homeland Security (DHS), which joined the program in 2004. This program initiative resulted in the publication of the Software Assurance (SwA) Common Body of Knowledge (CBK).[2] A working group drawn from industry, government, and academia was formed to examine two key questions:

1. What are the engineering activities or aspects of activities that are relevant to achieving secure software?
2. What knowledge is needed to perform these activities or aspects?

Based on the findings of this working group and a host of existing external documents and standards, the SwA CBK was developed and published to serve as a guideline. While this work has not yet been adopted as a standard or even a policy requirement of government agencies, it serves as a strongly recommended guide to developing more secure applications.

software assurance

A methodological approach to the development of software that seeks to build security into the development life cycle rather than address it at later stages.

The SwA CBK, which is a work in progress, contains the following sections:

- Nature of Dangers
- Fundamental Concepts and Principles
- Ethics, Law, and Governance
- Secure Software Requirements
- Secure Software Design
- Secure Software Construction
- Secure Software Verification, Validation, and Evaluation
- Secure Software Tools and Methods
- Secure Software Processes
- Secure Software Project Management
- Acquisition of Secure Software
- Secure Software Sustainment[3]

The following sections provide insight into the stages that should be incorporated into the software SDLC.

Software Design Principles

Good software development should result in a finished product that meets all of its design specifications. Information security considerations are a critical component of those specifications, though that has not always been true. Leaders in software development J. H. Saltzer and M. D. Schroeder note that:

> *The protection of information in computer systems [. . . and] the usefulness of a set of protection mechanisms depends upon the ability of a system to prevent security violations. In practice, producing a system at any level of functionality that actually does prevent all such unauthorized acts has proved to be extremely difficult. Sophisticated users of most systems are aware of at least one way to crash the system, denying other users authorized access to stored information. Penetration exercises involving a large number of different general-purpose systems all have shown that users can construct programs that can obtain unauthorized access to information stored within. Even in systems designed and implemented with security as an important objective, design and implementation flaws provide paths that circumvent the intended access constraints. Design and construction techniques that systematically exclude flaws are the topic of much research activity, but no complete method applicable to the construction of large general-purpose systems exists yet.[4]*

This statement could be about software development in the early part of the 21st century, but it actually dates back to 1975, before information security and software assurance became critical factors for many organizations. In the same article, the authors provide insight into what are now commonplace security principles:

- *Economy of mechanism: Keep the design as simple and small as possible.*
- *Fail-safe defaults: Base access decisions on permission rather than exclusion.*
- *Complete mediation: Every access to every object must be checked for authority.*
- *Open design: The design should not be secret, but rather depend on the possession of keys or passwords.*
- *Separation of privilege: Where feasible, a protection mechanism should require two keys to unlock, rather than one.*
- *Least privilege: Every program and every user of the system should operate using the least set of privileges necessary to complete the job.*
- *Least common mechanism: Minimize mechanisms (or shared variables) common to more than one user and depended on by all users.*
- *Psychological acceptability: It is essential that the human interface be designed for ease of use, so that users routinely and automatically apply the protection mechanisms correctly.[5]*

Many of the common problems associated with programming approaches that don't follow the software assurance methodology are discussed in Module 2.

For more information on software assurance and the national effort to develop an SA common body of knowledge and supporting curriculum, visit *https://buildsecurityin.us-cert.gov/dhs/dhs-software-assurance-resources*.

The NIST Approach to Securing the SDLC

NIST has adopted a simplified SDLC for its approach, based on five phases: initiation, development/acquisition, implementation/assessment, operation/maintenance, and disposal. These loosely map to the SDLC approach described earlier, as shown in Table 11-1.

Each phase of the SDLC should include consideration for the security of the system being assembled as well as the information it uses. Whether the system is custom-made and built from scratch, purchased and then customized, or *commercial off-the-shelf software (COTS)*, the implementing organization is responsible for ensuring its secure use. This means that each implementation of a system is secure and does not risk compromising the confidentiality, integrity, and availability of the organization's information assets. The following section, adapted from NIST Special Publication 800-64, Rev. 2, provides an overview of the security considerations for each phase of the SDLC.

While the following section offers advice from NIST expressed in the context of traditional methods (the waterfall methodology), note that these principles are equally valid when the effort uses RAD, JAD, Agile, XP, and other approaches to systems development. Development projects that make use of nontraditional development methodologies must still build in the requirements dictated by sound security practices. Software development should always include meeting security requirements.

> To be most effective, information security must be integrated into the SDLC from system inception. Early integration of security in the SDLC enables agencies to maximize return on investment in their security programs, through:
>
> - Early identification and mitigation of security vulnerabilities and misconfigurations, resulting in lower cost of security control implementation and vulnerability mitigation;
> - Awareness of potential engineering challenges caused by mandatory security controls;
> - Identification of shared security services and reuse of security strategies and tools to reduce development cost and schedule while improving security posture through proven methods and techniques; and
> - Facilitation of informed executive decision making through comprehensive risk management in a timely manner. [. . .]

Initiation

> During this first phase of the development life cycle, security considerations are key to diligent and early integration, thereby ensuring that threats, requirements, and potential constraints in functionality and integration are considered. At this point, security is looked at more in terms of business risks with input from the information security office. For example, an agency may identify a political risk resulting from

Table 11-1   Comparison of Waterfall and NIST SDLC Phases

Waterfall SDLC Phase	Equivalent NIST SDLC Phase
Investigation	Initiation
Analysis	
Logical Design	Development/Acquisition
Physical Design	
Implementation	Implementation/Assessment
Maintenance and Change	Operation/Maintenance
	Disposal

a prominent Web site being modified or made unavailable during a critical business period, resulting in decreased trust by citizens.

Key security activities for this phase include:

- *Initial delineation of business requirements in terms of confidentiality, integrity, and availability;*
- *Determination of information categorization and identification of known special handling requirements to transmit, store, or create information such as personally identifiable information; and*
- *Determination of any privacy requirements.*

Early planning and awareness will result in cost and time saving through proper risk management planning. Security discussions should be performed as part of (not separately from) the development project to ensure solid understandings among project personnel of business decisions and their risk implications to the overall development project. [. . .]

These activities and their related outputs are illustrated in Figure 11-2. The key aspect of this illustration is the alignment of the system design to enterprise architecture (EA) and information assurance (IA) design goals.

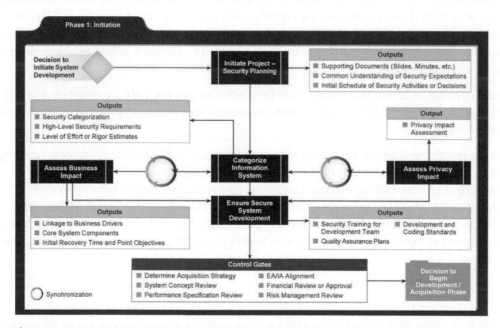

Figure 11-2 Relating security considerations in the Initiation phase

Source: NIST SP 800-64 Rev. 2: "Security Considerations in the System Development Life Cycle."

Development/Acquisition

This section addresses security considerations unique to the second SDLC phase. Key security activities for this phase include:

- *Conduct the risk assessment and use the results to supplement the baseline security controls;*
- *Analyze security requirements;*
- *Perform functional and security testing;*
- *Prepare initial documents for system certification and accreditation; and*
- *Design security architecture.*

Although this section presents the information security components in a sequential top-down manner, the order of completion is not necessarily fixed. Security analysis of complex systems will need to be iterated until consistency and completeness is achieved. [. . .]

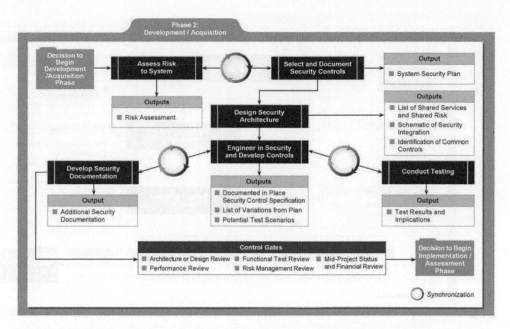

Figure 11-3   Relating security considerations in the Development/Acquisition phase

Source: NIST SP 800-64 Rev. 2: "Security Considerations in the System Development Life Cycle."

These activities and their related outputs are illustrated in Figure 11-3.

Implementation/Assessment

Implementation/Assessment is the third phase of the SDLC. During this phase, the system will be installed and evaluated in the organization's operational environment.

Key security activities for this phase include:

- *Integrate the information system into its environment;*
- *Plan and conduct system certification activities in synchronization with testing of security controls; and*
- *Complete system accreditation activities. [. . .]*

Note that the Certification and Authorization (C&A) approach to systems formerly used by the federal government has evolved into a comprehensive Risk Management Framework (RMF). As such, the performance of a risk assessment on the system under development would replace the C&A process. These activities and their related outputs are illustrated in Figure 11-4. The *POA&M* in the figure refers to a plan of action and milestones (POA&M), which is a document that identifies tasks to be accomplished.

Operations and Maintenance

Operations and Maintenance is the fourth phase of the SDLC. In this phase, systems are in place and operating, enhancements and/or modifications to the system are developed and tested, and hardware and/or software is added or replaced. The system is monitored for continued performance in accordance with security requirements and needed system modifications are incorporated. The operational system is periodically assessed to determine how the system can be made more effective, secure, and efficient. Operations continue as long as the system can be effectively adapted to respond to an organization's needs while maintaining an agreed-upon risk level. When necessary modifications or changes are identified, the system may reenter a previous phase of the SDLC.

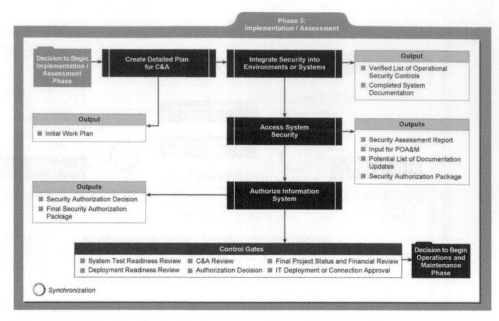

Figure 11-4   Relating security considerations in the Implementation/ Assessment phase

Source: NIST SP 800-64 Rev. 2: "Security Considerations in the System Development Life Cycle."

Key security activities for this phase include:

- *Conduct an operational readiness review;*
- *Manage the configuration of the system;*
- *Institute processes and procedures for assured operations and continuous monitoring of the information system's security controls; and*
- *Perform reauthorization as required. [. . .]*

These activities and their related outputs are illustrated in Figure 11-5. Note that the CCB indicated in this figure is the change control board, the organizational unit that coordinates changes to systems across the organization.

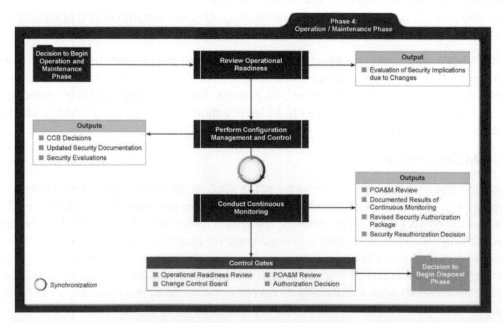

Figure 11-5   Relating security considerations in the Operations/Maintenance phase

Source: NIST SP 800-64 Rev. 2: "Security Considerations in the System Development Life Cycle."

Disposal

Disposal, the final phase in the SDLC, provides for disposal of a system and closeout of any contracts in place. Information security issues associated with information and system disposal should be addressed explicitly. When information systems are transferred, become obsolete, or are no longer usable, it is important to ensure that government resources and assets are protected.

Usually, there is no definitive end to a system. Systems normally evolve or transition to the next generation because of changing requirements or improvements in technology. System security plans should continually evolve with the system. Much of the environmental, management, and operational information should still be relevant and useful in developing the security plan for the follow-on system.

The disposal activities ensure the orderly termination of the system and preserve the vital information about the system so that some or all of the information may be reactivated in the future, if necessary. Particular emphasis is given to proper preservation of the data processed by the system so that the data is effectively migrated to another system or archived in accordance with applicable records management regulations and policies for potential future access.

Key security activities for this phase include:

- *Building and executing a disposal/transition plan;*
- *Archival of critical information;*
- *Sanitization of media; and*
- *Disposal of hardware and software.*[6]

These activities and their related outputs are illustrated in Figure 11-6.

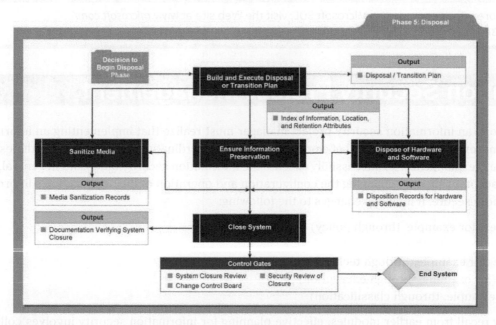

Figure 11-6   Relating security considerations in the Disposal phase

Source: NIST SP 800-64 Rev. 2: "Security Considerations in the System Development Life Cycle."

It is imperative that information security be designed into a system from its inception, rather than being added during or after the implementation phase. Information systems that were designed with no security functionality, or with security functions added as an afterthought, often require constant patching, updating, and maintenance to prevent risk to the systems and information. A well-known adage holds that "an ounce of prevention is worth a pound of cure." With this in mind, organizations are moving toward more security-focused development approaches, seeking to improve not only the functionality of existing systems but consumer confidence in their products. In early 2002, Microsoft effectively suspended development work on many of its products to put its OS developers, testers, and program managers through an intensive program that focused on secure software development. It also delayed release of its flagship server operating system to address critical security issues. Many other organizations followed Microsoft's lead in putting security into the development process. Since that time, Microsoft has developed its own Security Development Lifecycle, which uses a seven-phase, 17-step methodology that culminates in an executed incident response plan, as shown in Figure 11-7.[7]

Training	Requirements	Design	Implementation	Verification	Release	Response
Core security training	Establish security requirements	Establish design requirements	Use approved tools	Dynamic analysis	Incident response plan	Execute incident response plan
	Create quality gates/bug bars	Analyze attack surface	Deprecate unsafe functions	Fuzz testing	Final security review	
	Security and privacy risk assessment	Threat modeling	Static analysis	Attack surface review	Release archive	

Figure 11-7   Microsoft's SDL[8]

Source: Microsoft. Used with permission.

 For more information on the Microsoft SDL, visit the Web site at *www.microsoft.com/en-us/securityengineering/sdl/*.

Information Security Project Management

First and foremost, an information security project manager must realize that implementing an information security project takes time, effort, and a great deal of communication and coordination. This module continues the discussion from Module 3 and explains how to successfully execute the information security blueprint. In general, the implementation phase is accomplished by changing the configuration and operation of the organization's information systems to make them more secure. It includes changes to the following:

- Procedures (for example, through policy)
- People (for example, through training)
- Hardware (for example, through technology like firewalls)
- Software (for example, through encryption)
- Data (for example, through classification)

As you may recall from earlier modules, effective planning for information security involves collecting information about an organization's objectives, its technical architecture, and its information security environment. These elements are used to form the information security blueprint, which is the foundation for protecting the confidentiality, integrity, and availability of the organization's information. The realization of these objectives will require an organization to define and execute a project. Successful projects require the application of a management specialty known as **project management**.

project management

The process of identifying and controlling the goals, objectives, tasks, scheduling, and resources of a project.

During the implementation phase, the organization translates its blueprint for information security into a **project plan**. The project plan instructs the people who are executing the implementation phase. These instructions focus on the security control changes needed to improve the security of the hardware, software, procedures, data, and people that make up the organization's information systems. The information security project plan as a whole must describe how to acquire and implement the needed security controls and create a setting in which those controls achieve the desired outcomes.

> **project plan**
>
> The documented instructions for participants and stakeholders in a project that provide details on its goals, objectives, tasks, scheduling, and resource management.

As the opening scenario of this module illustrates, organizational change is not easily accomplished. The following sections discuss the issues a project plan must address, including project leadership; managerial, technical, and budgetary considerations; and organizational resistance to the change.

The major steps in executing the project plan are as follows:

- Planning the project
- Supervising tasks and action steps
- Wrapping up

The project plan can be developed in any number of ways. Each organization has to determine its own project management methodology for IT and information security projects. Whenever possible, information security projects should follow the organization's project management practices. Many organizations now make use of a *project office*—a centralized resource to maximize the benefits of a standardized approach to project management. One such benefit is the leveraging of common project management practices across the organization to enable reallocation of resources without confusion or delays.

Developing the Project Plan

Planning for the implementation phase requires the creation of a detailed project plan, which is often assigned either to a project manager or the project champion. This person manages the project and delegates parts of it to other decision makers. Often, the project manager is from the IT community of interest because most other employees lack the requisite information security background, management authority, and technical knowledge.

The project plan can be created using a simple planning tool such as the **work breakdown structure (WBS)**. An example is shown in Table 11-2. To use the WBS approach, you first break down the project plan into its major tasks. The major project tasks are placed into the WBS, along with the following attributes for each:

> **work breakdown structure (WBS)**
>
> A list of the tasks to be accomplished in a project, the skill sets or individual employees needed to perform the tasks, the start and end dates for tasks, the estimated resources required, and the dependencies among tasks.

- Work to be accomplished (activities and deliverables)
- The people or skill sets assigned to perform the task
- Start and end dates for the task, when known
- Amount of effort required for completion, in hours or work days
- Estimated capital expenses for the task
- Estimated noncapital expenses for the task
- Identification of dependencies between and among tasks

Each major task in the WBS is then further divided into either smaller tasks (subtasks) or specific action steps. For the sake of simplicity, the sample project plan outlined in the table and described in the following sections divides each major task into action steps. In an actual project plan, major tasks are often much more complex and must be divided into subtasks before action steps can be identified and assigned to a specific person or skill set. Given the variety of possible projects, there are few formal guidelines for determining the appropriate level of detail—that is, the level at which a task or subtask should become an action step. However, one hard-and-fast rule can help you make this determination: A task or subtask becomes an action step when it can be completed by one person or skill set and has a single deliverable. (A deliverable is a completed document or program module that can serve either as the beginning point for a later task or become an element in the finished project.)

Table 11-2 Example Work Breakdown Structure for a Project Plan

Task or Subtask	Resources	Start (S) & End (E) Dates	Estimated Effort in Hours	Estimated Capital Expense	Estimated Noncapital Expense	Dependencies
1. Contact field office and confirm network assumptions	Network architect	S: 9/22 E: 9/22	2	$0	$200	
2. Purchase standard firewall hardware						
2.1 Order firewall through purchasing group	Network architect	S: 9/23 E: 9/23	1	$0	$100	1
2.2 Order firewall from manufacturer	Purchasing group	S: 9/24 E: 9/24	2	$4,500	$100	2.1
2.3 Firewall delivered	Purchasing group	E: 10/3	1	$0	$50	2.2
3. Configure firewall	Network architect	S: 10/3 E: 10/5	8	$0	$800	2.3
4. Package and ship firewall to field office	Student intern	S: 10/6 E: 10/15	2	$0	$85	3
5. Work with local technical resource to install and test firewall	Network architect	S: 10/22 E: 10/31	6	$0	$600	4
6. Penetration test						
6.1 Request penetration test	Network architect	S: 11/1 E: 11/1	1	$0	$100	5
6.2 Perform penetration test	Penetration test team	S: 11/2 E: 11/12	9	$0	$900	6.1
6.3 Verify that results of penetration test were passing	Network architect	S: 11/13 E: 11/15	2	$0	$200	6.2
7. Get remote office sign-off and update all network drawings and documentation	Network architect	S: 11/16 E: 11/30	8	$0	$800	6.2

projectitis

A situation in project planning in which a project manager spends more time manipulating and adjusting aspects of the project management software than accomplishing meaningful project work.

The WBS can be prepared with a simple spreadsheet program. The use of more complex project management software often leads to **projectitis**, in which the project manager spends more time working with the project management software than accomplishing meaningful project work. Recall Kelvin's slides from the opening scenario, which were loaded with dates and details. His case of projectitis led him to develop an elegant, detailed plan before gaining consensus for the required changes. Because he was new to project management, he did not realize that simpler software tools could help him focus on organizing and coordinating with the project team.

Work to Be Accomplished

The work to be accomplished encompasses both activities and *deliverables*. Ideally, the project planner provides a label to identify the task and provides a thorough description for the task. The description should be complete enough to avoid ambiguity during the tracking process later, yet should not be so detailed as to make the WBS unwieldy. For instance, if the task is to write firewall specifications for the preparation of a *request for proposal (RFP)*, the planner should note that the deliverable is a specification document suitable for distribution to vendors.

Assignments

The project planner should describe the skills or personnel, often referred to as *resources*, needed to accomplish the task. The naming of individual employees should be avoided in early planning efforts, a rule Kelvin ignored when he named employees for every task in the first draft of his project plan. Instead of making individual assignments, the project plan should focus on organizational roles or known skill sets. For example, if any of the engineers in the networks group can write the specifications for a router, the assigned resource would be noted as "network engineer" in the WBS. As planning progresses, however, specific tasks and action steps should be assigned to individual employees. For example, when *only* the manager of the networks group can evaluate responses to the RFP and make an award for a contract, the project planner should assign the network manager as the resource for this task.

Start and End Dates

In the early stages of planning, the project planner should attempt to specify completion dates only for major project *milestones*. For example, the date for sending the final RFP to vendors is a milestone because it signals that all RFP preparation work is complete. Assigning too many dates to too many tasks early in the planning process exacerbates projectitis. This is another mistake Kelvin made, and was a significant cause of the resistance he faced from his coworkers. Planners can avoid this pitfall by assigning only key or milestone start and end dates early in the process. Later, planners may add start and end dates as needed.

Amount of Effort

Planners need to estimate the effort required to complete each task, subtask, or action step. Estimating effort hours for technical work is a complex process. Even when an organization has formal governance, technical review processes, and change control procedures, it is always good practice to ask the people who are most familiar with the tasks to make these estimates. After these estimates are made, the people assigned to action steps should review the estimated effort hours, understand the tasks, and agree with the estimates. Had Kelvin collaborated with his peers more effectively and adopted a more flexible planning approach, much of the resistance he encountered in the meeting would not have emerged.

Estimated Capital Expenses

Planners need to estimate the capital expenses required for the completion of each task, subtask, or action item. While each organization budgets and expends capital according to its own established procedures, most differentiate between capital outlays for durable assets and expenses for other purposes. For example, a firewall device that costs $5,000 may be a capital outlay for an organization, but it might not consider a $5,000 software package to be a capital outlay because its accounting rules classify all software as expense items, regardless of cost.

Estimated Noncapital Expenses

Planners need to estimate the noncapital expenses for the completion of each task, subtask, or action item. In business, capital expenses are those for revenue-producing projects that are expected to yield a return on investment, usually more than a year in the future. Noncapital expenses do not meet the criteria for capital expenditures. Some organizations require that current expenses for a project include a recovery charge for staff time, while others exclude employee time and consider only contract or consulting time used by the project as a noncapital expense. As mentioned earlier, it is important to determine the cost accounting practices for which the plan is to be used. For example, at some companies, a project to implement a firewall may charge only the costs of the firewall hardware as capital and consider all costs for labor and software as expense; the hardware element is regarded as a durable good that has a lifespan of many years. Another organization might use the aggregate of all cash outflows associated with the implementation as the capital charge and make no charges to the expense category for everything needed to complete the project. The justification behind using this aggregate of all costs—which might include charges for items like hardware, labor, and freight—is that the newly implemented capability is expected to last for many years and is an improvement to the organization's infrastructure. A third company may charge the whole project as expense if the aggregate amount falls below a certain threshold, under the theory that small projects are a cost of ongoing operations.

Task Dependencies

Whenever possible, planners should note the dependencies of other tasks or action steps on the one at hand, including task *predecessors* and *successors*. Predecessors are tasks that precede the current task, and successors are tasks that come after the current task and are dependent upon it. Multiple types of dependencies can exist, but such details are typically covered in courses on project management and are beyond the scope of this text.

A process for developing a simple WBS-style project plan is provided in the following steps. In this example, a small information security project has been assigned to Jane Smith for planning. The project is to design and implement a firewall for a small office. The hardware is a standard organizational product and will be installed at a location that already has a network connection.

Jane's first step is to list the major tasks:

1. Contact field office and confirm network assumptions.
2. Purchase standard firewall hardware.
3. Configure firewall.
4. Package and ship firewall to field office.
5. Work with local technical resource to install and test firewall.
6. Coordinate vulnerability assessment by penetration test team.
7. Get remote office sign-off and update all network drawings and documentation.

After all the people involved review and refine Jane's plan, she revises it to add more dates to the tasks listed, as shown in Table 11-2.

 For more information on project management certifications in the federal sector, visit *www.fai.gov/certification/program-and-project-managers-fac-ppm*.

Project Planning Considerations

As the project plan is developed, adding detail is not always straightforward. The following sections discuss factors that project planners must consider as they decide what to include in the work plan, how to break tasks into subtasks and action steps, and how to accomplish the objectives of the project.

Financial Considerations

Regardless of an organization's information security needs, the amount of effort that can be expended depends on the available funds. A cost-benefit analysis (CBA), as described in Module 4, is typically prepared and must be reviewed and verified prior to the development of the project plan. The CBA determines the impact that a specific technology or approach can have on the organization's information assets and what it may cost.

Each organization has its own approach to the creation and management of budgets and expenses. In many organizations, the information security budget is a subsection of the overall IT budget. In others, information security is a separate budget category that may have the same degree of visibility and priority as the IT budget. Regardless of where information security items are located in the budget, monetary constraints determine what can and cannot be accomplished.

Public organizations tend to be more predictable in their budget processes than private organizations because the budgets of public organizations are usually the product of legislation or public meetings. This makes it difficult to obtain additional funds once the budget is determined. Also, some public organizations rely on temporary or renewable grants for their budgets and must stipulate their planned expenditures when the grant applications are written. If new expenses arise, funds must be requested via new grant applications. Also, grant expenditures are usually audited and cannot be misspent. In addition, many public organizations must spend all budgeted funds within the fiscal year—otherwise, the subsequent year's budget is reduced by the unspent amount. As a result, these organizations often conduct "spend-a-thons" at the end of the fiscal year. This is often the best time to acquire a remaining piece of technology needed to complete the information security architecture.

Private (for-profit) organizations have budgetary constraints that are determined by the marketplace. When a for-profit organization initiates a project to improve security, the funding comes from the company's capital and expense budgets. Each for-profit organization has different methods for determining its capital budget and its rules for managing capital spending and expenses. In almost all cases, however, budgetary constraints affect the planning and actual expenditures for information security. For example, a preferred technology or solution may be sacrificed for a less desirable but more affordable solution. The budget ultimately guides the information security implementation.

To justify the amount budgeted for a security project at either a public or for-profit organization, it may be useful to benchmark expenses of similar organizations. Most for-profit organizations publish the components of their expense reports. Similarly, public organizations must document how funds are spent. A savvy information security project manager might find a number of similarly sized organizations with larger expenditures for security to justify planned spending. While such tactics may not improve this year's budget, they could improve future budgets. Ironically, attackers can also help information security project planners justify the information security budget. If attacks successfully compromise secured information systems, management may be more willing to support the information security budget.

Priority Considerations

In general, the most important information security controls in the project plan should be scheduled first. Budgetary constraints may have an effect on the assignment of a project's priorities. As you learned in Module 5, the implementation of controls is guided by the prioritization of threats and the value of the threatened information assets. A less important control may be prioritized if it addresses a group of specific vulnerabilities and improves the organization's security posture to a greater degree than other high-priority controls.

Time and Scheduling Considerations

Time and scheduling can affect a project plan at dozens of points, including the time between ordering and receiving a security control, which may not be immediately available; the time it takes to install and configure the control; the time it takes to train the users; and the time it takes to realize the control's return on investment. For example, if a control must be in place before an organization can implement its electronic commerce product, the selection process is likely to be influenced by the speed of acquisition and implementation of the various alternatives.

Staffing Considerations

The need for qualified, trained, and available personnel also constrains the project plan. An experienced staff is often needed to implement technologies and to develop and implement policies and training programs. If no staff members are trained to configure a new firewall, for example, the appropriate personnel must be trained or hired.

Procurement Considerations

There are often constraints on the selection of equipment and services—for example, some organizations require the use of particular service vendors or manufacturers and suppliers. These constraints may limit which technologies can be acquired. For example, in a recent budget cycle, the author's lab administrator was considering selecting an automated risk analysis software package. The leading candidate promised to integrate everything, including vulnerability scanning, risk weighting, and control selection. Upon receipt of the RFP, the vendor issued a bid to meet the desired requirements for a staggering $75,000, plus a 10 percent annual maintenance fee. If an organization has an annual information security budget of $30,000, it must eliminate a package like this from consideration. Also, consider the chilling effect on innovation when an organization requires elaborate supporting documentation and complex bidding for even small-scale purchases. Such procurement constraints, which are designed to control losses from occasional abuses, may actually increase costs when the lack of operating agility is taken into consideration.

Organizational Feasibility Considerations

Whenever possible, security-related technological changes should be transparent to system users, but sometimes such changes require new procedures—for example, additional authentication or validation. A successful project requires that an organization be able to assimilate the proposed changes. New technologies sometimes require new policies, employee training, and education. Scheduling training after the new processes are in place—and after the users have had to deal with the changes without preparation—can create tension and resistance, and might undermine security operations. Users who are untrained in a new technology may develop ways to work around unfamiliar security procedures, and their bypassing of controls may create additional vulnerabilities. Conversely, users should not be prepared so far in advance that they forget the new training techniques and requirements. The optimal time frame for training is usually one to three weeks before the new policies and technologies come online.

Training and Indoctrination Considerations

The size of the organization and the normal conduct of business may preclude a large training program for new security procedures or technologies. If so, the organization should conduct a phased-in or pilot implementation, such as roll-out training for one department at a time. See the "Conversion Strategies" section later in the module for details about various implementation approaches. When a project involves a change in policies, it may be sufficient to brief supervisors on the new policy and assign them the task of updating end users in regularly scheduled meetings. Project planners must ensure that compliance documents are also distributed and that all employees are required to read, understand, and agree to the new policies.

Scope Considerations

The scope of any given project plan should be carefully reviewed and kept as small as possible, given the project's objectives. To control project scope, organizations should implement large information security projects in stages, as in the bull's-eye approach discussed later in this module.

For several reasons, the scope of information security projects must be evaluated and adjusted with care. First, in addition to the challenge of handling many complex tasks at one time, the installation of information security controls can disrupt the ongoing operations of an organization and may also conflict with existing controls in unpredictable ways. For example, if you install a new packet-filtering router and a new application proxy firewall at the same time and users are blocked from accessing the Web as a result, which technology caused the conflict? Was it the router, the firewall, or an interaction between the two? Limiting the project scope to a set of manageable tasks does not mean that the project should only allow change to one component at a time, but a good plan carefully considers the number of tasks that are planned for the same time in a single department.

Recall from the opening scenario that all of Kelvin's change requests are in the area of networking, where the dependencies are particularly complex. If the changes in Kelvin's project plan are not deployed exactly as planned, or if unanticipated complexities arise, there could be extensive disruption to Sequential Label and Supply's daily operations. For instance, an error in the deployment of the primary firewall rules could interrupt all Internet connectivity, which might make detection and recovery from the error more difficult.

The Need for Project Management

Project management requires a unique set of skills and a thorough understanding of a broad body of specialized knowledge. In the opening scenario, Kelvin's inexperience as a project manager makes this all too clear. Realistically, most information security projects require a trained project manager—a CISO or a skilled IT manager who is trained in project management techniques. Even experienced project managers are advised to seek expert assistance when needed—for example, when engaging in a formal bidding process to select advanced or integrated technologies or outsourced services.

When projects are being implemented to support information security objectives, the project manager and others associated with the project should have an appropriate skill set in security or prior experience with the topic. The need for information security to be built into development efforts means that project leaders and other key participants should understand the security environment.

Supervised Implementation

Although it is not an optimal solution, some organizations designate a champion from the general management community of interest to supervise the implementation of an information security project plan. In this case, groups of tasks are delegated to individuals or teams from the IT and information security communities of interest. An alternative is to designate a senior IT manager or the CIO of the organization to lead the implementation. In this case, the detailed work is delegated to cross-functional teams.

The best solution is to designate a suitable person from the information security community of interest. In the final analysis, each organization must find the project leadership that best suits its specific needs and the personalities and politics of the organizational culture.

Executing the Plan

Once a project is under way, it is managed using a process known as **gap analysis** (also known as a negative feedback loop or cybernetic loop), which ensures that progress is measured periodically. When significant deviation occurs, corrective action is taken to bring the deviating task back into compliance with the project plan; otherwise, the project is revised in light of the new information. See Figure 11-8 for an overview of this process.

gap analysis

The process of comparing measured results against expected results and then using the resulting "gap" as a measure of project success and as feedback for project management.

Corrective action is taken in two basic situations: Either the estimate is flawed or performance has lagged. When an estimate is flawed, as when the number of effort hours required is underestimated, the plan should be corrected and downstream tasks updated to reflect the change. When performance has lagged— for example, due to high turnover of skilled employees—corrective action may take the form of adding resources, making longer schedules, or reducing the quality or quantity of the deliverable. Corrective action decisions are usually expressed in terms of trade-offs. Often, a project manager can adjust one of the three following planning parameters for the task being corrected:

- Effort and money allocated
- Elapsed time or scheduling impact
- Quality or quantity of the deliverable

When too much effort and money are being spent, you may decide to take more time to complete the project tasks or to lower the deliverable's quality or quantity. If the task is taking too long to complete, you should probably add more resources in staff time or money or decrease the deliverable's quality or quantity. If the quality of the deliverable is inadequate, you must usually add more resources in staff time or money or take longer to complete the task. Of course, there are complex dynamics among these variables, and these simplistic solutions do not serve in all cases, but this simple trade-off model can help the project manager analyze available options.

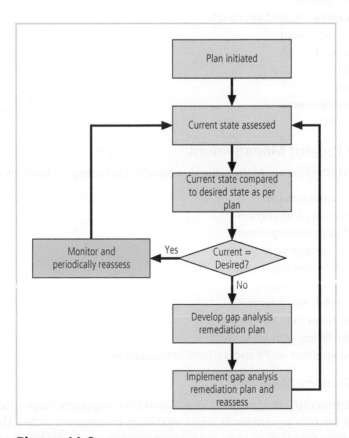

Figure 11-8   Gap analysis

Project Wrap-Up

Project wrap-up is usually handled as a procedural task and assigned to a mid-level IT or information security manager. These managers collect documentation, finalize status reports, and deliver a final report and a presentation at a wrap-up meeting. The goal of the wrap-up is to resolve any pending issues, critique the overall project effort, and draw conclusions about how to improve the process for the future.

 For more information on project management, visit the Project Management Institute's Web site at *www.pmi.org*.

Security Project Management Certifications

For information security professionals who seek additional credentials and recognition for their project management experience, some certifications are available.

GIAC Certified Project Manager

The SANS Institute offers a program that focuses on security professionals and managers who have project management responsibilities and seek to demonstrate their mastery of project management methods and strategies.[9] Candidates for the certification may either study on their own or enroll in the SANS IT Project Management course. The program focuses on the following topic areas:

- Earned value technique (EVT)
- Leadership and management strategy
- Project communication management
- Project cost management
- Project human resource management
- Project integration management
- Project management framework and approach
- Project procurement management
- Project quality management
- Project risk management
- Project scope management
- Project stakeholder management
- Project time management[10]

EC-Council IT Security Project Management

The EC-Council offers the Certified Project Management program. This program focuses on the following topics:

- Introduction to project management
- Project scope and technology integration
- Project scheduling and time management
- Project cost and budget management
- Project sourcing and vendor management
- Project controls and quality assurance
- Project opportunity and risk management
- Project governance and team management
- Project visualization, analytics, and reporting
- Project stakeholder engagement and expectations management[11]

SIA Certified Security Project Manager

The Security Industry Association (SIA) is a consortium focused predominantly on physical security, but it also incorporates information security into its programs. It has a certification program called the Certified Security Project Manager (CSPM), which signifies completion of its project manager course, a body of self-study, and the completion of a final examination.

For more information on the SANS GIAC Certified Project Manager certification, visit *www.giac.org/certification/certified-project-manager-gcpm*. For more information on the EC-Council's PM course, visit *www.eccouncil.org*. For more information on the SIA certification, visit *www.securityindustry.org*.

PMI Project Management Professional

The Project Management Institute offers training and an examination for the very prestigious Project Management Professional (PMP) certification. Many experts in project management believe the PMP is the premier certification in the field and proves you have the specific skills and experience employers seek.

 For more information on the Project Management Institute and the PMP certification, visit *www.pmi.org/certifications/project-management-pmp*.

Technical Aspects Of Implementation

Some aspects of the implementation process are technical and deal with the application of technology, while others deal with the human interface to technical systems. The following sections discuss conversion strategies, prioritization among multiple components, outsourcing, and technology governance.

Conversion Strategies

As the components of the new security system are planned, provisions must be made for the changeover from the previous method of performing a task to the new method. Just like IT systems, information security projects require careful conversion planning. This section discusses the four basic approaches for changing from an old system or process to a new one. The approaches are illustrated in Figure 11-9.

Direct Changeover

Also known as going "cold turkey," a **direct changeover conversion strategy** involves stopping the old method and beginning the new one. This approach could be as simple as having employees follow the existing procedure one week and then use a new procedure the next. Some cases of direct changeover are simple, such as requiring employees to begin using a new password with a stronger degree of authentication on an announced date. Some may be more complex, such as requiring the entire company to change procedures when the network team disables an old firewall and activates a new one. The primary drawback to the direct changeover approach is that if the new system fails or needs modification, users may be without services while the system's bugs are worked out. Complete testing of the new system in advance of the direct changeover reduces the probability of such problems.

> **direct changeover conversion strategy**
> The conversion strategy that involves stopping the old system and starting the new one without any overlap.

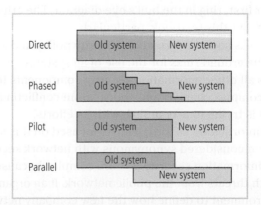

Figure 11-9   Conversion strategies

phased implementation conversion strategy

The conversion strategy that involves a measured rollout of the planned system; only part of the system is brought out and disseminated across an organization before the next piece is implemented.

pilot implementation conversion strategy

The conversion strategy that involves implementing the entire system into a single office, department, or division and dealing with issues that arise before expanding to the rest of the organization.

parallel operations conversion strategy

The conversion strategy that involves running the new system concurrently with the old system.

bull's-eye model

A method for prioritizing a program of complex change that requires issues to be addressed from the general to the specific and focuses on systematic solutions instead of individual problems.

Phased Implementation

A **phased implementation conversion strategy** is the most common and involves a measured rollout of the planned system, with only part of the system being brought out and disseminated across an organization before the next piece is implemented. For example, this could mean that the security group implements only a small portion of the new security profile, giving users a chance to get used to it and resolving issues as they arise. This is usually the best approach to security project implementation. As another example, if an organization seeks to update both its VPN and IDPS systems, it may first introduce the new VPN solution that employees can use to connect to the organization's network while they're traveling. Each week another department will be allowed to use the new VPN, with this process continuing until all departments are using the new approach. Once the new VPN has been phased into operation, revisions to the organization's IDPS can begin.

Pilot Implementation

In a **pilot implementation conversion strategy**, the entire security system is put in place in a single office, department, or division before expanding to the rest of the organization. The pilot implementation works well when an isolated group can serve as the "guinea pig," which prevents any problems with the new system from dramatically interfering with the performance of the organization as a whole. The operation of a research and development group, for example, may not affect the real-time operations of the organization and could assist security in resolving issues that emerge.

Parallel Operations

The **parallel operations conversion strategy** involves running two systems concurrently; in terms of information systems, it might involve running two firewalls concurrently, for example. Although this approach is complex, it can reinforce an organization's information security by allowing the old system(s) to serve as a backup for the new systems if they fail or are compromised. Drawbacks usually include the need to deal with both systems and maintain both sets of procedures.

The Bull's-Eye Model

A proven method for prioritizing a program of complex change is the **bull's-eye model**. This methodology, which goes by many different names and has been used by many organizations, requires that issues be addressed from the general to the specific and that the focus be on systematic solutions instead of individual problems. The increased capabilities—that is, increased expenditures—are used to improve the information security program in a systematic and measured way. As presented here and illustrated in Figure 11-10, the approach relies on a process of project plan evaluation in four layers:

1. *Policies*—This is the outer, or first, ring in the bull's-eye diagram. The critical importance of policies has been emphasized throughout this textbook, particularly in Module 3. The foundation of all effective information security programs is sound information security policy and information technology policy. Because policy establishes the ground rules for the use of all systems and describes what is appropriate and inappropriate, it enables all other information security components to function correctly. When deciding how to implement complex changes and choose from conflicting options, you can use policy to clarify what the organization is trying to accomplish with its efforts.
2. *Networks*—In the past, most information security efforts focused on this layer, so until recently, information security was often considered synonymous with network security. In today's computing environment, implementing information security is more complex because networking infrastructure often comes into contact with threats from the public network. If an organization is new to the Internet and examines its policy environment to define how the new company networks should be defended, it will soon find that designing and implementing an effective DMZ is the primary way to secure those networks.

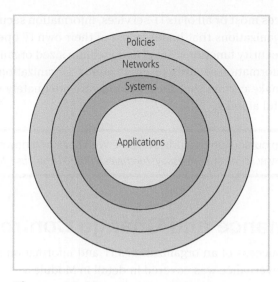

Figure 11-10   The bull's-eye model

Secondary efforts in this layer include providing the necessary authentication and authorization when allowing users to connect over public networks to the organization's systems.

3. *Systems*—Many organizations find that the problems of configuring and operating information systems in a secure fashion become more difficult as the number and complexity of these systems grow. This layer includes computers used as servers and desktop computers and systems used for process control and manufacturing systems.

4. *Applications*—The layer that receives attention last deals with the application software systems used by the organization to accomplish its work. This includes packaged applications, such as office automation and e-mail programs, as well as high-end enterprise resource planning (ERP) packages that span the organization. Custom application software developed by the organization for its own needs is also included.

By reviewing the information security blueprint and the current state of the organization's information security efforts in terms of these four layers, project planners can determine which areas require expanded capabilities. The bull's-eye model can also be used to evaluate the sequence of steps taken to integrate parts of the information security blueprint into a project plan. As suggested by its bull's-eye shape, this model dictates the following:

- Until sound and usable IT and information security policies are developed, communicated, and enforced, no additional resources should be spent on other controls.
- Until effective network controls are designed and deployed, all resources should go toward achieving that goal, unless resources are needed to revisit the policy needs of the organization.
- After policies and network controls are established, implementation should focus on the information, process, and manufacturing systems of the organization. Until there is well-informed assurance that all critical systems are being configured and operated in a secure fashion, all resources should be spent on reaching that goal.
- Once there is assurance that policies are in place, networks are secure, and systems are safe, attention should move to assessing and remediating the security of the organization's applications. This is a complicated and vast area of concern for many organizations, and most neglect to analyze the impact of information security on existing systems and their own proprietary systems. As in all planning efforts, attention should be paid to the most critical applications first.

To Outsource or Not

Not every organization needs to develop an information security department or program of its own. Just as some organizations outsource part or all of their IT operations, so too can organizations outsource their information security programs. The expense and time required to develop an effective information security program may be beyond the means of some organizations, so it may be in their best interest to hire professional services to help their IT departments implement such a program.

When an organization outsources most or all of its IT services, information security should be part of the contract arrangement with the supplier. Organizations that handle most of their own IT operations may choose to outsource the more specialized information security functions. Small and medium-sized organizations often hire outside consultants for penetration testing and information security program audits. Organizations of all sizes frequently outsource network monitoring functions to make certain that their systems are adequately secured and to gain assistance in watching for attempted or successful attacks.

 For an interesting article on outsourcing security, visit the Web page of renowned security consultant and author Bruce Schneier at *https://www.schneier.com/essays/archives/2002/01/the_case_for_outsour.html*.

Technology Governance and Change Control

Other factors that determine the success of an organization's IT and information security programs are technology governance and change control. Governance was covered in detail in Module 3.

technology governance

A process that organizations use to manage the effects and costs of technology implementation, innovation, and obsolescence.

Technology governance guides how frequently technical systems are updated and how technical updates are approved and funded. Technology governance also facilitates communication about technical advances and issues across the organization.

Medium-sized and large organizations deal with the impact of technical change on their operations through a **change control** process. By managing the process of change, the organization can do the following:

change control

A method of regulating the modification of systems within the organization by requiring formal review and approval for each change.

- Improve communication about change across the organization.
- Enhance coordination between groups within the organization as change is scheduled and completed.
- Reduce unintended consequences by having a process to resolve conflict and disruption that change can introduce.
- Improve quality of service as potential failures are eliminated and groups work together.
- Assure management that all groups are complying with the organization's policies for technology governance, procurement, accounting, and information security.

Effective change control is an essential part of the IT operation in all but the smallest organizations. The information security group can also use the change control process to ensure that the organization follows essential process steps that protect confidentiality, integrity, and availability when systems are upgraded across the organization.

The Center for Internet Security's Critical Security Controls

To provide guidance for the implementation of security controls in the organization, the Center for Internet Security (CIS) operates the Multi-State Information Sharing & Analysis Center (MS-ISAC), which serves as a sponsor and host of a concise, prioritized list of the most critical and widespread cyberattacks and a library of methods that can be used to control them. The MS-ISAC was created in response to industry practices that have seen security standards and requirement frameworks come and go; it makes an effort to address the risks that organizations face when using enterprise systems. These efforts often seem to devolve into a set of rote compliance reports to address past threats, resulting in a diversion of resources that may have been better spent making actual improvements in the security posture to meet evolving threats. This state of affairs was noted in 2008 by the U.S. National Security Agency (NSA), which undertook an "offense must inform defense" approach that sought to enable the selection and implementation of controls based on a prioritization model with an intention to block actual threats instead of generating compliance documentation. The result was the emergence of a global consortium drawn from industry and government that became known as the Critical Security Controls (the Controls). MS-ISAC was charged with a coordinating role in this process.

The CIS Controls sought to deliver functionality that focused on emerging advanced targeted threats, placing an emphasis on practical control approaches. The Controls were offered in a framework that emphasized standardization of approach and the use of automated techniques where possible, seeking to deliver a high degree of effectiveness and an essential efficiency to operations. The Controls are recognized as a subset of the controls enumerated in NIST SP 800-53 (currently in Draft Rev. 5) and are not intended to supplant the NIST directives, including the Cybersecurity Framework developed in response to Executive Order 13636. The order directed federal agencies to take steps to improve the security infrastructure of critical federal systems. One of those steps was the development and implementation of the Cybersecurity Framework. The Controls are a means of implementing a smaller number of actionable controls that deliver maximum results from a modest set of resource inputs using a structured list of priorities.

The Controls are informed by actual attacks and effective defenses, reflecting the knowledge of a broad range of experts in both the public and private sectors. These experts include threat responders, threat analysts, vulnerability finders, solution providers, defenders, policy makers, and users who work within government and academia as well as industries such as power, defense, finance, transportation, consulting, security, and IT.

The Controls are the most effective set of technical measures available to detect, prevent, respond to, and mitigate damage from attacks. The Controls work to block the initial compromise of systems and to prevent or disrupt further attacks on already compromised machines.[12]

The CIS Controls from Version 7.1, which was released in 2019, are as follows:

Basic Controls

1. *Inventory and Control of Hardware Assets*
2. *Inventory and Control of Software Assets*
3. *Continuous Vulnerability Management*
4. *Controlled Use of Administrative Privileges*
5. *Secure Configuration for Hardware and Software on Mobile Devices, Laptops, Workstations, and Servers*
6. *Maintenance, Monitoring, and Analysis of Audit Logs*

Foundational Controls

7. *E-mail and Web Browser Protections*
8. *Malware Defenses*
9. *Limitations and Control of Network Ports, Protocols, and Services*
10. *Data Recovery Capabilities*
11. *Secure Configuration for Network Devices such as Firewalls, Routers, and Switches*
12. *Boundary Defense*
13. *Data Protection*
14. *Controlled Access Based on the Need to Know*
15. *Wireless Access Controls*
16. *Account Monitoring and Control*

Organizational Controls

17. *Security Awareness and Training Program*
18. *Application Software Security*
19. *Incident Response and Management*
20. *Penetration Tests and Red Team Exercises.*[13]

Nontechnical Aspects Of Implementation

Some aspects of information security implementation are not technical in nature but deal instead with the human interface to technical systems. The sections that follow discuss the topics of creating a culture of change management and considerations for organizations facing change.

The Culture of Change Management

The prospect of change, the familiar shifting to the unfamiliar, can cause employees to resist the change, either unconsciously or consciously. Regardless of whether the changes are perceived as good or bad, employees tend to prefer the old way of doing things. Even when employees embrace changes, the stress of actually making the changes and adjusting to new procedures can increase the probability of mistakes or create vulnerabilities in systems. By understanding and applying some basic tenets of change management, project managers can lower employee resistance to change and can even build resilience for it, thereby making ongoing change more palatable to the entire organization.

The basic foundation of change management requires people who are making the changes to understand that organizations typically have cultures that represent their mood and philosophy. Disruptions to this culture must be properly addressed and their effects minimized. One of the oldest models of change is the Lewin change model, which consists of three simplistic stages:[14]

- *Unfreezing*—Thawing hard-and-fast habits and established procedures. Preparing the organization for upcoming changes facilitates the implementation of new processes, systems, and procedures. Training and awareness programs assist in this preparation.
- *Moving*—Transitioning between the old way and the new. The physical implementation of new methods, using the strategies outlined earlier in this module, requires the organization to recognize the cessation of old ways of work and reinforces the need to use the new methods.
- *Refreezing*—The integration of the new methods into the organizational culture. This integration is accomplished by creating an atmosphere in which the changes are accepted as the preferred way of accomplishing the necessary tasks.

Considerations for Organizational Change

An organization can take steps to make its employees more amenable to change. These steps reduce resistance to change at the beginning of the planning process and encourage members of the organization to be more flexible as changes occur.

Reducing Resistance to Change from the Start

The level of resistance to change affects the ease with which an organization can implement procedural and managerial changes. The more ingrained the existing methods and behaviors are, the more difficult it will probably be to make the change. It's best, therefore, to improve interactions between the affected members of the organization and project planners in the early phases of an information security improvement project. These interactions can be improved through a three-step process in which project managers communicate, educate, and involve.

Communication is the first and most critical step. Project managers must communicate with employees so they know a new security process is being considered and that their feedback is essential to making it work. Project managers must also constantly update employees on the progress of the project's changes and provide information on the expected completion dates. This ongoing series of updates keeps the process from being a last-minute surprise and primes people to accept the change more readily when it finally arrives.

At the same time, project managers must update and educate employees about exactly how the proposed changes will affect them individually and within the organization. While detailed information may not be available in earlier stages of a project plan, details that can be shared with employees may emerge as the project progresses. Education also involves teaching employees to use the new systems once they are in place. As discussed earlier, this means delivering high-quality training programs at the appropriate times.

Finally, project managers can reduce resistance to change by involving employees in the project plan. This means getting key representatives from user groups to serve as members of the project development process, as illustrated in the JAD methodology described earlier. Identifying a liaison between the IT team, information security subject matter experts, and the organization's general population can serve the project team well in early planning stages, when unforeseen problems with acceptance of the project may need to be addressed.

Developing a Culture That Supports Change

An ideal organization fosters resilience to change. This means the organization understands that change is a necessary part of the culture and that embracing change is more productive than fighting it. To develop such a culture, the organization must successfully accomplish many projects that require change. A resilient culture can be either cultivated or undermined by management's approach. Strong management support for change, with a clear executive-level champion, enables the organization to recognize the necessity for change and its strategic importance. Weak management support, with overly delegated responsibility and no champion, sentences the project to almost certain failure. In such a case, employees sense the low priority assigned to the project and do not communicate with the development team because the effort seems useless.

 For a sample change management and control policy template, visit the ISO 27001 security Web page at *www.iso27001security.com/ISO27k_Model_policy_on_change_management_and_control.docx*.

Closing Scenario

Charlie looked across his desk at Kelvin, who was absorbed in the sheaf of handwritten notes from the meeting. Charlie had asked Kelvin to come to his office and discuss the change control meeting from earlier that day.

"So what do you think?" Charlie asked.

"I think I was blindsided by a bus!" Kelvin replied. "I thought I had considered all the possible effects of the change in my project plan. I tried to explain this, but everyone acted as if I had threatened their lives."

"In a way you did, or you threatened their jobs, at least," Charlie stated. "Some people believe that change is the enemy."

"But these changes are important."

"I agree," Charlie said. "But successful change usually occurs in small steps. What's your top priority?"

"All the items on this list are top priorities," Kelvin said. "I haven't even gotten to the second tier."

"So what should you do to accomplish these top priorities?" Charlie asked.

"I guess I should reprioritize within my top tier, but what then?"

"The next step is to build support before the meeting, not during it," Charlie said, smiling. "Never go into a meeting where you haven't done your homework, especially when other people in the meeting can reduce your chance of success."

Discussion Questions

1. What project management tasks should Kelvin perform before his next meeting?
2. What change management tasks should Kelvin perform before his next meeting, and how do these tasks fit within the project management process?
3. Had you been in Kelvin's place, what would you have done differently to prepare for this meeting?

Ethical Decision Making

Kelvin has seven controls listed as the top tier of project initiatives. Suppose that at his next meeting with Charlie, he provides a rank-ordered list of these controls with projected losses over the next 10 years for each if the controls are not completed. Also, he has estimated the 10-year cost for developing, implementing, and operating each control. Kelvin has identified three controls as being the most advantageous for the organization *in his opinion*. As he prepared the slides for the meeting with Charlie, he "adjusted" most of the projected losses upward to the top end of the range estimate given by the consultant who prepared the data. For the projected costs of his preferred controls, he chose to use the lowest end of the range provided by the consultant.

1. Do you think Kelvin has had an ethical lapse by cherry-picking the data for his presentation?
2. Suppose that instead of choosing data from the range provided by the consultant, Kelvin simply chose better numbers, based on his experience, in support of his favorite initiatives. Is this an ethical lapse?

3. Suppose Kelvin has a close friend who works for a firm that makes and sells software for a specific control objective on the list. When Kelvin prioritized the list of his preferences, he made detailed adjustments to the data presented so the specific control was at the top of the list. Kelvin planned to provide his friend with internal design specifications and the assessment criteria to be used for vendor selection for the initiative. Has Kelvin committed an ethical lapse?

Selected Readings

- *Information Technology Project Management*, 5th Edition, by Kathy Schwalbe. Course Technology. 2007. Boston.
- *The PMI Project Management Fact Book*, 2nd Edition, by the Project Management Institute. 2001. Newtown Square, PA.
- NIST SP 800-37, Rev. 1, "Guide for Applying the Risk Management Framework to Federal Information Systems: A Security Life Cycle Approach."
- NIST DRAFT SP 800-39, "Managing Risk from Information Systems: An Organizational Perspective."

Module Summary

- Information security should be implemented in every major system. One approach is to ensure that security is a part of the organization's system development methodology. DevOps and SecDevOps are emerging accelerated development models that merge development and operational skills.
- Software assurance is a methodological approach to the development of software that seeks to build security into the development life cycle rather than address it at later stages.
- The implementation phase of the security systems development life cycle involves modifying the configuration and operation of the organization's information systems to make them more secure. Such changes include those to procedures, people, hardware, software, and data. During the implementation phase, the organization translates its blueprint for information security into a concrete project plan.
- Before developing a project plan, management should articulate and coordinate the organization's information security vision and objectives with the involved communities of interest.
- The major steps in executing the project plan are planning the project, supervising tasks and action steps within the plan, and wrapping up the plan.
- Each organization determines its own project management methodology for IT and information security projects. Whenever possible, an organization's information security projects should be in line with its project management practices.
- Planning for the implementation phase involves the creation of a detailed project plan. The project plan can be created by using a simple planning tool such as the work breakdown structure (WBS). The plan can be prepared with a simple desktop PC spreadsheet program or with more complex project management software. The WBS involves addressing major project tasks and their related attributes, including the following:
  - ○ Work to be accomplished (activities and deliverables)
  - ○ Individual employees or skill sets assigned to perform the task
  - ○ Start and end dates for the task, when known
  - ○ Amount of effort required for completion, in hours or days
  - ○ Estimated capital expenses for the task
  - ○ Estimated noncapital expenses for the task
  - ○ Identification of task interdependencies
- Constraints and considerations should be addressed when developing the project plan. Considerations include those for finances, procurement, priority, time and scheduling, staffing, scope, organizational feasibility, training and indoctrination, change control, and technology governance.

- Organizations usually designate a professional project manager to lead a security information project. Alternatively, some organizations designate a champion from a senior level of general management or a senior IT manager, such as the CIO.
- Once a project is under way, it can be managed to completion using a process known as a negative feedback loop or cybernetic loop. This process involves measuring variances from the project plan and then taking corrective action when needed.
- As the components of the new security system are planned, provisions must be made for the changeover from the previous method of performing a task to the new method(s). The four common conversion strategies for performing this changeover are as follows:
  - Direct changeover
  - Phased implementation
  - Pilot implementation
  - Parallel operations
- The bull's-eye model is a proven method for prioritizing a program of complex change. Using this method, the project manager can address issues from the general to the specific and focus on systematic solutions instead of individual problems.
- When the expense and time required to develop an effective information security program is beyond the reach of an organization, it should outsource the program to competent professional services.
- Technology governance is a complex process that an organization uses to manage the impacts and costs of technology implementation, innovation, and obsolescence.
- The change control process is a method that medium-sized and large organizations use to deal with the impact of technical change on their operations.
- As with any project, certain aspects of change must be addressed. In any major project, the prospect of moving from the familiar to the unfamiliar can cause employees to resist change, consciously or unconsciously.

Review Questions

1. What is a methodology in the context of implementing secure systems?
2. What is a systems development life cycle (or SDLC)?
3. What is a project plan? List what a project plan can accomplish.
4. What categories of constraints to project plan implementation are noted in the module? Explain each of them.
5. List and describe the three major steps in executing the project plan.
6. What is a work breakdown structure (WBS)? Is it the only way to organize a project plan?
7. What is projectitis? How is it cured or its impact minimized?
8. List and define the common attributes of tasks within a WBS.
9. How does a planner know when a task has been subdivided to an adequate degree and can be classified as an action step?
10. What is a deliverable? Name two uses for deliverables.
11. What is a resource? What are the two types?

12. Why is it a good practice to delay naming specific people as resources early in the planning process?
13. What is a milestone, and why is it significant to project planning?
14. Why is it good practice to assign start and end dates sparingly in the early stages of project planning?
15. Who is the best judge of effort estimates for project tasks and action steps? Why?
16. Within project management, what is a dependency? What is a predecessor? What is a successor?
17. What is a negative feedback loop? How is it used to keep a project in control?
18. When a task is not being completed according to the plan, what two circumstances are likely to be involved?
19. List and describe the four basic conversion strategies that are used when converting to a new system. Under which circumstances is each strategy the best approach?
20. What is technology governance? What is change control? How are they related?

Exercises

1. Using the Web, explore the emerging approach of SecDevOps (Security/Development/Operations). An earlier and alternative approach is DevSecOps. What is the difference implied in the two names?

2. Create a first draft of a WBS from the following scenario. Make assumptions as needed based on the section about project planning considerations and constraints in this module. In your WBS, describe the skill sets required for the tasks you have planned.

3. If you have access to commercial project management software, such as Microsoft Project, use it to complete a project plan based on the data shown in Table 11-2. Prepare a simple WBS report or Gantt chart that shows your work.

4. Write a job description for Kelvin Urich, the project manager described in the opening scenario of this module. Be sure to identify key characteristics of the ideal candidate, as well as work experience and educational background. Also, justify why your job description is suitable for potential candidates for this position.

5. Search the Web for job descriptions of project managers. You can use any number of Web sites, including *www.monster.com* or *www.dice.com*, to find at least 10 IT-related job descriptions. What common elements do you find among the job descriptions? What is the most unusual characteristic among them?

References

1. Adapted from Dewitz, Sandra D. *Systems Analysis and Design and the Transition to Objects*. 1996. New York: McGraw Hill Publishers, 94.

2. Redwine, Samuel T., Jr. (Editor). "Software Assurance: A Guide to the Common Body of Knowledge to Produce, Acquire, and Sustain Secure Software," Version 1.1. U.S. Department of Homeland Security. September 2006.

3. Ibid.

4. Saltzer, J. H., and Schroeder, M. D. "The Protection of Information in Computer Systems." Proceedings of the IEEE, vol. 63, no. 9 (1975), pp. 1278–1308. Accessed November 1, 2020, from *http://cap-lore.com/CapTheory/ProtInf/*.

5. Ibid.

6. Kissel, R., Stine, K., Scholl, M., Rossman, H., Fahlsing, J., and Gulick, J. Special Publication 800-64, Rev. 2, "Security Considerations in the System Development Life Cycle." National Institute of Standards and Technology. Accessed November 1, 2020, from *https://nvlpubs.nist.gov/nistpubs/Legacy/SP/nistspecialpublication800-64r2.pdf*.

7. Microsoft. "Microsoft Security Development Lifecycle (SDL) Process Guidance – Version 5.2." Accessed November 1, 2020, from *www.microsoft.com/en-us/download/confirmation.aspx?id=29884*.

8. Ibid.

9. The SANS Institute. "GIAC Certified Project Manager (GCPM)." Accessed October 24, 2020, from *www.giac.org/certification/certified-project-manager-gcpm*.

10. Ibid.

11. EC-Council. "Certified Project Management (CPM)." Accessed October 24, 2020, from *https://iclass.eccouncil.org/our-courses/certified-project-management/*.

12. "CIS Controls® Download." Version 7.1. Accessed November 1, 2020, from *www.cisecurity.org/controls/*.

13. Ibid.

14. Schein, E.H. "Kurt Lewin's Change Theory in the Field and in the Classroom: Notes Toward a Model of Managed Learning." *Systems Practice* 9, 27–47 (1996). *https://doi.org/10.1007/BF02173417*.

Information Security Maintenance

Upon completion of this material, you should be able to:

1. Discuss the need for ongoing maintenance of the information security program

2. Describe recommended security management models

3. Define a model for a full maintenance program

4. Identify the key factors involved in monitoring the external and internal environment

5. Describe how planning, risk assessment, vulnerability assessment, and remediation tie into information security maintenance

6. Explain how to build readiness and review procedures into information security maintenance

7. Discuss physical security controls

> *To improve is to change; to be perfect is to change often.*
>
> —Winston Churchill

Opening Scenario

Charlie Moody leaned back in his chair. It was Monday morning, the first workday after the biggest conversion weekend in the implementation of Sequential Label and Supply's information security project. Charlie had just reviewed the results. So far, everything had gone according to plan. The initial penetration tests run on Sunday afternoon were clean, and every change request processed in the past three months had gone through without any issues. Charlie was eager to return to the routine he had enjoyed before the attack on the company's network triggered the changes of the past few months.

Kelvin Urich tapped on the open door of Charlie's office. "Hey, Charlie," he said, "have you seen the e-mail I just sent? There's an urgent vulnerability report on Bugtraq about the version of OpenSSL we use. Something called the Bebop bug. The open-source community just released a critical patch to be applied right away. Should I get the system programming team started on it?"

"Absolutely! Get them to pull the download from the distribution site as soon as they can," said Charlie. "But remember we need to follow our quality assurance steps carefully. Before they install it on a single production system, I want you to review the test results and QA report yourself. If you sign off, have them patch the servers for the HQ development team. Oh, and don't forget you need to get change orders into change control ASAP if we go forward on the patch and you plan to hit tonight's critical systems change window."

"I'll get right on it," Kelvin said.

After Kelvin left, Charlie pulled up Bugtraq on his PC. He was reading about the new vulnerability when he heard another knock on the door. It was Iris Majwubu.

"Hi, Charlie," Iris said. "Got a second?"

"Sure, Iris. How have you been? Settling in with Kelvin's team okay?"

She smiled and nodded. "Yeah, they're a good group. They have me studying the documentation trail from the time before the security program was implemented. I came to see you about the reassessment of the information asset inventory and the threat-vulnerability update that you asked for."

Charlie was confused for a second, but then he remembered the task he had assigned to Iris. "Oh, right," he said, with a slight grimace. "Sorry—I had put the quarterly asset and threat review out of my mind while we were busy implementing the blueprint. I suppose it's time to start planning for the regular reviews, isn't it?"

Iris handed him a folder and said, "Here's the first draft of the plan for the review project. Kelvin has already seen it, and he suggested I review it with you. Could you take a look and let me know when you would like to go over it?"

Introduction To Information Security Maintenance

After successfully implementing and testing a new and improved information security profile, an organization may feel more confident about the level of protection it provides for its information assets. But it shouldn't, really. In all likelihood, a good deal of time has passed since the organization began implementing changes to the information security program. In that time, the dynamic aspects of the organization's environment will have changed. Almost all aspects of a company's environment are dynamic, meaning threats that were originally assessed in the early stages of the organization's risk management program have probably changed, and new priorities have emerged. New types of attacks such as viruses, worms, ransomware, and denial-of-service attacks have been developed, and new variants of existing attacks have likely emerged as well. In addition, a host of other variables outside and inside the organization have probably changed.

Developing a comprehensive list of dynamic factors in an organization's environment is beyond the scope of this text. However, the following changes may affect an organization's information security environment:

- The acquisition of new assets and the divestiture of old assets
- The emergence of vulnerabilities associated with new or existing assets
- Shifting business priorities
- The formation of new partnerships
- The dissolution of old partnerships
- The departure of personnel who are trained, educated, and aware of policies, procedures, and technologies
- The hiring of personnel

As this list shows, by the time a cycle of the risk management program is completed, the environment of an organization has probably changed considerably. The information security leadership team, usually led by the CISO, needs to be able to assure management periodically that the information security program is accommodating these changes. If the program is not adjusting adequately to change, it may be necessary to begin the cycle again. If an organization deals successfully with change and has created procedures and systems that can be adjusted to the environment, the existing security improvement program can continue to work well. Deciding whether to continue with the current improvement program or to renew the investigation, analysis, and design phases depends on how much change has occurred and how well the organization and its program for information security maintenance is adapting to its evolving environment.

Before learning about the maintenance model that the authors recommend, you need some background on the management and operation of an information security program. In this module, you will learn about the methods organizations use to monitor the three primary aspects of information security risk management, which are sometimes called the security triple: threats, assets, and vulnerabilities. You will also learn about the physical security component of information security: protecting the hardware and facilities associated with information assets.

Security Management Maintenance Models

To manage and operate the ongoing security program, the information security community must adopt a management maintenance model. In general, management models are frameworks that structure the tasks of managing a particular set of activities or business functions on an ongoing basis. Integral to any effective management maintenance model is the concept of continuous improvement—the cyclic, repetitive approach to improving, assessing, evaluating, and repeating changes and improvements in a life cycle. Information security is no different. It is critical that any effort performed within the security program follows a continuous improvement approach involving periodic review and assessment of any implemented change. Coupled with a strategic plan to move the status of any project toward its goal by closing the "gap," improvements become more than just change; they provide real progress toward making the security program better. Remember, "Good now is better than perfect never."

NIST SP 800-100, "Information Security Handbook: A Guide for Managers"

NIST Special Publication (SP) 800-100, "Information Security Handbook: A Guide for Managers," provides managerial guidance for the establishment and implementation of an information security program. In particular, the handbook addresses the ongoing tasks expected of an information security manager once the program is working and day-to-day operations are established.[1]

For each of the 13 areas of information security management presented in SP 800-100, there are specific monitoring activities—tasks that security managers should perform on an ongoing basis to monitor the function of the security program and take corrective actions when issues arise. Not all issues are negative, as in the opening scenario. Some are normal changes in the business environment, while others are changes in the technology environment—for example, the emergence of new technologies that could improve security or new security standards and regulations to which the organization should subscribe.

The following sections describe monitoring actions for the 13 information security areas. These sections were adapted from NIST SP 800-100.

 For more information on NIST SP 800-100 and other NIST special publications, visit *https://csrc.nist.gov/publications/sp*.

1. Information Security Governance

As you discovered in Module 3, an effective information security governance program requires constant review. Organizations should monitor the status of their programs to ensure the following:

- Ongoing information security activities are providing appropriate support to the organization's mission.
- Policies and procedures are current and aligned with evolving technologies, if appropriate.
- Controls are accomplishing their intended purpose.

Over time, policies and procedures may become inadequate because of changes in an organization's mission and operational requirements, threats, or the environment; deterioration in the degree of compliance; or changes in technology, infrastructure, or business processes. Periodic assessments and reports on activities can identify areas of noncompliance, remind users of their responsibilities, and demonstrate management's commitment to the security program. While an organization's mission does not frequently change, it may expand its mission to secure its programs and assets and require modification to its information security requirements and practices.

Table 12-1 provides a broad overview of key ongoing activities that can assist in monitoring and improving an organization's information governance activities.

Table 12-1 Ongoing Monitoring Activities of Information Security Governance[2]

Activities	Description of Activities
Plans of Action and Milestones (POA&Ms)	POA&Ms assist in identifying, assessing, prioritizing, and monitoring the progress of corrective efforts for security weaknesses found in programs and systems. The POA&M tracks the measures implemented to correct deficiencies and to reduce or eliminate known vulnerabilities. POA&Ms can also assist in identifying performance gaps, evaluating an organization's security performance and efficiency, and conducting oversight.
Measurement and Metrics	Metrics are tools designed to improve performance and accountability through the collection, analysis, and reporting (measurement) of relevant performance data. Information security metrics monitor the accomplishment of goals and objectives by quantifying the implementation level of security controls and their efficiency and effectiveness, by analyzing the adequacy of security activities, and by identifying possible improvements. The terms *metric* and *measurement* seem to have some overlap in their meanings. A metric is usually meant to be a more abstract, higher-level, or subjective value, while measures tend to be more objective and concrete.
Continuous Assessment (CA)	The CA process monitors the initial security accreditation of an information system to track changes to it, analyzes the security impact of those changes, makes appropriate adjustments to the security controls and the system security plan, and reports the system's security status to appropriate organizational officials.
Configuration Management (CM)	CM is an essential component of monitoring the status of security controls and identifying potential security problems in information systems. This information can help security managers understand and monitor the evolving nature of vulnerabilities that appear in a system under their responsibility, thus enabling managers to direct appropriate changes as required.
Network Monitoring	Information about network performance and user behavior on the network helps security program managers identify areas in need of improvement and point out potential performance improvements. This information can be correlated with other sources of information, such as the POA&M and CM, to create a comprehensive picture of the security program.
Incident and Event Statistics	Incident statistics are valuable in determining the effectiveness of implemented security policies and procedures. Incident statistics provide security program managers with further insights into the status of security programs under their purview, help them observe performance trends in program activities, and inform them about the need to change policies and procedures.

Source: NIST SP 800-100.

2. Systems Development Life Cycle

As you learned in Module 11, the systems development life cycle (SDLC) is the overall process of developing, implementing, and retiring information systems through a multistep approach—initiation, analysis, design, implementation, and maintenance to disposal. Each phase of the SDLC includes a minimum set of information security activities required to effectively incorporate security into a system.

SP 800-64, Rev. 2, "Security Considerations in the System Development Life Cycle," presents a framework for incorporating security into all phases of the SDLC to ensure the selection, acquisition, and use of appropriate and cost-effective security controls. These considerations are summarized in Table 12-2.

During the continuous monitoring phase, the organization should review system performance to ensure that it is consistent with established user and security requirements and that needed system modifications are incorporated.

Table 12-2   Ongoing Information Security Activities in the SDLC[3]

A. Initiation Phase

Needs Determination	• Define a problem that might be solved through product acquisition. • Establish and document the need and purpose of the system.
Security Categorization	• Identify information that will be transmitted, processed, or stored by the system and define applicable levels of categorizing information, especially the handling and safeguarding of personally identifiable information.
Preliminary Risk Assessment	• Establish an initial description of the system's basic security needs. A preliminary risk assessment should define the threat environment in which the system or product will operate.

B. Development/Acquisition Phase

Requirements Analysis/ Development	• Conduct a more in-depth study of the need that draws on and further develops the work performed during the initiation phase. • Develop and incorporate security requirements into specifications. • Analyze functional requirements that may include the system security environment (such as enterprise information security policy and enterprise security architecture) and security functional requirements. • Analyze assurance requirements for acquisition and product integration activities and evidence that the product will provide required information security correctly and effectively.
Risk Assessment	• Conduct a formal risk assessment to identify system protection requirements. This analysis builds on the initial risk assessment performed during the initiation phase, but it is more in-depth and specific.
Cost Considerations and Reporting	• Determine how much of the product's acquisition and integration cost can be attributed to information security over the life cycle of the system. These costs include hardware, software, personnel, and training.
Security Planning	• Fully document agreed-upon security controls, whether they are planned or in place. Develop the system security plan. • Develop documents that support the organization's information security program, such as the CM plan, contingency plan, incident response plan, security awareness and training plan, rules of behavior, risk assessment, security test and evaluation results, system interconnection agreements, security authorizations and accreditations, and plans of action and milestones. • Develop awareness and training requirements, including user manuals, operating manuals, and administrative manuals.
Security Control Development	• Develop, design, and implement security controls described in the respective security plans. For information systems that are currently in operation, their security plans may call for developing additional security controls to supplement existing controls or for modifying ineffective controls.
Developmental Security Test and Evaluation	• Test security controls developed for a new information system or product to ensure its proper and effective operation. • Develop the test plan, script, and scenarios.
Other Planning Components	• Ensure that all necessary components of product acquisition and integration are considered when incorporating security into the life cycle.

(continues)

Table 12-2   Ongoing Information Security Activities in the SDLC[3] (*Continued*)

C. Implementation Phase

Security Test and Evaluation	• Develop test data.
	• Test the unit, subsystem, and entire system.
	• Ensure that the system undergoes technical evaluation according to applicable laws, regulations, policies, guidelines, and standards.
Inspection and Acceptance	• Verify and validate that the functionality described in the specification is included in the deliverables.
System Integration/ Installation	• Integrate the system at the site where it will be deployed for operation. Enable security control settings and switches in accordance with vendor instructions and proper guidance for security implementation.
Security Certification	• Ensure that the controls are effectively implemented through established verification techniques and procedures, which gives the organization confidence that appropriate safeguards and countermeasures are in place to protect its information.
Security Accreditation	• Provide the necessary security authorization for an information system to process, store, or transmit information.

D. Operations/Maintenance Phase

Configuration Management and Control	• Ensure adequate consideration of potential security impacts due to changes in an information system or its surrounding environment.
	• Develop the CM plan.
	○ Establish baselines
	○ Identify configuration
	○ Describe configuration control process
	○ Identify schedule for configuration audits
Continuous Monitoring	• Monitor security controls to ensure that they continue to be effective in their application through periodic testing and evaluation.
	• Perform self-administered audits, independent security audits, or other assessments periodically. Use automated tools, internal control audits, security checklists, and penetration testing.
	• Monitor the system and/or users by reviewing system logs and reports, using automated tools, reviewing change management, monitoring trade publications and other external sources, and performing periodic reaccreditation.

E. Disposal Phase

Information Preservation	• Retain information as necessary to conform to current legal requirements and to accommodate future technology changes that may render the retrieval method obsolete.
	• Consult with the appropriate agency for information on retaining and archiving federal records. Ensure the long-term storage of cryptographic keys for encrypted data. Determine whether to archive, discard, or destroy information.
Media Sanitization	• Determine the sanitization level (overwrite, degauss, or destroy). Delete, erase, and overwrite data as necessary.
Hardware and Software Disposal	• Dispose of hardware and software as directed by the governing organization's policy.

Source: NIST SP 800-64, Rev. 2.

For **configuration and change management (CCM)**, also known as **configuration management (CM)**, it is important to document proposed or actual changes in the system security plan. Information systems are typically in a constant state of evolution, with upgrades to hardware, software, and firmware and possible modifications to the system's surrounding environment. Documenting information system changes and assessing their potential impact on system security is an essential part of continuous monitoring and key to avoiding a lapse in system security accreditation. Monitoring security controls helps to identify potential security problems in the information system that are not identified during the security impact analysis. This analysis is conducted as part of the CM and control process.

> **configuration and change management (CCM)**
>
> An approach to implementing system change that uses policies, procedures, techniques, and tools to manage and evaluate proposed changes, track changes through completion, and maintain systems inventory and supporting documentation.[4]

> **configuration management (CM)**
>
> See *configuration and change management (CCM)*.

3. Awareness and Training

As discussed in Module 3, once the program has been implemented, processes must be put in place to monitor compliance and effectiveness. An automated tracking system should be designed to capture key information about program activity, such as courses, dates, audience, costs, and sources. The tracking system should capture this data at an organizational level so it can be used to provide enterprise-wide analysis and reporting about awareness, training, and education initiatives.

Tracking compliance involves assessing the status of the program as indicated by the database information and mapping it to standards established by the organization. Reports can be generated and used to identify gaps or problems. Corrective action and necessary follow-up can then be taken. This follow-up may take the form of formal reminders to management; additional awareness, training, or education offerings; and the establishment of a corrective plan with scheduled completion dates. As the organization's environment changes, the security policies must evolve, and all awareness and training material should reflect these changes.

4. Capital Planning and Investment Control

Increased competition for limited resources requires that departments allocate available funding toward their highest-priority information security investments to afford the organization the appropriate degree of security for its needs. This goal can be achieved through a formal enterprise capital planning and investment control (CPIC) process designed to facilitate the expenditure of organizational funds.

NIST SP 800-65, Rev. 1 (DRAFT), "Recommendations for Integrating IT Security into the Capital Planning and Investment Control Process," provides a seven-step process for prioritizing security activities and corrective actions for funding purposes:

1. Identify the baseline—Use information security measurements or other available data to baseline the current security posture.
2. Identify prioritization requirements—Evaluate the security posture against legislative requirements, other requirements from the chief information officer (CIO), and the organization's mission.
3. Conduct enterprise-level prioritization—Prioritize potential information security investments at the enterprise level against the organization's mission and prioritize the financial impact of implementing appropriate security controls.
4. Conduct system-level prioritization—Prioritize potential system-level corrective actions against the system category and corrective action impact.
5. Develop supporting materials—For enterprise-level investments, develop an initial conceptual business plan, business case analysis, and capital asset plan. For system-level investments, adjust the capital asset plan to request additional funding that mitigates prioritized weaknesses.
6. Implement an investment review board (IRB) and portfolio management—Prioritize organization-wide business cases against requirements and CIO priorities and determine the investment portfolio.
7. Submit any required budget approval paperwork.[5]

5. Interconnecting Systems

A system interconnection is defined as the direct connection of two or more information systems for sharing data and other information resources. Organizations choose to interconnect their information systems for a variety of reasons based on their needs. For example, they may interconnect information systems to exchange data, collaborate on joint projects, or securely store data and backup files.

Interconnecting information systems can expose the participating organizations to risk. For instance, if the interconnection is not properly designed, security failures could compromise the connected systems and their data. Similarly, if one of the connected systems is compromised, the interconnection could be used as a conduit to compromise the other system and its data.

NIST SP 800-47 details a four-phase life cycle management approach for interconnecting information systems that emphasizes information security:

- Phase 1—Planning the interconnection
- Phase 2—Establishing the interconnection
- Phase 3—Maintaining the interconnection
- Phase 4—Disconnecting the interconnection[6]

Table 12-3 provides a checklist for organizations that are considering interconnecting multiple systems when developing an interconnection security agreement (ISA). While many parts of this agreement are specified for a federal government agency, referring to associated Special Publications and Federal Information Processing Standards (FIPS) can assist organizations in identifying issues to be resolved.

Table 12-3   ISA Checklist for Interconnecting Systems[7]

		YES	NO
1	**ISA Requirements:**		
A	Is there a formal requirement and justification for connecting two systems?		
B	Are there two systems being interconnected? If YES, have the systems been specified? If NO, the two systems need to be specified.		
C	Is there a list of benefits of required interconnection(s)?		
D	Is the name of the organization that initiated the requirement listed?		
2	**System Security Considerations:**		
A	Has a security certification and accreditation of the system been completed?		
B	Has the security certification and accreditation status been verified?		
C	Are there security features in place to protect the confidentiality, integrity, and availability of the data and the systems being interconnected?		
D	Has each systems security categorization been identified per FIPS 199?		
E	Have minimum controls been identified for each system in accordance with NIST SP 800-53?		
F	Have both parties answered each subject item regardless of whether the subject item only affects one party? If NO, both parties must go back and answer each item.		
G	Is there a general description of the information/data being made available, exchanged, or passed?		

(continues)

Table 12-3   ISA Checklist for Interconnecting Systems[7] (*Continued*)

		YES	NO
H	Is there a description of the information services offered over the interconnected system by each participating organization? Such services include e-mail, file transfer protocols, database queries, file queries, and general computational services.		
I	Have system users been identified and has an approval been put in place?		
J	Is there a description of all system security technical services pertinent to the secure exchange of information and data among the systems in question?		
K	Are there documented rules of behavior for users of each system in the interconnection?		
L	Are there titles of the formal security policy or policies that govern each system?		
M	Are there procedures for incidents related to the interconnection?		
N	Are there audit requirements?		
3	**Topological Drawing:**		
A	Is there a descriptive technical specification for the connections?		
4	**Signatory Authority:**		
	The ISA is valid for one year after the last date on either signature. At that time, it will be reviewed, updated if necessary, and revalidated. This agreement may be terminated upon 30 days of advance notice by either party or in the event of a security exception that would necessitate an immediate response.		

Source: NIST SP 800-47.

6. Performance Measurement

InfoSec performance management is the process of designing, implementing, and managing the use of collected data elements (called *measurements* or **metrics**) to determine the effectiveness of the overall security program. **Performance measurements** (or **performance measures**) are the data points or trends computed from such measurements that may indicate the effectiveness of security countermeasures or technical and managerial controls implemented in the organization. Some countermeasures, as you have learned, are technical, while others are managerial. Both types require some method of assessing the results of their use. Control approaches that are not effective should be modified or replaced, and those that are effective should be supported and continued. Measurement supports managerial decision making, increased accountability, and improved effectiveness of the InfoSec function. Also, by enabling the collection, analysis, and reporting of critical performance data, measurements help organizations align InfoSec performance and objectives with the organization's overall mission.[8]

Organizations use three types of measurements:

- Those that determine the effectiveness of the execution of InfoSec policy, most commonly issue-specific security policies.
- Those that determine the effectiveness and/or efficiency of the delivery of InfoSec services, whether they be managerial services, such as security training, or technical services, such as the installation of antivirus software.
- Those that assess the impact of an incident or other security event on the organization or its mission.[9]

InfoSec performance management

A process of designing, implementing, and managing the use of specific measurements to determine the effectiveness of the overall security program.

metric

A term traditionally used to describe any detailed statistical analysis technique on performance, but now commonly synonymous with performance measurement. See *performance measurements*.

performance measurements

Data or the trends in data that may indicate the effectiveness of security countermeasures or technical and managerial controls implemented in the organization. Also known as *performance measures* or *metrics*.

performance measures

See *performance measurements*.

need more detailed measurement, perhaps including the number of new users added, number of access control changes, number of users removed or de-authorized, number of access control violations, number of awareness briefings, number of systems by type, number of incidents by category (such as virus or worm outbreaks), number of malicious code instances blocked by filters, or many other possible measurements.

Collecting measurements about project activities may be even more challenging. Unless the organization is satisfied with a simple tally of who spent how many hours doing what tasks (which is more project management than performance measurement), it needs some mechanism to link the outcome of each project to the resources consumed, in terms of loss control or risk reduction. This is not a trivial process. Most organizations rely on narrative explanation rather than measurement-driven calculations to justify project expenditures.

Collecting InfoSec Measurements   The prospect of collecting performance measurements is daunting to some organizations. At large organizations, merely counting the number of computing systems in a production state may be a time-consuming project. Some thought must go into the processes used for data collection and record keeping. Once the question of what to measure is answered, the "how, when, where, and who" of metrics collection must be addressed. Designing the collection process requires thoughtful consideration of the intent of the measurement along with a thorough knowledge of how production services are delivered.

One of the priorities in building an InfoSec process measurement program is determining whether these measurements will be macro- or micro-focused. Macro-focus measurements examine the performance of the overall security program. Micro-focus measurements examine the performance of an individual control or group of controls within the InfoSec program. Some organizations may want to conduct a limited assessment using both types of measurements.

What is important is that the measurements are specifically tied to individual InfoSec goals and objectives. Implementing InfoSec process measurement just for the sake of collecting data wastes valuable resources. Therefore, the process measurement program must be driven by specific needs in the organization and not by the whims of any one manager.

Establishing Performance Targets   Performance targets make it possible to define success in the security program. For example, a goal of 100 percent employee InfoSec training as an objective for the training program validates the continued collection of training measurements. A periodic report indicating the status of employee training represents progress toward the goal. Many InfoSec performance measurement targets are represented by a 100 percent target goal. Other types of performance measurements, such as those used to determine relative effectiveness or efficiency or the impact of InfoSec on the organization's goals, tend to be more subjective and will require management to assess the purpose and value of such measurements. For example, the increase in relative or perceived security of the organization's information after the installation of a firewall requires a completely different perspective from that required for assessing personnel training performance through empirical measurement of attendance at training sessions or the evaluation of post-training quiz scores.

This example highlights one of the fundamental challenges in InfoSec performance measurement—namely, defining effective security. When is InfoSec effective? Researchers who study InfoSec success continue to grapple with this question. There is little agreement about how to define a successful program; some argue that simply avoiding losses is the best measurement, while others argue that any valid measure must be provable. The avoidance of losses may be attributed to luck or other nonprogram factors. This dilemma remains unresolved.

A number of example candidate measurements are provided in Table 12-4. Additional details on these measurements, including how they are calculated and used, are provided in NIST SP 800-55, Rev. 1.

Implementing InfoSec Performance Measurement   Once developed, InfoSec performance measurements must be implemented and integrated into ongoing InfoSec management operations. For the most part, it is insufficient simply to collect these measurements once (although some activities only require the collection of data for one particular purpose, such as certification and accreditation, as described later in this module). Performance measurement is an ongoing, continuous improvement operation. The collection of all measurement data should be part of standard operating procedures across the organization.

The process for implementing performance measurement recommended in NIST SP 800-55, Rev. 1, involves six subordinate tasks, as shown in Figure 12-2:

Phase 1—Prepare for data collection; identify, define, develop, and select InfoSec measures.

Phase 2—Collect data and analyze results; collect, aggregate, and consolidate metric data collection and compare measurements with targets (gap analysis).

Table 12-4 Examples of Possible Security Performance Measurements

Field	Example Data
Measurement ID	Security training coverage
Goal	Strategic goal: Ensure a high-quality workforce supported by modern and secure infrastructure and operational capabilities. InfoSec goal: Ensure that organizational personnel are adequately trained to carry out their assigned InfoSec-related duties and responsibilities.
Measurement	The percentage of InfoSec personnel who have received security training
Measure type	Implementation
Formula	Number of InfoSec personnel who have completed security training within the past year divided by the total number of InfoSec personnel, then multiplied by 100
Target	100 percent

Implementation evidence	1. Are significant security responsibilities defined with qualifications criteria and documented in policy? Yes/No
	
	2. Are records kept regarding which employees have significant security responsibilities? Yes/No
	
	3. How many employees in your department have significant security responsibilities?
	
	4. Are training records maintained? Yes/No
	
	5. How many of those with significant security responsibilities have received the required training?
	
	6. If all personnel have not received training, document all reasons that apply:
	  a. Insufficient funding
	  b. Insufficient time
	  c. Courses unavailable
	  d. Employee not registered
	  e. Other (specify)

Frequency	Collected as training is delivered Reported annually
Responsible parties	Information owner: training division Information collector: training division Information customer: CIO
Data source	Training and awareness tracking records
Reporting format	Pie chart illustrating the percentage of security personnel who have received training versus those who have not received training. If performance is below target, pie chart illustrating causes of performance falling short of targets.

Phase 3—Identify corrective actions; develop a plan to serve as the road map for closing the gap identified in Phase 2. This includes determining the range of corrective actions, prioritizing corrective actions based on overall risk mitigation goals, and selecting the most appropriate corrective actions.

Phase 4—Develop the business case.

Phase 5—Obtain resources; address the budgeting cycle for acquiring resources needed to implement the remediation actions identified in Phase 3.

Phase 6—Apply corrective actions; close the gap by implementing the recommended corrective actions in the security program or in the security controls.[15]

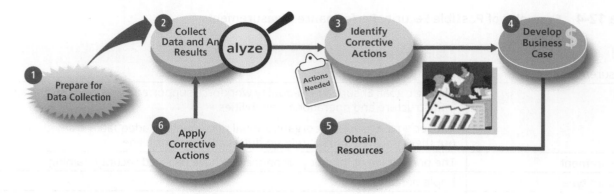

Figure 12-2 Implementing the information security measurement program

 For more information on developing and managing security performance measurements, read NIST SP 800-55, Rev. 1, "Performance Measurement Guide for Information Security," available from *https://csrc.nist.gov/publications/sp800*.

7. Security Planning

Planning for information security was discussed in detail in Module 3. Planning is one of the most crucial ongoing responsibilities in security management. Strategic, tactical, and operating plans must be developed that align with and support organizational and IT plans, goals, and objectives.

This section of SP 800-100 focuses on the controls available to address shortfalls identified in the planning process. FIPS 200, "Minimum Security Requirements for Federal Information and Information Systems," specifies federal security requirements in 17 areas. In addition to reviewing the minimum security requirements in FIPS 200, private organizations would benefit from studying the controls in NIST SP 800-53, "Recommended Security Controls for Federal Information Systems." NIST SP 800-18, Rev. 1, "Guide for Developing Security Plans for Federal Information Systems," provides a template for a systems security plan in Appendix A of the document.

8. Information Technology Contingency Planning

Contingency planning, covered in Module 5, consists of a process for recovery and documentation of procedures for conducting recovery. The ongoing responsibilities of security management involve the maintenance of the contingency plan. The contingency plan must always be in a ready state for use immediately upon notification. Periodic reviews of the plan must be conducted to ensure currency of key personnel and vendor information, system components and dependencies, the recovery strategy, vital records, and operating requirements. While some changes may be obvious, such as personnel turnover or vendor changes, others require analysis. The business impact analysis should be reviewed periodically and updated with new information to identify new contingency requirements and priorities. Changes to the plan are noted in a record of changes, dated, and signed or initialed by the person making the change. The revised plan or plan sections are circulated to those with plan responsibilities. Because of the impact that plan changes may have on interdependent business processes or information systems, the changes must be clearly communicated and properly annotated at the beginning of the document.

9. Risk Management

Risk management, covered in Module 4, is an ongoing effort as well. Risk identification, analysis, and management are cyclic and fundamental parts of continuous improvement in information security. The principal goal of risk management is to protect the organization and its ability to perform its mission, not just protect its information assets. Risk management is an essential management function of the organization that is tightly woven into the SDLC. Because risk cannot be eliminated entirely, the risk management process allows information security program managers to balance operating and economic costs of protective measures and achieve gains in mission capability. By employing practices and procedures designed to foster informed decision making, organizations help protect their information systems and the data that support their own mission.

Many risk management activities are conducted during a snapshot in time—a static representation of a dynamic environment. All the changes that occur to systems during normal, daily operations have the potential to adversely affect system security in some fashion. The goal of the evaluation and assessment process in risk management is to ensure that the system continues to operate safely and securely. This goal can be partially reached by implementing a strong configuration management program. In addition to monitoring the security of an information system on a continuous basis, organizations must track findings from the security control assessment to ensure they are addressed appropriately and do not pose risks to the system or introduce new ones.

The process of managing risk permeates the SDLC, from the early stages of project inception through the retirement of the system and its data. From inception forward, organizations should consider possible threats, vulnerabilities, and risks to the system so they can better prepare it to operate securely and effectively in its intended environment. During the security certification and accreditation process, a senior organization official determines whether the system is operating within an acceptable risk threshold.

10. Certification, Accreditation, and Security Assessments

Certification and accreditation is radically changing for federal systems not designated as national security information systems. Some organizations need to review their own systems for certification and accreditation to be compliant with banking, healthcare, international, or other regulations. Others may want the recognition offered by certifications like the ISO 27000 series. The security certification and accreditation process is designed to ensure that an information system operates with the appropriate management review, that there is ongoing monitoring of security controls, and that reaccreditation occurs periodically.

The continuous monitoring of a security assessment program, as a function of certification and accreditation, is an essential component of any security program. During this phase, the status of security controls in the information system is checked on an ongoing basis. An effective continuous monitoring program can be used to support the annual requirement specified in the Federal Information Security Management Act (FISMA) for assessing security controls in information systems. At a minimum, an effective monitoring program requires the following:

- Configuration management and configuration control processes for the information system
- Security impact analyses of changes to the information system
- Assessment of selected security controls in the information system and reporting of the system's security status to appropriate organization officials

To determine which security controls to select for review, organizations should first prioritize testing on "plan of action" items and milestone items that become closed. These newly implemented controls should be validated. Organizations should test against system-related security control changes that did not constitute a major change or require new certification and accreditation. Organizations should identify all security controls that are continuously monitored as annual testing and evaluation activities. Once this is complete, organizations should look at remaining controls that have not been tested that year and make a decision about further annual testing based on risk, the importance of the control, and the date of the last test. The results of continuous monitoring should be reviewed regularly by senior management and any necessary updates should be made to the system security plan. An example of a continuous monitoring reporting form is provided in NIST SP 800-53A.

Auditing systems is part of the ongoing security assessment. Most computer-based systems used in information security can create logs of their activity. These logs are a vital part of the detective functions associated with determining what happened, when it happened, and how. Managing system logs in large organizations is a complex process and is sometimes considered an art unto itself. Unless security or system administrators are vigilant, the logs can pile up quickly because systems are constantly writing the activity that occurs on them. Fortunately, automated tools known as log analyzers can consolidate system logs, perform comparative analysis, and detect common occurrences or behavior of interest. Behavior of interest may include port scanning and other anomalous network activity, malware signatures, hacking attempts, and illicit use of controlled network resources or computer systems. Log analyzers, a component of some intrusion detection and prevention systems (IDPSs), can detect activities in real time. Each type of IDPS—whether host-, network-, or application-based—also creates logs. These logs are invaluable records of events and should be archived and stored for future review as needed. System intruders have been known to attempt to cover their tracks by erasing entries in logs, so wise administrators configure their systems to create duplicate copies of the logs and store the copies on sources that cannot be easily modified, like optical disk technologies such as CD-R and DVD-R. Many vendors offer log consolidation and analysis features that allow for integration of log files from multiple products, such as firewalls, network equipment, and even products from other vendors.

To assist organizations in meeting their reporting requirements, the information security assessment survey shown in Table 12-5 covers many of the areas typically required for inclusion in reports. The questionnaire can be customized for an organization or program and can be completed by the CIO, the CISO, or an independent assessor of the organization's information security program.

Each question should be answered for each level of IT security maturity.

- To answer "Yes" at the Policy maturity level, the topic should be documented in the organization's policy.
- To answer "Yes" at the Procedures maturity level, the topic should be documented in detailed procedures.
- To answer "Yes" at the Implemented maturity level, the implementation is verified by examining the procedures and program area documentation and interviewing key personnel.
- To answer "Yes" at the Tested maturity level, documents should be examined and interviews should be conducted to verify that the policies and procedures covered by the question are implemented, operating as intended, and providing the desired level of security.
- To answer "Yes" at the Integrated maturity level, policies, procedures, implementation, and testing are continually monitored, and improvements are made as a normal business process of the organization.

Table 12-5   Information Security Program Questions[16]

Program Questions	Policy	Procedures	Implemented	Tested	Integrated
1. Security Control Review Process Does management ensure that corrective information security actions are tracked using the plan of action and milestones (POA&M) process?					
2. Capital Planning and Investment Control Does the organization require the use of a business case, capital asset plan, and IT portfolio to record the resources required for security at an acceptable level of risk for all programs and systems in the organization?					
3. Investment Review Board Is there an investment review board or similar group designated and empowered to ensure that all investment requests include the security resources needed or that all exceptions to this requirement are documented?					
4. Integrating Information Security into Capital Planning and Investment Control (CPIC) Is there integration of information security into the CPIC process?					
5. Budget and Resources Are information security resources, including personnel and funding, allocated to protect information and information systems in accordance with assessed risks?					
6. Systems and Projects Inventory Are IT projects and systems identified in an inventory, and is the information about the IT projects and systems relevant to the investment management process? Is there a detailed inventory of systems?					

(continues)

Table 12-5   Information Security Program Questions[16] (*Continued*)

Program Questions	Policy	Procedures	Implemented	Tested	Integrated
7. IT Security Measurements					
Are IT security measurements collected organization-wide and reported?					
8. Enterprise Architecture and the Enterprise Architecture Security and Privacy Profile					
Are system- and enterprise-level information security and privacy requirements and capabilities documented within the organization's enterprise architecture? Is that information used to understand the current risks to the organization's mission? Is that information used to help program and organization executives select the best security and privacy solutions to enable the mission?					
9. Critical Infrastructure Protection Plan					
If required in your organization, Is there a documented critical infrastructure and key resources protection plan?					
10. Life Cycle Management (LCM)					
Is there a system life cycle management process that requires each system to be certified and accredited? Is each system officially approved to operate? Is the system LCM process communicated to appropriate people?					

Source: NIST SP 800-100.

11. Security Services and Products Acquisition

Information security services and products are essential elements of an organization's information security program. Such products are widely available in the marketplace and are frequently used by federal agencies. Security products and services should be selected and used to support the organization's overall program to manage the design, development, and maintenance of its information security infrastructure and to protect its mission-critical information. Organizations should apply risk management principles to help identify and mitigate risks associated with product acquisition.

When acquiring information security products, organizations are encouraged to conduct a cost-benefit analysis—one that also includes the costs associated with risk mitigation. This analysis should include a life cycle cost estimate for current products and one for each identified alternative while highlighting the benefits associated with each alternative. NIST SP 800-36, "Guide to Selecting Information Technology Security Products," defines broad security product categories and then specifies product types, product characteristics, and environment considerations within those categories. The guide also provides a list of pertinent questions that organizations should ask when selecting products.

The process of selecting information security products and services involves numerous people throughout an organization. Each person or group involved in the process should understand the importance of security in the organization's information infrastructure and the security impacts of their decisions. Personnel might be included from across the organization to provide relevant perspective on information security needs that must be integrated into the solution.

Just as the SDLC supports the development of products, the security services life cycle (SSLC) provides a framework to help decision makers organize and coordinate their security efforts from initiation to completion. Figure 12-3 depicts the SSLC for obtaining security services at a high level. Table 12-6 provides a brief summary of each phase.

Vulnerabilities in IT products surface nearly every day, and many ready-to-use exploits are available on the Internet. Because IT products are often intended for a wide variety of audiences, restrictive security controls are usually not enabled by default, so many IT products are immediately vulnerable out of the box. Security program managers should review NIST SP 800-70, Rev. 4, (2018) "National Checklist Program for IT Products: Guidelines for Checklist Users and

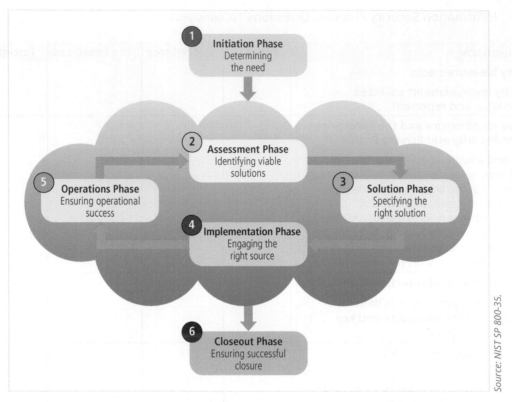

Source: NIST SP 800-35.

Figure 12-3 Information security services life cycle[17]

Table 12-6 The Information Security Services Life Cycle[18]

Phase	Activity
Phase 1—Initiation	• Begins when the need to initiate the services life cycle is recognized • Consists of needs determination, security categorization, and the preliminary risk assessment
Phase 2—Assessment	• Involves developing an accurate portrait of the current environment before decision makers can implement a service and a service provider • Baselines the existing environment; metrics creation, gathering, and analysis; and total cost of ownership • Analyzes opportunities and barriers • Identifies options and risks
Phase 3—Solution	• Requires decision makers to choose the appropriate solution from the viable options identified during the assessment phase • Develops the business case • Develops the service arrangement • Develops the implementation plan
Phase 4—Implementation	• Requires implementation of service providers • Identifies the service provider and develops the service agreement • Finalizes and executes the implementation plan • Manages expectations
Phase 5—Operations	• Oversees the services life cycle becoming iterative; the service is working, the service provided is fully installed, and a constant assessment must be made of the service level and source performance • Monitors and measures organization performance • Evaluates current operations and directs actions for continuous improvement

(continues)

Table 12-6   The Information Security Services Life Cycle[18] (*Continued*)

Phase	Activity
Phase 6—Closeout	• Requires consideration that the iterative nature of the life cycle might mean the service and service provider could continue indefinitely, but this is unlikely
	• Requires consideration that if the environment changes, information security program managers will identify triggers that initiate new and replacement services for information security
	• Selects the appropriate exit strategy
	• Implements the selected exit strategy

Developers," which helps them develop and disseminate security checklists so that organizations and individual users can better secure their IT products. In its simplest form, a security configuration checklist is a series of instructions for configuring a product to a particular operating environment. This checklist is sometimes called a lockdown or hardening guide or benchmark.

 For more information on any of the NIST Special Publications listed in this section, visit *https://csrc.nist.gov/publications/sp800*.

12. Incident Response

As illustrated throughout this text, attacks on information systems and networks have become more numerous, sophisticated, and severe in recent years. While preventing such attacks would be the ideal course of action, not all security incidents can be prevented. Every organization that depends on information systems and networks should identify and assess the risks to its systems and reduce those risks to an acceptable level. An important component of this risk management process is the trending analysis of past computer security incidents and the identification of effective ways to deal with them. A well-defined incident response capability helps the organization detect incidents rapidly, minimize loss and destruction, identify weaknesses, and restore IT operations rapidly.

As you learned in earlier modules, the first clue that an attack is under way often comes from reports by observant users. Similarly, the first clue that a security system has a fault or error may also come from user feedback. In many organizations, help desks handle these user reports as well as other system problems. If an organization does not have a help desk, it should probably consider establishing one, or at least make other provisions to allow users to report suspicious system behavior. The nearby feature discusses the function and organization of help desks.

The Help Desk

With a relatively small investment in an IT help desk, an organization can improve the quality of its IT support and information security function. A small help desk with only a few call agents can provide service for an organization of several hundred users. Large organizations can also improve customer service through the use of a help desk, as long as it receives adequate funding and effective management.

Although it may function differently depending on the organization, a help desk commonly provides the following services:

- A single point of contact for service requests from users
- Initial screening of requests, answering common questions, solving common problems, and dispatching other types of calls to other units
- Entering all calls into a tracking system
- Dispatching service providers to respond to calls
- Reporting and analysis of call volumes, patterns, and process improvement
- Early detection of adverse events, which could escalate to incidents or foreshadow disasters

Other services that may be integrated into the help desk include the following:

- Desk-side support for common IT applications such as Windows tools, end-user computing tools, and common applications
- Managing new users
- Timely removal of users who no longer need system access
- Password management
- Smart card management
- Knowledge management for service requests and optimum resolutions
- Server configuration
- Network monitoring
- Server capacity monitoring
- Virus activity monitoring and virus pattern management

While each organization has its own approach to creating and developing a help-desk solution, many help desks evolve and alter their mix of services over time.[19]

Help-desk personnel must be trained to distinguish a security problem from other system problems. As help-desk personnel screen problems, they must also track the activities involved in resolving each complaint in a help-desk information system. The tracking process is commonly implemented using a trouble ticket. A trouble ticket is opened when a user calls about an issue and is closed when help-desk or technical support personnel resolve the issue. One key advantage to having formal help-desk software is the ability to create and develop a knowledge base of common problems and solutions. This knowledge base can be searched when a user problem comes up; if it is like a problem that was already reported and resolved, complaints can be resolved more quickly. This knowledge base can also generate statistics about the frequency of problems by type, by user, or by application, and thus can detect trends and patterns in the data. Incidentally, some user problems may be created or influenced by a security program because modifications to firewalls, implementations of IDPS rules, or new systems policies in the network can directly affect how users interact with the systems. A significant number of help-desk trouble tickets are the result of user access issues involving passwords and other mechanisms of authentication, authorization, and accountability. Proper user training and ongoing awareness campaigns can reduce these problems but not eliminate them.

To resolve a problem, a support technician may need to visit a user's office to examine equipment or observe the user's procedures, or the technician might need to interact with other departments or workgroups. The help-desk team sometimes includes a dedicated security technician. In any case, the person working to resolve the trouble ticket must document both the diagnosis and the resolution, as they are invaluable components of the knowledge base. Once the problem has been resolved and the results are documented, the ticket is closed.

13. Configuration and Change Management

The purpose of configuration and change management is to manage the effects of changes or differences in configurations in an information system or network. In some organizations, configuration management is the identification, inventory, and documentation of the current information systems—hardware, software, and networking configurations. Change management is sometimes described as a separate function that only addresses modifications to this base configuration. Here, the two concepts are combined to address the current and proposed states of the information systems and the management of any needed modifications.

 To see an example framework for software product line practice—a best-practice configuration management approach—visit the Software Engineering Institute's Web site at *www.sei.cmu.edu/productlines/frame_report/config.man.htm.*

Just as documents should have version numbers, revision dates, and other features designated to monitor and administer changes made to them, so too should the technical components of systems, such as software, hardware, and firmware. Several key terms are used in the management of configuration and change in technical components, as shown in the following hypothetical example.

Assume that XYZ Security Solutions Corporation has developed a new software application called Panacea, the Ultimate Security Solution. Panacea is the *configuration item*. Panacea's *configuration* consists of three major software components: See-all, Know-all, and Cure-all. Thus, Panacea is *version* 1.0, and it is built from its three components. The *build list* is See-all 1.0, Know-all 1.0, and Cure-all 1.0, as this is the first *major release* of the complete application and its components. The *revision date* is the date associated with the first *build*. To create Panacea, the programmers at XYZ Security Solutions pulled information from their *software library*. Suppose that while the application is being used in the field, the programmers discover a minor flaw in a subroutine. When they correct this flaw, they issue a *minor release*, Panacea 1.1. If at some point they need to make a major revision to the software to meet changing market needs or fix more substantial problems with the subcomponents, they would issue a *major release*, Panacea 2.0. In addition to the challenge of keeping applications at the current version level, administrators face the release of newer versions of operating systems and ongoing rollouts of newer hardware versions. The combination of updated hardware, operating systems, and applications is further complicated by the constant need for bug fixes and security updates to these elements.

CCM assists in streamlining change management processes and prevents changes that could adversely affect the security posture of a system. In its entirety, the CCM process reduces the risk that any changes to a system will compromise the system or data's confidentiality, integrity, or availability, because the process provides a repeatable mechanism for effecting system modifications in a controlled environment. In accordance with the CCM process, system changes must be tested prior to implementation to observe the effects of the changes and minimize the risk of adverse results.

NIST SP 800-64, Rev. 2, "Security Considerations in the System Development Life Cycle," states:

> *Configuration management and control procedures are critical to establishing an initial baseline of hardware, software, and firmware components for the information system and subsequently to controlling and maintaining an accurate inventory of any changes to the system. Changes to the hardware, software, or firmware of a system can have a significant impact on the security of the system . . . changes should be documented, and their potential impact on security should be assessed regularly.*[20]

NIST SP 800-53, Rev. 4, "Security and Privacy Controls for Federal Information Systems and Organizations," defines seven CM controls that organizations are required to implement based on an information system's security categorization. The required CM controls are defined in Table 12-7.

The CM process identifies the steps required to ensure that all changes are properly requested, evaluated, and authorized. The CM process also provides a detailed, step-by-step procedure for identifying, processing, tracking, and documenting changes. An example CM process is described in the following sections.

Table 12-7   NIST SP 800-53, Rev. 4, Configuration Management Control Family[21]

Identifier	Title	Control
CM-1	Configuration Management Policy and Procedures	The organization: a. Develops, documents, and disseminates a CM policy that addresses purpose, scope, roles, responsibilities, management commitment, coordination among organizational entities, and compliance; and develops, documents, and disseminates procedures to facilitate the implementation of the CM policy and associated CM controls b. Reviews and updates the current CM policy and CM procedures
CM-2	Baseline Configuration	Under configuration control, the organization develops, documents, and maintains a current baseline configuration of the information system.

(continues)

Table 12-7   NIST SP 800-53, Rev. 4, Configuration Management Control Family[21] (*Continued*)

Identifier	Title	Control
CM-3	Configuration Change Control	The organization: a. Determines the types of changes to the information system that are configuration-controlled b. Reviews proposed configuration-controlled changes to the information system and approves or disapproves such changes with explicit consideration for security impact analyses c. Documents configuration change decisions associated with the information system d. Implements approved configuration-controlled changes to the information system e. Retains records of configuration-controlled changes to the information system for a specified time period f. Audits and reviews activities associated with configuration-controlled changes to the information system g. Coordinates and provides oversight for configuration change control activities through the organization's configuration change control committee or board
CM-4	Security Impact Analysis	The organization analyzes changes to the information system to determine potential security impacts prior to change implementation.
CM-5	Access Restrictions for Change	The organization defines, documents, approves, and enforces physical and logical access restrictions associated with changes to the information system.
CM-6	Configuration Settings	The organization establishes and documents configuration settings for information technology products employed within the information system, using security configuration checklists that reflect the most restrictive mode consistent with operating requirements; implements the configuration settings; identifies, documents, and approves any deviations from established configuration settings for the organization's information system components based on operating requirements; and monitors and controls changes to the configuration settings in accordance with the organization's policies and procedures.
CM-7	Least Functionality	The organization configures the information system to provide only essential capabilities, and prohibits or restricts the use of certain functions, ports, protocols, and services.

Source: NIST SP 800-53, Rev. 4.

Step 1: Identify Change—The first step of the CM process begins when a person or process associated with the information system identifies the need for a change. The change can be initiated by numerous people, such as users or system owners, or it may be identified by audit findings or other reviews. A change may consist of updating the fields or records of a database or upgrading the operating system with the latest security patches. Once the need for a change has been identified, a change request should be submitted to the appropriate decision-making body.

Step 2: Evaluate Change Request—After initiating a change request, the organization must evaluate possible effects that the change may have on the system or other interrelated systems. An impact analysis of the change should be conducted using the following guidelines:

- Whether the change is viable and improves the performance or security of the system
- Whether the change is technically correct, necessary, and feasible within the system constraints
- Whether system security will be affected by the change
- Whether associated costs for implementing the change were considered
- Whether security components are affected by the change

Step 3: Implementation Decision—Once the change has been evaluated and tested, one of the following actions should be taken:

- Approve—Implementation is authorized and may occur at any time after the appropriate authorization signature has been documented.
- Deny—The request is immediately denied regardless of circumstances and the information provided.
- Defer—The immediate decision is postponed until further notice. In this situation, additional testing or analysis may be needed before a final decision can be made.

Step 4: Implement Approved Change Request—Once the decision has been made to implement the change, it should be moved from the test environment into production. If required, the personnel who update the production environment are not the same people who developed the change. This requirement provides greater assurance that unapproved changes are not implemented into production.

Step 5: Continuous Monitoring—The CCM process calls for continuous system monitoring to ensure that it is operating as intended and that implemented changes do not adversely affect the system's performance or security posture. Organizations can achieve the goals of continuous system monitoring by performing configuration verification tests to ensure that the selected configuration for a given system has not been altered outside the established CCM process. In addition to configuration verification tests, organizations can also perform system audits. Both require an examination of system characteristics and supporting documentation to verify that the configuration meets user needs and is the approved system configuration baseline.[22]

As part of the overall CCM process, organizations should also perform patch management during this step. Patch management helps lower the potential risk to a network by "patching" or repairing known vulnerabilities in any of the network or system environments. Increasingly, vendors are proactive in developing fixes or antidotes to known vulnerabilities and releasing them to the public. Organizations must remain vigilant to ensure that they capture all relevant fixes as they are released, test their implementation for adverse effects, and implement the fixes after testing is concluded. Patching is associated with phases 2, 3, and 4 of the life cycle. In phase 2, patch management relates to risk management to prevent any vulnerability from being exploited and compromised. Phase 3 contains the testing to ensure that patching and any other changes do not negatively affect the system.

In general, configuration and change management should not interfere with use of the technology. One person on the security team should be appointed as the configuration manager or change manager and made responsible for maintaining appropriate data elements in the organization's cataloging mechanism, such as the specific version, revision date, and build associated with each piece of implemented hardware and software. In some cases, people outside the implementation process might be better suited to this role because they might not be distracted by the installation, configuration, and troubleshooting of the new implementation. In the case of minor revisions, it may be simpler to have a procedure that requires documenting the machines on which a revision is installed, the date and time of the installation, and the name of the installer. While the documentation procedures required for configuration and change management may seem onerous, they enable security teams to quickly and accurately determine which systems are affected when a new vulnerability arises. When stored in a comprehensive database with risk, threat, and attack information, configuration information enables organizations to respond quickly to new and rapidly changing threats and attacks.

The Security Maintenance Model

While management models such as the ISO 27000 series and NIST SP 800-100, "Information Security Handbook: A Guide for Managers," deal with methods to *manage* and *operate* systems, a maintenance model is designed to focus the organization's effort on *maintaining* systems. Figure 12-4 illustrates an approach recommended for dealing with change caused by information security maintenance. The figure diagrams a full maintenance program and serves as a framework for the discussion that follows.

The recommended maintenance model is based on five subject areas or domains:

- External monitoring
- Internal monitoring
- Planning and risk assessment
- Vulnerability assessment and remediation
- Readiness and review

The following sections explore each of these domains and their interactions.

Monitoring the External Environment

During the Cold War, the Western alliance, led by the United States and Great Britain, confronted the Soviet Union and its allies. A key component of the Western alliance's defense was maintaining the ability to detect early warnings of attacks. The image of an ever-vigilant team of radar operators scanning the sky for incoming attacks could also represent the current world of information security, where teams of security personnel must guard their organizations against dangerous and debilitating threats. While the stakes for modern organizations are not as critical as preventing nuclear war, they are nevertheless very high, especially at organizations that depend on information.

The objective of the **external monitoring domain** within the maintenance model is to provide early awareness of new and emerging threats, threat agents, vulnerabilities, and attacks so the organization can mount an effective and timely defense. Figure 12-5 shows the primary components of the external monitoring process.

external monitoring domain

The component of the maintenance model that focuses on evaluating external threats to the organization's information assets.

External monitoring entails collecting intelligence from various data sources and then giving the intelligence context and meaning for use by decision makers within the organization.

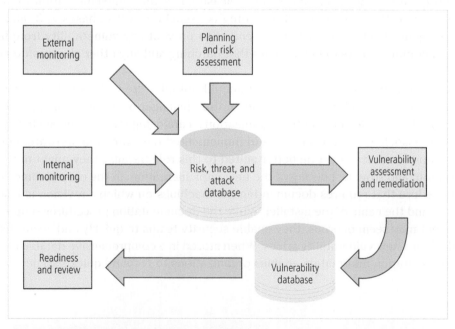

Figure 12-4   The maintenance model

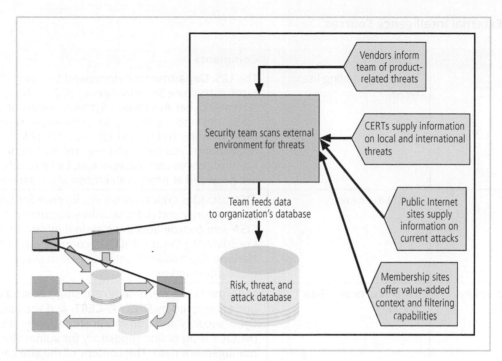

Figure 12-5   External monitoring

Data Sources

Acquiring data about threats, threat agents, vulnerabilities, and attacks is not difficult. There are many sources of raw intelligence and relatively few costs associated with gathering it. The challenge is to turn this flood of good and timely data into information that decision makers can use. For this reason, many organizations outsource this component of the maintenance model. Service providers can deliver a tailored supply of timely processed intelligence to organizations that can afford their subscription fees.

As shown in Figure 12-5, external intelligence can come from these classes of sources:

- *Vendors*—When an organization uses specific hardware and software as part of its information security program, the vendor often provides either direct support or indirect tools that allow user communities to support each other. This support often includes intelligence on emerging threats.
- *CERT organizations*—Computer emergency response teams (CERTs) exist in varying forms around the world. Often, US-CERT (*https://us-cert.cisa.gov/*) is viewed as the definitive authority. Many states have CERT agencies, and many countries have CERT organizations to deal with national issues and threats. Your local, state, or national government may have a CERT outreach program to provide notification services at no direct cost. The U.S. Department of Homeland Security's Cybersecurity & Infrastructure Security Agency (CISA) coordinates the services at US-CERT. The US-CERT Web site collects information on incidents, phishing attacks, malware, and vulnerabilities.
- *Public network sources*—Many publicly accessible information sources, including mailing lists and Web sites, are freely available to organizations and people who have the time and expertise to use them. Table 12-8 lists some of these information security intelligence sources.
- *Membership sites*—Various groups and organizations provide value to subscribers by adding contextual detail to publicly reported events and offering filtering capabilities that allow subscribers to quickly pinpoint the possible impact to their own organizations.

Note that the list in the preceding table is not comprehensive. There are hundreds of security Web sites, blogs, and news sites.

(i)   For more information about the US-CERT program, visit the Web site at *https://us-cert.cisa.gov/*.

Table 12-8 External Intelligence Sources

Source Name	Type	Comments
US-CERT	Web site, mailing list, news	The U.S. Department of Homeland Security's Cybersecurity & Infrastructure Security Agency (CISA) provides the National Cyber Awareness System, which can send e-mail advisories and supporting information to registered organizations and individuals. You can select the type of notifications you need and register for the desired advisory list at *https://us-cert.cisa.gov/ncas*. Links to other resources are provided at *https://us-cert.cisa.gov/resources*.
DHS' CISA	Web site, news	CISA provides critical threat intelligence for both the cybersecurity and national infrastructure communities. CISA also coordinates the National Infrastructure Coordinating Center (NICC) in cooperation with the DHS National Operations Center. See *https://www.cisa.gov/* for more information.
National Vulnerability Database (NVD)	Web site, news, data feeds	NVD, the U.S. government repository hosted by NIST and sponsored by DHS, US-CERT, and the National Cybersecurity and Communications Integration Center (NCCIC), is an online repository for vulnerability management data. The content of the site can be used to support automation of vulnerability detection. NVD includes several databases of security-related software flaws, information on misconfigurations, checklists for assessment of vulnerabilities, and other related content like impact metrics. The contents of this database are synchronized with the CVE database at *https://cve.mitre .org/*. NVD is available at *https://nvd.nist.gov/*.
CERT/CC	Web site, blogs, news	CERT/CC is a center of Internet security expertise at the Software Engineering Institute, a federally funded research and development center operated by Carnegie Mellon University. CERT/CC and DHS support the Web site, which is usually considered the definitive authority to be consulted when emerging threats become demonstrated vulnerabilities. See CERT/CC's information page at *https://www.sei.cmu.edu/about/divisions/cert/*.
IBM's X-Force	Web site, news	This is a commercial site with a focus on the vendor's own commercial IDPS and other security products. The site also provides breaking news about emerging threats and allows individuals to subscribe to alerts. See *www.ibm.com/security/services/ibm-x-force-incident-response-and-intelligence*.
Insecure.org	Web site, mailing lists, blog	*Insecure.org* is the creation of the well-known hacker Fyodor. He and his associates operate the site and provide the Internet community with software and information about vulnerabilities. Nmap is the best known of the *insecure.org* tools. Many topics are covered in the available lists at *https://seclists.org/*.
Mitre	Web site, news	Common Vulnerabilities and Exposures (see *https://cve .mitre.org/*) is an online database managed by the Mitre Corporation. The site offers information and news on current vulnerabilities and related exploitation methods.
Packet Storm	News	This commercial site provides news and discussion focusing on current security events and tools (see *packetstormsecurity.com*).

(continues)

Table 12-8   External Intelligence Sources (*Continued*)

Source Name	Type	Comments
SecurityFocus	Web site, mailing lists	This commercial site provides general coverage and commentary on information security (see *www.securityfocus.com/*). The site includes multiple information sources: • Bugtraq mailing list—The industry standard repository of detailed, full-disclosure discussions and announcements about computer security vulnerabilities. There are also multiple mailing lists of specialized categories under Bugtraq, like Focus on Microsoft, Focus on Apple, Focus on Virus, and Forensics. • The SecurityFocus Vulnerability Database • SecurityFocus Mailing Lists
SourceForge	Blogs	*SourceForge.net* maintains a large number of blogs and downloadable products for open-source software like Snort. To search for a particular topic, visit *https://sourceforge.net*.
Tenable	Web site, blog	Tenable's Web site is dedicated to the Nessus vulnerability scanner. The site has information about emerging threats and how to test for them. The blog is at *https://www.tenable.com/blog*.
Center for Internet Security	Web site, tools, blog	CIS provides cyberthreat intelligence, best practices, and tools to detect and react to security threats. The site is at *www.cisecurity.org/*.

Regardless of where or how external monitoring data is collected, it is not useful unless it is analyzed in the context of the organization's security environment. To perform this evaluation and take appropriate actions in a timely fashion, the CISO must do the following:

- Staff the function with people who understand the technical aspects of information security, have a comprehensive understanding of the organization's complete IT infrastructure, and have a thorough grounding in the organization's business operations.
- Provide documented and repeatable procedures.
- Train the primary and backup staff assigned to perform the monitoring tasks.
- Equip assigned staff with proper access and tools to perform the monitoring function.
- Cultivate expertise among monitoring analysts so they can cull meaningful summaries and actionable alerts from the vast flow of raw intelligence.
- Develop suitable communication methods for moving processed intelligence to designated internal decision makers in all three communities of interest—IT, information security, and general management.
- Integrate the incident response plan with the results of the external monitoring process to produce appropriate, timely responses.

Monitoring, Escalation, and Incident Response

The basic function of the external monitoring process is to monitor activity, report results, and escalate warnings. The best approach for escalation is based on a thorough integration of the monitoring process into the IRP, as you learned in Module 5. The monitoring process has three primary deliverables:

- Specific warning bulletins issued when developing threats and specific attacks pose a measurable risk to the organization. The bulletins should assign a meaningful risk level to the threat to help decision makers in the organization formulate the appropriate response.
- Periodic summaries of external information. The summaries present statistical results, such as the number of new or revised CERT advisories per month, or itemized lists of significant new vulnerabilities.

- Detailed intelligence on the highest-risk warnings. This information prepares the way for detection and remediation of vulnerabilities in the later steps of vulnerability assessment. This intelligence can include identifying which vendor updates apply to specific vulnerabilities and which types of defenses have been found to work against the specific vulnerabilities reported.

Data Collection and Management

Over time, the external monitoring processes should capture information about the external environment in a format that can be referenced throughout the organization as threats emerge and then referenced for historical use. This data collection can use e-mail, Web pages, databases, or even paper-and-pencil recording methods, if the essential facts are communicated, stored, and used to create queries when needed. In the final analysis, external monitoring collects raw intelligence, filters it for relevance to the organization, assigns it a relative risk impact, and communicates these findings to decision makers in time to make a difference.

Monitoring the Internal Environment

The primary goal of the **internal monitoring domain** is an informed awareness of the state of the organization's networks, information systems, and information security defenses. This awareness must be communicated and documented, especially for components that are exposed to the external network. Internal monitoring is accomplished by the following:

- Building and maintaining an inventory of network devices and channels, IT infrastructure and applications, and elements of information security infrastructure.
- Leading the IT governance process within the organization to integrate the inevitable changes found in all network, IT, and information security programs.
- Monitoring IT activity in real time using IDPSs to detect and respond to actions or events that introduce risk to the organization's information assets.
- Monitoring the internal state of the organization's networks and systems. To maintain awareness of new and emerging threats, this recursive review is required of network and system devices that are online at any given moment and of any changes to services offered on the network. This review can be accomplished through automated difference-detection methods that identify variances introduced to the network or system hardware and software.

The value of internal monitoring is increased when knowledge gained from the network and system configuration is fed into the vulnerability assessment and remediation domain. However, this knowledge becomes invaluable when incident response processes are fully integrated with the monitoring processes.

Figure 12-6 shows the component processes of the internal monitoring domain, which are discussed in the sections that follow.

Network Characterization and Inventory

Organizations should maintain a carefully planned and fully populated inventory of all their network devices, communication channels, and computing devices. This inventory should include server hardware, desktop hardware, and software, including operating systems and applications. The inventory should also include *partner interconnections—* network devices, communications channels, and applications that may not be owned by the organization but are essential to its continued partnership with another company. The process of collecting this information is often referred to as *characterization*.

internal monitoring domain

The component of the maintenance model that focuses on identifying, assessing, and managing the configuration and status of information assets in an organization.

Once the characteristics of the network environment have been identified and collected as data, they must be carefully organized and stored using a manual or automated mechanism that allows for timely retrieval and rapid integration of disparate facts. For all but the smallest network environments, this requires a relational database. The attributes of network devices such as systems, switches, and gateways were discussed in earlier modules. In contrast to the attributes collected for risk management, which are important for economic and business value, the characteristics collected here—manufacturer and software

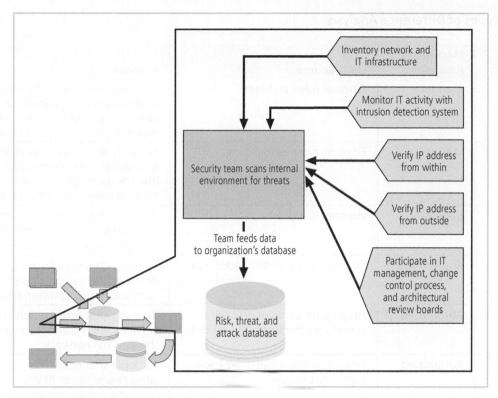

Figure 12-6   Internal monitoring

versions—relate to technical functionality, so they should be kept accurate and up to date. Also, the technology needed to store this data should be stand-alone and portable because if the data is needed to support incident response and disaster recovery, server or network access may be unavailable.

Making IDPSs Work

To be used most effectively, the information that comes from an IDPS must be integrated into the maintenance process. An IDPS generates a seemingly endless flow of alert messages that often have little bearing on the immediate effectiveness of the information security program. Except for an occasional real-time alert that is not a false positive, the IDPS reports events that have already occurred. Given this, the most important value of raw intelligence provided by the IDPS is that it can be used to prevent future attacks by indicating current or imminent vulnerabilities. Whether the organization outsources IDPS monitoring, staffs IDPS monitoring 24/7, staffs IDPS monitoring during business hours, or merely ignores the real-time alerts from the IDPS, the log files from the IDPS engines can be mined for information that can be added to the internal monitoring knowledge base.

Another element of IDPS monitoring is *traffic analysis*. Analyzing the traffic that flows through a system and its associated devices can often be a critically important process because the traffic identifies the most frequently used devices. Also, analyzing attack signatures from unsuccessful system attacks can help identify weaknesses in various security efforts. An example of the type of vulnerability exposed by traffic analysis occurs when an organization tries to determine if all its device signatures have been adequately masked. In general, the default configuration setting of many network devices allows them to respond to any request with a device signature message that identifies the device's make and model and perhaps even its software version. In the interest of greater security, many organizations require that all devices be reconfigured to conceal their device signatures. Suppose that an organization performs an analysis of unsuccessful attacks and discovers that lesser-known UNIX attacks are being launched against one of its servers. This discovery might inform the organization that the server under attack is responding to requests for OS type with its device signature.

Detecting Differences

One approach that can improve the awareness of the information security function uses a process known as **difference analysis** to quickly identify changes to the internal environment. Any unexpected differences between the current state and

difference analysis

A procedure that compares the current state of a network segment against a known previous state of the same network segment (the baseline of systems and services).

Table 12-9 Types of Difference Analysis

Suggested Frequency	Method of Analysis	Data Source	Purpose
Quarterly	Manual	Firewall rules and logs	To verify that new rules follow all risk assessment and procedural approvals, identify illicit rules, ensure removal of expired rules, and detect tampering
Quarterly	Manual	Edge router rules and logs	To verify that new rules follow all risk assessment and procedural approvals, identify illicit rules, ensure removal of expired rules, and detect tampering
Quarterly	Manual	Internet footprint	To verify that public Internet addresses registered to the organization are accurate and complete
Monthly	Automated	Fingerprinting of all IP addresses	To verify that only known and authorized devices offering critical services can be reached from the internal network
Weekly	Automated	Fingerprint services on critical servers on the internal network	To verify that only known and approved services are offered from critical servers in the internal network
Daily	Automated	Fingerprinting of all IP addresses from the outside	To verify that only known and approved servers and other devices can be reached from the public network
Hourly	Automated	Fingerprint services on critical servers exposed to the Internet	To enable e-mail notification of administrators if unexpected services become available on critical servers exposed to the Internet

planning and risk assessment domain

The component of the maintenance model that focuses on identifying and planning ongoing information security activities and identifying and managing risks introduced through IT information security projects.

the baseline state could indicate trouble. Table 12-9 shows how several kinds of difference analyses can be used. Note that the table lists suggestions for *possible* difference analyses; each organization should identify the differences it wants to measure and its criteria for action.

The value of difference analysis depends on the quality of the baseline, which is the initial snapshot portion of the difference comparison. The value of the analysis also depends on the degree to which the notification of discovered differences can induce action.

Planning and Risk Assessment

The primary objective of the **planning and risk assessment domain** is to keep an eye on the entire information security program, in part by identifying and planning ongoing information security activities that further reduce risk. In fact, the bulk of the security management maintenance model could fit in this domain. Also, the risk assessment group identifies and documents risks introduced both by IT projects and information security projects. It also identifies and documents risks that may be latent in the present environment. The primary objectives of this domain are as follows:

- Establishing a formal review process for the information security program that complements and supports both IT planning and strategic planning
- Instituting formal project identification, selection, planning, and management processes for follow-up activities that augment the current information security program
- Coordinating with IT project teams to introduce risk assessment and review for all IT projects so that risks introduced by the launches of new IT projects are identified, documented, and factored into decisions about the projects
- Integrating a mindset of risk assessment throughout the organization that encourages other departments to perform risk assessment activities when any technology system is implemented or modified

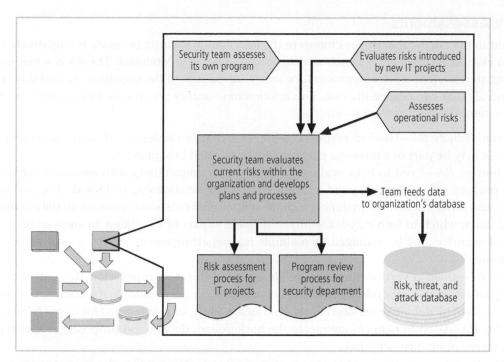

Figure 12-7 Planning and risk assessment

Figure 12-7 illustrates the relationships between the components of this maintenance domain. Note that there are two pivotal processes: the planning needed for information security programs and evaluation of current risks using operational risk assessment.

Information Security Program Planning and Review

An organization should periodically review its ongoing information security program and any planning for enhancements and extensions. The strategic planning process should examine the future IT needs of the organization and their impact on information security.

A recommended approach is to take advantage of the fact that most larger organizations have annual capital budget planning cycles. Thus, the IT group can develop an annual list of project ideas for planning and then prepare an estimate for the effort needed to complete the projects, the estimated amount of capital required, and a preliminary assessment of the risks associated with performing each project or not. These assessments become part of the organization's project planning process. When capital and expense budgets are made final, the projects to be funded are chosen using the planning information on hand. This allows executives to make informed decisions about which projects to fund. The IT group then follows up with quarterly reviews of progress, which include an updated project risk assessment. As each project nears completion, an operational risk assessment group reviews the impact of the project on the organization's risk profile. The sponsors of the project and perhaps other executives then determine if the risk level is acceptable, if the project requires additional risk remediation, or if the project must be aborted.

Projects that organizations might fund to maintain, extend, or enhance the information security program will arise in almost every planning cycle. Larger information security projects should be broken into smaller, incremental projects, which is important for several reasons:

- Smaller projects tend to have more manageable impacts on the networks and users. Larger projects tend to complicate the change control process in the implementation phase.
- Shorter planning, development, and implementation schedules reduce uncertainty for IT planners and financial sponsors.
- Most large projects can easily be broken into smaller projects, giving the security team more opportunities to change direction and gain flexibility as events occur and circumstances change.

Security Risk Assessments

A key component in the engine that drives change in the information security program is a relatively straightforward process called a risk assessment (RA), which was described in detail in Module 4. The RA is a method of identifying and documenting the risk that a project, process, or action introduces to the organization, and it may also offer suggestions for controls that can reduce the risk. The information security group coordinates the preparation of many types of RA documents, including the following:

- *Network connectivity RA*—Used to respond to network change requests and network architectural design proposals. It may be part of a business partner's RA or be used to support it.
- *Business partner RA*—Used to help evaluate a proposal for connectivity with business partners. Note that business partner risks extend beyond a direct contractual relationship to include the partner's vendors, landlords, and other clients. For instance, a cloud vendor may outsource some or all data center operations to a third party, which in turn may lease physical space in part of a building. In such an arrangement, part of physical security may be managed by a simple leasing arrangement, not by a professional data center security team.
- *Application RA*—Used at various stages in the life cycle of a business application. Its content depends on the project's position in the life cycle when the RA is prepared. Usually, multiple RA documents are prepared at different stages. The definitive version is prepared as the application is readied for conversion to production.
- *Vulnerability RA*—Used to help communicate the background, details, and proposed remediation as vulnerabilities emerge or change over time.
- *Privacy RA*—Used to document applications or systems that contain protected personal information that must be evaluated for compliance with the organization's privacy policies and relevant laws.
- *Acquisition or divestiture RA*—Used when planning for reorganization as units of the organization are acquired, divested, or moved.
- *Other RA*—Used when a statement about risk is needed for any project, proposal, or fault that is not contained in the preceding list.

The RA process identifies risks and proposes controls. Most RA documents are structured to include the components shown in Table 12-10. Most training programs on information security include training sessions for the preparation of RA documents.

Table 12-10   Risk Assessment Documentation Components

Component	Description	When and How Used
Introduction	A standard opening description to explain the RA to readers who are unfamiliar with the format. The exact text varies for each RA template. Here is an example: "The primary purpose of the security risk assessment is to identify computer and network security risks to information assets that may be introduced to the organization by the issue described in this document. This security risk assessment is also used to help identify security controls planned or proposed. Further, the sections below may identify risks that are not adequately controlled by the planned controls."	Found in all RA document templates
Scope	A statement of the boundaries of the RA. Here is an example: "To define the security and control requirements associated with project X running application Y with access via Internet and the migration of that application into the organization's environment."	Found in all RA document templates

(continues)

Table 12-10   Risk Assessment Documentation Components (*Continued*)

Component	Description	When and How Used
Disclaimer	A statement that identifies limits in the risk assessment based on when the report was developed in the project life cycle. The information that was available at different times during the project affects the comprehensiveness and accuracy of the report. Often, risk assessments are the most imprecise at the earliest stages of a project, so decision makers must be made aware of this lack of precision when the risk assessment is based on incomplete information. This statement is sometimes removed from the final RA when all information about the project is available, but it may be left in to provide awareness that some imprecision is inherent in the process. Here is an example: "The issues documented in this report should not be considered all-inclusive. A number of strategic and tactical decisions will be made during the development and implementation stages of the project, and therefore the security control deliverables may change based on actual implementation. Any changes should be reassessed to ensure that proper controls will still be enacted."	Found in all draft RA document templates; some issues may remain in the disclaimer in some final RA templates
Information security resources	A list of information security team members who collected information, analyzed risk, and documented the findings.	Found in all RA document templates
Other resources	A list of other organization members who provided information, assisted in analyzing risk, and documented the findings.	Found in all RA document templates
Background	Documentation of the proposed project, including network changes, application changes, and other issues or faults.	Found in all RA document templates
Planned controls	Documentation of all controls that are planned in the proposed project, including network changes, application changes, and other issues or faults.	Found in all RA document templates
IRP and DRP planning elements	Documentation of the incident response and disaster planning elements prepared for this proposed project, including network changes, application changes, and other issues or faults.	Recommended in all document templates
Opinion of risk	A summary statement of the risk introduced to the organization by the proposed project, network change, application, or other issue or fault. For example: "This application as it currently exists is considered high risk. IMPORTANT NOTE: Because of the high risk of the current implementation and the potential for harming the organization if system or data is compromised in any way, this notification needs to be escalated to the director or manager who would be held responsible for the added expense or loss of revenue associated with such a compromise. In addition, an acknowledgment of the risk and the urgency of correcting it must be signed and returned to the CISO."	Found in all RA document templates
Recommendations	A statement of what needs to be done to implement controls within the project to limit risk from it. For example: "A project team should be formed to assist the operating unit and technical support team in creating a comprehensive plan to address the security issues within application X. Specific areas of concern are authentication and authorization. The corrections of configuration errors found in the platform security validation process must continue. All user accounts need to be reviewed and scrubbed to determine whether the user or service account requires access. All user accounts need to be reviewed and assigned the appropriate privileges. The Web server of the application needs to be separated from the application and database server."	Found in all RA document templates

(continues)

Table 12-10   Risk Assessment Documentation Components (*Continued*)

Component	Description	When and How Used

Information security controls recommendations summary	A summary of the controls that are planned or needed, using the system's security architecture elements as an organizing method. The following categories of information should be documented in tabular form:
	
	• Security architecture elements and what they provide.
	   ○ Authentication—The user is verified as authentic.
	   ○ Authorization—The user is allowed to use the facility or service.
	   ○ Confidentiality—Content must be kept secret from unintended recipients.
	   ○ Integrity—Data storage must be secure, accurate, and precise.
	   ○ Accountability—Actions and data usage can be attributed to specific people.
	   ○ Availability and reliability—Systems work when needed.
	   ○ Privacy—Systems comply with the organization's privacy policy.
	
	• Security requirement written for a general audience in terms of the organization's information security policies, using the following core principles of information security:
	   ○ Authentication—Must conform to the organization's authentication policies.
	   ○ Authorization—Must conform to the organization's authorization and usage policies.
	   ○ Confidentiality—Must comply with the requirement to protect data in transit from interception and misuse by using hard encryption.
	   ○ Integrity—Must process data with procedures that ensure freedom from corruption.
	   ○ Accountability—Must track usage to allow actions to be audited later for policy compliance.
	   ○ Availability and reliability—Must be implemented to ensure availability that measures up to the organization's expectations.
	   ○ Privacy—Must process, store, and transmit data using procedures that meet legal privacy requirements.
	
	• Security controls planned or in place—Identify controls for each architectural element.
	• Planned completion date when the control will be fully operational.
	• Who is responsible—Which group or individual employees are accountable for implementing the control?
	• Status—What is the status of the control implementation?
		Recommended in all document templates

A risk assessment's identification of systemic or latent vulnerabilities that introduce risk to the organization can provide the opportunity to create a proposal for an information security project. When used as part of a complete risk management maintenance process, the RA can be a powerful and flexible tool that helps identify and document risk and remediate the underlying vulnerabilities that expose the organization to risks of loss.

Vulnerability Assessment and Remediation

The primary goal of the **vulnerability assessment and remediation domain** is to identify specific, documented vulnerabilities and remediate them in a timely fashion. This is accomplished by the following:

- Using documented vulnerability assessment procedures to safely collect intelligence about internal and public networks; platforms, including servers, desktops, and process control; and wireless network systems
- Documenting background information and providing tested remediation procedures for reported vulnerabilities
- Tracking vulnerabilities from the time they are identified until they are remediated or the risk of loss has been accepted by an authorized member of management
- Communicating vulnerability information, including an estimate of the risk and detailed remediation plans to the owners of vulnerable systems
- Reporting on the status of vulnerabilities that have been identified
- Ensuring that the proper level of management is involved in deciding to accept the risk of loss associated with unrepaired vulnerabilities

Figure 12-8 illustrates the process flow of the vulnerability assessment and remediation domain. Using the inventory of environment characteristics stored in the risk, threat, and attack database, the vulnerability assessment identifies and documents vulnerabilities. They are stored, tracked, and reported in the vulnerability database until they are remediated.

As shown in Figure 12-8, there are four common **vulnerability assessment (VA)** processes: Internet VA, intranet VA, platform security validation, and wireless VA. While the exact procedures associated with each can vary, these

vulnerability assessment and remediation domain

The component of the maintenance model focused on identifying specific, documented vulnerabilities and remediating them in a timely fashion.

vulnerability assessment (VA)

The process of identifying and documenting specific and provable flaws in the organization's information asset environment.

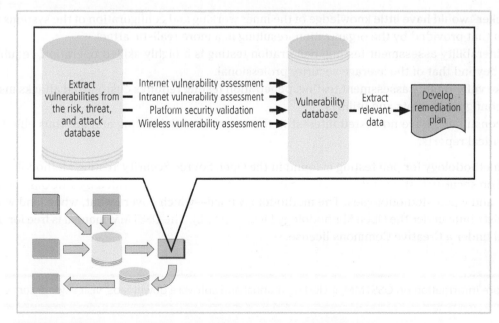

Figure 12-8   Vulnerability assessment and remediation

four processes can help many organizations balance the intrusiveness of vulnerability assessment with the need for a stable and effective production environment. Some organizations pursue a strategy of monthly vulnerability assessments that involve all four processes. Others perform an Internet vulnerability assessment every week and rotate the other three processes on a monthly or quarterly basis. These choices depend on the quantity and quality of resources dedicated to vulnerability assessments.

 For a list of the "top 125 security tools," including vulnerability assessment tools, visit *sectools.org*, a Web site hosted by *insecure.org*.

penetration testing

A set of security tests and evaluations that simulate attacks by a hacker or other malicious external source.

Penetration Testing

Penetration testing is a level of sophistication beyond vulnerability testing. A penetration test, or *pen test*, is usually performed periodically as part of a full security audit. In most security tests, such as vulnerability assessments, great care is taken not to disrupt normal business operations, but in pen testing, the analyst tries to get as far as possible by simulating the actions of an attacker. Unlike the attacker, however, the pen tester's ultimate responsibility is to identify weaknesses in the security of the organization's systems and networks and then present findings to the systems' owners in a detailed report.

While vulnerability testing is usually performed inside the organization's security perimeter with complete knowledge of the networks' configuration and operations, pen testing can be conducted in one of two ways—black box pen testing and white box pen testing. In black box pen testing, or blind testing, the "attacker" has no prior knowledge of the systems or network configurations and thus must investigate the organization's information infrastructure from scratch. In white box testing, also known as full-disclosure testing, the organization provides information about the systems to be examined, allowing for a faster, more focused test. White box pen testing is typically used when a specific system or network segment is suspect and the organization wants the pen tester to focus on a particular aspect of the target. Variations of black box and white box testing, known as grey box or partial-disclosure tests, involve partial knowledge of the organization's infrastructure.

Organizations often hire private security firms or consultants to perform penetration testing for several reasons:

- The "attacker" would have little knowledge of the inner working and configuration of the systems and network other than that provided by the organization, resulting in a more realistic attack.
- Unlike vulnerability assessment testing, penetration testing is a highly skilled operation, requiring levels of expertise beyond that of the average security professional.
- Also, unlike vulnerability assessment testing, penetration testing requires customized attacks instead of standard, preconfigured scripts and utilities.
- External consultants have no vested interest in the outcome of the testing and are thus able to offer more honest, critical reports.

A common methodology for pen testing is found in the Open Source Security Testing Methodology Manual (OSSTMM), a manual on security testing and analysis created by Pete Herzog and provided by ISECOM, the nonprofit Institute for Security and Open Methodologies. The methodology itself—which covers what, when, and where to test—is free to use and distribute under the Open Methodology License (OML). The OSSTMM manual is free for noncommercial use and released under a Creative Commons license.

 For more information on OSSTMM, including manual and software downloads, visit *www.isecom.org/*.

There are several penetration testing certifications available for those who are interested in this aspect of security testing. For example, the Information Assurance Certification Review Board (IACRB) offers a pen testing certification known as the Certified Penetration Tester (CPT). The CPT requires that the applicant pass a multiple-choice exam as well as a take-home practical exam that includes a penetration test against live servers. Subject areas on the multiple-choice exam include the following:

- Penetration testing methodologies
- Network protocol attacks
- Network reconnaissance
- Vulnerability identification
- Windows exploits
- UNIX/Linux exploits
- Covert channels and rootkits
- Wireless security flaws
- Web application vulnerabilities

Other penetration testing exams and approaches use the term *ethical hacking*. While these penetration testing certifications and efforts are valid, the use of the term is problematic, as described in the nearby feature.

An Etymological View of Ethical Hacking[23]

How we describe something defines it. A specific choice of words can cause irreparable damage to an idea or immortalize it. Part of the foundation of the field of information security is the expectation of ethical behavior. Most modern certifications and professional associations in information security, and to a lesser extent information technology in general, require their members to subscribe to codes of ethics. These canons ("a body of rules, principles, or standards accepted as axiomatic and universally binding in a field of study or art"[24]) provide guidance to the members and associates of an organization. They also represent an agreement between the members and their constituencies to provide service that is ethical ("being in accordance with the rules or standards for right conduct or practice, especially the standards of a profession"[25]).

If there is any doubt about the validity of these ethical codes or the conduct of professionals who subscribe to them, the entire discipline suffers. One such dubious area that has gained notoriety in the field of computing is the concept of the "hacker."

When the computer era began, *hacker* was a term for a computer enthusiast who enjoyed pushing the boundaries of computer technologies and who frequently applied unorthodox techniques to accomplish his goals. In the mid-1950s, the term *hacker* was reportedly associated with members of the MIT Model Railroad Club—"one who works like a hack at writing and experimenting with software, one who enjoys computer programming for its own sake."[26]

Today, the term has a much more sinister definition. According to the *American Heritage Dictionary*, to hack is:

a. "*Informal* To alter (a computer program)
b. To gain access to (a computer file or network) illegally or without authorization"[27]

The problem with hacking is not merely that some people actively seek to gain unauthorized access to others' information assets. The problem is much deeper; society seems to have an inexplicable fascination with the disreputable. This phenomenon is widespread, and one has only to reflect on our popular culture to find "felonious heroes" like Jesse James, Al Capone, and Bonnie and Clyde. We are enthralled by their apparent disregard for authority; many of them are portrayed as wrongfully accused. Some argue that we live vicariously through those who display no apparent regard for proper behavior or society's bonds. Others seek the attention afforded to "public enemies" made notorious by the media. Whatever the psychological attraction, the result is that some segments of our society turn a blind eye to certain crimes. A notable example in recent generations is the growing notoriety of computer hacking.

Computer hacking is portrayed in the media with a mixed message. Movies like *Ferris Bueller's Day Off*,[28] *WarGames*,[29] and *Hackers*[30] portray teenage hackers as idols and heroes. Unfortunately, this mixed message is being perpetuated into the modern information security society. We as the stoic guardians of information assets should condemn the entire hacker genre and culture.

This brings us to the point—the *ethical hacker*. The phrase itself is an oxymoron ("a figure of speech by which a locution produces an incongruous, seemingly self-contradictory effect"[31]). The MIT/Stanford "hacker ethic" written by

Stephen Levy attempted to justify the actions of the hacker, and stated that "access to computers should be unlimited and total." All information should be free; authority should be mistrusted. Levy also promoted the concept that hacking should encourage individual activity over any form of corporate authority or system of ideals.[32] Yet it is unlikely that Levy is willing to make his personal financial information "free" to everyone. This manifesto that "information wants to be free" seems to encourage an environment designed to promote and encourage illicit activity. Even in the information security community, there is some dissent over the true meaning of hacking. However, it is generally accepted that a hacker does not intend to follow the policies, rules, and regulations associated with fair and responsible use of computer resources.

Therefore, a distinction exists between hacking and *penetration testing*, or simply *pen testing*—the actions taken by an information security professional to thoroughly test and assess an organization's information assets and their security posture, including gaining access to the root information by bypassing security controls. Most professional information security organizations offer pen testing, and many information security professionals receive training in the craft.

Some will argue that the mindset of the penetration tester is sufficiently different from that of, say, the firewall administrator, because they say different skills are needed to break into a server or network as opposed to protecting it. They argue that people with a "hacker mentality" have a unique perspective on this activity, regardless of whether they have acted on their abilities illegally. This begs the question: Are hackers the only people who can master such skills? Is it not possible to undergo professional training, building upon the ingenuity and natural curiosity of the human psyche, to investigate and solve these puzzles? Or must one "walk on the dark side" to gain this knowledge? To follow the logic of this argument, must all law enforcement professionals "serve time" to better understand the mindset of the criminal? Far too many information security professionals perform penetration testing to claim that they are "reformed" or "converted" hackers.

The heart of the distinction between the pen tester and the hacker is really the issue of *authorization*. With authorization ("permission or power granted by an authority; sanction"[33]), pen testers can identify and recommend remediation for faults in the organization's information protection strategy. They can determine the presence of vulnerabilities and exposures and demonstrate the techniques used by hackers to attack them. But, at the day's end, pen testers are responsible for documenting their actions and making recommendations to resolve flaws in the defense posture. The hacker, being irresponsible, has no expectation of obligation or responsibility—only motives that are dubious at best. Some will argue that this is a futile semantic debate, and that what matters is the intent, not the title, when defining the difference between the white hat and the black hat or the hacker and cracker. Yes, the business world judges harshly on the face value of a professional.

For information security professionals, the (ISC)² code of ethics is their version of the Hippocratic oath ("I will prescribe regimens for the good of my patients according to my ability and my judgment and never do harm to anyone"[34]) The code includes the following:

> *The safety and welfare of society and the common good, duty to our principals, and to each other, requires that we adhere, and be seen to adhere, to the highest ethical standards of behavior.*
>
> - *Protect society, the common good, necessary public trust and confidence, and the infrastructure.*
> - *Act honorably, honestly, justly, responsibly, and legally.*
> - *Provide diligent and competent service to principals.*
> - *Advance and protect the profession.*[35]

The fundamental assertion of this discussion is that any professional—"a person who belongs to one of the professions, especially one of the learned professions; a person who is expert at his or her work"[36]—should be held to higher moral standards than the average employee. Information security professionals are expected to be above reproach as the true guardians of the organization's information assets. Any doubt as to our true beliefs, motives, and ethics undermines the efforts of us all. Adopting the juvenile moniker and attitude of a "hacker" is a cry for attention, to belong to a group of social outcasts. Even though an information security professional may not be a member of the (ISC)², the fundamental lesson is what is important: Above all else, do no harm.

Internet Vulnerability Assessment

The **Internet vulnerability assessment** is designed to find and document vulnerabilities that may be present in the organization's public network. Because attackers from this direction can take advantage of any flaw, this assessment is usually performed against all public addresses using every possible penetration testing approach. The steps in the process are as follows:

Internet vulnerability assessment

An assessment approach designed to find and document vulnerabilities that may be present in the organization's public-facing networks.

- *Planning, scheduling, and notification of penetration testing*—To execute the data collection phase of this assessment, large organizations often need an entire month, using nights and weekends but avoiding change control blackout windows—periods when changes are not allowed on the organization's systems or networks. This testing yields vast quantities of results and requires many hours of analysis, as explained in the following section. A rule of thumb is that every hour of scanning results in two to three hours of analysis. Therefore, scanning times should be spread out so that analysis is performed on fresh scanning results over the course of the assessment period. Also, the technical support communities should be given the detailed plan so they know when each device is scheduled for testing and what tests are used. This makes disruptions caused by invasive penetration testing easier to diagnose and recover from.
- *Target selection*—Working from the network characterization elements stored in the risk, threat, and attack database, the organization selects its penetration targets. As previously noted, most organizations choose to test every device that is exposed to the Internet.
- *Test selection*—This step involves using external monitoring intelligence to configure a test engine (such as Nessus) for the tests to be performed. Selecting the test library to employ usually evolves over time and matches the evolution of the threat environment. After the ground rules are established, there is usually little debate about the risk level of the tests used. After all, if a device is placed in a public role, it must be able to take everything the Internet can send its way, including the most aggressive penetration test scripts.
- *Scanning*—The penetration test engine is unleashed at the scheduled time using the planned target list and test selection. The results of the entire test run are logged to text files for analysis. This process should be monitored so that if an invasive penetration test causes a disruption to a targeted system, the outage can be reported immediately and recovery activities can be initiated. Note that the log files generated by this scanning, along with all data generated in the rest of this maintenance domain, must be treated as highly confidential.
- *Analysis*—A knowledgeable and experienced vulnerability analyst screens the test results for possible vulnerabilities logged during scanning. During this step, the analyst must perform three tasks:
  - Classify the risk level of the possible vulnerability as needing attention or as an acceptable risk.
  - Validate the existence of the vulnerability when it is deemed to be a significant risk—that is, the risk is greater than the risk appetite of the organization. This validation is important because it establishes the reality of the risk; the analyst must therefore use manual testing, human judgment, and a large dose of discretion. The goal of this step is to tread lightly and cause as little disruption and damage as possible while removing false positive candidates from further investigation. Proven cases of real vulnerabilities can now be considered vulnerability instances.
  - Document the results of the verification by saving a trophy (usually a screenshot) that can be used to convince skeptical system administrators that the vulnerability is real.
- *Record keeping*—In this phase, the organization must record the details of the documented vulnerability in the vulnerability database, identifying logical and physical characteristics and assigning a response risk level to differentiate the truly urgent vulnerability from the merely critical. When coupled with the criticality level from the characteristics in the risk, threat, and attack database, these records can help system administrators decide which items they need to remediate first.

As the list of documented vulnerabilities is identified for Internet information assets, confirmed items are moved to the remediation stage.

intranet vulnerability assessment

An assessment approach designed to find and document selected vulnerabilities that are present on the organization's internal networks.

Intranet Vulnerability Assessment

The **intranet vulnerability assessment** is designed to find and document selected vulnerabilities within the organization's internal networks. Intranet attackers are often internal members of the organization, affiliates of business partners, or automated attack vectors, such as viruses and worms. This assessment is usually performed against critical internal devices with a known, high value and thus requires the use of selective penetration testing.

Many employees and others are now allowed to access an organization's networks using their own devices. This type of environment is often referred to as "bring your own device" (BYOD). BYOD implies that all devices connected to the network, whether owned by the organization or individual workers within it, are in scope for the vulnerability assessment.

The steps in the assessment process are almost identical to those in the Internet vulnerability assessment, except as noted in the rest of this section:

- *Planning, scheduling, and notification of penetration testing*—Most organizations are amazed at how many devices exist inside even a moderately sized network. Bigger networks contain staggering numbers of networked devices. To plan a meaningful assessment, the planner should be aware that any significant degree of scanning will yield vast quantities of test results and require many hours of analysis. The same rule of thumb for Internet vulnerability assessment applies: Every hour of scanning results in two to three hours of analysis, so organizations must plan accordingly. As in Internet scanning, the technical support communities should be notified, although they are probably different from those notified for Internet scanning. The intranet support teams use this information to make any disruptions caused by invasive penetration testing easier to diagnose and recover from. In contrast to Internet system administrators, who prefer penetration testing to be performed during periods of low demand, such as nights and weekends for commercial operations, intranet administrators often prefer that penetration testing be performed during working hours. The best process accounts for the system administrator's planning needs when the schedule is built.
- *Target selection*—Like the Internet vulnerability assessment, the intranet scan starts with the network characterization elements stored in the risk, threat, and attack database. Intranet testing has so many target possibilities, however, that a more selective approach is required. At first, penetration test scanning and analysis should focus on the most valuable and critical systems. As the configuration of these systems is improved and fewer possible vulnerabilities are found in the scanning step, the target list can be expanded. The list of targeted intranet systems should eventually reach equilibrium so that it scans and analyzes as many systems as possible, given the resources dedicated to the process.
- *Test selection*—The testing for intranet vulnerability assessment typically uses different, less stringent criteria from those for Internet scanning. Test selection usually evolves over time and matches the evolution of the perceived intranet threat environment. Most organizations focus their intranet scanning efforts on a few critical vulnerabilities at first, and then expand the test pool to include more test scripts and detect more vulnerabilities. The degree to which an organization is willing to accept risk while scanning and analyzing also affects the selection of test scripts. If the organization is unwilling to risk disruptions to critical internal systems, test scripts that pose such risks should be avoided in favor of alternate means that confirm safety from those vulnerabilities.
- *Scanning*—Intranet scanning is the same process used for Internet scanning. The process should be monitored so that if an invasive penetration test causes disruption, it can be reported for repair.
- *Analysis*—Despite the differences in targets and tested vulnerabilities, the intranet scan analysis is essentially identical to the Internet analysis. It follows the same three steps: classify, validate, and document.
- *Record keeping*—This step is identical to the one followed in Internet vulnerability analysis. Organizations should use similarities between the processes to their advantage by sharing the database, reports, and procedures used for record keeping, reporting, and follow-up.

By leveraging the common assessment processes and using difference analysis on the data collected during the vulnerability assessment, an organization can identify a list of documented internal vulnerabilities, which is the essential information needed for the remediation stage.

Platform Security Validation

The **platform security validation (PSV)** is designed to find and document vulnerabilities in misconfigured systems used in the organization. These misconfigured systems fail to comply with company policy or standards that are adopted by the IT governance groups and communicated in the information security and awareness program. Fortunately, automated measurement systems are available to help with the intensive process of validating the compliance of platform configuration with policy.

- *Product selection*—Typically, an organization implements a PSV solution when deploying the information security program. That solution serves for ongoing PSV compliance as well. If a product has not yet been selected, a separate information security project selects and deploys a PSV solution.
- *Policy configuration*—As organizational policy and standards evolve, the policy templates of the PSV tool must be changed to match. After all, the goal of any selected approach is to be able to measure how well the systems comply with policy.
- *Deployment*—All systems that are mission critical should be enrolled in PSV measurement. If the organization can afford the associated licensing and support costs and can dedicate sufficient resources to the PSV program, it should enroll all of its devices. Security personnel should remember that attackers often enter a network using the weakest link, which may not be a critical system itself but a device connected to critical systems.
- *Measurement*—Using the PSV tools, the organization should measure the compliance of each enrolled system against the policy templates. Deficiencies should be reported as vulnerabilities.
- *Exclusion handling*—Some provision should be made for the exclusion of specific policy or standard exceptions. For instance, one measurement identifies user accounts that never expire. Some organizations assume the risk of having service accounts that do not expire or that have longer change intervals than standard user accounts. If the proper decision makers have made an informed choice to assume such risks in an organization, the automated PSV tool should be able to exclude the assumed risk factor from the compliance report.
- *Reporting*—Using the standard reporting components in the PSV tool, most organizations can inform system administrators of deficiencies that need remediation.
- *Remediation*—Noncompliant systems need to be updated with configurations that comply with policy. When the PSV process shows an outstanding configuration fault that has not been promptly remedied, the information should flow to the vulnerability database to assure remediation.

The ability of PSV software products to integrate with a custom vulnerability database is not a standard feature, but most PSV products can provide data extracts that an organization can import to its vulnerability database for integrated use in the remediation phase. If this degree of integration is not needed or cannot be justified, the stand-alone reporting capabilities of the products can generate sufficient reports for remediation functions.

Wireless Vulnerability Assessment

The **wireless vulnerability assessment** is designed to find and document vulnerabilities in the organization's wireless networks. Because attackers from this direction are likely to take advantage of any flaw, this assessment is usually performed against all publicly accessible areas using every possible approach to wireless penetration testing. This process can sometimes be described as **war driving** because it could be done with a laptop while an attacker drives around. War driving can be done using a laptop, tablet, or even a mobile phone. The steps in the process are as follows:

- *Planning, scheduling, and notification of wireless penetration testing*—This is a noninvasive scanning process that can be done almost any time without notifying system administrators. Even if company culture requires that administrators be notified, the organization should still consider scheduling some unannounced scans, as administrators have been known to turn off their wireless access points on scheduled test days to avoid detection and the resulting remediation effort. Testing times and days should be rotated over time to detect wireless devices that are used for intermittent projects.

- *Target selection*—All areas on the organization's premises should be scanned with a portable wireless network scanner, with special attention to the following: all areas that are publicly accessible, all areas in range of commonly available products, such as 802.11b, and areas where visitors might linger without attracting attention. Because the radio emissions of wireless network equipment can act in surprising ways, all locations should be tested periodically.
- *Test selection*—Wireless scanning tools should look for all wireless signals that do not meet the organization's minimum level of encryption strength.
- *Scanning*—The walking scan should survey the entire target area and identify all wireless local area network (WLAN) access points that are not cryptographically secure.
- *Analysis*—A knowledgeable and experienced vulnerability analyst should screen the test results for WLANs that have been logged, as previously described. During this step, the analyst should do the following:
  - ○ Remove false-positive candidates from further consideration as vulnerabilities while causing as little disruption or damage as possible.
  - ○ Document the results of the verification by saving a screenshot or other documentary evidence (often called a trophy). This serves a double purpose: It can convince skeptical system administrators that the vulnerability is real, and it documents wireless access points that are transient devices and thus may be off the air later.
- *Record keeping*—Good reporting makes the effort to communicate and follow up much easier. As in earlier phases of the vulnerability assessment, effective reporting maximizes results.

At this stage in the process, wireless vulnerabilities are documented and ready for remediation.

Now that each group of vulnerability assessments has been described, a discussion of the record-keeping process is in order.

Documenting Vulnerabilities

The vulnerability database, like the risk, threat, and attack database, both stores and tracks information. It should provide details about the vulnerability being reported and link to the information assets characterized in the risk, threat, and attack database. While this can be done through manual data storage, the low cost and ease of use associated with relational databases makes them a more realistic choice.

The data stored in the vulnerability database should include the following:

- A unique vulnerability ID number for reporting and tracking remediation actions
- Linkage to the risk, threat, and attack database based on the physical information asset underlying the vulnerability; the IP address is a good choice for this linkage
- Vulnerability details, which are usually based on the test script used during the scanning step of the process; if the Nessus scanner is used, each test script has an assigned code (NASL, or Nessus attack scripting language) that can identify the vulnerability effectively
- Dates and times of notification and remediation activities
- Current status of the vulnerability, such as found, reported, or repaired
- Comments, which give analysts the chance to provide system administrators with detailed information for fixing the vulnerability
- Other fields as needed to manage the reporting and tracking processes in the remediation phase

The vulnerability database is an essential part of effective remediation because it helps organizations keep track of specific vulnerabilities as they are reported and remediated.

Remediating Vulnerabilities

The final process in the vulnerability assessment and remediation domain is the remediation phase. The objective of **remediation** is to repair the flaw that caused a vulnerability or remove the risk associated with the vulnerability.

remediation

The processes of removing or repairing flaws in information assets that cause a vulnerability or reducing or removing the risk associated with the vulnerability.

Alternatively, informed decision makers with the proper authority may decide to accept the risk as a last resort.

When approaching the remediation process, it is important to recognize that the key to success is building relationships with those who control the information assets. In other words, success depends on the organization adopting a team approach to remediation in place of push and pull between departments or divisions.

Vulnerabilities can be remediated by accepting or transferring the risk, removing the threat, or repairing the vulnerability, as described in Module 4. The best solution in most cases is to repair the vulnerability, often by applying patch software or implementing a permanent alternative work practice. Many recent vulnerabilities have exploited Web servers on Windows operating systems, so simply updating the version of the installed Web server removes the vulnerability. Simple repairs are possible in other cases, too. For instance, if an account is flagged as a vulnerability because it has a password that has not been changed within the specified time interval, changing the password removes the vulnerability. Of course, the most common repair is the application of a software patch; this usually makes the system function in the expected fashion and removes the vulnerability.

Organizations must be careful to avoid expedient but temporary solutions that are done at low cost and within short time frames. Any quick workarounds must be noted and periodically reviewed to ensure efficacy, to check for side effects and other risks, and to find a way to replace the workarounds with permanent and durable solutions.

Readiness and Review

The primary goal of the readiness and review domain is to keep the information security program functioning as designed and improve it continuously over time. This goal can be accomplished by doing the following:

- *Policy review*—Policy needs to be reviewed and refreshed from time to time to ensure its soundness—in other words, it must provide a current foundation for the information security program.
- *Program review*—Major planning components should be reviewed on a periodic basis to ensure that they are current, accurate, and appropriate.
- *Rehearsals*—When possible, major plan elements should be rehearsed.

The relationships among the sectors of the readiness and review domain are shown in Figure 12-9. As the diagram indicates, policy review is the primary initiator of this domain. As policy is revised or current policy is confirmed, the planning elements are reviewed for compliance, the information security program is reviewed, and rehearsals are held to make sure all participants are capable of responding as needed.

Policy Review and Planning Review

Policy needs to be reviewed periodically, as you learned in Module 3. The planning and review process for incident response, disaster recovery, and business continuity planning (IRP, DRP, and BCP) were also covered in Module 5.

As policy needs shift, a thorough and independent review of the entire information security program is needed. While an exact timetable for review is not proposed here, many organizations find that the CISO should conduct a

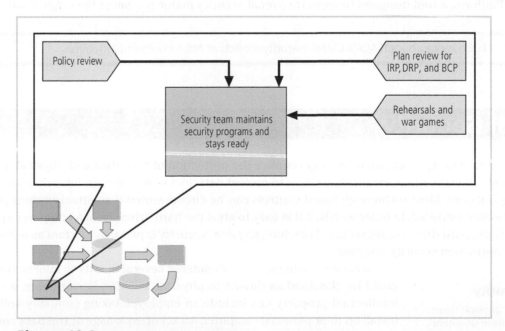

Figure 12-9   Readiness and review

formal review annually. Earlier in this module, you learned about the role of the CISO in the maintenance process. The CISO uses the results of maintenance activities and the review of the information security program to determine if the status quo is adequate against the threats at hand.

If the current information security program is not up to the challenges, the CISO must determine if incremental improvements are possible or if it is time to restructure the information security function within the organization.

Whenever possible, major planning elements should be rehearsed. Rehearsal adds value by exercising procedures, identifying shortcomings, and providing security personnel with the opportunity to improve the security plan before it is needed. In addition, rehearsals make people more effective when an actual event occurs. A type of rehearsal known as a *war game* or simulation exercise puts a subset of plans in place to create a realistic test environment. This adds to the value of the rehearsal and can enhance training.

Organizations can also gain assurance that their information security programs are reliable by using a capability maturity model (or CMM) to track how well the programs function and stay current.

Maturity models have been used in software engineering for many decades. Originally, the CMM was used to gauge the likelihood that an organization's processes could deliver a successful software project. In general, the higher the maturity score, the better the processes will deliver and maintain high-quality results. More capable and mature processes result in a greater likelihood that established processes will be used to design, develop, test, and build software. Continual self-review will also help maintain a high level of quality.

Because early CMM approaches were intended to improve the software development process, their use in assessing and improving security management systems was somewhat limited. Since then, capability maturity models have appeared in numerous disciplines, such as ICT infrastructure, service management, business process management, manufacturing, civil engineering, and cybersecurity. These approaches help organizations measure their processes' effectiveness and identify how to improve them over time.

Capability Maturity Model Integration (CMMI) helps organizations quickly understand their current level of capability and performance, both within the context of their own business objectives and when compared with those of similar organizations. CMMI is now widely used by organizations that supply government products or services; these organizations are often asked to meet CMMI level 3 across their core delivery processes. Level 3 is a level of maturity that requires the use of formal methods of design, development, testing, and delivery. CMMI has five maturity levels; level 5 is an ideal target state in which processes are fully optimized across the business and managed under a regime of continuous process improvement.

CMMI is flexible and applies to any business processes, so tailoring its framework for information security management was an obvious step. One example of an adapted CMMI solution for cybersecurity is the CMMI Institute's Cybermaturity Platform, a tool designed to measure overall security maturity against the original model.

 You can learn more about ISACA's CMMI maturity models at *https://cmmiinstitute.com/*.

Physical Security

As you learned in Module 1, information security requires the protection of both data and physical assets. You have already learned about many of the mechanisms used to protect data, including firewalls, intrusion detection systems, and monitoring software. Most technology-based controls can be circumvented if an attacker gains physical access to the devices being controlled. In other words, if it is easy to steal the hard drives from a computer system, then the information on those hard drives is not secure. Therefore, **physical security** is just as important as logical or computer security to an information security program.

physical security

The protection of physical items, objects, or areas from unauthorized access and misuse.

In earlier modules, you encountered several threats to information security that could be classified as threats to physical security. For example, a compromise to intellectual property can include an employee taking company software home to install on their personal computer. An act of espionage or trespass could be committed by a competitor sneaking into a facility with a camera. Sabotage or vandalism can be physical attacks on individuals or property. Theft includes employees stealing computer equipment, credentials, passwords, and laptops. Quality-of-service deviations from service providers, especially power and water utilities, also represent physical security threats, as do various environmental anomalies. In his book *Fighting Computer Crime*, Donn B. Parker lists the following "Seven Major Sources of Physical Loss":

1. Extreme temperature—Heat, cold
2. Gases—War gases, commercial vapors, humid or dry air, suspended particles
3. Liquids—Water, chemicals
4. Living organisms—Viruses, bacteria, people, animals, insects
5. Projectiles—Tangible objects in motion, powered objects
6. Movement—Collapse, shearing, shaking, vibration, liquefaction, flow waves, separation, slide
7. Energy anomalies—Electrical surge or failure; magnetism; static electricity; aging circuitry; radiation, including sound, light, radio, microwave, electromagnetic, and atomic[37]

As with all other areas of security, the implementation of physical security measures requires sound organizational policy. Physical security policies guide users in the appropriate use of computing resources and information assets, as well as in protecting their own safety in day-to-day operations.

Physical Access Controls

Several physical access controls are uniquely suited to governing the movement of people within an organization's facilities—specifically, controlling their physical access to company resources. While logical access to systems in the Internet age is a very important subject, the control of physical access to an organization's assets is also of critical importance. Some of the technology used to control physical access is also used to control logical access, including biometrics, smart cards, and wireless-enabled keycards.

Before learning more about physical access controls, you need to understand what makes a facility secure. An organization's general management oversees physical security. Commonly, a building's access controls are operated by a group called **facilities management**. Larger organizations may have an entire staff dedicated to facilities management, while smaller organizations often outsource these duties.

In facilities management, the term **secure facility** might suggest military bases, maximum-security prisons, and nuclear power plants. While securing a facility does require adherence to rules and procedures, the environment does not necessarily have to be that constrained. A facility does not have to resemble a fortress to minimize risk from physical attacks. In fact, a secure facility can sometimes use its natural terrain, local traffic flow, and surrounding development to enhance its physical security, along with protection mechanisms such as fences, gates, walls, guards, and alarms.

A secure facility includes the same defense-in-depth strategy as logical network security. Any intrusion attempt, whether natural or human-made, should be confronted with multiple layers of defense, including those for the facility's location, the drive to and onto the facility grounds, and multiple layers of physical access controls needed to gain access to information. This could start with a facility guard at the employee parking lot, continue through a keycard mantrap (explained later in this module), and end in the lock-and-key process necessary to access employees' individual offices. Although every business does not need such an extensive or expensive strategy, this module describes many affordable, feasible, and secure methods of protecting an organization's physical presence.

Physical Security Controls

An organization's communities of interest should consider several physical security controls when implementing physical security inside and outside the facility. Some of the major controls are as follows:

- Walls, fencing, and gates
- Guards and dogs
- ID cards and badges
- Locks and keys
- Electronic monitoring

facilities management

The aspect of organizational management focused on the development and maintenance of buildings and physical infrastructure.

secure facility

A physical location with access barriers and controls in place to minimize the risk of attacks from physical threats.

- Alarms and alarm systems
- Computer rooms and wiring closets
- Interior walls and doors

Some of these controls are discussed in the following sections.

Walls, Fencing, and Gates

While not every organization needs to implement external perimeter controls, walls and fences with suitable gates are an essential starting point when employees require access to physical locations the organization owns or controls. Each exterior perimeter control requires expert planning to ensure that it fulfills security goals and presents an image appropriate to the organization.

Guards and Dogs

Controls like fences and walls with gates are static, and are therefore unresponsive to actions unless they are programmed to react to specific stimuli, such as opening for someone who has the correct key. Guards, on the other hand, can evaluate each situation as it arises and make reasoned responses. Most guards have clear *standard operating procedures (SOPs)* that help them act decisively in unfamiliar situations. An issue with human guards, beyond the high cost, is the human tendency to boredom and distraction, making supervision and oversight of guards a management concern.

For an organization that is protecting valuable resources, dogs can be an important part of physical security if they are integrated into the plan and managed properly. Guard dogs are useful because their keen senses of smell and hearing can detect intrusions that human guards cannot, and they can be placed in harm's way when necessary to avoid risking the life of a person.

ID Cards and Badges

An identification (ID) card is typically carried concealed, whereas a badge is worn and visible. Both devices can serve multiple purposes. They serve as simple forms of biometrics in that they use the cardholder's picture to authenticate access to the facility. Some organizations choose a card or badge that displays the wearer's name and other information; others show nothing except the wearer's photograph. The cards may be visibly coded to specify which buildings or areas may be accessed. ID cards that have a magnetic strip or radio chip can be read by automated control devices and allow an organization to restrict access to sensitive areas within the facility.

tailgating

The process of gaining unauthorized entry into a facility by closely following another person through an entrance and using the credentials of the authorized person to bypass a control point.

ID cards and badges are not foolproof, however; even the cards designed to communicate with locks can be duplicated, stolen, or modified. Because of this inherent weakness, such devices should not be an organization's only means of controlling access to restricted areas. Another inherent weakness of cards and badges is the human factor. **Tailgating** occurs when an authorized person opens a door and other people also enter (see Figure 12-10). The problem becomes especially dangerous when the tailgater is not authorized to enter. Making employees aware of tailgating through a security awareness program is one way to combat this problem. There are

Figure 12-10   Tailgating

also technological means of discouraging tailgating, such as turnstiles or **mantraps**. These extra levels of control are usually expensive because they require floor space and construction, and they are inconvenient for the people who are required to use them. Consequently, anti-tailgating controls are used only where there is a significant security risk from unauthorized entry.

> **mantrap**
>
> A small room or enclosure with separate entry and exit points, designed to restrain a person who fails an access authorization attempt.

Locks and Keys

There are two types of lock mechanisms: mechanical and electromechanical. The mechanical lock may rely on a physical key. Electromechanical locks can accept a variety of inputs as keys, including magnetic strips on ID cards, radio signals from badges, personal identification numbers (PINs) typed into a keypad, or some combination of these to activate an electrically powered locking mechanism.

As described previously, some locks use smart cards—keys that contain computer chips. These smart cards can carry critical information, provide strong authentication, and offer other features. Keycard readers based on smart cards are often used to secure computer rooms, communications closets, and other restricted areas. The card reader can track entry and provide accountability. In a locking system that uses smart cards, employees' access levels can be adjusted according to their status so that personnel changes do not necessarily require replacement of a lock.

The most sophisticated locks are biometric locks. Finger, palm, and hand readers, iris and retina scanners, and voice and signature readers fall into this category. The technology that underlies biometric devices was discussed in Module 8.

The management of keys and locks is fundamental to fulfilling general management's responsibility to secure an organization's physical environment. As discussed in Module 7, when people are hired, fired, laid off, or transferred, their physical or logical access controls must be appropriately adjusted. Otherwise, employees can clean out their offices and take more than their personal effects.

Sometimes locks fail, so facilities need to have alternative procedures in place for controlling access. These procedures must take into account that locks fail in one of two ways. A door lock that fails and causes the door to become unlocked is called a fail-safe lock; a door lock that fails and causes the door to remain locked is called a fail-secure lock. In practice, the most common reasons that technically sophisticated locks fail are loss of power and activation through fire control systems. A fail-safe lock is normally used to secure an exit when a door must be unlocked in case of fire or another event. A fail-secure lock is used when human safety is not the dominant factor in the area being controlled. For example, in a situation in which the security of nuclear or biological weapons is vital, preventing a loss of control of the facility or the weapons is more critical to security than protecting the personnel guarding the weapons.

Computer Rooms and Wiring Closets

Computer rooms and wiring and communications closets require special attention to ensure the confidentiality, integrity, and availability of information.

 For more information on considerations for designing high-performance data centers, visit *http://hightech.lbl .gov/* and read the Pacific Gas and Electric Data Center Best Practices Guide at *www.pge.com/includes/docs/pdfs/ mybusiness/energysavingsrebates/incentivesbyindustry/DataCenters_BestPractices.pdf*.

Logical access controls are easily defeated if an attacker gains physical access to the computing equipment. Custodial staff members are often the least scrutinized people who have access to an organization's offices, yet custodians are given the greatest degree of unsupervised access. They are often handed the master keys to the entire building and then ignored, even though they collect paper from every office, dust many desks, and move large containers from every area. Therefore, it is not difficult for a custodian to gather critical information and computer media or copy proprietary and classified information. An organization's custodians should not be under constant suspicion of espionage, but their wide-reaching access can be a vulnerability that attackers exploit to gain unauthorized information. Factual accounts exist of technically trained agents working as custodians in the offices of their competition. Thus, custodial staff should be carefully supervised not only by the organization's general management but by information security management.

Fire Security and Safety

The most important security concern is the safety of the people in an organization's physical space—workers, customers, clients, and others. The most serious threat to that safety is fire. Fires account for more property damage, personal injury, and death than any other threat to physical security. Physical security plans must implement strong measures to detect and respond to fires and fire hazards.

 For more information on fire safety, including discussions of detection and response systems, visit the National Fire Protection Association's Web site at *www.nfpa.org*.

Fire suppression systems typically work by denying an environment one of the three requirements for a fire to burn: temperature (an ignition source), fuel, and oxygen. While the temperature of ignition, or *flame point*, depends on the material, it can be as low as a few hundred degrees. Paper, the most common combustible in an office, has a flame point of 451 degrees Fahrenheit, a fact used to dramatic effect in Ray Bradbury's novel *Fahrenheit 451*. Paper can reach its flame point when exposed to a carelessly dropped cigarette, malfunctioning electrical equipment, or other accidental or purposeful acts.

Water and water mist systems, which are described later in this section, work to reduce the temperature of the flame in order to extinguish it and to saturate some types of fuels (such as paper) to prevent ignition. Carbon dioxide (CO_2) systems rob fire of its oxygen. Soda acid systems deny fire its fuel, preventing the fire from spreading. Gas-based systems, such as halon and its approved replacements by the Environmental Protection Agency (EPA), disrupt the fire's chemical reaction but leave enough oxygen for people to survive for a short time. Before a fire can be suppressed, however, it must be detected.

Failure of Supporting Utilities and Structural Collapse

Supporting utilities, such as heating, ventilation, air conditioning, power, and water, have a significant impact on a facility's safe operation. Extreme temperatures and humidity levels, electrical fluctuations, and the interruption of water, sewage, and garbage services can create conditions that inject vulnerabilities in systems designed to protect information. Thus, each of these utilities must be properly managed to prevent damage to information and information systems.

Heating, Ventilation, and Air Conditioning

Although traditionally a responsibility of facilities management, the operation of the heating, ventilation, and air conditioning (HVAC) system can have a dramatic impact on information, information systems, and their protection. Specifically, the temperature, filtration, humidity, and static electricity controls must be monitored and adjusted to reduce risks to information systems.

Temperature and Filtration

Computer systems are electronic, and therefore are subject to damage from extreme temperatures and particulate contamination. Temperatures as low as 100 degrees Fahrenheit can damage computer media, and at 175 degrees Fahrenheit, computer hardware that has not been specifically designed and engineered to handle temperature extremes can be damaged or destroyed. When the temperature approaches 32 degrees Fahrenheit, most media that are not based on solid-state electronics are susceptible to cracking and computer components can actually freeze together. Rapid changes in temperature from hot to cold or vice versa can produce condensation, which can create short circuits or otherwise damage systems and components. The optimal temperature for most computing environments and for people without protective clothing is between 70 and 74 degrees Fahrenheit. Properly installed and maintained systems keep the environment within the manufacturer-recommended temperature range.

In the past, people thought it was necessary to fully filter all particles from the air flow of the HVAC system. Modern computing equipment is designed to operate in typical office environments, so the need to provide extensive filtration for air conditioning is now limited to particularly sensitive environments such as chip fabrication and component assembly areas. In other words, filtration is no longer as significant as it once was for most commercial data processing facilities.

Humidity and Static Electricity

High humidity levels create condensation problems, and low humidity levels can increase the amount of static electricity in the environment. With condensation comes the short-circuiting of electrical equipment and the potential for mold and rot in paper-based information storage. Static electricity is caused by triboelectrification, which occurs when two materials make contact and exchange electrons. As a result, one object becomes more positively charged and the other more negatively charged. When a third object with an opposite charge or ground is encountered, electrons flow again, and a spark is produced. One of the leading causes of damage to sensitive circuitry is electrostatic discharge (ESD). Integrated circuits in a computer are designed to use between two and five volts of electricity; any voltage level above this range introduces a risk of microchip damage. Static electricity is not noticeable to human beings until levels approach 1,500 volts, and the spark can't be seen until the level approaches 4,000 volts before being discharged. Moreover, a person can generate a discharge of up to 12,000 volts merely by walking across a carpet.[38]

In general, ESD damage to chips produces two types of failures. Immediate failures, also known as catastrophic failures, occur right away, are often totally destructive, and require chip replacement. Latent failures or delayed failures can occur weeks or even months after the damage occurs. The chip may suffer intermittent problems, although given the overall poor quality of some popular operating systems, this type of damage may be hard to notice. As a result, an optimal level of humidity between 40 percent and 60 percent must be maintained in the computing environment. Humidity levels below this range create static, and levels above it create condensation. Humidification or dehumidification systems can regulate humidity levels.

Ventilation Shafts

While the ductwork in residential buildings is quite small, it may be large enough for a person to climb through in large commercial buildings. This is one of Hollywood's favorite methods for having villains or heroes enter buildings, but ventilation shafts are not quite as negotiable as the movies would have you believe. In fact, with moderate security precautions, these shafts can be completely eliminated as a security vulnerability. In most new buildings, the ducts to individual rooms are no larger than 12 inches in diameter and are composed of flexible, insulated tubes. The size and nature of the ducts precludes most people from using them, but access may be possible via the plenum. If the ducts are much larger, the security team can install wire mesh grids at various points to compartmentalize the runs.

Power Management and Conditioning

Electrical power is another aspect of the organization's physical environment that is usually considered within the realm of physical security. Power systems used by information-processing equipment must be properly installed and correctly grounded. Because computers sometimes use the normal 60-Hertz cycle of electricity in alternating current to synchronize their clocks, noise that interferes with this cycle can result in inaccurate time clocks or, even worse, unreliable internal clocks inside the CPU.

Grounding ensures that the returning flow of current is properly discharged to the ground. If the grounding elements of the electrical system are not properly installed, anyone who touches a computer or other electrical device could become a ground source, which can cause damage to the equipment and injury or death to the person. In areas where water can accumulate, computing and other electrical equipment must be uniquely grounded using ground fault circuit interruption (GFCI) equipment. GFCI is capable of quickly identifying and interrupting a ground fault—for example, a situation in which a person comes into contact with water and becomes a better ground than the electrical circuit's current source.

The primary power source for an organization's computing equipment is most often the electric utility that serves the area where the buildings are located. This source of power can experience interruptions. Therefore, organizations should identify the computing systems that are critical to their operations and that must continue to operate during interruptions, and then make sure those systems are connected to a device that assures the delivery of electric power without interruption. This device is called an uninterruptible power supply (UPS).

The capacity of UPS devices is measured using the volt-ampere (or VA) power output rating. UPS devices typically run up to 1,000 VA and can be engineered to exceed 10,000 VA. A typical PC might use 200 VA, and a server in a computer room may need 2,000 to 5,000 VA, depending on how much running time is required. The big distinction for security professionals is ensuring that the organization has enough power backup to keep its critical systems online long enough to shut down safely.

and on off-site media. To ensure a secure process, the computers that telecommuters use must be made *more* secure than the organization's systems, because they are outside the security perimeter. An attacker who breaks into someone's home would probably find a much lower level of security than at an office. Most office systems require users to log in, but the telecommuter's home computer is probably a personal machine. Thus, it has a much less secure operating system or may not require a password. Teleworkers must use a securable device with a client operating system that can be configured to require password authentication. They must store all loose data in locking filing cabinets and loose media in locking fire safes. They must handle data at home more carefully than they would at the office because the general level of security for the average home is much less than that of a commercial building.

The same principles apply to workers using portable computing devices on the road. Employees who use tablets, smartphones, and notebook computers in public locations and in hotel rooms should presume that their unencrypted transmissions are being monitored, and that any unsecured notebook computer can be stolen. The off-site worker using leased facilities does not know who else is attached to the network and who might be listening to his or her data conversations. VPNs are a must in all off-site to on-site communications, and the use of associated advanced authentication systems is strongly recommended.

Although it is possible to secure remote sites, organizations cannot assume that employees will invest their own funds for security. Many organizations barely tolerate telecommuting for a number of reasons, foremost among them that such employees generally require two sets of computing equipment, one for the office and one for the home. This extra expense is difficult to justify, especially when the employee is the only one gaining the benefit from telecommuting. In rare cases in which allowing employees or consultants to telecommute is the only way for them to gain extremely valuable skills, the organization is usually willing to do what is necessary to secure its systems. Only when additional research into telecommuting clearly displays a bottom-line advantage do organizations begin to invest sufficient resources into securing telecommuting equipment.

Special Considerations for Physical Security

An organization must account for several special considerations when developing a physical security program. The first is the question of whether to handle physical security in-house or to outsource it. As with any aspect of information security, the make-or-buy decision should not be made lightly. Many qualified and professional agencies can provide physical security consulting and services. The benefits of outsourcing physical security include gaining the experience and knowledge of these agencies, many of which have been in the field for decades. Outsourcing unfamiliar operations always frees an organization to focus on its primary objectives rather than support operations. The disadvantages include the expense, the loss of control over individual components of physical security, and the need to trust another company to perform an essential business function. An organization must trust the processes used by the contracted company and its ability to hire and retain trustworthy employees who respect the security of the contracting company, even though they have no allegiance to it. This level of trust is often the most difficult aspect of the decision to outsource because the reality of outsourcing physical security is that an outside agency will be providing a safeguard that the organization administers only marginally.

Another physical security consideration is social engineering. As you learned in previous modules, social engineering involves using people skills to obtain confidential information from employees. While most social engineers prefer to use the telephone or computer to solicit information, some attempt to access the information more directly. Technically proficient agents can be placed in janitorial positions at a competitor's office, and an outsider can gain access to an organization's resources in other ways. For example, most organizations do not have thorough procedures for authenticating and controlling visitors who access their facility. When no procedure is in place, no one gives the wandering repairman, service worker, or city official a second look. It is not difficult to get a clipboard, dress like a repairman or building inspector, and move freely throughout a building. If you look like you have a mission and appear competent, most people will leave you alone. Organizations can combat this type of attack by requiring all people who enter the facility to display appropriate visitor badges and be escorted in restricted areas.

Closing Scenario

Remember from the beginning of this book how Amy's day started? Now imagine how it could have gone with better planning:

For Amy, that day had begun like any other at the Sequential Label and Supply Company (SLS) help desk. Taking calls and helping office workers with computer problems was not glamorous, but she enjoyed the work; it was challenging and paid well enough. Some of her friends in the industry worked at bigger companies, some at cutting-edge tech companies, but they all agreed that technology jobs were a good way to pay the bills.

The phone rang, as it did about four times an hour and 28 times a day. The first call of the day, from a user hoping Amy could help him out of a jam, seemed typical. The call display on her monitor showed some of the facts: the user's name, his phone number and department, where his office was on the company campus, and a list of his past calls to the help desk.

"Hi, Bob," Amy said. "Did you get that document formatting problem squared away?"

"Sure did, Amy. Hope we can figure out what's going on this time."

"We'll try, Bob. Tell me about it."

"Well, I need help setting a page break in this new spreadsheet template I'm working on," Bob said.

Amy smiled to herself. She knew spreadsheets well, so she would probably be able to close this call on the first contact. That would help her call statistics, which was one method of measuring her job performance.

Little did Amy know that roughly four minutes before Bob's phone call, a specially programmed computer at the edge of the SLS network had made a programmed decision. This computer was generally known as *postoffice.seqlbl.com*, but it was called the "e-mail gateway" by the networking, messaging, and information security teams at SLS. The decision was just like many thousands of other decisions the computer made in a typical day—that is, to block the transmission of a file that was attached to an e-mail addressed to *Bob.Hulme@seqlbl.com*. The gateway had determined that Bob did not need an executable program that had been attached to the e-mail message. The gateway had also determined that the message originated from somewhere on the Internet but contained a forged reply-to address from Davey Martinez at SLS. In other words, the gateway had delivered the e-mail text to Bob Hulme, but not the attachment.

When Bob got the e-mail, all he saw was another unsolicited commercial e-mail with an unwanted executable that had been blocked. He had deleted the nuisance message without a second thought. Had the malware interception not taken place automatically, Bob would have been asking Amy about an entirely different concern.

While she was talking to Bob, Amy looked up to see Charlie Moody walking down the hall. As you might recall from earlier modules, Charlie was the senior manager of the server administration team and the company's chief information security officer. Kelvin Urich and Iris Majwubu were trailing behind Charlie as he headed from his office to the door of the conference room. Amy thought, "It must be time for the weekly security status meeting."

She was the user representative on the company information security oversight committee, so she was due to attend this meeting. Amy continued talking Bob through the procedure for setting up a page break and decided she would join the information security team for coffee and bagels as soon as she was finished.

Discussion Questions

1. In the opening scenario, it seems there is always something to be done next. When does the information security program end?
2. What recommendations would you give SLS for how it might select a security management maintenance model?

Ethical Decision Making

Referring back to the opening scenario of this module, suppose Charlie had just finished a search for a new job and knew that he would soon be leaving the company. When Iris came in to talk about the tedious and time-consuming review process, he put her off and asked her to schedule a meeting with him "in two or three weeks," knowing full well that he would be gone by then. Do you think this kind of action is unethical because Charlie knows he is leaving soon?

Selected Readings

- *Fighting Computer Crime: A New Framework for Protecting Information*, by Donn B. Parker. 1998. John Wiley and Sons.
- *Digital Evidence and Computer Crime*, 3rd Edition, by Eoghan Casey. 2011. Academic Press.
- *Guide to Computer Forensics and Investigations*, 4th Edition, by Amelia Phillips and Christopher Steuart. 2010. Course Technology.

Module Summary

- Change is inevitable, so organizations should have procedures to deal with changes in the operation and maintenance of the information security program.
- The CISO decides whether the information security program can adapt to change as it is implemented or whether the process of the risk management program must be started anew.
- To stay current, the information security community of interest and the CISO must constantly monitor the three components of the security triple—threats, assets, and vulnerabilities.
- To assist the information security community in managing and operating the ongoing security program, the organization should adopt a security management maintenance model. These models are frameworks that are structured by the tasks of managing a particular set of activities or business functions.
- NIST SP 800-100, "Information Security Handbook: A Guide for Managers," outlines managerial tasks performed after the program is operational. For each of the 13 areas of information security management presented in SP 800-100, there are specific monitoring activities:
  1. Information security governance
  2. Systems development life cycle
  3. Awareness and training
  4. Capital planning and investment control
  5. Interconnecting systems
  6. Performance measures
  7. Security planning
  8. Information technology contingency planning
  9. Risk management
  10. Certification, accreditation, and security assessments
  11. Security services and products acquisition
  12. Incident response
  13. Configuration and change management
- The maintenance model recommended in this module is made up of five subject areas or domains: external monitoring, internal monitoring, planning and risk assessment, vulnerability assessment and remediation, and readiness and review.
- The objective of the external monitoring domain in the maintenance model is to provide early awareness of new and emerging threats, threat agents, vulnerabilities, and attacks so that an effective and timely defense can be mounted.
- The objective of the internal monitoring domain is an informed awareness of the state of the organization's networks, information systems, and information security defenses. The security team documents and communicates this awareness, particularly when it concerns system components that face the external network.
- The primary objective of the planning and risk assessment domain is to keep an eye on the entire information security program.
- The primary objectives of the vulnerability assessment and remediation domain are to identify specific, documented vulnerabilities and remediate them in a timely fashion.
- The primary objectives of the readiness and review domain are to keep the information security program functioning as designed and keep improving it over time.
- Physical security requires the design, implementation, and maintenance of countermeasures that protect the physical resources of an organization.
- An organization's policy should guide the planning for physical security throughout the development life cycle.
- In facilities management, a secure facility is a physical location that has controls to minimize the risk of attacks from physical threats. A secure facility can use natural terrain, traffic flow, and urban development, and can complement these environmental elements with protection mechanisms such as fences, gates, walls, guards, and alarms.
- The management of keys and locks is a fundamental part of general management's responsibility for the organization's physical environment.
- A fail-safe lock is typically used on an exit door when human safety in a fire or other emergency is the essential consideration. A fail-secure lock is used when human safety is not the dominant factor.

- Fire suppression systems typically work by denying an environment one of the three requirements for a fire to burn: temperature (an ignition source), fuel, and oxygen.
- Four environmental variables controlled by HVAC systems can cause damage to information systems: temperature, filtration, humidity, and static electricity.
- Computer systems depend on stable power supplies to function; when power levels are too high, too low, or too erratic, computer circuitry can be damaged or destroyed. The power provided to computing and networking equipment should contain no unwanted fluctuations and no embedded signaling.
- As with any phase of the security process, the implementation of physical security must be constantly documented, evaluated, and tested. Once the physical security of a facility is established, it must be diligently maintained.
- Data can be intercepted electronically and manually. The three routes of data interception are direct observation, interception of data transmission, and interception of electromagnetic radiation.
- With the increased use of laptops, tablets, and smartphones, organizations should be aware that mobile computing requires even more security than the average in-house system.
- Remote site computing requires a secure extension of the organization's internal networks and special attention to security for any connected home or off-site computing technology.

Review Questions

1. List and define the factors that are likely to shift in an organization's information security environment.
2. Who decides if the information security program can adapt to change adequately?
3. Is information security risk management usually a static or dynamic process?
4. What is a management maintenance model? What does it accomplish?
5. What changes need to be made to the model in SP 800-100 to adapt it for use in security management maintenance?
6. What ongoing responsibilities do security managers have in securing the SDLC?
7. What is vulnerability assessment?
8. What is penetration testing?
9. What is the difference between vulnerability assessment and penetration testing?
10. List and briefly describe the five domains of the general security maintenance model, as identified in the text.
11. What is the objective of the external monitoring domain of the maintenance model?
12. List and describe four vulnerability intelligence sources. Which seems the most effective? Why?
13. What does CERT stand for? Is there more than one CERT?
14. What is the primary objective of the internal monitoring domain?
15. What is the objective of the planning and risk assessment domain of the maintenance model? Why is this important?

16. What is the primary goal of the vulnerability assessment and remediation domain of the maintenance model? Is this important to an organization with an Internet presence? Why?
17. List and describe the five vulnerability assessments described in the text. Can you think of other assessment processes or variations that might exist?
18. What is physical security?
19. What are the roles of an organization's IT, security, and general management with regard to physical security?
20. Define a secure facility. What is the primary objective of designing such a facility? What are some secondary objectives of designing a secure facility?
21. What are the two possible modes of locks when they fail? What implications do these modes have for human safety? In which situation is each preferred?
22. What is a mantrap? When should it be used?
23. What is considered the most serious threat within the realm of physical security? Why is it valid to consider this threat the most serious?
24. What is the relationship between HVAC and physical security? What four physical characteristics of the indoor environment are controlled by a properly designed HVAC system? What are the optimal temperature and humidity ranges for computing systems?
25. List and describe the three fundamental ways that data can be intercepted. How does a physical security program protect against each of these data interception methods?

Exercises

1. Perform a Web search for "common vulnerabilities and exposures." What is a common vulnerability and exposure, and why is it significant to an information security practitioner?

2. Perform a Web search for "security mean time to detect." Read at least two results from your search. Quickly describe what the measurement means. Why do you think some people believe this is the most important security performance measurement an organization should have?

3. Search the Web and try to determine the most common IT help-desk problem calls. Which of these are security related?

4. Assume that your organization is planning to have an automated server room that functions without human assistance. Such a room is often called a lights-out server room. Describe the fire control system(s) you would install in that room.

5. Assume that you have converted an area of general office space into a server room. Describe the factors you would consider for each of the following components:

   - Walls and doors
   - Access control
   - Fire detection
   - Fire suppression
   - Heating, ventilation, and air conditioning
   - Power quality and distribution

6. Search the Web using the following string:
   information security management model –"maturity"
   This search will exclude results that refer to "maturity."
   Read the first five results and summarize the models they describe. Choose one you find interesting, and determine how it is similar to the NIST SP 800-100 model. How is it different?

References

1. Bowen, P., Hash, J., and Wilson, M. Special Publication (SP) 800-100, "Information Security Handbook: A Guide for Managers." National Institute of Standards and Technology. Accessed November 12, 2020, from *https://csrc.nist.gov/publications/sp800*.

2. Ibid.

3. Kissel, R., Stine, K., Scholl, M., Rossman, H., Fahlsing, J., and Gulick, J. SP 800-64, Rev. 2, "Security Considerations in the System Development Life Cycle." National Institute of Standards and Technology. October 2008. Accessed November 17, 2020, from *https://nvlpubs.nist.gov/nistpubs/Legacy/SP/nistspecialpublication800-64r2.pdf*.

4. "Configuration Management." Wikipedia. Accessed November 12, 2020, from *en.wikipedia.org/wiki/Configuration_management*.

5. Bowen, P., Kissel, R., Scholl, M., Robinson, W., Stansfield, J., and Voldish, L. SP 800-65, Rev. 1 (Draft), "Recommendations for Integrating IT Security into the Capital Planning and Investment Control Process." National Institute of Standards and Technology. July 2009. Accessed November 12, 2020, from *https://csrc.nist.gov/CSRC/media/Publications/sp/800-65/rev-1/archive/2009-07-14/documents/draft-sp800-65rev1.pdf*.

6. Grance, T., Hash, J., Peck, S., Smith, J., and Karow-Diks, K. SP 800-47, "Security Guide for Interconnecting Information Technology Systems." National Institute of Standards and Technology. August 2002. Accessed November 12, 2020, from *https://csrc.nist.gov/publications/sp800*.

7. Ibid.

8. Chew, E., Swanson, M., Stine, K., Bartol, N., Brown, A., and Robinson, W. SP 800-55, Rev. 1, "Performance Measurement Guide for Information Security." National Institute of Standards and Technology. July 2008. Accessed November 12, 2020, from *https://csrc.nist.gov/publications/sp800*.

9. Ibid.

10. Ibid.

11. Ibid.

12. Kovacich, Gerald L. *The Information Systems Security Officer's Guide*, 2nd ed. Elsevier Science, 2003: 196.

13. Chew, E., Swanson, M., Stine, K., Bartol, N., Brown, A., and Robinson, W. SP 800-55, Rev. 1, "Performance Measurement Guide for Information Security." National Institute of Standards and Technology. July 2008. Accessed November 12, 2020, from *https://csrc.nist.gov/publications/sp800*.

14. Ibid.

15. Avolio, Frederick. "Best Practices in Network Security." *Network Computing*. March 20, 2000.

16. Bowen, P., Hash, J., and Wilson, M. SP 800-100, "Information Security Handbook: A Guide for Managers." National Institute of Standards and Technology. Accessed November 12, 2020, from *https://csrc.nist.gov/ publications/sp800*.

17. Grance, T., Hash, J., Stevens, M., O'Neal, K., and Bartol, N. SP 800-35, "Guide to Information Technology Security Services." National Institute of Standards and Technology. October 2003. Accessed November 15, 2020, from *https://csrc.nist.gov/publications/sp800*.

18. Ibid.

19. Cuff, Jeanne. "Grow Up: How Mature Is Your Help Desk?" Compass America, Inc. Accessed November 15, 2020, from *fsz.ifas.ufl.edu/HD/GrowUpWP.pdf*.

20. Kissel, R., Stine, K., Scholl, M., Rossman, H., Fahlsing, J., and Gulick, J. SP 800-64, Rev. 2, "Security Considerations in the System Development Life Cycle." National Institute of Standards and Technology. October 2008. Accessed November 17, 2020, from *https://nvlpubs.nist.gov/nistpubs/Legacy/SP/ nistspecialpublication800-64r2.pdf*.

21. Joint Task Force Transformation Initiative. SP 800-53, Rev. 4, "Security and Privacy Controls for Federal Information Systems and Organizations." National Institute of Standards and Technology. September 2020. Accessed November 17, 2020, from *https://csrc.nist.gov/publications/sp800*.

22. Kissel, R., Stine, K., Scholl, M., Rossman, H., Fahlsing, J., and Gulick, J. SP 800-64, Rev. 2, "Security Considerations in the System Development Life Cycle." National Institute of Standards and Technology. October 2008. Accessed November 17, 2020, from *https://nvlpubs.nist.gov/nistpubs/Legacy/SP/ nistspecialpublication800-64r2.pdf*.

23. Whitman, Michael E., and Mattord, Herbert J. *Readings and Cases in the Management of Information Security: Legal and Ethical Issues*. 2010. Course Technology.

24. "Canon." Accessed November 17, 2020, from *www.dictionary.com/browse/canon*.

25. "Ethical." Accessed November 17, 2020, from *www.dictionary.com/browse/ethical*.

26. Multiple references, including *www.edu-cyberpg.com/Technology/ethics.html*. Accessed November 17, 2020.

27. "Hacking." Accessed November 17, 2020, from *www.dictionary.com/browse/hacking*.

28. © 1986 Paramount Pictures.

29. © 1983 Metro-Goldwyn-Mayer Studios Inc./United Artists.

30. © 1995 Metro-Goldwyn-Mayer Studios Inc.

31. "Oxymoron." Accessed November 17, 2020, from *www.dictionary.com/browse/oxymoron*.

32. Levy, S. *Hackers: Heroes of the Computer Revolution*. 1984. Putnam, NY: Penguin.

33. "Authorization." Accessed November 17, 2020, from *www.dictionary.com/browse/authorization*.

34. "Hippocratic Oath." Accessed November 11, 2017, from *en.wikipedia.org/wiki/Hippocratic_Oath*.

35. (ISC)² Code of Ethics. Accessed November 17, 2020, from *www.isc2.org/Ethics*.

36. "Professional." Accessed November 17, 2020, from *www.dictionary.com/browse/professional*.

37. Parker, Donn B. *Fighting Computer Crime*. 1998. New York: John Wiley and Sons Inc., 250–251.

38. "Static Electricity and Computers." Webopedia. Accessed November 19, 2020, from *www.webopedia.com/ DidYouKnow/Computer_Science/static.asp*.

39. Van Eck, Wim. "Electromagnetic Radiation from Video Display Units: An Eavesdropping Risk?" *Computers & Security* 4 (1985): 269–286.

40. Loughry, Joe, and Umphress, David A. "Information Leakage from Optical Emanations." *ACM Transactions on Information and System Security* 7, no. 7 (March 2002).

41. Metropolitan Police of the District of Columbia. "Tips for Preventing Theft of Laptops and Personal Electronics." Government of the District of Columbia Online. Accessed November 19, 2020, from *https:// mpdc.dc.gov/page/tips-preventing-theft-laptops-and-personal-electronics*.

GLOSSARY

3-2-1 backup rule A backup strategy that recommends the creation of at least three copies of critical data (the original and two copies) on at least two different media, with at least one copy stored off-site.

10.4 password rule An industry recommendation for password structure and strength that specifies passwords should be at least 10 characters long and contain at least one of the following four elements: an uppercase letter, one lowercase letter, one number, and one special character.

A

acceptance risk treatment strategy The risk treatment strategy that indicates the organization is willing to accept the current level of residual risk and, as a result, the organization makes a conscious decision to do nothing else to protect an information asset from risk and to "live with" the outcome from any resulting exploitation.

access A subject or object's ability to use, manipulate, modify, or affect another subject or object.

access control The selective method by which systems specify who may use a particular resource and how they may use it.

access control list (ACL) Specifications of authorization that govern the rights and privileges of users to a particular information asset; includes user access lists, matrices, and capabilities tables.

access control matrix An integration of access control lists (focusing on assets) and capability tables (focusing on users) that results in a matrix with organizational assets listed in the column headings and users listed in the row headings; contains ACLs in columns for a particular device or asset and capability tables in rows for a particular user.

accountability The access control mechanism that ensures all actions on a system—authorized or unauthorized—can be attributed to an authenticated identity; also known as *auditability*.

accuracy An attribute of information that describes how data is free of errors and has the value that the user expects.

active vulnerability scanner An application that scans networks to identify exposed usernames and groups, open network shares, configuration problems, and other vulnerabilities in servers.

address restrictions Firewall rules designed to prohibit packets with certain addresses or partial addresses from passing through the device.

Advanced Encryption Standard (AES) The current federal standard for the encryption of data, as specified by NIST; based on the Rijndael algorithm.

advance-fee fraud (AFF) A form of social engineering, typically conducted via e-mail, in which an organization or some third party indicates that the recipient is due an exorbitant amount of money and needs only to send a small advance fee or personal banking information to facilitate the transfer.

adverse event An event with negative consequences that could threaten the organization's information assets or operations; also referred to as an incident candidate.

adware Malware intended to provide undesired marketing and advertising, including pop-ups and banners on a user's screens.

affidavit Sworn testimony that certain facts are in the possession of an investigating officer and that they warrant the examination of specific items located at a specific place; the affidavit specifies the facts, the items, and the place.

after-action review (AAR) A detailed examination and discussion of the events that occurred during an incident or disaster, from first detection to final recovery.

agent See *sensor*.

aggregate information Collective data that relates to a group or category of people and that has been altered to remove characteristics or components that make it possible to identify individuals within the group. Not to be confused with *information aggregation*.

alarm An indication or notification that a system has just been attacked or is under attack.

alarm clustering and compaction A process of grouping almost identical alarms that occur nearly at the same time into a single higher-level alarm.

alarm filtering   The process of classifying IDPS alerts so they can be more effectively managed.

alert   See *alarm*.

alert message   A description of the incident or disaster that usually contains just enough information so that each person knows what portion of the IR or DR plan to implement without slowing down the notification process.

alert roster   A document that contains contact information for personnel to be notified in the event of an incident or disaster.

algorithm   The mathematical formula or method used to convert an unencrypted message into an encrypted message; sometimes refers to the programs that enable the cryptographic processes.

annualized failure rate (AFR)   The probability of a failure of hardware based on the manufacturer's data of failures per year.

annualized loss expectancy (ALE)   In a cost-benefit analysis, the product of the annualized rate of occurrence and single loss expectancy.

annualized rate of occurrence (ARO)   In a cost-benefit analysis, the expected frequency of an attack, expressed on a per-year basis.

anomaly-based detection   An IDPS detection method that compares current data and traffic patterns to an established baseline of normalcy; also known as *behavior-based detection*.

application firewall   See *application layer proxy firewall*.

application layer proxy firewall   A device capable of functioning both as a firewall and an application layer proxy server.

application protocol verification   The process of examining and verifying the higher-order protocols (HTTP, FTP, and Telnet) in network traffic for unexpected packet behavior or improper use.

apprehend and prosecute   The organizational CP philosophy that focuses on an attacker's identification and prosecution, the defense of information assets, and preventing reoccurrence; also known as "pursue and punish."

asset   The organizational resource that is being protected. An asset can be logical or physical.

asset valuation   The process of assigning financial value or worth to each information asset.

asymmetric encryption   A cryptographic method that incorporates mathematical operations involving both a public key and a private key to encipher or decipher a message; either key can be used to encrypt a message, but the other key is required to decrypt it.

asynchronous token   An authentication component in the form of a card or fob that contains a computer chip and a display that shows a computer-generated number used to support remote login authentication; the token does not require calibration of the central authentication server but uses a challenge/response system instead.

attack   An intentional or unintentional act that can damage or otherwise compromise information and the systems that support it. Attacks can be active or passive, intentional or unintentional, and direct or indirect.

attack protocol   A logical sequence of steps or processes used by an attacker to launch an attack against a target system or network.

attack surface   The functions and features that a system exposes to unauthenticated users.

attribute   A characteristic of a subject (user or system) that can be used to restrict access to an object; also known as a *subject attribute*.

attribute-based access control (ABAC)   An access control approach whereby the organization specifies the use of objects based on some attribute of the user or system.

auditability   See *accountability*.

authentication   The access control mechanism that requires the validation and verification of an entity's unsubstantiated identity.

authentication factors   Mechanisms that provide authentication based on something an unauthenticated entity knows, has, and is.

authentication header (AH) protocol   In IPSec, a protocol that provides system-to-system authentication and data integrity verification but does not provide secrecy for the content of a network communication.

authenticity   An attribute of information that describes how data is genuine or original rather than reproduced or fabricated.

authorization   The access control mechanism that represents the matching of an authenticated entity to a list of information assets and corresponding access levels.

availability   An attribute of information that describes how data is accessible and correctly formatted for use without interference or obstruction.

availability disruption An interruption or disruption in service, usually from a service provider, which causes an adverse event within an organization.

B

back door A malware payload that provides access to a system by bypassing normal access controls or an intentional access control bypass left by a system designer to facilitate development.

back hack The process of illegally attempting to determine the source of an intrusion by tracing it and trying to gain access to the originating system.

bastion host A device placed between an external, untrusted network and an internal, trusted network; also known as a *sacrificial host*, as it serves as the sole target for attack and should therefore be thoroughly secured.

behavior-based detection See *anomaly-based detection*.

biometric access control The use of physiological characteristics to provide authentication for a provided identification; also referred to as *biometrics*.

bit stream cipher An encryption method that involves converting plaintext to ciphertext one bit at a time.

blacklist A list of systems, users, files, or addresses that have been associated with malicious activity; it is commonly used to block those entities from systems or network access.

blackout A long-term interruption (outage) in electrical power availability.

block cipher An encryption method that involves dividing the plaintext into blocks or sets of bits and then converting the plaintext to ciphertext one block at a time.

boot virus Also known as a boot sector virus, a type of virus that targets the boot sector or Master Boot Record (MBR) of a computer system's hard drive or removable storage media.

bot An abbreviation of *robot*, an automated software program that executes certain commands when it receives a specific input; also known as a *zombie*.

bottom-up approach A method of establishing security policies and/or practices that begins as a grassroots effort in which systems administrators attempt to improve the security of their systems.

brownout A long-term decrease in quality of electrical power availability.

brute force password attack An attempt to guess a password by attempting every possible combination of characters and numbers in it.

buffer overrun (or buffer overflow) An application error that occurs when more data is sent to a program buffer than it is designed to handle.

bull's-eye model A method for prioritizing a program of complex change that requires issues to be addressed from the general to the specific and focuses on systematic solutions instead of individual problems.

business continuity (BC) An organization's set of efforts to ensure its long-term viability when a disaster precludes normal operations at the primary site; typically includes temporarily establishing critical operations at an alternate site until operations can be resumed at the primary site or a new permanent site.

business continuity plan (BC plan) The documented product of business continuity planning; a plan that shows the organization's intended efforts to continue critical functions when operations at the primary site are not feasible.

business continuity planning (BCP) The actions taken by senior management to develop and implement the BC policy, plan, and continuity teams.

business continuity planning team (BCPT) The team responsible for designing and managing the BC plan of relocating the organization and establishing primary operations at an alternate site until the disaster recovery planning team can recover the primary site or establish a new location.

business continuity policy (BC policy) The policy document that guides the development and implementation of BC plans and the formulation and performance of BC teams.

business e-mail compromise (BEC) A social engineering attack involving the compromise of an organization's e-mail system followed by a series of forged e-mail messages directing employees to transfer funds to a specified account, or to purchase gift cards and send them to an individual outside the organization.

business impact analysis (BIA) An investigation and assessment of adverse events that can affect the organization, conducted as a preliminary phase of the contingency planning process; it includes a determination of how critical a system or set of information is to the organization's core processes and its recovery priorities.

business process A task performed by an organization or one of its units in support of the organization's overall mission and operations.

business resumption planning (BRP) The actions taken by senior management to develop and implement a combined DR and BC policy, plan, and set of recovery teams.

C

capabilities table A lattice-based access control with rows of attributes associated with a particular subject (such as a user).

centralized IDPS control strategy An IDPS implementation approach in which all control functions are managed in a central location.

certificate authority (CA) In PKI, a third party that manages users' digital certificates.

certificate revocation list (CRL) In PKI, a published list of revoked or terminated digital certificates.

chain of custody See *chain of evidence*.

chain of evidence The detailed documentation of the collection, storage, transfer, and ownership of evidentiary material from the crime scene through its presentation in court and its eventual disposition.

change control A method of regulating the modification of systems within the organization by requiring formal review and approval for each change.

chief information officer (CIO) An executive-level position that oversees the organization's computing technology and strives to create efficiency in the processing and access of the organization's information.

chief information security officer (CISO) The title typically assigned to the top information security manager in an organization.

C.I.A. triad The industry standard for computer security since the development of the mainframe; the standard is based on three characteristics that describe the attributes of information that are important to protect: confidentiality, integrity, and availability.

cipher When used as a verb, the transformation of the individual components (characters, bytes, or bits) of an unencrypted message into encrypted components or vice versa (see *decryption* and *encryption*); when used as a noun, the process of encryption or the algorithm used in encryption, and a term synonymous with *cryptosystem*.

ciphertext The unintelligible encrypted or encoded message resulting from an encryption.

cleartext See *plaintext*.

clipping level A predefined assessment level that triggers a predetermined response when surpassed. Typically, the response is to write the event to a log file, notify an administrator, or both.

code The process of converting components (words or phrases) of an unencrypted message into encrypted components.

cold site A BC facility that provides only rudimentary services, with no computer hardware or peripherals.

command injection An application error that occurs when user input is passed directly to a compiler or interpreter without screening for content that may disrupt or compromise the intended function.

community of interest A group of individuals who are united by similar interests or values within an organization and who share a common goal of helping the organization to meet its objectives.

competitive intelligence The collection and analysis of information about an organization's business competitors through legal and ethical means to gain business intelligence and competitive advantage.

computer security In the early days of computers, this term specified the protection of the physical location and assets associated with computer technology from outside threats, but it later came to represent all actions taken to protect computer systems from losses.

computer security incident response team (CSIRT) An IR team composed of technical IT, managerial IT, and InfoSec professionals who are prepared to detect, react to, and recover from an incident; may include members of the IRPT.

confidence value The measure of an IDPS's ability to correctly detect and identify certain types of attacks.

confidentiality An attribute of information that describes how data is protected from disclosure or exposure to unauthorized individuals or systems.

configuration and change management (CCM) An approach to implementing system change that uses policies, procedures, techniques, and tools to manage and evaluate proposed changes, track changes through completion, and maintain systems inventory and supporting documentation.

configuration management (CM) See *configuration and change management (CCM)*.

configuration rules The instructions a system administrator codes into a server, networking device, or security device to specify how it operates.

content filter A software program or hardware/software appliance that allows administrators to restrict content that comes into or leaves a network.

contingency planning (CP) The actions taken by senior management to specify the organization's efforts and actions if an adverse event becomes an incident or disaster; CP typically includes incident response, disaster recovery, and business continuity efforts, as well as preparatory business impact analysis.

contingency planning management team (CPMT) The group of senior managers and project members organized to conduct and lead all CP efforts.

control, safeguard, or countermeasure Security mechanisms, policies, or procedures that can successfully counter attacks, reduce risk, resolve vulnerabilities, and otherwise improve security within an organization.

corporate governance Executive management's responsibility to provide strategic direction, ensure the accomplishment of objectives, oversee that risks are appropriately managed, and validate responsible resource use.

cost avoidance The financial savings from using the mitigation risk treatment strategy to implement a control and eliminate the financial ramifications of an incident.

cost-benefit analysis (CBA) The formal assessment and presentation of the economic expenditures needed for a particular security control, contrasted with its projected value to the organization; also known as an economic feasibility study.

covert channels Unauthorized or unintended methods of communications hidden inside a computer system.

cracker A hacker who intentionally removes or bypasses software copyright protection designed to prevent unauthorized duplication or use.

cracking Attempting to reverse-engineer, remove, or bypass a password or other access control protection, such as the copyright protection on software (see *cracker*).

crisis management (CM) An organization's set of planning and preparation efforts for dealing with potential human injury, emotional trauma, or loss of life as a result of a disaster.

crisis management plan (CM plan) The documented product of crisis management planning; a plan that shows the organization's intended efforts to protect its personnel and respond to safety threats.

crisis management planning (CMP) The actions taken by senior management to develop and implement the CM policy, plan, and response teams.

crisis management planning team (CMPT) The individuals from various functional areas of the organization assigned to develop and implement the CM plan.

crisis management policy (CM policy) The policy document that guides the development and implementation of CM plans and the formulation and performance of CM teams.

crossover error rate (CER) The point at which the rate of false rejections equals the rate of false acceptances; also called the *equal error rate*.

cross-site scripting (XSS) A Web application fault that occurs when an application running on a Web server inserts commands into a user's browser session and causes information to be sent to a hostile server.

cryptanalysis The process of obtaining the plaintext message from a ciphertext message without knowing the keys used to perform the encryption.

cryptogram See *ciphertext*.

cryptography The process of making and using codes to secure information.

cryptology The field of science that encompasses cryptography and cryptanalysis.

cryptovariable See *key*.

cultural mores The fixed moral attitudes or customs of a particular group.

cyberactivist See *hacktivist*.

cyberextortion See *information extortion*.

cybersecurity The affirmation or guarantee of the confidentiality, integrity, and availability of information in storage, processing, and transmission; often used synonymously with "information security."

cyberterrorism The conduct of terrorist activities via networks or Internet pathways.

cyberterrorist A hacker who attacks systems to conduct terrorist activities via networks or Internet pathways.

cyberwarfare Formally sanctioned offensive operations conducted by a government or state against information or systems of another government or state; sometimes called information warfare.

D

data Items of fact collected by an organization; includes raw numbers, facts, and words.

database A collection of related data stored in a structured form and usually managed by specialized systems.

database security A subset of information security that focuses on the assessment and protection of information stored in data repositories.

database shadowing A backup strategy that transfers duplicate online transaction data and duplicate databases to a remote site on a redundant server, combining electronic vaulting with remote journaling by writing multiple copies of the database simultaneously to two locations.

data classification scheme A formal access control methodology used to assign a level of confidentiality to an information asset and thus restrict the number of people who can access it.

data custodians Individuals who are responsible for the storage, maintenance, and protection of information.

data loss prevention A strategy to ensure that the users of a network do not send high-value information or other critical information outside the network without authorization.

data owners Individuals who control, and are therefore ultimately responsible for, the security and use of a particular set of information.

data stewards See *data custodians*.

data trustees Individuals who are assigned the task of managing a particular set of information and coordinating its protection, storage, and use.

data users Internal and external stakeholders (customers, suppliers, and employees) who interact with information in support of their organization's planning and operations.

decipher See *decryption*.

decryption The process of converting an encoded or enciphered message (ciphertext) back to its original readable form (plaintext); also referred to as *deciphering*.

de facto standard A standard that has been widely adopted or accepted by a public group rather than a formal standards organization.

defense in depth A strategy for the protection of information assets that uses multiple layers and different types of controls to provide optimal protection; typically, implementation of many different types of controls.

de jure standard A standard that has been formally evaluated, approved, and ratified by a formal standards organization.

demilitarized zone (DMZ) An intermediate area designed to provide servers and firewall filtering between a trusted internal network and the outside, untrusted network.

denial-of-service (DoS) attack An attack that attempts to overwhelm a computer target's ability to handle incoming communications, prohibiting legitimate users from accessing those systems.

deperimeterization The recognition that there is no clear information security boundary between an organization and the outside world, meaning that the organization must be prepared to protect its information both inside and outside its digital walls.

desk check The CP testing strategy in which copies of the appropriate plans are distributed to all individuals who will be assigned roles during an actual incident or disaster; each individual reviews the plan and validates its components.

dictionary password attack A variation of the brute force password attack that attempts to narrow the range of possible passwords guessed by using a list of common passwords and possibly including attempts based on the target's personal information.

difference analysis A procedure that compares the current state of a network segment against a known previous state of the same network segment (the baseline of systems and services).

Diffie–Hellman key exchange A hybrid cryptosystem that facilitates exchanging private keys using public-key encryption.

digital certificates Public-key container files that allow PKI system components and end users to validate a public key and identify its owner.

digital forensics Investigations that involve the preservation, identification, extraction, documentation, and interpretation of computer media for evidentiary and root cause analysis, following clear, well-defined methodologies.

digital malfeasance A crime involving digital media, computer technology, or related components.

Digital Signature Standard (DSS) The NIST standard for digital signature algorithm usage by federal information systems; based on a variant of the ElGamal signature scheme.

digital signatures Encrypted message components that can be mathematically proven as authentic.

direct changeover conversion strategy The conversion strategy that involves stopping the old system and starting the new one without any overlap.

disaster classification The process of examining an adverse event or incident and determining whether it constitutes an actual disaster.

disaster recovery (DR) An organization's set of planning and preparation efforts for detecting, reacting to, and recovering from a disaster.

disaster recovery plan (DR plan) The documented product of disaster recovery planning; a plan that shows the organization's intended efforts in the event of a disaster.

disaster recovery planning (DRP) The actions taken by senior management to develop and implement the DR policy, plan, and recovery teams.

disaster recovery planning team (DRPT) The team responsible for designing and managing the DR plan by specifying the organization's preparation, response, and recovery from disasters, including reestablishment of business operations at the primary site after the disaster.

disaster recovery policy (DR policy) The policy document that guides the development and implementation of DR plans and the formulation and performance of DR teams.

discretionary access controls (DACs) Access controls that are implemented at the judgment or option of the data user.

distributed denial-of-service (DDoS) attack A form of attack in which a coordinated stream of requests is launched against a target from multiple locations at the same time using bots or zombies.

Domain Name System (DNS) cache poisoning The intentional hacking and modification of a DNS database to redirect legitimate traffic to illegitimate Internet locations; also known as DNS spoofing.

downtime The percentage of time a particular service is not available.

doxing A practice of using online resources to find and then disseminate compromising information, perhaps without lawful authority, with the intent to embarrass or harm the reputation of an individual or organization. The term originates from *dox*, an abbreviation of *documents*.

due care Reasonable and prudent measures that an organization takes to ensure it is in compliance with a law, regulation, or requirement.

due diligence Measures taken to ensure that an organization *continues* to meet the obligations imposed by laws, regulations, and requirements; the management of due care.

dumb card An authentication card that contains digital user data, such as a personal identification number, against which user input is compared.

dynamic packet filtering A firewall type that can react to network traffic and create or modify its configuration rules to adapt.

E

electronic vaulting A backup strategy that transfers data in bulk batches to an off-site facility.

encapsulating security payload (ESP) protocol In IPSec, a protocol that provides secrecy for the contents of network communications as well as system-to-system authentication and data integrity verification.

encipher See *encryption*.

encryption The process of converting an original message (plaintext) into a form that cannot be used by unauthorized individuals (ciphertext); also referred to as *enciphering*.

enterprise information security policy (EISP) The high-level information security policy that sets the strategic direction, scope, and tone for all of an organization's security efforts; also known as a security program policy, general security policy, IT security policy, high-level InfoSec policy, or simply an InfoSec policy.

enticement The act of attracting attention to a system by placing tantalizing information in key locations.

entrapment The act of luring a person into committing a crime in order to get a conviction.

ethics The branch of philosophy that considers nature, criteria, sources, logic, and the validity of moral judgment.

evasion The process by which attackers change the format or timing of their activities to avoid being detected by an IDPS.

evidentiary material (EM) Any information that could potentially support an organization's legal or policy-based case against a suspect; also known as items of potential evidentiary value.

exclusive OR operation (XOR) A function within Boolean algebra used as an encryption function in which two bits are compared; identical bits result in a binary 0 while different bits result in a binary 1.

exit interview A meeting with an employee who is leaving the organization to remind the employee of contractual obligations, such as nondisclosure agreements, and to obtain feedback about the employee's tenure.

expert hacker A hacker who uses extensive knowledge of the inner workings of computer hardware and software to gain unauthorized access to systems and information, and who often creates automated exploits, scripts, and tools used by other hackers; also known as an *elite hacker*.

exploit A technique used to compromise a system; may also describe the tool, program, or script used in the compromise.

exposure A condition or state of being exposed; in information security, exposure exists when a vulnerability is known to an attacker.

external monitoring domain The component of the maintenance model that focuses on evaluating external threats to the organization's information assets.

extranet A segment of the DMZ where additional authentication and authorization controls are put into place to provide services that are not available to the general public.

F

facilities management The aspect of organizational management focused on the development and maintenance of buildings and physical infrastructure.

false accept rate The rate at which fraudulent users or nonusers are allowed access to systems or areas as a result of a failure in the biometric device; also known as a Type II error or a false positive.

false attack stimulus An event that triggers an alarm when no actual attack is in progress.

false negative The failure of a technical control (such as an IDPS) to react to an actual attack event.

false positive An alert or alarm that occurs in the absence of an actual attack.

false reject rate The rate at which authentic users are denied or prevented access to authorized areas as a result of a failure in the biometric device; also known as a Type I error or a false negative.

fault A short-term interruption in electrical power availability.

fingerprinting The systematic survey of a targeted organization's Internet addresses collected during the footprinting phase to identify the network services offered by the hosts in that range.

firewall In information security, a combination of hardware and software that filters or prevents specific information from moving between the outside network and the inside network.

footprinting The organized research and investigation of Internet addresses owned or controlled by a target organization.

forensics The coherent application of methodical investigatory techniques to present evidence of crimes in a court or similar setting.

full-interruption testing The CP testing strategy in which all team members follow each IR/DR/BC procedure, including those for interruption of service, restoration of data from backups, and notification of appropriate individuals.

fully distributed IDPS control strategy An IDPS implementation approach in which all control functions are applied at the physical location of each IDPS component.

G

gap analysis The process of comparing measured results against expected results and then using the resulting "gap" as a measure of project success and as feedback for project management.

goals A term sometimes used synonymously with *objectives*; the desired end of a planning cycle.

governance The set of responsibilities and practices exercised by the board and executive management with the goal of providing strategic direction, ensuring that objectives are achieved, ascertaining that risks are managed appropriately, and verifying that the enterprise's resources are used responsibly.

governance, risk management, and compliance (GRC) An approach to information security strategic guidance from a board of directors' or senior management perspective that seeks to integrate the three components of information security governance, risk management, and regulatory compliance.

guidelines Nonmandatory recommendations the employee may use as a reference in complying with a policy.

H

hacker A person who accesses systems and information without authorization and often illegally.

hacktivist A hacker who seeks to interfere with or disrupt systems to protest the operations, policies, or actions of an organization or government agency.

hash algorithms Public functions that create a *hash value*, also known as a message digest, by converting variable-length messages into a single fixed-length value.

hash functions Mathematical algorithms that generate a message summary or digest (sometimes called a fingerprint) to confirm the message's identity and integrity.

hash value See *message digest*.

honeynet A monitored network or network segment that contains multiple honeypot systems.

honeynet farm See *honeynet*.

honeypot An application that entices people who are illegally perusing the internal areas of a network by providing simulated rich content while the software notifies the administrator of the intrusion.

honeytoken Any system resource that is placed in a functional system but has no normal use in the system, and that instead serves as a decoy and alarm, similar to a honeypot.

host-based IDPS (HIDPS) An IDPS that resides on a particular computer or server, known as the host, and monitors activity only on that system; also known as a system integrity verifier.

hot site A fully configured BC facility that includes all computing services, communications links, and physical plant operations.

hybrid VPN A combination of trusted and secure VPN implementations.

I

identification The access control mechanism whereby unverified or unauthenticated entities who seek access to a resource provide a label or username by which they are known to the system.

identity theft The unauthorized taking of personally identifiable information with the intent of committing fraud and abuse of a person's financial and personal reputation, purchasing goods and services without authorization, and generally impersonating the victim for illegal or unethical purposes.

impact An understanding of the potential consequences of a successful attack on an information asset by a threat.

incident An adverse event that could result in a loss of information assets but does not threaten the viability of the entire organization.

incident candidate See *adverse event*.

incident classification The process of examining an adverse event or incident candidate and determining whether it constitutes an actual incident.

incident detection The identification and classification of an adverse event as an incident, accompanied by the notification of the CSIRT and the activation of the IR reaction phase.

incident response (IR) An organization's set of planning and preparation efforts for detecting, reacting to, and recovering from an incident.

incident response plan (IR plan) The documented product of incident response planning; a plan that shows the organization's intended efforts in the event of an incident.

incident response planning (IRP) The actions taken by senior management to develop and implement the IR policy, plan, and computer security incident response team.

incident response planning team (IRPT)   The team responsible for designing and managing the IR plan by specifying the organization's preparation, reaction, and recovery from incidents.

incident response policy (IR policy)   The policy document that guides the development and implementation of IR plans and the formulation and performance of IR teams.

incident response procedures (IR procedures)   Detailed, step-by-step methods of preparing, detecting, reacting to, and recovering from an incident.

industrial espionage   The collection and analysis of information about an organization's business competitors, often through illegal or unethical means, to gain an unfair competitive advantage; also known as *corporate spying*.

information   Data that has been organized, structured, and presented to provide additional insight into its context, worth, and usefulness.

information aggregation   Pieces of nonprivate data that, when combined, may create information that violates privacy. Not to be confused with *aggregate information*.

information asset   The focus of information security; information that has value to the organization and the systems that store, process, and transmit the information.

information assurance   See *cybersecurity*.

information extortion   The act of an attacker or trusted insider who steals or interrupts access to information from a computer system and demands compensation for its return or for an agreement not to disclose the information.

information security   Protection of the confidentiality, integrity, and availability of information assets, whether in storage, processing, or transmission, via the application of policy, education, training and awareness, and technology.

information security blueprint   In information security, a framework or security model customized to an organization, including implementation details.

information security framework   In information security, a specification of a model to be followed during the design, selection, and initial and ongoing implementation of all subsequent security controls, including information security policies, security education and training programs, and technological controls.

information security governance   The application of the principles and practices of corporate governance to the information security function, emphasizing the responsibility of the board of directors and/or senior management for the oversight of information security in the organization.

information security model   A well-recognized information security framework, usually promoted by a government agency, standards organization, or industry group.

information security policy   Written instructions provided by management that inform employees and others in the workplace about proper behavior regarding the use of information and information assets.

information system (IS)   The entire set of software, hardware, data, people, procedures, and networks that enable the use of information resources in the organization.

InfoSec performance management   A process of designing, implementing, and managing the use of specific measurements to determine the effectiveness of the overall security program.

inline sensor   An IDPS sensor intended for network perimeter use and deployed in close proximity to a perimeter firewall to detect incoming attacks that could overwhelm the firewall.

integer bug   A class of computational error caused by methods that computers use to store and manipulate integer numbers; this bug can be exploited by attackers.

integrity   An attribute of information that describes how data is whole, complete, and uncorrupted.

intellectual property (IP)   Original ideas and inventions created, owned, and controlled by a particular person or organization; IP includes the representation of original ideas.

internal monitoring domain   The component of the maintenance model that focuses on identifying, assessing, and managing the configuration and status of information assets in an organization.

Internet vulnerability assessment   An assessment approach designed to find and document vulnerabilities that may be present in the organization's public-facing networks.

intranet vulnerability assessment   An assessment approach designed to find and document selected vulnerabilities that are present on the organization's internal networks.

intrusion   An adverse event in which an attacker attempts to gain entry into an information system or disrupt its normal operations, almost always with the intent to do harm.

intrusion detection and prevention system (IDPS)   The general term for a system that can both detect and modify its configuration and environment to prevent intrusions. An IDPS encompasses the functions of both intrusion detection systems and intrusion prevention technology.

intrusion detection system (IDS)   A system capable of automatically detecting an intrusion into an organization's networks or host systems and notifying a designated authority.

IP Security (IPSec)   The primary and dominant cryptographic authentication and encryption product of the IETF's IP Protocol Security Working Group; provides application support for all uses within TCP/IP, including virtual private networks.

IP spoofing   A technique for gaining unauthorized access to computers using a forged or modified source IP address to give the perception that messages are coming from a trusted host.

issue-specific security policy (ISSP)   An organizational policy that provides detailed, targeted guidance to instruct all members of the organization in the use of a resource, such as one of its processes or technologies.

J

jailbreaking   Escalating privileges to gain administrator-level or root access control over a smartphone operating system; typically associated with Apple iOS smartphones. See also *rooting*.

job rotation   The requirement that every employee be able to perform the work of another employee.

jurisdiction   The power to make legal decisions and judgments; also, the domain or area within which an entity such as a court or law enforcement agency is empowered to make legal decisions and perform legal actions.

K

Kerberos   An authentication system that uses symmetric key encryption to validate an individual user's access to various network resources by keeping a database containing the private keys of clients and servers that are in the authentication domain it supervises.

key   The information used in conjunction with the algorithm to create the ciphertext from the plaintext; it can be a series of bits used in an algorithm or the knowledge of how to manipulate the plaintext.

keyspace   The entire range of values that can be used to construct an individual key.

knowledge-based detection   See *signature-based detection*.

known vulnerability   A published weakness or fault in an information asset or its protective systems that may be exploited and result in loss.

L

lattice-based access control (LBAC)   A variation on mandatory access controls that assigns users a matrix of authorizations for particular areas of access, incorporating the information assets of subjects such as users and objects.

laws   Rules that mandate or prohibit certain behavior and are enforced by the state.

least privilege   The data access principle that ensures no unnecessary access to data exists by regulating members so they can perform only the minimum data manipulation needed; least privilege implies a need to know.

liability   An entity's legal obligation or responsibility.

likelihood   The probability that a specific vulnerability within an organization will be attacked by a threat.

link encryption   A series of encryptions and decryptions between a number of systems, wherein each system in a network decrypts the message sent to it, re-encrypts the message using different keys, and sends it to the next neighbor.

log file monitor (LFM)   An attack detection method that reviews log files generated by computer systems looking for patterns and signatures that may indicate an attack or intrusion is in process or has already occurred.

long-arm jurisdiction   The ability of a legal entity to exercise its influence beyond its normal boundaries by asserting a connection between an out-of-jurisdiction entity and a local legal case.

loss   A single instance of an information asset suffering damage or destruction, unintended or unauthorized modification or disclosure, or denial of use.

M

macro virus   A type of virus written in a specific language to target applications that use the language, and activated when the application's product is opened; typically affects documents, slideshows, e-mails, or spreadsheets created by office suite applications.

mail bomb   An attack designed to overwhelm the receiver with excessive quantities of e-mail.

maintenance hook   See *back door*.

malicious code   See *malware*.

malicious software   See *malware*.

malware   Computer software specifically designed to perform malicious or unwanted actions.

malware hoax   A message that reports the presence of nonexistent malware and wastes valuable time as employees share the message.

managerial controls   Information security safeguards that focus on administrative planning, organizing, leading, and controlling, and that are designed by strategic planners and implemented by the organization's security administration; they include governance and risk management.

managerial guidance SysSP   A policy that expresses management's intent for the acquisition, implementation, configuration, and management of a particular technology, written from a business perspective.

mandatory access control (MAC)   A required, structured data classification scheme that assigns a sensitivity or classification rating to each collection of information as well as each user.

man-in-the-middle   A group of attacks whereby a person intercepts a communications stream and inserts himself in the conversation to convince each of the legitimate parties that he is the other communications partner; some of these attacks involve encryption functions.

mantrap   A small room or enclosure with separate entry and exit points, designed to restrain a person who fails an access authorization attempt.

maximum tolerable downtime (MTD)   The total amount of time the system owner or authorizing official is willing to accept for a business process outage or disruption. The MTD includes all impact considerations.

McCumber Cube   A graphical representation of the architectural approach used in computer and information security; commonly shown as a cube composed of 3×3×3 cells, similar to a Rubik's Cube.

mean time between failure (MTBF)   The average amount of time between hardware failures, calculated as the total amount of operation time for a specified number of units divided by the total number of failures.

mean time to diagnose (MTTD)   The average amount of time a computer repair technician needs to determine the cause of a failure.

mean time to failure (MTTF)   The average amount of time until the next hardware failure.

mean time to repair (MTTR)   The average amount of time a computer repair technician needs to resolve the cause of a failure through replacement or repair of a faulty unit.

media   As a subset of information assets, the systems, technologies, and networks that store, process, and transmit information.

media access control layer firewall   A firewall designed to operate at the media access control sublayer of the network's data link layer (Layer 2).

memory-resident virus   A virus that is capable of installing itself in a computer's operating system, starting when the computer is activated, and residing in the system's memory even after the host application is terminated; also known as a resident virus.

message authentication code (MAC)   A key-dependent, one-way hash function that allows only specific recipients (symmetric key holders) to access the message digest.

message digest   A value representing the application of a hash algorithm on a message that is transmitted with the message so it can be compared with the recipient's locally calculated hash of the same message; also known as a *hash value*.

methodology   A formal approach to solving a problem based on a structured sequence of procedures.

metric   A term traditionally used to describe any detailed statistical analysis technique on performance, but now commonly synonymous with performance measurement. See *performance measurements*.

minutiae   In biometric access controls, unique points of reference that are digitized and stored in an encrypted format when the user's system access credentials are created, and are then used in subsequent requests for access to authenticate the user's identity.

mirror port   See *monitoring port*.

misuse detection   See *signature-based detection*.

mitigation risk treatment strategy   The risk treatment strategy that attempts to eliminate or reduce any remaining uncontrolled risk through the application of additional controls and safeguards in an effort to change the likelihood of a successful attack on an information asset; also known as the *defense strategy*.

monitoring port   A specially configured connection on a network device that can view all the traffic that moves through the device; also known as a *switched port analysis (SPAN) port* or *mirror port*.

monoalphabetic substitution   A substitution cipher that incorporates a single alphabet in the encryption process.

mutual agreement   A BC strategy in which two organizations sign a contract to assist the other in a disaster by providing BC facilities, resources, and services until the organization in need can recover from the disaster.

N

need to know   The principle of limiting users' access privileges to the specific information required to perform their assigned tasks.

Network Address Translation (NAT)   A networking scheme in which multiple real, routable external IP addresses are converted to special ranges of internal IP addresses, usually on a one-to-one basis; that is, one external valid address directly maps to one assigned internal address.

network-based IDPS (NIDPS)   An IDPS that resides on a computer or appliance connected to a segment of an organization's network and monitors traffic on that segment, looking for indications of ongoing or successful attacks.

network security   A subset of communications security; the protection of voice and data networking components, connections, and content.

Next Generation Firewall (NextGen or NGFW)   A security appliance that delivers Unified Threat Management capabilities in a single integrated device.

noise   In incident response, alarm events that are accurate and noteworthy but do not pose significant threats to information security; also, the presence of additional and disruptive signals in network communications or electrical power delivery.

nondiscretionary access controls (NDACs)   Access controls that are implemented by a central authority.

non-memory-resident virus   A virus that terminates after it has been activated, infected its host system, and replicated itself; does not reside in an operating system or memory after executing and is also known as a non-resident virus.

nonrepudiation   The process of reversing public-key encryption to verify that a message was sent by the user and thus cannot be refuted.

novice hacker   A relatively unskilled hacker who uses the work of expert hackers to perform attacks; also known as a neophyte, n00b, newbie, script kiddie, or packet monkey.

O

objectives   A term sometimes used synonymously with *goals*; the intermediate states obtained to achieve progress toward a goal or goals.

operational controls   Information security safeguards focusing on lower-level planning that deals with the functionality of the organization's security; they include disaster recovery planning, incident response planning, and SETA programs.

operational plan   The documented product of operational planning; a plan for the organization's intended operational efforts on a day-to-day basis for the next several months.

operational planning   The actions taken by management to specify the short-term goals and objectives of the organization in order to obtain specified tactical goals, followed by estimates and schedules for the allocation of resources necessary to achieve those goals and objectives.

P

packet-filtering firewall   A networking device that examines the header information of data packets that come into a network and determines whether to drop them (deny) or forward them to the next network connection (allow), based on its configuration rules.

packet monkey   A novice hacker who uses automated exploits to engage in denial-of-service attacks.

packet sniffer   A software program or hardware appliance that can intercept, copy, and interpret network traffic.

padded cell system   A protected honeypot that cannot be easily compromised.

parallel operations conversion strategy   The conversion strategy that involves running the new system concurrently with the old system.

partially distributed IDPS control strategy   An IDPS implementation approach that combines the best aspects of the centralized and fully distributed strategies.

passive mode   An IDPS sensor setting in which the device simply monitors and analyzes observed network or system traffic.

passive vulnerability scanner   A scanner that listens in on a network and identifies vulnerable versions of both server and client software.

passphrase   A plain-language phrase, typically longer than a password, from which a virtual password is derived.

password   A secret word or combination of characters that only the user should know; it is used to authenticate the user.

penetration tester   An information security professional with authorization to attempt to gain system access in an effort to identify and recommend resolutions for vulnerabilities in those systems; also known as a *pen tester*.

penetration testing   A set of security tests and evaluations that simulate attacks by a hacker or other malicious external source.

pen register   An application that records information about outbound communications.

pen tester   See *penetration tester*.

performance measurements   Data or the trends in data that may indicate the effectiveness of security countermeasures or technical and managerial controls implemented in the organization. Also known as *performance measures* or *metrics*.

performance measures   See *performance measurements*.

permutation cipher   See *transposition cipher*.

personally identifiable information (PII)   Information about a person's history, background, and attributes that can be used to commit identity theft. This information typically includes a person's name, address, Social Security number, family information, employment history, and financial information.

pharming   The redirection of legitimate user Web traffic to illegitimate Web sites with the intent to collect personal information.

phased implementation conversion strategy   The conversion strategy that involves a measured rollout of the planned system; only part of the system is brought out and disseminated across an organization before the next piece is implemented.

phishing   A form of social engineering in which the attacker provides what appears to be a legitimate communication (usually e-mail), but it contains hidden or embedded code that redirects the reply to a third-party site in an effort to extract personal or confidential information.

phreaker   A hacker who manipulates the public telephone system to make free calls or disrupt services.

physical security   The protection of material items, objects, or areas from unauthorized access and misuse.

pilot implementation conversion strategy   The conversion strategy that involves implementing the entire system into a single office, department, or division and dealing with issues that arise before expanding to the rest of the organization.

plaintext   The original unencrypted message that is encrypted and the message that results from successful decryption.

planning and risk assessment domain   The component of the maintenance model that focuses on identifying and planning ongoing information security activities and identifying and managing risks introduced through IT information security projects.

platform security validation (PSV)   An assessment approach designed to find and document vulnerabilities if misconfigured systems are used within the organization.

policy   Guidelines that dictate certain behavior within an organization.

policy administrator   An employee responsible for the creation, revision, distribution, and storage of a policy in an organization.

polyalphabetic substitution   A substitution cipher that incorporates two or more alphabets in the encryption process.

polymorphic threat   Malware that over time changes the way it appears to antivirus software programs, making it undetectable by techniques that look for preconfigured signatures.

Port Address Translation (PAT) A networking scheme in which multiple real, routable external IP addresses are converted to special ranges of internal IP addresses, usually on a one-to-many basis; that is, one external valid address is mapped dynamically to a range of internal addresses by adding a unique port number to the address when traffic leaves the private network and is placed on the public network.

port scanner A type of tool used both by attackers and defenders to identify or fingerprint active computers on a network, the active ports and services on those computers, the functions and roles of the machines, and other useful information.

possession An attribute of information that describes how the data's ownership or control is legitimate or authorized.

practices Examples of actions that illustrate compliance with policies.

pretexting A form of social engineering in which the attacker pretends to be an authority figure who needs information to confirm the target's identity, but the real object is to trick the target into revealing confidential information; commonly performed by telephone.

privacy In the context of information security, the right of individuals or groups to protect themselves and their information from unauthorized access, providing confidentiality.

Privacy-Enhanced Mail (PEM) A standard proposed by the IETF that uses 3DES symmetric key encryption and RSA for key exchanges and digital signatures.

private-key encryption See *symmetric encryption*.

privilege escalation The unauthorized modification of an authorized or unauthorized system user account to gain advanced access and control over system resources.

procedures Step-by-step instructions designed to assist employees in following policies, standards, and guidelines.

process communications The necessary information flow within and between the governance group, RM framework team, and RM process team during the implementation of RM.

process monitoring and review The data collection and feedback associated with performance measures used during the conduct of the process.

professional hacker A hacker who conducts attacks for personal financial benefit or for a crime organization or foreign government; not to be confused with a penetration tester.

projectitis A situation in project planning in which a project manager spends more time manipulating and adjusting aspects of the project management software than accomplishing meaningful project work.

project management The process of identifying and controlling the goals, objectives, tasks, scheduling, and resources of a project.

project plan The documented instructions for participants and stakeholders in a project that provide details on its goals, objectives, tasks, scheduling, and resource management.

protect and forget The organizational CP philosophy that focuses on the defense of information assets and preventing reoccurrence rather than the attacker's identification and prosecution; also known as "patch and proceed."

protection profile The entire set of controls and safeguards—including policy, education, training and awareness, and technology—that the organization implements to protect the asset.

protocol stack verification The process of examining and verifying network traffic for invalid data packets—that is, packets that are malformed under the rules of the TCP/IP protocol.

proxy server A server that exists to intercept requests for information from external users and provide the requested information by retrieving it from an internal server, thus protecting and minimizing the demand on internal servers; some are also cache servers.

public-key encryption See *asymmetric encryption*.

public key infrastructure (PKI) An integrated system of software, encryption methodologies, protocols, legal agreements, and third-party services that enables users to communicate securely through the use of digital certificates.

R

rainbow table A table of hash values and their corresponding plaintext values that can be used to look up password values if an attacker is able to steal a system's encrypted password file.

ransomware   Computer software specifically designed to identify and encrypt valuable information in a victim's system in order to extort payment for the key needed to unlock the encryption.

rapid-onset disasters   Disasters that occur suddenly, with little warning, taking people's lives and destroying the means of production.

recovery point objective (RPO)   The point in time before a disruption or system outage to which business process data can be recovered after an outage, given the most recent backup copy of the data.

recovery time objective (RTO)   The maximum amount of time that a system resource can remain unavailable before there is an unacceptable impact on other system resources, supported business processes, and the maximum tolerable downtime.

redundancy   The use of multiple types and instances of technology that prevent the failure of one system from compromising the security of information; typically, multiple instances of the same type of control.

reference monitor   Within the trusted computing base, a conceptual piece of the system that manages access controls.

registration authority (RA)   In PKI, a third party that operates under the trusted collaboration of the certificate authority and handles day-to-day certification functions.

remediation   The processes of removing or repairing flaws in information assets that cause a vulnerability or reducing or removing the risk associated with the vulnerability.

Remote Authentication Dial-In User Service (RADIUS)   A computer connection system that centralizes the management of user authentication by placing the responsibility for authenticating each user on a central authentication server.

remote journaling   A backup strategy that transfers only transaction data in near real time to an off-site facility.

residual risk   The risk to information assets that remains even after current controls have been applied.

restitution   A legal requirement to make compensation or payment resulting from a loss or injury.

reverse firewall   See *content filter*.

reverse proxy   A proxy server that most commonly retrieves information from inside an organization and provides it to a requesting user or system outside the organization.

risk   The probability of an unwanted occurrence, such as an adverse event or loss.

risk acceptance   See *acceptance risk treatment strategy*.

risk analysis   A determination of the extent to which an organization's information assets are exposed to risk.

risk appetite   The quantity and nature of risk that organizations are willing to accept as they evaluate the trade-offs between perfect security and unlimited accessibility.

risk appetite statement   A formal document developed by the organization that specifies its overall willingness to accept risk to its information assets, based on a synthesis of individual risk tolerances.

risk assessment   The identification, analysis, and evaluation of risk as initial parts of risk management.

risk avoidance   See *termination risk treatment strategy*.

risk control   See *risk treatment*.

risk defense   See *mitigation risk treatment strategy*.

risk evaluation   The process of comparing an information asset's risk rating to the numerical representation of the organization's risk appetite or risk threshold to determine if risk treatment is required.

risk identification   The recognition, enumeration, and documentation of risks to an organization's information assets.

risk management   The process of identifying risk, assessing its relative magnitude, and taking steps to reduce it to an acceptable level.

risk management (RM) plan   A document that contains specifications for the implementation and conduct of RM efforts.

risk mitigation   See *mitigation risk treatment strategy*.

risk sharing   See *transference risk treatment strategy*.

risk termination   See *termination risk treatment strategy*.

risk threshold   See *risk tolerance*.

risk tolerance The assessment of the amount of risk an organization is willing to accept for a particular information asset, typically synthesized into the organization's overall risk appetite.

risk transfer See *transference risk treatment strategy*.

risk treatment The application of safeguards or controls to reduce the risks to an organization's information assets to an acceptable level.

RM framework The overall structure of the strategic planning and design for the entirety of the organization's RM efforts.

RM process The identification, analysis, evaluation, and treatment of risk to information assets, as specified in the RM framework.

role-based access control (RBAC) A nondiscretionary control where privileges are tied to the role or job a user performs in an organization and are inherited when a user is assigned to that role.

rolling mobile site A BC strategy that involves contracting with an organization to provide specialized facilities configured in the payload area of a tractor-trailer.

root cause analysis The determination of the source or origin of an event, problem, or issue like an incident.

rooting Escalating privileges to gain administrator-level control over a computer system (including smartphones); typically associated with Android OS smartphones. See also *jailbreaking*.

S

sacrificial host See *bastion host*.

sag A short-term decrease in electrical power availability.

screened host architecture A firewall architectural model that combines the packet-filtering router with a second, dedicated device such as a proxy server or proxy firewall.

screened subnet architecture A firewall architectural model that consists of one or more internal bastion hosts located behind a packet-filtering router on a dedicated network segment, with each host performing a role in protecting the trusted network.

script kiddies Novice hackers who use expertly written software to attack a system; also known as skids, skiddies, or script bunnies.

search warrant Permission to search for evidentiary material at a specified location or to seize items to return to an investigator's lab for examination.

secret key A key that can be used in symmetric encryption both to encipher and decipher the message.

Secure Electronic Transactions (SET) A protocol developed by credit card companies to protect against electronic payment fraud.

secure facility A physical location with access barriers and controls in place to minimize the risk of attacks from physical threats.

Secure Hash Standard (SHS) A standard issued by the National Institute of Standards and Technology (NIST) that specifies secure algorithms, such as SHA-1, for computing a condensed representation of a message or data file.

Secure HTTP (HTTPS) An extended version of Hypertext Transfer Protocol that provides for the encryption of protected Web pages transmitted via the Internet between a client and server.

Secure/Multipurpose Internet Mail Extensions (S/MIME) A security protocol that builds on the encoding format of the Multipurpose Internet Mail Extensions (MIME) protocol and uses digital signatures based on public-key cryptosystems to secure e-mail.

Secure Sockets Layer (SSL) A security protocol developed by Netscape to use public-key encryption to secure a channel over the Internet.

secure VPN A VPN implementation that uses security protocols to encrypt traffic transmitted across unsecured public networks.

security A state of being secure and free from danger or harm; also, the actions taken to make someone or something secure.

security domain An area of trust within which information assets share the same level of protection; communication between these trust areas requires evaluation of communications traffic.

security education, training, and awareness (SETA) A managerial program designed to improve the security of information assets by providing targeted knowledge, skills, and guidance for an organization's employees.

security information and event management (SIEM) An information management system specifically tasked to collect and correlate events and other log data from a number of servers

task-based access control (TBAC) A nondiscretionary control where privileges are tied to a task or temporary assignment a user performs in an organization and are inherited when a user is assigned to that task.

task rotation The requirement that all critical tasks can be performed by multiple employees.

TCP hijacking A form of man-in-the-middle attack whereby the attacker inserts himself into TCP/IP-based communications.

technical controls Information security safeguards that focus on the application of modern technologies, systems, and processes to protect information assets; they include firewalls, virtual private networks, and IDPSs.

technical specifications SysSP A policy that expresses technical details for the acquisition, implementation, configuration, and management of a particular technology, written from a technical perspective; usually includes details on configuration rules, systems policies, and access control.

technology governance A process that organizations use to manage the effects and costs of technology implementation, innovation, and obsolescence.

termination risk treatment strategy The risk treatment strategy that eliminates all risk associated with an information asset by removing it from service.

theft The illegal taking of another's property, which can be physical, electronic, or intellectual.

threat Any event or circumstance that has the potential to adversely affect operations and assets.

threat agent The specific instance or a component of a threat.

threat assessment An evaluation of the threats to information assets, including a determination of their likelihood of occurrence and potential impact of an attack.

threat event An occurrence of an event caused by a threat agent.

threat intelligence A process used to develop knowledge that allows an organization to understand the actions and intentions of threat actors and develop methods to prevent or mitigate cyberattacks.

threat source A category of objects, people, or other entities that represents the origin of danger to an asset—in other words, a category of threat agents.

threshold A value that sets the limit between normal and abnormal behavior. See also *clipping level*.

timeshare A continuity strategy in which an organization co-leases facilities with a business partner or sister organization, which allows the organization to have a BC option while reducing its overall costs.

timing channels TCSEC-defined covert channels that communicate by managing the relative timing of events.

top-down approach A methodology of establishing security policies and/or practices that is initiated by upper management.

transference risk treatment strategy The risk treatment strategy that attempts to shift risk to other assets, processes, or organizations.

transport mode In IPSec, an encryption method in which only a packet's IP data is encrypted, not the IP headers themselves; allows intermediate nodes to read the source and destination addresses.

transposition cipher A cryptographic operation that involves simply rearranging the values within a block based on an established pattern; also known as a *permutation cipher*.

trap-and-trace application An application that combines the function of honeypots or honeynets with the capability to track the attacker back through the network.

trap door See *back door*.

trespass Unauthorized entry into the real or virtual property of another party.

Trojan horse A malware program that hides its true nature and reveals its designed behavior only when activated.

true attack stimulus An event that triggers an alarm and causes an IDPS to react as if a real attack is in progress.

trusted computing base (TCB) Under the Trusted Computer System Evaluation Criteria (TCSEC), the combination of all hardware, firmware, and software responsible for enforcing the security policy.

trusted network The system of networks inside the organization that contains its information assets and is under the organization's control.

trusted VPN Also known as a legacy VPN, a VPN implementation that uses leased circuits from a service provider who gives contractual assurance that no one else is allowed to use these circuits and that they are properly maintained and protected.

tuning The process of adjusting an IDPS to maximize its efficiency in detecting true positives while minimizing false positives and false negatives.

tunnel mode In IPSec, an encryption method in which the entire IP packet is encrypted and inserted as the payload in another IP packet; requires other systems at the beginning and end of the tunnel to act as proxies to send and receive the encrypted packets and then transmit the packets to their ultimate destination.

two-person control The organization of a task or process so that at least two employees must work together to complete it. Also known as dual control.

U

uncertainty The state of having limited or imperfect knowledge of a situation, making it less likely that organizations can successfully anticipate future events or outcomes.

Unified Threat Management (UTM) Networking devices categorized by their ability to perform the work of multiple devices, such as stateful packet inspection firewalls, network intrusion detection and prevention systems (IDPSs), content filters, spam filters, and malware scanners and filters.

untrusted network The system of networks outside the organization over which the organization has no control, such as the Internet.

uptime The percentage of time a particular service is available.

utility An attribute of information that describes how data has value or usefulness for an end purpose.

V

Vernam cipher A cryptographic technique developed at AT&T and known as the "one-time pad," this cipher uses a set of characters for encryption operations only once and then discards it.

Vigenère cipher An advanced type of substitution cipher that uses a simple polyalphabetic code.

virtual password A stream of characters generated by taking elements from an easily remembered phrase.

virtual private network (VPN) A private, secure network operated over a public and insecure network; it uses encryption to protect the data between endpoints.

virus A type of malware that is attached to other executable programs and, when activated, replicates and propagates itself to multiple systems, spreading by multiple communications vectors.

vulnerability A potential weakness in an asset or its defensive control system(s).

vulnerability assessment (VA) The process of identifying and documenting specific and provable flaws in the organization's information asset environment.

vulnerability assessment and remediation domain The component of the maintenance model focused on identifying specific, documented vulnerabilities and remediating them in a timely fashion.

W

war dialer An automatic phone-dialing program that dials every number in a configured range and checks whether a person, voicemail, or modem picks up.

war driving The use of mobile scanning techniques to identify open wireless access points.

warm site A BC facility that provides many of the same services and options as a hot site, but typically without installed and configured software applications.

waterfall model A type of SDLC in which each phase of the process "flows from" the information gained in the previous phase, with multiple opportunities to return to previous phases and make adjustments.

whitelist A list of systems, users, files, or addresses that are known to be benign; it is commonly used to expedite access to systems or networks.

wireless vulnerability assessment An assessment approach designed to find and document vulnerabilities in the organization's wireless local area networks.

work breakdown structure (WBS) A list of the tasks to be accomplished in a project, the skill sets or individual employees needed to perform the tasks, the start and end dates for tasks, the estimated resources required, and the dependencies among tasks.

work factor The amount of effort (usually expressed in units of time) required to perform cryptanalysis on an encoded message.

work recovery time (WRT) The amount of effort (expressed as elapsed time) needed to make business functions work again after the technology element is recovered. This recovery time is identified by the RTO.

worm A type of malware that is capable of activation and replication without being attached to an existing program.

Z

zero-day attack An attack that makes use of malware that is not yet known by the antimalware software companies.

zero-day vulnerability An unknown or undisclosed vulnerability in an information asset or its protection systems that may be exploited and result in loss; once it is discovered, there are zero days to identify, mitigate, and resolve the vulnerability.

zero-tolerance risk exposure An extreme level of risk tolerance whereby the organization is unwilling to allow any successful attacks or suffer any loss to an information asset.

zombie See *bot*.

INDEX

Note: Page numbers followed by *f* and *t* indicate figures and tables, respectively.